Of the Making of Books

Malcolm Beckwith Parkes

Of the Making of Books

Medieval Manuscripts, their Scribes and Readers
Essays presented to M. B. Parkes

Edited by

P. R. ROBINSON and RIVKAH ZIM

SCOLAR
PRESS

Published by
SCOLAR PRESS
Gower House
Croft Road
Aldershot
Hants GU11 3HR
England

Ashgate Publishing Company
Old Post Road
Brookfield
Vermont 05036–9704
USA

British Library Cataloguing in Publication Data
Of the Making of Books: Medieval Manuscripts, their
   Scribes and Readers: Essays presented to M. B. Parkes.
   1. Manuscripts, Medieval.
   I. Robinson, P. R. (Pamela R.). II. Zim, Rivkah.
   091
ISBN 1–85928–079–X

Library of Congress Cataloguing-in-Publication Data
Of the making of books: medieval manuscripts, their scribes and
   readers: essays presented to M. B. Parkes/edited by P. R. Robinson
   and Rivkah Zim.
       p.   cm.
   Includes bibliographical references and index.
   ISBN 1–85928–079–X (hb: acid-free paper)
   1. Manuscripts, Medieval—England.   2. Manuscripts, Medieval—
Europe.   3. Books and reading—England—History.   I. Robinson,
Pamela.   II. Zim, Rivkah.   III. Parkes, M. B. (Malcolm Beckwith).
Z106.5.G7035   1997
091′.096—dc21
                                                     96–51680
                                                        CIP

ISBN 1 85928 079 X

This book is printed on acid free paper

Typeset in Sabon by Joshua Associates Ltd., Oxford and printed in Great Britain by Ipswich Book Company Ltd.

Contents

Foreword

Once an *ancilla* for the study of documents and classical literature, palaeography has become an independent discipline, of which Malcolm Parkes is a leading proponent and developer. This discipline has for some time been joined by parallel work in codicology (a twentieth-century neologism), art history, and all aspects of the history of creating books. These distinctive developments are notably illustrated in the works of the scholar to whom the following essays are presented: their range mirrors his own imagination, erudition and humour.

Malcolm Parkes's work began of course with literal palaeography, the historical study of the craft of writing. Tracing the evolution of cursive bookhands in England from 1250–1500, he established the dating and terminology for all subsequent discussion of English scripts. From scripts he went on to examine the development of manuscripts: the ordering and compiling of their components, their illustration, copying and dissemination – that is, codicology and the history of the book. In another direction, studies of scripts led him to individual scribes and scribal innovations, the grammar of legibility, and a history of punctuation. In recent years he has also contributed chapters on the palaeography of a number of important literary and historical manuscripts published in facsimile.

Along with all his personal study and writing, Malcolm has always been a challenging teacher, at home in Oxford and widely abroad, sharing his findings and expertise with colleagues and aspiring inquirers at conferences, seminars, and lectures. Many are the acknowledgements of this in other people's publications; especially lively are their recollections of personal discussions at jolly meals with this generous and convivial scholar.

Ruth J. Dean
New York

List of Plates and Tables, and Acknowledgements

Plates

Tables

Acknowledgements

Photographs are reproduced here by kind permission of the following:

Cambridge, Corpus Christi College, Pls 18, 19, 20, 22(a), 22(b), 23(a), (b), (c)
Cambridge, Trinity College, Pl. 9
Cambridge, University Library, Pls 10, 11
Glasgow, University Library, Department of Special Collections, Pls 8, 16, 17
London, The British Library, Pls 12, 21, 30
Oxford, The Bodleian Library, Pls 5, 6, 24, 25, 26, 27, 28, 29
Norwich, Norfolk Record Office, Pls 13, 14, 15
Garrett Collection of Medieval and Renaissance Manuscripts, Manuscripts Division, Department of Rare Books and Special Collections, Princeton University Libraries, Pls 1, 2, 3, 4.

The picture of MBP reproduced as a frontispiece is courtesy of Mr Alan Blackwood.

The editors would like to thank Professor Peter Ganz, Dr Lynne Grundy, Mr Sean Magee and Mrs Joan Templeton for their kind assistance in the preparation of this volume.

Principal Abbreviations and Conventions

App. Appendix
ASE *Anglo-Saxon England*
Bibl. mun. Bibliothèque municipale
BL [London] British Library
BN [Paris] Bibliothèque nationale
Bodl. Lib. [Oxford] Bodleian Library
c. *circa*
Cat. Royal MSS G. F. Warner and J. P. Gilson, *Catalogue of Western Manuscripts in the Old Royal and King's Collections in the British Museum*, 4 vols (London, 1921)
CCCM Corpus Christianorum, continuatio mediaevalis (Turnhout, 1966–)
CCSL Corpus Christianorum, series latina (Turnhout, 1953–)
CLA E. A. Lowe, *Codices latini antiquiores: a Palaeographical Guide to Latin Manuscripts prior to the Ninth Century* (Oxford, 1934–72)
col(s) column(s)
Coll. College
CSEL Corpus scriptorum ecclesiasticorum latinorum (Vienna, 1866–)
DNB *Dictionary of National Biography*
ed. edited by
edn edition
EEMF Early English Manuscripts in Facsimile
EETS (OS) Early English Text Society, Original Series
EETS (SS) Early English Text Society, Supplementary Series
facs. facsimile
HBS Henry Bradshaw Society
James, *Ancient Libraries* M. R. James, *The Ancient Libraries of Canterbury and Dover* (Cambridge, 1903)
Jnl *Journal*
Ker, *Catalogue* N. R. Ker, *Catalogue of Manuscripts containing Anglo-Saxon* (Oxford, 1957; repr. with supplement, 1990)
Ker, *English Manuscripts* N. R. Ker, *English Manuscripts in the Century after the Norman Conquest* (Oxford, 1960)
Ker, *MLGB* N. R. Ker, *Medieval Libraries of Great Britain*, Royal

	Historical Society Guides and Handbooks, 3, 2nd edn (London, 1964)
Ker, *MMBL*	N. R. Ker, *Medieval Manuscripts in British Libraries*, I–III (Oxford, 1969–83)
Ker and Piper, *MMBL*, IV	N. R. Ker and A. J. Piper, *Medieval Manuscripts in British Libraries*, IV (Oxford, 1992)
Lib.	Library
Manly and Rickert	J. M. Manly and E. Rickert, *The Text of the Canterbury Tales*, 8 vols (Chicago, 1940)
Medieval Book Production ed. Brownrigg	*Medieval Book Production: Assessing the Evidence* ed. L. L. Brownrigg (Los Altos Hills, CA, 1990)
MED	*Middle English Dictionary*, ed. H. Kurath and S. M. Kuhn (Ann Arbor MI, 1956–)
MGH	Monumenta Germaniae Historica
New Pal. Soc., 2nd ser.	New Palaeographical Society, *Facsimiles of Ancient Manuscripts Etc.*, ed. E. M. Thompson, G. F. Warner, F. G. Kenyon and J. P. Gilson, 2nd series (London, 1913–30)
n.s.	new series/nouvelle séries
OE	Old English
OED	*Oxford English Dictionary*
PL	*Patrologiae cursus completus*, series latina, accurante J. P. Migne (Paris, 1844–55)
Pl(s)	Plate(s)
Proc.	*Proceedings*
Riverside Chaucer	*The Riverside Chaucer*, ed. L. D. Benson (Oxford, 1988)
RS	Rolls Series; i.e. Rerum Britannicarum medii aevi scriptores (London, 1858–96)
SC	*A Summary Catalogue of Western Manuscripts in the Bodleian Library at Oxford* (Oxford, 1895–1953)
Scribes, Scripts and Readers	M. B. Parkes, *Scribes, Scripts and Readers; Studies in the Communication, Presentation and Dissemination of Medieval Texts* (London and Rio Grande, OH, 1991)
ser.	series
sig(s)	signature(s)
s.n.	*sub nomine*
STC	A. W. Pollard and G. R. Redgrave, *A Short-Title Catalogue of Books Printed in England, Scotland, and Ireland and of English Books Printed Abroad 1475–1640*, 2nd edn, revised and enlarged by W. A.

	Jackson, F. S. Ferguson and K. F. Pantzer, 3 vols (London, 1976–91)
suppl.	supplement/supplément
s.v.	*sub verbo*
TCBS	*Transactions of the Cambridge Bibliographical Society*
Trans.	*Transactions*
tr.	translator; translated by; translation
Watson, *Supplement*	A. G. Watson, *Medieval Libraries of Great Britain: Supplement to the Second Edition*, Royal Historical Society Guides and Handbooks, 15 (London, 1987)

The following conventions have been observed:

Fol. 21 indicates the recto of a leaf, fol. 21^v indicates the verso of a leaf.

When the date of a manuscript is expressed in terms of the formula in, for example, *s.* xii *med* or *s.* xii *ex*, the date is based on palaeographical opinion. This formula may be explained as follows: *s.* xii *in* ('*saeculo* xii *ineunte*'), *s.* xii^1 (i.e. 'first half of the twelfth century'), *s.* xii *med* ('*saeculo* xii *medio*'), *s.* xii^2 (i.e. 'second half of the twelfth century'), *s.* xii *ex* ('*saeculo* xii *exeunte*'), and *s.* xii/xiii (i.e. 'about the turn of the twelfth century to the thirteenth century').

In transcriptions of Latin, abbreviations are expanded silently; in transcriptions of English, expanded abbreviations are indicated by italics. The following symbols have been used: ` ´ to indicate marginal insertions or interlineations; [ ] to indicate editorial additions and emendations; and where text is damaged and the reading is conjectural, words are enclosed in ⟨ ⟩.

Introduction

Malcolm Parkes is the first holder of the title Professor of Palaeography in the University of Oxford. This title, conferred on him in 1996, is a tribute to his personal distinction as a scholar and a teacher: a man whom colleagues in Europe (and elsewhere) have long recognized (and referred to in print) as 'le grand médiéviste' and 'one of the great palaeographers of our century'. He belongs to a great tradition of Oxford palaeographers which includes Humfrey Wanley in the late seventeenth century, E. A. Lowe and Neil Ker in our own century. In recent years he has been honoured with a fellowship of the British Academy and a corresponding fellowship of the Medieval Academy of America.

This volume of essays is a more tangible tribute offered by a representative group of senior colleagues, former pupils and good friends – the categories are overlapping – in recognition of this scholar's rare personal qualities and in gratitude for his exemplary contributions to so many different aspects of medieval manuscript studies.

MBP is a practical man: he prefers to ask 'so what?' or 'what for?', rather than 'why?' in the abstract. He gathers examples and mulls over the details but these are not ends in themselves, rather they are the building blocks for ingenious, and often elegant, intellectual structures created by interpreting carefully sifted evidence. His published work is stimulating and informative because it is a judicious blend of speculation and minute observation: imagination and experience. He seldom loses sight of the wood for the trees, he never blinds an audience, or reader, with science but the prose style is as terse and remorseless as the lecturing style is expansive and encouraging. 'Logic, simplicity and clarity, these three; but the greatest of these is clarity', is his favourite piece of advice to those writing up their research. A celebrated American novelist reviewing *Pause and Effect: An Introduction to the History of Punctuation in the West* in the *New York Review of Books* confessed 'it is not an easy book to read in bed' and then explained how the square format imposed an angle of approach to the text by a recumbent reader, which gradually made the spaces between words seem to disappear giving the whole text the appearance of *scriptio continua*. Malcolm's readers tend to get involved with what he writes in more than one sense.

Over the years he has quietly developed new applications for traditional approaches to palaeography. His range of reference and expertise is enormous – one of the practical benefits of a long teaching career. Malcolm discourses with knowledgeable enthusiasm not only about Latin and vernacular literary texts from late Antiquity to the Renaissance, with Old and Middle English, French, German and Italian as particular favourites, but also about theology, history, linguistics and music, and specialist colleagues in these disciplines listen. Continuous contact with the lively minds and youthful intellectual curiosity of intelligent undergraduates has developed and tested not only Malcolm's remarkable stamina but also safeguarded his own lively independence of mind and a responsible but often unconventional approach to all kinds of questions and problems. Only a dedicated and experienced teacher whose pupils have always been encouraged to ask awkward questions can retain his patience, good-humour and essential modesty.

Teaching and research have always gone together for him and have enabled him to switch, one moment to the next, from the mundane to the esoteric in order to refocus on such fundamental issues as the authority of authors, or the conventions of verse layout, or what comes first – the reader or the text? Malcolm has taught all the beginning graduate students in English medieval studies at Oxford for some thirty years. A succession of research students from home and abroad – at one point in the late 1970s there must have been a dozen of them receiving Malcolm's guidance and supervision for their theses – have found their supervisor as eager to debate their research problems as he was willing to share his own, by way of example, with intellectual equals. After all, what we all need, in one of Malcolm's favourite phrases, is 'a good haggle'. Perhaps the secret of his success is his willingness and ability to learn from everyone. The results have been classic studies of punctuation generally and the layout of verse in particular, of the concepts of *ordinatio* and *compilatio*, of the 'grammar of legibility' and of the literacy of the laity, alongside the usual bread and butter palaeography of scripts, the description, dating and provenance of manuscripts, and specific studies of the dissemination of texts by Boniface, Chaucer and Gower.

As several of the contributors to this volume know he is a generous but demanding collaborator, and even an advantage of twenty years' youth cannot compensate for the effects of Malcolm's enormous reserves of energy, his capacity for working late into the night, his minute attention to detail.

Malcolm's wit and wisdom, kindness and tactful self-deprecation have helped to make him a legend in his own lifetime. Parkes historiography is developing into an art form; already there are several substantive variants in a familiar type of story which involves a research student, or a collaborator, being driven home in a yellow, or white, Volvo – variants in colour and size of car indicate several stemmata but the Volvo marque is constant. The subject is then deposited on his or her doorstep either at dawn, or with the milk bottles, feeling exhausted but exhilarated after a marathon session in Keble fighting thesis dragons – or similar species – with MBP.

A different subtextual tradition, also prevalent in many versions from all periods, involves the subject being comforted and strengthened for the academic fray by an excellent dinner at the 'Luna Caprese'. An eyewitness account of a more spiritual exchange exists. It concerns MBP offering the season's greetings to a nun in a brown habit who was seen crossing the quad during the first week in January. He approached and kissed her in greeting, on both cheeks, saying boldly, 'Parkes vobiscum', to which the scholarly sister responded, in a trice, 'et Benedicta tua'. By contrast there is no external evidence for the story of the English medievalist who locked himself out of his car – a great yellow Volvo doubling as a mobile library – in the village where Joan of Arc was born and who announced in a broad English accent to the assembled company watching him break in, with a coat-hanger poked through the quarter light, 'Je suis cambrioleur spécialist'. No one was arrested.

The cartoon collection pinned up outside his door in Keble has fallen into disrepair of late, but in its heyday it enlivened the interminable wait for Malcolm to finish one tutorial before proceeding with the next. The buxom grinning lady astride an embarrassed horse had a bubble coming out of her mouth and the words 'I'm the Wife of Bath but you can call me Bubbles!' above her hat. One further example of this genre must suffice; it was aimed at innocent undergraduates who equated sin with sex, and depicted two small furry creatures hanging upside down from the branch of a tree with one saying to the other, 'When you suggested living in sin I didn't think you meant sloth'.

Fellowship in Teaching: Malcolm and I could have known each other as under-graduates, but in fact we first met when we became jointly responsible for the teaching of English at Mansfield College. He had been working at Lambeth Palace and I had had a Quaker education, but neither of us, perhaps, were quite the sort of tutors one might then have expected to find at a theological college. Mansfield, however, had decided to introduce a secular element (as a step in the movement, now complete, towards full University integration). It was a congenial mandate, and we found a common interest trying to fulfil it. Our partnership continued when we both became Fellows of Keble, and has lasted for more than thirty years with never a cross word; I could not have wished for a more understanding colleague.

As Mansfield was outside the University entrance system, we had to admit candidates who for one reason or another had slipped through the usual nets (several of whom now hold chairs at home or abroad), and this both concentrated our minds and made us more aware of what it was that we were looking for. Although Malcolm taught the 'language' part of the syllabus (i.e. Old and Middle English literature and the history of the English language) and I looked after the 'literature', our desiderata turned out to be surprisingly compatible. In these matters, as in others, Malcolm's refusal to be impressed by the conventional, the proper, and the routine (however plausibly presented) and his insistence on making candidates justify their interpreta-tions of a text by detailed examination of its linguistic features, was the basis of an interviewing technique which often threatened to become tutorial. It was hardly economical in terms of time, but it was a practice that we subsequently clung to because a capacity for close examination of the words on the page seemed a better guide to individual potential in all branches of the subject than the orthodox deployment of derived judgements however fluent. It was at entrance that many of Malcolm's pupils first realized that where the problems of literary language and translation are concerned there is no substitute for thinking for oneself.

As a tutor, Malcolm's aim has been the classical one of teaching his students not what, but how, to think. He didn't mind – would even affect not to care – what the argument was, as long as it was coherently constructed. Authority is not there to be deferred to but to be checked against the evidence of the text, whether printed or in manuscript. This rigour as to method was balanced by an undogmatic open-mindedness; large ideas must proceed from local readings, but otherwise thought is free. It is no good, when writing an essay for Malcolm, playing to the gallery of the tutor's known prejudices: he insists that you get it right, not that he was. He was quite ready to be persuaded; pupils are there to be learnt from, as well as taught. Another aspect of this hospitality was his unwillingness to see 'language' (in the Oxford sense) set against 'literature' (literary criticism). When we gave joint seminars on Shakespeare, for instance, I was often struck by how complementary our approaches turned out to be – how, for instance, thinking about fringe meanings in the lexical sense revealed subtextual associations in a character's mind, or how syntax betrayed motivation.

The originality of Malcolm's scholarship clearly involves an integrity of procedure not necessarily enthralled by received ideas, and the value of this combination has not been lost on his pupils. A man whose revisionist views on punctuation appeared on the faculty lecture list as 'What's the Point?' (and who once claimed to be so overworked that he'd fallen asleep during one of his own lectures), can hardly be accused of pretension. His imaginative sense of the human, never absent in his own writing even at its most technical, is as informally accessible to his present-day pupils as it is available to a fourteenth-century scribe, if not more so, since unlike the former the latter couldn't call at any unscheduled time to discuss his or her problems and expect a good measure of whisky while doing so. Like il Penseroso's, Malcolm's lamp is often seen at midnight hour, but as much for pastoral as for studious reasons. The trouble he will take over an individual case is wholehearted as well as exhaustive, and freely available not only to his own college charges but to many graduates throughout the University – one reason why his influence has been so widely felt and acknowledged. As his colleague for so long I naturally owe him much, and in all sorts of ways – I recall with pleasure, for instance, that he first introduced me to F. W. Bateson, who had been his tutor, and whose successor as editor of his journal *Essays in Criticism* I subsequently became. There can be few of Malcolm's pupils who would not feel, looking back, a similar sense of gratitude for the energy of his attention, the wisdom of his advice, and the individuality of his example.

                                                                    Stephen Wall

Not all Malcolm's colleagues are aware that in Germany he is considered to be one of the outstanding palaeographers. He has twice been invited to come to the University of Konstanz as a visiting professor which gave him the chance to visit and work in the medieval library of St Gall and to study the manuscript collection of Reichenau which is now deposited at Karlsruhe. When the Herzog August Bibliothek in Wolfenbüttel, which possesses one of the most important collections of medieval manuscripts in Germany, decided to establish a permanent group of medievalists to stimulate and direct research there, Malcolm was considered the obvious person to represent palaeography. It was a pleasure to watch him listen to the sometimes chaotic arguments put forward in discussion and then make a brief but decisive proposal which would be accepted by everyone. It was due to his interventions that a short-title catalogue of medieval manuscript holdings in Lower Saxony was started and is now almost complete. And again, when one of the oldest and most respected German philological journals was looking for someone to review Bernhard Bischoff's Palaeography, Malcolm was recognized as the only one who could assess the great man's works with the proper pietas and also criticize shortcomings (where necessary) without causing offence. He is seen there as the ideal representative of an idealized university.

Anon.

Malcolm Parkes mi è sempre apparso come l'immagine dello studioso inglese nello stesso tempo legato alla tradizione e aperto ad ogni novità culturale. Nella sua figura intellettuale il gusto dello spirito e della 'battuta' si mescolano con la più ferrea serietà nello studio e nella ricerca, la massima concentrazione con la conversazione brillante. Lo ricordo in un incontro in Vaticana del 'Comité de paléographie latine' ove l'ho visto alternare momenti di lettura solitaria con divertenti passeggiate accompagnate dal fumo della pipa. La novità dei suoi studi, l'eccezionale larghezza dei suoi interessi, l'assoluto dominio del metodo paleografico e del panorama variato delle fonti da lui studiate ne fanno un paleografo originalissimo e moderno, tipico esponente di una tradizione pragmatica formatasi più nelle sale di studio delle biblioteche e degli archivi che non nei corridoi delle istituzioni universitarie. Purtroppo in Italia i contributi di Malcolm Parkes sono ancora relativamente poco conosciuti; e ciò è segno negativo di estraneità fra diverse tradizioni di studi. Spero che questa situazione possa cambiare e che la ricchezza di spunti presenti nei saggi raccolti sotto il titolo di *Scribes, Scripts and Readers* e soprattutto nello straordinario libro dedicato a *Pause and Effect*, possa risultare utile a vivacizzare gli studi paleografici anche nell'Europa continentale e in Italia. Grazie, Malcolm.[1]

Armando Petrucci

---

[1] Malcolm Parkes has always seemed to me the very image of the English scholar, at once aware of tradition, yet alert to cultural innovation. In his intellectual character a delight in the battle of wits mingles with an iron seriousness in study and research, the greatest concentration with sparkling conversation. I remember him in a meeting at the Vatican of the Comité de paléographie latine, where I watched him alternate periods of solitary reading with relaxing strolls enveloped in the smoke of his pipe. The originality of his work, the exceptional breadth of his interests, his absolute control of palaeographical method and of the varied panorama of the sources he has studied have made him a

Those who know Malcolm Parkes primarily in his eyrie with bookes clad in blak and reed may not know that this Clerk of Oxenford has on many occasions undertaken for to seken straunge transatlantic strondes in order to teach the rigours and delights of palaeography to American faculty and graduate students. He has taught intensive summer courses at the University of Pennsylvania (1976), University of California at Los Angeles (1978), and Harvard University (1988), and he was James J. Hill Visiting Professor at the University of Minnesota (Twin Cities) in 1991. He has also seen more of North America than have most North Americans in the course of innumerable guest lectures in the United States, and in Canada, especially at Toronto.

Few who participated in his summer seminars have forgotten either the pleasure or exhaustion attendant on their labours in those often-sweltering circumstances. Instruction began in the morning with daily sheafs of xeroxes for transcription and continued into late-night bonhomie where personal anecdote was the pedagogy for palaeographical and codicological instruction. George Brown speaks for many in observing that Malcolm 'wore all of us out'. These summer seminars also provided the opportunity to observe Malcolm at work with codices in American libraries (such as the Ellesmere Chaucer and the Stafford Gower at the Huntington) and observers on those occasions learned the respect without codicolotry due to manuscripts.

Malcolm encountered the other, septentrional, extremes of the North American climate as a visiting professor at the University of Minnesota in 1991, a sojourn that has produced many fond Minneapolis memories of the English don in his green John Deere baseball cap (later exchanged for a Minnesota Twins cap, after a suitable initiation into the rituals of change passing at baseball games; the winning streak that culminated in the World Series began in his presence). Malcolm's last momentous lecture for the Medieval Center's 1991 season was accompanied by the lamenting howls and driving rain of a tornado. His audience stayed and strained to listen to him speak about the history of reading, but sensibly moved away from the windows. It was this visit that elicited from Rutherford Aris the macaronic verse – suitably written out in Anglicana – beginning:

> Great decypherer of markes
> Is our Hill Professor Parkes
> Esse quite the best of them
> Puto Professor Parkem

---

palaeographer who is extremely original and contemporary, the typical exponent of a pragmatic tradition formed in the reading rooms of libraries and archives rather than in the corridors of universities. Unfortunately, in Italy his contributions are as yet relatively little known, and this is a regrettable sign of the divergences between different traditions of scholarship. I hope that this situation will change, and that the richness of ideas in the essays collected under the title *Scribes, Scripts and Readers* and, above all, the extraordinary book *Pause and Effect* will help to revitalize palaeographic studies both in continental Europe and in Italy. Grazie, Malcolm.

tr. Germaine Warkentin

Americans who studied palaeography in North America with this Clerk of Oxenford have found him subsequently most willing to support, reprimand, and encourage their scholarly efforts by means of telephone, fax, and intense discussions in his upstairs room – a medievalist's library – at Keble. Not only does he continue gladly to teche, but also finds himself sought out as a friend: for felaweshipe wel koude he laughe and carpe.

Linda Voigts

Publishing Parkes – a role I enjoyed through working with Malcolm on *Medieval Scribes, Manuscripts and Libraries* (published in 1978), the Keble manuscripts catalogue (1979), the new edition of *English Cursive Book Hands 1250–1500* (also 1979) and into the early stages of *Pause and Effect* (eventually published in 1992) – proved a deeply character-forming experience.

From our first encounter in 1976, through that fug of pipe smoke in his room above the main gate of Keble, working with Malcolm was always a delight. The editorship of *Medieval Scribes, Manuscripts and Libraries* – the Festschrift for N. R. Ker – cast Malcolm as gags merchant to Andrew Watson's straight man, Morecambe to his Wise, and it is a measure of the great affection in which both editors were held at Scolar that upon publication of the book we presented them with a fully typeset and illustrated spoof contribution to the book which examined 'the relationship between two scribes working for a commercial scriptorium in London in the last quarter of the twentieth century'. Malcolm – there identified as Scribe P – is described as having an 'obsessive and idiosyncratic concern with hyphens and commas in the texts he worked on', and there are allusions to the bright red shirt which characterized his sartorial style in the late 1970s: a manuscript is cited which describes 'scriptor in tunicae rubrissimae qui loquitur per diem et noctem.' (The particularly lurid shade of that shirt, incidentally, provided a colour swatch for the endpapers to the catalogue of manuscripts in Keble College.)

To their credit, neither Malcolm nor Andrew lodged a formal complaint with the Publishers' Association.

Just as a jockey has to adapt to the quirks and foibles of each individual mount, so a publisher adjusts to each author, a process compounded in Malcolm's case by his eccentric working habits: I could never reach him at college before lunch (and in those days few publishing houses did much work after), but as compensation he might well phone me at home at 2 a.m. for an hour's discussion on this or that contributor's attitude to the serial comma.

Even without the strain of such an unusual routine, few books reach the shelves of Blackwell's or Heffer's without at least some hint of difficulty, some cross word from either side, some umbrage taken, and I have run the whole gamut of author–publisher relationships – including one author who, nervous of how his text might be treated after delivery, wrote 'THIS WAY UP' in large letters on his typescript. But publishing Parkes never once (he might remember differently) occasioned a cross word between us.

Malcolm's authorial demeanour combined a professionalism which bordered on zealotry (he once took the trouble to acquire a pica rule and measure the x-height of a letter in a proof so that he could instruct us to make the correction with the right size of type) with a deep-rooted conviction that however serious the venture might be, and however dedicated to its execution we were, we could still enjoy ourselves while we pursued it. Adapting the adage about the advisability of keeping a dog and barking yourself, his avowed (and often repeated) philosophy of authorship was simple: 'Why keep a publisher and worry yourself?'

This imbued MBP the author with a sort of serenity, a blithe confidence in the capabilities of his publisher, which allowed him more time to appreciate the sheer fun of the whole enterprise – as, for example, when a simple typo in the proofs of the Keble manuscripts catalogue provided the caption, 'Bathsheba bathing receives a massage', a moment of human frailty over which he will still guffaw, nearly two decades on.

Hearing Malcolm on the end of the phone – ''Allo, sunshine!' was (still is) his perennial greeting to me – signalled a marathon conversation which would combine the smallest detail of editing with a lecture on an arcane nicety of punctuation, academic gossip, and advice regarding hangover cures or some aspect of personal hygiene. His keynote phrase 'To cut a long story short' was itself a sort of conversational punctuation mark, a paragraph indentation before continuing the same theme.

And could he continue! For some years there sat high on a shelf in his room at Keble a pencil drawing of myself slumped in my office chair listening on the phone – a sketch executed by my secretary at Scolar Press and entitled by her: 'Still Life: MBP talking to SM'.

These leviathan conversations contained nuggets of information which could have reached me from no other source. When in 1984 I announced that I was leaving Scolar to work for Basil Blackwell in Oxford, and would be moving to the Oxfordshire village of Chadlington, Malcolm uttered the most quintessentially donnish remark I have ever heard: 'You're getting into Digby 86 country out there.' I imagined a road sign somewhere beyond Charlbury – 'WELCOME TO DIGBY 86 COUNTRY: PLEASE DRIVE CAREFULLY' – but the exact significance of the remark was to elude me until I discovered that Robert de Pendock (*fl.* 1268–90), a member of the Worcestershire family associated with the manuscript, had held two virgates of the Earl of Warwick in Chadlington in 1278–79.Whenever I walk the dogs across those very virgates I think of MBP.

His talk may have been peppered with shelf-marks, but Malcolm the author was no tunnel-visioned academic, and he understood that the emotional and practical needs of his publisher went well beyond the confines of medieval studies. On the day of the launch party in Oxford for the Ker Festschrift, he made a point of allowing me access to the JCR at Keble so that I could watch Shirley Heights win the 1978 Derby by a head; and for years when all parking spaces in central Oxford were full I would slip my car into the fellows' car-park at Keble and leave it there with a note fibbing 'VISITING MR PARKES', knowing that he would never blow my alibi.

A more lasting benefit was Malcolm's generosity with regard to other scholars as potential authors, an invaluable boon to an editor building a list: Alastair Minnis's *Medieval Theory of Authorship* and Benedicta Ward's *Miracles and the Medieval Mind*, both works of exceptional quality, are just two of the books which came Scolar's grateful way through Malcolm. And my early travel round the medieval studies departments of the USA and Canada was much facilitated by the label which the always avuncular MBP had figuratively placed, Paddington Bear-style, round my neck: 'PLEASE LOOK AFTER THIS EDITOR'.

Were all authors like Malcolm, fewer books would be published, which may or may not be a good thing. But publishing Parkes himself was a joy, no better summed up than in his inscription in my own copy of *Medieval Scribes, Manuscripts and Libraries*: 'Explicit opus longissimum prolixissimum et iocundissimum faciendi.'

Sean Magee

In September 1997 MBP officially retires from his teaching posts in the University of Oxford and at Keble College; we all wish him well in his new life as a full-time, unofficial peripatetic: business as usual.

I
Of the Making of Books and of their Provenances

Origin and Provenance of Anglo-Saxon Manuscripts: the Case of Cotton Tiberius A.III

Helmut Gneuss

The significance of what we know about the origin and provenance of medieval English manuscripts is manifold. Whatever we can ascertain about the place where a manuscript was written, or where it was kept and, presumably, read and regularly consulted, can provide us with valuable information on the history and transmission of individual texts, on the development of handwriting and book illustration, on the intellectual climate in the institution – monastic or otherwise – and the scriptorium where it was produced, on the history of a particular library. Moreover, the study of English dialects, especially in the early Middle Ages, has profited greatly from research on manuscript origins and will no doubt continue to do so.

It is well-known that often enough the attempt to establish the origin, or at least the provenance of a manuscript is fraught with difficulties and may even appear a hopeless task. This is particularly so with regard to manuscripts written or owned in Anglo-Saxon England, and it does not seem surprising, therefore, that not a few among the recent, increasingly numerous studies in our field tend to question previous assumptions about the attribution of particular books to particular scriptoria or libraries in Anglo-Saxon England. What we can say with more or less certainty about the home of an Anglo-Saxon manuscript depends on the application of several criteria and the careful examination of all available evidence. In what follows I hope to be able to show how such a procedure can produce convincing results in the case of a complex manuscript on whose place of origin scholars no longer seem to be agreed.

London, BL, Cotton MS Tiberius A.III was written about the middle of the eleventh century or somewhat later; its contents, at first sight, might simply be called 'miscellaneous'. According to the latest and authoritative full description of the manuscript by Neil Ker[1] they consist of 91 items, and this figure alone should make it clear that it will be impossible to deal here with each of these pieces in detail. I list

---

[1] Ker, *Catalogue*, pp. 240–49 nos 186 and 187. For the earlier printed descriptions of the manuscript by Hickes, Thomas Smith, Wanley, Planta, Henri and Willem Logeman and Förster see L. Kornexl, *Die Regularis Concordia und ihre altenglische Interlinearversion* (München, 1993), pp. cxxi–cxxii; for Förster see also below, pp. 16–17. All references to the contents of Tiberius A.III in this essay follow Ker's article numbering. For printed editions and collations published after the appearance of Ker's *Catalogue*, see App. 1, below. For an addition to the analysis of scribal hands by

below the main items, together with the number assigned to them in Dr Ker's *Catalogue*, and the folio number of the beginning of each item (* in Old English; ** Latin with Old English interlinear gloss; all other texts in Latin):

Ker, see H. Sauer, 'Zwei spätaltenglische Beichtermahnungen aus Hs. Cotton Tiberius A.iii', *Anglia*, 98 (1980), 1–33, at 4–5.

Ker no.:		Fol.:
29.	Ælfric, *Pastoral Letter* III*	106
30.	Office of the Virgin	107ᵛ
31 a–c.	Prayers and verses, added *s.* xi/xii	116
31 d–g.	Prayers and verses, added *s.* xii	116

The number and diversity of subjects treated in the manuscript will be apparent from this simplified list, and will also have highlighted the problem of how to assess and interpret the character, purpose and use of Tiberius A.III. There would be next to no problem if we only had to deal with articles one to seven, a compendium of the Benedictine reform movements in Carolingian Francia and in tenth-century England.[2] Other items would fit into this group: articles 10a, 22, 25, perhaps 29, and certainly 30. But what about the rest? Mary Clayton suggested at first that our manuscript 'seems to have been compiled to preserve texts of interest and could perhaps have been used as a teaching book', but she and Magennis now think of Tiberius as primarily 'a type of reference book, preserving texts of interest to the community'.[3] This seems more convincing, since a few of the texts do not seem to belong in a teaching book, especially the *Examinatio episcopi* (art. 20),[4] which should only have been of special interest to an archbishop and his assistants. In any case, the collection of texts is not as haphazard and incoherent as may appear at first sight; thus, Charles D. Wright has recently pointed out the generic affinity of items 15 and 18, and possibly 17, which deal with encounters between a saint or hermit and the devil, and with accounts of the Otherworld.[5]

In this essay I assume that Cotton Tiberius A.III, as presently constituted, with the exception of fols 174–179, formed a composite but single volume – not a collection of booklets[6] – from the second half of the eleventh century onwards, or rather immediately after it was written about the middle of that century or somewhat later;

---

[2] On this compendium and its texts see now esp. *Initia Consuetudinis Benedictinae: Consuetudines saeculi octavi et noni*, ed. K. Hallinger et al., *Corpus Consuetudinum Monasticarum*, I (Siegburg, 1963); Wulfstan of Winchester, *The Life of St Æthelwold*, ed. M. Lapidge and M. Winterbottom (Oxford, 1991), pp. lv–lx; Kornexl, *Regularis Concordia*, and for the compilation in Tiberius A.III, R. Deshman, 'Benedictus Monarcha et Monachus: Early Medieval Ruler Theology and the Anglo-Saxon Reform', *Frühmittelalterliche Studien*, 22 (1988), 204–40, at 229.

[3] M. Clayton, *The Cult of the Virgin Mary in Anglo-Saxon England* (Cambridge, 1990), p. 76; M. Clayton and H. Magennis, *The Old English Lives of St Margaret* (Cambridge, 1994), pp. 85–6. See also D. Dumville, *Liturgy and the Ecclesiastical History of Late Anglo-Saxon England: Four Studies* (Woodbridge, 1992), p. 137.

[4] On this text see below, pp. 33–7.

[5] C. D. Wright, *The Irish Tradition in Old English Literature*, (Cambridge, 1993) p. 176 and notes 6 and 7. I owe this reference to Joyce Hill.

[6] For the concept of the booklet see P. R. Robinson, 'The "Booklet": a Self-Contained Unit in Composite Manuscripts', *Codicologica, 3: Essais typologiques*, ed. A. Gruys and J. P. Gumbert (Leiden, 1980), pp. 46–69, and her 'Self-Contained Units in Composite Manuscripts of the Anglo-Saxon Period', *ASE*, 7 (1978), 231–8.

a dating on which the experts in palaeography and art history now seem to be agreed.[7]

Evidence for the assumption of a one-volume unit comes from several sources: from an early-twelfth-century list of contents on fol. 117 and an entry in Prior Eastry's fourteenth-century catalogue of the library of Christ Church, Canterbury, to be discussed below; from entry no. 155 in the oldest catalogue of the Cotton library, extant in London, BL, MS Harley 6018, and from the so-called Cotton Elenchus, drawn up by Richard James, on fol. 2 of our manuscript; finally from Dr Ker's analysis of the distribution of the work of various hands in different parts of Tiberius. Dr Ker has also presented compelling evidence for what he has established as the original order of the parts of the manuscript (later disturbed by Sir Robert Cotton); this was: fols 117-173 followed by fols 2–116.

Apart from this it is clear from Ker's reconstruction of the quiring of Tiberius that almost everywhere the individual texts cut across quire boundaries, so that separate booklets or books could only be assumed for fols 117–173 + 2–56; fols 57–64; and fols 65–116. However, the distribution of the work of the several scribes speaks against this assumption and against an earlier attempt by Max Förster to distinguish originally independent parts of Tiberius. (The present fols 174–179 come from other manuscripts and were added by Cotton.)

The best scholarly treatment of the make-up and contents of Tiberius A.III after Wanley and before Ker was provided by Max Förster.[8] According to him, Tiberius consists of six originally independent *Manuskripte*, which were bound together by Cotton: I, fols 2–56; II, fols 57–116; III, fols 117–173; IV, fols 174–177; V, fol. 178; VI, fol. 179.

Förster was certainly right about his *Manuskripte* IV–VI. His number IV, with an Old English prose version of sections 14–19 of the *Regularis Concordia* (fols 174–176^v), and the end of section 68 of the *Regularis Concordia* in Latin, followed by two variant texts of letters announcing the death of a monk of Christ Church (fol. 177^{r-v}), was originally part of London, BL, Cotton MS Faustina B.III, fols 158–198, a mid-eleventh-century manuscript from Christ Church, Canterbury.[9] His number V, fol. 178, with a West-Saxon royal genealogy, was part of London, BL, Cotton MS Tiberius A.VI (as Wanley had already noticed), a copy of the Anglo-Saxon Chronicle (MS 'B'), probably written between *c*.977 and 979, perhaps at Abingdon. Förster's VI, fol. 179, with a horologium and a Latin prayer written in the late tenth century, must also have come from another manuscript.[10]

---

[7] But D. H. Turner has suggested the second half of the eleventh century: *The Golden Age of Anglo-Saxon Art 966–1066*, ed. J. Backhouse, D. H. Turner and L. Webster (London, 1984), p. 47, no. 28.

[8] Humfrey Wanley, *Librorum Vett. Septentrionalium . . . Catalogus Historico-Criticus* (Oxford, 1705), pp. 193–9; M. Förster, 'Beiträge zur mittelalterlichen Volkskunde III', *Archiv für das Studium der neueren Sprachen und Literaturen*, 121 (1908), 30–46.

[9] For this part of Tiberius A.III see now Kornexl, *Regularis Concordia*, pp. cxii–cxvi.

[10] Ker, *Catalogue*, no. 187.

Förster's division of fols 2–173 into three separate books or booklets would not conflict with Ker's collation, which had to be based on evidence like pricking and ruling, since Tiberius A.III was damaged in the Cotton fire of 1731, and its leaves are now mounted on paper frames. But three of the hands identified by Ker occur in Förster's *Manuskripte* I and II, and one of them probably in the gloss in Förster's III. Moreover, the list of contents on fol. 117 makes it clear that at least Förster's I and III must have been together in one volume by the early twelfth century. Although Tiberius A.III, fols 2–173, may not appear to modern eyes as a carefully and systematically planned collection, we will have to build on the assumption that it formed a single volume about the time of the Norman Conquest.

Though it may seem self-evident, I should like to stress that in what follows I am solely concerned with the origin of the Tiberius manuscript as such, and not with the origin of its various texts (or of particular variant forms of these), nor with the origin of the Old English glosses. It has been shown that a number of items in Tiberius must derive – either immediately or at several removes – from exemplars that did not originate in Canterbury. Thus – to mention just a few examples – the two well-known full-page illustrations in the manuscript have been thought to go back to archetypes devised by Bishop Æthelwold at Winchester;[11] the Old English glosses to the *Regula S. Benedicti* and the *Memoriale qualiter* are obviously based on Winchester – or Winchester school – exemplars, as a painstaking examination of their vocabulary has shown,[12] although the Tiberius gloss to the Rule is wholly independent of Æthelwold's prose translation. In view of the role that Winchester played in the Benedictine reform movement in England, it seems hardly surprising that there are other textual links with the Winchester monasteries and their surviving manuscripts. An instructive case is the Office of All Saints in Tiberius (art. 10 a), where in the *Preces* for Vespers Birinus, Swithun, Iudoc and Æthelthryth of Ely (a house refounded by Æthelwold) are invoked; it seems clear that this form of the supplementary Office of All Saints must have found its way from Winchester to Canterbury.[13] On the other hand, the possibility of an Anglian origin for the Old English life of St Margaret (art. 15) has been considered.[14]

Let us return to what has been suggested in the title of this essay. I hope to be

---

[11] Deshman, '*Benedictus Monarcha*', pp. 210, 220.

[12] W. Hofstetter, *Winchester und der spätaltenglische Sprachgebrauch. Untersuchungen zur geographischen und zeitlichen Verbreitung altenglischer Synonyme* (München, 1987), pp. 117–26, and his 'Winchester and the Standardization of Old English Vocabulary', *ASE*, **17** (1988), 139–61, at 159–60.

[13] H. Gneuss, *Hymnar und Hymnen im englischen Mittelalter* (Tübingen, 1968), p. 111; Lapidge, in Wulfstan of Winchester (as n. 2 above), pp. lxxv–lxxvii. A comprehensive study of liturgical links between Winchester and Canterbury would seem rewarding. For benedictionals, see A. Prescott, 'The Structure of English Pre-Conquest Benedictionals', *British Library Jnl*, **13** (1987), 118–58, at 132–3.

[14] See Clayton and Magennis (as n. 3 above), pp. 97–103; Hofstetter, *Winchester*, p. 236; L. Herbst, *Die altenglische Margaretenlegende in der Hs. Cotton Tiberius A.III*, Dr phil. Dissertation (Göttingen, 1975), pp. 9–46.

able to show that the origin and provenance of Cotton Tiberius A.III must be sought at Christ Church, the cathedral priory of Canterbury. This seems a promising and rewarding task, not only because it will be necessary and possible to demonstrate how to apply different tests and criteria, but especially because scholars do not seem to be agreed on where the Tiberius manuscript was written and utilized, and where it remained before it came into the hands of the sixteenth-century antiquarians and, finally, into Sir Robert Cotton's library.

A considerable number of scholars in various fields of study have expressed their opinion on where Tiberius A.III, or certain parts of it, may have been written. It would seem pointless to list all their names and the pertinent publications, but at present there certainly is no unanimity on the question. Humfrey Wanley appears to have been the first who looked for an answer: in his remarkably accurate description of the book, he noted that in the Marian Office (art. 30), his number LX, was to be found 'Litania in qua memoratur inter alios S. DVNSTANVS' (reproducing the manuscript capitals); he also printed the final formula of the *Examinatio episcopi* with its reference to the 'Archiepiscopus Christi aecclesiæ'.[15]

When philologists had succeeded in establishing the characteristics of the south-eastern or 'Kentish' dialect in Old English,[16] editors of texts and glosses from the Tiberius manuscript pointed out the occurrence of such characteristics; Friedrich Kluge in his edition of the treatise on monastic sign language (art. 22) was apparently the first to do so, and it is somewhat disappointing to find that the most recent editor of the same text has nothing at all to say about its language.[17] Kluge, and others, such as Henri Logeman in his edition of the Benedictine Rule with the Old English interlinear gloss,[18] did not, however, attribute the texts to a particular place. In our century, the majority of scholars, particularly art historians, were inclined to consider Christ Church, Canterbury, the original home of the manuscript. This came after Edward S. Dewick had published a facsimile and edition of the Marian Office (art. 30) with its characteristic litany, and after M. R. James had identified Tiberius A.III with an entry in Prior Eastry's library catalogue.[19] Shortly afterwards Förster, following James and noting south-eastern English dialectal forms, considered at least his first *Manuskript* (fols 2–56) as having probably ('wohl') been written at Christ Church.[20]

More recently, a number of scholars have expressed themselves more cautiously,

---

[15] Wanley, *Catalogus*, pp. 197–8.

[16] Cf. A. Campbell, *Old English Grammar* (Oxford, 1959), p. 4, n. 1.

[17] F. Kluge, 'Zur Geschichte der Zeichensprache. Angelsächsische Indicia Monasterialia', *Internationale Zeitschrift für allgemeine Sprachwissenschaft*, 2 (1885), 116–37, at 130; *Monasteriales Indicia. The Anglo-Saxon Monastic Sign Language*, ed. D. Banham (Pinner, Middx, 1991).

[18] *The Rule of S. Benet*, ed. H. Logeman, EETS (OS), 90 (1888).

[19] *Facsimiles of Horae de Beata Maria Virgine*, ed. E. S. Dewick, HBS, 21 (1902); James, *Ancient Libraries*, pp. 50 and 508.

[20] Förster (as n. 8 above), p. 31.

qualifying their attribution of the book to Christ Church by a query, or by adverbs like 'probably' – as Förster did – or 'almost certainly'. 'I should . . . quibble about the precise sense in which BM Cott. Tib. A.iii is a Christ Church book' was the dictum of Christopher Hohler, a distinguished liturgiologist.[21] Such a guarded approach is presumably – among other considerations – an expression of doubt as to the significance of the Eastry identification which, if it is correct, provides evidence for the provenance of the manuscript, but not for its place of origin.

Few scholars nowadays seem willing to say outright that this place is unknown, and no one, as far as I can see, has seriously and definitely suggested a place of origin outside Kent. The scriptorium of St Augustine's in Canterbury may have been thought a possibility by some, and recently a case has been made out, by Dr Mildred Budny, for accepting at least the illustrations in Tiberius A.III if not the manuscript itself as work from St Augustine's.[22] Finally, as Dr Ker has pointed out, 'some of the OE pieces are very corrupt'.[23] Is this what we would expect from Canterbury cathedral scribes around 1050?

In what follows, I will attempt to review and interpret the evidence we have for determining the origin of Tiberius A.III, the place, or places, where it was written and read. Whenever such an attempt is made, however, it seems advisable to remember that any evidence, of whatever kind – marks of ownership, entries in medieval library catalogues, script, decoration, liturgical pieces, textual affiliation and the dialectal features of Old English texts and glosses – may not be as conclusive as it appears. A scribe or an artist may have worked in more than one place or may have produced a book intended for another house; a book may have changed owners, although one with texts in Old English, or one written before c.1100, perhaps did not very often do so after the end of the Anglo-Saxon period; apparently localizable liturgical items (and references to local saints) may have been copied inadvertently in places where different liturgical practices obtained.

Ownership: names and libraries

The evidence for a Christ Church provenance of Tiberius A.III that is most often adduced are two entries in the library catalogue compiled in the 1320s at the bidding

---

[21] 'Some Service Books of the Later Saxon Church', in *Tenth-Century Studies. Essays in Commemoration of the Millennium of the Council of Winchester and Regularis Concordia*, ed. D. Parsons (London, 1975), pp. 60–83 and 217–27, at 220, n. 10.

[22] M. O. Budny, 'British Library Manuscript Royal 1 E.VI: The Anatomy of an Anglo-Saxon Bible Fragment', unpublished PhD thesis, University of London (1984), pp. 246–53, and her 'Additions and Corrections to the *Index to Iconographic Contents*', *Old English Newsletter*, 17 (1984), A.41–2. I am grateful to Dr Budny for kindly presenting me with a copy of her thesis.

[23] Ker, *Catalogue*, p. 240.

of Prior Henry of Eastry.[24] This evidence, however, is somewhat confusing and has to be reviewed briefly. The contents of two volumes listed in Eastry's catalogue, now preserved in London, BL, Cotton MS Galba E.IV, need to be considered; they are numbers 296 and 297 in the edition by M. R. James (the continuous numbering of the items, in square brackets, is mine):

296. [1?]   Batte super Regulam beati Benedicti.
             In hoc uol. cont.:
      [2]   Regula Aluricii glosata Anglice.
      [3]   Liber sompniorum.
      [4]   De obseruacione Lune in rebus agendis.
      [5]   Oraciones Anglice.

297.   Batte secundus.
             In hoc uol. cont.:
      [6]   Expositiones de Prisciano exposite Anglice.
      [7]   Locutio latina glosata Anglice ad instruendos pueros.
      [8]   Prophecia sibille.
      [9]   Excepciones de gradibus Ecclesie.
      [10]   Epistole Paschasii pape de ordinacione Radulfi Archiepiscopi.
      [11]   Epistola Johannis pape ad sanctum Dunstanum.
      [12]   Examinacio Episcopi antequam consecretur.
      [13]   Regula beati Benedicti glosata, Anglice.
      [14]   Omelie et Sermones quedam.
      [15]   Consuetudines de faciendo seruicio diuino per annum, glosate Anglice.

There appears to be good reason for equating the items in Eastry's 296 with the contents of Tiberius A.III and with a twelfth-century list of contents on fol. 117 of this manuscript (printed below on p. 23), originally the recto of its first leaf, whose wording is remarkably close to the entry in Eastry. Thus:

Eastry 296	*Tiberius fol. 117*	*Ker 186, art. no.*
[1]	1.	1
[2]	2.	6
[3]	3.	7a
[4]	4.	7b/7b, 7e, or 7b seqq.
[5]	5.?	9/8 seqq.

This would presuppose that the heading of Eastry 296 also refers to a particular text, and that the cataloguer of Eastry 296 had ignored not only the diversity of articles 7a–7r, but also article 8 and everything that follows article 9, whereas the compiler of the twelfth-century contents list had at least admitted that he had capitulated by

---

[24] James, *Ancient Libraries*, p. 50. For the Eastry catalogue see ibid., pp. xxxv–xliv, and now N. Ramsay, 'The Cathedral Archives and Library', in *A History of Canterbury Cathedral*, ed. P. Collinson, N. Ramsay and M. Sparks (Oxford, 1995), pp. 341–407, at 355–60.

describing everything that followed articles 7b and 7e as 'Item alia plura tam anglice quam latine' (his no. 5).

But what about Eastry's 297? It looks like a curious mixture of the texts in Tiberius A.III and others that may have had nothing to do with this book:

[6] This was almost certainly a copy of Ælfric's *Grammar*, but no such copy, with one or more of items [7]–[15] is extant; but compare item [7]. I am sure, however, that *Expositiones* is in error for *Excerptiones* (caused by *exposite* in the entry), taken from the beginning of Ælfric's first preface to his work.[25]

[7] No doubt Ælfric's *Colloquy* with its Old English gloss (cf. Tiberius A.III, art. 11). It may be noted that an unglossed, expanded version of this colloquy follows a copy of Ælfric's *Grammar* in Oxford, St John's College, MS 154 (*s.* xi *in.*).

[8] One of the versions of the *Oracula Sibyllina* known to the Anglo-Saxons.[26]

[9] One of several Latin and Old English texts dealing with the holy orders.[27]

[10] This entry I cannot explain; was there a connection with the following item?

[11] This is the privilege that Dunstan received from the hands of Pope John XII in 960, granting him the papal pallium. The earliest and best copy is preserved in the late-tenth-century pontifical in Paris, BN, MS lat. 943, a book that may have been intended for Dunstan's own use.[28]

[12] This corresponds to article 20 in Tiberius A.III; it is discussed in more detail below, pp. 33–7.

[13] This can only refer to a glossed copy of the Rule like article 1 in Tiberius

---

[25] See H. Gneuss, 'The Study of Language in Anglo-Saxon England', *Bulletin of the John Rylands Lib.*, 72 (1990), 3–32, at 13–17.

[26] No doubt one of the Latin poems based upon the *Oracula Sibyllina*. See B. Bischoff, 'Die lateinischen Übersetzungen und Bearbeitungen aus den Oracula Sibyllina', in *Mittelalterliche Studien*, I (Stuttgart, 1966), pp. 150–71, and B. McGinn, '*Teste David cum Sibylla*: The Significance of the Sibylline Tradition in the Middle Ages', in *Women of the Medieval World. Essays in Honor of John M. Mundy*, ed. J. Kirschner and S. F. Wemple (Oxford, 1985), pp. 7–35. It seems noteworthy that the Sibylline poem beginning *Iudicii signum, tellus sudore madescet*, first quoted in St Augustine's *De civitate Dei*, XVIII.23, is found in a manuscript written at Christ Church, Canterbury (*s.* x/xi or xi[1]), Boulogne, Bibl. mun., MS 189, fol. 1, and even in a much earlier manuscript, possibly from Kent (*s.*viii): Cambridge, Corpus Christi Coll., MS 173, fols 57–83, at fols 82[v]–83[v], in two versions; a tenth-century copy, possibly from Worcester, is preserved in Cambridge, Corpus Christi Coll., MS 448, fol. 87. For the poem see Bischoff, p. 154, McGinn, pp. 14–15, and D. Schaller and E. Köngsen, *Initia Carminum Latinorum Saeculo Undecimo Antiquorum* (Göttingen, 1977), no. 8495.

[27] For these see *Die Hirtenbriefe Ælfrics*, ed. B. Fehr (1914), repr. with a suppl. by P. Clemoes (Darmstadt, 1966), pp. 256–8; *Die 'Institutes of Polity, Civil and Ecclesiastical'*, ed. K. H. Jost (Bern, 1959), pp. 223–47; R. E. Reynolds, 'The De Officiis VII Graduum: its Origin and Early Medieval Development', *Medieval Studies*, 34 (1972), 113–51, and his 'At Sixes and Sevens – and Eights and Nines: the Sacred Mathematics of Sacred Orders in the Early Middle Ages', *Speculum*, 54 (1979), 669–84.

[28] Edited in *Councils and Synods with other Documents Relating to the English Church I. A.D. 871–1204. Part I: 871–1066*, ed. D. Whitelock, M. Brett and C. N. L. Brooke (Oxford, 1981), pp. 88–92; cf. D. Whitelock, 'The Appointment of Dunstan as Archbishop of Canterbury', in her *History, Law and Literature in 10th–11th Century England* (London, 1981), no. IV.

A.III and not, as Förster[29] suggested, to the bilingual copy of chapter 4 of the Rule that occurs as article 25 in Tiberius.

[14] If there is any connection with Tiberius, then its article 19 and others would answer this description.

[15] Very probably a glossed copy of the *Regularis Concordia*, rather than a glossed *De ecclesiasticis officiis* by Amalarius.[30]

Max Förster made an attempt to explain entry number 297 in the Eastry catalogue as a description of what he considered an originally independent manuscript that was later to form the second part (fols 57–116) of Tiberius A.III; accordingly, loss of leaves or quires would have caused the disappearance of items [6], [8–11] and [15] in the manuscript. The weaknesses of this hypothesis have recently been pointed out by Lucia Kornexl,[31] and we should perhaps follow, at least for Eastry 297, the more sober assessment of Dom Thomas Symons who thought that 'Batta's volumes and Tib A. 3 are probably sister codices'.[32] Yet some doubts remain: the contents as listed in Eastry 297 seem suspiciously close to those of Tiberius A.III, and – as I am going to point out later on – the *Examinatio episcopi* is an unusual item in its textual surroundings. How precise and trustworthy was the compiler of the Eastry catalogue?

Two personal names are connected with the history of Tiberius A.III and have to be considered: Eadwi and Ælfric Bata. A late-eleventh-century hand has entered in the margin of fol. 164 – 'Eadwi m[. . .] me ah', convincingly restored by Professor Pfaff to *Eadwi munuc me ah*.[33] Identifying individual Anglo-Saxons by means of their names is a tricky business; there are no surnames, and bynames, if they existed, were probably not used consistently. Nevertheless, there are good reasons for thinking that the inscription – at the beginning of the *Memoriale qualiter* – refers to somebody who must have been highly respected as scribe and scholar at Christ Church, Canterbury: *Eaduuius cognomento Basan*, as he calls himself on fol. 183[v] of the Gospel manuscript at Hanover (Kestner-Museum W. M. XXIa, 36). He was active at Christ Church from not later than 1018 and certainly in the twenties and thirties of the eleventh century; we owe our knowledge of this excellent scribe to T. A. M. Bishop, who was able to identify his work in 11 manuscripts or records.[34]

[29] See Kornexl, *Regularis Concordia*, p. cxxix and n. 65.

[30] As was suggested by R. M. Wilson, *The Lost Literature of Medieval England*, 2nd edn (London, 1970), p. 78.

[31] M. Förster, 'Vom Fortleben antiker Sammellunare', *Anglia*, 67–68 (1944), 1–171, at 49, and cf. n. 29, above.

[32] *Regularis Concordia*, ed. T. Symons (London, 1953), p. lvii.

[33] R. W. Pfaff, 'Eadui Basan: Scriptorum Princeps?', in *England in the Eleventh Century*, ed. C. Hicks (Stamford, 1992), pp. 267–83, esp. 280–81.

[34] T. A. M. Bishop, *English Caroline Minuscule* (Oxford, 1971), p. 22, nos 24 and 25; see also T. A. Heslop, 'The Production of *De Luxe* Manuscripts and the Patronage of King Cnut and Queen Emma', *ASE*, 19 (1990), 151–95, and D. N. Dumville, *English Caroline Script and Monastic History: Studies in Benedictinism A.D. 950–1030* (Woodbridge, 1993), ch. 4. For attempts to explain Eadwi's byname see Dumville, pp. 123–4, and Pfaff, 'Eadui Basan', p. 280.

We do not know if Eadwi was still alive by the time Tiberius A.III was written, and he certainly was not among its scribes, but it does not seem impossible that he was involved somehow in its production or, perhaps, even owned it (*'me ah'*). In any case, there is a great deal to be said for Richard Pfaff's claim that Eadwi's reputation at Canterbury lasted even into the twelfth century;[35] apart from this, it seems possible now to show not only that Eadwi was a member of the Christ Church community, but that he came from somewhere in South East England, judging by a text he had written apparently without having to follow an exemplar.[36]

Ælfric Bata is a more problematic figure. We have seen his name in the headings of numbers 296 and 297 of the Eastry catalogue, and it is even more prominent at the head of and in the contents table on fol. 117 of Tiberius A.III, preceding the Rule of St Benedict (my italics):

Eluricus Bate (head of page, *s.* xi/xii)
(Table *s.* xii *in.*; references to corresponding articles of Tiberius in square brackets):
Hec continentur in hoc uolumine
Regula sancti Benedicti glosata anglice [1]
Regula *elurici bate* glosata anglice [6]
De significationibus somniorum per ordinem alphabeti [7a]
De obseruacione lune in rebus agendis et in natalibus puerorum [7b, etc.]
Item alia plura tam anglice quam latine [8–31?].

Here we are on safer ground because we have a proper name and a byname, and we may assume that the Eastry catalogue and the manuscript entries refer to the same person, who is known to have composed several colloquies designed for teaching purposes, and who at the beginning of one of these called himself a pupil of the great Ælfric 'qui meus fuit magister'. But he has also been suspected of foul practices, trying to despoil Christ Church, Canterbury, as we are told in an incident reported by Dunstan's biographers Osbern and Eadmer.[37] Neither is his byname particularly flattering; Gösta Tengvik[38] relates it to OE *batt* 'bat, cudgel' and suggests that it denotes a person of stout and heavy appearance. What does he have to do with Tiberius A.III? It seems certain that Ælfric Bata taught in a monastic school in the first half of the eleventh century, and he may have served for a time as master at

---

[35] Cf. n. 33 above, and R. W. Pfaff, 'The Calendar', in *The Eadwine Psalter. Text, Image and Monastic Culture in Twelfth-Century Canterbury*, ed. M. Gibson, T. A. Heslop and R. W. Pfaff (London, 1992), pp. 62–87, at 85–7.

[36] Printed by F. E. Harmer, *Anglo-Saxon Writs* (Manchester, 1952), pp. 181–2, no. 26; cf. N. Brooks, *The Early History of the Church of Canterbury* (Leicester, 1984), pp. 288–90.

[37] Kornexl, *Regularis Concordia*, pp. cxxx–cxxxiv, has dealt with what is known about Ælfric Bata, and what he may have had to do with Tiberius A.III.

[38] *Old English Bynames*, Nomina Germanica, 4 (Uppsala, 1938), pp. 287–8. For other interpretations of *Bata* see Kornexl, *Regularis Concordia*, p. cxxx, n. 68.

Christ Church, Canterbury.[39] His name at the top of fol. 117 in Tiberius A.III (and in the headings of Eastry 296 and 297, but these may simply derive from the Tiberius entry) would indicate that he owned or assembled this collection of texts, but why he should have been considered the author of the *Regularis Concordia* (item 2 in the contents list) is difficult to explain.

Handwriting and illustrations

In a book dedicated to one of the great palaeographers of our century one would naturally expect a word about possible conclusions as to the origin of our manuscript, based on the handwriting of its scribes. Apart from the fact that any such pronouncements should be left to experts in the field it would appear that so far no pertinent evidence has been found. The study of Anglo-Saxon handwriting has made great progress in the last fifty years or so, and it has become possible to identify individual scribes in a considerable number of books written in the tenth and eleventh centuries in England. However, as Richard Gameson has recently noted, 'none of the various hands represented in the manuscript [Tiberius A.III] has yet been identified elsewhere'.[40]

Of some interest for our question are the syntactical glosses in the copy of the Rule of St Benedict in Tiberius A.III. This type of glossing was first systematically studied by Fred Robinson and Michael Korhammer. It seems remarkable that most of the eleventh-century English manuscripts employing the sequential, alphabetic system of syntactical glossing (Korhammer's *S-Konstruktionshilfen*) come from Canterbury, and it may be even more remarkable that Korhammer found within this group three manuscripts linked by the specific method of using the same letter for indicating syntactically closely related words; these three are Cambridge, Corpus Christi College, MS 214, fols 45–46[v], an early-eleventh-century Boethius, probably from Canterbury; Cambridge, University Library, MS Gg.5.35, the well-known mid-eleventh-century 'classbook' from St Augustine's, Canterbury , and Tiberius A.III.[41]

Much has been written about the two full-page illustrations in the Tiberius manuscript, and they have been frequently reproduced, mostly in black and white.[42]

---

[39] See Brooks, *Early History*, p. 266.

[40] R. Gameson, 'English Manuscript Art in the Late Eleventh Century: Canterbury and its Context', in *Canterbury and the Norman Conquest, Churches, Saints and Scholars 1066–1109*, ed. R. Eales and R. Sharpe (London, 1995), pp. 95–144, at 111–12, n. 55.

[41] M. Korhammer, 'Mittelalterliche Konstruktionshilfen und altenglische Wortstellung', *Scriptorium*, 34 (1980), 18–58, at 36.

[42] For a bibliography of earlier work (before 1976), discussion and reproductions see E. Temple, *Anglo-Saxon Manuscripts 900–1066* (London, 1976), pp. 118–19, no. 100, and pls 313 and 314; good reproductions, also of the two closely related pictures in Arundel 155 and Durham B.III.32, are in C. R. Dodwell, *The Canterbury School of Illumination 1066–1200* (Cambridge, 1954), pls 2 and 3. For

This is not the place to review the extensive discussion of these pictures, but there can be no doubt that they represent work produced at Canterbury. The first picture, on fol. 117ᵛ, in full colour, but now badly damaged, serves as a frontispiece to the glossed Rule of St Benedict. It depicts St Benedict enthroned, expounding his Rule to a group of three monks standing on his left. Below on the left, a kneeling monk is seen embracing the saint's feet, while to the right a fifth monk, falling to his knees, holds a long, winding scroll.

The second illustration, on fol. 2ᵛ, a tinted drawing, is also a frontispiece, this time to the *Regularis Concordia*, showing a king seated together with an archbishop (on his left) and a bishop (on his right) holding a winding scroll, while another scroll is being held by a genuflecting monk underneath. There can hardly be any doubt that the seated figures are King Edgar, Dunstan and Æthelwold, and that the monk is intended as a representative of the English monastic communities receiving the *Regularis Concordia* which, together with the Rule of St Benedict, was to become the guidebook of their daily lives.

The two miniatures in Tiberius A.III were not the original creations of one or two artists working at Canterbury around 1050. They probably continue an iconographic tradition that goes back to the tenth-century English Benedictine reform. Professor Deshman has argued convincingly that it was Æthelwold himself who, at Winchester, devised the prototypes of the two pictures: the one to serve as the frontispiece for his bilingual edition of the Rule, the other to go with a dedication copy of the *Regularis Concordia*. John Higgitt would prefer to link the archetypes of the illustrations with Glastonbury, but his evidence appears less compelling.[43]

For our purpose here, however, we want to be certain about the place where the Tiberius pictures were executed. Considering the evidence we have for a close relationship with illustrations in other near-contemporary English manuscripts, and considering what else is known about the history and contents of Tiberius A.III, only one of the two Canterbury houses seems likely to be the place where the frontispieces could have been drawn and painted. Dr Budny has brought forward arguments for identifying the artist of both Tiberius pictures with the one who, at St Augustine's about the middle of the eleventh century, supplied a full-page painted representation of the evangelist Mark on fol. 30ᵛ of London, BL, MS Royal 1.E.vi, a Gospel-book written in the first half of the ninth century; this artist's work is also found in three other manuscripts, two of them with a St Augustine's provenance. I must leave the consideration of Dr Budny's claim to the professional art historians, one of whom,

---

descriptions and more recent work see T. H. Ohlgren, *Insular and Anglo-Saxon Illuminated Manuscripts. An Iconographic Catalogue c. A.D. 625 to 1100* (New York, 1986), p. 271, no. 205; Kornexl, *Regularis Concordia*, pp. cxxxviii–cxli, and the references in the following notes.

[43] Deshman, see n. 2 above, and now also in his *The Benedictional of Æthelwold* (Princeton, 1995), ch. 6; J. Higgitt, 'Glastonbury, Dunstan, Monasticism and Manuscripts', *Art History*, 2 (1979), 275–90, esp. 283–7.

at least, has expressed some doubts.[44] But I feel, at any rate, that we must not ignore the close links between the Tiberius illustrations and pictures in two further manuscripts.

In London, BL, MS Arundel 155, a psalter written between 1012 and 1023 at Christ Church, Canterbury, by Eadwi Basan, we find on fol. 133, preceding the canticles, a full-page miniature partly painted and partly in tinted outline drawing, probably made by Eadwi.[45] The subject is the same as that of the Benedict group on fol. 117[v] of Tiberius A.III, and the correspondence between the two illustrations is such that one is tempted to believe that the Tiberius artist copied and adapted the Arundel miniature; this, apparently, is what Reginald Dodwell and Elzbieta Temple thought. Others have been more cautious, but Robert Deshman's suggestion that in Arundel we have an earlier copy of the archetype of the picture is the least we can assume[46] – and if so, it seems reasonable to think that this archetype must have been available in some form at Christ Church, Canterbury, when the Tiberius painter was active.

A similar problem of relationship, this time pointing in the opposite direction, obtains in the case of the Tiberius illustration preceding the *Regularis Concordia*, and here the arguments for a direct relationship are even stronger. In Durham, Dean and Chapter Library, MS B.III.32, a Latin hymnal and monastic canticles, all glossed in Old English, followed by a copy of Ælfric's *Grammar* (both written about the middle of the eleventh century and combined into one volume from the beginning), a full-page drawing introduces the *Grammar* on fol. 56[v], i.e. the verso of the first folio of the first of the 11 quires of this text.[47] This picture, again a tinted outline drawing, corresponds to that on fol. 2[v] of Tiberius A.III in nearly every detail, except that the king – no doubt King Edgar – has been eliminated from the composition. The omission appears logical and necessary, since a 'disputation picture', as it has been called by Mrs Temple, even involving two haloed ecclesiastics, must have appeared a more adequate frontispiece for what by the time it was copied had become the standard handbook of Latin grammar and general linguistics (if one may choose this modern term) in Anglo-Saxon England.[48] For those who might, understandably, find a picture of Dunstan and Æthelwold prefacing Ælfric's *Grammar* somewhat incongruous, it seems helpful to notice that Ælfric, close to the beginning of his work, dealing with the parts of speech in general, refers to *Eadgarus, Aðelwoldus* and *Dunstan*, and that he also expressly names the two bishops in his two Prefaces.[49]

It has recently been stated that the Durham book 'has been assigned to Christ

---

[44] Gameson, see n. 40 above. (Cambridge, Corpus Christi Coll., MS 389 and London, BL, Cotton MS Claudius B.IV are the manuscripts with a St Augustine's provenance.)

[45] Temple, *Anglo-Saxon MSS*, no. 66; Ohlgren (as n. 42 above), no. 171.

[46] Temple, *Anglo-Saxon MSS*, p. 118; Dodwell, *Canterbury School*, p. 4; Deshman, 'Benedictus Monarcha', p. 211.

[47] Temple, *Anglo-Saxon MSS*, no. 101; Ohlgren (as n. 42 above), no. 206.

[48] See Gneuss (as n. 25 above), pp. 13–18.

[49] *Ælfrics Grammatik und Glossar*, ed. J. Zupitza, 2nd edn with intro. by H. Gneuss (Berlin, 1966), pp. 1, 3, and 8.

Church on the strength of this very similarity',[50] i.e. of the illustrations in Durham, B.III.32 and Tiberius A.III, but as I pointed out nearly thirty years ago,[51] there is enough independent evidence that enables us to locate the Durham hymnal and grammar at Canterbury: the Kentish dialectal forms in the glosses to the hymns, and in Ælfric's *Grammar*; the textual relationship between the copies of the *Grammar* in Durham B.III.32 and London, BL, MS Harley 107 (contemporary with Durham, and also with Kentish forms); the structure of the Durham hymnal, a developed form of the earlier Canterbury hymnal of the Bosworth Psalter (London, BL, Additional MS 37517); the hymn for St Dunstan, *Ave Dunstane presulum*, found only in manuscripts of the eleventh to fourteenth centuries written and used at Christ Church, Canterbury; three hymns for St Augustine of Canterbury, which, as far as we know, are not identical with those used at St Augustine's; a textual change in a hymn for the dedication of a church, introducing St Augustine and his companions. Even if an origin at St Augustine's[52] for the Durham manuscript cannot be excluded, the combined evidence speaks for Christ Church, and this is also where its miniature on fol. 56ᵛ may well have been copied from that on fol. 2ᵛ of Tiberius A.III.

Finally, it should be mentioned that Dr Ker in his admirable description of Tiberius A.III noted that 'The two leaves containing drawings, [fols] 2, 117, were probably single half-sheets'. If we assume that relations between Christ Church and St Augustine's in the decades before the Norman Conquest were not as strained as has sometimes been thought,[53] we should not be surprised to find an artist at St Augustine's employed to work on an illustration commissioned by Christ Church. So far as the two pictures in Tiberius A.III are concerned, the evidence seems to me to be greatly in favour of a Christ Church origin, or at least a commission for inclusion in a Christ Church manuscript.

Contents and textual affiliations

While the later medieval provenance of Tiberius A.III seems fairly clear, and while its illustrations no doubt point to Canterbury as its place of origin, it is now time to look more closely at its contents in general and at the affiliation of its texts in particular, and especially at the liturgical evidence.

More than half of the manuscript is taken up by texts, largely glossed in Old

---

[50] Gameson, see n. 40 above.

[51] Gneuss, *Hymnar und Hymnen*, esp. pp. 85–90; see now also the edition of the hymnal by I. B. Milfull, *The Hymns of the Anglo-Saxon Church* (Cambridge, 1996). The canticles were edited by M. Korhammer, *Die monastischen Cantica im Mittelalter und ihre altenglischen Interlinearversionen* (München, 1976).

[52] This is what Christopher Hohler would support, see n. 21 above.

[53] See R. Sharpe, 'The Setting of St Augustine's Translation, 1091', in *Canterbury and the Norman Conquest* (as n. 40 above), pp. 1–13, at 4.

English, that are meant to serve the needs of a monastic community: the Rule of St Benedict and the four texts accompanying and supplementing it, the Admonition by Pseudo-Fulgentius, *Memoriale qualiter, De festivitatibus anni*, the compilation known as *Collectio capitularis* of 818 or 819,[54] followed by the *Regularis Concordia*. Other items that certainly belong in this category are the *Indicia monasterialia* (art. 22), the chapter from the Rule (art. 25), and most probably Ælfric's *Colloquy*. Also, it seems reasonable to assume that vespers and lauds of All Saints (art. 10a) and the full Office of the Virgin (art. 30) at the time of writing of Tiberius A.III would hardly be performed outside a Benedictine house in England. I shall demonstrate later on why the *Examinatio episcopi* (art. 20) must have been employed in the context of a monastic institution.

All this would certainly strengthen the case for a possible origin of the Tiberius manuscript at Christ Church, Canterbury. Exactly when the southern metropolitan's cathedral became a monastic house has been debated for quite some time,[55] but whatever the differing opinions have been, it seems certain that by the time Tiberius A.III was written, Christ Church had become a cathedral priory served by monks and not by secular canons, and our manuscript would therefore provide reading and reference material apt to serve such a community.

Examining the textual relationship of the various items in our manuscript might promise to afford us some information on where to look for its place of origin. However, certain conditions would have to be met before any such information could be regarded as trustworthy: several Anglo-Saxon copies of a particular text, or continuous interlinear gloss, would have to be extant, with three of these as a minimum; the stemmatic relationship of these copies would have to be clear, even if we were to deny that a stemma in the traditional sense could be drawn up; there must also be some certainty about the places of origin of the other copies.

Tiberius A.III contains several texts – some of them rare – in common [1.] with the New Minster Prayerbook of Ælfwine, London, BL, Cotton MSS Titus D.XXVI and D.XXVII, probably written between 1023 and 1035 (arts 7a–g; 8b; 12; 13); [2.] with additions made in the first half of the eleventh century to the Psalter manuscript London, BL, MS Royal 2.B.v, which certainly was at Christ Church, Canterbury in the eleventh century (arts 9a–b, 9d–f); [3.] with the Wulfstan Portiforium, Cambridge, Corpus Christi College, MS 391 (arts 7c, 7h, 9d) written at Worcester in the later eleventh century. Relations with the Royal Psalter are fairly close, but they are not direct relations, and it is uncertain where the Royal manuscript originated about the middle of the tenth century (Winchester?) and when exactly it reached Canterbury.[56]

---

[54] See now also H. Mordek, *Bibliotheca capitularium regum Francorum manuscripta*, MGH Hilfsmittel, 15 (München, 1994), pp. 223–5.

[55] On this difficult problem see now Brooks, *Early History*, pp. 251–60.

[56] For the texts and the relationship with the three manuscripts see Ker, *Catalogue*; Ælfric's *De Temporibus Anni*, ed. H. Henel, EETS (OS), 213 (1942), pp. xii–xiii; *Ælfwine's Prayerbook*, ed. B.

There is some more compelling evidence available, however. This comes first of all from the Latin text of the Rule of St Benedict. It is the kind of text that would be particularly subject to contamination,[57] and no stemma of the surviving 12 Anglo-Saxon copies can be drawn up. But by calculating the percentage of shared readings for all possible combinations of two manuscripts, Mechthild Gretsch has been able to show that the copy closest to the text of Tiberius is that in London, BL, MS Harley 5431, written *c.*1000 at St Augustine's, Canterbury.[58] This may not be conclusive proof in order to establish a Canterbury origin of the text of the Rule in Tiberius A.III, and the supplements to the Rule even point in a different direction: the Tiberius texts of the *Memoriale qualiter* and the *Collectio capitularis* are closest to those in the Abingdon manuscript (Cambridge, Corpus Christi College, MS 57 (*s.* x/xi)) and differ from Harley 5431 and London, BL, Cotton MS Titus A.IV (*s.* xi *med.*, from Winchester?), while the still unlocalized Cambridge, University Library, MS Ll.1.14 (*s.* xi²) shares readings with the *Collectio* in Tiberius, but not with its *Memoriale*.[59]

There is still clearer evidence. The *Traumlunar* in Tiberius (art. 7h) is closely related to another manuscript from Christ Church, Canterbury, London, BL, Cotton MS Caligula A.XV, fols 120–153 (with the *Lunar* on fols 131ᵛ–132), whereas the text preserved in Corpus 391, pp. 720–721, differs considerably from the two others.[60] Heinrich Henel has noted that among the seven manuscripts containing Ælfric's *De temporibus anni* Tiberius A.III and Caligula A.XV, fols 120–153, belong in the same branch of transmission.[61] While here the relationship is not close enough in order to draw definite conclusions, we find that two other texts by Ælfric are considered as being derived from south-eastern exemplars by experts in the field of Ælfric studies: the Homily for Palm Sunday and the second Old English Pastoral Letter to Archbishop Wulfstan (arts 16 and 29).[62]

Günzel, HBS, **108** (1993), and *The Portiforium of Saint Wulstan*, ed. A. Hughes, HBS, **89** and **90** (1958–60).

[57] Owing to the daily reading of a section of the Rule in the chapter office, and possibly to learning the text of the Rule by heart, as prescribed in the *Collectio capitularis* (art. 5 in Tiberius A.III), section II: 'Ut monachi omnes qui possunt *memoriter* regulam discant' (my italics; Mechthild Gretsch drew my attention to this injunction).

[58] M. Gretsch, *Die Regula Sancti Benedicti in England und ihre altenglische Übersetzung* (München, 1973), pp. 94–107, and her 'Æthelwold's Translation of the *Regula Sancti Benedicti* and its Latin Exemplar', *ASE*, 3 (1974), 125–51. An exceptional case of agreement in the text of the Rule between Tiberius and CCCC, MS 56 is the long addition in ch. VII.55, noted by P. Meyvaert, 'Towards a History of the Textual Transmission of the *Regula S. Benedicti*', *Scriptorium*, 17 (1963), 83–110, at 101, and by Hanslik (see App. 1 below, art. 1), p. lxiii.

[59] See the critical editions of arts 3 and 5 listed in App. 1 below. For the place of the English manuscripts in the transmission of the *Collectio capitularis*, see now Mordek (as n. 54 above), p. 416.

[60] See M. Förster, 'Die altenglischen Traumlunare', *Englische Studien*, 60 (1925–6), 58–93, at 79–86.

[61] Henel (as n. 56 above), pp. xxxv–xxxviii.

[62] *Ælfric's Catholic Homilies. The Second Series*, ed. M. Godden, EETS (SS), 5 (1979), p. lvi; P. Clemoes in his supplement to the reprint of *Die Hirtenbriefe Ælfrics* (as n. 27 above), p. cxliv.

The results so far obtained from textual evidence are not negligible and yet may seem disappointing when one considers the overall number of texts in Tiberius A.III. The reasons for this are not far to seek. Many of these texts are either unique or extant in not more than two or three Anglo-Saxon copies; where more copies have survived, we have to reckon with the loss of others, representing various intermediate stages of the respective textual transmission. As so often, we shall see, however, that the evidence coming from liturgical texts is far more informative and, as I shall argue, in not a few cases even incontrovertible.

Horae BVM and the litany

For the liturgiologist, Tiberius A.III is of utmost importance in being the first witness of a full Marian Office (art. 30) in England, and it is here that I find conclusive evidence for the usage of Christ Church, Canterbury, in the hymns, in two prayers and an antiphon, and in the litany following the collect at compline.[63]

For the hymns, it is instructive to compare them with those in the contemporary or somewhat later Office BVM in London, BL, MS Royal 2.B.v (probably from the Nunnaminster, Winchester), and with the earlier but much shorter Marian Office in Titus D.XXVII. Of the eight hymns required for a complete cursus, Tiberius and Royal have only four in common, but all are used for different hours. Tiberius has four hymns that do not occur in the Winchester-type hymnals in tenth- and eleventh-century England, and only one of them is in Royal 2.B.v, but all are found in other Canterbury manuscripts: (90) Prime: *Maria mater domini* (in Royal for nocturns); (91) Terce: *Gabrihel dei archangelus*; (92) Sext: *Maria celi regina*; (93) None: *Maria virgo virginum*. Moreover, Royal 2.B.v employs *Ave maris stella* for vespers (Tiberius for lauds), and the same hymn in the short Office in Titus D.XXVII, a Winchester (New Minster) manuscript, no doubt comes from a vespers Office. Finally, the version of this hymn in Royal 2.B.v, but not in Tiberius, lacks stanzas 2 and 6, as in other Winchester-type books, whereas the full version in Tiberius agrees with that in other Canterbury manuscripts.[64]

In the same Marian Office in Tiberius, both Dunstan and Ælfheah, the archbishop of Canterbury martyred in 1012, are invoked three times (not including the litany which I am going to discuss separately): first, in an antiphon belonging to the suffrage of All Saints, following lauds of the Virgin, fol. 110; secondly, in a collect for

---

[63] For a facs. and printed edn of the Office, see n. 19 above; for its analysis, see J. B. L. Tolhurst, *Introduction to the English Monastic Breviaries*, HBS, 80 (1942; repr. 1993), 120–29, and Clayton, *Cult of the Virgin*, pp. 65–81.

[64] For the hymns in the Marian Office see Gneuss, *Hymnar und Hymnen*, pp. 109–13, 349–50, 374–7. The numbers in parentheses refer to this edn.

All Saints at the end of the vespers of the Virgin, fol. 112[65]; thirdly, in one of the prayers following the litany at compline, fol. 114[r-v].

In the case of the prayer after the litany it can be shown conclusively that this was specially adapted for no other place than Christ Church, Canterbury, while we can exclude St Augustine's, as the name of one of its patrons – Augustinus – is not found in any of the three liturgical pieces just listed, and as the litany, too, speaks against such an attribution. As for the prayer on fol. 114[r-v], this is the text in Tiberius A.III (my punctuation):

> Familiam huius sacri cenobii quesumus, Domine, intercedente beato Benedicto abbate et sancto Dunstano archipresule nostro atque sancto Ælfego martiro tuo cum omnibus sanctis, perpetuo guberna moderamine ut adsit nobis et in securitate cautela et inter aspera fortitudo. per.

This prayer is frequently found elsewhere. It appears as a collect for a mass *pro congregatione* or similarly designated in the Leofric Missal (Oxford, Bodl. Lib., MS Bodley 579), the Winchcombe Sacramentary (Orléans, Bibl. mun., MS 127), the 'Missal' of Robert of Jumièges (Rouen, Bibl. mun., MS 274 [Y.6]), the St Augustine's 'Missal' (Cambridge, Corpus Christi Coll., MS 270) and much later in the Westminster Missal (London, Westminster Abbey, MS 37, datable 1383–84), and it serves as a private prayer in London, BL, Cotton MS Galba A.XIV (s. xi[1]), in Titus D.XXVI, and in Corpus 391. Intercessions of various saints and of the Virgin are invoked in the versions of these manuscripts, but nowhere do we find either Dunstan or Ælfheah or both among them.

On fols 112[v]–113[v] of Tiberius A.III, the collect for compline in the Marian Office is followed by a litany.[66] The names here invoked are, as usual, in five sections: (1) the Trinity, the Virgin and the archangels; (2) the apostles and evangelists; (3) martyrs; (4) confessors; (5) virgins. Those that are of interest for our enquiry in sections three to five are, in their vocative forms:

(3) Ælfeage (third of eighteen martyrs) and, at the end, Albane, Eadmunde, Eadwarde;

(4) Benedicte (in first place), Gregorii (sixth place), AUGUSTINE, DUNSTANE (seventh and eighth, both in capitals), Audoene, Pauline, Swyðune, Fursee, Cuthberhte (nos 9–13 of fifteen confessors);

---

[65] This prayer is also found in services for the day (14 Sept.) of Saints Cornelius and Cyprianus in the Leofric Missal (Oxford, Bodl. Lib., MS Bodley 579), the Missal of Robert of Jumièges (Rouen, Bibl. mun., MS 274 [Y.6]), the Winchcombe Sacramentary (Orléans, Bibl. mun., MS 127), the New Minster Missal (Le Havre, Bibl. mun., MS 330), the Canterbury Missal (Cambridge, Corpus Christi Coll., MS 270) – in the corresponding prayer text in all these the intercession of the two saints is expressly invoked – and in the Wulfstan Portiforium (CCCC, MS 391).

[66] Pr. M. Lapidge, *Anglo-Saxon Litanies of the Saints*, HBS, 106 (1991), 174–7, no. XVIII.

(5) MARGARETA (tenth place, in capitals), Astroberhta, Æðeldryða, Mildryða, Brigida, Columchilla[67] (nos 12–16 of sixteen virgins).

There can hardly be any doubt that this is a litany compiled for Christ Church, Canterbury. This is indicated by the position of Ælfheah and by the capitals for Augustine (here certainly St Augustine of Canterbury) and Dunstan, and it is confirmed when one compares other Canterbury evidence for the liturgical role of the saints listed above, and also for Saints Blasius and Salvius, who occur among the sixteen martyrs of Tiberius A.III. Such evidence is found in:

1. Litanies in eleventh-century manuscripts from Christ Church, Canterbury: London, BL, MS Arundel 155 (an early-twelfth-century addition, recopied from an earlier litany?); Cotton MS Claudius A.III, fols 9–18 and 87–105 ('Claudius Pontifical II'); Cambridge, Corpus Christi College, MS 44, a pontifical that may have been written at St Augustine's, Canterbury, but apparently for use at the Cathedral.[68]

2. Calendars from Christ Church, Canterbury: MS Arundel 155,[69] and Cambridge, Trinity College, MS R.17.1, the Eadwine Psalter, a twelfth-century book whose calendar, however, according to Richard Pfaff, has an eleventh-century basis.[70]

3. The sanctorale of the eleventh-century Christ Church Benedictional in London, BL, MS Harley 2892,[71] which includes new compositions for feasts of saints with cults at Canterbury Cathedral and also appearing in the Tiberius litany: St Stephen (two new blessings), St Ælfheah (five), St Edward the martyr, St Benedict (two blessings for the translation), St Gregory, St Augustine of Canterbury, St Dunstan (three), St Ouen (Audoenus), St Cuthbert, St Agnes (two), St Lucia, St Austroberhta, St Etheldreda, St Mildred.

4. Evidence for relics of saints owned by Christ Church, Canterbury. These include apart, of course, from Dunstan and Ælfheah – King Edmund of East Anglia, Saints Ouen, Swithun, Fursey and Austroberhta.[72]

---

[67] Presumably in error for *Columcille* (St Columba of Iona).

[68] Lapidge, *Anglo-Saxon Litanies*, nos XIII, XV, and II.

[69] Printed by F. Wormald, *English Kalendars before 1100 A.D.*, HBS, 72 (1934; repr. 1988), 169–81.

[70] See the excellent treatment by Pfaff, 'The Calendar' (as n. 35 above). The twelfth-century Christ Church calendar in Oxford, Bodl. Lib., MS Add. C.260 has now been edited by T. A. Heslop, 'The Canterbury Calendars and the Norman Conquest', in *Canterbury and the Norman Conquest* (as n. 40 above), pp. 53–85, at 70–77. The origin of the calendar written presumably at Christ Church, *c.*1000, and prefixed to the Bosworth Psalter, London, BL, Add. MS 37517, appears to remain controversial; see now N. Orchard, 'The Bosworth Psalter and the St. Augustine's Missal', *Canterbury and the Norman Conquest*, pp. 87–94, who opts for St Augustine's abbey.

[71] Edited by R. M. Woolley, *The Canterbury Benedictional*, HBS, 51 (1917; repr. 1995). Cf. Prescott (as n. 13 above), pp. 132–3 and 148–55.

[72] See D. H. Farmer, *The Oxford Dictionary of Saints*, 3rd edn (Oxford, 1992); J. W. Legg and W. H. St John Hope, *Inventories of Christ Church, Canterbury* (London, 1902). For the relics of Audoenus (St Ouen) see also T. A. Heslop (as n. 34 above), pp. 183–4.

There is thus nothing to contradict Francis Wormald's view, expressed in a letter to Heinrich Henel about sixty years ago: 'Personally I am convinced that it is a litany of Christ Church, Canterbury'.[73] Nevertheless, as so often happens with liturgical manuscripts, the evidence in Tiberius A.III is not as clear-cut as one could wish. Thus I cannot explain why Wilfrid, some of whose relics had been translated to Canterbury in the tenth century, is not included in the Tiberius litany; however, the main problem appears to lie in the fact that the names of only three saints are in capitals: St Augustine, St Dunstan and, in the tenth place of 17 virgins, 'Sancta MARGARETA'. This treatment of her name should probably be linked to the Old English life of St Margaret on fols 73ᵛ–77ᵛ of our manuscript; there are other indications of the veneration of St Margaret in Canterbury or Kent from the later tenth century onwards, especially in the entry of her feast (together with that of St Wulmar) on 20 July in the calendar of Arundel 155, datable before 1203, marked 'xii lc.', i.e. nocturns of 12 lessons, which presumably refers to the feast of St Margaret. Another Old English life of the saint is extant in Cambridge, Corpus Christi College, MS 303, written in the first half of the twelfth century, probably at Rochester, with traces of Kentish dialect forms in the text.[74] By the time Tiberius A.III was written, the cult of St Margaret had become widespread in England, and there were relics of her in several places. If such relics could be shown to have existed in pre-Conquest Canterbury, an explanation for the saint's entry in the Tiberius litany and for the inclusion of her Old English life might be found. It is perhaps of some interest that Margaret's name also appears in capitals in the calendar of Oxford, Bodleian Library, MS Douce 296, written about the middle of the eleventh century, probably for use at Crowland in Lincolnshire.[75]

The *Examinatio episcopi*

The liturgical evidence presented so far is reinforced by a text (art. 20)[76] that seems somewhat oddly placed, between Old English homiletic pieces and directions for a confessor, on fols 93ᵛ–94ᵛ of Tiberius A.III. It begins with the rubric 'Incipit ordo uel examinatio in ordinatione episcopi' and is part of the ordination services found – together with other rites and ceremonies – in pontificals and, earlier, in sacramentaries. Why was this piece from a liturgical book copied into our manuscript?

In the Gallican liturgy, the actual ordination and consecration of a bishop, in the form of an extended mass, was preceded by an examination of the future bishop, in which he was made to promise to fulfil his episcopal duties, to lead an exemplary life

---

[73] Printed by Henel (as n. 56), p. xii, n. 2.
[74] See Clayton and Magennis (as n. 3 above), esp. ch. 5 and pp. 93–4, 105–6.
[75] Wormald, *Kalendars*, p. 260.
[76] Printed by M. Richter, *Canterbury Professions*, Canterbury and York Society, 67 (1973), 118–20.

and to be charitable to the poor; he had to confirm, among other things, his belief in the doctrine of the Trinity and in the divine authorship of the Scriptures.[77] It can easily be seen that such an examination would serve the same purpose as the professions of faith and obedience which survive in considerable numbers from Canterbury, having been deposited there between c.796 and 870 (and probably much earlier), and from 1070 onwards, when the practice may have been reintroduced by Archbishop Lanfranc.[78]

From the tenth century onwards, in England and on the continent, we find pontificals in the form of separate liturgical books, often beautifully executed, and a remarkable number of such books written in England in the second half of the tenth and in the eleventh centuries are still extant.[79] A thorough, systematic study of these is still needed, and especially, for our purpose, a study examining the form and development of the ordination of a bishop. What follows can therefore only be of a tentative character, but should be sufficient to explain the significance of the *Examinatio* text in Tiberius A.III here to be discussed.

We encounter the ordination of a bishop in all those English pontifical copies that are complete, but only very few exhibit the *Examinatio*, which clearly was not part of the originally English ceremonial collections. It was, however, included in a pontifical newly compiled around the middle of the tenth century, probably at Mainz, and this type of book soon gained the status of an authoritative collection that was widely copied and observed. This is the so-called *Pontificale Romano-Germanicum*,[80] of which copies written in Germany in the first half or middle of the eleventh century also reached England: London, BL, Cotton MS Vitellius E.XII, fols 116–152, from Cologne, now fragmentary, which came to York and later to Exeter; Cotton MS Tiberius C.I, fols 43–203, which found its way to Sherborne and from there to Salisbury and whose extensive late-eleventh-century supplement, written in England, includes the *Examinatio episcopi*.[81] An English copy of the Romano-German

---

[77] See V. Leroquais, *Les pontificaux manuscrits des bibliothèques publiques de France, I* (Paris, 1938), pp. lxxxiii–lxxxvi.

[78] For these professions, see Richter, *Canterbury Professions*; Brooks, *Early History*, pp. 165–7; D. Whitelock, *English Historical Documents, c.500–1042*, 2nd edn (London, 1979), pp. 628–9, and in *Councils and Synods* (as n. 28 above), I.i, pp. 81–4.

[79] For a list of these, see H. Gneuss, 'Liturgical Books in Anglo-Saxon England and their Old English Terminology', in *Learning and Literature in Anglo-Saxon England. Studies Presented to Peter Clemoes on the Occasion of his Sixty-Fifth Birthday*, ed. M. Lapidge and H. Gneuss (Cambridge, 1985), pp. 91–141, at 132.

[80] Ed. C. Vogel and R. Elze, *Le Pontifical Romano-Germanique du dixième siècle*, Studi e testi, 226–7, 269 (Rome, 1963–72); the *Examinatio episcopi* (sections LXIII.12–17) is printed in vol. I, pp. 200–12. See also *Les Ordines Romani du haut moyen âge*, ed. M. Andrieu (Louvain, 1931–61), I, 191–2 and 496–8; III, 616–17; IV, 101–4.

[81] See M. Lapidge, 'Ealdred of York and MS. Cotton Vitellius E.XII', *Yorkshire Archaeological Jnl*, 55 (1983), 11–25, repr. with additions in his *Anglo-Latin Literature 900–1066* (London, 1993), pp. 453–67 and 492; N. R. Ker, 'Three Old English Texts in a Salisbury Pontifical, Cotton Tiberius C i',

Pontifical, written perhaps at the Old Minster, Winchester, about the middle of the eleventh century, and closely related to Vitellius E.XII, is preserved in Cambridge, Corpus Christi College, MS 163.[82] I do not consider here English eleventh-century manuscripts, or parts of these, that contain only shorter excerpts from the Romano-Germanic Pontifical: the Leofric Missal (MS Bodley 579) and Cambridge, Corpus Christi College, MS 265. It is clear then that the *Examinatio* of a bishop based upon a fixed scheme – although allowing some textual variation – of questions and answers found its way to England in the context of the Romano-German Pontifical and is thus recorded in Tiberius C.I and Corpus 163, while it almost certainly formed part of the lost portion of Vitellius E.XII.

The *Examinatio* may have appeared among the most important and useful innovations of the Romano-German Pontifical to the English archbishops, to those on the continent as well, and perhaps to secular rulers, too. Consequently, where copies of the older pontificals were used, the *Examinatio* might be added, or was kept at hand. This can be seen in the well-known but misnamed 'Benedictional of Archbishop Robert' (Rouen, Bibl. mun., MS 369 [Y.7]), actually a pontifical and benedictional, written probably at Winchester in the 980s, but subsequently taken to Normandy, where, in the eleventh century, at the end of the book the *Ordinatio* together with the *Examinatio* (demanding obedience to the Archbishop of Rouen) were added, although an *Ordinatio* had already been provided in the Anglo-Saxon core of the book, on fols 144^v–150^v.[83] The same thing happened in England at about the same time, when in Corpus 44, fols 2^v–5^v the *Examinatio* was placed in front of a pontifical written in the second quarter of the eleventh century at St Augustine's, Canterbury, but probably for use at Christ Church there; the actual *Ordinatio* in this manuscript follows much later in its proper place.

These analogues provide the explanation for the somewhat unexpected copy of the *Examinatio* in Tiberius A.III, and they may even give us a hint as to who would have consulted this book. If, as seems likely, the archbishops of Canterbury continued to employ one or more pontificals of the traditional Anglo-Saxon type, they may have wanted to supplement the ordination ceremony of a bishop by prefixing the *Examinatio*, presumably a public ceremony apt to strengthen their position as metropolitans. Accordingly, the text of the *Examinatio* had to be copied for them from a manuscript of the Romano-Germanic Pontifical, and that this happened in the case of Tiberius A.III can be seen from the incipit quoted above: the scribe (or his predecessor) had a rubric before him that covered both the *Examinatio* and the *Ordinatio* of a bishop, but as the formulae for the ordination were readily available in the Canterbury books there was no need to copy these together with the *Examinatio*.

---

in *The Anglo-Saxons, Studies in some Aspects of their History and Culture Presented to Bruce Dickins*, ed. P. Clemoes (London, 1959), pp. 262–79, at 266.

[82] M. Lapidge, 'The Origin of Corpus Christi College Cambridge 163', *TCBS*, 8 (1981–85), 18–28.

[83] *The Benedictional of Archbishop Robert*, ed. H. A. Wilson, HBS, 24 (1903), 125–30 and 162–5.

Here we return to the original argument of this essay and look at two passages in the *Examinatio* as found in Tiberius A.III. Most of the manuscripts representing the *Pontificale Romano-Germanicum* insert a passage, in different positions, in the section dealing with the duties and conduct of a future bishop. This passage demands that the candidate is to pledge his subjection and obedience to the metropolitan bishop and his successors. The formula on fol. 94 of Tiberius A.III, already noted by Dr Ker, is:

> Interrogatio. Uis subiectus esse et obediens in diuinis negotiis. sancte Dorober-
> nensi ęcclesie. Responsio. Uolo.

Exactly the same formula is found in Corpus 44, fol. 3ᵛ, and a similar formula in the so-called Magdalen College Pontifical (Oxford, Magdalen College, MS 226) of the twelfth century from the province of Canterbury.[84]

Even more telling is the Tiberius text (fol. 94ᵛ) of the formula concluding the *Examinatio*, which had already caught the attention of the great Humfrey Wanley[85] 300 years ago:

> Ita quoque examinatus. et pleniter instructus. cum consensu monachorum siue
> clericorum et laicorum. a conuentu totius provincię episcoporum. maximeque
> archiepiscopi Christi aecclesie ab auctoritate aut presentia ordinetur. Explicuit.

A variant form of this concluding statement occurs in all the copies of the *Examinatio*, but in the two Canterbury books, Tiberius A.III and Corpus 44, we have the express reference to the archbishop of Canterbury and, what seems far more important, the reference to *monachi* present at the procedures, whereas in all other versions so far printed or collated only *clerici* and *laici* are mentioned. Consequently, the wording in the two manuscripts points to an archbishop's church in England where a monastic community existed, and this, in the eleventh century and later on, could only be Christ Church, Canterbury.

Here it could be objected that similar or identical references would be expected, copied from a Canterbury exemplar in all English pontificals, from the later eleventh century onwards, that included the *Examinatio* and had been produced for, and were kept at, any of the bishops' sees in the Canterbury province, as can be seen in the Magdalen College Pontifical; however, none of these bishops, except the archbishop of Canterbury, could have conducted the ceremony. The respective evidence will have to be examined. But in my view, the *Examinatio*, recorded as an excerpt, as it occurs in Tiberius A.III, points to a place where this addition to the pontifical, documenting an innovative ceremony, was needed for practical purposes: there can be no doubt that the public profession of faith and obedience by the bishops of the English

---

[84] *The Pontifical of Magdalen College*, ed. H. A. Wilson, HBS, 39 (1910), 71.
[85] *Catalogus* (as n. 8 above), p. 197.

southern and Midland dioceses would effectively underpin the authority of the archbishop of Canterbury.

Old English dialectal features

To draw conclusions about the origin of a manuscript, based on the dialect, or dialectal elements, of its Old English texts or glosses may seem problematic if not impracticable, for several reasons.

First of all, copyists of texts or glosses in Old English may simply reproduce, more or less consistently, dialectal features of their exemplars, features that are not necessarily representative of the type of language the copyist speaks and writes, and presumably not that of the members of the community to which he belongs. Conversely, the dialect character or, more usually, dialect traces of a text have often been introduced by copyists, as can be seen in the Old English continuous gloss to the Rule of St Benedict in Tiberius A.III. This gloss points back to a Winchester exemplar,[86] although here as elsewhere the facts may be even more complex: our scribe may have had a Canterbury copy of a Winchester manuscript before him, and the Kenticisms in his gloss may then well be those of his immediate exemplar.[87]

Another problem is that we know very little about where the members of monastic and other religious communities came from: would a monastery recruit its inmates, novices and oblates, mainly in its immediate surroundings or in a particular dialect area,[88] and would monastic and cathedral scribes often or rarely move from one place to another? The available evidence needs to be surveyed systematically. We are probably justified in assuming a certain mobility in the foundation phase of the reformed monasteries in the tenth century; an instructive example is provided by Wulfstan of Winchester, who, in his *Vita S. Æthelwoldi*, tells us what happened when Æthelwold had been appointed abbot of Abingdon:

> Venit ergo seruus Dei ad locum sibi commissum: quem protinus secuti sunt quidam clerici de Glastonia, scilicet Osgarus, Foldbirthus, Frithegarus, et Ordbirthus de Wintonia, et Eadricus de Lundonia, eius discipulatui se subdentes. Congregauitque sibi in breui spacio gregem monachorum . . .

It seems noteworthy that Osgar later accompanied Æthelwold to Winchester and

---

[86] See above, p. 17.

[87] On the whole difficult problem, see J. Pope, ed., *Homilies of Ælfric. A Supplementary Collection I*, EETS (OS), 259 (1967), pp. 177–82, and J. P. Crowley, 'The Study of Old English Dialects', unpublished PhD dissertation, University of North Carolina at Chapel Hill (1980), ch. 4. For the example of the well-known Canterbury scribe Eadwi who employed – and presumably spoke – the regional Kentish dialect, see above, p. 23.

[88] On this question see D. Knowles, *The Monastic Order in England*, 2nd edn (Cambridge, 1963), pp. 417–25.

afterwards became abbot of Abingdon, while Ordbriht was entrusted with Chertsey Abbey and later became bishop of Selsey.[89] There can hardly be any doubt that newly appointed bishops and archbishops would come to their sees with trusted companions, including scribes, who would work for and with them, and that books, too, would find a new home under such circumstances.[90] Also, we know of individual scribes who moved from one religious house to another, like the one who may have gone from Abingdon to New Minster, Winchester, around 966,[91] and another who left York for Exeter in the later eleventh century.[92]

The main problem, however, in any attempt to relate dialect features in Old English to the possible place of origin of a manuscript is our severely restricted knowledge of Old English dialects, which prevents us from employing anything like the methods developed so successfully by the authors of the *Linguistic Atlas of Late Medieval English*.[93] Such features as we do know may be characteristic of particular periods or places, and these places are often not even known. Phonological or lexical characteristics considered 'Anglian' may be representative of an area stretching from the Thames to Northumberland and so are practically useless for our purpose. We encounter even greater difficulties with what is considered the West-Saxon dialect, which in the course of the tenth century developed into a nation-wide standard that could have been written – though not, of course, spoken – anywhere in the country.

But there is one exception that we should not ignore, and this is what our historical grammars call 'Kentish', actually a south-eastern dialect some of whose features certainly reached beyond the confines of Kent into Surrey, Sussex, Middlesex, Essex and Suffolk, if we can trust our Middle English evidence.[94] This then is a comparatively small dialect area, and one in which, for the period from the Benedictine reform onwards, we can locate only very few institutions with active scriptoria, or where we think such scriptoria may have existed: the cathedrals of Canterbury, Rochester, and St Paul's in London, and the monasteries at Canterbury (St Augustine's), Chertsey, Westminster, St Albans, and the nunnery at Barking. As it turns out, we have no manuscripts, Latin or Old English, written before the late eleventh century that can with certainty be attributed to these houses except for the

---

[89] See Wulfstan of Winchester (as n. 2 above), p. 20 and notes.

[90] Cf. Deshman, '*Benedictus Monarcha*', p. 219, and the evidence for Winchester texts and books at Canterbury.

[91] Bishop, *English Caroline Minuscule*, p. xxi; cf. Wulfstan of Winchester (as n. 2 above), p. 36, ch. 20.

[92] Lapidge, 'Ealdred of York', pp. 23–4.

[93] A. McIntosh, M. L. Samuels and M. Benskin, *A Linguistic Atlas of Late Medieval English*, 4 vols (Aberdeen, 1986).

[94] For an important 'Kentish' feature, the spelling *e* as the reflex of OE short and long *u* + *i*-Umlaut, see now K. Dietz, 'Die historische Schichtung phonologischer Isoglossen in den englischen Dialekten: Altenglische Isoglossen', *Anglia*, 107 (1989), 295–329, at 311–14, and G. Kristensson, *A Survey of Middle English Dialects 1290–1350: The East Midland Counties* (Lund, 1995), pp. 57–75.

two at Canterbury.[95] The provenance of two or three Old English eleventh-century homiliaries may be Rochester, but the place of origin of these books could have been Rochester or Canterbury.[96]

There is then good reason at least to suspect that a manuscript displaying 'Kentish' features may have something to do with Canterbury, and we have in fact quite a number of manuscripts with such features whose origin or at least provenance at Christ Church or St Augustine's can be proved by means of evidence other than linguistic. Unfortunately, we do not yet have a reliable inventory of Anglo-Saxon manuscripts containing at least traces of Kentish speech; the few attempted listings are incomplete and not always reliable.[97] Here we also have to note a serious deficiency in our historical grammars of English: when they refer to 'Kentish' texts and glosses, they exclusively mention what they consider to be in more or less 'pure' Kentish:[98] names and forms in eighth- and ninth-century charters, which do not concern us here; a number of glosses added before 900 to London, BL, Cotton MS Tiberius C.II, a copy of Bede's *Historia ecclesiastica*, and, above all, the more than 1200 interlinear glosses to the Parabolae Salomonis and the so-called Kentish Hymn and Kentish Psalm, all in BL, Cotton MS Vespasian D.VI, written about the middle of the tenth century and showing (on fol. 2) the fourteenth-century pressmark and *ex libris* of St Augustine's, Canterbury. What the grammarians just mention is the fact that the two poems in Vespasian D.VI are less consistently Kentish in their phonology than the glosses. What they simply ignore is the not inconsiderable number of manuscripts with scattered Kentish forms; only the great Karl Luick duly noted: 'Spuren kentischer Schreiber sind in anderen Handschriften recht häufig.'[99]

One of these manuscripts is Cotton Tiberius A.III. A systematic study of the language of all its Old English texts and glosses has not so far been attempted, but

---

[95] Cf. H. Gneuss, 'A Preliminary List of Manuscripts Written or Owned in England up to 1100', *ASE*, 9 (1981), 1–60; a thoroughly revised and updated version is in preparation.

[96] Oxford, Bodl. Lib., MSS Bodley 340, 342; and Cambridge, CCC, MS 162. See the introductions to their editions of Ælfric's homilies by Pope (as n. 87 above) and Godden (as n. 62 above).

[97] For such listings see M. Ångström, *Studies in Old English MSS with Special Reference to the Delabialization of y̆ (< ŭ + i) to ĭ*, dissertation (Uppsala, 1937), pp. 103–46 and 151–2. Crowley, 'Study of Old English Dialects', pp. 111–12. A more comprehensive yet not definitive list will be found below, in App. 2.

[98] Only the most important references can be here given: K. D. Bülbring, *Altenglisches Elementarbuch. I. Teil: Lautlehre* (Heidelberg, 1902), §§ 21 and 26; K. Luick, *Historische Grammatik der englischen Sprache* (Leipzig, 1914–40), § 23; K. Brunner, *Altenglische Grammatik nach der angelsächsischen Grammatik von Eduard Sievers*, 3rd edn (Tübingen, 1965), § 2, n. 7; Campbell, *Old English Grammar*, §§ 14–15, see also §§ 288–91 and p. 363; R. M. Hogg, *A Grammar of Old English. Vol. 1: Phonology* (Oxford, 1992), p. 7.

[99] See Luick, *Historische Grammatik*, p. 33. For Elmar Seebold's recently developed concepts of Jutish Kentish and a Jutish substratum in West-Saxon see the survey and references in H. Sauer, 'Old English Word Geography: Some Problems and Results', in *Anglistentag 1991 Düsseldorf: Proceedings*, ed. W. G. Busse (Tübingen, 1992), pp. 307–26, at 322–3, and Kornexl, *Regularis Concordia*, p. ccxxxv.

what I have found in a cursory survey tends to confirm convincingly the observations made in the previous sections of this essay. Of the ninety-odd items in this manuscript, 73 are partly or wholly in Old English, or have been supplied with continuous interlinear glosses, and at least more than forty of these, including all the longer prose texts and the extensive interlinear glosses, exhibit Kenticisms, from occasional traces to frequent instances. Among these items are the glosses to the Rule of St Benedict, to the *Regularis Concordia*, to the *Somniale Danielis* and to the following prognostic texts (arts 7b–7g), the confessional prayers and texts (arts 9a, 9e–9f, 9h, 9i, 9k), the extract from King Alfred's version of Augustine's *Soliloquia* (art. 9g), the gloss to Ælfric's *Colloquy*, Ælfric's *De temporibus*, the commonplaces on fol. 73^{r-v} (art. 14), the Life of St Margaret, the version of Ælfric's Homily for Palm Sunday, the 'Sunday letter' (art. 17), the Devil's Account of the Next World (art. 18), some of the homiletic pieces (art. 19, also art. 24), the *Indicia monasterialia*, the Old English Lapidary, the Old English prose translations of chapter 4 of the Rule of St Benedict and chapters 14 and 26 of Alcuin's *De virtutibus et vitiis*, and, finally, Ælfric's second Old English letter to Archbishop Wulfstan (arts 22, 23, 25–27, and 29).

This is not a suitable place for a full documentation of the Kenticisms in the texts listed; moreover, the dialectal features in a number of them have already been noticed in editions and investigations,[100] although a comprehensive treatment of this aspect of Tiberius A.III, recommended by Max Förster as early as 1910,[101] is still needed.

As to the criteria employed in identifying Kentish forms in texts and glosses, it seems safe to say that phonological tests still yield the most reliable results. What we can consider the characteristics of Kentish phonology has been recorded in our historical grammars and need not be repeated here in any detail; also, we are only concerned with the state that south-eastern English had reached by the tenth century. Few spellings – assumed to be representative of dialectal sound changes – occur only in Kentish; the unrounding and lowering of short and long *y* (from *i*-Umlaut of *u*) to *e* is the safest feature, as well as inverted spellings (caused by this and other developments) like *fyt* (in art. 16) or *fæt* (in art. 9f) for *fet*. Other typically Kentish developments are the merger of short and long *eo* and *io* in *io*, and spellings with *ea* for short and long *eo*. Further Kentish spelling characteristics are shared with

---

[100] Pertinent studies have been listed and supplemented by P. Kitson, 'Lapidary Traditions in Anglo-Saxon England: Part I', *ASE*, 7 (1978), 9–60, at 34, n. 4; Sauer, 'Beichtermahnungen' (as n. 1 above), p. 18, n. 28; P. Lendinara, 'Donne bibliche da Venanzio Fortunato ad un ignoto compilatore anglosassone', *Studi di filologia classica in onore di Giusto Monaco*, IV (Palermo, 1992), pp. 1497–1510, at 1508, n. 49. To these lists should be added W. Hermanns, *Lautlehre und dialektale Untersuchung der Interlinearversion der Benediktinerregel*, Dr phil. Dissertation (Bonn, 1906), and Kornexl, *Regularis Concordia*, pp. cxcvii–ccxii.

[101] Förster, 'Beiträge zur mittelalterlichen Volkskunde IV', *Archiv für das Studium der neueren Sprachen und Literaturen*, 125 (1910), 39–70, at 45, n. 2.

Anglian, and so their evidence needs to be strengthened by other dialect features. Most important and in contrast to West-Saxon is the raising of all *æ* sounds to *e*: short *æ* (also in Mercian), *æ*₁ from WGmc. *ā* (also in Anglian), *æ*₂ from WGmc. *ai* + *i*-Umlaut (only in Kentish).[102] Also frequent, and shared with Anglian, is *e* (long and short) as the result of *i*-Umlaut of *ea*. All these spellings, as well as their inverted counterparts, are found in Tiberius A.III.

Other notable spellings that occur in our manuscript may be either late or not specifically Kentish, or both, like *dæig* (for *dæg*), and loss of initial *h*, or inorganic initial *h*. There is one type of spelling, however, that may not be exclusively south-eastern, but should definitely be considered as a frequently occurring characteristic feature of Kentish texts in the eleventh century, even though Professor Campbell would exclude Kent from its area of distribution.[103] This is the representation of short *a* + nasal + *i*-Umlaut by *æ*, as in *acænned* (in art. 8a). The explanation of such forms as inverted spellings (in texts in which *e* for West Saxon *æ* rarely turns up, or not at all), seems less convincing to me than the view that they were chosen for phonetic reasons; but in any case these spellings are common in manuscripts with other south-eastern traits and should therefore definitely be included in a list of the Old English dialect characteristics of Kent and the surrounding shires.[104]

As was pointed out above, we cannot be certain whether Kentish spellings in our texts and glosses are due to the scribes of Tiberius A.III, or to their exemplars. What seems significant, however, is the fact that these spellings are to be found in the work of all four scribes (Ker's nos 1, 3, 4 and 5) who wrote Old English texts or glosses.

Phonological criteria do not provide the only evidence for the dialectal provenance of our manuscript. I leave aside inflexional morphology, which is of very limited use here, and turn to the vocabulary. Ever since Richard Jordan published his pioneer work in 1906, considerable progress has been made in the study of Old English dialect words or preferred usage,[105] though the aim so far has mainly been to distinguish between what James Murray called 'common words' and 'dialect words'.[106] The emphasis has been almost exclusively on identifying words used only in Anglian, or only in West-Saxon, with a distinction sometimes being made

---

[102] 'Kentish Raising' is, however, regarded as a process entirely distinct from West Mercian Second Fronting by R. M. Hogg, 'On the Impossibility of Old English Dialectology', in *Luick Revisited. Papers Read at the Luick-Symposium at Schloß Liechtenstein, 15–18. 9. 1985*, ed. D. Kastovsky and G. Bauer (Tübingen, 1989), pp. 183–203.

[103] Campbell, *Old English Grammar*, § 193(d).

[104] A great deal has been written about this. For earlier views see Gneuss, *Hymnar und Hymnen*, pp. 160–61; for more recent work cf. esp. Pope (as n. 87 above), pp. 79–80 and 181 with n. 3; I. Carlson, *The Pastoral Care, Edited from British Museum MS. Cotton Otho B.ii*, Pt I (Stockholm, 1975), pp. 38–9; *The Stowe Psalter*, ed. A. C. Kimmens (Toronto, 1979), p. xxx and n. 44; Hogg, *Grammar of Old English*, p. 126.

[105] R. Jordan, *Eigentümlichkeiten des anglischen Wortschatzes*, Anglistische Forschungen, 17 (Heidelberg, 1906). For a review of twentieth-century research, see Sauer (as n. 99 above).

[106] In *OED*, I, xxvii, diagram rev. C. T. Onions, *Shorter OED*, 3rd edn (Oxford, 1944), I, viii.

between Early and Late West-Saxon; more recently the word usage of the so-called Winchester school from the later tenth century onwards has met with special interest.[107] A few years ago, however, Walter Hofstetter was able to show that a certain number of words occur only in interlinear glosses written at Christ Church, Canterbury, in the first half or about the middle of the eleventh century.[108] These are glosses to seven Latin texts, three of them in Tiberius A.III, but there written by two different hands:

> *Liber Scintillarum* (London, BL, MS Royal 7.C.iv);
> *De vitiis et peccatis* (BL, MS Royal 7.C.iv);
> Prayers (BL, MS Arundel 155);
> Prudentius, Works (Boulogne-sur-Mer, Bibl. mun., MS 189);
> *Regularis Concordia* (Tiberius A.III, art. 6);
> *Somniale Danielis* (Tiberius A.III, art. 7a);
> 'Sammellunar' (Tiberius A.III, art. 7b).

Lucia Kornexl was able to add to Hofstetter's list, which now includes *bewerung* 'defensio', *dysigdom* 'imperitia', *fordimmian* 'obnubilare', *forgyting* 'oblivio', *forlæting* 'intermissio', *fyndel* 'adinventio', *halbære* 'salubris', *oferprut* 'tumidus', *reafol* 'rabidus', *togang* 'accessus', *þeoging* 'profectus' all these occur in the *Regularis Concordia*, glossing the Latin lemmata here given, and in one or more of the other glossed texts.[109]

What we have before us here may not necessarily be south-east English dialect vocabulary; at least some of these words may well be representative of specific usage followed in the Christ Church scriptorium, somewhat like the usage of the Winchester school, although the evidence here is not as overwhelming as it is for Winchester. In any case we should not ignore what these 'Canterbury words' can tell us about the Tiberius manuscript.

Cotton Tiberius A.III, in view of the number and diversity of its texts, is an extremely complex Anglo-Saxon book, and it may not therefore seem surprising that scholars have been in some doubt about its place of origin. Future research may help to answer questions that had to remain open in this essay, especially the poor quality, mentioned above, of some of the Old English pieces, but I believe

---

[107] W. Hofstetter, 'Winchester and the Standardization of Old English Vocabulary', and his *Winchester* (as n. 12 above).

[108] Ibid., pp. 109–10 and 433–48.

[109] Kornexl, *Regularis Concordia*, pp. ccxxxii–ccxxxv, and 'The *Regularis Concordia* and its Old English gloss', *ASE*, 24 (1995), 95–130, at 128–30. For further words that point to Canterbury usage, including words in the glosses to *Somniale Danielis* and 'Sammellunar' in Tiberius A.III (arts 7a, 7b) and to the Canterbury hymnal in Durham B.III.32, see Hofstetter, *Winchester*, pp. 109–10 and 442–5.

that the evidence here presented will allow us to regard with more certainty than before the scriptorium of Christ Church, Canterbury, as the place where Cotton Tiberius A.III was written.[110]

[110] This essay is a revised and expanded version of a paper (or, rather, notes) read at a workshop on MS Tiberius A.III at the British Library on 9 August 1993, organized by the Research Group on Manuscript Evidence at the Parker Library, Corpus Christi College, Cambridge. I am grateful to Professor Michael Lapidge, who kindly examined the texts of the *Examinatio episcopi* in Corpus MSS 44 and 163 for me; I wish to thank Mechthild Gretsch and Lucia Kornexl for reading a draft version of this paper and for suggesting improvements, and Helene Feulner for computerizing the final version.

Appendix 1: texts from Cotton Tiberius A.III edited or collated after the publication of Ker's *Catalogue of Manuscripts Containing Anglo-Saxon* **(1957)**

Initial references are to the numbering of the articles in Ker, *Catalogue*, no. 186.

Art. 1: *Benedicti Regula*, ed. R. Hanslik, 2nd edn, CSEL, 75 (1977); Latin collated as *i*. For shortcomings of Hanslik's collation see P. Meyvaert, 'Towards a History of the Textual Transmission of the *Regula S. Benedicti*', *Scriptorium*, 17 (1963), 83–110, and M. Gretsch, *Die Regula Sancti Benedicti in England und ihre altenglische Übersetzung* (München, 1973), pp. 60–1.

Art. 2: H. Sauer, 'Die Ermahnung des Pseudo-Fulgentius zur Benediktinerregel und ihre altenglische Glossierung', *Anglia*, 102 (1984), 419–25; much more informative than P. Pulsiano, 'BL Cotton MS Tiberius A.iii: Fulgentius, Injunction', *American Notes and Queries*, n.s., 1 (1988), 43–4.

Art. 3: *Memoriale qualiter*, ed. D. C. Morgand, in *Corpus Consuetudinum Monasticarum I: Initia Consuetudinis Benedictinae*, ed. K. Hallinger (Siegburg, 1963), pp. 177–261; Latin collated as *H*.

Art. 4: J. E. Cross, '*De festiuitatibus anni* and Ansegisus, *Capitularum* [*sic*] *Collectio* (827) in Anglo-Saxon manuscripts', *Liverpool Classical Monthly*, 17.8 (Oct. 1992), 119–20; collated with text of London, BL, Cotton MS Titus A.IV. For two earlier editions of the Latin text see ibid., notes 6 and 10.

Art. 5: *Regula Sancti Benedicti Abbatis Anianensis sive Collectio Capitularis*, ed. J. Semmler, in *Corpus Consuetudinum Monasticarum I* (see art. 3), pp. 501–36; collated as *G5*.

Art. 6: *Regularis Concordia Anglicae Nationis*, ed. T. Symons, S. Spath, M. Wegener and K. Hallinger in *Corpus Consuetudinum Monasticarum VII/3: Consuetudinum saeculi X/XI/XII monumenta non-Cluniacensia*, ed. K. Hallinger (Siegburg, 1984), pp. 61–147; L. Kornexl, *Die Regularis Concordia und ihre altenglische Interlinearversion* (München, 1993).

Art. 7(a): L. T. Martin, *Somniale Danielis. An Edition of a Medieval Latin Dream Interpretation Handbook* (Frankfurt am Main, 1981); Latin only.

Art. 7(a) and 7(q): S. R. Fischer, *The Complete Medieval Dreambook. A Multilingual Alphabetical Somnia Danielis Collection* (Bern, 1982); Latin and Old English.

Art. 7(a), 7(i) and 7(q): A. Epe, *Wissensliteratur im angelsächsischen England: das Fachschrifttum der vergessenen artes mechanicae und artes magicae. Mit besonderer Berücksichtigung des Somniale Danielis* (Münster in Westphalen, 1995).

Art. 8(b): H. L. C. Tristram, *Sex aetates mundi: Die Weltzeitalter bei den Angelsachsen und Iren* (Heidelberg, 1985), p. 301.

Art. 8(d): B. Günzel, *Ælfwine's Prayerbook*, HBS, 108 (1993), 64–5.

Arts 9(a), 9(d), 9(e) and 9(f): P. Pulsiano and J. McGowan, 'Four Unedited Prayers in London, British Library Cotton Tiberius A.iii', *Medieval Studies*, 56 (1994), 189–216.

Arts 9(e) and 9(f): L.-G. Hallander, 'Two Old English Confessional Prayers', *Stockholm Studies in Modern Philology*, n.s., 3 (1968), 87–110; collated with text of London, BL, MS Royal 2.B.v.

Arts 9(h) and 9(i): H. Sauer, 'Zwei spätaltenglische Beichtermahnungen aus Hs. Cotton Tiberius A.iii', *Anglia*, 98 (1980), 1–33.

Arts 9(j)–9(l) and 21(a)–21(g): R. Fowler, 'A Late Old English Handbook for the Use of a Confessor', *Anglia*, 83 (1965), 1–34; collated as *N*, except 9(j), which is printed from Tiberius A.III.

Art. 10(a): Wulfstan of Winchester, *The Life of St. Æthelwold*, ed. M. Lapidge and M. Winterbottom (Oxford, 1991), pp. lxxv–lxxvii; previously edited in shortened form by J. B. L. Tolhurst, *Introduction to the English Monastic Breviaries* [= *The Monastic Breviary of Hyde Abbey, Winchester*, vol. VI], HBS, 80 (1942; repr. 1993), 114–19.

Art. 10(d): P. Pulsiano, 'British Library, Cotton Tiberius A.iii, fol. 59^{rv}: An Unrecorded Charm in the Form of an Address to the Cross', *American Notes and Queries*, n.s., 4 (1991), 3–5.

Art. 10(e): A parallel version is printed from London, BL, Cotton MS Titus D.XXVII by Günzel, see art. 8(d) above, p. 126.

Art. 11: For editions in anthologies and collections see L. M. Reinsma, *Ælfric: an Annotated Bibliography* (New York, 1987).

Art. 15: L. Herbst, *Die altenglische Margaretenlegende in der Hs. Cotton Tiberius A.III*, Dr phil. Dissertation, Göttingen (1975) (privately printed); superseded, except for the treatment of the language, by M. Clayton and H. Magennis, *The Old English Lives of St Margaret* (Cambridge, 1994).

Art. 16: *Ælfric's Catholic Homilies. The Second Series: Text*, ed. M. Godden, EETS (SS), 5 (1979), 381–90.

Art. 18: F. C. Robinson, 'The Devil's Account of the Next World: An Anecdote from Old English Homiletic Literature', *Neuphilologische Mitteilungen*, 73 (1972), 362–71, repr. with 'Afterword' in his *The Editing of Old English* (Oxford, 1994), pp. 196–

205; also edited in *The Vercelli Homilies and Related Texts*, ed. D. G. Scragg, EETS (OS), 300 (1992), pp. 169–83.

Arts 19(a) and 19(b): collated as 'K' in D. Bethurum, *The Homilies of Wulfstan* (Oxford, 1957), no. XIII.

Art. 19(j): collated as 'K', ibid., no. VIIa.

Arts 19(k) and 19(l): *Die 'Institutes of Polity, Civil and Ecclesiastical'*, ed. K. H. Jost (Bern, 1959), pp. 85–102.

Art. 20: *Canterbury Professions*, ed. M. Richter, Canterbury and York Society, 67 (1973), pp. 118–20.

Art. 21: See above, art. 9.

Art. 22: *Monasteriales Indicia. The Anglo-Saxon Monastic Sign Language*, ed. D. Banham (Pinner, Middx, 1991).

Art. 23: P. Kitson, 'Lapidary Traditions in Anglo-Saxon England: Part I, the Background; the Old English Lapidary', *ASE*, 7 (1978), 9–60.

Art. 25: M. A. d'Aronco: 'Il IV capitolo della *Regula Sancti Benedicti* del Ms. Londra, B.M., Cotton Tiberius A.III', in *Feor ond neah: Scritti di Filologia Germanica in memoria di Augusto Scaffidi Abbate*, ed. P. Lendinara and L. Melazzo (Palermo, 1983), pp. 105–28.

Arts 26–27: P. E. Szarmach, 'Cotton Tiberius A.iii, Arts. 26 and 27', in *Words, Texts and Manuscripts: Studies in Anglo-Saxon Culture Presented to Helmut Gneuss*, ed. M. Korhammer (Cambridge, 1992), pp. 29–42.

Art. 30: *Anglo-Saxon Litanies of the Saints*, ed. M. Lapidge, HBS, 106 (1991), 174–7: litany on fols 112^v–113^v; I. B. Milfull, *The Hymns of the Anglo-Saxon Church* (Cambridge, 1996): hymns collated.

Appendix 2: Anglo-Saxon manuscripts with south-eastern dialectal features

The following, preliminary list should not be considered complete or definitive. Early charters (s. viii and ix) with names or texts in the Kentish dialect have not been included; for these see A. Campbell, *Old English Grammar* (Oxford, 1959), §14. The two late copies of the West-Saxon Gospels, London, BL, MS Royal 1.A.xiv and Oxford, Bodleian Library, MS Hatton 38, have also been omitted, as their language now tends to be regarded as East-Saxon. Latin texts with Old English interlinear glosses are marked by an asterisk. Most of the texts and glosses listed are in late West-Saxon, with south-eastern spellings occurring more or less frequently.

Boulogne, Bibliothèque municipale, 189 (s. xi[1])
   Prudentius, Works*

Brussels, Bibliothèque royale, 1650 (s. xi[1])
   Aldhelm, *De laudibus virginitatis* (prose)*, especially Goossens' hand CD

Cambridge, Corpus Christi College:
162 (s. xi *in.*)
   Homilies (mainly by Ælfric): additions and alterations (s. xi)
198 (s. xi[1], xi[2])
   Homilies (most by Ælfric)
303 (s. xii[1])
   Lives of St Margaret, St Aegidius, and St Nicolas

Durham, Dean and Chapter Library, B.III.32 (s. xi *med.*)
   Hymnal*, monastic canticles*; Ælfric's *Grammar* (MS D)

London, British Library:
Arundel 155 (s. xi[1])
   Prayers* (Canterbury vocabulary)
Cotton Domitian VIII, fols 30–70 (s. xi/xii)
   Anglo-Saxon Chronicle F
Cotton Julius A.II, fols 10–135 (s. xi *med.*)
   Ælfric's *Grammar* (MS J)
Cotton Julius A.VI (s. xi *med.*)
   Expositio hymnorum*, monastic canticles*.
Cotton Otho A.VI (s. xi *med.*)
   Alfred, Boethius.
Cotton Otho C.I, vol. 2 (s. xi *in.*, xi *med.*)
   Wærferth, Gregory's *Dialogi*.
Cotton Tiberius A.III (s. xi *med.*)
   Various texts and continuous glosses, see above, pp. 14 and 39–40.

Cotton Tiberius A.VII, fols 165–166 (s. xi[1])
  Prosper, *Epigrammata** and *Versus ad coniugem**
Cotton Tiberius C.II (s. ix)
  Glossaries inserted in Beda, *Historia ecclesiastica*
Cotton Vespasian A.I (s. xi?)
  Gloss added to Psalm 75.6
Cotton Vespasian D.VI, fols 2–77 (s. x *med.*)
  Parabolae Salomonis*; Alcuin, *De virtutibus et vitiis**; Kentish Hymn and Psalm
Cotton Vespasian D.XII (s. xi *med.*)
  Expositio hymnorum*, monastic canticles in prose versions*
Cotton Vespasian D.XIV, fols 4–169 (s. xii *med.*)
  Miscellany, mainly homilies by Ælfric
Harley 107 (s. xi *med.*)
  Ælfric, *Grammar and Glossary* (MS H)
Royal 1.D.ix, fol. 44[v] (s. xi[1])
  Writ (Harmer no. 26)
Royal 7.C.iv (s. xi *med.*)
  *Liber Scintillarum** (Canterbury vocabulary)

Oxford, Bodleian Library:
Bodley 180 (s. xii[1])
  Alfred, Boethius
Bodley 340 and 342 (s. xi *in.*)
  Homilies (most by Ælfric)
Digby 146 (s. xi *med.*)
  Aldhelm, *De laudibus virginitatis* (prose)*
Junius 85 and 86 (s. xi *med.*)
  Homilies, *Visio S. Pauli*

New Haven, Yale University, Beinecke Library:
401 and *membra disiecta* (s. x[2])
  Aldhelm, *De laudibus virginitatis* (prose)*
578 (s. xi[1])
  West-Saxon Gospels, fragment

Paris, Bibliothèque nationale:
lat. 943 (s. xi *in.*)
  Homily (Ker 364, art. c)
lat. 9561 (s. x)
  Glosses to Gregory, *Regula pastoralis.*

CHAPTER TWO

Mixed Blessings: A Twelfth-Century Manuscript from Waverley

Jean F. Preston

Princeton University Library's MS Garrett 71, a book from the Cistercian monastery of Waverley,[1] is of particular interest because it is the earliest of only four (or probably five) surviving manuscripts from the first Cistercian abbey in England. Consisting of three booklets, it dates from the late twelfth to the first quarter of the thirteenth century, and contains works by Bernard, Bede, and Augustine, all suitable reading for Cistercian monks. Unfortunately, there were some errors of scribe and binder, confusing the contents, but these errors too can be of interest to the modern scholar. And it is also instructive to consider what may have happened to the book after the Dissolution, when so much was destroyed.

The Abbey of the Blessed Virgin Mary at Waverley was founded on 24 November 1128, with 12 brethren and their abbot brought over from the abbey of L'Aumône in Normandy, by William Giffard, Bishop of Winchester, shortly before his death on 23 January 1129. Established during the lifetime of Bernard of Clairvaux (1090–1153), not long after the foundation of Clairvaux in 1115, Waverley was built about two miles south of Farnham in Surrey, where Henry of Blois (brother of King Stephen and Giffard's successor as Bishop of Winchester, 1129–71) rebuilt and fortified Farnham Castle in 1138 as one of the bishop's residences. Thus influential Norman church leaders would have had easy contact with England's first Cistercian house. For many years there were close and friendly relations between the bishops of Winchester and the abbey, which flourished as a result of its good connections.[2] During the next 25 years after Waverley's foundation, some 50 more Cistercian abbeys were established in this country, and others followed.[3]

Very little is known about the contents of Cistercian libraries in England and Wales, as catalogues or inventories have survived from only three of them: two from the North (Rievaulx and Meaux in Yorkshire) and one from the South (Flaxley in

---

[1] See S. de Ricci and W. J. Wilson, *Census of Medieval and Renaissance Manuscripts in the United States and Canada*, (New York, 1935), I, p. 877: listed as no. 71 in the library of Robert Garrett of Baltimore, Maryland; A. Bennett, J. F. Preston and W. P. Stoneman, *Summary Guide to Western Medieval and Renaissance Manuscripts at Princeton University* (Princeton, 1991), p. 8, no. 18.

[2] *Victoria County History, Surrey*, II (London, 1905), pp. 77–88; also D. Knowles and R. N. Hadcock, *Medieval Religious Houses: England and Wales* (London, 1971), pp. 127–8.

[3] See further B. D. Hill, *English Cistercian Monasteries and their Patrons in the Twelfth Century* (Urbana, IL, 1968).

Gloucestershire). Rievaulx had 225 books in its library catalogue, datable *c.*1190–1200, Meaux 363 books in 1396, while in the early thirteenth century Flaxley owned 80.[4] These three libraries seem to have concentrated on theological works, with hardly any classical texts and rarely any law or secular literature in their collections. With so few surviving lists, it is impossible to judge the size or variety of contents of individual houses' libraries, or how far these three were typical. According to the extant catalogues, only Meaux possessed any of the several texts in the Princeton manuscript: St Bernard's *De praecepto et dispensatione* was included with other sermons in one volume and the *Liber exhortationis* (attributed to St Augustine) in another.[5] However, the catalogues do not usually provide a full listing of all of the items in a book, so there may well have been copies elsewhere of other works in the Princeton manuscript. We cannot tell how many books were once at Waverley in the absence of a catalogue, although it seems likely that one was available when John Leland compiled his *Collectanea* (*c.*1536–42). His list of five Waverley volumes has comments on three that 'clearly indicate' to David Bell that Leland consulted a catalogue rather than the books themselves.[6] Four of the five volumes Leland mentions contained sermons and other theological works (by Palladius, Odo of Canterbury, John of Cornwall, and Robert of Cricklade), and one contained Bede on the equinox (*Epistola ad Wicthedum de aequinoctio vel de pasche celebratione*). Not one of these five volumes can be identified today.

Neil Ker could trace only four manuscripts from the house: the Princeton manuscript (the earliest); and one each in Cambridge (University Library, MS Additional 5368), Oxford (Bodl. Lib., MS Bodley 527), and London (BL, Cotton MS Vespasian A.XVI.[7]

The Cambridge manuscript (Add. 5368), contains Origen's homilies on Genesis, Exodus and Leviticus, and is dated by Ker to the end of the twelfth century. It was written by more than one scribe, the hands looking similar to each other, and some of them very close to those in the Princeton manuscript. The Cambridge manuscript is written throughout in long lines whereas two of the booklets in Princeton are in double columns. Instructions to the rubricator are written vertically up or down the very edge of the outer margin (not horizontally as in the first booklet of Princeton), and have often been trimmed in the binding. There are a few scribal errors, such as the omission of several rubrics on fols 48, 57 and 62, the red running heads giving out after fol. 14, and the replacement of a large red initial S by a large green N painted over it, to read 'Nuper' instead of 'Super' on fol. 168. The manuscript has a

---

[4] See D. N. Bell, *The Libraries of the Cistercians, Gilbertines and Premonstratensians*, Corpus of British Medieval Library Catalogues, 3 (London, 1992).

[5] Ibid., p. 56, no. 166e and p. 42, no. 52b; see also his *Index of Authors and Works in Cistercian Libraries in Great Britain* (Kalamazoo, 1992).

[6] Bell, *The Libraries*, pp. 149–50; cf. *J. Leland de rebus Britannici collectanea*, ed. T. Hearne, 2nd edn (London, 1774), IV, 148.

[7] Ker, *MLGB*.

fourteenth-century *ex libris* on fol. 4ᵛ with the same wording as on fol. 92 of Princeton, but written in a different and decorative hand: 'Wauerlea liber tuus est hic crimine liber Non erit ante deum qui tollet eum'. The volume still has the upper oak board with three bands and stitching of its medieval binding but has lost the lower board and last quire of text. The book, acquired by the University Library for £4.15s in 1913, came from the Cope library at Bramshill, Hampshire, as did Princeton's.[8]

Oxford, Bodleian Library, MS Bodley 527 (*SC* 2219) contains Juvencus, *Evangeliorum libri IV*, in hexameters, together with various other works in verse, including some attributed to Bernard and Augustine. It is written in many different thirteenth-century hands, some very tiny; it has no quire signatures or catchwords but all the leaves were trimmed for the book's eighteenth-century leather rebinding. There is a Waverley *ex libris* and list of contents added by a later medieval hand. The manuscript was given by Sir George More of Loseley, Surrey, to the Bodleian Library in 1604.

London, BL, Cotton MS Vespasian A.XVI contains a kalendar and episcopal lists as well as the *Annales abbatiae* of Waverley, written between the late twelfth and the end of the thirteenth century, by a large number of different hands. Ker noted that in the entry for 1236 on fol. 133 the scribes changed from writing above to below top line.[9] The annals (fols 24–200) cover the years 1–1291, beginning with the birth of Christ, and have rather skimpy entries for the first thousand years.[10] The founding of Waverley in 1128 is noted on fol. 79 and that of Fountains in 1133 on fol. 80, and both abbeys have their names written in red in the margin. Waverley's centenary in 1228 is noted on fol. 121. The annals become fuller after 1202, with longer contemporaneous entries written by a large number of different scribes; they stop abruptly in 1291, in the middle of a copy of the written submission (in French) to Edward I of the claimants to the crown of Scotland. The text is incomplete despite the following blank leaves, which probably form part of another quire. The manuscript has no *ex libris*; it was acquired by Sir Robert Cotton (1571–1631), who perhaps added the identification 'Annales monasterii de Waverley', but it is not known where he obtained it.[11]

Another manuscript in the British Library may well come from Waverley: MS Harley 1229. This Cistercian missal is a very large volume written in thick letters in dark ink by a number of late-twelfth-century scribes, on coarse parchment. There are numerous plain, coloured initials alternately blue, red and green; these are similar to

---

[8] Below p. 61.

[9] N. R. Ker, 'From "Above Top Line" to "Below Top Line": a Change in Scribal Practice', in his *Books, Collectors and Libraries: Studies in the Medieval Heritage*, ed. A. G. Watson (London, 1985), p. 73.

[10] *Annales Monastici*, ed. H. R. Luard, ii, RS, 36 (1865), 129–411, with discussion of the manuscript, pp. xxix–l, and facs. of fol. 155 (the annal concerning Simon de Montfort).

[11] For Cotton as a collector, see C. G. C. Tite, *The Manuscript Library of Sir Robert Cotton*, The Panizzi Lectures 1993 (London, 1994).

some initials in Princeton, but such initials were very common in twelfth-century books. There are also four decorated initials: an opening feathery blue **A** on fol. 1, and red decoration within a blue **P** and a green **B**, and blue decoration on a red **T**, all at the beginning of the Canon of the Mass on fols 115ᵛ–116. The book has been tightly rebound in red half-calf in 1960. Andrew Watson dated it after 1192 because of the inclusion of a collect for the feast of St Malachy (fol. 195), first celebrated at Clairvaux in that year, but before 1202 since special collects of St Bernard, ordered then by the General Chapter, appear on an added slip (fol. 171).[12] The presence of Winchester saints in the text suggested to him that the volume may have originated at Waverley, then the only Cistercian house in the Winchester diocese. There is however no *ex libris*.[13]

To turn to the Princeton manuscript itself, this is a composite volume of three booklets, written in the South of England, perhaps at Waverley itself, by several different scribes writing at various times during the late twelfth to the first quarter of the thirteenth century. The volume was certainly in the abbey library by the mid-thirteenth century, when the Waverley *ex libris* and anathema were written on fol. 1ᵛ. The first booklet (containing Bede and Bernard) consists of the present fols 2–50 and 63–70; the second booklet (Augustine) is misbound in the middle of the first as fols 51–62; and the third booklet (mostly Bernard) follows the first on fols 71–93. Fourteenth-century music has been added on the formerly blank endleaves, fols 92ᵛ–93ᵛ. The contents are not straightforward, for besides the misbound booklet, there are several losses and repetitions of text, lost and cancelled leaves, and two missing quires, all suggesting errors by scribe and binder. We will examine the book in detail, noting its contents and losses.

Fol. 1 (the former flyleaf is a singleton) has later scribbles and occasional words or phrases in Latin and English, also to be found inside the pastedown on the front cover. Fol. 1ᵛ bears the Waverley *ex libris* and anathema written in a thirteenth-century hand 'Hic Waurelea liber tuus est. anathemate liber. Non erit ante deum. qui tibi tollet eum'. This is followed by a list of contents, written in the same hand:

> In hoc volumine continentur ista.
> Beda super actus apostolorum. Liber retractacionis eiusdem.
> Augustinus de vera et falsa penitencia.
> Bernardus de precepto et dispensacione.
> Meditaciones eiusdem. de miseria hominis.

Each line of this list, including the *ex libris* and anathema, opens with a simple one-line painted initial, alternately red or green. The list of contents shows that the three

---

[12] *Catalogue of Dated and Datable Manuscripts c.700–1600 in the Department of Manuscripts The British Library* (London, 1979), no. 641 and pl. 111, but Professor Watson informs me that he 'did not think the evidence was strong enough to justify inclusion' under Waverley in Watson, *Supplement*.

[13] There is no mention of Harley 1229 in C. E. Wright, *Fontes Harleiani* (London, 1972).

booklets were already bound in their present order by the thirteenth century, although they were written at different times by four different scribes with different layouts. The volume was rebound in the fourteenth century.

The first booklet (fols 2–50 and 63–70) was made up of nine quires, two of which are missing: the collation is: 1^8 (fols 2–9) 2^{10} (8 canc., fols 10–18) 3^8 (fols 19–26) quire 4 lacking 5–7^8 (fols 27–50) + quire 9 lacking 10^{10} (4, 6 canc., fols 63–70).[14] It was written by two different scribes, A and B, who both wrote 27 long lines per page. Scribe A copied fols 1–19, 50^v (part), and 70^v, while scribe B copied fols 19^v–50^v (part) and 63–70.

Scribe A began, as the contents list indicates, with Bede: after the preface to his *Expositio Actuum Apostolorum* on fols 2–3, the text follows on fols 3–26^v.[15] However, signs of carelessness appear from the start. Despite clear scribal instructions to the rubricator, written in a small cursive hand at the bottom of fol. 3, not enough room was allowed at the end of the preface: only half a line, room for the brief explicit of the preface, but not enough for the longer incipit of the main text. Thus this rubric had to be completed on four lines written inside the large red painted P which began the text ('Primum quidem sermonem'), with symbols in red ink in both the margin and inside the P to show where the rest of the rubric could be found (see Pl. 1).

On fol. 13 the first scribe, A, must have lost his place, as he re-copied 20 lines he had already copied on fol. 12^v and had to cancel or vacate them, by drawing wiggly dark ink lines down both sides of the page and beneath fol. 13, line 20, with 'va' written at the top and 'cat' on line 20 in both margins; he also provided a symbol to indicate this cancellation. On fol. 15^v he omitted a sentence which was added in the left margin by a slightly different hand, with symbols in the margin and in the body of the text, to show where the omitted passage should be inserted.

Perhaps because of A's carelessness, the second scribe B took over on fols 19^v–50^v and 63–70. He wrote a tighter script, getting more onto the page, and seems rather more professional; his h has a longer limb, his d may have a sloping ascender at the end of a word. Bede's *Exposito Actuum Apostolorum* stops abruptly at the foot of fol. 26^v, at chapter 17, verse 24 'cum ergo unum deum esse'. Although the text on fol. 27 looks continuous since it is written by the same hand, the 8 leaves of quire 4 are missing between fols 26/27, as the quire numbering indicates. Only four quires in the manuscript are numbered, quires 2, 3, 5 and 6 (all in the first booklet): fol. 26^v is signed 'III' and fol. 34^v (the last leaf of the following quire) is signed 'V'. Moreover, a trimmed catchword at the bottom of fol. 26^v does not agree with the opening words of fol. 27.[16] This starts abruptly in the middle of a different but associated work on

---

[14] Quire 8 is the misbound second booklet.

[15] *Bedae venerabilis expositio actuum apostolorum et retractio*, ed. M. L. W. Laistner (Cambridge, MA, 1939), pp. 3–66; see his comments on Princeton, pp. xxvi–xxvii, xxxiv and xxxvii.

[16] As with the quire signatures, there are catchwords only in the first booklet: fols 26^v, 34^v, 42^v.

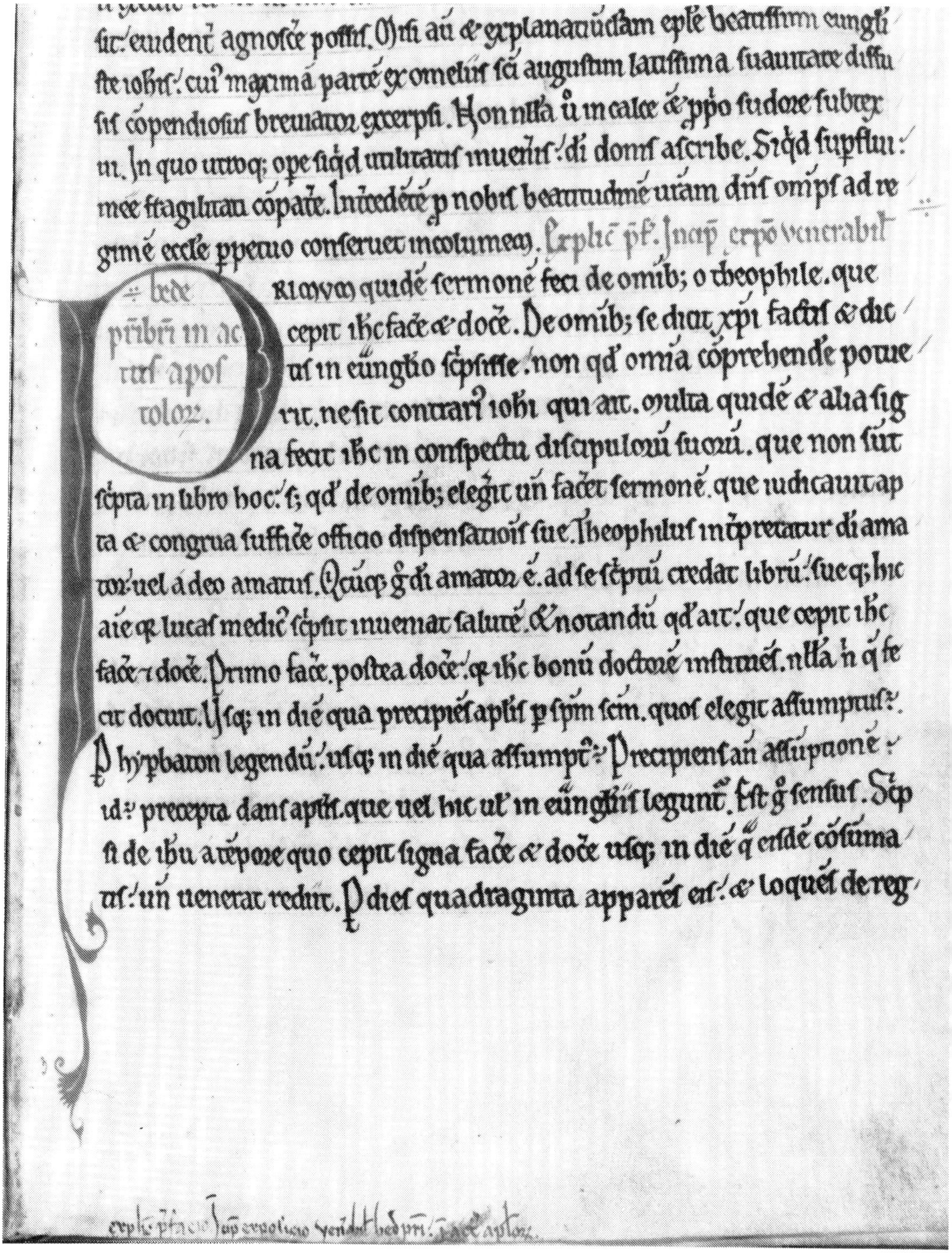

Plate 1   Princeton University Library, MS Garrett 71, fol. 3, actual size. The hand of scribe A

Acts, Bede's *Nomina regionum atque locorum de Actibus Apostolorum*, in the middle of the section on Libya 'libiam habet cuius inferiorem partem nilus'.[17] This ends on fol. 30 followed by the rubric 'Explicit liber iv in dei nomine expositionis venerabilis Bede presbyteri in actus apostolorum'. It is followed immediately by the prologue to Bede's *Retractatio in Actus Apostolorum* (the second item in the list of contents), the text itself beginning on fol. 30[v] (see Pl. 2) and ending on line 4 of fol. 50[v].[18] Then, after an erased rubric,[19] scribe A resumed copying with Bernard's Prologue to *De praecepto et dispensacione* (listed as the fourth item).[20] Scribe A must have been expecting this work (copied by his collaborator, scribe B) to follow, as it would have done, had not the second booklet been inserted or misbound in the middle of the first by the mid thirteenth century.[21]

The second booklet (fols 51–62) is a single gathering of twelve leaves (8[12]) written by scribe C. It looks quite different from the first because the text is copied in double columns of 31 lines per page rather than long lines, and there are green as well as the red initials of the first booklet. Scribe C wrote slightly later than the scribes of booklet one; C's letter forms include round-backed **d** (instead of the upright **d** of scribes A and B) and an **a** which is almost closed up to make the two-compartment form as well as the trailing-headed **a** (Pl. 3).

This booklet contains *De vera et falsa penitencia* (the third item in the contents list), attributed in the rubric to St Augustine: 'Incipit liber aurelii augustini de vera et falsa penitencia'.[22] It is the main item in this booklet and ends on fol. 62[v], line 13, leaving a column and a half blank. In this space a fourth scribe, D, the latest of the scribes, recopied the prologue to Bernard's *De praecepto* which scribe A had previously written on fol. 50[v]. Although the Bernard work thus introduced follows this preface (in the second part of the first booklet), there were problems for the medieval binder: all 8 leaves of the quire which contained the beginning of item 4 were missing. As there are no quire numbers or catchwords here, there is no obvious indication of this large loss of text.

The first booklet returns on fol. 63, with scribe B writing in long lines. *De praecepto* begins abruptly 'infirmari per carnem quia spiritus non adiuvat' and

---

[17] Laistner, App., pp. 149–58; the manuscript begins abruptly in line 9.

[18] Laistner, pp. 93–146, and p. xxxiv where this manuscript is classified as Class II.

[19] This perhaps called for a different work by Bernard but it is impossible to read the erased title.

[20] *Sancti Bernardi opera III: Tractatus et opuscula*, ed. J. Leclercq and H. M. Rochais (Rome, 1963), pp. 253–54. The same prologue is repeated on fol. 62[v] by a different hand, and the main text begins abruptly on fol. 63, following the missing quire 9.

[21] It is possible that booklet II (the present quire 8) was placed here deliberately by the binder, to fill the gap before the beginning of quire 10, quire 9 having already been lost.

[22] *PL*, 40, 1113–30; the text is now considered to be 'perhaps by Gilbert the Minorite', according to R. Sharpe, *List of Identifications*, Corpus of British Medieval Library Catalogues, 2nd edn (London, 1995), p. 36. His source for this statement was probably *Clavis patristica pseudepigraphorum medii aevi*, 2 (Turnhout, 1994), p. 709, no. 3081, according to Andrew Watson.

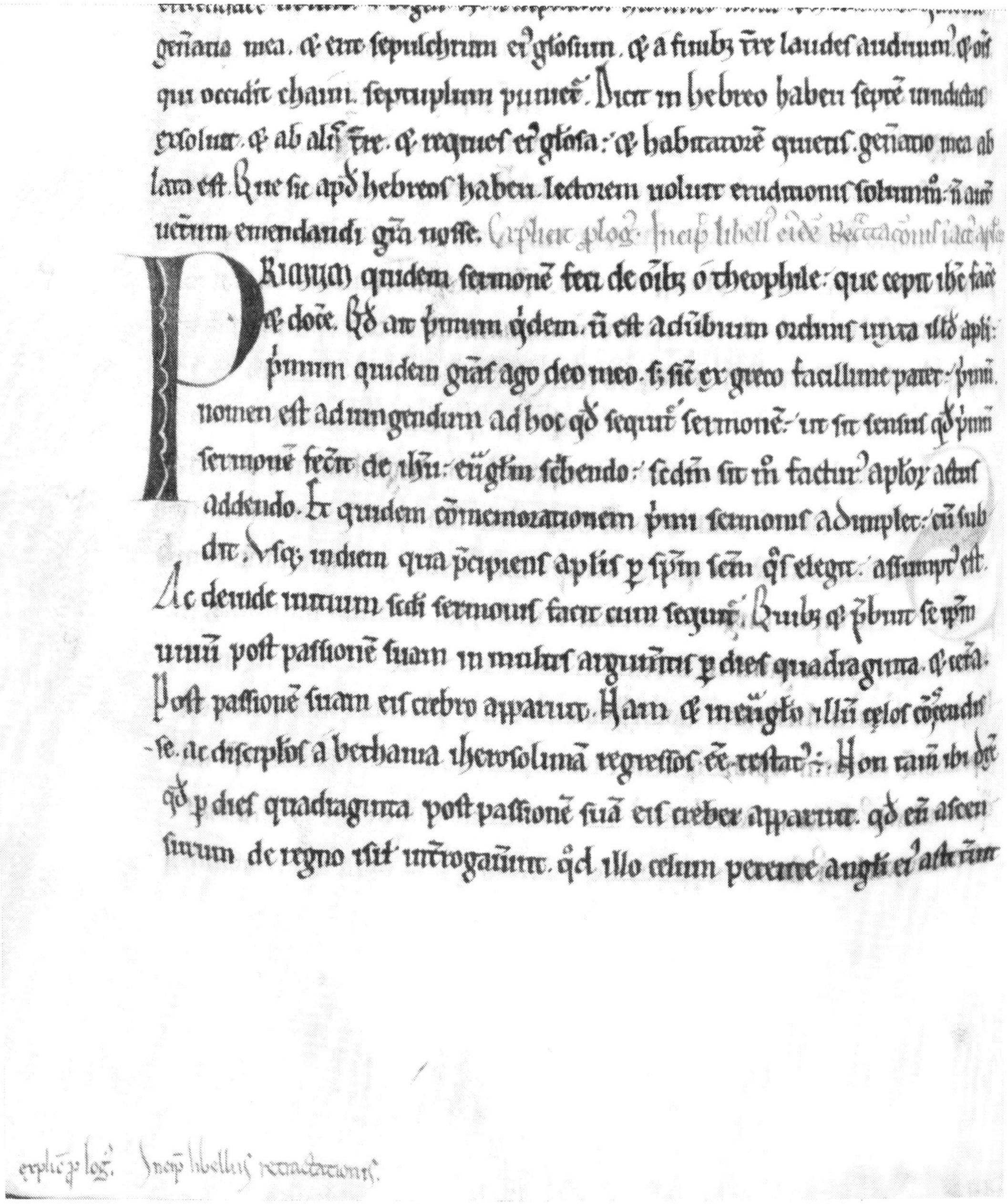

Plate 2   Princeton University Library, MS Garrett 71, fol. 30ᵛ, actual size. The hand of scribe B

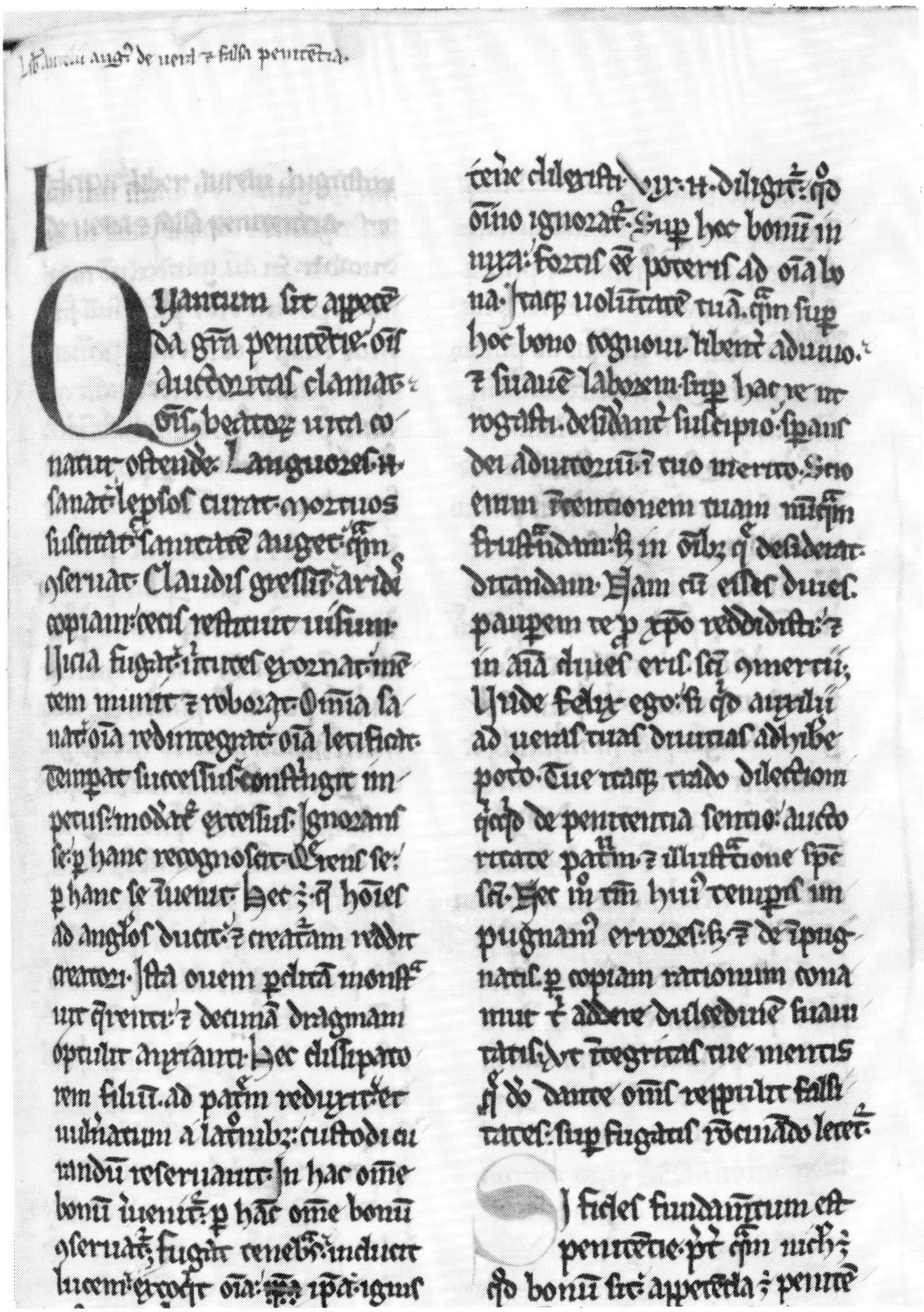

Plate 3   Princeton University Library, MS Garrett 71, fol. 51, actual size. The hand of scribe C

finishes on fol. 70 without any explicit, despite several lines' space available for one.[23] On fol. 70ᵛ scribe A added a short text, another Bede work, *De loquela per gestum digitorum: libellum*, without any identifying rubric, incipit or explicit.[24]

The third booklet (fols 71–93) consists of three quires of 8 leaves each (11–12⁸) (fols 71–86) 13⁸ (lacks 7, fols 87–93) written slightly later than the others by scribe D, and contains the 'meditationes beati Bernardi abbatis de miseria hominis', ending on fol. 84.[25] As in the second booklet, the text is written in double columns of 31 lines per page, but because it is more tightly written with a slightly finer pen, it looks different; there is also more frequent use of colour. The *meditationes* begin with a six-line red and green painted **M**, decorated with fine foliate red pen decoration (Pl. 4), and end with a rubricated explicit added in the margin. It is followed by items not given in the contents: a short piece (fols 84–85) attributed to Augustine in a marginal rubric 'Quedam excerpta ex libro exhortacionis sancti augustini',[26] and three parables of Bernard: *Parabola V, De fide, spe et charitate* (fols 85–86ᵛ),[27] *Parabola VI, De Ethiopissa* (fols 86ᵛ–89ᵛ),[28] and *Parabola II, De pugna spirituali* (fols 89ᵛ–92).[29]

All the texts in the third booklet have a little more pen decoration than there is in the others. Initials are in two colours, green and red, or divided red and black as on fols 71 and 85, and red touches occur on some small capitals. Not every text was at first identified by a rubric supplied at its beginning or end: these were sometimes added in the margins in a larger hand. For instance, in the outer margin of fol. 84 there is a rubricated explicit to the *meditationes* followed by the incipit to 'Quedam excerpta'. The **Q** is a large green initial. An omitted passage in the second of the Parables had to be added at the foot of the second column of fol. 87. They finish on fol. 92, and the rest of the page (formerly left blank) was filled by many later scribbles and pen trials, as well as the Waverley *ex libris* copied by a fourteenth-century hand. Sixteenth-century scribbles include a few words in English: 'god kepe you in good hele'.

The music added to fols 92ᵛ–93ᵛ in the fourteenth century was written in square notation on a 4-line stave. These leaves contain antiphons for St Edmund of Abingdon, archbishop of Canterbury, beginning 'eadmundo archiepiscopo. ad i

---

[23] It lacks pp. 254–75 of the text as edited by J. Leclercq and H. M. Rochais, beginning p. 275, line 24, to p. 294.

[24] *PL*, 90, 689–92.

[25] *PL*, 184, 485–508, a pseudonymous work; cf. Sharpe, *List*, p. 50.

[26] *PL*, 40, 1047–78, as Augustine; *PL*, 99, 197–282, as Paulinus of Aquilea. Cf. Sharpe, *List*, pp. 37 and 147.

[27] Cf. *Sancti Bernardi opera VI: 2 Sermones III*, ed. J. Leclercq and H. M. Rochais (Rome, 1972), pp. 282–85, with title 'De tribus filiabus regus'. Princeton's rubric reads 'Parabola sancti Bernardi de Rege nobili et filiabus eius'.

[28] Ibid., pp. 288–95, preceded by *Introductio* not in this manuscript.

[29] Ibid., pp. 267–73, with title 'De conflictu duorum regum' and with textual variants.

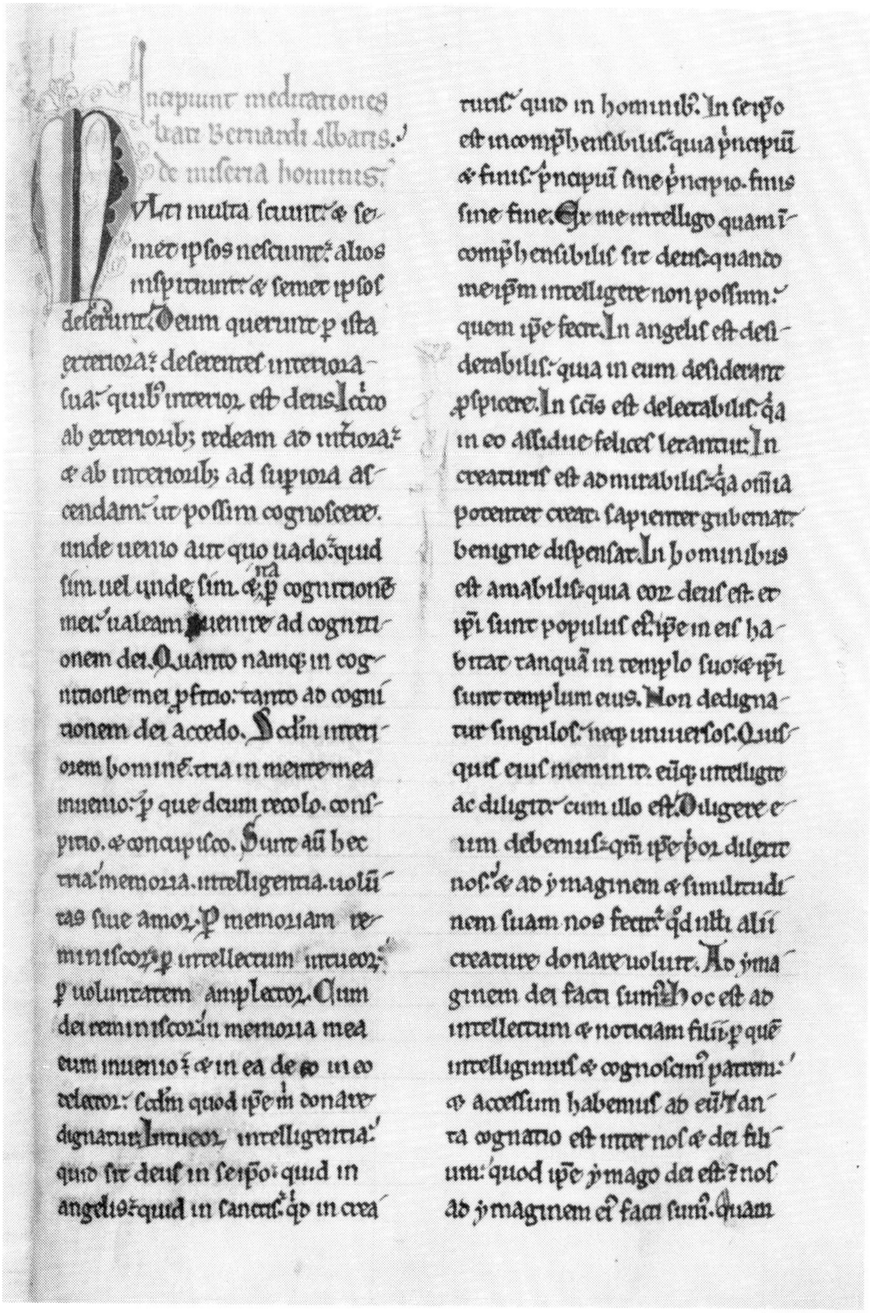

Incipiunt meditationes beati Bernardi abbatis de miseria hominis.

Multi multa sciunt et semetipsos nesciunt. alios inspiciunt et semetipsos deserunt. Deum querunt per ista exteriora. deserentes interiora sua. quibus interior est deus. Idcirco ab exterioribus redeam ad interiora. et ab interioribus ad superiora ascendam. ut possim cognoscere. unde venio aut quo vado. quid sim. vel unde sim. et ita per cognitionem mei. valeam pervenire ad cognitionem dei. Quanto namque in cognitione mei proficio. tanto ad cognitionem dei accedo. Secundum interiorem hominem. tria in mente mea invenio. per que deum recolo. conspicio. et concupisco. Sunt autem hec tria. memoria. intelligentia. voluntas sive amor. Per memoriam reminiscor. per intellectum intueor. per voluntatem amplector. Cum dei reminiscor. in memoria mea eum invenio. et in ea de eo in eo delector. secundum quod ipse mihi donare dignatur. Intueor intelligentia. quid sit deus in seipso. quid in angelis. quid in sanctis. quid in creaturis. quid in hominibus. In seipso est incomprehensibilis. quia principium et finis. principium sine principio. finis sine fine. Ex me intelligo quam incomprehensibilis sit deus. quando meipsum intelligere non possum. quem ipse fecit. In angelis est desiderabilis. quia in eum desiderant prospicere. In sanctis est delectabilis. quia in eo assidue felices letantur. In creaturis est admirabilis. quia omnia potenter creat. sapienter gubernat. benigne dispensat. In hominibus est amabilis. quia eorum deus est. et ipsi sunt populus eius. et ipse in eis habitat tanquam in templo suo. et ipsi sunt templum eius. Non dedignatur singulos. neque universos. Quisquis eius meminit. eumque intelligit ac diligit. cum illo est. Diligere eum debemus. quoniam ipse prior diligit nos. et ad ymaginem et similitudinem suam nos fecit. quod nulli alii creature donare voluit. Ad ymaginem dei facti sumus. hoc est ad intellectum et notitiam filii. per quem intelligimus et cognoscimus patrem. et accessum habemus ad eum. Tanta cognatio est inter nos et dei filium. quod ipse ymago dei est. et nos ad ymaginem eius facti sumus. Quam

Plate 4 Princeton University Library, MS Garrett 71, fol. 71, actual size. The hand of scribe D

antiphona. Gaude syon ornata tympano . . . fecit crucis ludibrus'. Unfortunately, a leaf has been lost between fols 92 and 93 so that the antiphons are incomplete: they restart abruptly on fol. 93 'caritatis ut iubar ethereum, pluit verbum . . . ', and end equally abruptly on fol. 93ᵛ '. . . ac cherubim glorie. Plus ignes'. Possibly they once continued on a now lost pastedown on the back cover.

The book was rebound in the fourteenth century and still has its binding of oak boards covered with alum-tawed skin, rebacked and restored in the early twentieth century. The faint impression of the medieval title can be seen near the top of the lower cover 'Beda. Super [actus] apostolorum', as well as the marks of a strap and pin fastening.[30] A rough pen sketch of a cavalier was added to the front cover in the seventeenth century.

Despite its imperfections, the volume was clearly part of Waverley's library for over three centuries. The two ownership inscriptions (fols 1ᵛ, 92ᵛ) show that it certainly belonged there in the thirteenth and fourteenth centuries. After four centuries, Waverley was suppressed with the lesser monasteries in 1536. It is difficult to determine what subsequently happened to the books in its library. We can trace ownership of the land, but we do not know whether the property might have included contents such as books.

Henry VIII granted dissolved monastic estates to his favourites. On 20 July 1537 Sir William Fitzwilliam, KG, received from the king the property of the lately dissolved abbey of Waverley, with the manor, the church and churchyard, all messuages and lands and the rectory and advowson of the same.[31] Sir William, a close friend of Henry's, was Lord High Admiral and Treasurer of the King's household; he was created Earl of Southampton in 1537. After his death in 1542, the properties of Waverley passed to his half-brother, Sir Anthony Browne (d. 1548), guardian to Prince Edward and Princess Elizabeth. Sir Anthony had received Battle Abbey in 1538, and many other church lands and manors. Anthony Browne (1526–92), eldest of his seven sons, inherited in 1548. A Roman Catholic, he was an ambassador and loyal servant of the Crown under both Mary and Elizabeth, and was created Viscount Montague in 1554, on the occasion of Mary's marriage to Philip of Spain.

During the first Lord Montague's time, the great pillaging of Waverley's buildings began. Between 1562 and 1568 Sir William More who was building his new house at nearby Loseley 'brought there many waggonloads of building material (mostly stone) from Waverley, which then belonged to his friend Lord Montague . . . As a part of the abbey buildings was occupied as a dwelling house, this must have been brought from the Church and from those monastic buildings which were not suitable for domestic

---

[30] Marks of the strap from upper to lower cover, with nail-hole for catchpin on lower cover. According to Michael Gullick, the binding is 'Pollard stage xx'.

[31] *Letters and Papers Foreign and Domestic of the Reign of Henry VIII*, ed. J. Gairdner, XI (London, 1888), no. 202 (37).

use'.[32] Books may also have been moved out at that time, when the buildings were being dismantled, and possibly some were taken to Loseley. In 1604 Sir William's son, Sir George (1553–1632) presented 26 manuscripts to the Bodleian Library, including Waverley's copy of Juvencus (now MS Bodley 527).[33]

Were all Waverley's manuscripts dispersed in the 1560s or did some remain in the possession of the Browne family? Lord Montague's heir in 1592 was his grandson, Anthony Maria Browne, second Viscount (1573/4–1629).[34] A Roman Catholic like his grandfather, he regularly sheltered priests, and both men may well have 'protected' medieval books of Catholic interest. The second Viscount was a known scholar and booklover, who translated St Bonaventura's *Legenda S. Francisci*.[35] In 1609 Anthony and his brother John Browne conveyed the Waverley estate to John Coldham, and the land remained in the Coldham family for four generations.

In the eighteenth century the Princeton manuscript is to be found with other medieval manuscripts in the library of the Cope family of Bramshill Park. Bramshill is only some 12 miles distant from Waverley, across the county boundary in Hampshire; it was purchased in 1700 by John Cope, later 6th baronet (d. 1749). We do not know how or when the medieval books known to have been at Bramshill arrived there. It is possible that they came through the collecting activities of John Cope's collateral ancestor, Sir Walter Cope (d. 1615).[36] Sir Walter had collected at least 215 manuscript volumes from across the length and breadth of England. In 1600 his friend Thomas James published his *Ecloga Oxonio-Cantabrigiensis*, primarily a catalogue of Oxford and Cambridge college libraries, but with separate lists of theological and philosophical manuscripts with reference to two private libraries: that of John, first Baron Lumley (1534?–1609)[37] and that of Sir Walter Cope. Many of these privately-owned manuscripts had come from former monastic houses, and

---

[32] *Victoria County History, Surrey*, II, pp. 623-24.

[33] *SC*, I, 88–9. An inventory of Sir William's books, drawn up 20 August 1566, includes several chronicles, statutes, the classics and works in English (including Chaucer and Lydgate); see J. Evans, 'Extracts from the Private Account Book of Sir William More, of Loseley, in Surrey, in the Time of Queen Mary and Queen Elizabeth', *Archaeologia*, 36 (1855), 284–310, at 290–92.

[34] Isaac Oliver painted a portrait of him in 1598, aged 24, with his two younger brothers John and William Browne. It is now in the Burghley House Collection, formerly at Cowdray, Sussex, the Montague family seat; see *Dynasties: Painting in Tudor and Jacobean England, 1530–1630*, ed. K. Hearn, Catalogue of an Exhibition held at the Tate Gallery, London, 12 October 1995–7 January 1996 (London, 1995), no. 81, p. 134. The National Portrait Gallery, London, owns a portrait of his grandfather, painted in 1569 by Hans Eworth, painter of many Catholic sympathisers.

[35] As *The Life of the Holie Father S. Francis written by Saint Bonaventure, and as it is related by . . . Aloysius Lipomanus*, Douai, L. Kellam, 1610 (*STC* 3271); facs. ed. D. M. Rogers, English Recusant Literature, 1558–1640 (Menston, 1972).

[36] For Sir Walter's library, see A. G. Watson, 'The Manuscript Collection of Sir Walter Cope, d. 1615', *Bodleian Library Record*, 12 (1987), 262–97.

[37] Lumley had inherited the library of his father-in-law, the Earl of Arundel, who had acquired Archbishop Cranmer's books; see further S. Jayne and F. R. Johnson, *The Lumley Library: the Catalogue of 1609* (London, 1956).

Cope gave 40 of them to the Bodleian Library in 1602. James's list does not seem to include the Princeton manuscript, but not all the items in it can be identified with extant volumes.

A manuscript 'Catalogue of the Books in the Library at Bramshill', dated January 1772, was drawn up during the time of Sir John Mordaunt Cope, 8th baronet (d. 1779). Now Oxford, Bodleian Library, MS Eng. misc. C.307, it lists several hundred printed books (pp. 1–147), followed by a list of 27 manuscripts (pp. 149–53). Nos 1–18 in the latter list are Latin manuscripts, nos 19–27 English manuscripts (or described in English), including a few Elizabethan and Stuart records. The very first manuscript listed is the Princeton volume, for the contents given correspond exactly with those of Garrett 71:

> Prefatio Venerabilis Bedae in Actus Apostolorum acce Episcopo. Expositio Venerabilis Bedae Presbyteri in Actus Apostolorum. Libellus ejusdem Retractationis in Actus Apostolorum. Liber Aurelii Augustini de Vera et falsa Poenitentia. Meditationes Sancti Bernardi Abbatis de Miseria Hominis. Quaedam excerpta ex Libro Exhortationis Sancti Augustini. Parabola Sancti Bernardi de Æthiopissa quam Filius Regis duxit in Uxorem. De guerra inter Babylonem et Jerusalem. Folio.

Thus the manuscript was certainly at Bramshill by 1772. No information about provenance is given in the catalogue, for this or any other book. If the book had once belonged to Sir Walter it could well have passed from one generation to another of the Cope family, since his brother Sir Anthony (d. 1614) was the great-great-great-great-grandfather of John Mordaunt Cope.

Another possibility is suggested by the close personal connections that existed between the Elizabethan and Jacobean owners of Waverley and Eversley, a manor adjoining Bramshill. Sir William Fitzwilliam, the first post-Dissolution owner of Waverley, had married Lucy Norris, the heiress of Eversley; after his death, Lucy remarried Sir William's half-brother and heir, Sir Anthony Browne. His son later sold Eversley, which was eventually acquired along with Bramshill by John Cope in 1700.[38] Books could thus have been moved from Waverley to Eversley and perhaps thence to Bramshill. Two of the surviving Waverley manuscripts certainly found their way there: Garrett 71 and the Origen manuscript now at Cambridge,[39] and there may have been others.

The Reverend Sir William Henry Cope, 12th baronet (1811–92), inherited Bramshill in 1851 from his fifth cousin Sir John who had died without issue. Sir William's collection of manuscripts described as 'ancient volumes formerly belonging to Waverley Abbey and the monastery of Winchelcombe [the Benedictine abbey of St

---

[38] Sale in 1582 to Deodatus Staverton, whose descendant Richard Staverton sold in 1669 to Sir Andrew Henley, 1st baronet; his nephew, also Sir Andrew, 3rd baronet, sold Bramshill to Cope for £21,500 in 1700.

[39] See above, p. 50.

Kenelm, Winchcombe, Glos.] and Wytham Abbey [outside Oxford]' was listed in 1872 for the Historical Manuscripts Commission.[40] According to this listing, the Cope collection had grown in a hundred years, from the 27 volumes listed in the 1772 catalogue to 86 volumes. Like his forebears, Sir William was a bibliophile and scholar: in 1848 he edited, with a biographical preface, the *Meditations on Twenty Select Psalms* of his Tudor ancestor, Sir Anthony Cope (d. 1551).[41] After Sir William's death, Bramshill and its library was inherited by his son, Sir Anthony, but after the latter's death without issue in 1912 the books were sold.

The Princeton manuscript was lot 17 in Sotheby's sale of 4 March 1913 and sold for £13 to Quaritch, who sold it on to the American bibliophile, Robert Garrett of Baltimore. Garrett, who was an omnivorous collector, acquired 172 medieval manuscripts from various sources, of which nine were English monastic books. In 1942 he gave his medieval collection to Princeton University, his *alma mater*, along with several thousand Arabic and other manuscripts he had collected.

Thus after over three centuries at Waverley, this monastic manuscript survived the Dissolution, cared for by Catholic families and remaining in the same geographical locality for a further four centuries. Members of both the Browne and Cope families were book lovers and collectors, who would have wished to preserve books from the past. In this century the book crossed the Atlantic, and for over 50 years has been in the safe keeping of a university library, where it is available for research by present and future generations.[42]

---

[40] *Royal Commission on Historical Manuscripts*, 3rd Report (London, 1872), p. xvi and app., p. 242; the Princeton MS is no. VI in the collection, while the Cambridge volume is no. I.

[41] Sir Anthony also published *The Historie of . . . Anniball and Scipio, translated out of Titus Livius and other authoures* in 1554. The Bramshill/Cope library contained two manuscripts ascribed to him, an abbreviated chronology and a commentary on the first two gospels, dedicated to Edward VI. Cf. *DNB*. Sir William published *Bramshill: its History and Architecture* (London, 1883).

[42] Warm thanks to three friends, Professors Nancy Pollard Brown, Jeanne Krochalis and Barbara Raw, who have read and commented helpfully on early versions of this essay, and to Professor Andrew Watson for his later comments.

CHAPTER THREE

'Quaderni simul ligati': Recherches sur les manuscrits en cahiers

Jean Vezin

Un nombre relativement important de manuscrits antérieurs au XVe siècle se présentent encore dans leur état d'origine. Sauf rares exceptions, ces volumes sont couverts par des ais de bois et par une peau en général plutôt épaisse. Ces reliures sont fort résistantes et devaient coûter très cher si l'on considère les prescriptions faites vers le milieu du XIIe siècle pour l'entretien des livres de monastères comme Corbie ou Fleury.[1] Différents textes montrent cependant que tous les livres n'étaient pas dotés de couvertures aussi solides. Des auteurs comme Alcuin et Raban Maur, pressés par le temps, ont pu expédier des exemplaires de leurs oeuvres sous forme de *quaterniones* ou de *schedulae* non encore reliés afin que leurs destinataires puissent les utiliser plus rapidement.[2] On connaît aussi des livres du XVe siècle qui sont restés 'non lyés ne historiez'[3] en attendant leur achèvement.

De nombreux textes, surtout des inventaires de bibliothèques, montrent que dès le haut Moyen Age on a pu conserver des livres non reliés ou couverts d'une simple feuille de cuir, de parchemin ou d'étoffe et dont les cahiers étaient cousus très légèrement. Il est question, dans ces inventaires, de *codicelli*, de *libelli* ou de *quaterniones* pour désigner un ensemble de cahiers simplement cousus: 'quaderni simul ligati'.[4] Ainsi, le catalogue carolingien de Murbach mentionne des 'Schedule diverse in quibus continentur passiones vel vitae sanctorum'.[5] Dans le catalogue de la bibliothèque de Saint-Gall, dressé vers 884-888, on rencontre des formules comme 'Vita sancti Hilarii in codicillo uno', 'quarternio unus de inventione corporis sancti

[1] J. Vezin, 'Les reliures carolingiennes de cuir à décor estampé de la Bibliothèque nationale de Paris', *Bibliothèque de l'Ecole des chartes*, **128** (1970), 88 et n. 3.

[2] E. Lesne, *Histoire de la propriété ecclésiastique en France. IV. Les livres, scriptoria et bibliothèques du commencement du VIIIe siècle à la fin du XIe siècle* (Lille, 1938), p. 373.

[3] A. De Schryver, 'Prix de l'enluminure et codicologie', dans *Miscellanea codicologica F. Masai dicata*, éd. P. Cockshaw, M.-C. Garand et P. Jodogne, (Gand, 1979), II, 471.

[4] F. Dolbeau, 'Noms de livres', dans *Vocabulaire du livre et de l'écriture au Moyen Age: actes de la table ronde, Paris 24–26 septembre 1987*, ed. O. Weijers (Turnhout, 1989), pp. 89 et 96. Sur le sens de *quaternio* ou *quaternus*, voir aussi L. Bataillon, 'Exemplar, pecia, quaternus', dans *Vocabulaire du livre*, pp. 208–11. Autres références dans P. R. Robinson, 'The Booklet, a Self-Contained Unit in Composite Manuscripts', dans *Codicologica 3. Essais typologiques*, réd. A. Gruijs et J. P. Gumbert (Leiden, 1980), pp. 52–4; Lesne, *Histoire de la propriété ecclésiastique*, pp. 372–3.

[5] W. Milde, *Der Bibliothekskatalog des Klosters Murbach aus dem 9. Jahrhundert* (Heidelberg, 1968), p. 46 et pl. 10.

Stephani', 'Liber I genesis in quaternionibus', 'Expositio in cantica canticorum in quaternionibus II'. La majorité des notices ne sont accompagnées d'aucune précision ou bien de la mention 'in volumine uno';[6] on peut supposer qu'il s'agit alors de volumes normalement reliés.

Toutefois, le vocabulaire employé dans ces inventaires est difficile à interpréter, comme le montre l'exemple du catalogue dressé au XIVe siècle de la bibliothèque du prieuré augustin de Lanthony à Hyde, près de Gloucester.[7] On trouve dans ce document des mentions comme 'quaternus simplex', 'parvus quaternus', 'quaternus magnus', 'albus quaternus', 'in uno nigro quaterno', 'quaternus magnus cum rubeo coreo'. Ces trois dernières mentions s'appliquent vraisemblablement à des ensembles de cahiers cousus et enveloppés par une simple feuille de cuir ou de parchemin blanc, noir ou rouge. La notice numérotée 269–270 par Henri Omont semble résoudre notre problème. Elle est en effet rédigée de la manière suivante: 'Casus Bernardi, libri duo, quorum unus ligatus et alter quaternus'. Malheureusement, un peu plus bas, sous le numéro 281, il est question d'un 'quaternus ligatus'. Pour le rédacteur de ce catalogue, le mot *quaternus* aurait-il deux sens, celui de cahier et celui de *codex*?

Même dans les bibliothèques princières, certains livres possèdent une couverture très modeste. C'est ce que l'on peut constater à la lecture de l'inventaire de la librairie de Charles V au Louvre.[8] D'après l'inventaire de la bibliothèque pontificale dressé en 1369, une quarantaine de volumes avaient reçu une simple couverture de parchemin ou de cuir sans ais: 'coopertus de pergameno sine postibus', 'coopertus corio rubeo sine postibus', ou même de tissus: 'coopertus sindone rubea sine postibus'.[9] La *Consignatio librorum* de la bibliothèque des Visconti-Sforza, datée de 1426, décrit des ouvrages, notamment des traités de médecine, dépourvus de reliure: 'Sexterni quinque scripti in medicina in magna forma sine assidibus et copertura', 'Iosephus hystoriographus non ligatus sexternorum decem et foliorum duorum'.[10] Le même inventaire cite aussi un manuscrit formé de cahiers simplement couverts de parchemin ou de cuir blanc: 'Certe autoritates medicine voluminis parvi in pluribus quaternis coperti carta sive corio albo veteri pauci valoris'.[11] Toujours dans le même inventaire, nombreux sont les cas où un livre est dit 'copertus carta', c'est à dire de parchemin. A plusieurs reprises, le rédacteur précise: 'copertus carta sine assidibus'.[12]

---

[6] P. Lehmann, *Mittelalterliche Bibliothekskataloge Deutschlands und der Schweiz*, 1 (München, 1918), *passim*.

[7] H. Omont, 'Catalogue des manuscrits du prieuré de Lanthony (Gloucestershire) (XIVe siècle)', *Centralblatt für Bibliothekswesen*, 9 (1892), 207–22.

[8] L. Delisle, *Recherches sur la librairie de Charles V* (Paris, 1907).

[9] P. Gasnault, 'Observations paléographiques et codicologiques tirées de l'inventaire de la librairie pontificale de 1369', *Scriptorium*, 34 (1980), 273.

[10] E. Pellegrin, *La bibliothèque des Visconti et des Sforza, ducs de Milan au XVe siècle* (Paris, 1955), pp. 19 et 251, nos A 801, 802, 804.

[11] Ibid., p. 169, no. A 430.

[12] Ibid., pp. 21, 83, nos A 49, 50; p. 105, no. A 150; p. 142, no. A 318 *et passim*.

Un volume est seulement couvert de papier: 'papiro albo',[13] ce qui semble le distinguer de trois volumes dotés de plats de carton couverts de cuir: 'cum assidibus papiri et copertura corii'.[14]

Plusieurs exemples, qu'il serait facile de multiplier, permettent d'illustrer ces textes. Le 'Book of Mulling', manuscrit copié dans le seconde moitié du VIIIe siècle en minuscule irlandaise est composé de quatre cahiers, un pour chaque évangile. Ces cahiers n'ont jamais été reliés et sont conservés dans un coffret de cuivre.[15] Le manuscrit 40 de Saint-Gall est un recueil factice relié entre deux ais de bois fort épais.[16] Ce recueil se compose de trois parties. La première page de la deuxième partie (pp. 168–299) est restée blanche depuis l'origine. Elle est fort sale, comme si elle avait servi de couverture, ce que confirme la présence d'un titre en capitales rustiques écrit sur deux lignes, sans doute au IXe siècle, parallèlement au grand côté, le bas des lettres étant tourné vers le dos: 'EXPOS IN EVANGL/MATH'. La première page de la troisième partie (pp. 300–57), restée blanche également, porte aussi un titre en capitales rustiques contemporaines des précédentes, disposé comme dans la seconde partie, mais sur une seule ligne: 'EXPOSITIO SUP MISSA'. On peut penser que ces deux parties sont restées un certain temps en cahiers avant d'être protégées par une reliure plus solide. Comme l'indique le cas de ce manuscrit de Saint-Gall, tôt ou tard, ces volumes *in quaternionibus*, trop fragiles, étaient reliés. Cependant quelques très rares exemples de manuscrits sont couverts d'une simple feuille de parchemin ou de cuir à laquelle les cahiers sont ordinairement cousus de façon très rudimentaire, ce qui permettait de les découdre facilement. Nous connaissons une vingtaine de ces reliures remontant à l'époque carolingienne, dont la moitié, environ, proviennent de Fulda.[17]

D'autres reliures par enveloppement réalisées pendant le Moyen Age sont encore

---

[13] Ibid., pp. 19 et 222, no. A 671.

[14] Ibid., pp. 19 et 263, no. A 853; p. 267, no. A 868; p. 270, no. A 884.

[15] S. Berger, *Histoire de la Vulgate* (Paris, 1893), p. 34; *CLA*, II, 276; P. McGurk, *Latin Gospel Books from A.D. 400 to 800* (Paris et Bruxelles, 1961), p. 83.

[16] A. Bruckner, *Scriptoria medii aevi Helvetica*, 2 (Genève, 1936), p. 57. Deux exemples analogues ont été relevés sur un manuscrit de Fulda par K. Christ, 'Karolingische Bibliothekseinbände', dans *Festschrift Georg Leyh: Aufsätze zum Bibliothekswesen u. zur Forschungsgeschichte dargebracht zum 60. Geburtstage*, éd. E. Leipprand (Leipzig, 1937), p. 84 et sur un manuscrit de Freising par B. Bischoff, *Die Südostdeutschen Schreibschulen und Bibliotheken in der Karolingerzeit*, I, *Die bayerischen Diözesen*, 3e édn (Wiesbaden, 1974), pp. 148–9.

[17] Christ, 'Karolingische Bibliothekseinbände', pp. 84–6; B. Van Regemorter, 'La reliure souple des manuscrits carolingiens de Fulda', *Scriptorium*, 11 (1957), 249–57; *CLA*, IX, 1381. Pour d'autres exemples, voir B. Van Regemorter, 'Evolution de la technique de la reliure du VIIIe au XIIe siècle', *Scriptorium*, 2 (1949), 283–4, pl. 22; B. Bischoff et J. Hoffmann, *Libri Sancti Kiliani, die Würzburger Schreibschule und die Dombibliothek im VIII. und IX. Jahrhundert* (Würzburg, 1952), p. 103; *CLA*, IX, 1428; B. Bischoff, *Mittelalterliche Studien*, 3 (Stuttgart, 1981), pp. 108–9; J. Vezin, 'Une reliure carolingienne de cuir souple (Oxford, Bodleian Library, Marshall 19), *Revue française d'histoire du livre*, 36 (1982), 235–41; *CLA*, IX, 1352.

conservées. La Hessische Landesbibliothek de Darmstadt en possède trois qui remontent au XIIᵉ siècle.[18] La Bibliothèque nationale de France en garde quelques unes du XIIᵉ ou du XIIIᵉ siècle.[19] Certaines de ces reliures sont très rudimentaires et les cahiers sont simplement fixés à la feuille de cuir ou de parchemin servant de couverture par de petits liens de parchemin. D'autres, en revanche, sont plus soignées. La couverture proprement dite est doublée de toile et un rabat protège la tranche de gouttière. Extrêmement rares jusqu'au XIVᵉ siècle, ces reliures se multiplient à la fin du Moyen Age, surtout, semble t-il, dans les régions germaniques. C'est du moins ce que les exemplaires subsistants laissent penser. Jouant avec les fils de couture et des renforts de cuir ou de corne, les relieurs réalisent alors des ouvrages de grande qualité dont le nom: 'ligaturae more studentium' indique assez la destination.[20]

Un cas particulièrement intéressant est celui du manuscrit A.IV.34 de la cathédrale de Durham. Ce tout petit volume, copié au XIIᵉ siècle, comprend 67 fols et mesure 185/190mm de haut sur 105/110mm de large. Il n'a jamais été relié. Chacun de ses cahiers a été constitué par pliage d'une feuille de parchemin découpée sans doute avant de recevoir l'écriture. Par un hasard extraordinaire, ces cahiers sont restés indépendants les uns des autres, nul n'ayant songé à les relier pendant les sept siècles qui ont suivi leur transcription. En revanche, à l'intérieur de chaque cahier, les doubles feuillets étaient rendus solidaires les uns des autres par deux petites bandes de peau qui les traversaient en tête et en queue du dos. Plusieurs de ces liens subsistent encore.[21] Ce livre est ainsi décrit dans le catalogue de la bibliothèque de la cathédrale de Durham: 'Notae super Cantica canticorum, in quaterno. Secundo folio *tituli est*'.[22] Cette notice confirme que l'expression *in quaterno* peut s'appliquer à un ensemble de plusieurs cahiers. On constate également que les feuillets constituant un cahier pouvaient être rendus solidaires par des liens passés en tête et en queue du dos. C'est sans doute ce que veut dire Alexandre Neckam quand il écrit: 'Cedula sive apendice tam superiori parte, quam inferiori folia habeat coniuncta'.[23]

---

[18] H. Knaus, 'Hochmittelalterliche Koperteinbände, *Zeitschrift für Bibliothekswesen und Bibliographie*, 8 (1961), 326–37.

[19] J. Vezin, 'Reliures souples des XIIᵉ et XIIIᵉ siècles', *Bulletin de la Société nationale des Antiquaires de France* (1976), 168–71; idem, 'Paléographie et codicologie', *Ecole pratique des Hautes Etudes, IVᵉ section, sciences historiques et philologiques, Annuaire* (1977–78), 583–6.

[20] B. Bischoff, *Paléographie de l'Antiquité romaine et du Moyen Age occidental*, tr. H. Astma et J. Vezin (Paris, 1993), p. 39; M. Mairold, 'Die gotischen Bucheinbände des Stiftes Seckau', *Codices manuscripti*, 1 (1975), 13–22, ill.; H. Alker, 'Wiener Kettenstich- und Langsticheinbände', *Gutenberg Jahrbuch*, 40 (1965), 368–73, ill.; idem. 'Ketten- und Langsticheinbände aus der Österreichischen Nationalbibliothek', *Gutenberg Jahrbuch*, 41 (1966), 331–35.

[21] A. I. Doyle, 'Further Observations on Durham Cathedral MS. A. IV. 34', dans *Litterae textuales, Essays Presented to G. I. Lieftinck, I. Varia codicologica* (Amsterdam, 1972), pp. 35–47, figs 1–3.

[22] P. R. Robinson, 'The Booklet', p. 53.

[23] Alexander Neckham, *De utensilibus*, ed. T. Wright (London, 1857), p. 116; il faut vraisemblablement traduire ce passage: 'le scribe doit disposer de cahiers dont les feuillets sont réunis en tête et en queue par des bandes de parchemin'. Le mot *cedula* est glosé par *agnice* qui a ce sens. Cf. A. Tobler et

On a encore pu observer des vestiges de cette pratique dans un certain nombre de
manuscrits portant encore leur reliure à ais de bois d'origine. Il est très vraisemblable
que les exemples se multiplieront maintenant que l'attention des chercheurs est
attirée sur cette particularité. Ainsi, dans un exemplaire de l'*Expositio in Matthaeum*
du pseudo-Bède conservé à Munich,[24] on voit, à quelques centimètres des extrémités
de tête et de queue de chaque cahier, deux trous distants de 5mm environ. Des fils
subsistent toujours dans certains de ces trous entre les fols 12^v–13, 28^v–29, 52^v–53.
Un autre manuscrit de la même bibliothèque, qui contient les Catégories d'Aristote et
le *de Trinitate* de Boèce,[25] présente la même particularité à la pliure de son troisième
cahier. On observe des trous vides destinés sans doute au même usage dans un
manuscrit provenant de Fulda.[26] Dans un manuscrit copié à Metz pendant la
première moitié du XIe siècle, à la pliure d'un cahier (fols 51^v–52), on voit, en
plus du fil de couture, un très mince lacet de cuir passé dans deux trous séparés par
quelques millimètres à environ 80 ou 85mm de la tête. Ce lacet a dû servir à assurer
la solidarité des feuillets du cahier avant la couture.[27] On peut faire des constatations
similaires dans un recueil de textes divers constitué au XIIIe siècle.[28]

Notre collègue, Mme Marie-Pierre Laffitte, nous a signalé la présence de petits
liens de parchemin en tête et en queue des cahiers du manuscrit latin 11995 de la
Bibliothèque nationale de France relié à Corbie au IXe siècle. Le Professeur Szirmai a
signalé le même phénomène à Saint-Gall.[29] Dans une communication faite de 12
novembre 1990 à Wolfenbüttel, Mme Aliza Cohen a montré qu'il y avait des trous en
haut et en bas des feuillets dans les Evangiles de Henri le Lion. Ces trous servaient
visiblement au passage de fils qui permettaient de rendre solidaires les feuillets d'un
même cahier. M. Michael Gullick nous a indiqué l'existence d'un petit lien de
parchemin entre les fols 13^v–14 d'un manuscrit du XIIIe siècle composé seulement de
deux cahiers,[30] qui porte un *ex libris* de Saint-Denis de Reims du XVe siècle.
M. Obbema a signalé des traces de ligatures de cahiers au moyen d'une cordelette de
parchemin dans un manuscrit italien de la seconde moitié du XIIe siècle.[31] M. Albert

---

E. Lommatzsch, *Altfranzösisches Wörterbuch*, 1 (Berlin, 1925), s.v. *Agniz. Apendice* est synonyme de
cedula; F. Godefroy, *Dictionnaire de l'ancienne langue française*, 1 (Paris, 1881), s.v. *Agni*.

[24] München, Bayerische Staatsbibl., Clm 6268.

[25] München, Bayerische Staatsbibl., Clm 6373.

[26] Kassel, Gesamthochschulbibl., HS Theol. Q. 10.

[27] J. Vezin, 'Un manuscrit de la première moitié du XIe siècle (Reims, Bibl. mun. 1429)', dans
Miscellanea codicologica F. Masai dicata, I, 157–64.

[28] J. Vezin, 'Une très ancienne reliure à claies de parchemin (Oxford, Bodleian Library, Ms. Bodley
807)', dans *De libris compactis miscellanea*, éd. G. Colin (Bruxelles, 1984), p. 12.

[29] J. A. Szirmai, 'Carolingian Bindings in the Abbey Library of St Gall', dans *Making the Medieval
Book: Techniques of Production*, éd. L. L. Brownrigg (Los Altos Hills, CA, 1995), pp. 162–3, fig. 11.

[30] Philadelphia, Free Library, Lewis 5. Voir aussi M. C. Garand, 'Le septième colloque international
de paléographie latine', *Scriptorium*, 40 (1986), 129.

[31] L. Gimbrere et P. F. J. Obbema, 'Restauratie van handschriften en codicologie', dans *Le respect de
l'oeuvre d'art* cité dans *Scriptorium*, 42 (1988), *Bulletin codicologique*, no. 208, par Claudine Lemaire.

Derolez a relevé dans l'inventaire de la boutique de Michele Baldini, libraire à Florence, dressé en 1426, une mention qui s'applique à des cahiers de papier: 'fogli reali rigati e ligati, in fol. e in 4°, quadern. 9s.' Il conjecture que cette mention indiquait 'l'utilisation d'une ficelle pour réunir les bifeuillets constituant les cahiers'.[32]

Les observations qui précèdent renseignent sur quelques aspects du travail des scribes. Il apparaît que ceux-ci ont pu copier des ouvrages en utilisant des cahiers dont les feuillets, qu'ils soient de parchemin ou de papier, étaient rendus solidaires par deux minces tortillons de parchemin ou par deux fils. Ceci expliquerait, entre autres, que, sauf très rares exceptions, les feuillets sont toujours disposés dans l'ordre convenable à l'intérieur des cahiers des manuscrits, que leur reliure soit médiévale ou moderne. Pourtant, durant tout le haut Moyen Age, il n'existe pas, sauf exceptions rarissimes, de système de numérotation des feuillets;[33] seuls les cahiers portent, ordinairement en bas de la dernière page, du moins dans le monde latin, un chiffre, une lettre ou une réclame permettant de les disposer selon l'ordre convenable pour la reliure. Ce n'est qu'à partir des années 1230 environ qu'est mis au point un système de numérotation des feuillets à l'intérieur des cahiers, au moins dans les volumes soignés réalisés dans des ateliers qui produisaient des livres pour ainsi dire en série et dans lesquels plusieurs artisans, scribes, rubricateurs, peintres d'initiales et enlumineurs pouvaient se répartir la tâche, ce qui obligeait à dépecer les cahiers qui ne pouvaient être reconstitués qu'après que tous les intervenants aient achevé leur travail. Nous savons aussi que quelques rares cahiers ont été copiés en au moins deux parties au cours de l'époque antérieure. Ainsi, au IXe siècle, le onzième cahier du manuscrit Vatican, Regina lat. 96 (fols 81–88[v]) a été copié par deux scribes travaillant simultanément. Le premier a transcrit les fols 81–82[v] et 87–88[v] et le second, les fols 83–86[v]. Le même phénomène a été observé dans le cahier qui occupe les fols 79–86[v] d'un manuscrit un peu plus récent, Zürich, Bibliothèque de la ville, C 43 (72). Chaque fois, il a été nécessaire de reconstituer le cahier après la fin de la copie.[34]

La présence d'ouvrages *in quaternionibus* dans les bibliothèques médiévales explique certainement que d'assez nombreux manuscrits aient été copiés par plusieurs scribes travaillant simultanément après s'être réparti les cahiers d'un modèle. Le meilleur exemple est sans doute celui du manuscrit de la Troisième

---

[32] A. Derolez, *Codicologie des manuscrits en écriture humanistique sur parchemin* (Turnhout, 1984), I, 35, n. 11.

[33] P. Lehmann, *Erforschung des Mittelalters* (Stuttgart, 1960), III, 1–59.

[34] J. Vezin, 'Une faute de copiste et le travail dans les scriptoria du haut Moyen Age', dans *Sous la Règle de saint Benoît, structures monastiques et société en France du Moyen Age à l'époque moderne*, Ecole pratique des Hautes Etudes, IVe section, sciences historiques et philologiques, V. Hautes Etudes médiévales et modernes, 47 (Genève et Paris, 1982), pp. 427–31; P. Cagin, 'L'observation paléographique dans l'étude du Sacramentarium triplex de Saint-Gall', dans *Mélanges offerts à M. Emile Chatelain* (Paris, 1910), pp. 96–8.

Décade de Tite Live transcrit vers 800 à Tours par huit copistes utilisant comme modèle un volume du Ve siècle en écriture onciale.[35] Il existe plusieurs autres exemples de cette pratique.[36] En revanche, une lettre de Philippe, prieur de Clairvaux, adressée au milieu du XIIe siècle à un abbé de Liessies signale la présence à Clairvaux de cinq traités de saint Augustin qui manquaient à Liessies; 'mais, écrit le prieur, ces ouvrages sont insérés dans des recueils de grand format, de sorte qu'ils ne peuvent en être séparés, ni vous être envoyés'.[37] L'attitude du prieur est doublement compréhensible. D'une part, les reliures des recueils du genre de celui qui se trouvait à Clairvaux étaient certainement fort coûteuses et, d'autre part, si l'on considère les reliures cisterciennes du XIIe siècle actuellement conservées, elles étaient d'une grande solidité et il était très difficile de défaire les coutures unissant les cahiers aux nerfs. Nos restaurateurs le savent bien qui conservent souvent ces coutures médiévales quand ils refont une reliure. Il ne pouvait donc pas être question de démonter des ouvrages dont les cahiers étaient cousus sur nerfs et protégés par des ais de bois couverts de cuir. Ainsi, selon toute vraisemblance, seuls des livres conservés dans les bibliothèques médiévales sous la forme sommaire de simples cahiers isolés ou simplement cousus ont pu faciliter le travail des scribes en permettant de répartir les cahiers d'un livre modèle entre plusieurs copistes, autorisant ainsi à réduire le temps consacré à sa transcription. Cet aspect positif, cependant, ne doit pas faire oublier que ce mode de conservation rudimentaire favorisait la perte de feuillets ou de cahiers entiers.

---

[35] Vatican, Bibl. apost., MS Reg. lat. 762 et Paris, BN, MS lat. 5730. Cf. E. Chatelain, 'Le Reginensis 762 de Tite Live', *Revue de philologie*, 14 (1890), 29–85.

[36] Lesne, *Histoire de la propriété ecclésiastique*, pp. 358–62; Bischoff, *Paléographie*, p. 50; J. Vezin, 'La répartition du travail dans les scriptoria carolingiens', *Journal des Savants* (1974), 218–22; idem, 'Hincmar de Reims et Saint-Denis, à propos de deux manuscrits du De Trinitate de saint Hilaire', *Revue d'histoire des textes*, 9 (1979), 289–98, ill. Ces questions ont été récemment étudiées par W. Noel, 'The Division of Work in the Harley Psalter', dans *Making the Medieval Book: Techniques of Production*, éd. L. L. Brownrigg (Los Altos Hills, CA, 1995), pp. 1–15.

[37] J.-F. Genest, 'La bibliothèque cistercienne', dans *Histoire de Clairvaux: actes du colloque de Bar-sur-Aube/Clairvaux, 22–23 juin 1990* (Bar-sur-Aube, 1991), p. 115; J.-P. Bouhot, 'L'homéliaire des sancti catholici patres, sources et composition', *Revue des études augustiniennes*, 24 (1978), 123–7.

II
Scribes and Scripts

CHAPTER FOUR

A Twelfth-Century *Scriptrix* from Nunnaminster

P. R. Robinson

Malcolm Parkes has suggested that a group of early-tenth-century manuscripts consisting of part of the Parker manuscript of the *Anglo-Saxon Chronicle*, the Junius Psalter, the Tollemache Orosius, a copy of Isidore of Seville's *Etymologiae*, and a fragment of a commentary attributed to Remigius of Auxerre on the *De Nuptiis Philologiae et Mercurii* of Martianus Capella, was produced in a scriptorium at St Mary's Abbey, Winchester, better known as the Nunnaminster.[1] These manuscripts are interrelated by their script and decoration, and two calendars which precede (and are copied by the same hand as) the Junius Psalter point to their common origin at Winchester. More specifically, Professor Parkes has identified the hands responsible for two separate additions in the 'Book of Nunnaminster', a ninth-century prayer book owned by the house,[2] with those of the first scribe of the Parker manuscript and the second scribe of the Isidore respectively. The existence of a flourishing scriptorium at Nunnaminster would not be surprising since a tradition of nuns copying books was probably well established in Anglo-Saxon England, even though there is no undisputed evidence, such as a colophon stating that a manuscript was copied by a woman, as there is from the continent. What appears to be the earliest, if not the only, English manuscript signed by a nun survives from the twelfth century – interestingly, from Nunnaminster.[3]

---

[1] M. B. Parkes, 'The Palaeography of the Parker Manuscript of the *Chronicle*, Laws and Sedulius, and Historiography at Winchester in the Late Ninth and Tenth Centuries' (1976) and 'A Fragment of an Early Tenth-Century Anglo-Saxon Manuscript and its Significance' (1983), both repr. in his *Scribes, Scripts and Readers*, pp. 143–69 and 171–85.

[2] London, BL, MS Harley 2965, on which see W. de Gray Birch, *An Ancient Manuscript of the Eighth or Ninth Century Formerly Belonging to St. Mary's Abbey, or Nunnaminster, Winchester*, Hampshire Record Society (1899); *CLA*, II, 199; and Ker, *Catalogue*, no. 237. For the date, see J. Morrish, 'Dated and Datable Manuscripts Copied in England during the Ninth Century', *Mediaeval Studies*, 50 (1988), 512–38.

[3] Both E. A. Lowe (*CLA*, VI, 738) and B. Bischoff ('Manuscripts in the Early Middle Ages', in his *Manuscripts and Libraries in the Age of Charlemagne*, tr. and ed. M. Gorman (Cambridge, 1994), p. 13) thought that an eighth-century manuscript, containing a copy of Apponius's commentary on the Song of Songs, was copied by the Burginda named in a verse letter at the commentary's end. However, P. Sims-Williams, 'An Unpublished Seventh- or Eighth-Century Anglo-Latin Letter in Boulogne-sur-Mer 74 (82)', *Medium Aevum*, 48 (1979), 1–22, has argued that the text of this letter is so corrupt it must have been a copy. Moreover, as the letter does not unequivocally state that Burginda copied rather than

Oxford, Bodleian Library, MS Bodley 451 (*SC* 2401) contains a copy of Smaragdus of Saint-Mihiel's *Diadema monachorum* (fols ii^v–71^v),[4] followed by an anonymous moral treatise in 36 chapters (fols 72–94^v)[5] and 14 miscellaneous sermons (fols 94^v–119^v). Despite the manuscript's attribution of these sermons to St Augustine, they are chiefly by St Caesarius of Arles.[6] All three items were written and rubricated by a single hand which concluded its copying with the colophon in verse 'Salva et incolomis maneat per secula scriptrix' (fol. 119^v). Although the scribe does not give her name, it is clear she was a nun at St Mary's. Additions on endleaves (fols ii, 120), one by the scribe herself, relate to St Edburga of Winchester, a nun of the house, whose cult was localized.[7] Moreover, a fragmentary account roll used as a pastedown (fol. 121) in the fourteenth-century binding probably concerned the hospital of poor sisters (later known as the Sisterne House) within the precincts of, and belonging to, St Mary's.[8]

This twelfth-century volume forms a striking contrast with the usual type of book extant from a medieval English nunnery: content and date as well as its female scribe

---

commissioned a manuscript, it cannot be argued that she had copied its lost exemplar instead of the extant volume. See further his *Religion and Literature in Western England 600–800* (Cambridge, 1990), pp. 199–208, 213–15.

[4] *PL*, **102**, 593–690. For Smaragdus and his work see R. Grégoire in *Dictionnaire de Spiritualité*, ed. M. Viller, 14 (Paris, 1988), cols 959–61; also J. Leclercq, 'Smaragdus', in *An Introduction to the Medieval Mystics of Europe*, ed. P. E. Szarmach (Albany, NY, 1984), pp. 37–51.

[5] M. W. Bloomfield, *Incipits of Latin Works on the Virtues and Vices, 1100–1500 A.D.* (Cambridge, MA, 1979), no. 1452.

[6] *Sancti Caesarii Arelatensis Sermones*, ed. G. Morin, CCSL, 103, 104 (Turnhout, 1953). Those of Caesarius's sermons which can be identified in the present manuscript (fols 96^v–116) are: 54 (103, pp. 235–40), 43 (103, pp. 189–94), 154 (104, pp. 628–31), 46 (103, pp. 205–11), 47 (103, pp. 211–15), 44 (103, pp. 195–200), 223 (104, pp. 882–5), 157 (104, pp. 641–5), 33 (103, pp. 143–7), 13 (103, pp. 64–8), 227 (104, pp. 897–900), and 41 (103, pp. 180–4). The first (fols 95–96^v), beginning 'O fratres dilectissimi in hac die letari debemus die magno die natalis domini nostri iesu christi qui de celis descendit . . .', is unidentified; for the last sermon (fols 116–119^v), see F. Römer, *Die handschriftliche Überlieferung der Werke des heiligen Augustinus*, II/2 (Wien, 1972), p. 239.

[7] These additions have been published by S. J. Ridyard, *The Royal Saints of Anglo-Saxon England: a Study of West-Saxon and East-Anglian Cults* (Cambridge, 1988), pp. 309–10; that on fol. ii has also been printed, inaccurately, by L. Braswell, 'Saint Edburga of Winchester: a Study of her Cult, A.D. 950–1500, with an Edition of the Fourteenth-Century Middle English and Latin Lives', *Mediaeval Studies*, 33 (1971), 304 n. 53. The date of Edburga's death is uncertain but, according to Ridyard, p. 104 n. 30, she probably died sometime in the early 950s.

[8] This roll evidently contained accounts (for the years 1331–34) for some small ecclesiastical institution in Hampshire as payments are recorded for Selborne stone and other local building materials, such as slates for roofing and white earth (or chalk) for rough flooring. Its income consisted mainly of offerings on the Feast of St Mary Magdalen, plus a few small legacies and 'entry payments' by individuals. This last suggests that the accounts were those of a hospital or almshouse, and Derek Keene has informed me that he believes the Sisterne House (on which see his *Survey of Medieval Winchester*, Winchester Studies, 2 (Oxford, 1985), p. 855) is the most likely institution to which they belong. I hope to publish these accounts elsewhere.

make it noteworthy.[9] The *Diadema monachorum*, as a standard work of spiritual and monastic guidance, might be expected to be found in any monastic library but it is remarkable to find a copy from Nunnaminster. Despite the widespread dissemination of this text (there are at least 121 manuscripts of the work ranging in date from the ninth to the sixteenth centuries),[10] Bodley 451 contains the only surviving copy established definitely to have come from a female house, either in England or on the continent. Judging from books known to have survived from other English houses, few nunneries owned any Latin works. This impression may be due partly to the fact that few early books can be shown to have belonged to any female foundation, even the earlier ones. Only Nunnaminster itself with ninth- and eleventh-century prayer books,[11] Barking with an eleventh-century Gospel book,[12] and possibly Shaftesbury with a late-tenth-century psalter,[13] are assigned books that predate the twelfth century. Similarly, few twelfth-century volumes have survived from any female house, and of those few, books other than psalters are rare. Barking owned both a *Vitae Sanctorum* and a *Song of Songs with Lamentations*, glossed,[14] but a copy of Ambrose, *De officiis*, presumed to have belonged to the Yorkshire house of Swine may not have come into Swine's possession until the end of the fourteenth or beginning of the fifteenth century along with other books given by the local vicar, Peter.[15] Exceptionally, Peter's gift included other volumes which may have dated from

---

[9] D. N. Bell, *What Nuns Read: Books and Libraries in Medieval English Nunneries* (Kalamazoo, 1995), conveniently abstracts from Ker, *MLGB*, and Watson, *Supplement*, lists of books surviving from nunneries.

[10] R. Grégoire's list, 'La Tradizione manoscritta del 'Diadema monachorum' di Smaragdo († *ca.* 830)', *Inter Fratres*, 34 (1984), 1–20, supersedes that of W. Witters, 'Smaragde au Moyen Âge. La diffusion de ses écrits d'après la tradition manuscrite', in *Études ligériennes d'histoire et d'archéologie médiévales*, Mémoires et exposés présentés à la semaine d'études médiévales de Saint-Benoit-sur-Loire du 3 au 10 juillet 1969, ed. R. Louis, Soc. des fouilles archéologiques de l'Yonne (Auxerre, 1975), pp. 361–76.

[11] Besides the ninth-century 'Book of Nunnaminster' (see n. 2 above), an eleventh-century prayer book consisting of London, BL, Cotton MSS Nero A.II, fols 3–13, + Galba A.XIV survives. See E. Bishop, 'About an Old Prayer Book', in his *Liturgica historica: Papers on the Liturgy and Religious Life of the Western Church* (Oxford, 1918), pp. 384–91; Ker, *Catalogue*, no. 157; M. Lapidge, 'Some Latin Poems as Evidence for the Reign of Athelstan', *ASE*, 9 (1981), 83–93; B. J. Muir, *A Pre-Conquest English Prayer-Book*, HBS, 103 (1988); and D. Dumville, 'On the Dating of some Late Anglo-Saxon Liturgical Manuscripts', *TCBS*, 10 (1991), 46–7. J. Hillaby, 'Early Christian and Pre-Conquest Leominster: an Exploration of the Sources', *Trans. Woolhope Naturalists' Field Club*, 45 (1987), 557–684, argues that this prayer book belonged to Leominster.

[12] Oxford, Bodl. Lib., MS Bodley 155 (*SC* 1974); Ker, *Catalogue*, no. 303.

[13] Salisbury Cathedral Library, MS 150; cf. Watson, *Supplement*.

[14] Cardiff, Central Public Library, MS 1.381, fols 81–146 (see Ker, *MMBL*, II, 348–9), and Oxford, Bodl. Lib., MS Laud lat. 19 (see H. O. Coxe, *Laudian Manuscripts*, repr. from 1858–85 edn, with corrections and additions, and an historical introduction by R. W. Hunt (Oxford, 1973), p. 13).

[15] Cambridge, King's College, MS 18: the list of books Peter gave, recorded on fol. 104ᵛ, has been published by M. R. James, *A Descriptive Catalogue of the Manuscripts Other than Oriental in the Library of King's College Cambridge* (Cambridge, 1895), pp. 34–5.

the twelfth century, such as Peter Comestor's *Historia scholastica*, and Mark's Gospel, glossed, but they are not known to have survived.

The Nunnaminster Smaragdus is a volume of quarto size (290 × 185 mm) consisting of 120 folios arranged in 15 quires of 8 leaves each (quires 8 and 9 both have an added leaf [$8^8 + 1$ (fol. 56) before 1; $9^8 + 1$ (fol. 65) before 1] while quire 15 wants the last leaf, probably blank; its present fifth leaf (fol. 118) was supplied by another hand). Its *scriptrix* wrote a legible Anglo-Caroline minuscule that increased only slightly in size during the course of her copying (the book's written space measures 217 × 126 mm with 27 long lines per page at the beginning and 30 long lines towards the end). Her hand is very neat with upright, rounded letter forms (see Pl. 5) and she left a generous space between lines. She was a careful copyist and any corrections to the text were effected tidily and unobtrusively. On fol. ii she also added a note concerning the genealogy of St Edburga, granddaughter of Nunnaminster's founders Alfred and his queen Eahlswith, but this note was probably written when our *scriptrix* was old. Although the general aspect of the hand is the same, its strokes are not so firm. Such shakiness could be due to cold or infirmity rather than to age,[16] but the volume does not appear to me to have been copied as late as the added note which is datable *c.*1150 ('A transitu uero Aluredi regis usque M.c.l. anno incarnationis domini computati sunt cc^{ti} .l. anni . . .'). Thus, the manuscript may have been written sometime around 1120, assuming that its *scriptrix*'s career did not span more than about thirty years.

As was the custom of twelfth-century scribes, the *scriptrix* was also responsible for rubricating and decorating the volume. The Rustic Capitals used for chapter headings and the colophon are identical with those she used for *litterae notabiliores* throughout all the texts. Coloured initials of red, blue or green occur at the beginnings of each item and chapter, often over-spilling the space allocated for them (see Pl. 5). In the margins next to these initials tiny letters in red ink indicate the colour to be used and such directions have been followed faithfully: **r** (*rubeus* or *rouge*) for red initials, **a** (*azurus* or *azure*) for blue initials, and, unusually, **g** for green initials (as, for example, on fols 60, 60^v and 61). In using **g** when she was planning the alternation of colour, the nun was using English; more commonly, when such colour notes are found, **v** (for *viridis* or *vert*) indicated green.[17]

The resulting volume is a handsome one in which it would have been easy to find one's place in the text. Thus, it would have admirably fulfilled the purpose Smaragdus had intended. Composed for his monks as a commentary on the Benedictine rule, he wished that, since it was monastic custom to read the rule at chapter each morning, the *Diadema* should similarly be read each evening: 'Et quia

---

[16] Thus the shakiness of the so-called 'tremulous hand' which glossed many Worcester manuscripts is now believed to be due to a congenital tremor rather than age; see C. Franzen, *The Tremulous Hand of Worcester: a Study of Old English in the Thirteenth Century* (Oxford, 1991).

[17] Cf. A. Petzold, 'Colour Notes in English Romanesque Manuscripts', *British Library Jnl*, 16 (1990), 16–25. Michelle Brown has suggested to me that **g** could be an abbreviation for *viride grecum*.

frs̄ km̄i non extra nos sed intus innobis cum dī gīa possint exerce
re si uolunt. Si enim peccata relinquim̄ & uirtut operam dan̄t.
de terra morientium feliciter egressi sint̄ & in terra uiuentiū
feliciter uenient. & ideo qui solebat maledicere benedicat. &
qui solebat detrahere. semp qd bonum ē studeat pferre. Qui
solebat uacundiam incorde seruare. pacientiam teneat. qui
res alienas solebat inuadere. de reb; pprus studeat erogare.
Qui innegotio fraudem facere. & p stateras ul mensuras duppli
ces lucra mundi conquirere solebat. ab omni fraude & ab omi
iniquitate suum animum pp acientiam ul inisediam conten
dit erogare. Hoc g agite frs̄ km̄i & dīs pacis & dilectionis erit uo
biscum. DE MARTYRIO QUOD IN PACE A ECCLE FIT.

E mo dicat frs̄ qd temporib; nr̄is martyrum certami
na ee. non possint. habet enim & pax nr̄a martyres suos.
Nam sicut frequenter suggessim̄ uacundiam mitigare. libidi
nem fugere. iusticiam custodire. auariciam contempnere. ua
cundiam mitigare. libidinem fugere. Contempnenda ē em̄
auaricia. que nobis ido iniqua lucra petitat ut nos suos faciat.
Nri enim essemus. si illa nob̄ esset contemnenda. Iniqua
ē auaricia. que uelut ignis quantum plus accipit tanto plus
querit. Iracundia uero mitiganda ē que prius noccuris im
pedit. quam nocendis. Qd autem libidinem fugiendam ē. sug
gerimus. aptīs paulus euidenter ostendit. qui cum omnibus
uiciis predicauerit resistendum. dum contra libidinem lo
queretur non dixit resistit. sed fugite fornicationem. ac sic
contra reliqua uicia dō auxiliante debem̄ inpresenti resistere.
libidinem uero fugiendo supare Ergo contra libidinis impe
tum apprehende fugam. si uis optinere uictoriam. nec tibi
uerecundum sit fugere. si castitatis palmam desideras optine
re Unde frs̄ km̄i ab omnib; xpianus precipue tamen a clericis

mos est monachorum, ut regulam beati Benedicti ad capitulum legant quotidie matutinum: volumus ut iste libellus ad eorum capitulum quotidie legatur vespertinum'.[18] At least ten other copies written in the twelfth century or earlier survive from England but none of them appears quite as suitable in size and appearance for such public reading as the copy produced by Nunnaminster's *scriptrix*. The largest copy (Cambridge, Corpus Christi College, MS 57 at 382 × 265 mm) belonged to Abingdon and, in addition to the *Diadema*, contains the Rule of St Benedict and Usuard's Martyrology.[19] Although size and content establish that this volume, written *c.*1000, was intended for reading aloud at collation, its scribe's choice of the Square minuscule script (set to become obsolete in the eleventh century for Latin texts) makes it appear less neat and this would have made it less attractive to read from by comparison with a book written in Caroline minuscule.[20] Apart from the Nunnaminster Smaragdus, the only other copy large enough to read aloud from comfortably (Cambridge, Clare College, MS 17 at 306 × 195 mm) was untidily written.[21]

The remaining English copies of the *Diadema* are all much smaller and seem more appropriate for library use than for lectern books. Thus, five twelfth-century copies range in size from only 202 × 135 mm to no bigger than 245 × 180 mm.[22] Two other copies, although slightly larger, were produced by scribes just learning to write. One (Cambridge, University Library, MS Ff.4.43 at 263 × 190 mm) was produced in the late tenth century at Christ Church Canterbury by a team of six scribes, four of

---

[18] *PL*, 103, 593. The *Diadema* frequently occurs in lists of books to be read at collation, see D. Nebbiai-Dalla Guardia, 'Les listes médiévales des lectures monastiques', *Revue bénédictine*, 96 (1986), 271–326.

[19] See M. R. James, *A Descriptive Catalogue of the Manuscripts in the Library of Corpus Christi College Cambridge* (Cambridge, 1912), I, 114–18; E. Temple, *Anglo-Saxon Manuscripts 900–1066* (London, 1976), no. 30 (x). M. G. Andersen, 'Missale- og martyrologietraditioner i dansk middelalder', Nordisk Kollokvium IV i Latinsk Liturgiforskning 15.–17. juni 1978, Lysebu/Oslo, Institutt for Kirkehistorie Universitetet i Oslo (1978), has identified the Martyrology as that of Usuard. D. N. Dumville, *English Caroline Script and Monastic History: Studies in Benedictinism, A.D. 950–1030* (Woodbridge, 1993), pl. XV(a), (b), illustrates both the original hand and the rather uncomfortable looking hand which sought to imitate the former when repairing text in the mid eleventh century.

[20] Cf. the comments of Ker, *Catalogue*, p. xxvi.

[21] See M. R. James, *A Descriptive Catalogue of the Western Manuscripts in the Library of Clare College Cambridge* (Cambridge, 1905), p. 35. The manuscript, of unknown provenance, dating from the end of the eleventh or beginning of the twelfth century, was copied by an eccentric hand which sometimes appears as if it had been influenced by Insular minuscule.

[22] Thus, Oxford, Bodl. Lib., MS e Musaeo 195 (*SC* 3608), from Kirkstall, is only 202 × 135 mm; Wisbech Town Lib., MS 9, of unknown provenance (Ker and Piper, *MMBL*, IV, 659–60), is 232 × 150 mm; London, BL, MS Royal 8.E.xviii, from Leominster (*Cat. Royal MSS*, I, p. 260 and IV, pl. 60b), is 234 × 165 mm; London, Lambeth Palace Lib., MS 373, from Lanthony (M. R. James, *A Descriptive Catalogue of the Manuscripts in the Library of Lambeth Palace* (Cambridge, 1932), pp. 514–17), is 245 × 150 mm; and Oxford, Bodl. Lib., MS Rawlinson C.330, from Holy Cross, Waltham (W. D. Macray, *Catalogi Codicum Manuscriptorum Bibliothecae Bodleianae*, v, fasc. ii (Oxford, 1897), p. 146), is 245 × 180 mm.

whom were only beginners;[23] the other (London, BL, MS Royal 8.D.xiii at 267 × 185 mm), from Worcester, was produced in the twelfth century by at least seven different learners.[24] While the choice of text was very suitable for Benedictine monks as an exercise in writing, for anyone who had to read it aloud the inexpert handwriting of some of the scribes involved in these two books might have caused problems. A third copy (Salisbury Cathedral Library, MS 12 at 245 × 153 mm) whose handwriting would render reading aloud difficult was made by one of the canons of Salisbury in the small 'academic' hand, heavily abbreviated, which was characteristic of books produced there between 1078 and 1099.[25]

There seems to have been two different traditions of the text in England. In the Nunnaminster Smaragdus, as in the copies extant from Christ Church, Salisbury, Kirkstall (Oxford, Bodl. Lib., MS e Musaeo 195), and Holy Cross, Waltham (Oxford, Bodl. Lib., MS Rawlinson C.330), the first chapter is provided with subheadings; these the *scriptrix* wrote in red Rustic Capitals. This confused a fifteenth-century reader who numbered each chapter in arabic numerals and who at first included the subheadings in chapter one in the numeration. Only at the beginning of the second chapter was it realized a mistake had been made and the numeration began again, correctly, with chapter two. The copies from Abingdon, Worcester, Leominster (London, BL, MS Royal 8.E.xviii), Lanthony (London, Lambeth Palace Library, MS 373) and two of unknown provenance (Clare College, MS 17 and Wisbech Town Library, MS 9) do not have subheadings in chapter one.

The Nunnaminster Smaragdus shows that it is impossible to determine the gender of medieval copyists from their handwriting. Although a difference in the *Schriftpyschologie* of male and female scribes has been postulated,[26] without the colophon it would be impossible to tell this scribe's gender from script alone. It is only her use of the form *scriptrix* which indicates she was female; there is nothing else unusual either in the script used or in the book production techniques. Her example does not support the contention that the habits of female scribes tended to be more conservative. Her letter forms compare with those of other scribes writing books in the first half of the twelfth century, and her handwriting displays no difference in duct from that of contemporaries known from the colophons they signed to be men.

---

[23] T. A. M. Bishop, *English Caroline Minuscule* (Oxford, 1971), no. 8 and pl. VI (illustrating the hand of one of the experts).

[24] *Cat. Royal MSS*, I, p. 249 and IV, pl. 58.

[25] Cf. T. Webber, *Scribes and Scholars at Salisbury Cathedral c.1075–c.1125* (Oxford, 1992), p. 13: written by scribe iv of her Group I scribes, i.e. those working during the episcopate of Bishop Osmund.

[26] By A. Bruckner, 'Weibliche Schreibtätigkeit im schweizerischen Spätmittelalter', *Festschrift Bernhard Bischoff zu seinem 65. Geburtstag*, ed. J. Autenrieth and F. Brunhölzl (Stuttgart, 1971), pp. 441–8; see also his 'Zum Problem der Frauenschriften im Mittelalter', in *Aus Mittelalter und Neuzeit: Gerhard Kallen zum 70. Geburtstag*, ed. J. Engel and H. M. Klinkenberg (Bonn, 1957), pp. 171–83. K. Schneider (*Gotische Schriften in deutscher Sprache, I. vom späten 12. Jahrhundert bis um 1300* (Wiesbaden, 1987), p. 249) detects a conservatism in the handwriting of German nuns when compared to the handwriting of their male contemporaries.

This anonymous Winchester *scriptrix* would appear to have had no *consoeur* in England. None of the limited number of other female scribes reported in *Colophons des manuscrits* comes from this country.[27] However, this lack of other colophon evidence for the involvement of English women in the production of books should not be taken as evidence they were not so involved, since colophons are found generally less often in English manuscripts than in manuscripts produced on the continent. Throughout the Middle Ages fewer English men signed the books they had copied than their counterparts on the mainland of Europe.[28]

The contribution of women to medieval book production has been recognized since at least the seventeenth century.[29] Even in the early church their skill as copyists had been praised. Eusebius informs us that Origen employed, with Ambrose's help, 'girls skilled in penmanship' to produce copies of his biblical commentaries.[30] Gerontius, chaplain and biographer of St Melania the Younger (d. 438), praised her for the accuracy of her copying. He tells us she copied manuscripts everyday, and while she was copying them a sister in one of the convents Melania had founded dictated ('legebat') to her. Melania listened so earnestly that she was able to correct any mistake made by the sister who was reading, even if the latter erred by a single letter: 'Scribebat etiam per totam septimam in membranis. Cum autem scribebat ipsa, una de sororibus ei legebat, et in tantum sensu sobrio audiebat, ut etiam emendaret eam quae legebat, vel si in una littera oberrasset'.[31] As the foundress of several houses, Melania's example may have helped to establish a precedent whereby copying manuscripts was considered as suitable a task for nuns as for monks. In the early eighth century, according to their ninth-century *Vita*, the sister-saints Harlindis and Relindis, of the abbey of Aldeneik in Flanders, copied a Gospel book.[32]

---

[27] *Colophons des manuscrits occidentaux des origines au xvie siècle*, compiled by the Benedictines of Le Bouveret, Spicilegii Friburgensis Subsidia, 2–6 (Fribourg, 1965–79).

[28] Similarly, English scribes were far less likely than continental scribes to date manuscripts they had copied; cf. my comments in *Catalogue of Dated and Datable Manuscripts c.737–1600 in Cambridge Libraries* (Cambridge, 1988), p. 5.

[29] Thus Jean Mabillon in his *Traité des études monastiques divisé en trois parties* (Paris, 1691), pt I, pp. 38–9, wrote: 'Il n'estoit pas mesme jusqu'aux Religeuses qui ne s'employassent à ce pieux exercice'. Mabillon cited St Melania the younger, Sts Harlindis and Relindis, and Abbess Eadburga (St Boniface's correspondent) as examples of female copyists. In the nineteenth century, both C. Cahier, *Nouveaux mélanges d'archéologie, d'histoire et de littérature sur le moyen âge*, IV, *Bibliothèques* (Paris, 1877), p. 70, and G. H. Putnam, *Books and their Makers during the Middle Ages: a Study of the Conditions of the Production and Distribution of Literature from the Fall of the Roman Empire to the Close of the Seventeenth Century* (New York and London, 1896), I, 52–3, praised the handwriting of nuns.

[30] Eusebius, *The Ecclesiastical History*, VI, xxiii, tr. J. E. L. Oulton, Loeb Classical Library, 265 (London, 1932; repr. Cambridge, MA, 1994), p. 69.

[31] *Vita Sanctae Melaniae*, c. xxiii, ed. Cardinal Rampolla, *Sancta Melania Giuniore Senatrice Romana*, Documenti Contemporanei e Note (Rome, 1905), pp. xxxvi and 15.

[32] Cf. *Acta Sanctorum*, March III, ed. J. Carnandet (Paris, 1865), p. 386. The traditional identification of their Gospel book with the Maaseik Gospels (Maaseik, Church of St Catherine, s.n.) is unlikely since the colophon, fol. 132ʳ, asks for prayers 'pro laboratore huius operis'. The

Early rules for women, such as the influential rule drawn up by St Caesarius of Arles (*c.*470–532), make it clear they were expected to be literate, although they do not explicitly stipulate that women should spend any of their time copying manuscripts.[33] Despite the absence of such provision in Caesarius's Rule, a contemporary life of the saint informs us that the nuns of the convent he founded for his sister Caesaria were excellent scribes of liturgical books: 'inter psalmos atque ieiunia, vigilias quoque et lectiones, libros divinos pulchre scriptitent virgines Christi'.[34] In England, there is no text of a rule definitely used by Anglo-Saxon nuns until the production of the *Regularis Concordia* in *c.*970.[35] Both this and the Rule of St Benedict which it elaborated are silent on the topic of book production, although the emphasis in the latter on the importance of reading presupposes a ready supply of books best met by scribal labour within a house.[36] In the case of male religious, notwithstanding the Rule's silence on the subject, monks evidently copied those books that they needed; nuns doubtless did the same.

By the early thirteenth century, when the Gilbertine Rule had evolved, it was laid down that nuns were not to copy or commission any books, prayers, or meditations without the assent of the Master of the order ('prioris omnium'), nor were they allowed to hire or bring scribes into their church without permission. However, they were permitted to copy service books:

> Nulla etiam de nostris praesumat libros aliquos, vel orationes, vel meditationes scribere vel scribi facere, sine assensu prioris omnium, vel scriptores conducere et retinere in ecclesiis monialium . . . [*penalties for disobedience follow*] . . . Libri tamen ad divinum officium scribi permittuntur.[37]

Maaseik Gospels were perhaps produced at the abbey of Echternach; see further A. Derolez, 'The Manuscript and its History' in *Codex Eyckensis: an Insular Gospel Book from the Abbey of Aldeneik*, introduced by C. Coppens, A. Derolez and H. Heymans (Maaseik, 1994), pp. 17–34, and N. Netzer, 'Willibrord's scriptorium at Echternach and its Relationship to Ireland and Lindisfarne', in *St Cuthbert, his Cult and Community to AD 1200*, ed. G. Bonner, D. Rollason and C. Stancliffe (Woodbridge, 1989), pp. 203–12.

[33] Cf. *Césaire d'Arles, Oeuvres monastiques*, I, ed. A. de Vogüé and J. Courreau, Sources Chrétiennes, 345 (Paris, 1988), p. 192, c. 18. Caesarius's provisions are repeated in the rules of Aurelian of Arles, d. 551 (*PL*, 68, 402) and Donatus of Besançon, d. *c.*660 (*PL*, 87, 281–2); see M. C. McCarthy, *The Rule for Nuns of St. Caesarius of Arles: a Translation with Critical Introduction* (Washington, DC, 1960), pp. 48 and 158. The rule of Leander of Seville, d. *c.*600, also stipulates that women should be literate (*PL*, 72, 883–4).

[34] *Vita S. Caesarii Arelatensis*, I, c. 58, ed. G. Morin, *Sancti Caesarii Arelatensis Opera Omnia*, II (Maredsous, 1942), p. 320; see also W. E. Klingshirn, *Caesarius of Arles: the Making of a Christian Community in Late Antique Gaul* (Cambridge, 1994), pp. 117–24.

[35] Cf. B. Yorke, '"Sisters under the skin"? Anglo-Saxon Nuns and Nunneries in Southern England', *Reading Medieval Studies*, 15 (1984), 95–117.

[36] Cf. *La Règle de Saint Benoît*, c. xlviii, ed. A. de Vogüé and J. Neufville (Paris, 1972).

[37] Cf. William Dugdale, *Monasticon Anglicanum: a history of the abbies and other monasteries, hospitals, frieries, and cathedrals and collegiate churches, with their dependencies in England and Wales,*

This injunction relating to nuns largely repeats one in the earlier part of the Rule concerned with the canons, yet it must have borne some relation to reality since the nuns were expected to follow the customs of the latter. In a later section of the Rule we find that although the nuns were not generally permitted to enter the kitchen an exception was made to allow female copyists to dry their parchment. 'Nulla ingrediatur coquinam, exceptis . . . scriptricibus ad siccandum percamenum'.[38] Furthermore, this provision suggests that the nuns were not just copying manuscripts but preparing the parchment themselves. In view of the prohibition against hiring outside scribes without special permission, a non-liturgical work such as the late-twelfth-century copy of Origen's homilies on the Old Testament which belonged to the Gilbertine nuns of Chicksands might have been copied by one of the sisters.[39]

Like any other religious, nuns would have required books in order to meet the basic liturgical needs of their community; however, books were also recommended to women for reading, meditation, and prayer. Aldhelm (d. 709) recommended the nuns of Barking to read holy Scripture, the Church Fathers, historians and chroniclers, grammarians, Cassian's *Collationes* and the *Moralia in Job*.[40] Unfortunately, the earliest manuscript known to survive from the house is a Gospel book from the eleventh century.[41] A recommended programme of reading nearer in date (*c.*1082–83) to the activity of the Nunnaminster *scriptrix* (in the 1120s) was drawn up by Goscelin of St Bertin in a letter he sent to the former nun Eve who had left Wilton to become a recluse. Goscelin's list included the scriptural commentaries of Jerome, Augustine, Gregory and others, the lives of the Fathers, Augustine's *Confessions* and *City of God*, Cassiodorus, *Historia ecclesiastica tripartita*, Eusebius, *Ecclesiastical History*, Orosius, *De Ornesta mundi*, and Boethius, *Consolation of Philosophy*.[42] His suggestions presuppose Eve had been well educated at Wilton; she

---

ed. J. Caley, H. Ellis and B. Bandinel, VI, pt ii (London, 1830), p. *lxxxiii. I owe this reference to Bella Millett. The Rule, which survives only in Oxford, Bodl. Lib., MS Douce 136, dating from between 1220 and 1223, is a composite work, containing additions and amendments; it is thus impossible to recover the original arrangements made by St Gilbert himself. See further B. Golding, *Gilbert of Sempringham and the Gilbertine Order c.1130–c.1300* (Oxford, 1995), pp. 71–137, esp. 81.

[38] Dugdale, *Monasticon*, VI, p ii, p. *lxxxiv.

[39] Oxford, Bodl. Lib., MS Auct. E infra 4 has the thirteenth-century *ex libris* '⟨liber sanctimo⟩nialium de Chikesand'.

[40] *De virginitate*, cc. 4, 13, ed. R. Ehwald, *Aldhelmi Opera*, MGH, Auctorum Antiquissimorum, 15 (Berlin, 1919), pp. 232, 242; tr. M. Lapidge in *Aldhelm: the Prose Works*, ed. M. Lapidge and M. Herren (Cambridge, 1979), pp. 62, 70.

[41] See above p. 75.

[42] See C. H. Talbot, 'The *Liber confortatorius* of Goscelin of Saint Bertin', *Analecta Monastica*, ser. 3, Studia Anselmiana, 37 (1955), 80–1; and cf. B. Millet, 'Women in No Man's Land: English Recluses and the Development of Vernacular Literature in the Twelfth and Thirteenth Centuries', *Women and Literature in Britain, 1150–1500*, ed. C. M. Meale (Cambridge, 1993), pp. 86–103.

may have been introduced to some of the books on his reading list there, although the only Wilton volumes known to have survived are two thirteenth-century psalters and an early fifteenth-century Life of St Edith in English.[43]

Such reading lists (one dating from the late seventh or early eighth century, the other from the late eleventh century) demonstrate that there was a continuing need for books in houses of English women and suggest that it is possible that their occupants combined the ability to copy the manuscripts they required with the ability to read them.

Circumstantial evidence exists to suggest that in the early Middle Ages it had been a fairly common practice for English nuns to be copyists. A prominent feature of Boniface's mission to Germany in the first half of the eighth century was the role of women in supplying him with books.[44] Writing home from abroad to an Abbess Eadburga he asked her to copy for him the Epistles of Peter in letters of gold, although when he wished to learn the whereabouts of suitable exemplars (as opposed to having copies made) Boniface wrote to a man, Abbot Duddo.[45] The abbess later received from Boniface's successor, Lul, a silver stylus: a present that would have been useless had she been unable to write. Eadburga has usually been identified with the abbess of Minster in Thanet (d. 751).[46] An eighth-century copy of Acts, written in English Uncial, that can plausibly be assigned to Thanet has the letters 'Eadb' (for Eadburga?) scratched on a leaf.[47] By the later Middle Ages this volume had come to belong to St Augustine's Canterbury but a prayer in the feminine gender, added to an originally blank leaf, suggests it had formerly belonged to a female house. Since St Augustine's is known to have acquired Thanet's property by the eleventh century, it could well have acquired the book from Thanet by the same time.[48] Elsewhere, there is the evidence of eighth- and early-ninth-century styli found at both Barking and Whitby.[49] Hence

---

[43] Respectively, Oxford, Bodl. Lib., MS Rawlinson G.23, London, Royal College of Physicians, MS 409, and BL, Cotton MS Faustina B.III, fols 199–280.

[44] Cf. *Die Briefe des heiligen Bonifatius und Lullus*, ed. M. Tangl, MGH, Epistolae selectae, 1 (Berlin, 1916), nos 30, 35, 70.

[45] Ibid., no. 34.

[46] But see Sims-Williams, *Religion and Literature*, p. 204, who has recently argued that Boniface's correspondent was abbess of Wimborne.

[47] Oxford, Bodl. Lib., MS Selden supra 30 (*CLA*, II, 257 and New Pal. Soc., 2nd ser., pl. 56).

[48] The added prayer on p. 70 speaks of 'indignam famulam tuam'. For the manuscript's later provenance, see James, *Ancient Libraries*, p. 210, no. 222; and for the transfer of Thanet's property to St Augustine's, see N. Brooks, *The Early History of the Church of Canterbury* (Leicester, 1984), pp. 203–6.

[49] For the finds at Barking, see *The Making of England, Anglo-Saxon Art and Culture*, ed. L. Webster and J. Backhouse, Catalogue of an Exhibition, British Museum/Library, 1991–92 (London, 1991), nos 67 (i)–(k); those at Whitby were found with other objects connected with book production in that area of the double house occupied by women, see C. Peers and C. A. Ralegh-Radford, 'The Saxon Monastery of Whitby', *Archaeologia*, 89 (1943), 27–88, and R. Cramp, 'Monastic Sites', in *The Archaeology of Anglo-Saxon England*, ed. D. M. Wilson (London, 1976), p. 229.

books must have been made in these two houses but no eighth- or ninth-century manuscripts have survived from either foundation.

Although such archaeological evidence cannot be substantiated by any known contemporary volumes from Barking or Whitby, other Anglo-Saxon books contain evidence that nuns were able to write. Content alone may not be adequate evidence of this but additions to books in female ownership demonstrate the likelihood of female scribes. For instance, the deliberate selection of content in an eleventh-century ordinal, where only those *ordines* for the consecration of women have been copied, might indicate – as has been suggested – that it had been copied by a nun for her house.[50] On the other hand, it could equally well be argued that a male scribe had tailored the material to suit the needs of the women who required it. It is more likely that where a manuscript was owned by a woman – especially one living in a convent – insertions or additions to it may be regarded as the work of a female scribe and/or attributed to the owner. Abbess Cuthswith of Inkberrow, Worcestershire, owned, *c*.700, a late-fifth- or early-sixth-century copy of Jerome's commentary on Ecclesiastes (a text specifically written for women). Her copy contains six supply leaves written in seventh-century English Uncial;[51] these were probably provided by one of the nuns at Inkberrow. Books with prayers in the main body of the text that use feminine forms could have been written by a male scribe for female ownership, but when added prayers use such forms it creates a strong presumption that their copyist was female. Thus the prayer in the feminine gender added to the copy of Acts later acquired by St Augustine's was likely to have been added by a woman, whether the Abbess Eadburga of Thanet or not.

Similarly, when the words 'ora pro me peccatrice' occur in a form of confession added in the tenth century (on fol. 41) to the 'Book of Nunnaminster',[52] it is reasonable to assume that the confession has been added by a female hand. Malcolm Parkes's identification of the hand which added this confession with the second scribe of the Isidore belonging to the Parker *Chronicle* group of manuscripts provides the crucial evidence for an active scriptorium at Nunnaminster since, a priori, the other scribes involved in the group also worked there.[53] Another addition in the same prayer book, describing the boundaries of land in Winchester on which the house

---

[50] Cf. M. Lapidge, 'The Origin of Corpus Christi College Cambridge 163', *TCBS*, 8 (1981–85), 18–28.

[51] Würzburg, Universitätsbibliothek, M.p.th.q.2 bears on fol. 1 the *ex libris* 'Cuthsuuithae boec thaerae abbatissan'; see *CLA*, IX, 1430a–b and E. A. Lowe, *English Uncial* (Oxford, 1960) pls I, V. She has been identified as Abbess of Inkberrow by P. Sims-Williams, 'Cuthswith, seventh-century abbess of Inkberrow, near Worcester, and the Würzburg manuscript of Jerome on Ecclesiastes', *ASE*, 5 (1976), 1–21; see also his *Religion and Literature*, pp. 191–7. Professor Parkes has also remarked on this manuscript in 'Archaizing Hands in English Manuscripts', in *Books and Collectors 1200–1700: Essays Presented to Andrew Watson*, ed. J. Carley and C. G. C. Tite (London, 1997), pp. 101–41, esp. 101.

[52] For which see above, p. 73, and n. 2.

[53] Cf. Parkes, *Scribes, Scripts and Readers*, pp. 173–8.

was established, was made by the first hand of the Parker *Chronicle* itself (Cambridge, Corpus Christi College, MS 173).

The inference from such earlier English evidence that the *scriptrix* of Bodley 451 belonged to a tradition of nuns copying manuscripts is supported by continental examples. Although she has no predecessor from this country who signed a book, books signed by female copyists survive from elsewhere. Thus Dulcia wrote an eighth-century copy of Isidore's works, concluding with the colophon 'Explicit liber premiorum Ego dulcia scripsi et subscripsi istum librum rotarum' (that is, the *De natura rerum*).[54] Dulcia used Laon **az** minuscule, a script derived from that of Luxeuil; it is therefore tempting to speculate that it was the Laonnais monastery of Notre-Dame-la-Profonde, founded from Luxeuil, which introduced **az** to Laon and that Dulcia was a nun of Notre-Dame-la-Profonde.[55] Eugenia copied a ninth-century grammatical miscellany; besides elementary schoolworks by Charisius and Tatwine, she included in it more advanced texts such as Phocas's *Ars de nomine et verbo* and Priscian's *Institutio de nomine, pronomine et verbo*.[56] Not only must Eugenia have known Latin grammar but she also knew a little Greek, since she transcribed her Latin colophon ('Eugenia scripsit') in the Greek alphabet. Other volumes bearing a female name believed to be that of their scribe include a copy of Augustine's *De Trinitate* with 'Madalberta' written within an initial.[57] Since David, scribe of the Gellone Sacramentary,[58] signed that manuscript in the same way, Madalberta can be presumed to be one of the scribes who collaborated on the Augustine. Its master scribe who began the text, corrected it and supplied chapter headings, was David himself.[59] Two Würzburg manuscripts, one with 'Abirhilt' written in the margin by the scribe of the latter part of a copy of Gregory's *Homiliae in evangelia*, the other with a scribal monogram decipherable as 'Guntza' at the end of a copy of Defensor's *Liber scintillarum*, were also likely to have been copied by women. The hands of these two have been identified in other volumes at Würzburg.[60]

---

[54] Laon, Bibl. mun., MS 423, fol. 79ᵛ (*CLA*, VI, 766; New Pal. Soc., 2nd ser., pl. 9(b)).

[55] Cf. J. J. Contreni, *The Cathedral School of Laon from 850 to 930: its Manuscripts and Masters*, Münchener Beiträge zur Mediävistik und Renaissance-Forschung, 29 (1978), pp. 16 n. 70, and 49.

[56] Paris, BN, MS lat. 7560; for which see C. Jeudy, 'L'*Institutio de nomine, pronomine et verbo* de Priscien: manuscrits et commentaires médiévaux', *Revue d'histoire des textes*, 2 (1972), 123. The colophon, fol. 54, has been edited by H. Omont, 'Note sur un recueil de grammairiens latins, copié par une femme au xe siècle', *Comptes rendus de séances de l'Année 1905 de l'Academie des Inscriptions et Belles-Lettres* (Paris, 1905), pp. 15–19 and pl; also P. Lehmann, 'Mitteilungen aus Handschriften, I', Sitzungsberichte der Bayerischen Akademie der Wissenschaften. Philosophische-historische Abteilung, I (1929), 19–20, who described it as bizarre.

[57] Cambrai, Bibl. mun., MS 300 (282); Madalberta's name occurs in fol. 155 (*CLA*, VI, 739).

[58] Paris, BN, MS lat. 12048 (*CLA*, V, 618).

[59] See C. R. Baldwin, 'The Scriptorium of the Sacramentary of Gellone', *Scriptorium*, 25 (1971), 3–17; B. Bischoff, 'Manuscripts in the Age of Charlemagne', *Manuscripts and Libraries*, p. 25.

[60] Abirhilt's name occurs on fol. 71ᵛ of Würzburg, Universitätsbibliothek, M.p.th.f.45 (*CLA*, IX, 1412), while Guntza's monogram is on fol. 57ᵛ of M.p.th.f.13 (*CLA*, IX, 1404). See further B. Bischoff

The best known of early *scriptrices* are the nuns of Chelles, near Paris, where between 785 and 819 Adruhic, Agelberta, Agnes, Altildis, Eusebia, Girbalda, Gisledrudis, Gislildis, Vera, and a tenth sister whose name has been lost, collaborated to produce a three-volume set of Augustine on the Psalms for Hildebald, Archbishop of Cologne.[61] To speed up production of copy their exemplar had been distributed among them, each sister signing with her name + *scripsit* the *portio* (or group of quires) which she had copied.[62] Two other copies of Augustine on the Psalms, one of them signed by some of the same sisters (Adruhic, Gisledrudis, Gislildis, and Girbalda), were produced in the same scriptorium.[63] Chelles itself would hardly have required multiple copies of the same work and, as the gift to Archbishop Hildebald suggests, perhaps copied volumes for export. As well as the Augustine text, the nuns of Chelles also copied an Evangeliary, a collection of the canons of the *Concilia Gallicae* (in which Altildis's hand again occurs), copies of Cassiodorus on the Psalms, the *Historia ecclesiastica* of Eusebius-Rufinus, Jerome's *Epistulae*, Isidore's *Etymologiae*, *Prooemia* and *De natura rerum*, Gregory's *Homiliae in evangelia*, and the oldest copy of Smaragdus, *Expositio Comitis*.[64] This busy scriptorium may have existed at Chelles for some time, if (as has been suggested) a mid-eighth-century copy of Augustine's *De trinitate* was written there also.[65] Chelles was clearly an establishment with skilled personnel by the time Adruhic and her sisters were working, since the manuscripts produced by them are well-written, elegant copies of works of major importance.

Chelles was probably not an isolated example. However, the existence of other early scriptoria staffed by women which have been suggested cannot be accepted without reservation. For instance, the suggestion that there was a scriptorium of

and J. Hofmann, *Libri Sancti Kyliani: die Würzburger Schreibschule und die Dombibliothek im VIII und IX. Jahrhundert*, Quellen und Forschungen zur Geschichte des Bistums und Hochstifts Würzburg, 6 (1952), pp. 7–9, 100, 102, 160. For the identification of Abirhilt's and Guntza's hands in other manuscripts, see R. McKitterick, 'Nuns' Scriptoria in England and Francia in the Eighth Century', in her *Books, Scribes and Learning in the Frankish Kingdoms 6th–9th Centuries* (Aldershot, 1994), VII, 1–35, esp. 22–3.

[61] Cologne, Dombibliothek, HSS 63, 65 and 67. L. W. Jones, *The Script of Cologne from Hildebald to Hermann* (Cambridge, 1932), pls 67–71, illustrates the handwriting of each of the sisters (the leaf that would have given the name of the tenth has been lost). For a study of the Chelles scriptorium, see B. Bischoff, 'Die Kölner Nonnenhandschriften und das Skriptorium von Chelles', in his *Mittelalterliche Studien*, I (Stuttgart, 1966), pp. 16–34.

[62] On the system of copying by *portiones*, see J. Vezin, 'Le répartition du travail dans les "scriptoria" carolingiens', *Journal des Savants* (Paris, 1973), 212–27.

[63] Berlin, Deutsche Staatsbibl., HS Phillipps 1657 is signed by Adruhic and her sisters while a third copy represented only by a single leaf (Cologne, Histor. Archiv. GB Frag. Kasten B. Nr. 155) has been assigned to Chelles; see *CLA*, VIII, 1170 and Bischoff, 'Die Kölner Nonnenhandschriften'.

[64] Ibid. For St Gall, Stiftsbibl. HS 345, see F. Rädle, *Studien zu Smaragd von Saint-Mihiel* (München, 1974), pp. 121, 131.

[65] Oxford, Bodl. Lib., MS Laud Misc. 126. Bischoff attributed this volume to Chelles but McKitterick, 'Nuns' Scriptoria', pp. 7–14, argues for its origin at Jouarre.

nuns, perhaps at Corbie, whose house-script was **ab** minuscule seems to me unfounded. This suggestion depends on a prayer in the feminine gender ('domine iesu christi inlumina cor ancille tue') which was added to the earliest complete copy of the *Regula magistri*.[66] This prayer was added in **ab** minuscule. Since the manuscript was at Corbie by the ninth century whence 14 books written in **ab** (or nearly half the extant number of manuscripts written in the script) come, the **ab** scriptorium has been located there.[67] As the arrangement of parchment in these 14 books differs from that in other books written at Corbie in Caroline minuscule, Alan Bishop suggested that a nuns' scriptorium, segregated from and independent of that of the monks, produced the books copied in **ab** while Corbie's monks produced those copied in Caroline minuscule. However, Corbie is not known to have been a double house and more probably acquired its **ab** manuscripts from elsewhere.[68] Moreover, wherever **ab** might have been written, the fact that one specimen of it (the added prayer) was by a woman does not (it seems to me) mean that all other specimens necessarily were. Such a situation would imply a gender-specific script for which there are no precedents or parallels.

Similarly, the argument for the existence of a nuns' scriptorium at Jouarre is doubtful. It is based on comparisons observed among a number of manuscripts, produced throughout the eighth century, in three different scripts (Uncial, Half Uncial and **b** minuscule), which are nevertheless linked by common stylistic features of decoration and display script.[69] However, in no two or more of the books concerned have two or more scribes and artists been identified as collaborating, and none of the books is known to have come from the same provenance.[70] Therefore the similarities perceived to exist among them can only be accepted with caution as evidence of their common origin in the same house. A style of script and decoration could become fashionable and spread beyond an immediate centre to others. This happened in the ninth century with the influential 'Martinian' style which spread

---

[66] Paris, BN, MS lat. 12205, fols 2, 158ᵛ. See R. P. Toustain and C. Tassin, *Nouveau traité de diplomatique*, III (Paris, 1757), pp. 244, 280, and pl. 49; also H. Vanderhoven, F. Masai and P. B. Corbett, *La Règle du Maître* (Paris and Brussels, 1953), p. 37 and n. 2.

[67] See T. A. M. Bishop, 'The Prototype of the *Liber glossarum*', in *Medieval Scribes, Manuscripts and Libraries: Essays Presented to N. R. Ker*, ed. M. B. Parkes and A. G. Watson (London, 1978), pp. 69–86; also 'The Scribes of the Corbie *a–b*', in *Charlemagne's Heir: New Perspectives on the Reign of Louis the Pious (814–840)*, ed. P. Godman and R. Collins (Oxford, 1990), pp. 523–36. For the total of ab manuscripts from Corbie, see D. Ganz, *Corbie and the Carolingian Renaissance* (Sigmaringen, 1990), p. 49.

[68] Ganz, *Corbie and the Carolingian Renaissance*, p. 53, suggests they came to Corbie from Soissons or Noirmoutier, while McKitterick, 'Nuns' Scriptoria', pp. 19–21, favours Jouarre.

[69] Cf. McKitterick, 'Nuns' Scriptoria', pp. 7–14.

[70] Cf. Professor Parkes's 'Patterns of Scribal Activity and Revisions of the Text in Early Copies of the Works of John Gower', in *New Science out of Old Books: Studies in Manuscripts and Early Printed Books in Honour of A. I. Doyle*, ed. R. Beadle and A. J. Piper (Aldershot, 1995), p. 81, on criteria for establishing the existence of a scriptorium.

beyond Tours,[71] and in the twelfth century with the so-called 'prickly hand' which spread from Christ Church Canterbury to both St Augustine's and Rochester.[72]

That nuns continued to copy manuscripts is probable, despite there being little concrete evidence provided by manuscripts signed by female scribes between the early examples from the eighth and ninth centuries and later examples from the twelfth century. For example, in 1093–94 Elsindis, a nun of Marcigny-sur-Loire, copied Ado's martyrology and the necrology of the house.[73] However, it is well to remind ourselves that it was unusual for any scribe to sign a book in the earlier Middle Ages. The practice only began to develop significantly in the twelfth century and the Nunnaminster *scriptrix* had a number of continental contemporaries.

In the first half of the twelfth century, at Munsterbilsen, near Maastricht, eight Benedictine nuns (Gertrude, Sibilia, Dierwic, Walderat, Hadewic, Lugart, Ota, and Cunigunt) collaborated to produce a volume containing Isidore's *Etymologiae* and *De natura rerum*; the colophon at its end names them all.[74] Other *scriptrices*, according to their colophons, worked independently. Thus Guta, canoness of the Augustinian house of Schwarzenthann, copied its necrology in 1154;[75] another woman called Guda, from an unknown house in the Rhineland, copied and painted an homiliary;[76] a 'soror Irmengart' copied two books (Haymo of Halberstadt's

---

[71] Cf. E. K. Rand, *A Survey of the Manuscripts of Tours* (Cambridge, MA, 1929), pp. 9 and 66–8; also Bischoff, 'Manuscripts in the Age of Charlemagne', p. 31.

[72] See Ker, *English Manuscripts*, pp. 26–32.

[73] Paris, BN, nouv. acq. lat. 348, for which see C. Samaran and R. Marichal, *Catalogue des manuscrits en écriture latine portant des indications de date, de lieu ou de copiste*, IV (Paris, 1981), and pl. 17; also J. Wollasch, 'A Cluniac Necrology from the Time of Abbot Hugh', in *Cluniac Monasticism in the Central Middle Ages*, ed. N. Hunt (London, 1971), pp. 143–90. Ende, who collaborated on the Gerona Apocalypse (Gerona, Archivo Catedralico, MS 7) in 975, was its *pintrix* rather than its scribe. For other, later, examples of female artists, see D. Miner, *Anastaise and Her Sisters: Women Artists of the Middle Ages* (The Walters Art Gallery, Baltimore, MD, 1974).

[74] London, BL, MS Harley 3099. The colophon on fol. 166 reads: 'Hec sunt nomina illarum que scripserunt librum istum. Gerdrut. Sibilia. Dierwic. Walderat. Hadewic. Lugart. Ota. Cunigunt. Ipse namque scripserunt monasteriensibus dominis quatinus deum pro eis rogent ut a penis eas liberet et in paradyso collocet. Quisque eis abstulerit anatematizatus sit'; cf. A. G. Watson, *Catalogue of Dated and Datable Manuscripts c.700–1600 in the Department of Manuscripts The British Library* (London, 1979), no. 729 and pls 72a and b. The date '1134' has been added to the colophon in modern arabic numerals.

[75] Strasbourg, Bibl. du Grand Séminaire, MS 37, fol. 4ᵛ: 'Perscriptum est autem hoc ipsum opusculum ab eadem predicta Gota miniatum vero siue illuminatum a quodam humili canonice 'marbacensi' et indigno presbitero. nomine Sintrammo et ad finem usque perductum anno ab incarnato dei uerbo Millesimo. Centesimo. Quinquagesimo. quarto Indictione II Epacta IIII concurrente IIII'; also fol. 4 'Ego peccatrix . . . Guta'. See C. Samaran and R. Marichal, *MSS datés*, V (Paris, 1965), I, p. 445 and II, pl. xv.

[76] Frankfurt am Main, Stadt- und Universitäsbibl., HS Barth. 42, fol. 110ᵛ where an initial with the accompanying inscription 'Guda peccatrix mulier scripsit et pinxit hunc librum' depicts her; reproduced by P. d'Ancona and E. Aeschlimann, *Dictionnaire des miniaturistes*, 2nd edn (Milan, 1949), pl. 51, and J. J. G. Alexander, 'Scribes as Artists: the Arabesque Initial in Twelfth-Century

Tractatus super epistolas et evangelia and Rupert of Deutz's *Liber de divinis officiis*) for Abbot Heinrich I (1164–1200) of the Premonstratensian house of Schäftlarn;[77] while Ermengard, from the Benedictine house of Lamspring, near Hildesheim, copied and signed Augustine's *Sermones*.[78]

The most prolific *scriptrix* of all was Diemot, 'ancilla dei', who copied 45 manuscripts for the Benedictine abbey of Saints Peter and Paul, Wessobrun.[79] A twelfth-century list of her work includes a two-volume Bible (exchanged by the abbey for a farm at Bissenberg) and 11 service books; two of these, a gradual and office book ('liber officialis') must have been thought very fine for they were presented to the bishops of Trier and Augsburg respectively. However, the books she copied for divine service represent only a small part of Diemot's output. As well as the 11 service books, the list informs us she also copied texts of major authors such as Augustine (a three-volume set of his commentary on the Psalms, his commentaries on John's Gospel and Epistles, his *Epistolae, De verbis Domini, Sermones* and *Confessiones*), Gregory (the *Moralia* and his commentary on Ezekiel), Jerome (*Epistolae* and *De hebraicis quaestionibus*), Origen (his commentaries on the Old Testament and Song of Songs), and an unidentified work by 'Johannes Chrysostomus'. Further, she copied two histories, Cassiodorus's *Historia ecclesiastica tripartita* and the *Ecclesiastical History* of Eusebius-Rufinus. Some of the books mentioned in this list still survive, signed by Diemot: a 'Liber cum evangelis', Gregory's *Moralia*, books 2 and 4–6, and his work on Ezekiel, Jerome's *De hebraicis quaestionibus*, and both the histories.[80] Thanks to her industry, Wessobrun acquired a substantial patristic collection, the desiderata of twelfth-century librarians.

Thus the *scriptrix* of the Nunnaminster Smaragdus was not alone in her ability to copy manuscripts. Nevertheless, apart from her tenth-century predecessors, were any

---

England', in *Medieval Scribes, Manuscripts and Libraries*, ed. Parkes and Watson, pl. 21. See further *Die Handschriften des Bartholomaeusstifts und Karmeliterklosters in Frankfurt am Main*, ed. G. Powitz and H. Buck, *Kataloge der Stadt- und Universitätsbibliothek Frankfurt am Main*, 2 (Frankfurt am Main, 1974), pp. 84–5.

[77] Munich, Bayerische Staatsbibl., Clm 17087 and Clm 17116 both have the colophon 'Scripsit soror Irmengart obtentu Hainrici praepositi'; see *Catalogus Codicum Latinorum Bibliothecae Regiae Monacensis*, II, pars iii (Munich, 1878), 80, 81; and P. Ruf, 'Die Handschriften des Klosters Schäftlarn', in *1200 Jahre Kloster Schäftlarn*, ed. S. Mitterer, Beiträge zur altbayerischen Kirchengeschichte, 22/3 (Munich, 1962), p. 43; Schneider, *Gotische Schriften*, I, 30 and II, abb. 4.

[78] Wolfenbüttel, Herzog August Bibl., MS 237, fol. 1ᵛ: 'Liber sancti Adriani martiris in Lamesprigge scriptus a domina Ermengarde in diebus domine Iuddtte priorisse et Gerhardi preposti [1178–91]. Sermones sancti Augustini episcopi'. See *Die Handschriften der Herzoglichen Bibliothek zu Wolfenbüttel*, ed. O. von Heinemann, I (Wolfenbüttel, 1884), p. 185.

[79] The list, extant in Munich Clm 22001, is printed by J. A. Schmeller, 'Über Bücherkataloge des xv. und früherer Jahrhunderte', *Serapeum*, II (Leipzig, 1841), 249–51.

[80] They are all to be found among the manuscripts from Wessobrun now in Munich, Staatsbibl.: thus, Clm 22039 is the 'Liber cum evangeliis' copied by Diemot; Clm 22009–12 contain the *Moralia*, books 2 and 4–6; Clm 22008 is the commentary on Ezekiel; Clm 22016, the Jerome; Clm 22015, the Cassiodorus; and Clm 22014, the Eusebius.

of her contemporaries at Nunnaminster also able to write, even if there is no evidence for organized production of books in the house? Since the manuscript remained in Nunnaminster's possession (as shown by the nature of the additions on the endleaves and the fragmentary account roll used in the later medieval binding), additions to it were likely to have been made by other nuns. In such a case the supply leaf (fol. 118) and the addition made on the endleaf (fol. 120) suggest the presence of at least two other *scriptrices*. The supply leaf, written in a larger, less regular hand (see Pl. 6) than that of the main *scriptrix*, replaces a leaf removed in the last quire; this supply leaf contains 58 lines of the final sermon.[81] The hand can be dated on palaeographical grounds to the first half of the twelfth century. The addition on fol. 120 was written (in my opinion) perhaps somewhat later, in a large, clumsy hand, and consists of an account of a miracle of St Edburga from a lost life of the saint.[82]

Unfortunately, it is impossible to identify these three hands elsewhere since no other twelfth-century books can be securely located to Nunnaminster. The twelfth-century addition of a prayer in the feminine gender and interlineation of feminine forms throughout an eleventh-century book of prayers and private devotions (London, BL, Cotton MSS Titus D.XXVI + XXVII) suggests that by the twelfth century it was owned by a woman. As this prayer book had been written at the neighbouring New Minster (Hyde Abbey), partly by the monk Aelsinus, scribe of the 'Liber vitae' of Hyde, and owned by the deacon Aelfwine before he became abbot of Hyde in 1032,[83] it is possible that its later female owner was a Nunnaminster nun. However, the hand of the addition and interlineations is not one of those which occur in Bodley 451. Likewise, the hand of the Nunnaminster *titulus* on the mortuary roll of Abbot Vitalis of Savigny, datable *c*.1122–23, is different.[84] The existence of Bodley 451's *scriptrix* shows it is unnecessary to assume that *tituli* for female houses could only have been made by their chaplains, and Nunnaminster's scribe on the mortuary roll could well have been another nun. Like the *scriptrix* of Bodley 451 who versified her colophon, the writer of the *titulus* composed a verse 'Sit semper Christi requies eterna Vitali'.[85] Her hand is a little shaky but those of the writers of the *tituli*

---

[81] Headed 'Sermo sancti Augustini de adam'; printed in full by D. A. B. Caillau, *Sancti Augustini, Opera omnia*, Collectio selecta SS. Ecclesiae Patrum, 131 (Paris, 1842), pp. 8–14; it is also printed, in part, among Paul the Deacon's works, *PL*, 95, 1208. E. Dekkers, *Clavis Patrum Latinorum*, Sacris Erudiri, 3 (Steenbrugge, 1961) no. 922, ascribes it to Pseudo-Chrysostom.

[82] See Ridyard, *Royal Saints*, pp. 28–9 nn. 66 and 69.

[83] Bishop, *English Caroline Minuscule*, pl. XXIII; Ker, *Catalogue*, no. 202; Watson, *Dated MSS British Library*, no. 561 and pl. 35a–c. The prayer is added on Titus D.XXVII, fol. 74; see *Aelfwine's Prayerbook*, ed. B. Günzel, HBS, 108 (1993), 128, 201 and cf. 3–4.

[84] Paris, Musée des Archives nationales, MS 138, for a facs. of which see L. Delisle, *Rouleau mortuaire du B. Vital de Savigni* (Paris, 1901); the Nunnaminster *titulus* is no. 184. The lost mortuary roll of Matilda, abbess of Sainte-Trinité de Caen (d. *c*.1110), extant only in a seventeenth-century copy (Paris, BN, MS lat. 12652), also contained a Nunnaminster entry.

[85] Delisle, *Rouleau mortuaire*, p. 23, argues that it was usual for whoever composed verses for the roll to copy them themselves.

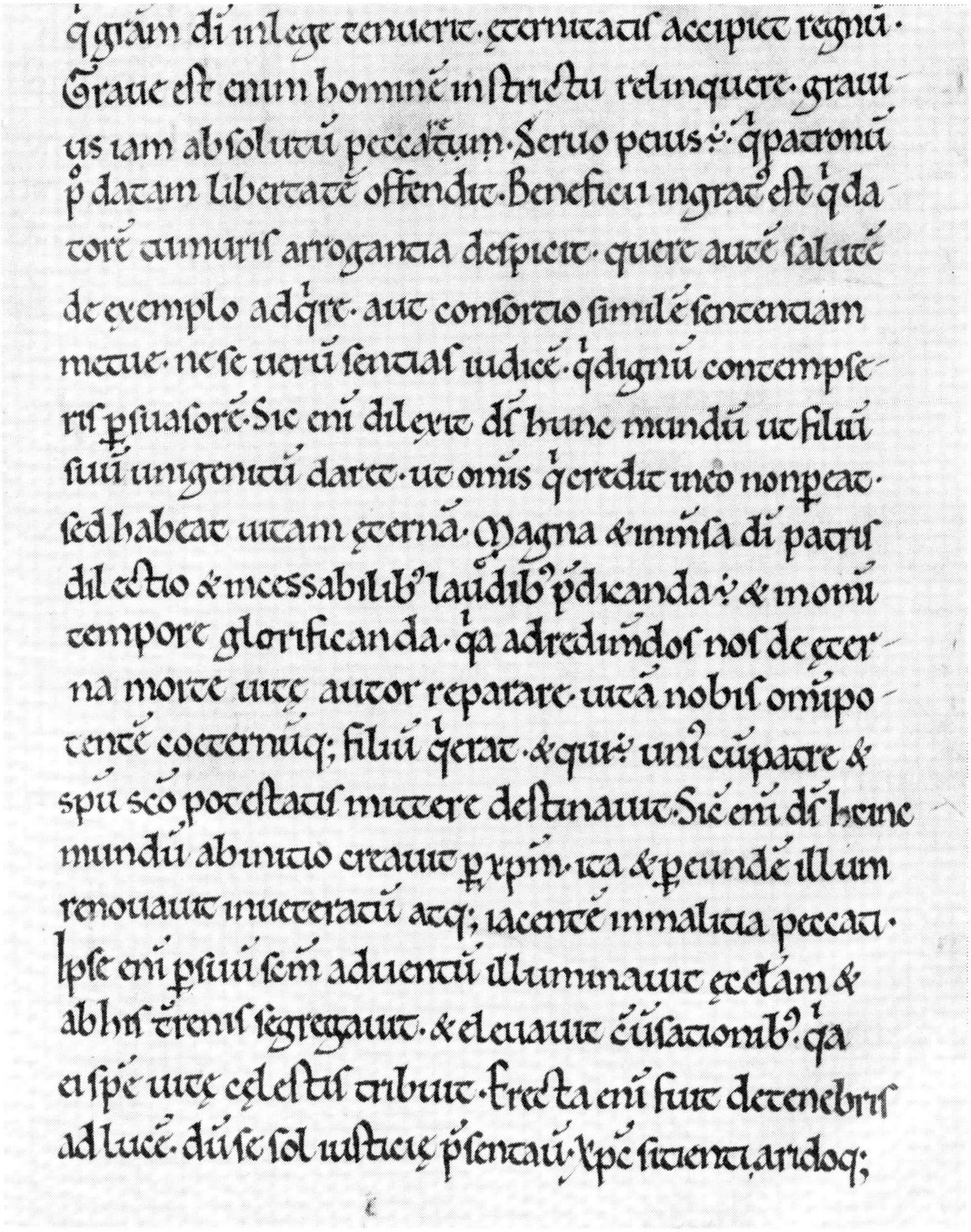

q gram di in lege tenuerit. eternitatis accipiet regnum. Graue est enim homine in stricto relinquere. gratius iam absolutum peccatum. Seruo peius est qui patronum p datam libertate offendit. Beneficii ingrat est qui datore cum iniuriis arrogantia despicit. quere aute salute de exemplo adquirit. aut consortio simile sententiam metuit. ne se uerum sentiat iudice qui dignum contempserit psuasore. Sic enim dilexit deus hunc mundum ut filii sui unigeniti daret. ut omnis qui credit in eo non pereat. sed habeat uitam eternam. Magna & inmensa dei patris dilectio & incessabilibus laudibus pdicanda & in omni tempore glorificanda. qa ad redimendos nos de eterna morte uitae autor reparare uitam nobis omipotente coeterniq; filiu qerat & qui uni cum patre & spu sco potestatis mittere destinauit. Sic enim deus hunc mundu abinitio creauit p xpin ita & per eunde illum renouauit inueteratu atq; iacente inmalitia peccati. Ipse enim psuii sem aduentu illuminauit ecctam & ab hiis tenis segregauit. & eleuauit eum sationibus qa ei spe uitae celestis tribuit. erecta enim sunt de tenebris ad luce. dum se sol iustitie psentauit. xpe siuenti aridoq;

Plate 6   Oxford, Bodleian Library, MS Bodley 451, part of fol. 118, actual size. The supply leaf added by a *scriptrix* at Nunnaminster

of Wilton and Shaftesbury, two of the other seven English nunneries included, are well formed and competent.

Evidence for further scribal activity by English nuns after this date is still to seek. It is generally agreed standards of convent literacy declined in the later Middle Ages, but the Abbess of Elstow's decision, in 1191 or 1192, to commission a professional scribe, Robert of Bedford, to make a copy of Peter Comestor's *Historia scholastica*[86] for the house need not be symptomatic of her nuns' inability to write. Increasingly, by the end of the twelfth century monastic houses tended to acquire new books from professional scribes rather than relying on their monks to produce them. So successful was this secularization of book production that one may too readily assume that a later medieval book surviving from a monastic library was bought rather than produced in the house.[87]

Scant numbers of books survive from medieval convents, yet a detailed examination of them may well provide evidence that later nuns continued to be able to write, even if they did not copy anything equivalent to the Nunnaminster Smaragdus. A devotional miscellany from Syon abbey, although mainly copied by men (including the well-known scribe William Darker), contains short English and Latin prayers added on endleaves by a 'scrybeler' who concludes with the request that the 'Good Syster' who owned the book should pray for the writer of the added prayers with these words 'iesu haue marcy on my wreched syster whose name by the marcy of god `j trust' shall be wrytyn in the book of lyfe'.[88] Such wording implies the scribbler was female. However, it would be unsafe to infer from the inclusion of recipes for making parchment and ink in a fifteenth-century 'household book', apparently from Barking abbey,[89] that this provided evidence that any of the nuns there were copyists. It is a

---

[86] London, BL, MS Royal 7.F.iii, for which see Watson, *Dated MSS British Library*, no. 878 and pl. 109. *Cat. Royal MSS*, pl. 56b illustrates the colophon.

[87] See the warning by A. I. Doyle, 'Book Production by the Monastic Orders in England (*c.*1375–1530): Assessing the Evidence', in *Medieval Book Production*, ed. Brownrigg, pp. 1–19.

[88] London, Lambeth Palace Lib., MS 546, consisting of two booklets; Darker copied the second (fols 57–77ᵛ). For other manuscripts by him, see M. B. Parkes, *English Cursive Book Hands 1250–1500*, 2nd edn (London, 1979), pl. 8 (ii). The first booklet (fols 1–56) was largely copied by John Warde and Robert Davemport, both of whom ask for the reader's prayers (fols 20ᵛ, 52). The prayers copied by the 'scrybeler' have been added at the end (fols 52ᵛ–55) of the first booklet. See further V. M. O'Mara, 'A Middle English Text Written by a Female Scribe', *Notes and Queries*, 235 (1990), 396–8, and C. de Hamel, 'The Medieval Manuscripts of Syon Abbey, and their Dispersal', *Syon Abbey: the Library of the Bridgettine Nuns and their Peregrinations after the Reformation*, Roxburghe Club (Otley, 1991), p. 98.

[89] London, BL, Cotton MS Julius D.VIII. For the term 'household book', see L. E. Voigts, 'Scientific and Medieval Books', in *Book Production and Publishing in Britain 1375–1475*, ed. J. Griffiths and D. Pearsall (Cambridge, 1989), p. 389 n. 18. It consists of four different booklets, one of which (fols 32–39) was written in the twelfth century; the other three (fols 1–31, 40–47 and 48–132) were written by three different fifteenth-century scribes. No single hand occurs in all four booklets which might enable us to establish when the volume was first put together.

composite volume, and the only item in it which suggests Barking provenance, 'the charche longynge to the office of the celeresse of þe Monestary of Barkinge', is contained in one booklet (fols 40–47) while the recipes occur in another copied by someone else (fols 48–132). It may be a post-medieval rather than a medieval collection; it is impossible to establish when the volume was first put together.

From Nunnaminster, no books survive of date later than the Smaragdus, except two sixteenth-century acquisitions. One of these is an early-fifteenth-century psalter written in the neighbourhood of Romsey Abbey and the other is a sixteenth-century *Ordo consecrationis sanctimonialium* given by Richard Fox, bishop of Winchester 1501–28.[90] Yet the Smaragdus itself indicates that some of the later sisters at Nunnaminster could write: in the thirteenth century someone copied out lines from the pages below into the top margins of fols 28ᵛ, 112ᵛ and 115; there are also pen trials by various thirteenth-century hands. Those on the originally blank first page (fol. ii) are of a suitably devotional nature: 'ama deum super omnia' and 'aue maria gracia plenus dominus'. That repeated several times on the last page (fol. 119ᵛ), also apparently a favourite epigram among religious, is known to us all from the motto occurring (somewhat ambiguously) on the gold brooch of Chaucer's Prioress: 'Amor vincit omnia'.[91]

---

[90] The psalter is at Romsey Parish Church: see Ker and Piper, *MMBL*, IV, 218–19. The *Ordo*, Cambridge, University Library, MS Mm.3.13, has been published by W. Maskell, *Monumenta Ritualia Ecclesiae Anglicanae* (London, 1846), II, 307–31.

[91] *Canterbury Tales*, I, 160–2 (cf. *Riverside Chaucer*). M. Madeleva, 'Chaucer's Nuns', in her *A Lost Language and Other Essays on Chaucer* (New York, 1951; repr. 1967), p. 43, stresses the motto's popularity among religious women. I am most grateful to Sally Thompson who first drew my attention to MS Bodley 451; to my audience at a meeting of the History of the Book Seminar in March 1996 for their helpful comments on an earlier version of this essay; and to Michelle Brown, Michael Clanchy, Helmut Gneuss, Jeanne Krochalis, and my co-editor who kindly read it and offered advice and criticism. I am solely responsible for the errors and omissions that remain.

CHAPTER FIVE

Stephen Dodesham of Witham and Sheen

A. I. Doyle

In 1967 I devoted most of my fourth Lyell lecture at Oxford to what I had by then identified as written by Stephen Dodesham; in 1969 and 1979 Malcolm Parkes included a specimen of Dodesham's hand and lists of work by him in the two editions of *English Cursive Book Hands*.[1] Since that time several scholars have published descriptions of a number of the manuscripts and discussed the conjectural circumstances of their making, notably Mr John Ayto and Dr Alexandra Barratt in their edition of translations of Aelred of Rievaulx, and more recently Professor A. S. G. Edwards on copies of John Lydgate's *Siege of Thebes*.[2] The number of identifications has increased considerably over the years and I have been repeatedly asked when my account of them might appear in print. The present occasion seems a particularly appropriate one.

There are only three manuscripts with contemporary attributions to Stephen Dodesham. Possibly the earliest of the three is a copy, measuring 145 × 100 mm (5¾ × 4 ins), in an expert Textura script, of the pseudo-Augustine *Sermones morales ad fratres suos in heremo*, with a fine illuminated initial of a mitred cleric (Pl. 7). This book, formerly the property of Sir Sydney Cockerell, had an inscription in a skilled Secretary hand: 'Liber Domus beate Marie de Wytham ordinis Cartusiensis quem scripsit Domnus Stephanus Dodesham monachus eiusdem Domus Anno Domini Millesimo quadragentesimo sexagesimo secundo'.[3] These words were not written by Dodesham himself, I think (on comparing his cursive script to be discussed below), but by another member of Witham Charterhouse (Somerset), who added similar *ex-libris* inscriptions to others of its books and wrote a portion of the list of gifts to it by John Blacman (after 1463 and before 1474).[4]

---

[1] M. B. Parkes, *English Cursive Book Hands 1250–1500* (Oxford, 1969), p. 6, pl. 6(ii); corr. repr. (London, 1979), p. 25, additions to list include London BL, Add. MS 10053, which is not by Dodesham: see A. J. Fletcher, *Notes and Queries*, n.s., 32 (1985), 10–11.

[2] *Aelred of Rievaulx's De Institutione Inclusarum: Two English Versions*, ed. J. R. Ayto and A. Barratt, EETS (OS), 287 (1984), pp. xxix–xxxii; A. S. G. Edwards, 'Beinecke MS 661 and Early Fifteenth-Century English Manuscript Production', *Yale University Library Gazette*, 66, Suppl. (1991), 181–6.

[3] S. C. Cockerell, 'Signed Manuscripts in my Collection', *Book Handbook*, 1 (1947–50), 432, 449, pl. 7, 7b; it was for sale in catalogues of A. G. Thomas, 1957, Dawsons of Pall Mall, 1960, and Philip C. Duschnes of New York, 1961, but was stolen from the latter and has not yet reappeared. My statement quoted by Sir Sydney that Dodesham was a visionary was through confusion with Stephen, monk of Hinton: cf. E. M. Thompson, *The Carthusian Order in England* (London, 1930), pp. 268–74.

[4] Ibid., pp. 317–21; R. Lovatt, 'The Library of John Blacman and Contemporary Carthusian Spirituality', *Jnl Ecclesiastical History*, 43 (1992), 195–230, esp. 201–2.

Plate 7 Former Cockerell/Duschnes Manuscript, fol. 1

Probably second in date, and the only book signed by Dodesham as scribe, Oxford, Trinity College, MS 46, contains a Latin choir Psalter, Canticles, litanies and lessons for the dead, prefaced by a Carthusian liturgical calendar, with English verses on calculating Easter: it measures 287×180 mm ($11\frac{1}{4} \times 7\frac{1}{4}$ ins), and is written in more than one size of the same Textura as the pseudo-Augustine, with an inscription on fol. 167^v in a smaller size: 'Orate pro anima domni Stephani Dodesham huius libri scriptoris. dicendo deuote Anima eius & anime omnium fidelium defunctorum per misericordiam dei requiescant in pace'. This follows lists of saintly British kings, which have led to the hypothesis that the book was made for Sheen Charterhouse, because it was founded by King Henry V.[5] Witham, however, had been founded by Henry II, and St Hugh, its first prior, is invoked here twice in the litanies. The calendar contains (in the original hand and ink) the feast of the Visitation authorized for the whole Carthusian order in 1468, though allowed much earlier in England; it does not have that of the Presentation of the BVM authorized in 1474.[6] The fine illuminated borders are in a Franco-Flemish style of the second half of the fifteenth century, which is perhaps more likely to have been employed in or near London than Somerset; yet the earlier-looking English illumination of the Cockerell book is also of metropolitan standard.[7]

The third and most consequential attribution is in Glasgow, University Library, Hunterian MS T.3.15 (77), a copy of Nicholas Love's *Mirror of the Life of Christ*, 280 × 205 mm (11 × 8 ins), by a large individual Anglicana Formata, with English illuminated initials and borders.[8] It contains a rough cursive inscription by a different hand: 'Thys Boke be longgyth on to the Chartter hows of schene wrettyn be þe hand[es?] of dane stephene doddzam monke of þe same plasse the ʒer of Kynge Edwarde the iiij[the] xiiij[the]', i.e. between 4 March 1474 and 3 March 1475.[9]

Stephen Dodesham is three times mentioned in the annual *cartae* (ordinances) of the General Chapter of the Carthusian order. First, in 1469 it is reported under Witham that, since he 'nimis confuse prolixe et irreverenter scripsit' to the Grande Chartreuse, he would not be answered for the present; next, in 1471, he is described as a professed monk of Sheen (Surrey) but writing against the prior of Witham, 'non solum inordinate sed eciam false prout sufficienter informati sumus, super suis scriptis et articulis perpetuum silencium imponimus sub pena inobediencie et carceris'.[10] Transfers from one Charterhouse to another, temporarily or permanently, were not unusual in cases of personal difficulties, but such a severe threat was less common. He

---

[5] H. O. Coxe, *Catalogus Codicum Manuscriptorum . . . in Collegiis Aulisque Oxoniensibus*, II (Oxford, 1852), p. 18; J. J. G. Alexander and E. Temple, *Illuminated Manuscripts in Oxford College Libraries* (Oxford, 1985), p. 58, no. 589, pl. XXXV; S. J. P. Van Dijk's typescript catalogue of liturgical manuscripts in the Bodleian, II, 29.

[6] A. A. King, *Liturgies of the Religious Orders* (London, 1955), p. 25; J. A. Gribbin, *Aspects of Carthusian Liturgical Practice in Later Medieval England*, Analecta Cartusiana, 99:33 (Salzburg, 1995), pp. 60, 73.

[7] Reduced reproduction of fol. 68[v] in R. Gameson and A. Coates, *The Old Library, Trinity College, Oxford* (Oxford, Trinity College, 1988), p. 15.

[8] Parkes (as n. 1 above), pl. 6(ii); N. Thorp, *The Glory of the Page: Medieval and Renaissance Illuminated Manuscripts from Glasgow University Library* (London, 1987), p. 96, no. 42, with reduced reproduction of fol. 3[v].

[9] J. Young and P. H. Aitken, *Catalogue of the Manuscripts in the Library of the Hunterian Museum* (Glasgow, 1908), p. 85, no. 77, with misreading 'doddram'; a downstroke on the last letter of 'hand' might mean the plural. Some scholars have been led by the spelling here to call him 'Doddesham' but in Trinity Coll., MS 46 he uses one *d*.

[10] J. Clark, ed. *The Chartae of the Carthusian General Chapter: London, Lambeth Palace MS 413*, pt 3, Analecta Cartusiana, 100:12 (Salzburg, 1991), pp. 117, 145.

presumably complied, since he was allowed to copy Hunterian T.3.15 in 1474/5. Finally, the *carta* for 1482 recorded his death, as a professed monk first of Witham and second of Sheen; he must have died within the 12 months up to Easter, after which information from England would go to the Grande Chartreuse for the General Chapter there, at which the annual *carta* was compiled.[11]

It is interesting that in two of Dodesham's books his brethren found it proper to name the copyist, in at least one case after he had been disciplined. The diligent and skilled performance of a task particularly encouraged in the order was perhaps thought to merit commendation as an example and to excite the prayers he asks for himself in the third book. It appears that anonymity was not then (unlike later times) obligatory for Carthusians, and there are a number (if not many) instances of their scribes being named in late medieval England and many more on the continent.[12]

The identification of other manuscripts by Dodesham relies on one's recognition of the repetition of an ensemble of palaeographical characteristics distinctive enough to be that of an individual, not simply a school or a type of script. Although the Textura Quadrata of the Cockerell and Trinity manuscripts is clearly of the same type (for instance in its formation of **a, d** and **g**), in comparison with examples of other types, the degree of conventionality in this script makes it more difficult to recognize unsigned individual performances on cursory inspection, and I have not noticed other instances; Dodesham also used a more common type of Textura Quadrata for purposes of emphasis[13] along with his Anglicana Formata, of which so many more instances have been identified. It is his version of this latter script, and of its display modes, which it is comparatively easy to recognize, proceeding from the specimens in the Glasgow manuscript. Dodesham's Anglicana Formata may vary from manuscript to manuscript and within each more or less noticeably in size and refinement, perhaps between some manuscripts owing to his comparative age but when variation occurs within a volume this was probably due to varying conditions of material, implements, light, urgency, comfort or health. We have (until more evidence emerges) limited clues to the dates and destinations of his different pieces of work, and so the chronology and circumstances of his career remain to a considerable degree speculative. I will consider first those pieces which are most closely datable, then those only

---

[11] G. Schwengel, *Apparatus ad annales S. O. Cartusiensis, British Library London Add. MS 17092*, Analecta Cartusiana, 90:9 (Salzburg, 1983); BL, Add. MS 17092, fol. 124 (obit for which the *carta* is lost).

[12] See A. I. Doyle, 'Book Production by the Monastic Orders in England (*c.*1375–1530)' in *Medieval Book Production*, ed. Brownrigg, pp. 13–15, for English instances; for the most thorough examination of contemporaneous foreign ones see J. P. Gumbert, *Die Utrechter Kartäuser und ihre Bücher im frühen fünfzehnten Jahrhundert* (Leiden, 1974).

[13] E.g. for the final colophon of Cambridge, University Library, MS Dd.7.10, fol. 330ᵛ: 'Explicit postilla super apocalipsim, Finito libro reddatur gloria Christo – Scriptoris anime te Christe precor misereri'.

more relatively so, and lastly those least certain, specifying there (after the illustrations from books not previously exemplified in print) some of the diagnostic details.

His earliest datable work, and one of his two largest, is represented by Karlsruhe, Badische Landesbibliothek, MS Sankt Georgen 12, the first of two original volumes of the *Sanctilogium salvatoris*, a compilation of saints' lives in the order of the months of their feasts, based chiefly on the *Sanctilogium* of John of Tynemouth, but said to include two extra books of additions (not known to survive), apparently compiled by a brother of Syon Abbey, and copied for it at the expense of Margaret Duchess of Clarence, who died in 1439.[14] Both volumes occur in the brethren's library catalogue as M1–2.[15] In the surviving volume (M1) of 198 leaves, 550 × 405 mm (22 × 16 ins), both the whole of the main text, in two columns of 65 lines each, and many of the separately ruled marginal additions, are in Dodesham's Anglicana Formata; on fol. 5 a neat Hybrida commences a martyrological kalendar which is completed by Dodesham, and it also makes a number of the marginal additions and annotations, evidently subsequent to his, because with uniform flourishing and illumination.[16] This second hand entered in a volume of the Syon brethren's rules, London, BL, Additional MS 5208, fol. 128ᵛ, their decision in 1431 concerning commemorations of deceased founders, members and benefactors. This hand was perhaps also responsible for another copy of that text, together with its confirmation of 1440, in their martyrology (London, BL, Add. MS 22285, fols 3– 4).[17] It is not impossible that this is the hand of Simon Wynter, brother of Syon by 1429, known as the spiritual counsellor of the Duchess of Clarence, and that the picture of the compiler on fol. 1 is meant to portray him.[18] The first professions were not made at Syon until 1420, and the earliest buildings were abandoned for new ones in 1431.[19] The lavish illumination of the Karlsruhe book includes historiated initials

---

[14] E. J. Beer, *Initial und Miniatur: Buchmalerei aus neun Jahrhunderten in Handschriften der Badischen Landesbibliothek, Karlsruhe*, 2. Aufl. (Basle, 1965), pp. 51, 87 (enlarged detail), no. 54.

[15] M. Bateson, ed. *Catalogue of the Library of Syon Monastery, Isleworth* (Cambridge, 1898), p. 96.

[16] January and February on fol. 5 and the names of the other months are in the hybrida, but the rest of the other months from fol. 5ᵛ onwards are by Dodesham; the compiler's prologue, copied by Dodesham, fol. 1ʳ⁻ᵛ, refers in the first person to having made marginal additions from exemplars he could not get all at one time, and also the kalendar.

[17] G. J. Aungier, *History and Antiquities of Syon Monastery* (London, 1840), pp. 54–6.

[18] Cf. G. R. Keiser, 'Patronage and Piety in Fifteenth-Century England: Margaret, Duchess of Clarence, Symon Wynter and Beinecke MS 317', *Yale University Library Gazette*, 60 (1985), 32–46; although she got Wynter licence to transfer from the Brigittines to a less strict order in 1429, it seems from the entry of his death in 1448 in the Syon Martiloge (BL, Add. MS 22285), and his gift of nine volumes to the brethren's library (including four of his own sermons) and his procuring another from the Duchess, in each of which he is described simply as a professed brother, that he may not in fact have moved: Bateson, *Catalogue*, p. xxvii; Ker, *MLGB*, pp. 185, 309.

[19] F. R. Johnston, 'Syon Abbey', *Victoria County History: Middlesex*, I (London, 1969), pp. 182–9.

in the style of the school of Herman Scheerre, the Annunciation being of the same design as that in Margaret's own *Horae ad usum Sarum*, made after the Duke's death in 1421 (now in private ownership), the Psalter and Hours of John Duke of Bedford (BL, Add. MS 42131, *c.*1414–23) and the 'Hours of Elizabeth the Queen' (BL, Add. MS 50001, *c.*1420–30).[20] If Dodesham also copied the whole of the missing second volume, the two, together with the marginal additions and decoration, must have taken at least a couple of years to complete, on the working days of a full-time scribe, even longer for a religious, so it seems likely that he was at work by the 1430s, if not before.[21]

His Anglicana Formata in the Karlsruhe volume can be compared with that in Hunterian T.3.15, datable at least 35, and possibly 45, years later in his career, where there is no loss of calligraphic skill, and with its characteristics as seen in the following manuscripts in which it appears alone or with other hands. His writing is, in Karlsruhe, as regular in its manner and details as in any other manuscript; it varies little in size (with a 5.6 mm vertical module, i.e. unit of ruling) and deteriorates, most conspicuously in smoothness, in some marginal additions on added ruling. The module is much smaller than that of Hunterian T.3.15 (6.6 mm) but the most noticeable other palaeographical difference is the employment of initial and medial long r in the text of Karlsruhe, as well as short r (with the latter preferred in headings), and 8-like s preferred to Secretary final s, whereas Hunterian prefers short r and Secretary s in its text. Both books have, besides more common punctuation, a mid-line curved *virgula* like the upper stroke of the *punctus elevatus*, an unusual short line-end filler like a hyphen, and two forms of the *punctus versus* or *positura*, which are all salient features of Dodesham's hand.[22]

The second most closely datable, and the longest work of Dodesham yet found, is Cambridge, University Library, MSS Dd. 7–10, comprising four volumes, of just over 1200 leaves, *c.*465–475 × 330–40 mm (19 × 13 ins). The work, Nicholas de Lyra on the Bible, is copied in two columns of 53 lines each of Anglicana Formata (on a module of 5.7 mm), elaborated in some headings, with Textura used for the opening

---

[20] Formerly the property of S. Eckman, Sotheby's auction 12 December 1967, lot 46, and then of Major J. R. Abbey, Sotheby's 19 June 1989, lot 3018, catalogue pp. 64–73; still in private ownership. For fragments of a breviary probably provided for Syon by the Duke of Bedford in 1426, by the same scribe as BL, Add. 42131, see C. de Hamel, *Syon Abbey: the Library of the Bridgettine Nuns and their Peregrinations after the Reformation*, Roxburghe Club (Otley, 1991), pp. 62–5 and on the Duchess of Clarence, pp. 58–60.

[21] Cf. A. I. Doyle (intro.), *The Vernon Manuscript* (Cambridge, 1987), p. 6, n. 16; C. Bozzolo and E. Ornato, *Pour une histoire du livre manuscrit au moyen âge: trois essais de codicologie quantitative* (Paris, 1980), pp. 46–8; repr. with *Supplément* (1983), p. 363; M. Gullick, 'How Fast Did Scribes Write? Evidence from Romanesque Manuscripts', in *Making the Medieval Book: Techniques of Production*, ed. L. L. Brownrigg (Los Altos Hills, CA, 1995), pp. 39–58; p. 48 details post-romanesque cases.

[22] Cf. M. B. Parkes, *Pause and Effect: an Introduction to the History of Punctuation in the West* (Aldershot, 1992), pp. 42–3, 132, 306–7; and see p. 113 below.

words of some chapters and for a final colophon.[23] The text has large illustrations to Exodus and Ezekiel, and inhabited initials in the New Testament, with illuminated initials, borders and sprays throughout, in more than one English style of the mid fifteenth century, but some strongly coloured curling acanthus branch-work is more like that in Germanic books of the same period.[24] In the front of two volumes there are contemporary copies of an indenture, 17 May 1457, which record the gift of the four volumes by Dame Eleanor Hull and Roger Huswyff, clerk, to the abbot and convent of St Albans, but reserving their use to Huswyff for the length of his life. The set would therefore seem to have been completed by that date, or earlier, and could have taken five years or so of full-time scribal activity, with naturally some variation in script (e.g. in the use of long and short r) and illumination.[25] Eleanor Hull was a devout lady (d. 1460) who had been associated with St Albans since 1417 and Roger Huswyff was her executor, a lawyer and priest, also closely connected with that house and with John Whethamstede, its abbot 1420–40 and 1451–65, whom he outlived. Whether the manuscript was made at St Albans or elsewhere is arguable.[26]

If Dodesham had been a Carthusian at the time of writing the *Sanctilogium salvatoris* for Syon Abbey, in collaboration with its editor, he could have done it in the neighbouring Charterhouse of Sheen; but the *cartae* do not mention his being temporarily there, which would have to have been for more than a year or two for that purpose. And the main source, John of Tynemouth's *Sanctilogium*, was particularly associated with St Albans, as was its probable adaptor, Simon Wynter, who explains in his preface that the various additions at the end and in the margins of the Syon manuscript were owing to delays in access to exemplars, of which Tynemouth's text itself was notably bulky. The work could have been done, at Syon or Sheen, from borrowed exemplars, if the owners had been willing to dispense with these books for reading and reference over lengthy periods, or else by the main copyist going to spend the requisite time on them *in situ*, hardly permissible for a Carthusian. The illumination of the set of Lyra looks distinctly later than that of the *Sanctilogium*, and appropriate for the 1440s or 1450s, though that does not of course

---

[23] *Catalogue of the Manuscripts Preserved in the University Library of Cambridge*, 5 vols (Cambridge, 1856–67), I, 327; P. R. Robinson, *Catalogue of Dated and Datable Manuscripts c.737–1600 in Cambridge Libraries* (Cambridge, 1988), I, no. 9; II, pl. 265 (Dd.7.7, fol. 191 detail). I am doubtful of D. R. Howlett's attribution of the marginal corrections by a small Secretary hand, many erased and implemented by Dodesham, as John Whethamstede's autograph; there is no reason to suppose that he was so intimately involved in the actual copying of the Lyra, though it was reported at St Albans 'idem Abbas suis in temporibus facit inchoari de manu satis sollempni postillam Nicholai de lira super totam bibliam' (London, BL, Cotton MS Nero D.VII, fol. 32): 'inchoari' may imply it was not completed at his expense, or even in his abbacy, or life, ending 1464–65. See n. 13 above for colophon.

[24] E.g. Dd.7.7, fols 176, 193ᵛ; Dd.7.10, fols 1, 57ᵛ, 70ᵛ, 99ᵛ, 281ᵛ, etc.

[25] In Dd.7.8 the catchwords have exaggerated ascenders and descenders; and the prevalence of long or short r, for instance, varies from volume to volume.

[26] *The Seven Psalms: a Commentary on the Penitential Psalms Translated from French into English by Dame Eleanor Hull*, ed. A. Barratt EETS (OS), 307 (1995), pp. xxiii–xxxiii.

mean that the writing could not be earlier in part or as a whole. In view of its greater bulk (four massive volumes) than the *Sanctilogium* an exemplar is less likely to have been available for lending over an even longer time span to a single Carthusian scribe, not able to work at it full-time. Like the *Sanctilogium* the Lyra was no doubt decorated by professional limners, and the size of these tasks of Dodesham and his equally high standards of performance suggest that he was probably a professional scribe at these stages in his career, and possibly peripatetic, as the limners could have been too.[27]

The likelihood that he was not a religious but a lay or clerical scribe for part of his career is strengthened by his copying of three surviving copies of Lydgate's *Siege of Thebes*: Boston (MA), Public Library, MS f.med.94 (275 × 180 mm, 10¾ × 7 ins); Cambridge, University Library, MS Additional 3137 (savagely cropped); and New Haven, Yale University, Beinecke Library, MS 661 (270 × 176 mm, 10½ × 7 ins).[28] The composition of this sequel to Chaucer's *Canterbury Tales* dates from 1421 and, although the author was a Benedictine monk, is quite secular in substance.[29] The repeated copying of the same text in such a case points to paid employment, and although there are instances, more clearly on the continent than in England, of religious writing books 'pro pretio' (as Lydgate himself in effect may have composed them), the austerity of Carthusian discipline would surely have drawn a line about content.[30] The three copies are all on good membrane and well-illuminated in the metropolitan style of *c.*1430–60, one limner's hand occurring in both Boston and Beinecke. The text of each, however, is from a different exemplar,[31] nor are they parallel page for page: Boston normally having 33 lines per page with a module of 5.7 mm approximately; Cambridge the same with 33 or 32 lines (thus getting out of step); and Beinecke 39 lines with a module of only 5 mm. Boston, interestingly, migrated from English to Scottish lay ownership by the early sixteenth century.[32]

---

[27] London, BL, Cotton MS Tiberius E.I (badly damaged), from St Albans, is the leading copy (*s.* xiv *med.*) of the *Sanctilogium*: it is in kalendar order, as is the Karlsruhe manuscript: *Nova Legenda Angliae*, ed. C. Horstman (Oxford, 1901), I, ix–xv. Only a few sets of the Lyra survive in manuscripts from England in the fourteenth and fifteenth centuries: F. Stegmüller, *Repertorium Biblicum Medii Aevi* (Madrid, 1940–80), IV, 52, nos 5829–923, omits Durham, Dean and Chapter Library MSS A.1.3–5 (from the medieval Priory) and New Haven, Yale University, Beinecke Library (ex-Mostyn).

[28] Edwards, 'Beinecke MS 661'; he first suggested to me that Add. 3137 was by Dodesham.

[29] D. A. Pearsall, *John Lydgate* (London, 1970), p. 151.

[30] For the basis and extent of Carthusian scribal work see P. Lehmann, 'Bücherliebe und Bücherpflege bei die Karthäusern', *Erforschung des Mittelalters*, 3 (Stuttgart, 1960), pp. 121–42; J. P. Gumbert, 'Over Kartuizer-bibliotheken in de Nederlanden', in *Contributions à l'histoire des bibliothèques et de la lecture aux Pays Bas*, special no. of *Archives et bibliothèques de Belgique* (1974), 159–86, esp. 162–3, 178–81.

[31] Edwards, 'Beinecke MS 661', figs 1–3 (reduced), pp. 187–9, 191–3, 195–6 nn. 33–8.

[32] Ibid., describing Boston (MA) Public Lib., MS f.med.94; Edwards does not note 'Dieu remembres vus de moy', fol. 76, in a mid-fifteenth-century English Secretary hand; cf. his reference, n. 6, to Agnes Paston lending a copy to the Earl of Arran (an exile in England) in 1472.

Three copies by Dodesham are also known of the Mountgrace Carthusian Nicholas Love's *Mirror of the Life of Christ*, one of which (Glasgow, Hunterian T.3.15, see above p. 96) was written in 1474–75 for Sheen Charterhouse; the others, of a book so frequently reproduced for readers of all classes since its archiepiscopal approval *c.*1410, could have been made either in the world or the cloister. Cambridge, Trinity College, B.15.16(352), 300 × 210 mm (11¾ × 8¼ ins), has 33 lines to the page and a module of 5.7 mm (like the Boston and Cambridge Lydgates), and more lavish mid-fifteenth-century illumination, by a different artist from any in them.[33] Oxford, Bodleian Library, MS Rawlinson A.387B is of mixed and inferior membrane on which the ink has not taken or held very well, and Dodesham's writing is larger and coarser, with varying ruled pages and number of lines (28–31), giving a module of 6.2–6.3 mm. There is a considerable number of corrections, some by Dodesham himself, but one omission on the first page of text, and some longer supplies, are by different fifteenth-century hands; the note 'corrigitur' occurs at the foot of a series of last pages of quires, indicative of systematic supervision, which is usually thought to be a commercial practice but was not necessarily so. Rawlinson may have been copied in haste, ill health or old age, and its illuminated initials and sprays have been dated by Kathleen Scott to *c.*1468–70.[34] The Glasgow manuscript, dated by the Sheen *ex libris* 1474–75, late in Dodesham's life, has an even larger module, 6.6 mm, for 26–30 ruled lines, in two columns except for the preliminary chapter list and memoranda; it is of good membrane and carefully written, with few corrections, neatly made by the scribe's hand, and good illumination of the period.[35] Michael Sargent, from his selective collations of the *Mirror* texts, puts Rawlinson and Hunterian together in a distinct branch (A3) of his Alpha stemma, but Trinity B.15.16, possibly earlier in Dodesham's career, is in a subordinate branch (B6) of Beta. Trinity belonged, before the dissolution of the monasteries, to a secular priest in Berkshire.[36]

Another book with earlier illumination, probably of the second rather than third quarter of the century, is Downside Abbey, MS 26542 (233 × 172 mm, 9¼ × 6¾ ins), containing the *Pricking of Love*, the *Poor Caitiff*, and three shorter texts (one in English and two in Latin), of which the penultimate is an extract (taken from Suso's *Horologium sapientie* and Mechthild of Hackeborn's Revelations) from the *Speculum*

---

[33] Ibid., fig. 4 (fol. 5, reduced), pp. 189–90; M. R. James, *The Western Manuscripts in the Library of Trinity College, Cambridge: a Descriptive Catalogue*, 4 vols (Cambridge, 1900–4), I, 479–80.

[34] In her lecture to the conference on Love's *Myrrour* at Waseda University, Tokyo, July 1995, in *Nicholas Love at Waseda*, ed. S. Oguro, R. Beadle and M. G. Sargent (Woodbridge, 1997). W. D. Macray, *Catalogi Codicum Manuscriptorum Bibliothecae Bodleianae*, V, fasc. i (Oxford, 1862), col. 384. Parkes, as n. 1 above (1979), p. 25, first identified Rawl. A.387B as Dodesham's.

[35] Ibid., pl. 6(ii); Thorp, as n. 8 above; Young and Aitken, as n. 9 above.

[36] M. Sargent, ed. *Nicholas Love's Mirror of the Blessed Life of Jesus Christ: a Critical Edition Based on Cambridge University Library Additional MSS 6578 and 6686* (New York, 1992), p. lxxxix, expanded with his paper to the Waseda conference; James, *Trinity MSS*, I, 479–80.

spiritualium, a compendium of Carthusian origin. It has 31 lines to the page and a module of 5.3 mm and there are corrections by the scribe. A subsequent inscription of gift to Betryce Chaumbre says that after her death the book was to stay with the Domincan nuns of Dartford Priory (Kent) 'to pray for hem that yeve yt'.[37] The plural could refer to family or friends, but they might simply have arranged for the volume to be made for this donation.

Oxford, Bodleian Library, MS Bodley 423, sections B and C, fols 128–243 (270 × 195 mm, $10\frac{1}{2}$ × $7\frac{3}{4}$ ins), contains 18 English religious items in prose and two in verse. They include the only known copy of one English translation of Aelred of Rievaulx's rule for a recluse. The pages of both sections are ruled for 37 lines of text, with a module of 5.8–6 mm, on good membrane, and it is clear from the contemporary quire-lettering that section C was intended to follow B. Although there are corrections both by Dodesham and another hand, there are several sorts of evidence (such as the underlay only for illumination of initials and for a border, in a mid-century style) that the manuscript was not fully finished. Its contents suggest devout and possibly female readers, though quite early in the sixteenth century it seems to have been in laymen's hands in London.[38]

There is no illumination to help in dating the rest of the present list of Dodesham's *oeuvre* but a variety of other evidence can assist our assessment of the period or circumstances in which it was produced. If changes are looked for in his writing of Anglicana, I can only offer the possibility that there may be an increasing preference for a larger module, which would go with naturally deteriorating eyesight, and a diminishing ease with the pen towards the end of his long career; such superficial impressions are however untrustworthy.

There is an approximate *terminus ante* from the content of the first of two now separated portions of what was once a single codex, as is clear from their uniformity, their quire-numbering and their post-medieval pagination. Glasgow, University Library, Hunterian MSS U.4.17 (259) and U.4.16 (258), (260 × 180 mm, $10\frac{1}{4}$ × $7\frac{1}{4}$ ins), in that order in the original codex, lack 57 leaves between them, which from that extent and the differing dimensions cannot be T.3.15 of the same collection, already discussed.[39] U.4.17 contains the English verse paraphrase of the *Parvus Cato*

---

[37] Ker, *MMBL*, II, 444–5.

[38] *SC*, no. 2322, incomplete in listing the contents; enlarged by Ayto and Barratt (as n. 2 above).

[39] Young and Aitken, *Catalogue*, pp. 209–11. N. R. Ker, 'William Hunter as a Collector of Medieval Manuscripts' (Glasgow, 1983), pp. 20–21, guessed that the original codex could have been broken up by Thomas Martin who wrote his name in both the present two portions, with his numbers 100 and 99; he sold part of his collection in 1769 to T. Payne, in one of whose catalogues, 1770, they appear as nos 7590–91, with no obvious candidates in the vicinity for the missing portion (which should be sig. ciij–kiij, in eights): it is not apparently any other manuscript listed here, though Oxford, Bodl. Lib., MS Bodley 549 is of similar dimensions.

and *Magnus Cato* by Benedict Burgh, a secular priest, probably not composed before 1440, followed by the verse *Dietary* by John Lydgate (d. *c*.1449), though neither author is named here.[40] Within the ruling of 31 lines per page the Latin distiches of the pseudo-Cato are in larger Bastard Anglicana alternating with the English stanzas, the module of the latter being about 5.4 mm but that of the Latin, of an English colophon, and the *Dietary* heading about 6 mm (Pl. 8). U.4.16, the second portion of the former codex, contains a copy of the English prose treatise *Benjamin minor*, here called *Studium sapiencie*, also on 31 lines with a module of 6 mm, and after it the beginning of an English poem on blood-letting added in a fifteenth-century Secretary hand.[41] This may seem a somewhat surprising selection of contents, and with unknown matter between, but the pseudo-Cato, traditionally used to teach Latin and good manners to the young, the advice on health, and the allegorical exposition of spiritual life would not have been discordant in either a pious secular household or the novitiate of a religious community. The large size of the writing could have been helpful to beginners in learning.

A more definite *terminus ante* is known for London, BL, MS Harley 630, the English *Gilt Legend* which in one manuscript is said to have been completed in 1438. Here Dodesham was responsible only for supplying fol. 163^{r-v}, two columns each side, of text omitted accidentally from fol. 164 by the main copyist who wrote a mixed set cursive of the middle of the century, hastily and on poor membrane, with various mistakes corrected by more than one other hand. The number of lines (38) for Dodesham were not his choice but effectually determined by the main scribe. The book, to which a Dutch-spelling scribe added a contents list, soon belonged to a London layman who died in 1495.[42] It looks as if Dodesham was one of several hands called on for piecemeal ameliorations, in what circumstances is uncertain, but possibly commercial.

London, BL Additional MS 11305 is a copy of the southern recension of the *Prick of Conscience* (270 × 170 mm, $10\frac{1}{2}$ × $6\frac{3}{4}$ ins, approx.), 31–32 lines to a page, all in Dodesham's Anglicana Formata. The writing varies in neatness and size within the book on a module of 6 mm; there is no illumination, only customary red-flourished blue initials and paraphs of alternating colour. The inferiorities in writing may reflect those of the varying membrane. Towards the end

---

[40] Henry, Lord Bourchier, for whose son and heir Caxton said it was composed, was married by 1426; William the son was married by 1467: G. E. C[okayne], *Complete Peerage*, V (London, 1926), 137–8; Burgh was beneficed in Essex from 1440 and by Bourchier's gift from 1450: R. Newcourt, *Repertorium Ecclesiasticum Diocesis Londinensis* (London, 1708–10) II, 323, 517.

[41] *Deonise Hid Diuinite and Other Treatises on Contemplative Prayer*, ed. P. Hodgson, EETS (OS), 231 (1955), pp. xvi, 12–76; C. Brown and R. H. Robbins, *Index of Middle English Verse* (New York, 1943), and R. H. Robbins, *Supplement* (Lexington, 1965), no. 3848.

[42] 'Hier beghint þe table of de⟨se⟩ bo⟨ec?⟩', fol. 366ᵛ; 'Edwardo Goldisburgh constat liber', fol. 234: cf. London, Guildhall Library, Commissary Court Register 8, fol. 101ᵛ, testament made 3 November 1484, probate 12 November 1495. Another inscription in large plummet Anglicana (*s*. xv), fol. 188, 'Beaugrand'.

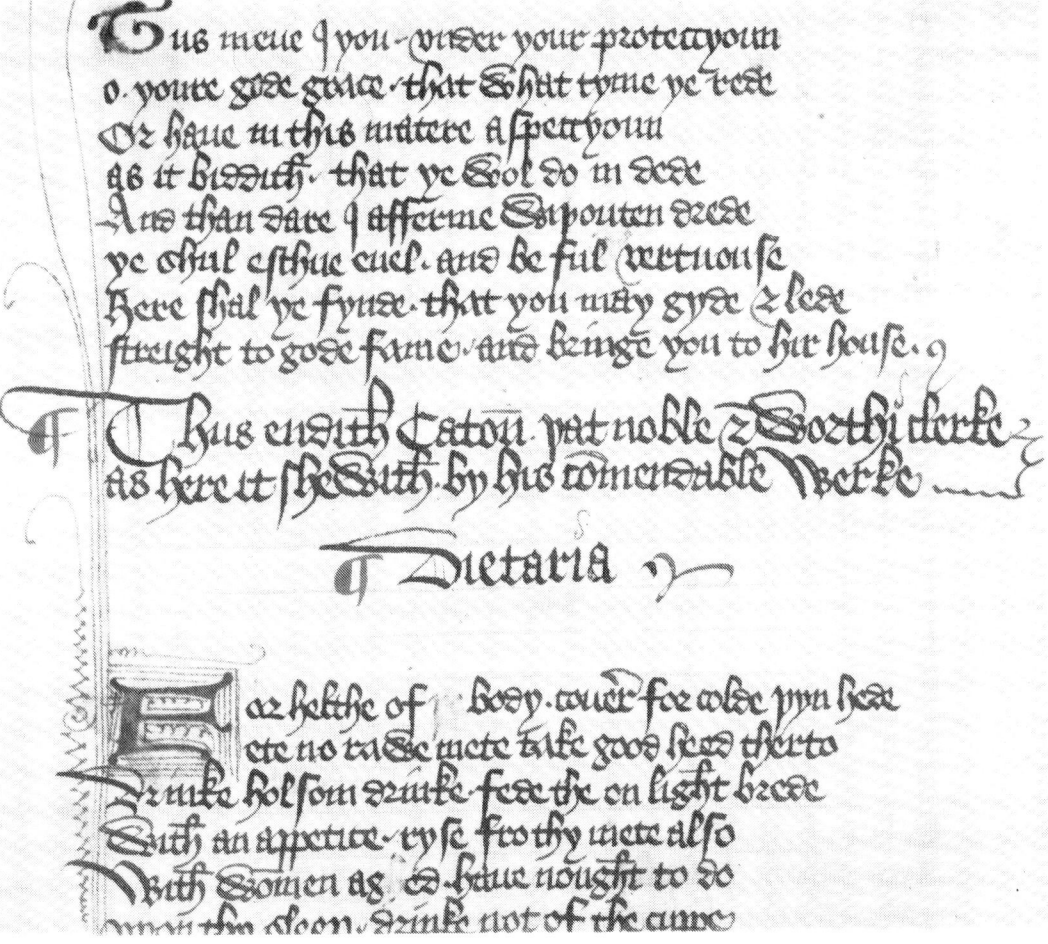

Plate 8   Glasgow, University Library, Hunterian MS U.4.17 (259), p. 50, top half

of the book a number of bifolia are palimpsest from a larger book in two columns: apparently in a smaller module and neater quality of Dodesham's Anglicana, identifiable as a Latin alphabetical index to Bartholomaeus Anglicus, *De Proprietatibus rerum*. If that was a work which he copied as a whole it would have been on a similar scale to a volume of the Cambridge manuscript of Lyra's *Postille*.[43] Such reject leaves

---

[43] R. E. Lewis and A. McIntosh, *Descriptive Guide to the Manuscripts of the Prick of Conscience*, Medium Aevum Monographs, 12 (Oxford, 1982), pp. 140–41; A. McIntosh, M. L. Samuels and M. Benskin, *Linguistic Atlas of Late Mediaeval English* (Aberdeen, 1986), I, 100; III, 302; LP 6440, Middlesex. The ruled writing space of the palimpsest is about 205 mm wide, implying a height of at least 300 mm: the Cambridge Lyra has 305 × 208 mm, the Karlsruhe book 370 × 258 mm. The lower margins were at least 80 mm deep, implying leaves at least 450 × 300 mm (17¾ × 12 ins); the

could have resulted from an error in the sequence of copying, or an omission, and their re-use from economy, when cost was crucial or adequate fresh supplies of membrane unobtainable. That this copy of the *Prick*, in origin a northern work, was later in the north is probably a coincidence.[44]

Cambridge, Trinity College, MS B.14.54 (337) is a small volume, 130 × 85 mm (5 × 3½ ins), containing brief English prose expositions of the elements of Christian doctrine, starting with the Creed, where some passages suggest a Lollard antecedent or interpolation.[45] With only 14 lines per page the module is 5.7 mm (Pl. 9). The quality of membrane and of the writing is good, and the marginal corrections are also in Dodesham's Anglicana. At the end of each quire is the note 'corrigitur' (as in Rawlinson A.387B above). The quires signed *l* and *m* are palimpsest of another manuscript copied by Dodesham, on larger leaves, in English prose; it recited the indulgences attached to a number of feasts and times of the year at Syon Abbey, and corresponds verbally with those in an English sermon in London, BL, MS Harley 2321, fols 17–63, probably that ascribed in the catalogue of the brethren's library to Simon Wynter (the possible adaptor of the *Sanctilogium salvatoris* described above). The Syon indulgences, which were widely advertised, such as that of the Portiuncula at Assisi, mentioned in Trinity B.14.54, had been obtained during the 1420s and this text could have been copied by *c.*1430, or any time subsequently.[46] Trinity B.14.54 itself is a book for an individual, from the contents probably made for a lay person, while the palimpsest shows that Dodesham had been working for Syon before he came to make Trinity.[47]

In contrast Cambridge, University Library, MS Additional 3042, an even smaller book, 115 × 70 mm (4½ × 2¾ ins), in a medieval binding, comprises separate portions and insertions written by ten or more different fifteenth-century hands, Textura and Anglicana, of Latin, English and French devotional items. In the core of the volume, the *Horae de Sancto Spiritu* are followed by a *memoria* of St Etheldreda (fol. 33), there is an added English confession for a religious mentioning St Augustine (fols 79–80ᵛ), and prayers to the Holy Cross for 'ego

---

Lyra is 475 × 340 mm. The visible indexing goes as far as initial **M** and to book 15 ch. 95 of Bartholomaeus.

[44] Lewis and McIntosh do not mention verses (on fol. 127) saying it was 'dame catryn Radcleffis boke . . . She bought me of ane herytike for sothe'; this must be the wife of Sir George of Dilston (Northumberland) *c.*1550–70: cf. W. N. Thompson, 'The Derwentwaters and the Radcliffes', *Trans. Cumberland and Westmorland Antiquarian and Archaeological Society*, n.s., 4 (1904), 288–322.

[45] James, *Trinity MSS*, I, 463.

[46] The palimpsest appears to have been written only on one side of its leaves or sheet, although the size of the script is scarcely large enough (being in his smallest module, 5 mm, Pl. 9) for it to be meant for display as a poster or on a panel. The cited indulgence of Ad Vincula (S. Petri), was granted to Syon in 1425: Johnston, 'Syon Abbey', p. 186.

[47] The name 'briȝtwelle' (cf. places in Berkshire and Suffolk) on fol. 100ᵛ, in a neat hand of s.xv, not Dodesham's, near the last 'corrigitur', could be that of a collaborator, or else an early owner.

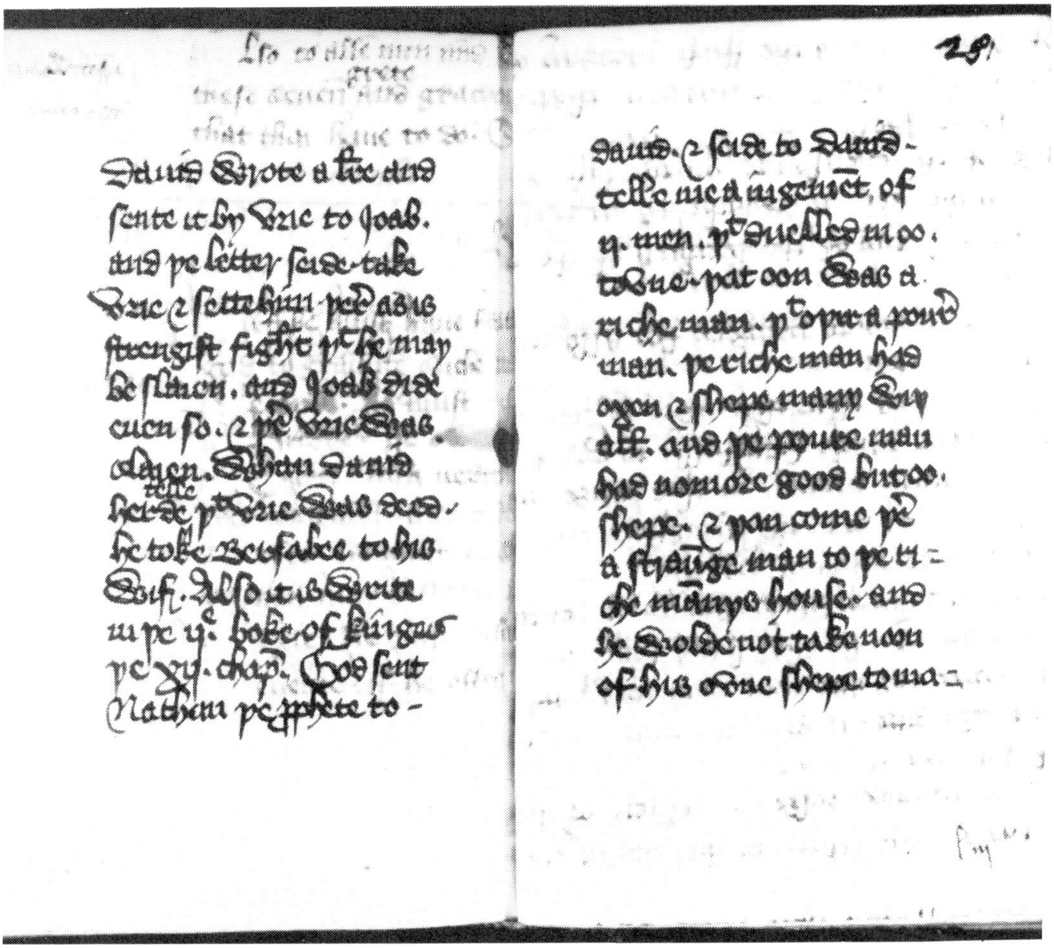

Dauid wrote a lettre and
sente it by Urie to Joab.
and þe letter seide take
Urie & sette hym þere as ys
strengist fight þat he may
be slayn. and Joab dide
euen so. & þe Urie was
slayn. Whan Dauid
herde þat Urie was deed.
he toke Bersabee to his
wif. Also it is wreten
in þe ij. boke of kingis
þe xij. chap. God sent
Nathan þe prophete to -

29

Dauid. & seide to Dauid -
telle me a iugement of
ij. men. þat duellid in oo.
toune. þat oon was a
riche man. þat oþer a pouere
man. þe riche man had
oxen & schepe many wiþ
all. and þe pouere man
had nomore good but oo.
schepe. & þan come þere
a straunge man to þe ri=
che mannys house. and
he wolde not take noon
of his owne schepe to ma=

Plate 9 Cambridge, Trinity College, MS B.14.54 (337), fols 27ᵛ–28, showing traces of palimpsest (reproduction about 90% of actual size)

miserrima peccatrix' with French rubrics. These point to an Augustinian nunnery; there was none in the diocese of Ely, the centre of the cult of Etheldreda, but it was spread through East Anglia and even Canonsleigh Abbey in Devon was dedicated to her, but the English spelling of the several hands and the later ownership suggest north-east Midland and East Anglian origins.[48] One quire of ten

[48] McIntosh, et al., *Linguistic Atlas*, I, 66; III, 279; LP 425: hands D and F (of those in English), Lincolnshire. In previous private communications Professor McIntosh judged hand A of the same area and the others 'less northerly'; in particular hand B (fols 36–78ᵛ) to be in the same language and text hand as Oxford, Bodl. Lib., MS Bodley 288 of a Wycliffite recension of Rolle on the Psalms and Canticles: ibid., I, 146; III, 182–3; LP 55, Huntingdonshire. The text in Add.3042 is the expanded

leaves, fols 116–25, is in Dodesham's Anglicana; however, fol. 125ᵛ has an English addition in a Textura hand which occurs previously in the book, proving the contemporaneous incorporation of the quire in the volume. The membrane of this quire is second-class, it is ruled for 19 lines per page, the module (4.5 mm) is unusually small, and the writing does not maintain an even course (Pl. 10). The text, in English with Latin prayers and hymns, offers counsel (in the first and second persons singular) on two kinds of praisings to God, preparation by purging of the soul, the three mights of the soul and the image of God, and ends with a Latin assertion of the compiler's experience in support of his advice to the devout soul. It would be interesting if this were Dodesham's own compilation, and it certainly could be a Carthusian's. Such small quires could have been assembled from various sources over a wide area as gifts for a member of a religious community and augmented within it.[49]

Cambridge, University Library, MS Kk.6.41 is another small volume (135 × 95 mm, $5\frac{1}{2}$ × $3\frac{3}{4}$ ins), a little bigger than Trinity B.14.54, but comprised entirely of short Latin spiritual treatises. It contains the *Speculum peccatoris* (wrongly ascribed to St Bernard), a sequence of nine sermons (questionably ascribed to St Augustine), the *Secreta meditacio beati Jeronimi* (in fact by Peter Damian), an extract from St Brigit's Revelations and a couple of other treatises found also notably in manuscripts of English Carthusian ownership or connections.[50] It is all in a very neat performance of Dodesham's Anglicana Formata (Pl. 11). In 18 lines per page at first, it changes to 15 lines towards the end, giving modules of 4.5 and 5.3 mm, on good thin membrane. The endleaves, originally ruled like the rest of the book, have (added in red plummet) rough first-person accounts of a receiver of large sums of money, most probably forced loans to Henry VI's government (*c.*1445–50) from towns, monasteries and individuals in Warwickshire, Gloucestershire, Worcestershire, and south Wales. These could indicate the area of the book's early ownership, not so far

---

version of Rolle's Meditations on the Passion, without northern rhymes but with one of the very few ascriptions of his works which give his surname, besides date of death: H. E. Allen, *Writings Ascribed to Richard Rolle and Materials for his Biography* (New York, 1927), pp. 278–9. Fols 109–13, in hand F, resembling that of fol. 125ᵛ, are devotions from the Revelations of St Brigit.

[49] Add.3042 is one of a small group of manuscripts from the former Brent Eleigh parish library, Suffolk, which may suggest Campsey as its source. But not all of these manuscripts were so local.

[50] *Catalogue* (Cambridge, 1856–67), III, 731–3. The *Tractatus de utilitate temptacionum et tribulacionum* (not William Flete's), fols 113ᵛ–24ᵛ, occurs as ch. 14 of pt 2 of the *Speculum spiritualium* and in the *Opusculum veni mecum in adiutorium* in Cambridge, St John's Coll., MS E.22 (125), copied by John Clerk, monk of Hinton Charterhouse (d. 1472), and in Oxford, St John's Coll., MS 77, John Dygon's, recluse at Sheen (*c.*1435–after 1445). The epistle of Venturinus da Bergamo against blasphemy is also in Oxford, St John's 77; and Westminster, Archdiocesan Archives, H.38, and Dublin, Trinity Coll. MS C.4.9 (321), for which see A. I. Doyle, 'English Carthusian Books not yet Linked with a Charterhouse', in '*A Miracle of Learning': Irish Manuscripts, their Uses and their Owners, 800–1760*, ed. T. C. Barnard, D. Ó Cróinín and K. Simms (Aldershot, 1997).

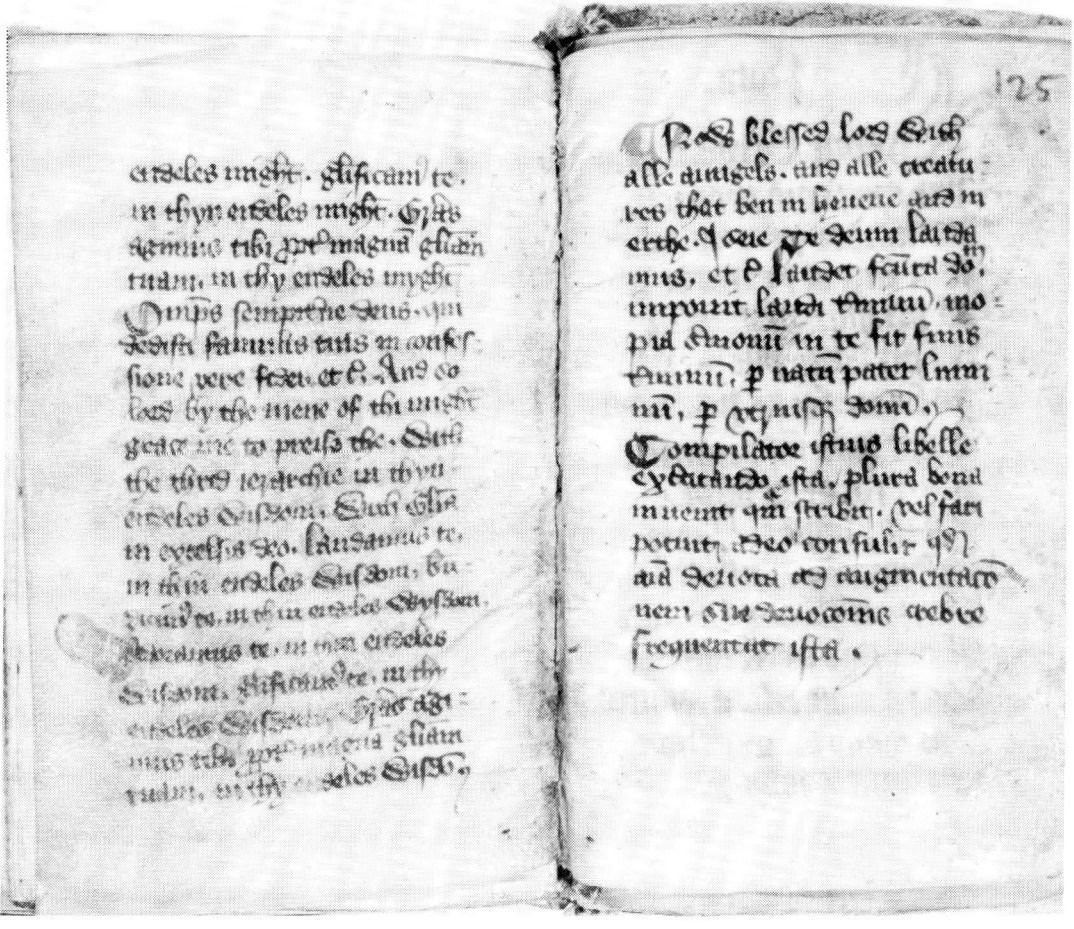

Plate 10   Cambridge, University Library, MS Additional 3042, fols 124ᵛ–25

from Witham as from Sheen or London. The contents suggest a monastic readership but the writer of the accounts is more likely to have been a clerk or layman.[51]

Oxford, Bodleian Library, MS Bodley 549, sections B (fols 25–97) and C (fols 98–198), constitute a more sizeable codex, 250 × 200 mm (10 × 8 ins, approx.), probably bound up with section A, fols 1–24, by the beginning of the sixteenth century: its content, the *Ars moriendi* from Suso's *Horologium sapientie*, book 2, in two early-fifteenth-century hands, is not inappropriate to the remainder, and the

---

[51] One is 'recepi de nanfan in die assumptionis sancte marie [?apu]t couintre vijs. iiijd.'; John Nanfan, 1400–59, of Worcestershire and Cornwall, was MP for the former and Chamberlain of the Exchequer 1445–46, and also Constable of Cardiff: J. C. Wedgwood and A. D. Holt, *History of Parliament: Biographies of Members of the Commons House 1439–1509* (London, 1936), pp. 621–3.

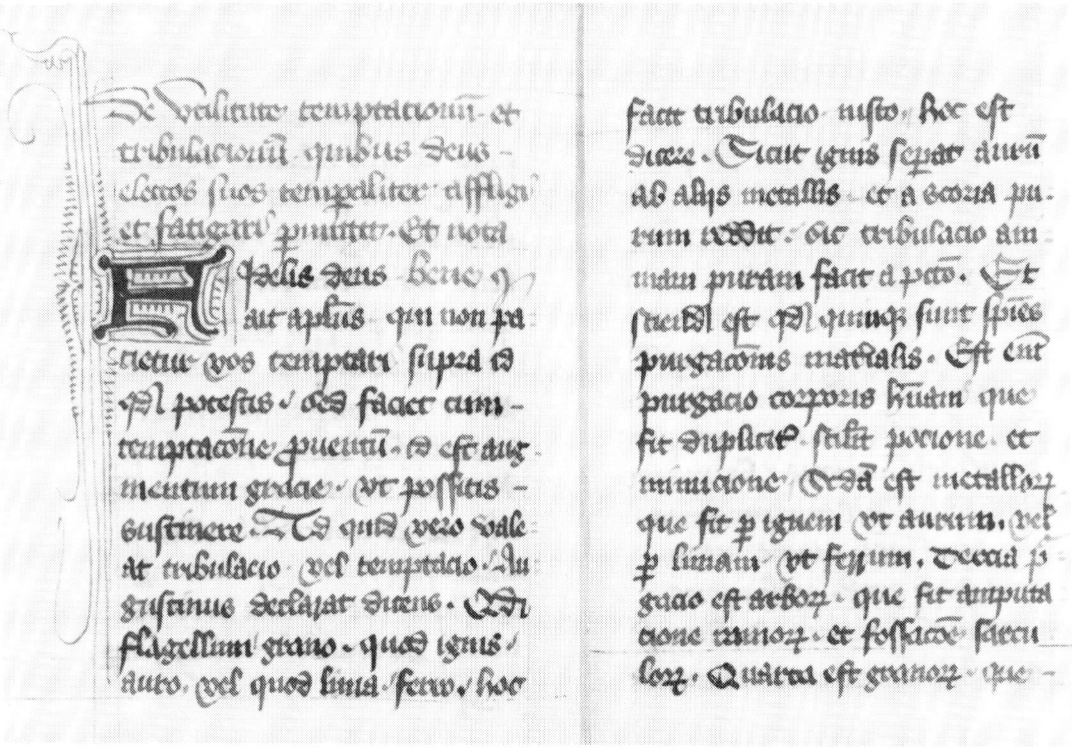

Plate 11　Cambridge, University Library, MS Kk.6.41, fols 113ᵛ–14

same marginal clef signs (for *nota*) appear in each section. B and C seem also to have been designed originally to be separate, with discrete sequences of quire-signatures and the contents of C only are listed by Dodesham at its end on fol. 198ᵛ.[52] There are 28 lines to the page, with a module of 6.6 mm, in B; C has 6.2–6.3 for 32 lines, partly in two columns. All of B is in Latin and a large size of Dodesham's Anglicana, except for fols 77ᵛ–79ʳ line 21, where English stanzas on elements of Christian doctrine and the five joys of Our Lady are written in another Anglicana Formata with a thinner nib. This hand was responsible also for a volume of English lives of saints once in the Fletewode collection (now divided in four), including that of Jerome elsewhere recorded as having been dedicated to the Duchess of Clarence by Simon Wynter of Syon.[53] From the way in which the English stanzas occur in the midst of a quire and between two consecutive chapters in Dodesham's copying of the *Tractatus*

---

[52] *SC*, no. 2298.

[53] The stanzas on the elements ed. G. H. Russell, *Jnl Religious History*, 2 (1962), 114–16; the prayer to angels and saints ed. R. H. Robbins, *Traditio*, 24 (1968), 462. For the broken-up volume see G. R. Keiser (as n. 18 above) pp. 41–2; C. W. Dutschke, *Guide to Medieval and Renaissance Manuscripts in the Huntington Library* (San Marino, CA, 1989), I, 152–3.

de origine et veritate perfecte religionis ad defendendum ordinem Cartusiensem (by Gulielmus de Yporegia)[54] they must have been inserted during a pause in the work, and so by someone with easy access to it, presumably in a Charterhouse. The rationale for the insertion (however out of place) was presumably that Carthusian lay brethren had to be taught to recite the elements of doctrine daily in their vernacular.[55] Section B starts with the *Declaratio optima regule Cartusie* (attributed to Boso), as one of a sequence of tracts on the order found in continental Carthusian manuscripts but not otherwise in English ones, so far as I know.[56] They are followed by a *Tractatus de regimine sanitatis* (by John of Toledo), of concern in a monastery, and a *Symbolum fidei* by John Barton (a London physician purged of Lollardy in 1416–17), a text copied elsewhere by another Sheen monk and by one of the Brigittines from Vadstena (Sweden) who helped to found Syon.[57]

Section C of Bodley 549 starts with Latin expositions of the Pater Noster, Ave Maria and Credo (elsewhere attributed to Richard Rolle), and includes the *Manuale sacerdotum* (by John Mirk), besides prayers and treatises on spirituality.[58] Dodesham's list on fol. 198[v] has 'AM' in blue above, which might be a library mark, and heads the contents list of section C expressly as if for a whole volume.[59] Section C could have been joined with B for the utility of the pastoral items for whoever had care of novices or lay brethren. It is of interest that the abbreviated 'corrigitur' is found near the catchwords of a number of the quires in this section, once (fol. 137[v]) in red as if by the rubricator, who was Dodesham himself, or by the supplier of the plain red initials, who may have been Dodesham. The size, comparable coarseness and details of Dodesham's writing in the two sections are sufficiently similar for it to be likely that they were made about the same time.

Dublin, Trinity College F.5.8 (678) is a copy of the first English translation of the *Imitatio Christi*, books I–III, under the title *Musica ecclesiastica*, 205 × 135 mm (8 × 5¼ ins). It is ruled for 24 lines of writing with a module of 5.4 mm, on second-class membrane, which seems to have given the scribe a good deal of difficulty, with some

---

[54] Cf. J. Hogg, in Analecta Cartusiana, 82:2 (Salzburg, 1980), pp. 84–118, esp. 104–6.

[55] Basle, Universitätsbibl., MS B.XI.19, *s*.xv, from the Charterhouse there, has the elements in German verse for the lay-brethren to repeat daily: G. Meyer and M. Burckhardt, *Die mittelalterlichen Handschriften der Universitätsbibliothek* (Basle, 1960–75), II, 1028–45.

[56] Hogg (as n. 54 above) pp. 91–109 and, not mentioned there, Brussels, Bibl. royale, MSS 298–306, J. Van den Gheyn, E. Bacha, E. Wagemans and F. Lyna, *Catalogue des manuscrits* (Brussels, 1901–48), V, no. 3133.

[57] C. H. Talbot and E. A. Hammond, *The Medical Practitioners in Medieval England* (London, 1965), p. 121; A. Hudson, *The Premature Reformation* (Oxford, 1988), pp. 132 n. 89, 250 n. 120, 309 n. 195; M. Hedlund, 'Vadstena kloster – ett fönster mot England', *Annales Academiae Regiae Scientiarum Upsaliensis*, 28 (1989–90), 84–96, esp. 91–4.

[58] Allen, *Rolle*, pp. 156–7; A. J. Fletcher, 'The Manuscripts of John Mirk's *Manuale Sacerdotis*', *Leeds Studies in English*, n.s., 19 (1988), 105–39, esp. 114–15.

[59] Evidence about Carthusian library marks is sadly wanting both in their books and from the lack of medieval catalogues.

running of ink which may be partly owing to subsequent damage by damp. There are many corrections, over erasures and in the margins, by Dodesham himself and also in the distinctive fere-textura of William Darker, monk of Sheen from about 1481 to 1513. Dr Brendan Biggs has established that Darker collated the text with a copy of the Latin nearer to the source than that used by the English translator, and incorporated the resulting improvements in the fair copy (Glasgow, University Library Hunterian MS T.6.18 (136)) which he wrote for Elizabeth Gibbs, abbess of Syon, in 1502.[60] From their comparative dates at Sheen, Darker may have corrected the Dublin manuscript shortly before or after Dodesham's death, but there can be little doubt the book was at Sheen and copied by Dodesham for the Charterhouse, possibly towards the end of his life.

The Edinburgh dialect survey had localised the spellings of the Dublin *Imitatio* in the south of Buckinghamshire, but by a comparison with the other three known copies (which all have characteristics of the 'home counties') Dr Biggs shows that it might be better placed in eastern Middlesex, where the survey put BL, Additional 11305 (see p. 104 above).[61] Further study by him of the language of Dodesham's other manuscripts does not disturb the impression that his English was consistently compatible with the broad metropolitan area. If he came from a Somerset family, as seems likely,[62] he must have adapted his spelling, as other scribes did in the fifteenth century, as a result of migration to that milieu.[63] It could have happened in a religious house, but the pressure to do so would be greater in paid employment as a scribe near London, because of the immediate market.

On the evidence of Dodesham's identified *oeuvre*, the bulk of some of his tasks and the repetition of others, together with their expensive illumination, suggest that he was in touch with the commercial book trade, either as an employee or else as a freelance, lay or clerical, in the earlier part of his career (from *c*.1430 to *c*.1460?). Perhaps influenced by some of his patrons and by some of the texts he was commissioned to copy, he may then have entered Witham, it being in his native region. After proving

[60] J. E. G. De Montmorency, *Thomas à Kempis, his Age and Book* (London, 1906), pl. opp. p. 247; B. Biggs, D.Phil. thesis, University of Oxford (1992), and new edition, EETS (OS) 309 (1997).

[61] B. Biggs, 'The Language of the Scribes of the First English Translation of the *Imitatio Christi*', *Leeds Studies in English*, n.s., 26 (1995), 79–111.

[62] Dr Alexandra Barratt drew my attention to Stephen Doddesham with his wife, Joan, 1394–95, in *Pedes Finium for the County of Somerset*, ed. E. Green, Somerset Record Society, 17 (1902), 160–61; and William Dodesham with his wife Joan, 1438–39, in *Pedes Finium*, ed. Green, Somerset Record Society, 22 (1906), 94–5; 1445, *Bishop Bekynton's Register*, ed. H. C. Maxwell-Lyte and M. C. B. Dawes, I, Somerset Record Society 49 (1934), no. 131; 1453, ibid., no. 792; and in *Medieval Wills*, ed. F. W. Weaver, Somerset Record Society 19 (1903), 118–19.

[63] Cf. A. I. Doyle, 'A Palaeographer's View', in *Speaking in Our Tongues*, ed. M. Laing and K. Williamson (Cambridge, 1994), pp. 93–7; discussion 112–13.

unsettled there and being moved to Sheen, he continued to exercise his skill, possibly not only for his brethren's benefit in his own house and order but also for members of other orders or people in the world outside. On this hypothesis we cannot assign a number of his products to either phase of his career with any certainty. His handwriting, like his language, is remarkably uniform in general and in detail throughout the great range of his output, despite variations in size or quality of execution, associable chiefly with inferior materials, if perhaps in some cases with haste, health or age.

His Anglicana Formata resembles most closely that used in documents of the royal Chancery during the reign of Henry VI (1422–71). Because a number of its forms are quite complex it gives an impression of considerable calligraphic skill. In a record of the making of the set of Lyra for St Albans it is described as 'satis sollempnis'. Dodesham's Anglicana Formata includes some forms and duct from Secretary script: in particular a variant of **A** with a horizontal slightly curved top stroke (e.g. Pl. 11, verso, line 11 'Ad'), **D** with a sharp left foot (Pl. 8, line 11 'Dietaria'; Pl. 11, verso, line 1 'De'), a very spiky **N** and **R**, a loopless **W** (Pl. 8, line 10 'werke'), tri- or quadrangular single-compartment **a** (Pl. 8, line 2 'grace', 'that'; Pl. 9, verso, line 10 'Bersabee'; Pl. 11, recto, line 1 'tribulacio'), invariably tapered and often slanting **f** and long **s** (Pl. 8, lines 6–7 'ful vertuose', 'shal', 'fynde'), final kidney-shaped (B-like) **s** (Pl. 8, line 3 'this', line 10 'his'; Pl. 9, verso, line 9 'was'; Pl. 10, recto, line 15 'deuocionis'; Pl. 11, verso, line 13 'dicens'). It does not have Secretary **g** except in the larger display script of a colophon (e.g. that of the Yale manuscript).

For display Dodesham sometimes uses a Bastard or, more exactly, enlarged Anglicana (Pl. 8, lines 9–10) with a broader nib and stronger feet to the minims. In any size minuscule **a** is mostly of the two-storey form. He uses both short and long **r** in varying proportions, apparently reflecting deliberation or speed in execution, apart from 2-like **r** in the usual positions after round forms. Final **s** is commonly 8-like (Pl. 8, line 10 'as'; Pl. 10, verso, lines 1–2 'endeles'; Pl. 11, verso, line 2 'quibus'), varying with the Secretary form; 6-like (sigma) **s** varies with long **s** in the initial position (Pl. 8, line 6 'shul'; Pl. 9, verso, line 8 'slaien'), and sometimes is found finally (Pl. 9, verso, line 12 'kinges'). He has more than one variant of looped **w**, one especially in Bodley 423 with pointed feet, and also of the simpler Secretary **w**, like the majuscule **W**. A casual practice (not often found with other scribes) is that of using **v** medially, as in 'tovne', 'ovne' (Pl. 9, recto, line 4 and last line), and finally, as in 'hov', where 'u' would be normal.

But the most distinctive characteristics of his writing are his non-alphabetic graphs: punctuation and space-fillers. The simple *punctus* is sometimes turned down slightly like a modern comma (Pl. 10, verso, lines 7, 11) and, in prose and verse, extended or replaced by a curved stroke rising to the right (Pl. 8, lines 1, 2; Pl. 9, verso, line 3; Pl. 11, verso, lines 8, 10, 14, 15) as a *virgula* or like the upper stroke of the full *punctus elevatus* which he also uses (Pl. 11, recto, line 4). The alternative *virgula* sometimes has a slanting approach stroke at the top right or a shorter horizontal one on its left. He frequently employs the 9-like *positura* or *punctus versus* at the end of major passages (Pl. 8, line 8), and even more often a similar form completing a clockwise loop at its foot (Pl. 8, line 11; Pl. 10, recto, line 9; Pl. 11, verso, line 5), which serves also when repeated as a line-filler, as do tremolo strokes and double virgules. Most conspicuously, as noticed by Neil Ker in the Downside manuscript, when the last word of a line of prose does not reach to the right-hand ruled edge, and he does not go on to hyphenate, he frequently fills the space with a short hyphen-like horizontal or rising stroke (Pl. 9, verso, last line; Pl. 11, verso, lines 2, 8, 10).

There are no close similarities between Dodesham's writing style or details and those of other known English Carthusian scribes of his time (John Feriby, William Mede, John Clerk, or later, William Darker and Robert Benet), nor those of St Albans where it has been surmised he might have worked for the Duchess of Clarence and Eleanor Hull. His closest congeners seem to be in certain royal charters of the 1440s and one may therefore guess that he might have had his training with their scribes.[64]

Dodesham has probably the most extensive extant *oeuvre* of a medieval English scribe yet identified: all or most of 23 or 24 volumes, large and small, and three shorter pieces. For his career of at least 35, very likely 45, quite possibly 50 years, the quantity of recognized manuscript by him approaches that of some famous contemporary Italian humanist scribes.[65] Lacking the special prestige of their style of handwriting and of the texts that they copied, subject moreover to the hostility of the English Reformation, many more pieces of his work have surely disappeared than have survived, even if some are still to be discovered. Well could the writer of an elegant Elizabethan italic note in both Cambridge, University Library, MSS Dd.7.7 and 8 say: 'Valde notabile est quod hic scriptor per omnes quatuor magnos libros non mutauerit formam scribendi, ita vt per vnum et eundem calamum scripta possunt videri. O diligentiam et nostrorum temporum socordiam.'[66]

---

[64] The King's College, Cambridge, and Eton charters from Henry VI, 1446: J. J. G. Alexander, 'William Abell "lymnour" and 15th-Century English Illumination', in *Kunsthistorische Forschungen Otto Pächt*, ed. A. Rosenauer and G. Weber (Salzburg, 1972), pp. 166–72, fig. 2; J. McConnell, ed. *Treasures of Eton* (London, 1977), p. 32. pl. 28; F. L. Harrison, *Music in Medieval Britain* (London, 1958), pl. IV. Cf. the royal charter to Ipswich of the same year, P. Lasko and N. J. Morgan, eds, *Medieval Art in East Anglia 1300–1520* (London, 1973), p. 46, fig. 68.

[65] B. L. Ullman, *The Origin and Development of Humanistic Script* (Rome, 1960), pp. 98–109, 111–23; J. Wardrop, *The Script of Humanism* (Oxford, 1963), pp. 23–35, 50–53. In England, scribe D of Cambridge, Trinity Coll., MS R.3.2 (581), may have done a larger number of words but in a more concentrated career.

[66] 'It is very remarkable that this scribe has not changed the form of his writing through four big books, so that they may seem to have been written with one and the same pen. What diligence, unlike the laziness of our times!'

Brief list of Dodesham's Manuscripts

Items 1–3 inclusive have contemporary attributions to Dodesham; items 4–11 are closely datable; items 12–19 are less securely datable.

 1 New York, formerly Cockerell/Duschnes (pseudo-Augustine), Witham, 1462
 2 Oxford, Trinity College, 46, signed, before 1474
 3 Glasgow, University Library, Hunterian T.3.15 (77), Sheen, 1474/75
 4 Karlsruhe, Badische Landesbibliothek, St Georgen 12, Syon, before 1439
 5 Cambridge, University Library, Dd.7.7–10, St Albans, before 1457
 6 Boston (MA), Public Library, f.med.94, Lydgate, not before 1421
 7 Cambridge, University Library, Add. 3137, Lydgate, not before 1421
 8 New Haven, Yale University Library, Beinecke 661, Lydgate, not before 1421
 9 Cambridge, Trinity College, B.15.16 (352), Love, not before 1410
10 Oxford, Bodl. Lib., Rawlinson A.387B, Love, not before 1410
11 Oxford, Bodl. Lib., Bodley 423 (B and C), miscellaneous
12 Glasgow, University Library, Hunterian U.4.17 (259) and U.4.16 (258), miscellaneous
13 London, BL, Harley 630, fol. 163, not before 1438
14 London, BL, Additional 11305 (part palimpsest)
15 Cambridge, Trinity College, B.14.54 (337) (part palimpsest)
16 Cambridge, University Library, Add. 3042, fols 116–25
17 Cambridge, University Library, Kk.6.41, miscellaneous
18 Oxford, Bodl. Lib., Bodley 549 (B and C), miscellaneous
19 Dublin, Trinity College, F.5.8 (678), corrected at Sheen
20 Oxford, Bodl. Lib., Eng. poet.e.15 (*SC*, 32401). While this essay was in proof Malcolm Parkes sent me a specimen photocopy of fol. 15 of this manuscript, another copy of Burgh's *Parvus* and *Magnus Cato*, as in Glasgow, University Library, Hunterian U.4.17, no. 12 above, but of smaller format (180 × 130 mm, 7 × 5 ins), the module of writing 5.6 mm, and with a Latin instead of an English explicit. It is undoubtedly in Dodesham's Anglicana, with his distinctive punctuation.

CHAPTER SIX

Geoffrey Spirleng (*c.*1426–*c.*1494): a Scribe of the *Canterbury Tales* in his Time

Richard Beadle

Copyists of later medieval English manuscript books rarely concluded a piece of work with the kind of informative colophon that is often found in manuscripts copied on the continental mainland of Europe, but the information engrossed at the end of a copy of the *Canterbury Tales* in Glasgow, University Library, Hunterian MS U. I. 1 (197) is by any standard unusually full:

> Orate pro salute animarum Galfridi Spirleng Ciuis Norwici Courtholder Clerici Maioratus et Communitatis dicte Ciuitatis ac Thome Spirleng filij sui qui scribendo hunc librum compleuerunt mense Januarij anno domini Millesimo CCCC^{mo} lxxvj^{to} quo tempore dictus Galfridus quasi quinquaginta et dictus Thomas quasi Sexdecim etatis extiterunt annorum (fol. 102^v)[1]

What became of the manuscript after it was completed early in 1476 remains uncertain, but it seems to have remained in East Anglia, passing through the hands of the noted local antiquaries Peter le Neve (*c.*1661–1729) and Thomas Martin of Palgrave (*c.*1697–1771), before finding its resting place in Dr William Hunter's museum in Glasgow, towards the end of the eighteenth century. It was described in some detail in the catalogue of the Hunterian manuscripts published in 1908, and investigated more extensively by Manly and Rickert, appearing in their *Text of the Canterbury Tales* (as it had done occasionally in earlier literature) under the siglum Gl.[2]

---

[1] For a facs. see New Pal. Soc., 2nd ser., pl. 178. Geoffrey Spirleng spelled his surname in a variety of ways, as did others who wrote it. The form followed here is that common to the colophon in the Glasgow manuscript and the three documents from the Norwich muniments reproduced in the plates.

[2] J. Young and P. Henderson Aitken, *A Catalogue of the Manuscripts in the Library of the Hunterian Museum in the University of Glasgow* (Glasgow, 1908), pp. 138–41; Manly and Rickert, I, 183–8. The manuscript was not known to the eighteenth-century editors of Chaucer, Urry and Tyrwhitt. Apart from a cutting from an untraced eighteenth-century sale catalogue pasted on one of the front flyleaves of Gl (and probably relating to one of the numerous sales of Thomas Martin's manuscripts), the earliest printed notices appear in G. Haenel, *Catalogum librorum manuscriptorum* (Leipzig, 1830), col. 793, and the App. to the *Royal Commission on Historical Manuscripts, 3rd Report* (London, 1872), p. 424, where its date and Geoffrey Spirleng's role as copyist are first noted. The Pardoner's Prologue and Tale were printed from Gl by J. Zupitza in *Parallel Text Specimens of all Accessible Unprinted Chaucer Manuscripts*, Chaucer Society, 1st ser., 85 (1892). A facs. of fol. 52 appears in New Pal. Soc. (see n. 1 above).

Gl contains an eccentrically ordered copy of the *Canterbury Tales* (fols 1–115) and a Latin text of the legend of St Patrick's Purgatory (fols 116–20), now placed at the end of the manuscript, but originally standing immediately after the colophon on fol. 102^v, quoted above. It consists entirely of paper, showing watermarks resembling examples dated by Briquet to the 1460s and 1470s, the leaves being of fairly generous dimensions (approximately 15 × 11 inches, or 380 × 280 mm). The layout of the text, on the other hand, is economical, with both prose and verse disposed in double columns of around 50 lines. Manly and Rickert were concerned principally with the quality of the text in the *Canterbury Tales* section, and in tracing its affiliations they established that approximately half Gl was derived directly from another extant manuscript, now Cambridge, University Library, Mm. 2. 5 (Mm), but in Spirleng's time apparently owned by another Norfolk man, Sir William Boleyn.[3] To be more precise, the first 46 leaves of Gl had as their immediate exemplar fols 1–115 of Mm, to a point a little way into the Wife of Bath's Prologue (probably up to III (D) 193),[4] in the irregular sequence of the tales shared by the two manuscripts. On fol. 47^v of Gl there was a change of exemplar, to a manuscript no longer extant, which possessed a different ordering of the tales. By the time the copying of Gl had progressed to the Parson's Tale and the Retraction, both the Shipman's and the Prioress's Tales had been copied twice, whilst the Clerk's Tale and the Canon's Yeoman's Tale had been omitted. These omissions were noticed only after the Parson's Tale and the Retraction had been completed and the colophon quoted above had been added. The copying of St Patrick's Purgatory had in the meantime taken place, as is evident from its appearance on paper from the same stock as that used for the last few leaves of the *Canterbury Tales* (fols 96–102). The second (unidentified) exemplar for the tales must by this time have passed out of Spirleng's hands, but he was nevertheless able to regain access to Mm and to make copies of the Clerk's Tale and the Canon's Yeoman's Tale on an additional quire (now fols 103–15), consisting of paper from a stock different from that used for fols 96–102 and what are now fols 116–20. The insertion of a quire carrying the two missing tales after the colophon on fol. 102^v spoiled its effect, so Spirleng added the following explanatory note, engrossed in red, at the end of the Parson's Tale: 'Be it remenbred that the tale of the Clerk of Oxenford and the tale of the Chanons Yoman folwen inmediatli in the next leef'. He also stroked out the careful Textura of his original colophon and wrote beneath in his usual small cursive hand: 'This writyng is drawen [i.e. deleted] for the book of Canterbury is nat yet ended and therfor these woord*es* arn writen in the xij leef folwyng by cause that ij tales arn yet folwyng inmediatly'. The colophon was accordingly repeated, again in Textura, on fol. 115^v, at the end of the Canon's Yeoman's Tale.

---

[3] Manly and Rickert, I, 183, give the relevant numbers in C. M. Briquet, *Les Filigranes*, 2nd edn (Leipzig, 1923), for the watermarks of the four stocks of paper used in Gl. For their description of Mm and reference to Sir William Boleyn see II, 365–71.

[4] Unless otherwise indicated, references to Chaucer's writings relate to *The Riverside Chaucer*.

These circumstances, only somewhat tedious to us to disentangle, were no doubt the occasion of some exasperation to Geoffrey Spirleng, who, as we shall see, was in his day-to-day occupations necessarily a methodical and tidy-minded individual. They also provide a rare direct glimpse of the kind of sudden and arbitrary shifts of exemplar which must lie behind so many puzzling episodes in the transmission of the *Canterbury Tales*. Manly and Rickert's assertion that a large part of Gl was copied directly from Mm, and not from a common ancestor, seems never to have been questioned, nor is there any call to question it. The annotated rotographs of all the manuscripts of the *Canterbury Tales* that they deposited in the Department of Manuscripts at the British Library enable one effectively to lay Gl and Mm side-by-side,[5] to compare them directly with other copies, and to see how, up to WBProl. III (D) 193, they alone share a particularly eccentric ordering of the tales, identical spurious material, links, headings and so forth; and further, that line-by-line and word-by-word, these two alone share the same omissions, disorderings, and a text where the one follows the other verbatim for large stretches at a time. Certain variant readings in Gl turn out to be palaeographically explicable only in terms of what was before the scribe in Mm. In all, about 10000 lines of Chaucer's verse were copied directly from Mm into Gl, and they offer us a rare and important insight into some of the processes involved in the transmission of a vernacular text from one generation to the next in this period.

'The relationship of a copy to its exemplar', wrote N. R. Ker, 'is always interesting'. Ker himself contributed valuable discussions of significant examples ranging from the eleventh to the fifteenth century, which demonstrate the breadth of that interest, extending to matters of layout, script, decoration, textual fidelity, punctuation, and the division of labour amongst scribes.[6] In general, however, issues arising from the relationship of exemplar and copy have not yet been made the object of systematic study. The known examples remain to be drawn together into a classified list that might provide a basis for some estimate of the frequency of the phenomenon, and a point of departure for a comparative assessment of the dynamics of scribal practice that such survivals uniquely disclose. Both of these factors have a significant part to play in areas that range beyond the purely palaeographical. For example, the frequency (or otherwise) at different times and

---

[5] MS Facs. 405(27) and 405(54) respectively. Copies of the rotographs held in the library of the University of Chicago were used by E. A. Golson in her valuable analysis of the Gl orthographical system, as it emerges in a comparison with that of the exemplar: 'The Spelling System of the Glasgow MS of the *Canterbury Tales*', PhD dissertation, University of Chicago (1942). Her investigation incidentally tended to confirm the accuracy of Manly and Rickert's observation that Gl fols 1–46 and 103–15 could only have been derived from Mm, and not from a common ancestor (p. 1, n. 3).

[6] N. R. Ker, 'Copying an Exemplar: Two Manuscripts of Jerome on Habbakuk' (1979), repr. in his *Books, Collectors and Libraries: Studies in the Medieval Heritage*, ed. A. G. Watson (London and Ronceverte, 1985), pp. 75–86, esp. 77; cf. Ker's 'Eton College MS 44 and its Exemplar' (1972), ibid., pp. 87–99; see also Ker, *English Manuscripts*, pp. 12–14.

in different places, of the survival of both exemplar and copy, may provide clues towards an answer to a large and difficult question that palaeographers and textual critics have seldom asked themselves: that is, what proportion of the total number of manuscripts produced before the age of print has come down to us? Or on a more specific front, what insights into the frequency and nature of errors and other types of variation introduced in the copying process can the study of copies in relation to their exemplars give us, and what contribution might these insights make to textual criticism, stemmatics, and (in vernacular contexts) the historical study of the language?

The present investigation moves towards the construction of a framework within which a particular instance of copy and exemplar might be addressed, taking account of the especially demanding medium of transmission represented by late Middle English, a language whose written form exhibited a very much wider range of graphemic and graphetic variation than (for example) the Latin or the Anglo-Norman of the time. The question of how many other instances of the survival of both exemplar and copy are to be found amongst the total number of Middle English manuscripts still in existence (certainly some thousands) will remain unresolved for some time to come, but one's initial impression is that it is likely to be decidedly small. As far as the 80 or so complete or fragmentary copies of the *Canterbury Tales* are concerned, Manly and Rickert point to Gl and Mm as the only surviving pair of exemplar and copy; and amongst Middle English manuscripts generally only a handful of other instances have been confirmed or suggested.[7] If indeed there proves to be a dearth of Middle English manuscripts that can be demonstrated to have been copied one from another, then estimates of the losses sustained will have to be set fairly high in relation to the total number of books that have survived.

---

[7] Passing mention has been made in a few places of the possible co-existence of exemplars and copies of Middle English writings, e.g. A. I. Doyle, 'A Text Attributed to Ruusbroec Circulating in England', in *Dr. L. Reypens-Album*, ed. A. Ampe (Antwerp, 1964), pp. 153–71 (p. 160, Oxford, Bodl. Lib., MS Douce 322 and London, BL, MS Harley 1706, first half, devotional texts); idem, 'Remarks on the Surviving Manuscripts of *Piers Plowman*', in *Medieval English Religious and Ethical Literature: Essays in Honour of George Russell*, ed. G. Kratzmann and J. Simpson (Cambridge, 1986), pp. 35–48 (p. 41, Oxford, Bodl. Lib., MS Bodley 814, and London, BL, Cotton MS Caligula A. XI); R. F. Hamer, report of discussion, in *Speaking in our Tongues: Proceedings of a Colloquium on Medieval Dialectology and Related Disciplines*, ed. M. Laing and K. Williamson (Cambridge, 1994), p. 110 (the *Gilte Legend*, in Oxford, Bodl. Lib., MS Douce 372, and London, BL, MS Harley 4775, by the scribe Ricardus Franciscus, and in Tokyo, Professor T. Takamiya, MS 45.17 (frag.) and London, BL, MS Egerton 876); G. M. Lester, 'The Earliest English Sailing Directions', in *Popular and Practical Science of Medieval England*, ed. L. M. Matheson (East Lansing, MI, 1994), pp. 331–59 (pp. 334–5, New York, Pierpont Morgan Lib., MS 775, and London, BL, MS Lansdowne 285, Sir John Paston's 'Grete Boke', mostly copied by William Ebesham).

Turning to the case in hand, it is necessary in the first place to establish the principal features of the external environment within which Gl came to be copied, in part, from Mm. The natural starting point is the colophon quoted above, which testifies rather ostentatiously to Geoffrey Spirleng's status as a civic official in late-fifteenth-century Norwich. This exceptionally explicit recording of personal and family details gives strong grounds for suspecting that Gl was made for the Spirlengs' own use, rather than on commission for another party; as such the manuscript would seem to belong to the para-professional category of book-making by literate laymen, practised increasingly, and to a variety of standards, during the fifteenth century.[8] As we shall see, Geoffrey Spirleng was not by profession a jobbing copyist of literary manuscripts, or manuscript books of any kind. Gl is nevertheless indistinguishable physically from the large numbers of other fifteenth-century English vernacular manuscripts that were undoubtedly produced in more formal or 'commercial' circumstances. Spirleng, for example, pricked the sheets (a point not noted by Manly and Rickert; see fols 16–22), ruled them throughout in a consistent two-column format, and gathered them in regular quires of eight leaves, inserting the normal apparatus of quire and leaf signatures and catchwords in the usual places. Like many professional makers of books at the time, he wrote the body of the text in his ordinary cursive 'business' hand, a variable mixture of forms from the Secretary and Anglicana repertoires, enlarging it for display purposes in headings and in the rubrication.

Outside Gl, there are a considerable number of sources of information about Geoffrey Spirleng, but almost none concerning his son. Geoffrey is mentioned occasionally in the Paston Letters, now mostly amongst the Additional manuscripts in the British Library, and in the records relating to the business affairs and estates of the renowned captain Sir John Fastolf (1380–1459), which are now mostly at Magdalen College, Oxford.[9] Geoffrey's name appears frequently in the later-fifteenth-century muniments of Norwich, now in the Norfolk Record Office. A considerable quantity of documentary writing by him has survived. From these sources it is clear that Geoffrey Spirleng's career had two phases, the first as an estate servant employed by Sir John Fastolf at and around Caister in north-east Norfolk, and the second, after Fastolf's death, as a civic and gild official in Norwich. The colophon in Gl indicates that he was born about 1426. In common with all of Fastolf's other East Anglian estate servants he was probably recruited locally, and he may have come from Norwich, where he later became a freeman, and where a number of men with the same surname are recorded during the fifteenth and

---

[8] Manly and Rickert, followed by others, have referred to Geoffrey Spirleng as a 'wealthy scrivener', but for reasons that will become apparent, I can find no grounds to endorse the suggestion that he was engaged in a trade involving the regular copying of literary or other manuscripts resembling Gl.

[9] Citations from the Paston Letters are, as indicated, from either J. Gairdner, ed. *The Paston Letters 1422–1509*, 6 vols (London and Exeter, 1904) or N. Davis, ed. *Paston Letters and Papers of the Fifteenth Century*, 2 vols (Oxford, 1971–76).

sixteenth centuries.[10] Spirleng's name begins to appear in the Fastolf papers in the mid 1440s, when he would have been in his late teens or early twenties.[11] Sir John Fastolf had by this time retired from military campaigning and was a very wealthy man, investing much of his profits from the wars in France in property in his native Norfolk, and building himself a lavishly appointed castle at Caister, where he eventually took up residence in 1454.[12] No direct information concerning Spirleng's early background or education has yet come to light, but the ambience in which we first see him is distinctive: that of what K. B. McFarlane styled the 'gentleman bureaucrat', a type of man often employed in the households of major landowners in the fifteenth century, 'lesser gentry, expert in accounting and estate management'.[13]

Fastolf was a formidable man who took a keen personal interest in the efficient administration of his estates. Much of Spirleng's time in the late 1440s and throughout the 1450s was spent out and about attending to Fastolf's numerous properties and business interests in Norfolk and Suffolk. Estate employees of this kind were sometimes known as 'riding servants'. He worked at first as an assistant to Fastolf's receivers, the clerk Thomas Howes, and Walter Shipdam. Fastolf wrote to the three of them jointly, and they to him, on matters of estate business.[14] Of

---

[10] F. Blomefield, *An Essay towards a Topographical History of the County of Norfolk*, 2nd edn, 11 vols (London, 1805–10), I, 540; IV, 376; V, 428; VII, 262; J. L'Estrange, *Calendar of the Freemen of Norwich from 1317 to 1603*, ed. W. Rye (London, 1888), p. 129; T. Hawes, *An Index to Norwich City Officers 1453–1835*, Norfolk Genealogy, 21 (Norwich, 1989), p. 144.

[11] Oxford, Magdalen Coll., Archives, EP 176/8 is an account roll showing arrears of manorial debts owed to Walter Shipdam, Sir John Fastolf's receiver general, from Michaelmas 1445 to Michaelmas 1446. It is mostly in Geoffrey Spirleng's hand, in Latin, and is signed by him at the end, with a counter signature by Fastolf himself.

[12] K. B. McFarlane, 'The Investment of Sir John Fastolf's Profits of War', *Trans. Royal Historical Society*, 5th ser., 7 (1957), 91–116, repr. in his *England in the Fifteenth Century: Collected Essays* (London, 1981), pp. 175–97; A. Smith, '"The greatest man of that age": the Acquisition of Sir John Fastolf's East Anglian Estates', in *Rulers and Ruled in Late Medieval England: Essays Presented to Gerald Harriss*, ed. R. E. Archer and S. Walker (London and Rio Grande, OH, 1995), pp. 137–53. The following picture of Spirleng's activities as an estate servant of Fastolf's has benefited greatly from Dr Anthony Smith's advice, and the very valuable chapter devoted to administration in his 'Aspects of the Career of Sir John Fastolf (1380–1459)', D.Phil. thesis, University of Oxford (1982), pp. 44–101.

[13] K. B. McFarlane, 'William Worcester: a Preliminary Survey', in *Studies Presented to Sir Hilary Jenkinson*, ed. J. Conway Davies (London, 1957), pp. 196–221, esp. 199, repr. in his *Collected Essays*, pp. 199–224, esp. 202. McFarlane associates Spirleng with William Worcester, antiquary, bibliophile and translator, who was Fastolf's personal secretary, and with Nicholas Bocking, one of his receivers-general, together with other professionally educated members of the household whose names appear frequently in Paston letters and Fastolf papers. William Worcester, writing to John Paston I in 1457, refers to him as 'my broþere Spyrlyng', which gives some idea of his status (Davis, no. 571). The intellectual and cultural milieu of Fastolf's household has been addressed by J. Hughes, 'Stephen Scrope and the Circle of Sir John Fastolf: Moral and Intellectual Outlooks', in *Medieval Knighthood IV: Papers from the Fifth Strawberry Hill Conference 1990*, ed. C. Harper-Bill and R. Harvey (Woodbridge, 1993), pp. 109–46.

[14] Oxford, Magdalen College, Archives, Titchwell 158, and Urbana-Champaign, University of

particular interest in this context are a set of Spirleng's personal accounts of expenses for the period from 29 September 1448 to 24 June 1451, drawn up in his own hand for Thomas Howes, to whom he was evidently acting as deputy. This long roll (which is in Latin) gives an interesting picture of an estate servant's varied activities. Amongst much else, it details the costs of many journeys to outlying manors and to Norwich on financial and legal business, including courtholding; it shows disbursements to builders at Caister, and mentions expenses for work at the time of a wreck on one of Fastolf's properties on the seashore. The roll also includes a note of Spirleng's annual stipend of 40 shillings, which, taking into account the free board and lodging he would have enjoyed at Caister Castle, was a handsome emolument for a young man at the outset of his career.[15] An important household document that was drawn up by Spirleng at this time is the extensive inventory of the sumptuous wardrobe, furnishings and other appurtenances of Caister, including a list of the French books used by Worcester and others of the community, its cover enigmatically endorsed 'Neuer trust ontryed quod Spirlyng'.[16] After several years of assisting the receivers, Spirleng progressed during the 1450s to the more senior post of auditor in Fastolf's service. As Denholm-Young remarked, the office of auditor required considerable technical knowledge. Fastolf's auditors, of whom there were usually two in post at any one time, had oversight not only of the financial affairs of minor

Illinois Library, MS xq822.33/DF26d are examples of letters, dated 1449 and 1451, addressed respectively by the receivers and Spirleng to Fastolf, and by Fastolf to them, mostly concerning litigation. A transcription of the latter, printed by K. G. Madison, 'Some Unused Sources Concerning the Litigation of Sir John Fastolf and John Paston III', *Iowa State Jnl of Research*, 56 (1981), 159–75, esp. 161–3, should be used with caution. Magdalen Coll., Archives, Hickling 140 is a letter of 1447 from Thomas Howes to Fastolf, mentioning that he has sent Spirleng to make legal enquiries about an inheritance. For a good impression of the volume and intricacy of the legal business involved in the administration of Fastolf's estates, see A. Smith, 'Litigation and Politics: Sir John Fastolf's Defence of his English Property', in *Property and Politics: Essays in Later Medieval English History*, ed. T. Pollard (Gloucester, 1984), pp. 59–75.
[15] Oxford, Magdalen Coll., Archives, EP 176/9. Spirleng's stipend was comparable to that of other Fastolf estate servants of similar rank. Fastolf received long and devoted service from them, as Dr Smith has shown, 'Career of Sir John Fastolf', p. 66. Mention of Spirleng in a letter from Fastolf to Thomas Howes of 1450 suggests that the young man might be over-zealous in defending his position: 'Item byasmoch as the greete besynesse of myne Audyt fallyth now I pray you to do sende for William Cole and that he wold see and hyre the examynyng and makyng of the accomptes yovyng hys gode avice thereto. And that Geffrey Spyrlyng forbere hym and gefe none occasion to displese hym' (London, BL, Additional MS 39848, fol. 9). Cole was one of Fastolf's most senior and long-serving auditors, whose duties would have included examining a deputy receiver's accounts; see n. 17 below.
[16] Oxford, Magdalen Coll., Archives, FP 43, dated 31 October 1448. Gairdner's less full version of this document (no. 389) derives from a lost roll; see *Archaeologia*, 21 (1827), 232–80. Various marginal annotations (e.g. 'caret' against certain items) show that it was put to practical use, and there are memoranda of 1454–55 in the hand of William Worcester towards the end. For the proverb on the cover see N. Davis, in *Medium Ævum*, 41 (1972), 166, and for the list of books, see App. to *Royal Commission on Historical Manuscripts, 8th report* (1881, repr. 1908), p. 268a.

manorial officials such as reeves and bailiffs, but also of the accounts of his receivers, and his household steward at Caister.[17]

In the Paston Letters, we continue to hear of Spirleng attending to the household accounts at Caister and to those of Fastolf's manors elsewhere, exercising power of attorney, and acting as a confidential messenger, especially to John Paston I, one of Fastolf's lawyers, and his principal ally in East Anglia.[18] Like most others close to Fastolf, Spirleng found himself, upon his master's death in November 1459, embroiled in the disputes that immediately arose between the Pastons and others about Fastolf's will, by which he had bequeathed to John Paston I all his large landholdings in Norfolk and Suffolk. Spirleng's only extant letter, written in his own hand to John Paston I (6 January 1460), puts into writing what he had understood of Fastolf's testamentary intentions in favour of Paston, and quotes some of his testy employer's conversation (Pl. 12).[19] The tone of the letter indicates that Spirleng was of the Pastons' party in the dispute, which dragged on into the 1470s, long after he had taken up civic duties in Norwich; subsequent references to him by the Pastons note that his sympathies continued to lie in their direction.[20] Occasionally he appears as an agent or an accountant for them in the administration of his former master's estates.[21]

In 1456–57, when he was about thirty years of age, and still in Fastolf's service, Spirleng became a freeman of Norwich, almost certainly by redemption (i.e.

---

[17] N. Denholm-Young, *Seignorial Administration in England* (Oxford, 1937), p. 5; for the conduct of audits, see pp. 145–51. Fastolf relied upon his auditors for the efficient management of his estates, since they gave him the means to monitor the performance of other officials; see Smith, 'Career of Sir John Fastolf', pp. 63–4. Where Spirleng first acquired the professional expertise to become one of Fastolf's senior estate team is not known. He may have been trained by Thomas Howes, or he could have earlier received schooling in business and estate management of the kind that was available, for example, in Oxford, see H. G. Richardson, 'Business Training in Medieval Oxford', *American Historical Review*, 45 (1941), 259–80. Numerous manuscripts containing instructional treatises on estate management and accounting were in circulation; see D. Oschinsky, 'Medieval Treatises on Estate Management', *Economic History Review*, 2nd ser., 8 (1955–56), 296–309.

[18] Gairdner, no. 157 (dated 1450); Davis, nos 523, 566, 569, 571, 572, 584, 585 (dated between 1455 and 1459). Unpublished Fastolf estate documents in the archives of Magdalen Coll., Oxford, shed similar light on Spirleng's activities in this period, e.g. Titchwell 72 and Norfolk and Suffolk 59 (granting Spirleng powers of attorney in 1456 and 1457), and EP 69/21 (assisting Walter Shipdam as auditor in 1456–57). FP 62 is a list of outstanding debts to Fastolf drawn up by Spirleng (in English) at Michaelmas 1457, mentioning a wide variety of manorial business in which he had been involved.

[19] Davis, no. 603; it also confirms that Spirleng was officially one of Fastolf's auditors at this time (ll. 11–14). Later in his life Spirleng came into possession of property in Norwich that had belonged to Fastolf; see n. 31 below. Oxford, Magdalen Coll., Archives FP 47 is a memorandum by Fastolf to his trustees and executors expressing the desire that his servants should 'aftir the contynuaunce of there longe service be rewardid as largely and more than I haue devised in my will and testament late made'; it is possible that Spirleng was a beneficiary of such a provision.

[20] Davis, nos 339, 341 (dated 1470).

[21] Davis, nos 164, 268, 318, 352 (dated between 1461 and 1472). In Davis no. 268, of 30 April 1472, John Paston III refers to Spirleng as an 'auditore of Norwyche'.

purchase), rather than by the other possible routes of patrimony or apprenticeship.[22] Freedom of the city was the normal prelude to membership of the gild of St George, effectively the oligarchy that controlled the civic administration in Norwich, most of the elected and appointed officials of the city being drawn from the ranks of this fraternity.[23] Spirleng evidently took up residence in Norwich at or about the time of Fastolf's death, and the birth of his son Thomas (cf. the colophon to Gl, quoted above). Soon afterwards, in 1464, he was appointed one of the city's auditors. He also accepted election annually as a councillor for the Coslany ward until 1471.[24] In 1469 he was made clerk to St George's gild, a lifetime appointment, having acted as one of its auditors for some years previously, and his hand appears frequently thereafter in the surviving muniments of the gild. Examples include St George's Gild Book A, 1441–1517, where an inventory of the gild's property dated 1469 and signed by Spirleng seems to be the first item in his hand (see Pl. 13). The minutes of gild meetings held between October 1469 and March 1491/2 are in his hand, and his name appears frequently in the business.[25] Few of the account rolls of the gild have survived from this period, and those that do are damaged and faded, but appear likewise to be in Spirleng's hand, as principal auditor.[26]

In May 1471 Spirleng took up appointment as common clerk (town clerk) to the city of Norwich, a post to which he was re-elected annually until 1490, not long before his death.[27] Amongst other things, the common clerk also acted as clerk of the

---

[22] L'Estrange, *Freemen of Norwich*, p. 128; Spirleng's appearance in the list of scriveners was merely nominal. From 1450 it was ordered that all those taking out the freedom of the city should be entered under the name of a trade, thus, e.g. John Paston III was listed as a mercer, which he manifestly was not. Thomas Grene, Spirleng's predecessor as common clerk, and Leonard Spencer, a successor, were both styled 'gentleman', but entered under the scriveners; see ibid., pp. ii–iii, 64, 106, 128. Grene may have been the Norfolk lawyer of that name whose name appears in the Paston Letters and Fastolf Papers. None of the Norwich scriveners active during Spirleng's adult lifetime are listed as having been apprenticed to him; there were some 25 enrolled *c.*1450–1490. Speculations about Spirleng's activities as a scrivener in R. Vance Ramsey, 'Palaeography and Scribes of Shared Training', *Studies in the Age of Chaucer*, 8 (1986), 107–44, seem baseless.

[23] See B. R. McRee, 'Religious Gilds and Civic Order: the Case of Norwich in the late Middle Ages', *Speculum*, 67 (1992), 69–97, esp. 81–2.

[24] Hawes, *Index to Norwich Officers*, p. 144.

[25] Norwich, Norfolk Record Office (NRO), Norwich City Records, St George's Gild Book A, pp. 226–69. The minute recording Spirleng's appointment (17 April 1469) reads: 'It is agreed that Geffrey Spirlyng shalbe discharged of the Fest of Saynt Georges Gilde for the good since that he hath doon in comptees makyng and upon this condicion that he shall yearly make the countes terme of his liff whill he is of abilite to make accountees and mor ouer he to be clerk of the same gylde and to attend at assembles set by the alderman by himself or by his depute he takyng yerly for his salary of the said Gilde vj s. viij d. and no more'; see *Records of the Gild of St George in Norwich, 1389–1547: a Transcript with an Introduction*, ed. M. Grace, Norfolk Record Society (Norwich, 1937), pp. 61–83, esp. 61.

[26] Norwich, NRO, Norwich City Records B/8/e, Gild of St George, Roll of Surveyors' Accounts, 1472–75.

[27] Norwich, NRO, Norwich City Records 16/d/1, Folio Book of the Proceedings of the Municipal

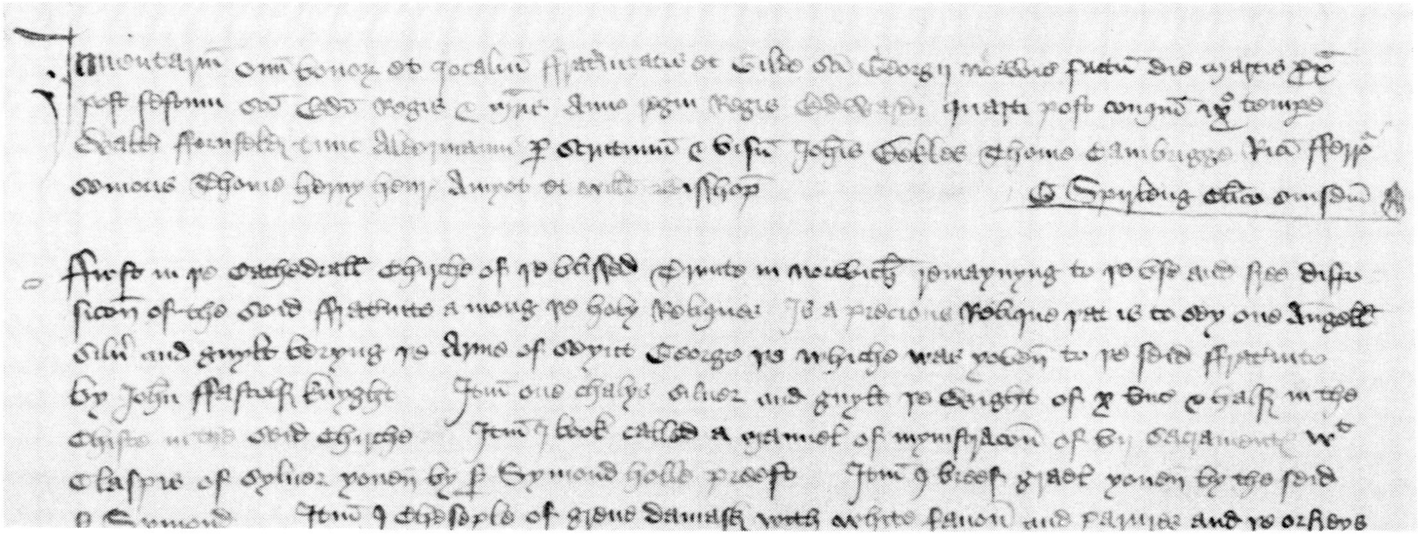

Plate 13 Norwich, Norfolk Record Office, Norwich City Records 17/b, St George's Gild Book A, 1441–1517, fol. 17, upper portion, actual size. Inventory, 1469, written and signed by Geoffrey Spirleng, with his paraph

peace, and was responsible for the custody of the city's documents. He recorded the proceedings of the city assembly, usually in Latin, and most of the entries in the minute book for the period of Spirleng's tenure are in his hand (see Pl. 14). Again, his own name often appears in the records of the city's business, and this, together with his gild responsibilities, must have occupied much of his time.[28] Copies of important documents in the Norwich Liber Albus (the city's official repository of its instruments) are often in Spirleng's hand at this period (see Pl. 15),[29] and much of the first half of the Chamberlains' Account Book for the period 1470 to 1490 is also by him. Of particular interest in the latter are the accounts for the reception of Queen Elizabeth Woodville at Norwich in late July 1469, including what sounds like a *tableau vivant* arranged by Spirleng, with explanatory speeches by him, depicting the Salutation of the Virgin.[30]

The successive phases of Geoffrey Spirleng's career as estate servant and civic official would undoubtedly repay much longer attention than they have been given above, and more work in his hand will certainly be identified. How far service in Fastolf's household encouraged him to develop the literary leanings that later expressed themselves in the composition of dramatic speeches and the copying of the *Canterbury Tales* can only be a matter for speculation, but daily association at Caister with cultivated and bookish men like William Worcester and Stephen Scrope is likely to have left its mark. On the other hand, an extended reading of the documentary sources associated with him leaves the consistent impression that Spirleng was throughout his life a very busy and highly competent professional man, in whom shrewd but demanding employers were keen to invest large responsibilities and trust. It is impossible to say whether he gave a period of undivided attention to the copying of Chaucer, and the natural assumption is that such work would be a

---

Assembly, 1434–91, fol. 91ᵛ, where the minute recording Spirleng's first election is in his own hand. The last record of his annual election is in May 1490 (fol. 142ᵛ), but later that year he is noted as being 'tunc absente', and a deputy is designated. In May 1491 the election of his successor, Andrew Pawe, was minuted (fol. 145).

[28] In this connexion, it may be significant that after 1472 he was only once more elected as a councillor; see Hawes, *Index to Norwich Officers*, p. 144.

[29] Norwich, NRO, Norwich City Records 17/b/1; see e.g. fols 52–53, copy of the charter of Edward IV for the worsted weavers of Norwich (1467), made and signed by Spirleng in 1474; fol. 117ʳ⁻ᵛ, copy of the agistment for the walls, of 1451, made and signed by Spirleng, undated. The latter is printed in W. Hudson and J. C. Tingey, *The Records of the City of Norwich*, 2 vols (Norwich and London, 1906), II, 313–15.

[30] Norwich, NRO, Norwich City Records 18/a, fols 10–14, accounts in Spirleng's hand, include payment to himself for paper on which to set the speeches down, and for the writing (ij d.); and further: 'Et in regardo datum Galfrido Spirleng pro sua diligencia in prouisione duarum stacionum ac pro factura loquelarum expositum ad faciem Regine ac salutacionis Marie et Elizabetham breuiter manifestate pro discrecionem iam auditorum et superuisorum duarum stacionum ijˡⁱ'. See also H. Harrod, 'Queen Elizabeth Woodville's Visit to Norwich in 1469', *Norfolk Archaeology*, 5 (1859), 32–7.

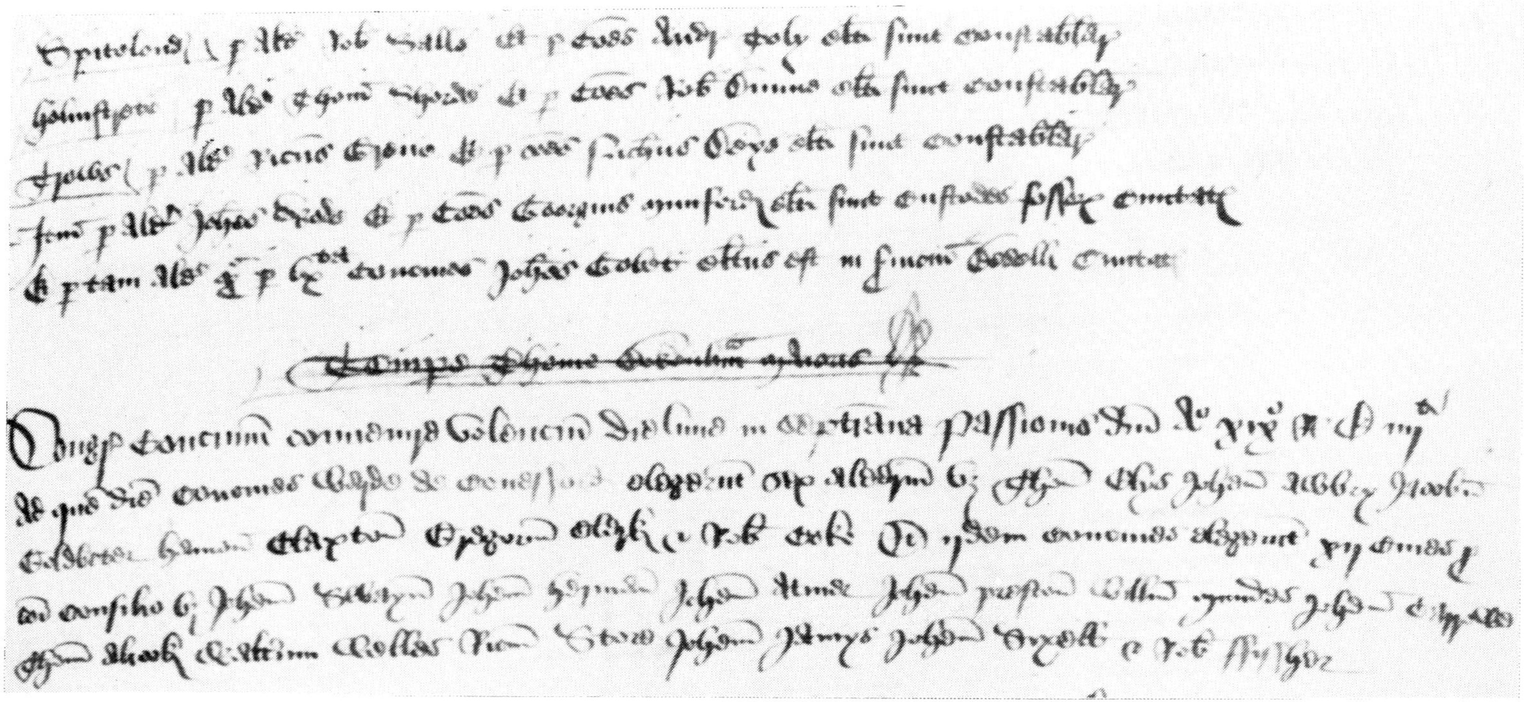

Plate 14 Norwich, Norfolk Record Office, Norwich City Records 16/d/1, Folio Book of Proceedings of the Municipal Assembly, 1434–91, fol. 107, upper portion, actual size. Minutes of the assembly, 1479, in the hand of Geoffrey Spirleng, including a deletion accompanied by his paraph

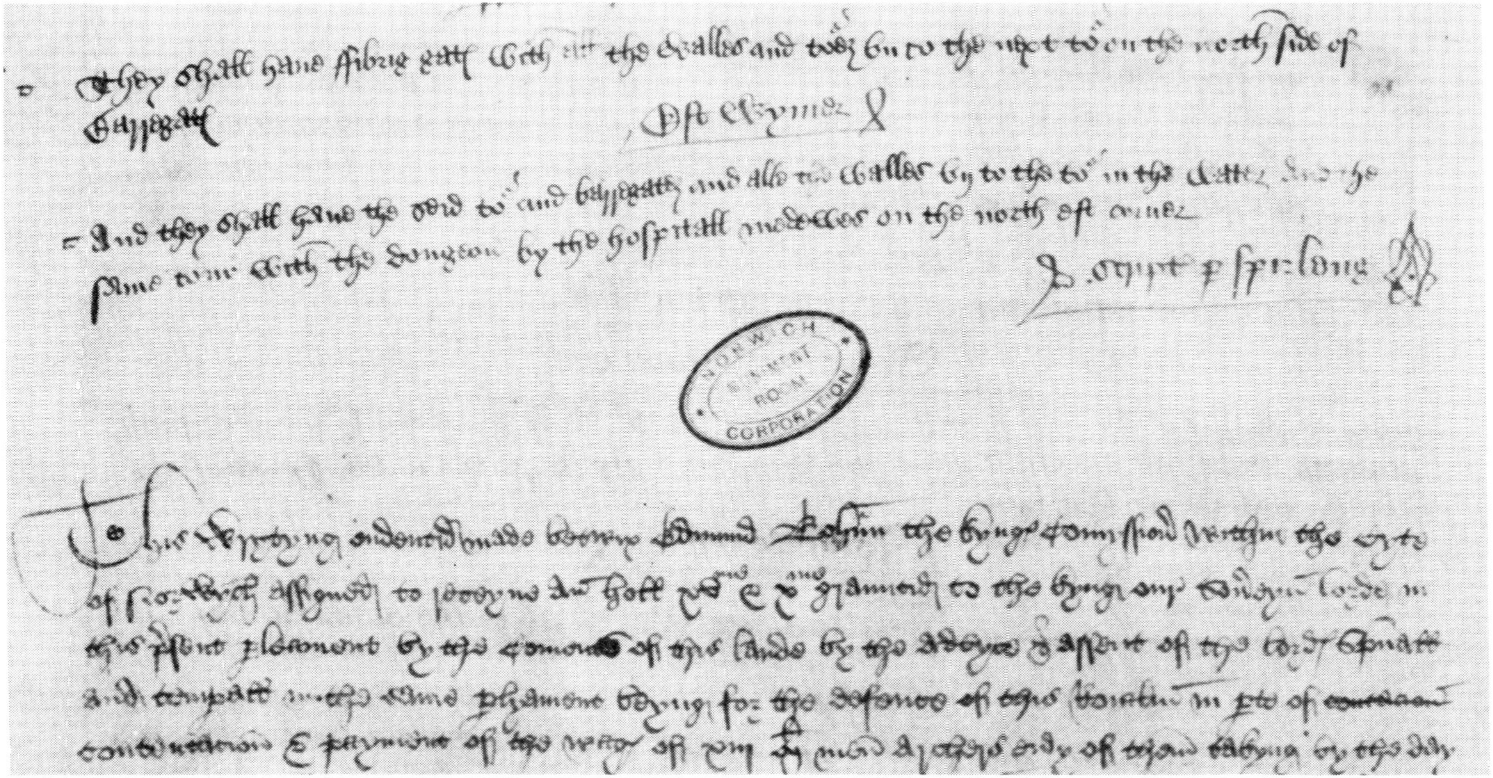

Plate 15 Norwich, Norfolk Record Office, Norwich City Records 17/b, Liber Albus, fol. 117ᵛ, upper portion, actual size. Copy of the agistment for the city walls (end), 1481, written and signed by Geoffrey Spirleng, with his paraph, followed by the beginning of a copy of an indenture in his hand

part-time undertaking, fitted in piecemeal amidst a variety of other activities. Spirleng's personal motivation for making his own copy of the *Canterbury Tales* (to say nothing of the Latin version of St Patrick's Purgatory) must have been strong, and as we shall see, despite the acknowledgement of his son's assistance in the colophon to Gl, he carried out most of the work himself. At his death, which seems to have occurred in 1493–94, Geoffrey Spirleng was plainly a man of some substance, leaving property in several Norwich parishes to his wife Leticia Terry (who was pregnant) and his son Thomas,[31] who seems not to have achieved anything of his father's prominence in the city. There appears to be no evidence of Thomas Spirleng's occupation, though he was presumably the man of that name who was constable for Conisford ward in 1496.[32] He died around 1514.

In order to have provided a part-exemplar for Gl, Mm must have been in Norwich or its neighbourhood for some time during 1475–76, when Spirleng had access to it. Amongst the early marks of presumed ownership in Mm is the name Wyllyam Boleyn (fol. 190) datable to the later fifteenth century, in dry point. Manly and Rickert suggest that this must have been Sir William Boleyn (d. 1505), of the prominent Norfolk family of that name, and grandfather of Anne Boleyn.[33] Their Norfolk seat was at Blickling, about twelve miles north of Norwich, a manor which Sir John Fastolf had sold to Boleyn's father in 1452. The estate and the family were certainly well known to Spirleng from his time in Fastolf's service, and accounts relating to his visits to Blickling on business survive among the Fastolf estate papers.[34] Sir William Boleyn also had an important residence in Norwich itself,[35] and Spirleng was presumably on friendly personal terms with him, such

---

[31] Geoffrey Spirleng's will is enrolled in Norwich City Court Roll 20, 1483–1508 (Norwich, NRO, Norwich City Records A/1/d), membr. 65, dorse, dated 16 June 1494. It mentions 'My ij Meses with the byldynges and gardeyns lying to gydre in Norwich in the parichesse of Seynt Marie and Seynt Martyn of Coslany wyth thappurtenaunces late wardes Syr John Fastolff knyght . . .', 'my tenement in the parysche of Seynt Gyle in Norwiche', and 'my tenement in the parysche of Seynt Georges Muspool'. Manly and Rickert, I, 187, say (without giving any reference) that Spirleng also 'had two shops by the Norwich Town Hall', but I have not been able to confirm this.

[32] Hawes, *Index to Norwich Officers*, p. 144. Constable was the most junior office in the civic hierarchy, and normally the first stepping stone towards higher things, but Thomas appears to have proceeded no further. For his will, see Manly and Rickert, I, 188.

[33] Manly and Rickert, I, 370.

[34] Blomefield, *Norfolk*, VI, 386–7, gave 1457 as the date at which Fastolf sold Blickling to Geoffrey Boleyn, but Dr Smith established that the sale took place in 1452 ('"The greatest man of that age"', p. 152, n. 64; cf. Davis, no. 144). Spirleng's work for Fastolf at Blickling included drawing up accounts of the manor's arrears in 1446, and visiting it several times between 1448 and 1451, on one occasion to hold a court there; Oxford, Magdalen Coll., Archives, EP176/8 and 176/9.

[35] Blomefield, *Norfolk*, IV, 84.

that he could have borrowed Mm (more than once) in order to start and eventually to complete a copy of the *Canterbury Tales* from it.

Mm is, in outward appearance, a good-quality copy of the Tales, in folio format, on vellum, the text disposed in a single column, and written in a professional-looking Anglicana Formata bookhand of the second quarter of the fifteenth century. The orthography, however, is provincial, with y being used consistently to represent þ, as well as having its normal signification, together with northern or north midland features such as *scho* for 'she', and unvoiced consonants in words like *luff* 'love', *liffed* 'lived' and *thof* 'though'. The scribe of Mm employed a spelling system very different from Geoffrey Spirleng's (which is discussed below); it has recently been identified with the language of documents and texts associated with north Leicestershire.[36] Throughout Mm there are good illuminated borders at the beginnings of the tales, together with many smaller illuminated initials elsewhere, and the signs are that it may have been commissioned from a commercial source by a well-to-do person. Although Gl is of roughly the same dimensions as Mm, it is made of cheaper material, and the text is more economically disposed on the page, in double columns, so that the contents of about two pages in the exemplar occupy about one side in the copy. There is of course no attempt to reflect the expensive decorative scheme of Mm in Gl. Spirleng plainly intended that his manuscript should represent only a compact copy of the text, but not the physical layout of the exemplar from which it was initially being made.

Before one can turn to some comparison of exemplar and copy on the level of textual detail, it is necessary to establish the division of labour between the two scribes whom we know to have been involved in the copying of Gl. Manly and Rickert found the hands of Geoffrey and Thomas Spirleng very much alike, and were mostly vague (perhaps deliberately so) about exactly who had written what. They offered no descriptive detail about the hand of either scribe, beyond the aesthetic remark that Geoffrey's was 'the freer and more graceful', and whilst they claimed to be able to distinguish the father's work from the son's at some points, they also found that for long stretches of the manuscript they could not tell the two apart.[37] My own examination of Gl, in the light of comparison with other examples of Geoffrey Spirleng's hand, indicates that although two distinct hands do appear in the manuscript, one of them was responsible for the great bulk of the work, whilst the other contributed very little.

Plates 13–15 show something of the range of variation to be seen in Geoffrey Spirleng's handwriting as it is represented in Norwich civic muniments dated within

---

[36] A. McIntosh, M. L. Samuels and M. Benskin, *A Linguistic Atlas of Late Mediæval English*, 4 vols (Aberdeen, 1986), I, 68. According to Manly and Rickert, I, 369–70, owners of Mm prior to Boleyn may have included members of the Brokesby family of Frisby, Leicestershire.

[37] Manly and Rickert, I, 184, attribute the two previously missing tales in the final quire to Geoffrey, and indicate that the two hands alternated recognizably in the course of the copying of the Parson's Tale.

five years or so of the time when Gl was copied. Earlier surviving pieces of writing by him include the letter to John Paston I of January 1460 (London, BL, Additional MS 27444, fol. 70, Pl. 12), and account rolls amongst Fastolf estate papers, dated 1446, 1451 and 1457 (Oxford, Magdalen College, Archives EP 176/8 and 9, and FP 62). In the letter his hand appears as a small *cursiva currens* whose range of letter forms is drawn almost exclusively from the Anglicana repertoire: double compartment **a**, which sometimes rises above the x-height; reverse **e**; 8-shaped **g** (usually); long **r** in certain positions; sigma-shaped **s**; and the elaborated form of **w**. The ascenders of **b**, **d**, **h** and **l** are looped, and **k** has an especially wide sweeping hook at the head of its vertical stroke. The descender of **y** sweeps to the right to form an approach stroke to the letter following, and the limb of **h** is looped to the left beneath the line, again forming an approach stroke where another letter follows. Secretary letter-forms are avoided, but the thick-thin alternations in the formation of groups of minims, and the appearance of tapering descenders to **f** and long **s** indicate at least some influence of the other variety of cursive script in use at the time. In the earlier account rolls, which are in both Latin and English, his hand is often untidier, but has a similar aspect, with only occasional use of Secretary graphs (usually the single compartment **a** and **g**) in this more informal setting.

Such evidence as we have in the letter to John Paston I suggests that in his mid thirties Geoffrey Spirleng chose a fairly pure variety of current Anglicana for the purposes of formal correspondence, and that this was perhaps the type of script that he had been brought up or trained to use in early life. If this was so, Anglicana remained the foundation of his hand, and all of its letter forms are strongly represented in his work in the Norwich documents and in Gl, with, however, varying admixtures of Secretary forms. In the inventory of the Gild of St George of 1469 (Pl. 13), which is also carefully and neatly written, Secretary forms appear quite frequently beside their Anglicana counterparts, notably the single compartment **a**, short **r**, kidney-shaped final **s**, and simplified **w**, though not Secretary **g**. Minutes of 1479 in the Municipal Assembly Book (Pl. 14), set down with greater haste and currency, and in Latin, include a line in the larger, near-formata type of writing that Spirleng sometimes employed for headings and other purposes of display, such as the rubricated matter in Gl; here, once again, no Secretary forms appear. The extract from the Liber Albus (Pl. 15), written in 1481, shows, in the copy of the agistment (above the Norwich Muniment Room stamp), the less current version of his hand. Below the stamp, in the indenture, is another of its more current manifestations. In both examples, selective use is made of Secretary graphs: single compartment **a** and short **r** (but not the simpler **w**) in the agistment, but by contrast the simpler form of **w**, beside Anglicana **w**, in the indenture. These examples suffice to show a general tendency in Geoffrey Spirleng's work. Depending on the purpose, content, and perhaps the language of what he was writing, he might use either the relatively unadulterated variety of Anglicana which he may have been taught in his youth, or alternatively he might adopt a mixed hand in which selected Secretary graphs (usually a, r, s, and w, but g rather seldom) could be introduced, alongside their Anglicana counterparts, on a basis that was to some extent, and significantly, systematic.

With these discriminations in mind we may now turn to the handwritings in Gl, illustrated in Plates 16 and 17, showing adjacent columns on folio 99ᵛ (part of the Parson's Tale), in the section of the manuscript where the two hands alternate for several pages. The hand of the column on the right (fol. 99ᵛ, col. b) is the one responsible for almost all of Gl, and is plainly that of Geoffrey Spirleng. The column on the left (fol. 99ᵛ, col. a) shows the hand of the minority contributor, which must be that of Thomas Spirleng. Thomas's hand, which appears only briefly in Gl, alternates in several places with Geoffrey's, between fols 91 and 99ᵛ, but his stints include rubrication and some insertions and corrections by his father.[38] For example, in the section of Thomas's contribution illustrated here, the words 'Putoures' (line 1), 'Auoutrie' (line 6) and 'Subdeken deken or prest or hospitaleɼs' (lines 23–4) are insertions by Geoffrey; line 30 shows a deletion and interlinear correction by him.

The shared generic affiliation of the hands of Geoffrey and Thomas Spirleng is clear enough from these examples, and sufficient has been said above, with reference to Geoffrey's, to characterize it. Their hands are indeed very similar to one another, but they are similar also to many other hands of like date and type. It is of course possible, as has been suggested, that the father taught the son to write, but this seems to me, on the evidence of their handwritings alone, by no means a necessary assumption, given the quite commonplace nature of the script on which both their hands are modelled. There are in fact signs that mixed hands of this type might be taught systematically in schools and other educational establishments, as is strikingly witnessed in Ker's investigation of Eton College MS 44.[39] Discriminating between the hands of Geoffrey and Thomas Spirleng may at first sight seem difficult, but attention to the respective ducts, aspects, slopes and ranges of letter form in their work reveals distinct and consistently observable differences.

In our examples, Thomas's hand is the more widely spaced, as between one line and another and between one word and the next. Within the word-unit itself his writing is also somewhat less current than his father's, for more of his individual

---

[38] The full extent of Thomas Spirleng's contribution to Gl seems to have been as follows: fol. 91, cols a–b, line 33; fol. 91ᵛ, col. a, line 17 to fol. 91ᵛ, col. b foot; fol. 92, col. a to line 19; fol. 92, col. b to line 22, and from line 29 to foot; fol. 92ᵛ, cols a–b; fol. 93, cols a–b; fol. 94, cols a–b; fol. 94ᵛ, col. a to line 18; fol. 94ᵛ, col. b; fol. 95, col. a from line 8 up to foot; fol. 95, col. b; fols 95ᵛ, col. a to 97, col. b; fol. 97ᵛ, col. a to line 21, and from line 9 up to foot; fol. 97ᵛ, col. b; fols 98, col. a to 99ᵛ, col. a.

[39] Ker estimated that some 53 young scribes, nearly all of whom wrote rather similar hands affiliated to a mixed cursive model, contributed to Eton Coll. MS 44 at Oxford in the 1480s, some of them having come up from Winchester: 'The scribes use single compartment *a* nearly always, two-compartment *a* very occasionally, 8-shaped *g* much more often than secretary *g*, 2-shaped *r* commonly, long-tailed *r* and short *r* occasionally. Who taught them this script?'; 'Eton College MS 44' (see n. 6 above), p. 90, n. 4.

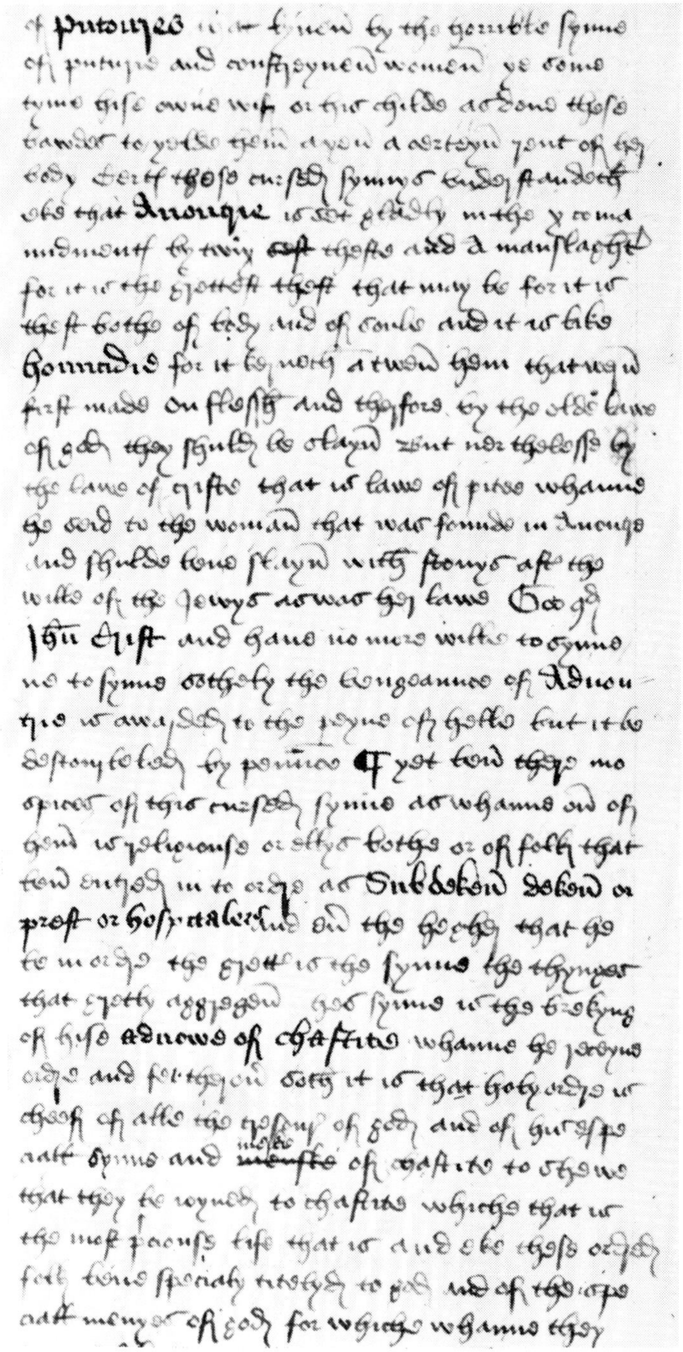

5

10

15

20

25

30

Plate 16   Glasgow, University Library, Hunterian MS U.I.1, fol. 99ᵛ, col. a, upper portion, actual size. Geoffrey Chaucer, *Canterbury Tales*, 'Parson's Tale', X(I), 885–93. Hand of Thomas Spirleng, 1476, with insertions by Geoffrey Spirleng (see p. 133)

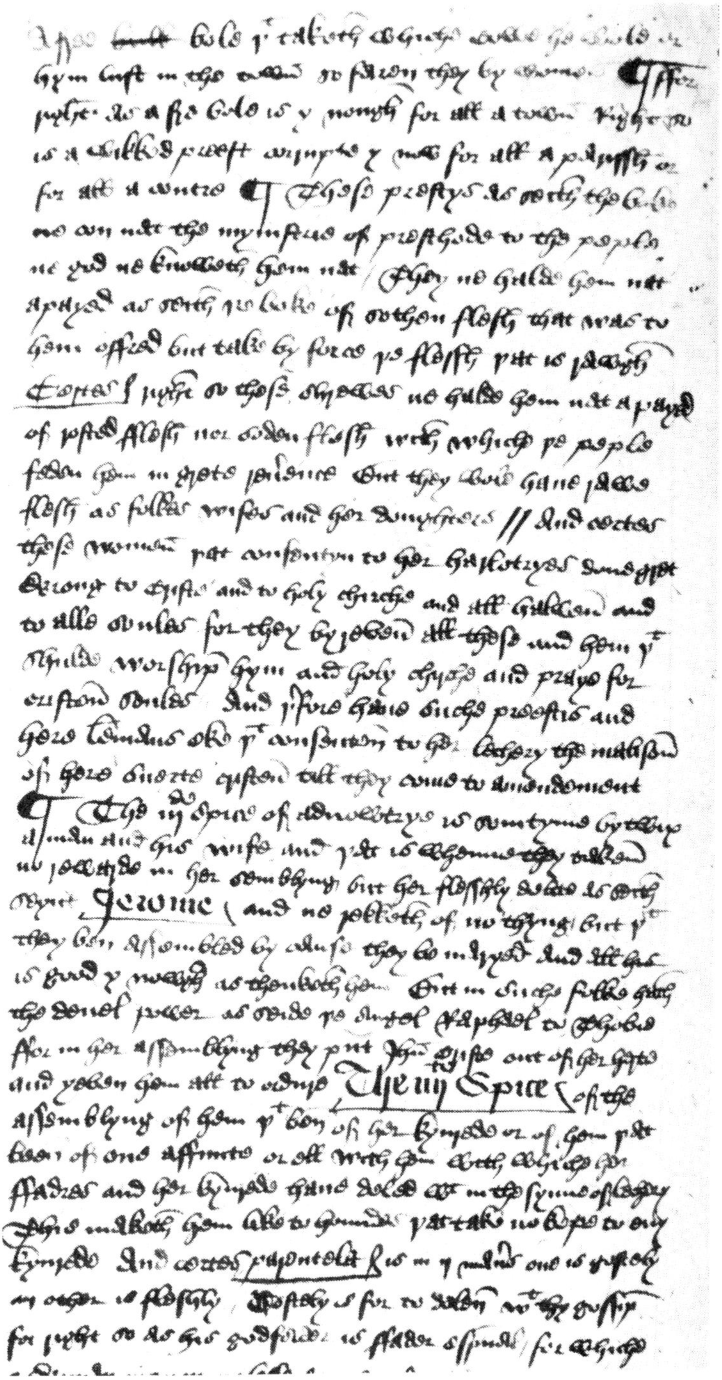

Plate 17 Glasgow, University Library, Hunterian MS U.I.1, fol. 99ᵛ, col. b, upper portion, actual size. Geoffrey Chaucer, *Canterbury Tales*, 'Parson's Tale', X(I), 897–908. Hand of Geoffrey Spirleng, 1476

graphic units are unligatured, and in the unligatured state he leaves more space between them. Geoffrey's hand here is more densely and compactly written, with the lines closer together, and much less space between words and between letters. His hand also slopes more markedly to the right than Thomas's, with minim strokes in particular tending to slope obliquely from right to left. The minims in Thomas's hand, by contrast, generally slope in the opposite direction. With certain significant exceptions, the range of letter forms in the two hands is similar, and there is little distinction to be made between them in their execution of a number of standard graphs, notably the Anglicana reverse e and long r, the looped letters (b, d, f, g, h, l), and y with its descender swept to the right. Other letter shapes, do, however, differ. The main distinctions are as follows: Thomas's k ('eke', line 6; 'folk', line 22) does not have the more ostentatious sweep at the head which is always characteristic of Geoffrey's ('kynrede', lines 30, 32), and his sigma-shaped final s ('as', line 3; 'was', line 16) is more carefully formed than his father's ('is', lines 3, 21). The treatment of a and w constitutes a marked difference between the two hands. It is notable that Thomas generally restricts himself to the simpler Secretary forms in each case ('was', line 16, 'whanne', line 34), using the Anglicana forms rather seldom, as if he were otherwise consciously avoiding them. Geoffrey, as we have seen elsewhere, uses both the Anglicana and the Secretary forms freely, the two types of w, seemingly in equal proportions, as alternatives ('women', line 14; 'wrong', line 15), but with a marked preference for the two-compartment Anglicana a over the Secretary form. A clear distinction between the formation of Geoffrey's Secretary w ('which', line 11; 'women', line 14) and that of Thomas's ('woman', line 14; 'which', line 34) can also be made. The marked approach stroke to Geoffrey's Secretary w is often matched by a similar anticipatory flourish in his formation of n ('nough', line 3; 'now', line 4); Thomas's work does not have these features. Finally, we may note a marked graphetic distinction between Thomas's work and that of his father: whereas Geoffrey makes frequent use of thorn, usually in *þe, þᵗ, þat, þᵘ* and *þou*, Thomas avoids it all but completely – an isolated tell-tale *þᵗ* instead of his usual *that* squeezed in a line-ending (fol. 91, col. a, line 31) suggests that he elsewhere sought to keep the obsolescent graph out of his active repertoire.

Although the attribution of all but a very small part of Gl to the hand of Geoffrey Spirleng may be confidently offered on the basis of an examination of the hand-writing, confirmation may be drawn from another feature of the manuscript, in comparison with his work elsewhere. Each of the examples of Spirleng's hand from the Norwich muniments reproduced in Plates 13, 14 and 15 illustrates his personal mark, a paraph that often accompanies his signature, and sometimes occurs by itself to authenticate his work. It often forms a terminating flourish to the underlining of a heading or a signature. The repeated appearance of the same mark throughout Gl was no doubt a matter of habit. It is found, for example, on fol. 110, after the heading for the late-copied Canon's Yeoman's Tale, after the running titles at the heads of fols 111ᵛ and 114, and also between the end of the first and the beginning of the second part of the Parson's Tale, at the foot of folio 89ᵛ, col. b, which is noteworthy because it was very shortly after this point that Spirleng temporarily handed over part of the task of copying to his son for several pages. More important, however, is Spirleng's systematic 'signing' of most of the catchwords at the ends of the quires in Gl with his paraph, confirming they were his work.[40]

The significance of establishing the precise division of labour between the scribes of Gl emerges as we come to consider the textual relationship between the Spirlengs' manuscript and its part-exemplar in Mm. For it is now clear that the entire section of Gl that was derived directly from Mm was the work of Geoffrey Spirleng alone, and it is to the issues of his accuracy and intelligence as a copyist, and their wider consequences, that we may now turn.

Depending on such factors as the character of the scripts, texts and languages involved, a comparison between a copy and its exemplar might be carried forward on several different but interrelated levels; and a full comparison would undoubtedly have to be developed at much greater length and in far more detail than is possible in the present context. As far as the relationship between Gl and Mm is concerned, a start may be made by addressing certain basic questions, the answers to which, whilst interesting in themselves, also have wider implications for the understanding of scribal practices, textual transmission, and the development of later Middle English. The first question to ask is how accurate a scribe was Geoffrey Spirleng? If what we see in the section of Gl that he derived directly from Mm differs from the exemplar, what explanations can be advanced for the variations that appear in his copy? In this context it is necessary to have regard to both the diachronic and the diatopic factors that could have drastic effects upon the transmission of any later Middle English text. By 1476 Chaucer's writings had already begun to look in some respects archaic to his readers and copyists, because of various rapid changes that had taken place in the English language during the fifteenth century, especially in its morphology and in its lexical complexion. In addition, Spirleng would immediately have seen, upon opening Mm, that it was the work of a scribe whose dialect, in its written form, was very different from his own. In embarking upon his copy of the *Canterbury Tales* he was faced in every line with a task which involved not only reproducing the substance of the text accurately but also choosing whether or not to preserve features of Chaucer's language that had since become obsolete, and deciding how to deal with the alien orthographical forms of the Mm scribe. Any of the 10 000 or so lines

---

[40] The catchwords on fols 5ᵛ, 26ᵛ, 34ᵛ, 47ᵛ, 55ᵛ, 63ᵛ, 71ᵛ, 79ᵛ and 87ᵛ are all accompanied by Spirleng's paraph. That on fol. 13ᵛ has his characteristic style of underlining and flourish, and only the one on fol. 21ᵛ is unadorned; there is no sign of a hand other than Geoffrey Spirleng's at work in the vicinity. A catchword in Thomas's stint (fol. 95ᵛ) is not marked.

that Spirleng copied from Mm will serve to investigate his procedures. In the present context, two passages are reproduced at length and analysed in detail, whilst four others (giving an overall total of 126 lines) have been analysed but not printed here, in order to provide some preliminary responses to the questions posed at the beginning of this paragraph.

The following passage reproduces lines 1785–1805 of the Knight's Tale, giving first the text of Mm (fol. 20), then that of Gl (fol. 8, cols a–b), and below in smaller type the received text, together with certain alternative readings at a few points:[41]

Mm	The godde of luff o benedicite	1785
Gl	The god of love o benedicite	
	The god of love a benedicite	
	Howe myȝhty and howe grete a lorde is he	1786
	How myghty and how grete a lorde is he	
	How myghty and how greet a lorde is he	
	Agayñ his miȝht yere agayneth non obstacles	1787
	Ageyn his myghte there gayneth non obstacles	
	Ayeyns his myght ther gayneth none obstacles	
	He may be cleped a godde for his miracles	1788
	He may be cleped a god for his myracles	
	He may be cleped a god for his myracles	
	For he cañ makeñ at his owñ gyse	1789
	For he can maken at hise oweñ guyse	
	For he kan maken at his owene gyse	
	Off eueriche herte as yat hym liste devise	1790
	Of eueryche herte as þat hym liste deuyse	
	Of everich herte as that hym list divyse	
	Loo here yis Arcite and yis Palemoñ	1791
	Lo heere þis Arcite and this Palamoñ	
	Lo heere this Arcite and this Palamoun	
	That quytely were oute of my prisoñ goone	1792
	That wightely were out of my prisoñ goñ	
	That quitly weren out of my prisoun	

---

[41] The received text is that of the *Riverside Chaucer*; the alternative readings are from the classificatory group of manuscripts designated d* by Manly and Rickert, to which Mm and Gl belong at this point. In the manuscripts a flourish on final **r** is transcribed as **e**, whereas a flourish on final **n** evidently has no abbreviatory function, and is represented by a macron.

And miȝht haue liffed in Thebes ryally   1793
And myght haue lyved in Thebes ryally
And myghte han lyved in Thebes roially

And wyten yat I am here mortell enmye   1794
And knoweñ þat I am there mortall enmye
And witen I am hir mortal enemy

And yat hire deeth is in myȝhte also   1795
And þat ther deth is in my myght also
And that hir deth lith [d* is] in my myght also

And ȝit hath loue / mawgre in yer eyeñ twoo   1796
And yet hath love magre in there eyeñ bothe twoo
And yet hath love maugree hir eyen two

Broȝht hem hider both for to dye   1797
Brought hem hider bothe for to dye
Broght hem hyder bothe for to dye

Nowe loketh / is not yis a grete folye   1798
Now loketh is nat this a grete folye
Now looketh is nat that [d* this] an heigh [d* grete] folye

Who may be a foole but if he loue   1799
Who may be a fole but yf he love
Who may been a fool but if he love

Beholde for godes loue yeit suteth alone   1800
Byholde for goddes love that sytteth above
Bihoold for Goddes sake [d* loue] that sit above

See howe yei bleede be / yei not wele araiede   1801
See how they blede be they nat weel arrayed
Se how they blede be they noght wel arrayed

Thus hath hire lorde ye god of luff hem paiede   1802
þus hath ther lorde þe god of love hem payed
Thus hath hir lord the god of love ypayed [d* hem payed]

Here wages ande her fees for here seruyse   1803
Here wages and here fees for here seruice
Hir wages and hir fees for hir servyse

And ȝit yei weneñ to bene full wyse   1804
And yet they wenen to beeñ full wyse
And yet they wenen for to been ful wyse

That *seruen* loue for ought yat may befalle   1805
þat *seruen* love for ought that may befalle
That serven love for aught that may bifalle

The passage as it is found in Mm consists of 169 words, of which Spirleng copies 96 (or 56.8 per cent) literatim, that is to say, his realization of them in terms of both substantive and accidental features (including abbreviations as well as spellings) is identical to what was before him in the exemplar.[42] A number of the words concerned, many of them of frequent occurrence, admit of little or no graphemic variation (e.g. 'a', 'he', 'is', 'of', and so on), and these contribute significantly to the literatim element of Spirleng's work. Nevertheless, all of the words reproduced literatim constitute a significant proportion – somewhat over half – of the overall number of words in the passage. There remains however a large proportion – over 40 per cent of the total number of words copied – where Spirleng departs from the exemplar either by setting down the same readings, but with different spellings or abbreviations (i.e. varying the accidentals), or, in a small number of cases, giving different substantive readings. This tendency may be quantified by saying that of the 169 words in the Mm passage, Spirleng reproduces 163 (or 96.4 per cent) verbatim, but with many of them (somewhat under half) 'translated' into his own system of spelling and abbreviation. In six places his text varies from that of the exemplar, and on two occasions he adds words that are not in Mm.

Before turning to the substantive differences between this copy of KtT lines 1785–1805 and its exemplar, it is necessary to draw attention to the relevance of E. A. Golson's extensive analysis of the spelling system displayed in Gl, which she contrasted with that of Mm. Contrary to the expectations aroused by Manly and Rickert's view, that the hands of the Spirlengs, father and son, alternated throughout Gl, Dr Golson was surprised to discover that all of the text in Gl derived from Mm had been converted into a single, self-consistent orthographical system, which – apart from a handful of East Anglian features – aligned closely with educated London usage of the latter half of the fifteenth century.[43] In the light of the palaeographical arguments advanced above, the fact that Dr Golson was able to identify only one spelling system becomes explicable, since her analysis focused upon work which we now see was exclusively in the hand of Geoffrey Spirleng.[44] When

---

[42] This figure ignores the graphetic variation whereby the Mm scribe writes þ in the form y, whilst Spirleng writes þ proper. Also disregarded is the presence or otherwise of non-abbreviatory flourishes on final n, signified by macrons in the transcription.

[43] Golson, 'Spelling System' (see n. 5 above), pp. 46, 60.

[44] She refers, quite correctly, to the spelling system of Gl fols 1–46 and 103–15 in the singular, but following Manly and Rickert, attributes it to two scribes. However, the hypothesis that it represents the work of two copyists whose work was palaeographically indistinguishable and orthographically identical, may now be set aside. Her tabulation (ibid., pp. 32–5) gives a comprehensive picture of Geoffrey's spelling system, with which Thomas's may be compared; see n. 45 below. Assuming that

Thomas's hand eventually does appear sporadically in Gl, between fols 91 and 99ᵛ, the orthographic similarities to his father's work are quite marked, but so are the differences, many of which consist of the kind of Norfolk forms that Geoffrey had schooled himself to avoid.[45]

In the light of most thinking about textual transmission, especially as regards the more open or fluid environment of a late Middle English text composed in a common idiom, it might be expected that the variant readings in Spirleng's copy of KtT lines 1785–1805 would all be errors or corruptions. However, this is not so. In four places (lines 1787, 1800), Spirleng substitutes readings, adopted in the received text, where Mm by the same token is itself in error; and in one place (line 1795) he adds a necessary word where Mm would otherwise transmit an error of omission if reproduced verbatim. On the other hand, in line 1796, Spirleng unnecessarily inserts a word not in Mm, and in two places (lines 1792, 1794) he substitutes readings different from those of the exemplar, which align with those of the received text – though in neither case does Gl stray very far from the general sense of what Chaucer is likely to have written.

A closer approach to what might have been going through Spirleng's mind when he introduced these departures from the readings of his exemplar must be in some degree speculative. The errors, which in this passage all appear to be of the determined rather than the mechanical or spontaneous type, fall into recognizable categories amongst the 'tendencies of substitution' that have been described by Kane and others as characteristic of the copyists of Middle English texts.[46] Gl 'eyeñ both

---

Geoffrey was of Norfolk origins, he must have chosen to avoid most of the distinctive spellings habitually used by a great many East Anglian scribes (e.g. *xal/xuld* for 'shall'/'should'; *qu-/qu-/w-* for 'wh-'; *-t-/-th-* instead of *-gh-* or yogh in '-ght' words; *i/y* lowered to *e* in many words) in favour of the nascent London standard usage. Such a process is seen in changes to their spelling systems, from the mid to late fifteenth century, by some of Spirleng's immediate associates amongst the Paston men; see N. Davis, 'The Language of the Pastons' (1954), revised in *Middle English Literature: British Academy Gollancz Lectures*, ed. J. A. Burrow (Oxford, 1989), pp. 45–70, esp. 60. A few tell-tale East Anglian forms remain in consistent use in Geoffrey's orthographic repertoire, e.g. *douter* for 'daughter'; *i* lowered to *e* in a few words, such as *pety*, *petous*, *dede*, *mankende*; *on-* for the 'un-' prefix; cf. Golson, 'Spelling System', pp. 61–2.

[45] A fully worked comparison of Thomas's spelling system with his father's, as set out by Dr Golson, would be of considerable interest. They share many identical preferences, some commonplace, others more idiosyncratic (e.g. *hise* for 'his'; *fier* for 'fire'; *netheless* for 'nevertheless'; *guylt* for 'guilt', a very rare form that approaches the modern spelling, usually not thought to be attested before the sixteenth century). Thomas, however, also uses numerous forms that were current amongst Norfolk scribes throughout the fifteenth century, of which the following are the most noticeable: in '-ght' words, *rite*, *knyte*, *cawt*, *tawt*, *bout*; *nout(e)*, *nowt(e)* for 'not'; in 'wh-' words, *wiche*, *werfore*; *e* for more general *i* in *wele* ('will' vb.), *dede*, *leke*, *leue* etc.; *wordle*, *wordly* for 'world', 'worldly'; *erdly* for 'earthly'; *owther* for 'either'; *noyther* for 'neither'; *silf* for 'self'; *thine* for 'thy' preceding consonants; for the currency and distribution of many of these forms in Norfolk see *Linguistic Atlas* (as n. 36 above), IV, *passim*. A noteworthy East Anglian lexical variant introduced by Thomas was *therknesse* for 'darkness' (fol. 99ᵛ, col. a, line 6 up).

[46] G. Kane, ed. *Piers Plowman: the A Version* (London, 1960), pp. 62, 125–43. For a Chaucerian

twoo' for Mm 'eyeñ twoo' (line 1796) could be construed as a common variant of the type that leads to an arbitrary increase of emphasis, though it might also have been unconsciously induced by 'bothe' in line 1797. Either way, it says little for Spirleng's metrical sense, in adding another syllable to an already corrupt and overloaded line. Gl 'knowen' for Mm (and received text) 'wyten' (line 1794) is plainly a lexical substitution for a word which Spirleng presumably regarded as obsolescent; several other scribes of late manuscripts arrived at this reading independently.[47] Gl 'wightely' for Mm's near-received form 'quytely' (line 1792) is however unique, most other erring scribes substituting for this hard word such readings as 'quikly', 'queyntly' and 'quietly'.[48] Spirleng's difficulty with it seems to have been different, and dialectal rather than lexical, for he evidently felt the need to remove what he mistook for provincial spellings. He thought he was looking at a word in which *qu*- had been written instead of *w*-, and the -*gh*- dropped from -*ght*- (both common with Norfolk scribes of provincial orthographic habits), and guessed that the original reading might have been 'wightely' (= briskly), though he may in any case not have known the rare and perhaps obsolete 'quitly' (= completely).

Of greater interest are the variations in which the readings substituted or inserted by Spirleng constitute corrections to or at least improvements upon what he found before him in Mm. They function in much the same way as a modern editor's emendations, and were arrived at by processes resembling those of textual criticism. Gl 'gayneth' for Mm 'agayneth' (line 1787), the latter doubtless induced by the proximity of 'Agayñ' earlier in the line, restores the received reading and the metre. Gl 'in my myght' for Mm 'in myȝht' (line 1795) corrects a commonplace and readily explicable type of omission. A more impressive emendation is Gl 'that sytteth above' for Mm's inexplicable and unrhyming 'yeit suteth alone' (line 1800), where Spirleng almost succeeds in restoring the reading of the received text, but for its uninflected form of the verb. In sum, KtT lines 1785–1805 deteriorates slightly in some places, but improves in others, at Spirleng's hands in the process of transmission.

A second passage, again chosen more or less at random, also shows that manuscript transmission is not necessarily or inevitably a one-way process of corruption. Lines 488–508 of the Prioress's Tale run as follows in Mm (fol. 64ᵛ) and Gl (fol. 28, col. a) respectively:

Mm	Ther was in Asye in a grete citee	488
Gl	Ther was in Asye in a grete cite	
	Ther was in Asye in a greet citee	

---

text, investigated with a view to indicating the varieties of scribal substitution that may underlie the variant readings in the manuscripts, see J. Cowen and G. Kane, eds, *Geoffrey Chaucer: the Legend of Good Women* (East Lansing, MI, 1995).

[47] Manly and Rickert, V, 172.

[48] Ibid., V, 171–2.

Amanges cristeñ folke and Jwrye   489
Among cristeñ folk and Jewerye
Amonges Cristene folk a Jewerye

Sustened by a lorde of yat cuntre   490
Sustened by a lord of þat cuntre
Sustened by a lord of that contree

For foule vsure and lucre of vylanye   491
For foule vsure and lucre of vilanye
For foule usure and lucre of vilenye

Hatfull to criste and and to his companye   492
Hateful to Criste and to his companye
Hateful to Crist and to his compaigne

And thurgh ye strete meñ myȝht ride or wende   493
And thurgh þe strete meñ myght ride or wende
And thurgh the strete men myghte ride or wende

For it was fre and open at euery ende   494
For it was frende and open at euery ende
For it was fre and open at eyther ende

A litill scole of cristeñ folke yer stode   495
A litel scole of cristen folk there stode
A litle scole of Cristen folk ther stood

Doun at ye feryer ende in whiche yer wer   496
Douñ at þe ferther ende in whiche there were
Doun at the ferther ende in which ther were

Children an hepe y com of cristes blode   497
Childreñ an hepe y comeñ of cristes blode
Children an heep ycomen of Cristen blood

That lerned in yat scole ȝere by ȝere   498
þat lerned in þat scole yeer by yeer
That lerned in that scole yeer by yere

Suche maner doctrine as meñ vseth yer   499
Suche manere doctrine as men vse ther
Swich manere doctrine as men used there

This is to sey syngeñ and to rede   500
This is to sey to syng and to Rede
This to seyn to syngen and to rede

As smale childreñ done in here childhede   501
As smale children done in ther childehede
As smale children doon in hire childhede

Amonge yis childreñ was a wydwes soñ   502
Among these children was a widows sone
Among thise children was a wydwes sone

A litell clergiouñ vij ȝere of age   503
A litel Clergioñ vij yeer of age
A litel clergeon seven yeer of age

That day be day to scole was he wone   504
þat day by day to scole was he wone
That day by day to scole was his wone

And eke also where he sagh ye ymage   505
And eke also where he saw the ymag
And eke also where as he saugh th'ymage

Of cristes moder had he in vsage   506
Of Cristes moder hadde he in vsage
Of Cristes mooder hadde he in usage

And hym was tauȝht to knele a douñ and seye   507
And hym was taught to knele a doun and seye
As hym was taught to knele adoun and seye

His Aue marie as he goith by ye waye   508
His Aue mary as he goth by the weye
His Ave Marie as he goth by the weye

This passage consists of 165 words, 117 (or 70.9 per cent) of which Spirleng copied literatim, and 163 (or 98.8 per cent) of which he reproduced verbatim. He also added one word. Though the substantive differences between the Mm and Gl versions are relatively minor and infrequent, the passage again illustrates that in Spirleng's hands textual variation could be for the better as well as for the worse. The word he added was the second 'to' in line 500, which rectifies Mm's obvious error of omission, though Spirleng's own failure to retain the old inflexion in Mm 'syngen' left his version of the line metrically lame. Two other departures from the exemplar also affect the sense. In line 492 Spirleng put right Mm's plainly erroneous repetition of 'and', but in line 494 he stumbled over the exemplar's slightly odd abbreviation in 'fre' (f + r with an upward flourish). His eye must have been caught by 'ende' later in the line, and if his nonsensical 'For it was frende . . .' had been pointed out to him immediately after he had written it, he would doubtless have put it right. Otherwise, Spirleng once again gives a highly accurate rendering of what was before him in Mm, translated where necessary into his preferred orthographical system, and accepting (as the copyists of other *Canterbury Tales* manuscripts did at the same places) a number of readings which are unlikely to have been original (e.g. 'and', line 489; 'cristes', line 497).[49]

Study of several other passages along these lines reveals minor fluctuations in Spirleng's literatim and verbatim fidelity to his exemplar, and again shows him in the acts both of committing a variety of the usual scribal errors, and of emending when he happened to spot what he thought were (and often are) mistakes in Mm. The following table shows the number of words in the four passages mentioned, the number of words reproduced by Spirleng literatim, and the number verbatim:

Table 1   Number of words in each passage

Passage	Actual	Literatim	Verbatim
KtT 2773–92	144	102 (70.8%)	140 (97.2%)
MilT 3187–207	148	101 (68.2%)	143 (96.6%)
MerT 2028–50	181	125 (69.0%)	180 (99.4%)
CYT 922–41	176	105 (59.6%)	169 (96.0%)[50]

The total number of words in all six passages examined for the present purpose is 983: Spirleng copied 646 (65.7 per cent) of them literatim, and 958 (97.4 per cent) verbatim.

An extended comparison of the 10 000 or so lines of Chaucer's verse that Geoffrey Spirleng copied from Mm into Gl would undoubtedly provide many concrete examples of the exact operations of scribal error, together with a quantification of its frequency, areas of investigation otherwise generally restricted to hypothesis. It would moreover shed light on other phenomena even less accessible to textual critics, by demonstrating in some detail that a given copy is neither necessarily nor axiomatically to be regarded as inferior to its exemplar, and that locally, if not

[49] Manly and Rickert, VII, 159–60.

[50] The passage from the Canon's Yeoman's Tale is from Gl, fol. 112, col. b, the second section of the manuscript copied from Mm by Geoffrey Spirleng, after he (and Thomas) had used a different exemplar for the Chaucerian material occupying fols 47–102. The signs are that Spirleng's further access to Mm was brief, since the copying shows signs of haste, and the conversion of the text into the Gl spelling system is slightly less extensive than in fols 1–46 (see Golson, 'Spelling System', pp. 4–5). The use of abbreviations is also more noticeable on fols 103–15.

generally, it may sometimes be better.[51] One concomitant of this demonstration would be that scribal correction or emendation could be firmly established (again, rather than hypothesized) as a regular source of the widespread coincident variation that seriously hampers the application of recension, the 'shared error' method of textual criticism, in tracing the exact descent of writings transmitted in late Middle English. Though, like all of us, Geoffrey Spirleng made mistakes, he also made attempts (some successful, some not) to rectify errors left by his predecessors. How representative of Middle English scribal practices his procedures were remains to be seen, in the light of comparison with other surviving examples of exemplar and copy. The Mm text of the *Canterbury Tales* that Spirleng inherited, and went on to reincarnate rather accurately in his own idiolect as Gl, provides all too ample evidence of the 'miswriting' and 'mismetring' (and worse) that Chaucer feared was the fate awaiting his verses. The poet might at least have been gratified to learn that, in the hands of another professional literate layman like himself, the process was not altogether irreversible.[52]

---

[51] It may eventually be necessary to qualify such assertions as 'the axiomatic deterioration of scribal transmission'; see G. Kane and E. T. Donaldson, eds, *Piers Plowman: the B Version* (London, 1975), p. 213.

[52] I am most grateful to the following for advice, information and practical assistance in pursuing and presenting this study: Dr A. I. Doyle, Dr J. Cottis (Archivist, Magdalen College, Oxford), Dr T. Hobbs (Keeper of Special Collections, Glasgow University Library), Miss J. Kennedy (County Archivist) and her staff at the Norfolk Record Office, Professor Colin Richmond, Dr Anthony Smith, Dr Jeremy Smith, Dr P. N. R. Zutshi, and the editors. Documents in the archives of Magdalen College, Oxford, are cited by permission of the President and Fellows.

CHAPTER SEVEN

A Testimonye of Verye Ancient Tyme? Some Manuscript Models for the Parkerian Anglo-Saxon Type-Designs

Peter J. Lucas

In modern libraries manuscripts and early printed books often have to be consulted in distinct reading rooms, even when they are the products of the same period, for example, 1455–1700.[1] Such bibliographical segregation did not usually apply at the time they were produced.[2] In late-fifteenth-century library catalogues, for example, manuscripts and printed books appear together, and they were sometimes bound together; some early printed books were passed on to a rubricator to be finished off by hand. Sometimes printed text and manuscript copy were combined according to a plan made in advance, and manuscript copies continued to be made even from printed texts.[3] While 'the advent of printing transformed the conditions under which texts were produced, distributed and consumed, . . . the *ars artificialiter scribendi* was first and foremost a duplicating process'.[4] The term itself could apply to the skills taught by writing masters before it came to be understood as 'the art of writing by mechanical means'.[5] In presenting their texts early printers such as Caxton:

---

[1] As well as the editors I should like to thank the friends and colleagues who have been most helpful while I was working on this essay. In the Parker Library I enjoyed constant courtesy and helpfulness from Mrs Gill Cannell, and Mrs Catherine Hall and Professor Ray Page each contributed information and encouragement in their different ways. On typographical matters I have had practical assistance from Mr John Lane, Mr James Mosley and Professor Dr Hendrik Vervliet. Dr David McKitterick kindly read a draft version and saved me from a number of errors, as well as suggesting additional references. When an earlier version of this essay was delivered at the Seminar in the History of the Book to 1500 in March 1996, other members of the seminar made constructive comments, and MBP in particular (all unwitting) offered stimulating discussion afterwards. I am solely responsible for the views expressed and for any errors.

[2] Ironically, in view of the topic of the present essay, an exception seems to have been the library of Corpus Christi (then Bene't) College, Cambridge, where Parker's bequest of his library was housed: see B. Dickins, 'The Making of the Parker Library', *TCBS*, 6 (1972–76), 19–34, at 29. Cf. Cotton's similar distinction, still 'fairly novel', in his library: see C. G. C. Tite, *The Manuscript Library of Sir Robert Cotton*, Panizzi Lectures 1993 (London, 1994), p. 99.

[3] See N. F. Blake, 'Manuscript to Print', in *Book Production and Publishing 1375–1475*, ed. J. Griffiths and D. Pearsall (Cambridge, 1989), pp. 403–32.

[4] E. L. Eisenstein, *The Printing Press as an Agent of Change. Communications and Cultural Transformations in Early-Modern Europe* (Cambridge, 1979), p. 168.

[5] A. Swierk, 'Was bedeutet "ars artificialiter scribendi"?', in *Der gegenwärtige Stand der Gutenberg-Forschung*, ed. H. Widmann (Stuttgart, 1972), pp. 243–50.

imitated the presentation and letter forms of manuscripts. For example, his vernacular texts are printed in a Flemish bâtarde type, while his liturgical and religious works are in a Gothic type; he did not employ title pages and only rarely did he include foliation; and his books were made up of quires marked with signature letters to ensure a correct binding sequence.[6]

The transformation brought about by printing was essentially an evolutionary process,[7] and written material was still distributed in manuscript form rather than print in the seventeenth century.[8]

Despite this large chronological overlap between the two means of distributing written text, in the case of Old English the process of transferring written material into printed form was what Anglo-Saxonists would probably prefer not to call a retarded development, beginning in 1566 with the first book printed with special Anglo-Saxon characters by John Day (1522–84).[9] There were two principal reasons for this delayed start, the first socio-historical, and the second technical.

First, it was not until the Elizabethan period that there was sufficient revival of interest in Anglo-Saxon materials, chiefly, in the first place, for the light that they might shed on the Church in England, which Henry VIII had separated from Rome. Day worked under the auspices of Matthew Parker, archbishop of Canterbury (1559–75),[10] who was much concerned to establish older precedents for the liturgy and doctrine being adopted in association with the new Book of Common Prayer and the establishment of the *Ecclesia Anglicana*. This thinking is clearly reflected in the title of Day's first production using Anglo-Saxon types: *A Testimonie of Antiquitie* (*STC* 159 and 159.5), which includes text and translation of Ælfric's *Sermo de Sacrificio in die Pascae* probably edited jointly by Parker and John Joscelyn (1529–1603), Parker's Latin secretary.[11]

Secondly, the revolution in written communication brought about by printing was still in progress in the sixteenth century, and, much more than manuscripts, brought

[6] Blake, 'Manuscript to Print', p. 404.

[7] Cf. Eisenstein, *Printing Press*, p. 22.

[8] H. Love, *Scribal Publication in Seventeenth-Century England* (Oxford, 1993).

[9] On whom see C. L. Oastler, *John Day, the Elizabethan Printer* (Oxford, 1975), and for his earlier career L. P. Fairfield, 'The Mysterious Press of "Michael Wood" (1553–1554)', *The Library*, 5th ser., 27 (1972), 220–32. The date of publication (1566?) of *A Testimonie* is problematical; it must have been after 20 October 1566, when Nicholas Robinson, bishop of Bangor, was consecrated, and before 26 June 1568, when Thomas Young, archbishop of York, died; cf. 1st edn sigs ¶1ʳ–¶2ᵛ; 2nd edn K3ʳ–4ᵛ.

[10] See *DNB*, s.n., and V. J. K. Brook, *A Life of Archbishop Parker* (Oxford, 1962); for a full collection of materials see John Strype, *The Life and Acts of Matthew Parker* (London, 1711), repr. in 3 vols (Oxford, 1821).

[11] See J. Bromwich, 'The First Book Printed in Anglo-Saxon Type', *TCBS*, 3 (1959–63), 265–91. For brief notices of Joscelyn see *DNB*, s.n., and C. H. Cooper and T. Cooper, *Athenae Cantabrigienses*, 2 vols (Cambridge, 1858–61), II, 366–7; for an overview see M. S. Hetherington, *The Beginnings of Old English Lexicography* (Spicewood, TX, 1980), pp. 25–51; see also nn. 31 and 32 below.

Englishmen into contact with the continent, because nearly all the tools of the printing trade were imported from there. Up to the 1570s continental craftsmen came to England because they alone could perform some of the more highly skilled tasks.[12] Although roman types were first used in England in 1509,[13] their use, long familiar on the continent, did not become widespread in England until the middle of the sixteenth century. Pica Roman first appeared in 1553.[14] The first book in the English language printed entirely in Roman type appeared in 1555.[15] Roman type-designs, which ultimately derived from the letter-forms of the continental Caroline minuscule script used at the end of the Anglo-Saxon period, offered the potential to print Old English alongside early Modern English or Latin, but distinctively, if special sorts were made for the specifically Anglo-Saxon characters. This potential for printing a language which used the Roman alphabet but required special sorts was exploited for Irish too,[16] and, as noted below, special sorts were cut for some early spelling reformers, though in this case to match italic founts. The purpose of the present essay is to observe and scrutinize one particular aspect of the process of transferring Old English from script to print, the dependence of the designs for the first Anglo-Saxon types on manuscript models.[17] Since the editors of *A Testimonie*, and Joscelyn in particular, were dealing directly with manuscript sources it is inherently likely that some of these manuscripts provided the basis for the models used for the type-designs.

Anglo-Saxon scribes used two alphabets: one for writing Latin, Caroline minuscule, and one for writing Old English, Anglo-Saxon square minuscule. They varied 'the forms of a, d, e, f, g, h, r, and s, according to the language they were writing', as, for example, in Oxford, Corpus Christi College, MS 197, art. 1 (*s.* x^2), a bilingual copy of the Rule of St Benedict.[18] This manuscript, a relatively early one compared with the majority of bilingual texts that have survived, distinguishes between Latin and Old English particularly scrupulously. 'For example, in Old English only, c and o begin, like e, with a slight projection or horn to the left, the bow of p is open, and the end of the bow of t is often curled up. Another less conspicuous difference is in the form of the shaft of t, which is more curved in Old English than it is in Latin.' In the eleventh century Anglo-Saxon rounded a contrasted with Latin Caroline a, Anglo-Saxon round-backed d contrasted with Latin Caroline d, Anglo-

---

[12] See esp. H. Carter, 'Huguenot Typography', *Proc. Huguenot Society of London*, 21 (1970), 532–44.

[13] T. B. Reed, *A History of the old English Letter Foundries*, rev. A. F. Johnson (London, 1952), p. 40.

[14] W. C. Ferguson, *Pica Roman Type in Elizabethan England* (Aldershot, 1989), p. 9.

[15] Carter, 'Huguenot Typography', p. 538 and n. 30.

[16] See D. McGuinne, *Irish Type Design* (Blackrock, Co. Dublin, 1992), and for Parker's interest in it B. Dickins, 'The Irish Broadside of 1571', *TCBS*, 1 (1949–53), 48–60.

[17] Although I differ from G. Wakeman ('The Design of Day's Saxon', *The Library*, 5th ser., 22 (1967), 283–98) in many particulars, his pioneering approach was praiseworthy.

[18] Ker, *Catalogue*, no. 353 and pl. II; see also p. xxvi for the following quotations.

Saxon horned **e** contrasted with Latin round-backed **e**, Anglo-Saxon long **f** contrasted with Latin Caroline tall **f**, Anglo-Saxon insular **ȝ** contrasted with Latin Caroline **g**, Anglo-Saxon **h** with the limb turned outwards contrasted with Latin Caroline **h** where the limb turns inwards, Anglo-Saxon insular long **r** contrasted with Latin Caroline short **r**, and Anglo-Saxon insular long **s** often contrasted with Latin tall **s** or round **s**. Later these distinctions were adhered to less strictly. 'In the twelfth century [scribes] usually employ[ed] the caroline form of **a** in Old English texts, and often ma[d]e no distinction in the forms of **e** and **h**, generalizing the forms used in Latin texts.' The letters **d**, **f**, **g**, **r**, and **s**, were generally distinguished. There were also the additional letter symbols, **þ**, **ð**, and **p**, 'thorn', 'eth'[19] and 'wynn'. As for capitals Anglo-Saxon scribes used square capitals or uncials rather than the rustic capitals generally used in Latin texts.[20]

When Anglo-Saxon script is viewed from a later period it is often noted that Anglo-Saxon dotted **y** is used in a given Old English text. In Anglo-Saxon manuscripts dotted **y** is used in both Latin and Old English. Sometimes scribes made a distinction, using rounded **y** for Latin, where it is rare but occurs from time to time, and straight-limbed dotted **y** for Old English, where it is, of course, frequent as a vowel-symbol, and this distinction may be observed in London, BL, Cotton MS Tiberius B.I, fol. 35, line 14, in 'babylonia' as against 'cyng', but it breaks down in 'þy ylcan' where rounded **y** is used for 'ylcan' (fol. 39, line 18) and is hardly a discernible trend.[21] Similarly, the 'undotted i' of Old English texts viewed with hindsight is a feature of both Latin and Old English in the original manuscripts.

From the sixteenth century onwards many transcripts were made of Anglo-Saxon materials. The first person to take a significant interest in Anglo-Saxon texts in this period was Robert Talbot (*c.*1505–58),[22] whose notebook survives as Cambridge, Corpus Christi College, MS 379.[23] A feature of Talbot's transcripts is that while he wrote Old English carefully, mostly letter by letter, he did not normally distinguish Latin and Old English letter-forms as in Anglo-Saxon manuscripts. His partial

---

[19] I have preferred the traditional (Icelandic) name for this letter, although the Anglo-Saxon name for it was **ðæt** 'that'.; see F. C. Robinson, 'Syntactical Glosses in Latin Manuscripts of Anglo-Saxon Provenance', *Speculum*, 48 (1973), 451.

[20] Ker, *Catalogue*, p. xxxvi.

[21] Dotted **y** is a feature of Middle English script through to early printed texts; cf. *OED*, s.v. Y.

[22] See *DNB*, s.n.; A. B. Emden, *A Biographical Register of the University of Oxford A.D. 1501 to 1540* (Oxford, 1974), p. 555; Ker, *Catalogue*, p. l; idem, 'Medieval Manuscripts from Norwich Cathedral Priory', in his *Books, Collectors and Libraries: Studies in the Medieval Heritage*, ed. A. G. Watson (London, 1985), ch. 18, esp. p. 246, n. 5, and pl. 29a; and T. Graham, 'Robert Talbot's "Old Saxonice Bede": Cambridge University Library MS Kk.3.18 and the "Alphabetum Narwagicum" of British Library, Cotton MS Domitian A.IX', in *Books and Collectors 1200–1700: Essays presented to Andrew Watson*, ed. J. P. Carley and C. G. C. Tite (London, 1997), pp. 295–316. After Talbot's death his books were acquired by Parker, see Strype, *Life of Parker*, p. 529.

[23] See M. R. James, *A Descriptive Catalogue of the Manuscripts in the Library of Corpus Christi College Cambridge*, 2 vols (Cambridge, 1912), II, 226–7.

transcript of Ælfric's Preface to his Old English translation of the biblical book of Genesis occurs in Corpus 379 on fols 10–12ᵛ, copied from London, BL, Cotton MS Claudius B.IV,[24] before it lost its first leaf. As can be seen from Plate 18 he did not distinguish Latin/Old English **d**, **f**, **g**, **r**, **s**, but he did reproduce the Old English special letters, as **æ**, **þ**, **ð**, **ƿ**, dotted y – **þ** (not illustrated) being rare only because the scribe of Claudius B.IV rarely used it. Once, however, Talbot does reproduce Anglo-Saxon **s**, on fol. 10ᵛ, line 15, in 'sæde', a tell-tale aberration which suggests he was making a conscious effort to avoid specific Anglo-Saxon forms of familiar letters.

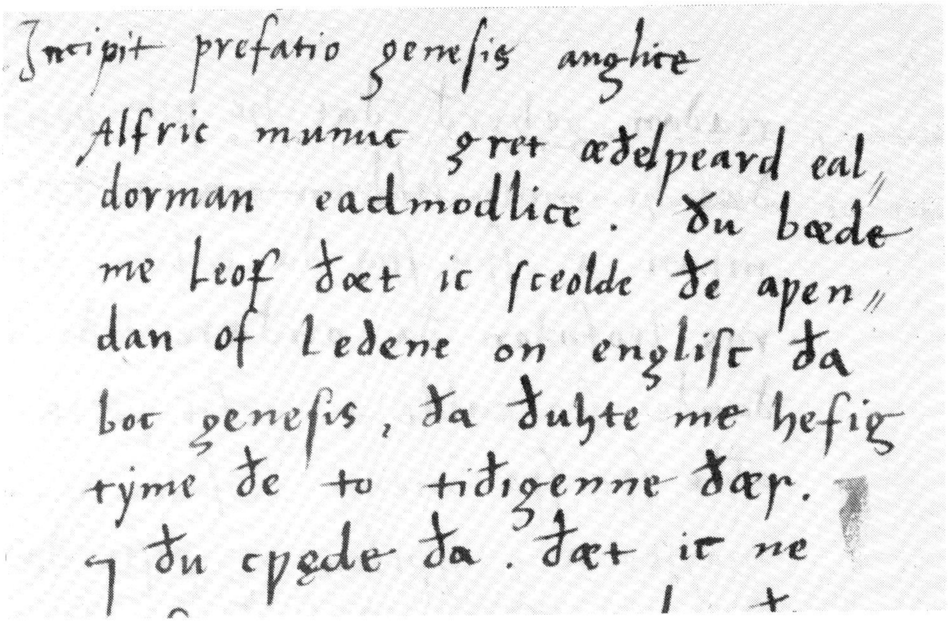
Incipit prefatio genesis anglice
Alfric munuc gret æðelƿeard eal
dorman eadmodlice. ðu bæde
me leof ðæt ic sceolde ðe aƿen//
dan of Ledene on englisc ða
boc genesis, ða ðuhte me hefig
tyme ðe to tiðigenne ðær.
7 ðu cƿede ða. ðæt ic ne

Plate 18 Cambridge, Corpus Christi College, MS 379, fol. 10, lines 1–8. Robert Talbot: Transcript of Ælfric's Preface to Genesis from London, BL, Cotton MS Claudius B.IV

If so, he was certainly bucking the trend. When his contemporary, Robert Recorde (*c.*1510–58), only five years younger than Talbot, annotated the thirteenth-century chronicle in Cambridge, Corpus Christi College, MS 138 with passages from the *Anglo-Saxon Chronicle* he used Anglo-Saxon letter-forms, **d** (sometimes), **f**, **g**, **r**, **s** (with occasional lapses), as well as the Old English special letters **æ**, **þ**, **ð**, **ƿ**, dotted y (see Pl. 19), and his manner of writing Old English is endorsed in a neat italic script

[24] See C. R. Dodwell and P. Clemoes, *The Old English Illustrated Hexateuch: British Museum Cotton Claudius B.IV*, EEMF, 18 (Copenhagen, 1974). For the text see S. J. Crawford, *The Old English Version of the Heptateuch, Ælfric's Treatise on the Old and New Testament and his Preface to Genesis*, EETS (OS), 160 (1922), pp. 76–80; Talbot transcribes Crawford's lines 1–41, 113–14.

of *s.* xvi² on the front endleaf (fol. [i]ᵛ): 'Robertus Recorde erat qui notauit hunc librum Characterib⟨us⟩ Saxonicis'.²⁵ The handwriting of this note, with its long descenders turned sharply and fully to the left, and its ascenders turned curvaciously to the right, resembles that of the annotations in Cambridge, Corpus Christi College, MS 583, 'Matthew Parker's Parchment Roll', an account of the great moments in the archbishop's life, written by an amanuensis but amended with great care in another hand which may well be that of Parker himself; the content is certainly personal and it is difficult to imagine how it could have been written by anyone else unless Parker were standing over him telling him not only the content but where to write the amendments.

Whether or not Parker wrote the note in Corpus 138 it has the tone of authority that bears his stamp, and indicates a complete reversal of policy towards reproducing Anglo-Saxon script from that manifested by Talbot. For under Parker's aegis great care was taken to imitate the distinctive letter forms to be found in Anglo-Saxon manuscripts. Parker's encouragement of this development can be seen from his letter to Sir William Cecil (later Lord Burghley) dated 24 January 1565/6, in which (to the consternation of modern conservationists) Parker is contemplating furnishing a Psalter with a more attractive opening folio to be taken from within the book:

> and methought the leaf going before the xxvith psalm would have been a meet beginning before the whole Psalter, having David sitting with his harp or psaltery, *decachordo vel ogdochordo*, with his ministers with *tubis ductilibus et cymbalis sonoris*, &c., and then the first psalm written on the back side: which I was in mind to have caused Lylye to have counterfeited in antiquity, &c., but that I called to remembrance that ye have a singular artificer to adorn the same, which your honour shall do well to have the monument finished, or else I will cause it to be done and remitted again to your library.²⁶

Parker endorsed the practice of imitating Anglo-Saxon script when he added his own 'tremulous hand' glosses on a supply leaf in Cambridge, Corpus Christi College, MS 178, p. 31.²⁷ In the Parkerian household (as well, apparently, as Cecil's) special

²⁵ Corpus 138 contains 'Alexandri Essebiensis epitome historiae Britanniae a Christo nato at annum 1255' annotated by Recorde with Old English from the copy of the *Anglo-Saxon Chronicle* in Cotton MS Tiberius B.I. Noted by R. I. Page, 'Anglo-Saxon Texts in Early Modern Transcripts', *TCBS*, 6 (1973), 69–85, esp. 75–9, and cf. also T. Graham, 'The Beginnings of Old English Studies: Evidence from the Manuscripts of Matthew Parker', in *Occasional Papers of the Centre for Medieval Studies Tokyo*, 1 (1997), 31.

²⁶ J. Bruce and T. T. Perowne, ed. *Correspondence of Matthew Parker, D.D. Archbishop of Canterbury*, Parker Society (Cambridge, 1853), no. 194. As stated in *The life off the 70. Archbishopp off Canterbury . . . Englished* ([Zürich, C. Froschauer?], 1574; *STC* 19292a), C1ᵛ, Parker's conservation policy, 'to the ende that these antiquities might last longe and be carefullye kept', was such that 'he caused them beinge broughte into one place to be well bounde and trymly couered'. For Parker's treatment of his books, see R. I. Page, *Matthew Parker and his Books* (Kalamazoo, 1993). On Peter Lyly, see A. G. Feuillerat, *John Lyly* (Cambridge, 1910), pp. 17–20 and 516–20 (his will).

²⁷ Page, *Matthew Parker*, pp. 54, 98, pl. 57; Page thought that the supply leaf was itself written by

Plate 19   Cambridge, Corpus Christi College, MS 138, p. 25, top right-hand corner. Robert Recorde: Copy-Extract from the *Anglo-Saxon Chronicle* used to annotate a later chronicle

scribes were employed to 'counterfeit' Anglo-Saxon script 'in antiquity'. Such scribes could be brought in specially to write a passage of Old English in a Latin work. A particularly clear example occurs in Cambridge, Corpus Christi College, MS 100 (*s.* xvi[2]). Pages 261–319 contain the *Annals of St Neots*, copied from Cambridge, Trinity College, MS R.7.28 (770).[28] *Bede's Death Song* occurs on p. 280 (see Pl. 20) in an imitation Anglo-Saxon minuscule apparently written in (in a darker shade of ink) after the main scribe had left a space for it, but that space was not enough so the last three words were added in the bottom margin together with the Latin paraphrase. The Latin script of this addition shows that the scribe of the Old English was not the same as the main scribe. There is a similar instance (possibly by another scribe, who starts with Caroline f and uses Caroline **a** throughout) on p. 29 of the same manuscript, where *Bede's Death Song* in Old English has been added in another hand in space provided by the main scribe; the same hand as wrote the Old English added 'Quod ita latine sonat'. The text in this instance is Symeon of Durham's 'Liber de exordio atque procursu Dunelmensis ecclesiae' (pp. 1–122) copied from Durham, Dean and Chapter Library, MS A.IV.36 (formerly Phillipps 9374; *s.* xii/xiii),[29] given to Parker by Robert Horne, dean of Durham, in 1568.[30] In this manuscript *Bede's Death Song* occurs on fol. 25[v], written by the main scribe, who imitates Anglo-Saxon insular letters, but makes the tell-tale mistake of writing

Parker, but the difference in the shade of the ink between the main text and the glosses (which are paler) indicates that they were written at different times and could therefore have been written by different hands, as argued by Graham, 'Beginnings', p. 46, n. 50. On the medieval 'tremulous hand' see C. Franzen, *The Tremulous Hand of Worcester* (Oxford, 1991).

[28] See D. Dumville and M. Lapidge, *The Annals of St Neots with Vita Prima Sancti Neoti*, The Anglo-Saxon Chronicle A Collaborative Edition 17 (Cambridge, 1985), and my description of MS R.7.28 for the series Anglo-Saxon Manuscripts in Microfiche Facsimile, forthcoming.

[29] See J. C. Davies, 'A Recovered Manuscript of Symeon of Durham', *Durham University Jnl*, **44** (1950–51), 22–8. For additional information about the text of *Bede's Death Song* in this manuscript I am grateful to Dr Ian Doyle.

[30] I am grateful to Professor David Rollason for supplying me with a print-out of the introduction to his forthcoming edition of Symeon's *Liber Dunelmensis* where information about this manuscript enabled me to identify it as the exemplar of the text in Corpus 100.

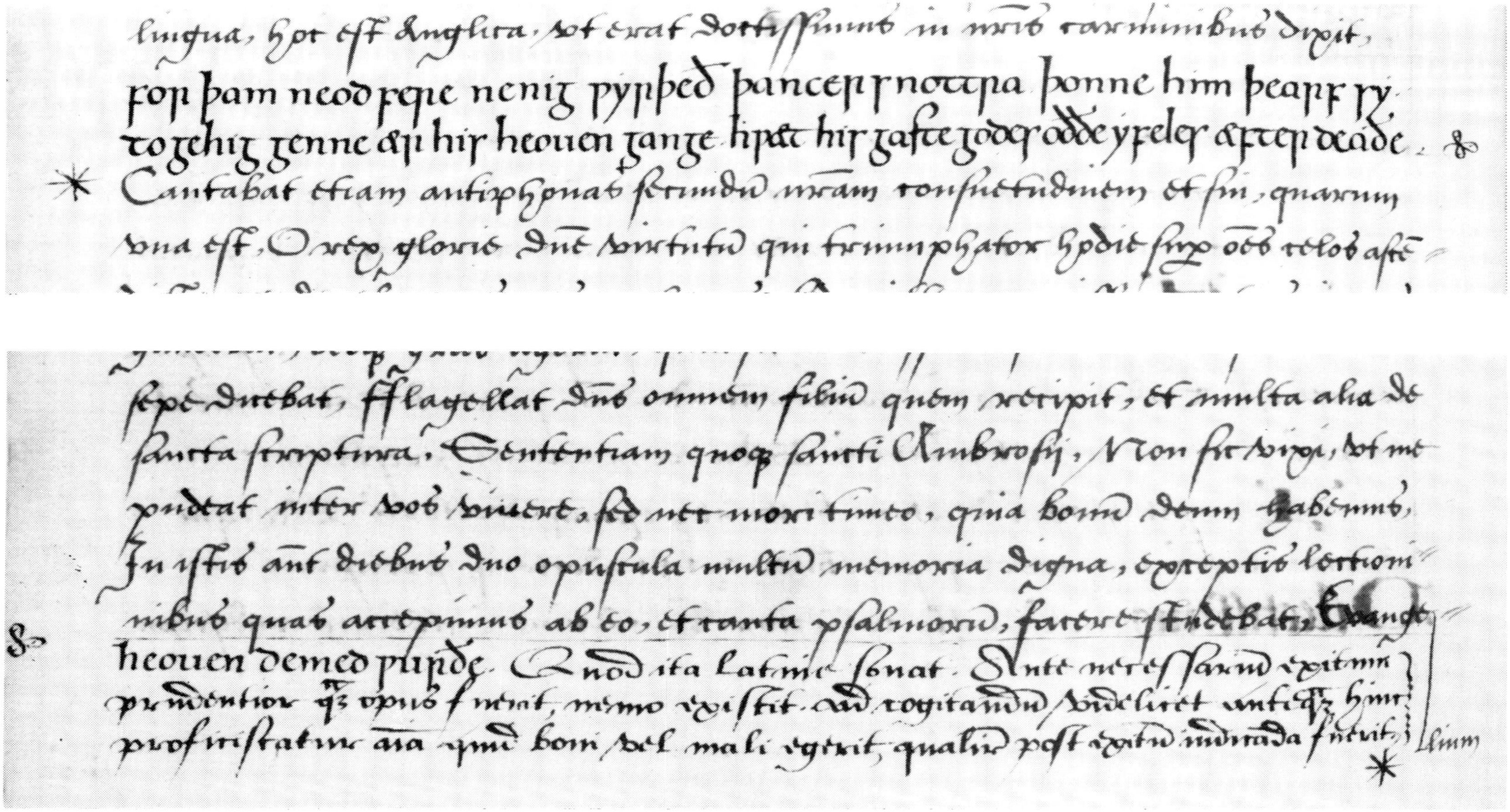

Plate 20 Cambridge, Corpus Christi College, MS 100, extracts from the bottom half of p. 280. Transcript of the Annals of St Neots, with *Bede's Death Song* copied in another hand

'þancer' with Gothic r. It would appear that, since this mistake is taken over in both versions of *Bede's Death Song* in Corpus 100, they are both based on the text in this Durham manuscript; presumably someone in Parker's household (rightly) thought it a better text than that in Trinity MS R.7.28, even though neither is Anglo-Saxon in date.

The most important of Parker's associates was Joscelyn. Although not a calligraphic penman, Joscelyn copied Old English frequently and made a dictionary that served as a foundation for that later published by Somner in 1659.[31] His notebook, much damaged by fire in 1731, survives as London, BL, Cotton MS Vitellius D. VII,[32] and contains, *inter alia*, his transcript of Ælfric's second letter to Wulfstan (archbishop of York 1002–23),[33] one of the texts from which excerpts appear in *A Testimonie of Antiquitie*. The surviving part of his transcript corresponding to that in *A Testimonie* occurs on fols 5–6 (see Pl. 21). As the reading *of þam gastlicum stane* indicates,[34] both derive from Oxford, Bodleian Library, MS Junius 121, fol. 117ᵛ, but since the beginning and end of the passage used for *A Testimonie* are marked in the manuscript with a cross and asterisk respectively, presumably by Joscelyn, it seems likely that the extract for the printed book was made before Joscelyn made his own transcript, which, unlike the extract in *A Testimonie*, does not omit Fehr's §96. Since Joscelyn played a vital role in the editing of *A Testimonie* it is important to examine how he treated Anglo-Saxon script. As can be seen from Pl. 21, although he did not distinguish a or d, he did distinguish the following Anglo-Saxon letters: f, g, r, long s (with occasional tall s), t, and the special sorts þ, ð, p. As noted above the distinction of Old English t from Latin t is rare in Anglo-Saxon manuscripts, and those cited above were apparently not used by Parker's household, but there is one source in particular where Joscelyn is likely to have seen this distinction. Cambridge, Corpus Christi College, MS 190 contains both the Latin and the Old English text of Ælfric's second letter to Wulfstan, and these texts (on p. 155, line 1–p. 156, line 22 and p. 341, line 12–p. 343, line 12 respectively) were seen by the editors of *A Testimonie*; indeed, a passage erased in Cambridge, Corpus Christi College, MS 265 on p. 177, lines 18–21 has been

---

[31] William Somner, *Dictionarium Saxonico-Latino-Anglicum. Voces, phrasesque præcipuas Anglo-Saxonicas* (Oxford, 1659); facs. ed. R. C. Alston, English Linguistics 1500–1800, 247 (Menston, 1970). Joscelyn's manuscript dictionary is London, BL, Cotton MSS Titus A.XV, XVI, on which see J. L. Rosier, 'The Sources of John Joscelyn's Old English-Latin Dictionary', *Anglia*, 78 (1960), 28–39. On Joscelyn see also n. 11 above, J. Bately, 'John Joscelyn and the Laws of the Anglo-Saxon Kings', in *Words, Texts and Manuscripts: Studies in Anglo-Saxon Culture Presented to Helmut Gneuss*, ed. M. Korhammer (Cambridge, 1992), pp. 435–66, A. Lutz, 'Das Studium der angelsächsischen Chronik im 16. Jahrhundert: Nowell und Joscelyn', *Anglia*, 100 (1982), 301–56, and R. I. Page, 'The Sixteenth-Century Reception of Alfred the Great's Letter to his Bishops', *Anglia*, 110 (1992), 36–64, esp. 47–8, 54.

[32] See J. S. Gale, 'John Joscelyn's Notebook: a Study of the Contents and Sources of B.L., Cotton MS. Vitellius D. VII', unpublished M.Phil thesis, University of Nottingham, 1978.

[33] B. Fehr, *Die Hirtenbriefe Ælfrics* (Hamburg, 1914, repr. suppl. P. Clemoes, Darmstadt, 1966), Brief III. The excerpts in the *Testimonie* correspond to Fehr's §§86–95, 97–109.

[34] Fehr, *Hirtenbriefe*, §105.

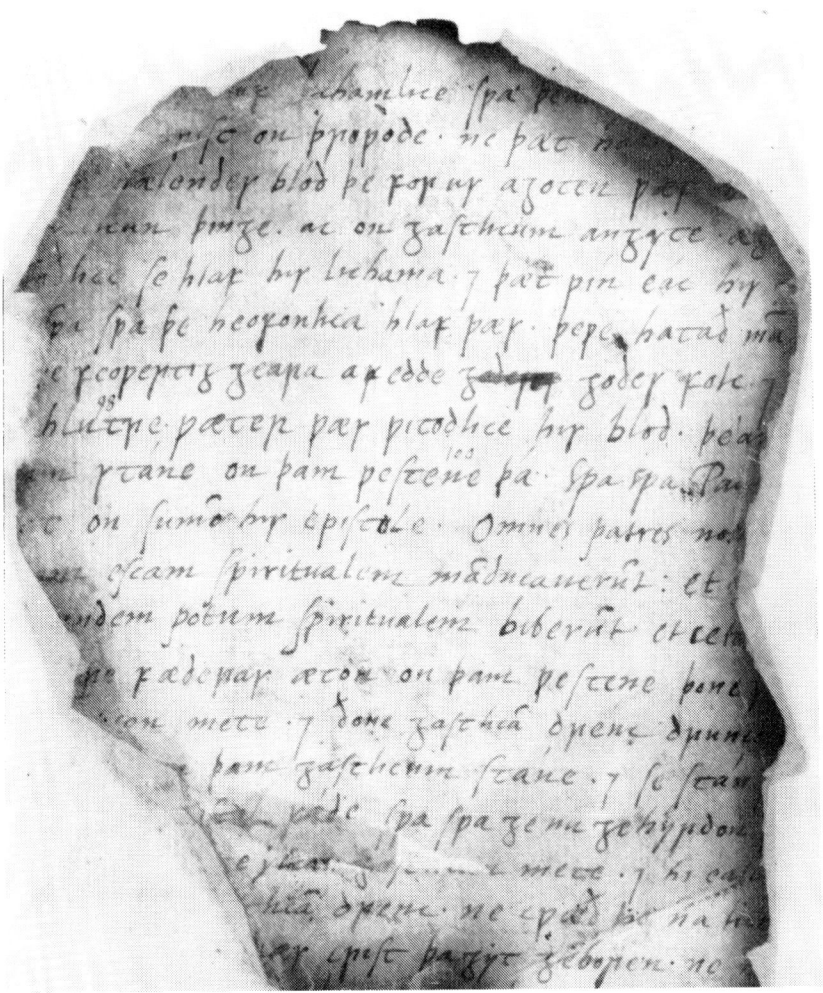

Plate 21   London, British Library, Cotton MS Vitellius D.VII, fol. 6. John Joscelyn's transcript of Ælfric's 2nd Letter to Wulfstan in Old English

supplied, with explanatory annotation in the margin by Joscelyn, from Corpus 190. Pages 341–2 of Corpus 190 have a membrane tag attached for ease of finding the Old English passage used for the printed book, and on p. 342 there is a cross-reference to p. 156 where the equivalent Latin passage is to be found; p. 156 also has a cross-reference to p. 342 (see Pl. 22(a)). In the Latin on p. 156 the stem of Latin t is often written with a c-stroke that shows above the head-stroke (e.g., Pl. 22(a): 'pluit', 'fluxit'), whereas on p. 342 (written by a different scribe) the stem of Old English t is a c-stroke that more or less consistently does not rise above the head-stroke (e.g., Pl. 22(b): 'ðæt', 'luttre'). Because these texts were equivalent Joscelyn evidently took

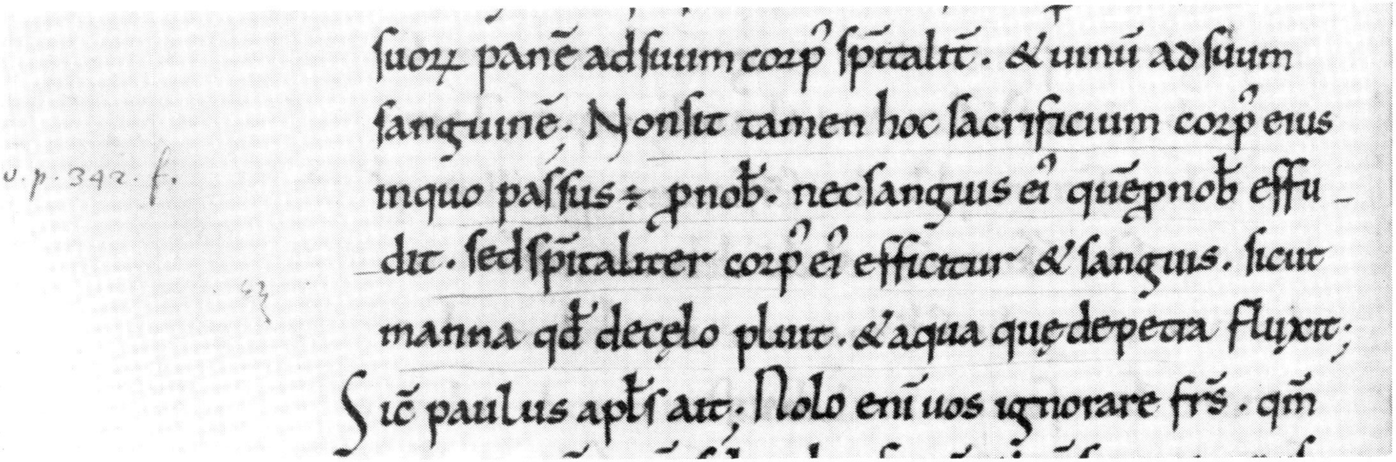

Plate 22(a) Cambridge, Corpus Christi College, MS 190, p. 156, lines 7–12. Latin text of Ælfric's 2nd Letter to Wulfstan with Joscelyn's underlining, cross-reference to the Old English text, and triquetra attention-mark

special note of the difference in script,[35] even though there is no distinction between Latin and Old English t on p. 342 itself (cf. Latin 'patres', line 28). The distinction between Latin and Old English t also occurs in sixteenth-century supply leaves in Cambridge, Corpus Christi College, MS 449 (e.g. fols 1ᵛ, 2ᵛ).

The process involved in having Anglo-Saxon types made was described by the first scholar, as opposed to printer, to carry out such a project, Franciscus Junius (1591– 1677).[36] In a letter of 8 May 1654 to John Selden (1584–1654) from Amsterdam Junius wrote:[37]

> In the meane while have I here Anglo-Saxonick types (I know not whether you call them Punchons) a cutting, and hope they will be matriculated, and cast within the space of seven or eight weeks at the furthest.[38]

In his deposition to a lawyer who was assisting him in his claim for remuneration from the family of the earl of Arundel, Junius's patron and employer until his death in 1646, Junius noted what must have been his considerable expenses ('les despens extraordinaires' as they had already been called in the sixteenth century) in equipping himself with printing types for the early Germanic languages;[39] he stated that prior to publication

> hee was first to undergoe the charges to have Anglo-Saxonike, Runike, & Gothike letters cutt & cast, to divulge his Observations the better,[40] by giving unto everie one of these dialects their owne auncient caracters & orthographie.

[35] By contrast, he ignored the distinction between Latin and Old English a. This distinction was perhaps one that the Elizabethans would have perceived as the difference between roman and italic.

[36] K. Aldrich, P. Fehl and R. Fehl, *Franciscus Junius, The Literature of Classical Art*, 2 vols (Berkeley, CA, 1991), I, xxvi–xlix; P. H. Breuker, 'On the Course of Franciscus Junius' Germanic Studies with Special Reference to Frisian', in *Aspects of Old Frisian Philology*, ed. R. H. Bremmer jr, G. van der Meer and O. Vries (Amsterdam, 1990), pp. 42–68; P. J. Lucas, *Franciscus Junius Cædmonis Monachi Paraphrasis Poetica Genesios ac praecipuarum Sacrae paginae Historiarum, abhinc annos M.LXX. Anglo-Saxonicè conscripta, & nunc primum edita* (Amsterdam, 1997), Introduction, §1.

[37] On Selden see *DNB*, s.n., also *The Bodleian Library in the Seventeenth Century: Guide to an Exhibition held during the Festival of Britain 1951* (Oxford, 1951), pp. 43–7.

[38] Pr. George Hickes, *Linguarum Vett. Septentrionalium Thesaurus* (Oxford, 1705), p. xliii. A specimen of Junius's types appears in *A Specimen of the Several Sorts of Letter given to the University by Dr. John Fell late Lord Bishop of Oxford. To which is Added the Letter Given by Mr. F. Junius* (Oxford, 1693), sigs D1–2. See further P. J. Lucas, 'Junius, his Printers and his Types: an Interim Report', in *Franciscus Junius and his Circle*, ed. R. H. Bremmer jr (Amsterdam, 1997).

[39] A transcript (by Reina Racz) of questions to Junius and his answers, Amsterdam Gemeentarchief, Not. Arch. 2435, pp. 37–47, was kindly lent to me by Dr Rolf Bremmer. The relevant part on p. 43 is quoted by Breuker, 'Junius' Germanic Studies', p. 50, and cf. also p. 68. It dates from 1654. Some idea of the costs involved in acquiring punches, etc., may be gauged from a letter from Henri du Tour (= Hendrik van der Keere, Ghent) to Christophe Plantin of 16 January 1576; cf. M. Rooses, ed. *Correspondance de Christophe Plantin*, 9 vols (Antwerp, 1883–1920, repr. Neudeln, Liechtenstein, 1968), V, 117–20, at 119.

[40] I.e. Junius's *Observationes in Willerami Abbatis Francicam Paraphrasin Cantici canticorum* (Amsterdam, Christoffel Cunrad, 1655); facs. edn N. Voorwinden (Amsterdam, 1992).

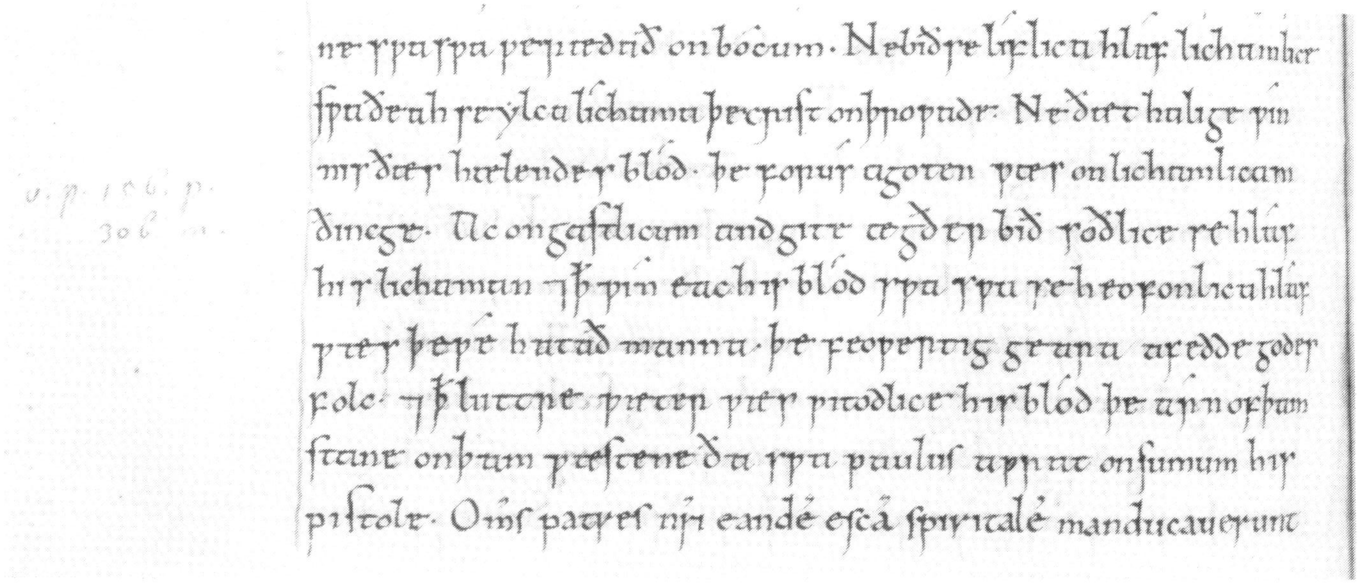

Plate 22(b) Cambridge, Corpus Christi College, MS 190, p. 342, lines 20–28. English text of Ælfric's 2nd Letter to Wulfstan with Joscelyn's cross-reference to the Latin text

Junius's threefold description of his 'types' ('cutting . . . matriculated, and cast') in his letter to Selden shows characteristic precision. 'Punchons' were punches, made of steel, at the end of which the required letter pattern was cut by hand, 'a most exacting occupation requiring the utmost expertness'.[41] Once the punch-cutter had been supplied with handwritten or hand-drawn designs,[42] the image of the character to be cut was transferred on to the face of the projected punch, and the inner shape was excavated and the outer shape filed away. The design on the punch could then be checked by means of a soot impression or 'smoke-proof'.[43] To 'matriculate' meant to make matrices by hammering the punch into small blocks of copper so as to make moulds from which types could be 'cast' in sufficient numbers to make up a fount adequate for the printer's needs.[44]

Only one design of Anglo-Saxon types was produced during Parker's lifetime. In body size it is a Great Primer, and it is used in *A Testimonie of Antiquitie* for the main Old English text. The method of assembling a complete set of types for a language such as Old English was to add special sorts to an existing fount.

> Of the capitals, eight only, including two diphthongs, are distinctively Saxon, the remaining eighteen letters being ordinary roman; while in the lower-case there are twelve Saxon letters as against fifteen of the roman.[45]

This statement applies to the type-specimen set out at the end of *A Testimonie* (Pl. 23(a)) for the reader's benefit, which shows 24 special sorts; besides the 12 lower-case letters there is a lower-case Tironian sign for 'and', and the abbreviation for *þæt*, and besides the eight upper-case letters, with two sorts for Æ, making nine in all, there is an upper-case Tironian sign for 'and'. Altogether there were 26 special sorts, of which this specimen lacks two. A *punctus versus* punctuation mark for a mid pause, to substitute for the semi-colon utilized in the *Testimonie* specimen, first appears in a specimen in William Lambarde's *Archaionomia* (*STC* 15142) printed by John Day in 1568 (Pl. 23(b)). The last special sort was a capital X, which first appears in a specimen (on sig. A1ᵛ) in Parker's edition (introduction by John Foxe) of the Old English gospels printed by John Day in 1571 (*STC* 2961), and is illustrated in the specimen from Parker's edition of Asser's *Ælfredi regis res gestæ* printed by John Day in 1574 (*STC* 863): see Pl. 23(c); although this latter specimen shows only 20

---

[41] S. Morison, in C. Enschedé, tr. and rev. H. Carter, *Typefoundries in the Netherlands from the Fifteenth to the Nineteenth Century by Charles Enschedé*, ed. L. Hellinga (Haarlem, 1978), p. 422.

[42] H. Carter, *A View of Early Typography up to about 1600* (Oxford, 1969), pp. 25, 43.

[43] Carter, *View of Typography*, frontispiece, also [Guillaume Le Bé II], *Sixteenth-Century French Typefounders: The Le Bé Memorandum*, ed. H. Carter (Paris, 1967), pl. [iv] following p. 52.

[44] For a reconstruction with photographs of the threefold process of making printing type see A. May, 'Making "Real" Type: Virtue Regained', *Printing Historical Society Bulletin*, 32 (1992), 4–8. For an account of the process contemporary with Parker see C. Plantin, *An Account of Calligraphy and Printing in the Sixteenth Century*, tr. R. Nash, intro. S. Morison (New York, 1949), pp. 3–4.

[45] Reed, *Old English Letter Foundries*, p. 91.

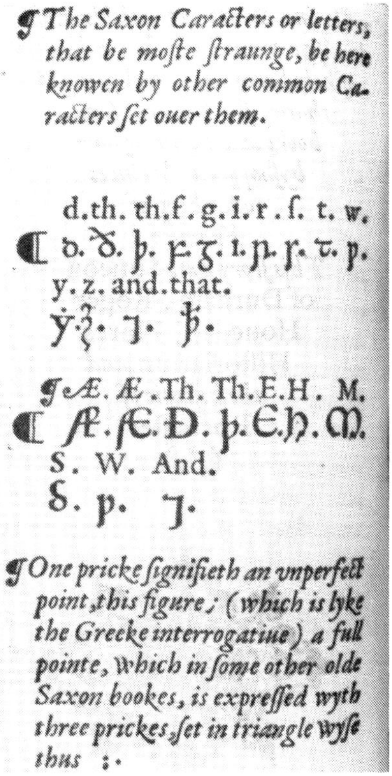

¶ *The Saxon Caraƈters or letters, that be moſte ſtraunge, be here knowen by other common Caraƈters ſet ouer them.*

d. th. th. f. g. i. r. ſ. t. w.

❡ ꝺ. ꝺ̄. þ. ꝼꞡ. ꞵ. ꝓ. ꞃ. ꞇ. ƿ.

y. z. and. that.

ẏꝽ. ⁊. ꝥ.

¶ Æ. Æ. Th. Th. E. H. M.

❡ Ǽ. ǽ. Ð. þ. Ꝺ. ꝺ. ꟽ.

S. W. And.

ꞅ. ƿ. ⁊.

¶ *One pricke ſignifieth an vnperfeƈt point, this figure; (which is lyke the Greeke interrogatiue) a full pointe, which in ſome other olde Saxon bookes, is expreſſed wyth three prickes, ſet in triangle wyſe thus ː·*

Plate 23(a)   Anglo-Saxon type specimen from *Testimonie of Antiquitie* (1566), sig. L7ᵛ (Cambridge, Corpus Christi College, SP.281)

special sorts, it has the benefit of clarity through citing the alphabet in both lower and upper cases in columns. The Anglo-Saxon sorts are combined with Pierre Haultin's English Roman,[46] which shows the same x-height, on a Great Primer body (four lines of Latin set in Roman in *A Testimonie* on sigs I3ʳ, I6ᵛ and I6ʳ). The body size is 112mm for 20 lines of printed matter, and the following sizes apply:[47]

Anglo-Saxon:	Body 112	Face 110 × 2.0: 4.3.
Roman:	Body 95	Face 92 × 2.0: 3.

---

[46] Illust. in H. D. L. Vervliet, *The Type Specimen of The Vatican Press 1628* (Amsterdam, 1967), no. 41, also F. Isaac, 'Elizabethan Roman and Italic Types', *The Library*, 4th ser., **14** (1933), 85–100, 212–28, fig. 5; for discussion see A. F. Johnson, 'Some Types Used by Paolo Manuzio', in his *Selected Essays on Books and Printing*, ed. P. H. Muir (Amsterdam, 1970), pp. 255–9.

[47] The first figure is the distance from the top of an ascender to the bottom of a descender multiplied by 20 to obtain the face size corresponding to the body size. The second figure is the x-height of a letter, and the third figure is the height of a capital letter. See further P. Gaskell, *A New Introduction to Bibliography* (Oxford, 1972), pp. 12–16.

Quò facilius lectores, nulloq̃ ferè negotio,
Saxonica legant, ac legentes aliquo modo edi-
ſcere poſſent, Alphabetum primò apponendum
duximus.

A	a	l	l	p	ƿ
b	b	ꟿ	m	x	x
c	c	n	n	ẏ	y
ꝺ	d	o	o	Æ	Æ
Є	e	p	p	Ǽ	æ
Ꝼ	f	q	q	Ð	th
ᵹ	g	ꞃ	r	ð	th
h	h	ꞃ	s	þ	th
ı	i	ꞇ	t	⁊	and
k	k	u	u	ꝥ	that

Comma apud illos hoc modo . notatur
Periodi forma hac ⁊ nos vſi ſumus.

❡ *Hæc igitur cum in perfacili cognitione verſentur, non eſt quòd
diffidant lectores ſe poſſe intelligere, ſi modo cupiant, ipſum
etenim literarum genus pro maiori partevel hodie vſitatũ,
Sermo itidem aut vulgaris eſt, aut nõ ità multùm a vulgari intelligentia remotus.*

Plate 23(b)   Anglo-Saxon type specimen from Lambarde's *Archaionomia* (1568), sig. B2ʳ
(Cambridge, Corpus Christi College, Y.7.14)

Anglo-Saxon 'types' are particularly interesting for the typographical historian
because they often offer evidence of punch-cutting at a time when most printers were
using founts that had been in existence for some time.[48] The punch-cutting involved
had to be particularly skilful because the special sorts to be cut should match all the

[48] Edward Rowe Mores, *A Dissertation upon English Typographical Founders and Founderies
(1778)*, ed. H. Carter and C. Ricks (Oxford, 1961), p. lxxii.

❧ Alphabetum Saxonicum ita defcriptum, vt fa-
cillima citiffimaȷ, inde ad eam perfectè legendam
ratio cuiuis eius linguȩ cupido patefiat.

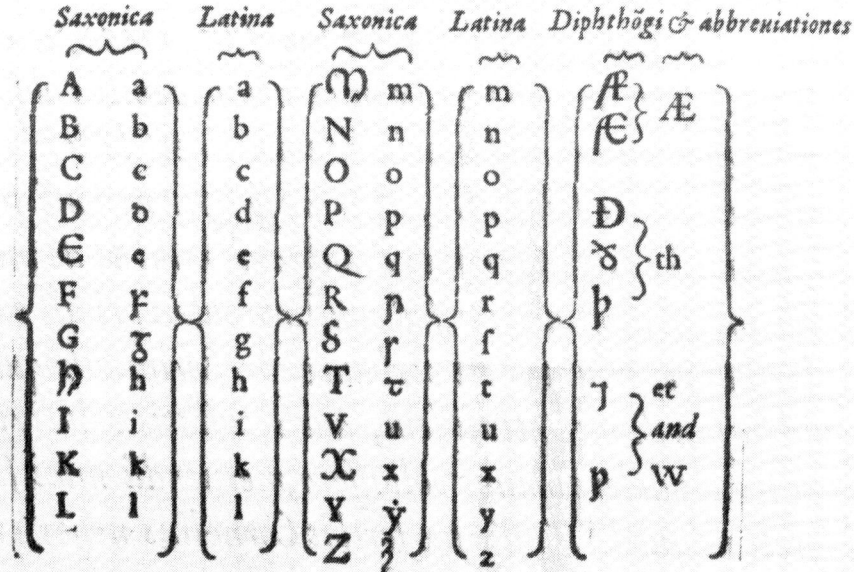

Præpofitiua particula ᵹe fæpiffimè apud Saxones eft fu-
perflua,& vbi communiter vtuntur duobus aut tribus nega-
tionibus,vt vehementiùs negent (ficut & Græci faciunt) tamen fecundùm phrafim Anglici fermonis, vnica tantùm
fufficit.

Plate 23(c)   Anglo-Saxon type specimen from *Ælfredi Regis Res Gestæ* (1574), sig. ¶1ᵛ
(Cambridge, Corpus Christi College, MS 176)

qualities of the design of the existing sorts.[49] There has therefore been considerable
interest in the statement in the preface to Parker's edition of Asser's *Ælfredi regis res
gestæ* (sig. A4ʳ):

> Iam verò cum Dayus Typographus primus (& omnium certè quod sciam solus)
> has formas æri inciderit: facilè quæ Saxonicis literis perscripta sunt, ijsdem typis

---

[49] For a discussion by a modern punch-cutter of what is involved in cutting Anglo-Saxon sorts
(lower-case ð, þ, and capital Ð) to match an existing fount see S. Nelson, 'Cutting Anglo-Saxon Sorts',
Fine Print, **12** (1986), 228–9.

diuulgabuntur. Quorum sanè lectio & veteris tibi linguæ, ac quondam domesticæ
memoriam renouabit, & haud paruam suppeditabit abstrusæ cognitionis
suppellectilem. Facile autem erit vocum vim, & verborum varietatem percipere,
præsertim cum tanta sit huius nostræ (qua nunc vtimur) linguæ & illius veteris
similitudo.

(For in as much as Day the printer [is the] first (and to my knowledge the only
one) [to have] indented these shapes (?moulds) in copper those things that are
written in Saxon letters will be easily published in these same types. The reading
of which [Anglo-Saxon letters in the new types] indeed will restore for you the
memory of the ancient but once familiar language, and will provide no little
household furniture for [previously] concealed knowledge. It will be easy to
perceive the meaning of utterances and the diversity of words, especially when
the similitude of this our language (which we now use) and of the old language is
so great.)

Two aspects of this important statement require discussion, first, the technical aspect
about the making of the first Anglo-Saxon types, and secondly, Parker's attitude to
their function.

In the past, as a result of a misreading of this statement in the preface to the Asser,
taking *æri inciderit* to mean 'cut from metal', Day has been credited with cutting the
Anglo-Saxon sorts in this fount; he was also credited with the Double Pica Roman
and Double Pica Italic found in the Asser,[50] both of which are attributable to
François Guyot.[51] This older reading caused some difficulty, as Parker's statement
might show ignorance of what Day really did,[52] or it could be interpreted as a form of
encouragement, giving Day the credit for what others in no position to object
actually did. It is now generally agreed that while Day may have organized the
making of the Anglo-Saxon types for Parker, he was a printer, not a punch-cutter,
nor even a type-founder.[53] If, however, *æri inciderit* is taken to mean 'indented in
copper' (i.e., made matrices) then the passage makes good sense. Although it is still
unlikely that Day made the matrices himself, he probably had them made and held
them, as suggested below. It was quite usual for a printer to be supplied with matrices

---

[50] See Reed, *Old English Letter Foundries*, pp. 90–93; Mores's *Dissertation*, pp. lxvi–lxviii; and
Wakeman's title, 'Day's Saxon'. For a suggestion leading to the present reading see Bromwich, 'First
Book', p. 271, n. 2.

[51] J. G. Dreyfus, *Type Specimen Facsimiles*, I (London, 1963), pl. 1.

[52] An informed writer might have been expected to signify the crucial information of what kind of
metal was involved; punch-cutters had to use steel, which could be relied upon to make an impression
when hammered into the (relatively soft) copper of the matrix. If *æri* means 'bronze' or 'brass' its use
suggests ignorance of the process of letter-founding.

[53] Oastler, *Day*, p. 35.

(which he could then hold) and for punch-cutters to hold the punches. As far as the punch-cutting was concerned, while the Anglo-Saxon sorts may have been cut in England, it is unlikely that they were cut by a native Englishman,[54] and it is possible that they were cut abroad.

At about the same time as Parker and his circle were looking to have Anglo-Saxon sorts made, two orthoepists also required and had made special sorts for their phonetic orthographic symbols which they wished to add to the roman alphabet for reforming English spelling. One was Sir Thomas Smith, Secretary of State (1548–49, 1572–76) and an associate of Parker's (and of Cecil's, with whom he was imprisoned in the Tower after the fall of Somerset in October 1549), whose *De recta & emendata Linguæ anglicæ scriptione, Dialogus* was printed at Paris by Robert (II) Estienne in 1568.[55] The other was John Hart, Chester Herald (1567–74), whose *An Orthographie, conteyning the due order and reason, howe to write or paint thimage of mannes voice, most like to the life or nature* was printed at London by [?Henry Denham for] William Seres in 1569,[56] and whose *A Methode or comfortable beginning for all vnlearned, to read English* was printed at London by Henry Denham in 1570 (*STC* 12889). As early as 1551 Hart had advocated making special sorts for his phonetic orthographic symbols. In his unpublished manuscript 'The opening of the unreasonable writing of our inglish toung' he noted that:

> mani will say that it were impossible to frame our commune writen hand . . . in souch a iust uniformite, as it mought be easili prynted . . . The cause of theis fayned impossibilities, is . . . (for making of new punchons) the lak of the first disbursing of (at most) one hundred pounds.[57]

Hart goes on to suggest that the work's dedicatee, Edward VI, should support such a project. Success apparently came when, as Chester Herald, he was a crown officer in the service of Sir William Cecil. Both Smith and Hart had special sorts made to complement an italic fount. Smith used several Anglo-Saxon letter-forms, viz. ſ, ᵹ, þ, ð, and also undotted ı, and dotted y, made to fit with Claude Garamont's Great Primer Italic.[58] Hart used modifications of roman letter-forms made to fit with two

---

[54] *Pace* Carter and Ricks's intro. to Mores, *Dissertation*, p. lxviii, and Wakeman, 'Day's Saxon', p. 283.

[55] *STC* 22856.5. Facs. ed. R. C. Alston, English Linguistics 1500–1800, 109 (Menston, 1958). For Smith's relations with Robert (II) Estienne see E. Armstrong, 'The Publication of the Royal Edicts and Ordinances under Charles IX: The Destiny of Robert (II) Estienne as King's Printer', *Proc. Huguenot Society*, 19 (1953–4), 41–59, esp. 48–52. See also M. Dewar, *Sir Thomas Smith A Tudor Intellectual in Office* (London, 1964).

[56] *STC* 12890. Facs. edn The English Experience, 40 (Amsterdam, 1968); also R. C. Alston, English Linguistics, 209 (Menston, 1969).

[57] B. Danielsson, *John Hart's Works* (Stockholm, 1955), quotation on p. 148 from BL, MS Royal 17.C.vii, pp. 168–9; cf. also Danielsson, p. 88.

[58] Illust. in J. Veyrin-Forrer and A. Jammes, *Les Premiers caractères de l'imprimerie royale. Étude sur un spécimen inconnu de 1643* (Paris, 1958), pl. 11, no. 2. The attribution to Garamont is moot.

sizes, a Pica Italic for the *Orthographie* in 1569,[59] and a 2-line Great Primer Italic for
the *Methode* in 1570,[60] which also utilizes the Pica Italic special sorts; the nearest he
came to an Anglo-Saxon letter-form was his symbol for /ʤ/, which was based on the
shape of an Anglo-Saxon **g**, or, more probably, its Middle English descendant ʒ
(yogh), with the tail looped right round crossing back over itself. As it happens we
have contemporary evidence that both had their special sorts made by aliens. In his *A
short Introduction or guiding to print, write, and reade Inglish speech*, printed at
London by Henry Denham in 1580 (2nd edn, 1581),[61] William Bullokar (*c*.1531–
1609) took Smith and Hart to task for employing foreign immigrants to cut their
special sorts,

> sir Thomas Smith and M. Chester [i.e. Hart] were driuen to seeke straungers to
> fashion their figures . . . for lack of helpe of skilfull men within the realme at that
> time . . . But now (thanks be to God) the Printer and workmen being Inglish, can
> aide the Aucthors meaning, in ioining perfect conference of the olde use and new
> togither, which was not possible to be done by straungers, . . .[62]

If Smith and Hart had to resort to foreign punch-cutters it is highly likely that Day
(working for Parker) had to do the same. Smith was Elizabeth's ambassador to France
in Paris from 1562 to 1566, and his book was published by a Paris printer in 1568, so
probably he had his special sorts cut in Paris, and in this respect he may have been a
special case. In England itself two family firms who operated mainly on the continent
could have provided the necessary technical expertise for making the Anglo-Saxon
special sorts, the Guyot family and the Haultin family. Hart probably used the punch-
cutting services of both. In the *Methode* (1570) the 2-line Great Primer, with which the
large special sorts are matched, is the bold variety of that size cut by François Guyot.[63]

---

[59] Illust. in Isaac, 'Elizabethan Types', fig. 11. This type-design differs from Isaac's fig. 6 (= H. D. L.
Vervliet, *Sixteenth-Century Printing Types of the Low Countries* (Amsterdam, 1968), IT10), and I
understand from Prof. Vervliet (private communication) that he would now modify his commentary to
IT1. See also n. 71 below.

[60] Illust. in Danielsson, *Hart's Works*, fig. 23 (reduced) on p. 249. I follow the size-designation of
Carter, *View of Typography*, p. 127.

[61] *STC* 4086.5; 2nd edn, *STC* 4086.7. Facs. ed. B. Danielsson and R. C. Alston, *The Works of William
Bullokar vol. I* (Leeds, 1966). Bullokar produced an edn of 'Aesops Fablz in tru ortŏgraphy' in 1585.

[62] Quoted from the 1581 edn, p. [21]; similarly the 1580 edn, p. [18]. Bullokar used a Textura
(Black Letter) fount and made only minor modifications to existing letter forms. See also
D. Abercrombie, 'Extending the Roman Alphabet: Some Orthographic Experiments of the Past
Four Centuries', in *Towards a History of Phonetics*, ed. R. E. Asher and J. A. Henderson (Edinburgh,
1981), pp. 206–24.

[63] Vervliet, *Printing Types*, IT1. The fullest illustration occurs in C. Axel-Nilsson, *Type Studies: the
Norstedt Collection of Matrices in the Typefoundry of the Royal Printing Office, a History and
Catalogue* (Stockholm, 1983), NS 174 on p. 116 (I am grateful to Sir David Wilson for drawing this
book to my attention). Also illustrated in J. Prijs, *Die Basler Hebräischen Drucke 1492–1866* (Olten,
1964), fig. 76. Another example occurs in Bartholomæus Đurđeviç (= Georgius), *De Turcarum ritu et
caeremoniis* (Antwerp, Gregorius Bontius, 1544).

We know that Day was on friendly terms with Guyot, who (with his family) stayed in Day's house in 1568,[64] evidence that fits well with the appearance of special sorts matching Guyot's type-design in Hart's publication of 1570; in 1576, Gabriel Guyot, second son of François, stayed with Day again.[65] Perhaps the first visit was on foot of business done earlier, when François Guyot was Christophe Plantin's regular type-caster in Antwerp.[66] Day was responsible for introducing some of Guyot's type-designs into England, his Double Pica Roman and Double Pica Italic already mentioned, and in *A Testimonie of Antiquitie* the translation facing the Old English text utilizes Guyot's Great Primer Italic.[67] Vervliet, not knowing of François Guyot's visit to Day in 1568, asked 'whether this specimen [i.e. example of Anglo-Saxon type-designs] was not originally sent by Guyot to John Day'.[68] The only evidence that might apparently confirm this suspicion that Guyot cut the Parkerian Anglo-Saxon type-designs is that of style, but to my eye the evidence looks insufficient.[69] In both his Double Picas Guyot apparently pioneered the cutting of a Roman and Italic designed to complement each other,[70] and this idea of complementarity is evident in the use of the Parkerian Great Primer Anglo-Saxon alongside Guyot's Great Primer Italic (he did not cut a Great Primer Roman), but it does not necessarily mean that Guyot cut the Anglo-Saxon sorts.

In both Hart's *Orthographie* (1569) and his *Methode* (1570) the Pica Italic with which the special sorts were made to fit was that cut by Pierre Haultin, the Parisian punch-cutter who transferred his business to the Huguenot stronghold of La Rochelle in 1571.[71] As far as we know the first foreign type-caster to come to London was Hubert d'Armillier, a former apprentice of Robert Granjon, who probably brought matrices of Granjon's Italics with him when he came to London not later than 1553.[72] Amongst his servants in 1568 was one Jérôme Haultin,[73] the nephew of Pierre. We know that Jérôme in London paid for matrices from his uncle in La Rochelle in 1575–76, and that he cast types to supply to London printers.[74] It seems probable that he was carrying out this work earlier than 1568, as such a supposition

---

[64] Oastler, *Day*, pp. 34 and 78, n. 28, quoting BL, MS Lansdowne 202, fol. 19ᵛ.

[65] E. J. Worman, *Alien Members of the Book-Trade during the Tudor Period* (London, 1906), p. 26.

[66] Carter, *View of Typography*, p. 95.

[67] Dreyfus, *Type Specimen*, I, pl. 1; Vervliet, *Printing Types*, IT3.

[68] Ibid., pp. 26–7. For the note of Guyot's visit to Day in 1568 as subsequent information see the preface by H. Carter, p. vii, n. 1.

[69] Cf. the remarks about the letters z, H, M in App. 1 below.

[70] Vervliet, *Printing Types*, p. 27, Carter, *View of Typography*, pp. 96–7.

[71] See L. Desgraves, *Les Haultin 1571–1623*, L'Imprimerie à La Rochelle 2 (Geneva, 1960). For the identification of the Pica Italic noticed in n. 59 above as Haultin's I am indebted to Professor Vervliet. It occurs in *Biblia Sacra Veteris & Noui Testamenti iuxta Vvlgatam, quam dicvnt, editionem*, ed. J. Benedictus (Paris, heirs of Carola Guillard widow of Claudius Chevallonius, 1558) on sigs *3ᵛ, *4ᵛ, in the 'Index Testimoniorum', and the whole of the 'Index Rerum et Sententiarum': sigs A⁸ B⁶ C⁶.

[72] Carter, *View of Typography*, p. 94.

[73] Oastler, *Day*, p. 33 and n. 6.

[74] Desgraves, *Les Haultin*, pp. xvii–xviii; Carter, *View of Typography*, pp. 86–7.

provides the most obvious explanation of the occurrence of Haultin type-designs in English books before this date. In the *Testimonie of Antiquitie* the preface is set in Pierre Haultin's Pica Roman,[75] and the English Roman with which the Anglo-Saxon sorts are combined is also his. He is thus the most obvious candidate to have cut the special sorts in Hart's works to match Haultin's Pica Italic (which Isaac records in England from 1566).[76] Is it not possible that the special sorts were cut by Pierre Haultin with Jérôme Haultin acting as the intermediary between Denham and Hart in London and the punch-cutter in France? Similarly with the Anglo-Saxon special sorts: if they were cut by Pierre Haultin Jérôme could have acted as the intermediary between Day and the type-designers in London, and the punch-cutter in France. Like Guyot, Haultin cut a Roman and Italic to complement each other, in this case in Nonpareil size,[77] but he did not cut an Italic larger than Pica,[78] so the pairing of Haultin's English Roman on a Great Primer body with Guyot's Great Primer Italic may have been a practical solution to the problem of finding types of an appropriate size to display the Old English text alongside an early Modern English translation.

When Parker said that Day alone 'indented' the new Anglo-Saxon type-designs, however inaccurate his statement about who 'matriculated' them may have been, he did not say, and could not have meant, that Day was to have exclusive use of them. Two more books containing them appeared within two years of *A Testimonie of Antiquitie*, one written or purportedly written by Parker himself, and one officially sanctioned by him. The second edition of Parker's *A Defence of priestes mariages* (STC 17519) was printed at London by Richarde Jugge and published in 1567; the material added on pp. 276–351 contains four passages in Anglo-Saxon type (on pp. 288, 306, 308, 346) of the same size and design, and with the same size and design of roman, as in *A Testimonie*. The first edition of the *De antiquitate Cantabrigiensis Academie* by John Caius (1510–73), authorized with Parker's approval in the year 22 July 1567 to 22 July 1568, was printed at London by Henry Bynneman and published in August 1568;[79] it too contains passages and marginal glosses in Anglo-Saxon type (on pp. 49, 181, 183, 229, 287, 288, 300) of the same size and design, and with the same size and design of roman, as in *A Testimonie*. Although one printer sometimes did work for another without receiving any credit (as was probably the case with Henry Denham and Hart's *Orthographie*), in these instances it appears more likely that the Anglo-Saxon types (probably the types rather than the matrices, as no great quantity was

---

[75] J. A. Lane, 'Identifying Typefaces', *The Library*, 6th ser., 14 (1992), 357–65, esp. 362, where the Pica Roman incorrectly attributed to Garamont in Ferguson, *Pica Roman* is reassigned to Haultin. Cf. Carter, *View of Typography*, p. 86.

[76] Isaac, 'Elizabethan Types', fig. 11.

[77] Illustrated in Christophe Plantin, [*Index sive Specimen characterum C. Plantini*], type-specimen issued from Antwerp, 1567, facs. intro. D. C. McMurtrie (New York, 1924), sig. D3, nos 1 and 2.

[78] On the type-designs cut by Pierre Haultin see *Sixteenth-Century French Typefounders*, ed. Carter, p. 31 and p. 42, n. 32.

[79] STC 4344.

required)[80] were made available to Jugge and Bynneman, presumably on Parker's instructions, or, at least, with his approval. Parker's statement about 'Dayus . . . solus' could therefore mean that Day alone held the matrices for the Anglo-Saxon type-designs;[81] in this way Parker could control their use through Day.[82]

Parker seems to have regarded Anglo-Saxon types as we regard reproduction furniture,[83] as virtue regained; they would provide a key of remembrance facilitating easier access to the authority of Anglo-Saxon writings. Even more than the archaizing hands that Parker advocated for transcripts, the new types were to be, in Malcolm Parkes's phrase 'emblematic of the past',[84] a past regarded as yielding authoritative guidance for the present and the future. Given this approach, Parker and his associates were bound to look for type-designs that reproduced the shape of letters in the original manuscripts. Since the manuscripts used by Parker and Joscelyn still bear the scars of their usage it is possible to study them with a view to determining where the models for the Parkerian Anglo-Saxon type-designs came from.

With the aid of Neil Ker's *Catalogue of Manuscripts containing Anglo-Saxon* I drew up a list of some 61 manuscripts containing Old English used and/or owned by Parker,[85] and a list of some 36 manuscripts containing Old English used and/or

---

[80] Cf. H. R. Plomer, 'Henry Bynneman, Printer, 1566–83', *The Library*, 1st ser., 9 (1908), 225–44, esp. 232. For a possible analogy with this usage cf. Ferguson, *Pica Roman*, p. 12.

[81] Oastler, *Day*, p. 34, argues that, like his contemporaries, Bynneman and Vautrollier, Day stocked matrices.

[82] No other Anglo-Saxon fount was cut in Parker's lifetime, whereas in 1576, one year after his death, two more appeared, both Pica in size, only one of which could have been sanctioned by Parker. This fount first appeared in John Foxe's *Actes and Monuments* (1576, *STC* 11224), printed by John Day, while the other first appeared in William Lambarde's *Perambulation of Kent* (*STC* 15175) printed by Henry Middleton in 1576.

[83] Cf. the preface to Parker's edn of Asser (pp. 163–4 above); I have taken the word *supellex* to have its usual meaning of 'household furniture', interpreting the context as indicating something familiar which provides the means of recreating something old and venerable. ('Furniture' as the wooden wedges used to hold blocks of type firmly in the forme is not recorded by *OED* until 1683 (Moxon), and could hardly apply in this instance.)

[84] M. B. Parkes, 'Archaizing Hands in English Manuscripts', in *Books and Collectors*, ed. Carley and Tite (1997), pp. 101–41, esp. 123. I am grateful to MBP for allowing me to see this article prior to publication and for (unwittingly) supplying helpful references. The phrase is based on Parker's statement in the Preface to the *Ælfredi Regis Res Gestæ* (1574) that he is printing the Latin text in Anglo-Saxon characters *ob venerandam . . . archetypi antiquitatem* 'for the purpose of revering the antiquity of the original' (A2ʳ). Since Anglo-Saxon Latin texts did not employ Insular script, Parker's use of his Anglo-Saxon types for printing Latin was described by Wakeman, 'Day's Saxon', p. 297, as 'a travesty'. But the inspiration for so doing was probably Irish manuscripts containing Latin texts, e.g. Lambeth Palace Library, MS 1370, the 'Gospels of MacDurnan' (*s.* ix), which Parker owned (see next note).

[85] Ker, *Catalogue*, nos 13–14, 17–21, 23, 29–43, 45–50, 53–73, *84, 86, 87–8, 89, 144,* 269, 312, 325, 338, 346; in the instances italicized the evidence for ownership is through John Parker, the

owned by Joscelyn.[86] Naturally, there is some overlap between these lists, amounting to 14 manuscripts, so the combined lists give a total of 82 manuscripts. Not all these manuscripts were available to Parker and Joscelyn before 1566, when the Anglo-Saxon types were first used. To narrow the list down to manuscripts that must have been in front of Parker and/or Joscelyn when the designs of the new Anglo-Saxon types were being considered, I therefore drew up a list of manuscripts used for the Old English texts and passages quoted in the first book containing Anglo-Saxon types, *A Testimonie of Antiquitie*.[87] The present list is based on close textual analysis of all the texts and passages concerned using the best modern editions with readings from all the variant manuscripts. I then checked all my findings against the original manuscripts, or in some cases facsimiles. (These findings are set out in Appendix 2.) I also checked the next two books containing Anglo-Saxon types, both issued with Parker's blessing, his own *A Defence of priestes mariages*, and Caius's *De antiquitate Cantabrigiensis Academie*, but nothing from the manuscripts that they drew on affects the argument here.[88] In Table 2 the first column on the left gives the institution holding the manuscript, the second the shelf-mark, the third the date when it was written, the fourth the contents (abbreviated), and the fifth the provenance.[89] Even this list of 13 manuscripts is quite long, reflecting the considerable amount of research that went into the making of *A Testimonie*. There is a notable preponderance in the list for manuscripts of the eleventh century.

A few other manuscripts must be added. In London, BL, Cotton MS Nero C.III, fol. 208 (formerly 191), there is a list entitled 'Libri Saxonica Lingua descripti qui ad manus John Gocelin venerunt',[90] which, as far as those actually containing Old

---

archbishop's son. This list excludes manuscripts queried by Ker, and is provisional. The only exception is Lambeth Palace Library, MS 1370 (Ker, no. 284) which has Parker's signature in red ochre on the recto of the front flyleaf, gospel chapter numbers added throughout in Parker's hand in red ochre, and a binding of a characteristic style used for some of Parker's books (cf. Cambridge, University Library, MS Ff.1.23).

[86] Ker, *Catalogue*, nos 17, 29, 32, 39, 41, 45–9, 53, 65, 67, 116, 140, 153, 155, 157, 163–4, 166, 177, 179, 181, 188, 191–2, 204–5, 207, 209, 240, 324, 331, 338, 343. This list excludes manuscripts queried by Ker, and is provisional.

[87] An earlier list of seven manuscripts by Ker, *Catalogue*, p. liii, item *h*, is incomplete, and its inclusion of Cambridge, Corpus Christi Coll. MS 162 is inaccurate. On p. 387 of Corpus 162 Parker saw a passage very similar to one printed in the *Testimonie* and noted in the margin 'pag. 10' (a reference to the text of the first edition of the *Testimonie*), and below this he wrote in red ochre 'in Libello Impresso', i.e. the *Testimonie*.

[88] The findings from these books will be set out in detail in my *Analytical Bibliographical Catalogue of Early Printed Books Containing Anglo-Saxon*, forthcoming.

[89] Following Ker, *Catalogue*, collated with Ker, *MLGB* and Watson, *Supplement*.

[90] Printed by C. E. Wright, 'The Dispersal of the Monastic Libraries and the Beginnings of Anglo-Saxon Studies. Matthew Parker and his Circle: a Preliminary Study', *TCBS*, 1 (1949–53), 208–37, esp. 218–19; Wright shows that the list owes much to Bale. See also Lutz, 'Studium der ASC', pp. 307–8, and cf. M. McKisack, *Medieval History in the Tudor Age* (Oxford, 1971), p. 45.

Table 2   MSS used for texts in the first printed book containing A-S types

Institution	Shelf-mark	Date	Contents	Provenance
Cambridge Univ. Lib.	Hh.1.10	s. xi$^{3/4}$/xii	Ælfric, Grammar	Exeter
	Ii.2.11	s. xi$^{3/4}$	Gospels	Exeter
Cambridge, Corpus Christi Coll.	173	s. ix/x–xi^2	AS Chronicle (A)	Canterbury Christ Church
	190	s. xi^1	Ecclesiastical Institutes	Exeter
	198	s. xi^1, xi^2	Homilies incl. *In die Pascæ*	Worcester
	265	s. xi^{med}	Ælfric, Letters, etc.	Worcester
Exeter Cath. Lib.	3501	s. x^2	Exeter Book of OE Poetry	Exeter
London, BL Cotton	Cleopatra B.XIII	s. xi$^{3/4}$	Pater Noster, Creed	Exeter
	Faustina A.IX	s. xii^1	Homilies incl. *In die Pascæ*	not known
	Nero A.I	s. xi^{med}	Laws, etc.	not known
	Vespasian D.XIV	s. xii^{med}	Homilies	not known
Oxford, Bodl. Lib.	Junius 121	s. xi$^{3/4}$	Eccl. Institutes, Homilies	Worcester
	Laud Misc. 636	s. xii^1, xii^{med}	AS Chronicle (E)	Peterborough

English is concerned, is confined to manuscripts of the *Anglo-Saxon Chronicle* known by Joscelyn. The historical orientation of the list is confirmed by what follows on fols 208^v–212: 'Catalogus Aucto⟨rum⟩ qui scripserunt Historiam Anglia quo⟨rum⟩ opera ad manus John Gocelin peruenerunt et vbi extant'.[91] According to Ivor Atkins, who adduces internal evidence, the first list 'dates from before 1567, and probably between 1560 and 1567'.[92] The *Anglo-Saxon Chronicle* manuscripts in this first list must therefore be included amongst those that could have influenced the type-designs. In addition to Cambridge, Corpus Christi College, MS 173 and Oxford, Bodleian Library, MS Laud Misc. 636 already noted they are as listed in Table 3.

The manuscripts now in Cambridge were all owned by Parker, but Joscelyn left his mark on all those used for the *Testimonie* except University Library Ii.2.11. Of those now not in Cambridge all, except apparently BL, Cotton MS Otho B.XI, were worked on by Joscelyn, but Parker's hand is found only in BL, Cotton MS Cleopatra B.XIII and Bodleian Library, MSS Junius 121 and Laud Misc. 636 (the 'Peterborough Chronicle'). MS Tiberius B.I was annotated by Robert Talbot and used by Robert

---

[91] Dated by C. E. Wright, in *The English Library before 1700*, ed. F. Wormald and C. E. Wright (London, 1958), pp. 157 and 173, n. 24, 'to 1565 or thereabouts', but he does not cite his evidence for so thinking. (In London, Lambeth Palace, MS 593, pp. 359–70, there is a list of historians used by Joscelyn, including on p. 370 a list of Anglo-Saxon historical books, but, as far as I am aware, it is not known at what stage these books became available to Joscelyn.)

[92] 'The Origin of the Later Part of the Saxon Chronicle Known as D', *English Historical Review*, 55 (1940), 8–26, esp. 25.

Table 3   Other MSS known by those involved in the first A-S type designs

Institution	Shelf-mark	Date	Contents	Provenance
London, BL Cotton	Otho B.XI	s. x^{med}–xi^1	AS Chronicle (G), etc.	Southwick
	Tiberius A.VI	s. x^2	AS Chronicle (B)	Canterbury, St Augustine's
	Tiberius B.I	s. xi^1–xi^2	Orosius, AS Chronicle (C)	Abingdon[93]
	Tiberius B.IV	s. xi^{med}, xi^2	AS Chronicle (D)	Worcester[94]

Recorde for his annotations in Corpus 138. One manuscript (BL, Cotton Faustina A.IX) apparently arrived in the Parkerian circle in time to be of use for the second edition only of *A Testimonie* (STC 159.5),[95] so it may not have been in front of Parker and Joscelyn when they (and others) were considering the type-designs, but I have included it in Table 4 in the interests of completeness.[96] As Bromwich demonstrated, the text of the Easter homily in Cambridge, Corpus Christi College, MS 198 was prepared more carefully (with thin vertical strokes to indicate word-divisions) than that in Faustina A.IX.[97] This preparation was probably intended for a copyist to make a transcript that was used by the printer. There is apparently no evidence that these original manuscripts were used in the printer's workshop.

The Parkerian Anglo-Saxon type-designs show particular features that may be related to features in the Anglo-Saxon script(s) on which they were modelled. The following eight features (see Pl. 23(a)–(c), pp. 161–3 above) are notable:

1. The descenders of **f**, long **r**, long **s**, **þ** and **p** are turned to the left at the bottom;
2. The letter **d** is round-backed with a short ascender turned up at the top;

---

[93] The manuscript was at Abingdon when the *Anglo-Saxon Chronicle* annals for 491–1048 were added.

[94] But D. Whitelock, *Peterborough Chronicle*, EEMF, 4 (Copenhagen, 1954), p. 28, argued that York is also possible.

[95] Bromwich, 'First Book', esp. pp. 281 and 284.

[96] Wakeman, 'Day's Saxon', mentions 12 manuscripts: Cambridge, University Library, MSS Ii.2.11, Ii.4.6, and Corpus Christi College MS 140; London, BL, Cotton MSS Faustina A.IX, Otho B.XI, Otho C.I(1), Tiberius B.I; Oxford, Bodl. Lib., MSS Bodley 441, Hatton 38 and 114, Junius 121, Laud Misc. 482. Five contain the Anglo-Saxon Gospels (Ii.2.11, Corpus 140, Otho C.I, Bodley 441, Hatton 38), but only Ii.2.11 was used for the *Testimonie*, as well as, later, with the others, for Foxe's edn of the Anglo-Saxon gospels (1571, STC 2961). Ii.4.6 was given to Parker 29 December 1567; Otho B.XI was used by Lawrence Nowell (in Cecil's household) in 1562, and Laud Misc. 482 was used by Joscelyn, so these manuscripts (with MSS Ii.2.11, Tiberius B.I, Hatton 114 and Junius 121) were available to influence the type-designs, but they show no features not already available in the manuscripts certainly used in preparing the *Testimonie* or listed as available to Joscelyn.

[97] Bromwich, 'First Book', esp. pp. 277–8.

3. The tail of **g** is closed;
4. The letter **ð** shows a long straight ascender (with cross bar (rather than a spur)) sloping steeply to the left (and slightly turned to the left at the tip), so much so that it requires a space in front of it that looks inappropriate when the letter is medial or final;
5. Capitals are round rather than square in shape, e.g., **Ð, þ, Þ, X**;
6. Capital **E, H**, and **M** are uncial;
7. Capital **S** is round and the lower half is almost closed.
8. Capital **Æ** shows two designs, **Æ¹** based on an uncial **E**, and **Æ²** apparently based on bringing together an angular **A** with tall **e**, or with square **E**.

For the purpose of trying to identify the probable manuscript models used by the type-designers the shape of the letter **ð** is particularly suggestive. Only in the eleventh century, especially the second half, was this letter so prominent with its long ascender sloping steeply to the left. This feature suggests that the preponderance of eleventh-century manuscripts in the list of manuscripts used by Joscelyn and others is significant. With this and the other features in mind I then examined the thirteen manuscripts used for the compilation of the *Testimonie* (i.e., including Faustina A.IX even though it may not have been available early enough) plus the extra four *Anglo-Saxon Chronicle* manuscripts from Joscelyn's list to see whether or not they showed similar features. The results are set out in Table 4. The material condensed here is generally representative of the usage in each manuscript concerned (except that for a few manuscripts there is more than one entry),[98] and, since more than one scribe may have been responsible, it relates as far as possible to that in the passage used for *A Testimonie*; sometimes the usage recorded for individual capitals indicates existence rather than the norm, to err on the side of inclusiveness. No attempt has been made to record exceptional usages, but none is significant for the present argument.

While some of the features, such as descenders turned to the left, or round rather than square capitals, are quite common in these manuscripts, others, such as the form of capital **S**, and capital **Æ** based on an uncial **E**, are rare, while others fall in between. Only one manuscript illustrates all the features indicated: Junius 121. This manuscript was written at Worcester together with two companion volumes in the same hand (Oxford, Bodl. Lib., MSS Hatton 113 and 114, formerly Junius 99 and 22; *SC* 5210 and 5134).[99] The secondary display capitals in this trio of manuscripts

---

[98] E.g. Cambridge, Corpus Christi College MS 190: one for Ker's art. 17, and one for his art. 3.

[99] A very similar (if not identical) hand occurs in Cambridge, University Library, MS Kk.3.18, which was also used by Parker and Joscelyn early on. Of the manuscripts used for the *Testimonie* Cambridge, Corpus Christi College MS 265, another Worcester manuscript, approaches nearest to Junius 121 in showing nearly all the features of the type-designs; Ker (*Catalogue*, p. 94) compares the script of pp. 222–7 with that of Hatton 113 and 114. See N. R. Ker, 'Hemming's Cartulary: a Description of the Two Worcester Cartularies in Cotton Tiberius A. XIII', in his *Books, Collectors and Libraries* (1985), ch. 4, at p. 41.

Table 4   Comparative summary of distinctive features in relevant A-S MSS

Source	Feature 1*	Feature 2	Feature 3	Feature 4	Feature 5	Feature 6			Feature 7	Feature 8
						E	H	M		
Cambridge Univ. Lib.										
Hh.1.10	√	×	√	×	√	√	√	√	×	√/2
Ii.2.11	√	×	√	×	√	√	√	√	×	×
Cambridge, Corpus Christi Coll.										
173	×	×	×	×	×	√	√	×	×	×
190 (17+3)										
pp. 295–308	√	√	√	√	√	×	√	×	×	×
pp. 336–49	√	×	√	√	√	√	×	×	×	√/2
198	×	×	√	√	√	×	√	√	×	√/2
265	√	√	√	√	√	√	√	×	×	√/2
Exeter Cath. Lib.										
3501	√	√	√	√	√	√	×	×	×	×
London, BL, Cotton										
Cleo. B.XIII	√	×	√	√	√	√	×	×	×	×
Faust. A.IX	×	×	×	×	√	×	√	×	×	×
Nero A.I	√	×	√	×	√	√	√	×	×	√/2
Otho B.XI + Add.										
34652 fol. 2	×	×	×	×	√	×	×	√	×	×
Tib. A.VI	×	×	×	√	√	√	√	—	×	×
Tib. B.I										
fols 3–32	×	×	×	×	√	√	√	√	×	√/1
fols 32ᵛ–34	×	×	×	×	√	√	×	×	×	√/2
fols 35–44ᵛ	×	×	×	×	√	√	√	√	×	√/1+2
fols 45ᵛ–111ᵛ	×	×	×	√	√	√	√	√	×	√/1
fols 112–18ᵛ	×	×	√	×	√	√	√	√	×	×
fols 119–58	√	×	×	√	√	√	√	√	×	√/2
Tib. B.IV										
fols 3–9ᵛ	×	√	×	×	√	—	√	—	×	√/2
fols 19–67ᵛ	×	√	√	√	√	√	√	√	×	—
fols 68–73	√	√	√	×	√	√	√	√	×	√/2
fols 74–75ᵛ, line 21	×	√	×	√	√	—	√	√	×	×
fols 76–90	√	√	√	×	√	√	√	√	×	×
Vesp. D.XIV	√	×	×	×	√	√	√	√	×	×
Oxford, Bodl. Lib.										
Junius 121	√	√	√	√	√	√	√	√	√	√/1+2
Laud Misc. 636	√	×	×	×	√	√	√	√	×	√/2

Note: * Column number key is in preceding numbered list (pp. 172–3).

are particularly fine, utilising colour (green, red and blue, with some silver). They were still at Worcester in 1622–23 when Patrick Young made his catalogue, in which they occur as nos 318 (Hatton 113), 319 (Hatton 114), and 321 (Junius 121).[100] We know that Joscelyn used these manuscripts, because he annotated them and also because he noted in the margins of Corpus 198 (the base-text manuscript for the edition of Ælfric's *Sermo in die Pascæ* in the *Testimonie*) where the corresponding texts occur in Hatton 113 and 114.[101] Since the features found in Junius 121 occur also in Hatton 113 and 114, I looked at these manuscripts too so as to have available the largest possible collection of examples with which to match the features of the first Anglo-Saxon type-designs. These features may be observed in the Plates as follows:

1. The descenders of **f**, **r**, long **s**, **þ** and **p** are turned to the left at the tip in 'scrift' (Pl. 24, line 20), 'syðþan' (lines 20 and 21), 'weofode' (line 23);
2. Round-backed **d** in 'unhadode' (line 15);
3. The letter **g** as in 'ænige' (line 23);
4. **ð** as in 'við' (line 22);
5. Round capitals as in 'OÐÐE' (Pl. 24, line 12), 'ÐROPODE' (Pl. 25, line 16), 'SERMO IN XL' (Pl. 26, line 14);[102]
6. Uncial E, H and M in 'GELEAHTROD', 'MÆSSEPREOST' (Pl. 24, line 6);
7. Capital S as in 'CRISTNUNGE' (Pl. 27, line 17);
8. The two designs of capital Æ, Æ[1] as in 'MÆSSEPREOST' (Pl. 24, line 17) and 'DÆGE' (Pl. 25, line 16), and Æ[2] as in 'ÐÆRE' (Pl. 27, line 17).[103]

Of particular interest in Hatton 113 is the occurrence on fol. i [v] of an Anglo-Saxon alphabet written out across the page in a sixteenth-century hand with the early Modern English equivalents set out in a parallel row below (Pl. 28). The various graphs for 'th' are set out separately and also together with the various vowels. This alphabet gives the impression of having been useful for a sixteenth-century reader who was becoming familiar with Old English. Since Joscelyn was, so far as other evidence indicates, the only sixteenth-century user of the manuscript who was interested in Old English, the most obvious explanation is that the Anglo-Saxon alphabet is by him. As it seems somewhat elementary it was presumably done fairly early in Joscelyn's career as an Anglo-Saxonist. The Anglo-Saxon letters are written carefully, and even hesitantly, one by one, but some of them match those in the more

---

[100] I. Atkins and N. R. Ker, '*Catalogus Librorum Manuscriptorum Bibliothecae Wigorniensis' Made in 1622–1623 by Patrick Young, Librarian to King James I* (Cambridge, 1944), p. 7.

[101] Graham, 'Beginnings', p. 41; cf. also Ker, *Catalogue*, p. 76.

[102] Capital **þ** is not common in this manuscript, but occurs, e.g., in 'þE þAS' (fol. 71, line 8), 'þa' (fol. 145, line 21).

[103] Æ[2] occurs in Junius 121 rarely, for example, 'Æfter' (fol. 113[v], line 7), and 'Ælc' (fol. 119[v], line 17). High **e** used as a capital occurs in 'Eal' (fol. 137, line 3).

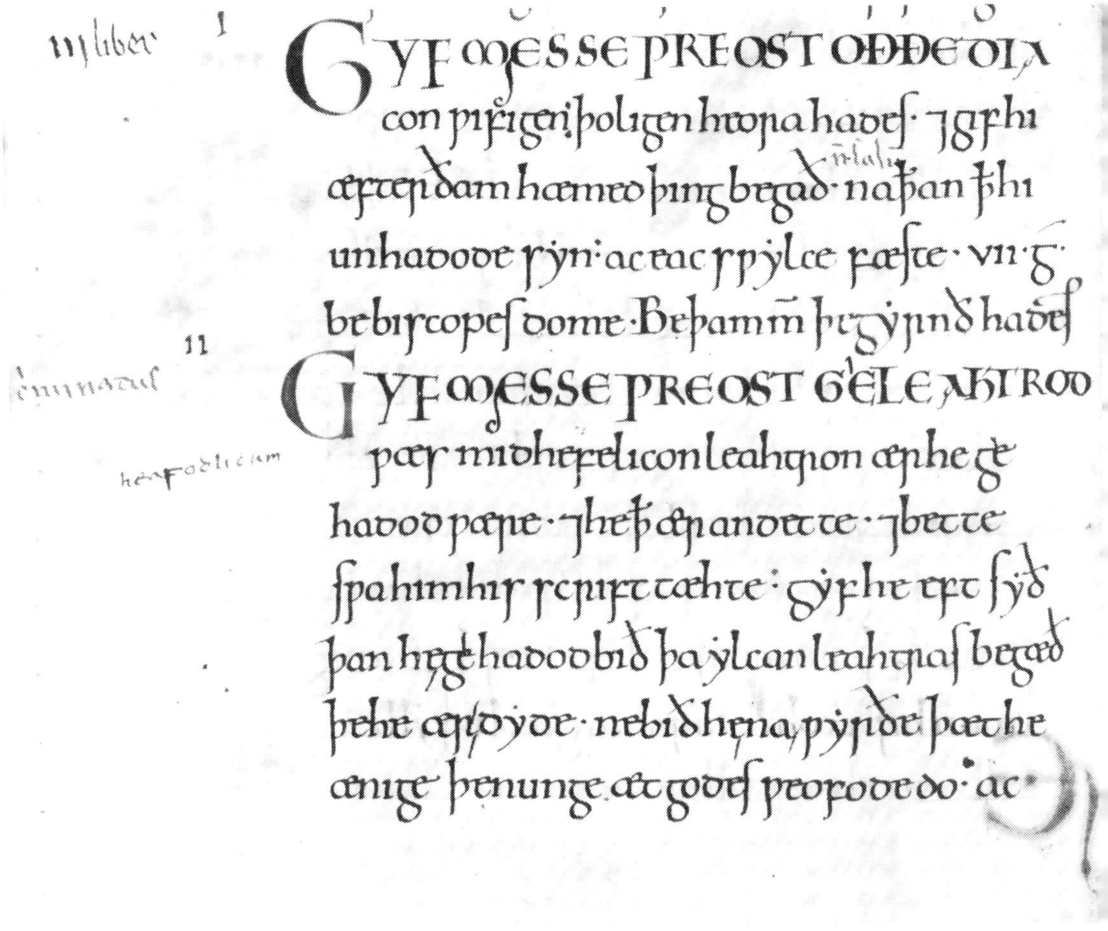

GYF MESSE PREOST OÐÐE OIX
con pifigri þoligen hwona haoef· ꝑ gfhi
æfteꝑ ðam hæmeo þing beꝯað· naþan þhi
unhavooe ꝑyn· aceac ꝑꝑylce ꝼæfte· vn g.
bebiꝑcopef oome·Beþam m̄ þꝯyꝑnð haoef
GYF MESSE PREOST GELE XHI ROO
ꝑæꝑ miohꝑeliconleahqion æphe ge
havoo pæpe· ꝯhꝛeþ æp anoecce· ꝯbecce
ſpahimhiꝑ ꝑcꝑiꝼc cæhce· gyꝼhe cꝼc ſyð
þan hꝯꝯhavoobið þaylcanleahqiaſ beꝯað
þehe æqoyoe· nebiðhꝛna ꝑyꝑiðe þæche
ænige þenunge·æcgooſ peoꝼovevo· ac

Plate 24   Oxford, Bodleian Library, MS Junius 121, fol. 80ᵛ, lines 12–23

quickly executed Plate 21 (see p. 156) quite closely, for example **a** in 'stane' (line 9), **i** in 'gastlicum' (line 4), **r** in 'for' (line 3), **s** in 'his' (line 10). The script of the early Modern English equivalent letters is a curious mixture of secretary and italic forms; for example **p** and **v** are secretary forms, while **g** and **l** are italic. Nevertheless it seems to me probable that the alphabet was written by Joscelyn.[104] The identification is made more difficult because, while Joscelyn wrote in different styles of handwriting, he did not, so far as I have discovered, use the letter-forms found in the alphabet together elsewhere. The **p** with the bowl made by intersecting the descender diagonally is characteristic of Joscelyn's Secretary **p** in his notebook (Cotton Vitellius

---

[104] For examples of Joscelyn's handwriting see Wright, 'Beginnings of Anglo-Saxon Studies', p. 234, facs. (e).

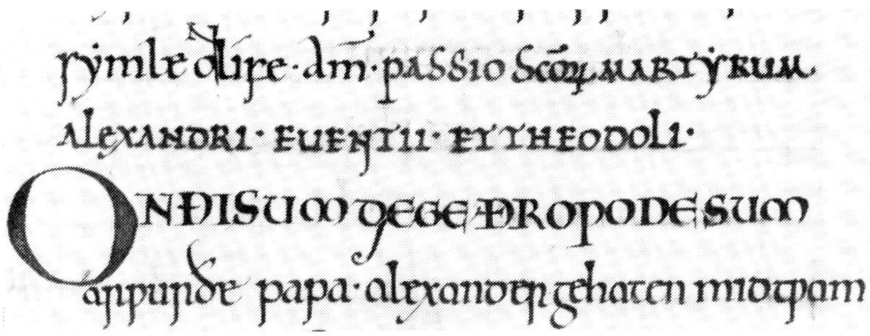

ꞃꞗmle ꝺliꞃe · ꝺm · pꜳ�731o Sꞔoꞡ.ꞁꞁꜳꞃꞇꞃꞃꞃꞅꞁꞁ.
Aⲗꞓꜳⲛꝺꞃ1 · EUⲉⲚꞇ11 · Eꞇ ꞇHEⲞꝺⲟⲖ1 ·
Ⲟ ⲚꝦ1SⳒꞁꞁ꜠ⲟⲟ ꝺEGE ꝒꞃⲟpⲟꝺE 7Ⳓꞁ꜠ⲟⲟ
ꜳꞃꞃuꞃꝺꞓ papa · aⲗⲧⲭꜳⲛⲟⲧꞃ ꞡ꜠ꜳⲧⲉⲛ ꞁꞁⲟⲟꞇꞃꜳⲙ

Plate 25 Oxford, Bodleian Library, MS Hatton 114, fol. 153, lines 14–17

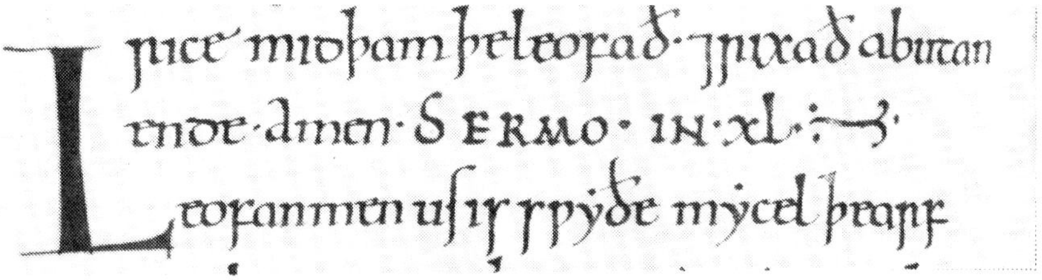

L ꞃꞁⲧꞓ′ ꞁꞁⲟⲟꝧꜳⲙ ꝧⲉꞇⲧⲟꞃꜳ ꝺ · ꞃꞃꞁⲧⲭꜳ ꝺ abⲩⲧꜳⲛ
ⲧⲛⲟꞇ · ꜳꞁⲟⲉⲛ · S ERⲙⲟ · 1Ⲛ · ⲭⲖ · ÷ꞃ ·
ⲧⲟꞃꜳⲛꞁꞁⲟⲉⲛ uꞅꞁꞃ ꞃꞃꞃⲭꝺꞓ ꞁꞁⲭⳇⲉⲗ ꝧⲧꜳꞃꞃꞃ

Plate 26 Oxford, Bodleian Library, MS Hatton 113, fol. 56ᵛ, lines 13–15

L ꞡⲟⲟꞃ ꞗⲉꞗⲟⲟꜳ ꞡꝥꞁꞇꞓ ꝧⲉ ꞡⲧⲟꞃⲛⲟꞃ ÷ ꞃ⟋ⲙⲟⲛ
ⲕⲁⲏꞃ ⲗꜳⲛꜳ ꞃ ⲗꜳꞡꜳ · ꝧⲉⲣⲩⲕ꜠Ⳝꞁⲧⲟⲛ ⲕⲧꜳⲗⲟⲧ · ⳑⲧⲉꞁꞁ
ⲧⲟⳑⲁⲏ ⲁⲗⲉⲏ ⲞⲚꝺⲆRE CR1SꞇⳘⳁⲚGE Ꝧⲉ
ⲙⲁⲛⲟⲧꞕ ꝺꝧⲓꝺaⲙ ꞃⳑⲗⳑⲩⲕⲧⲉ · 1ꞃ ꞁꞁⲭⳇⲉⲗ ꞡⲧⳇꜳⲩ

Plate 27 Oxford, Bodleian Library, MS Hatton 113, fol. 16ᵛ, lines 15–18

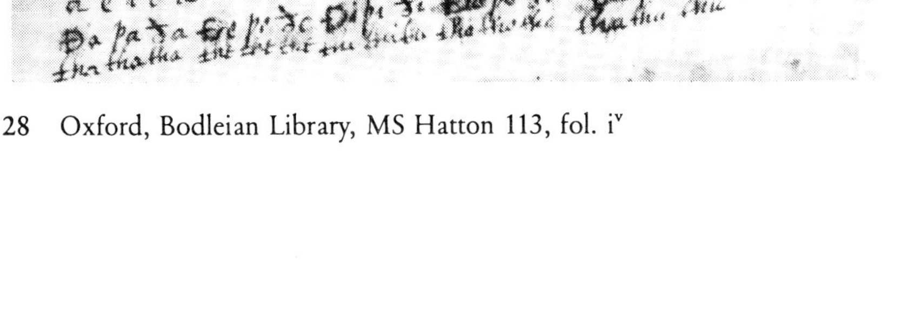

Plate 28 Oxford, Bodleian Library, MS Hatton 113, fol. iᵛ

D.VII, e.g., fols 146–147ᵛ) and the 'and' glossing the Tironian sign at the end of the Anglo-Saxon row of letters looks like Joscelyn's hand.[105] While not all the Anglo-Saxon letters in the alphabet are such as one could claim that the type-designs match them, the z included in the Anglo-Saxon row (and simply left out of the early Modern English row, presumably because writing it in would have been mere duplication) is exactly the kind of sixteenth-century z followed by the type-designers.[106] This tell-tale feature suggests that this Anglo-Saxon alphabet could have served as a trial version of some such set of models devised for the type-designs.

Since the crucial manuscripts for influencing the design of the first Anglo-Saxon types have Worcester provenance and show evidence of use by Joscelyn, it follows that Joscelyn probably used them in Worcester. On 4 October 1560 Joscelyn was instituted into the prebend of Gorwall and Overbury in the diocese of Hereford, a position obtained for him by Parker, and which he held until 1577, when he took possession of the living of Hollingbourn, Kent, which Parker bequeathed him.[107] From his base in Hereford diocese Joscelyn found at Worcester one of the finest collections of Anglo-Saxon manuscripts in any of the medieval cathedral libraries.[108] Work on Anglo-Saxon manuscripts continued during the second half of the eleventh century in Worcester, where Wulfstan II (d. 1095) was the longest serving Anglo-Saxon bishop after the Norman Conquest. Many of the manuscripts in this collection had been the subject of study much deeper into the Middle English period than in other centres, and perhaps in connection with Wulfstan's canonization in 1203 were glossed by the 'tremulous' hand in the early thirteenth century,[109] glosses which Joscelyn and his associates evidently found helpful, and which, as noted above, Parker thought important enough to copy in a transcript himself. Joscelyn's hand is found in 12 Worcester manuscripts, but the only one also to contain Parker's characteristic red ochre crayon is Junius 121. From the fact that Junius 121 is the only manuscript, amongst those definitely used early on by Parker and Joscelyn, to show all the features indicated above as those characterizing the Parkerian Anglo-Saxon fount, it seems reasonable to conclude that this manuscript was probably the main gateway through which the sixteenth-century type-designers passed to acquire the models used by the punch-cutters.[110] From the extent of his

[105] For advice on Joscelyn's handwriting I am indebted to Mr Tim Graham.

[106] See the notes on particular letters in App. 1, below.

[107] Bruce and Perowne, *Parker Correspondence*, p. xiii.

[108] As noted by James, *Corpus Catalogue*, p. xxx, Worcester is 'the principal contributor' of Anglo-Saxon manuscripts in the Corpus collection. For Anglo-Saxon manuscripts at Worcester in the Middle Ages see Ker, *Catalogue*, p. xlv, and cf. also p. xlviii; for those written at Worcester see p. lx.

[109] See Franzen, *Tremulous Hand* (1991); for the continued use of Anglo-Saxon manuscripts in the early Middle English period, see esp. pp. 183–7.

[110] This is not to overlook the suggestion above that the distinction between Latin and Old English t was observed by Joscelyn in Cambridge, Corpus Christi Coll. MS 190, an Exeter manuscript.

annotations in it, and from the fact that Joscelyn, but apparently not Parker, worked on the companion volumes Hatton 113 and 114, it seems reasonable to conclude that Joscelyn made an important contribution to this process, working closely with Parker and perhaps others more calligraphically skilled. In Joscelyn's epitaph there occur the following verses:

> In Learning tryde, whereto he did his mind alwaies incline.
> But others took the Fame and Praise of his deserving Witt,
> And his Inventions, as their owne, to printing did committ.[111]

This statement is usually interpreted as referring to the absence of Joscelyn's name as (co-)author of the *De Antiquitate Britannicæ*, attributed to Parker and privately printed by John Day in 1572 (*STC* 19292), taking *Inventions* as 'literary compositions';[112] it is, however, possible that the reference could be to Joscelyn's type-designs, if such they were, taking *Inventions* as 'something devised . . . by the ingenuity of some person, and previously unknown'.[113]

At this point it may be helpful to review the features distinguishing Old English from early Modern English in the lower case of the Parkerian Anglo-Saxon fount as against those distinguishing Old English from Latin in the original manuscripts; some further notes on particular letter-forms are added in Appendix 1.

Anglo-Saxon Manuscripts *s*.x:	a	d	e	f	g	h		r	s	t	æ þ ð p
Anglo-Saxon Manuscripts *s*.xii:		d		f	g			r	s		æ þ ð p
Parkerian Anglo-Saxon Types:		d		f	g		i	r	s	t	y æ þ ð p

In the eleventh century, the period from which the majority of surviving Anglo-Saxon manuscripts known in Parker's circle emanated, the usage with regard to a, e, and h was inconsistent. Those in Parker's circle were familiar with the twelfth-century position from manuscripts such as Vespasian D. XIV, where a, e, and h were not distinguished. The pattern established in this first Anglo-Saxon fount was to serve as the model for succeeding founts, and the usage with regard to t is particularly notable, as the forms of this letter in Latin and Old English were rarely distinguished in the manuscripts. Whoever was responsible for observing this distinction, and I have suggested above that it was John Joscelyn when he was studying Corpus 190, it had considerable repercussions. With regard to z the printed form appears to be based on a Textura form with a hooked terminal such as is found in Textura type-faces (see Appendix 1). In the 'hierarchy of types' Textura was pre-eminent, being used for the Bible and religious works, notably in

---

[111] Cooper and Cooper, *Athenae Cantabrigienses* (1858–61), II, 306.

[112] For example, by McKisack, *Medieval History*, pp. 47–8; though it could equally well have applied to other publications as well. For this interpretation of 'Invention' see *OED*, s.v., 7.

[113] *OED*, 'Invention', 9.

Parker's Bishops' Bible (1568).[114] The inclusion of this textura z in the Anglo-Saxon alphabet gives an indication of the kind of impact it was intended to make: it was a prestige type.

With regard to the capitals the Parkerian Anglo-Saxon fount distinguished nine letters, viz. E, H, M, S, X, plus Ð, þ, Ƿ and Æ (two forms). Apart from the specifically Anglo-Saxon graphs Ð, þ, Ƿ, there was no systematic distinction in the manuscripts between the forms of these letters used in Latin as opposed to Old English. In the Junius 121 group of manuscripts, for example, the forms of the capitals there employed occur in text in both languages (Pls 25, 27, and 29). The uncial E, H, M, the capital S, the curvacious X, and the two forms of Æ, both ornamental in style, all testify to Parker's purpose of producing a prestige type bearing the stamp of antique authority.[115] The fact that some Anglo-Saxon letters occurred in Latin as well would only have added to their *auctoritas* in the eyes of Parker and his circle.[116] Similarly the punctuation, utilizing the point, the *punctus versus*, and the triple point, and the abbreviation mark for 'and', utilizing the Tironian sign rather than the ampersand, are designed to add further verisimilitude to an already convincing display of antique features.

Plate 29   Oxford, Bodleian Library, MS Hatton 113, fol. vi[v]

As indicated above Parker regarded these Anglo-Saxon types as we regard reproduction furniture, providing a new substitute for old authenticity. They differed somewhat in their intended impact from archaizing hands, which were designed to mimic the features of an older script, to produce what May McKisack bluntly called 'a fake Old English hand',[117] to 'counterfeit in antiquity', as Parker himself put it. The types were more akin in their impact to some kinds of script that originated on the continent during the Middle Ages. In a period of script

---

[114] *STC* 2099.

[115] According to Wakeman, 'Day's Saxon', p. 298, these features 'seem to have been based on aesthetic principles'.

[116] In the Preface to *A Testimonie* (sig. A3) it is remarked that the homilies found in the original manuscripts 'were not first written in the olde Saxon tounge: but were translated into it . . . from the Lattyne', an observation (however incorrect it may be seen to be with the benefit of subsequent scholarship) that could only add to their authority.

[117] McKisack, *Medieval History*, p. 47.

reform older models were often resorted to. Thus, during the ninth century Lupus of Ferrières had supervised the development of a distinctive kind of Caroline minuscule from models in late-antique manuscripts;[118] and in their search for antique authenticity the fifteenth-century Italian humanists devised a new script based initially on antique models from the tenth or eleventh centuries.[119] *Littera antiqua* evolved and subsequently provided the basis of roman and italic type-design. As stated by Erasmus, it was part of the humanist ethos that what really improved a book was 'elegans, dilucida, distinctaque scriptura, Latinis elementis Latina uerba repraesentatibus',[120] (an elegant, clear, and readable script which presents Latin words in the Latin alphabet). This approach was inherited by Parker, who transferred it to Anglo-Saxon vernacular materials, taking (perhaps coincidentally) as the models for the Anglo-Saxon type-designs made under his direction script of the same period as had originally inspired the humanistic script reformers. The Parkerian designs became established through his authority as archbishop of Canterbury, just as *littera antiqua* became established in Italy through papal authority.[121] And just as the contents of the first book printed with the Parkerian Anglo-Saxon types were 'a testimonie of antiquitie', so the mode of presentation employed to communicate those contents was itself a 'testimonye of verye ancient tyme'. Parker's decision to print Old English in this way was to have an influence on the subject that lasted for centuries.

---

[118] B. Bischoff, *Manuscripts and Libraries in the Age of Charlemagne*, tr. M. Gorman (Cambridge, 1994), p. 126.

[119] B. Bischoff, *Latin Palaeography: Antiquity and the Middle Ages*, tr. D. Ó Cróinín and D. Ganz (Cambridge, 1990), pp. 145–9, and references, esp. B. L. Ullmann, *The Origin and Development of Humanistic Script* (Rome, 1960), also A. de la Mare, *The Handwriting of Italian Humanists* (Oxford, 1973).

[120] Erasmus, *De recta Latini Graecique sermonis pronuntiatione dialogus*, ed. J. Kramer, Beiträge zur Klassischen Philologie, 98 (Meisenheim am Glan, 1978), §924 on p. 52; tr. M. Pope in *Collected Works of Erasmus*, 26, ed. J. K. Sowards (Toronto, 1985), p. 391.

[121] For the establishment of *littera antiqua* see S. Morison, *Politics and Script*, ed. N. Barker, Lyell Lectures 1957 (Oxford, 1972), ch. 6, esp. p. 305.

Appendix 1

Some notes on particular letters:

Lower-case letters

i undotted. As noted by Wakeman ('Day's Saxon', p. 286) on the authority of C. L. Oastler the Anglo-Saxon undotted **i** is the same as the roman **i** with the dot filed off. The two can be seen and measured side by side in the *Testimonie*, 2nd edn, sigs I5ᵛ and I6ʳ.

ð. The choice of this form, with its long ascender sloping steeply to the left, led to considerable problems in setting the Old English in *A Testimonie*, and there is evidence of the substitution of **þ** for **ð** in medial and final positions in the revision of the setting between the first and second editions, e.g. M3ᵛ line 18 'oðer' becomes 'oþer' H5ᵛ line 18 (cf. Bromwich, 'First Book', p. 288). Eventually this problem was solved by recasting the type from the matrix in such a way that it would fit snugly against the preceding letter. The recast variety is first seen in John Foxe (intro.), *The Gospels of the fower Euangelistes translated in the olde Saxons tyme out of Latin into the vulgare toung of the Saxons*, London, John Day, 1571(*STC* 2961) between sigs Gg and Hh. Up to Gg4ᵛ line 26 'þencð' the **ð** shows a space in front of it which distances it from the letter it follows. From Hh1ʳ line 2 'doð' the **ð** fits snugly against its preceding letter.

z. This form is matched by the **z** in the Parkerian Anglo-Saxon alphabet in Hatton 113 (Pl. 28, see above p. 177), but not, as far as I have been able to observe, by anything authentic in Anglo-Saxon manuscripts, where the usual form of **z** is roughly similar to the modern printed form. For several examples together, see London, BL, MS Harley 3376, fol. 53 where words beginning with **z** are collected for glossing. Other examples can be seen in Cambridge, Corpus Christi College, MS 188, p. 429 and Trinity College, MS B.10.4, fol. 90ᵛ. The Parkerian written **z** resembles a Secretary **z** of the period (G. E. Dawson and L. Kennedy-Skipton, *Elizabethan Handwriting 1500–1650* (London, 1968, repr. Chichester, 1981), pl. 2A), and the printed version appears to be based on a Textura form with a hooked terminal such as is found in the Pica Textura (sometimes called 'Black Letter' or 'English') used, for example, for Parker's *Defence of priestes mariages* (cf. F. Isaac, *English Printers' Types of the Sixteenth Century* (London, 1936), pl. 54), or in the Pica Textura tentatively attributed to Guyot (Vervliet T34), or in the *lettres de forme, lettre bastarde,* and *lettres tourneures* of Geofroy Tory (*Champ Fleury* (Paris, G. Gourmont, 1529), sigs O2ᵛ and O3). Another possibility is that the use of a sixteenth-century Secretary or Textura **z** was inspired by the shape of **z** sometimes found in Irish manuscripts. In Lambeth Palace MS 1370 (the 'Gospels of MacDurnan' of *s.* ix) (see above p. 169–

70, n. 84–5) z sometimes occurs with the lower limb turned down and round to form a tail, e.g. in 'nazarenum' on fol. 209ᵛ line 10 at John 18: 7, although, unlike sixteenth-century z, the diagonal extends beyond the juncture with the lower limb.

Capitals

In the *Testimonie* Roman capitals are very occasionally taken from a Great Primer fount, e.g. Great Primer F on sig. F2ᵛ line 18 beside English F on sig. E3ᵛ line 12. This practice is commoner in *The Gospels* (STC 2961), e.g. on sig. Dd2ᵛ Great Primer D and G (line 2) beside English D (line 18) and G (line 3).

Æ. In the *Testimonie*, but not in subsequent specimens, Æ¹ and Æ² are shown as equivalent to roman and swash italic Æ respectively. Æ¹ in particular is quite rare in the manuscripts, but, besides the Junius 121 group, is found notably in Tiberius B.I, throughout the Orosius (fols 3–111), as a full display capital, but also as a secondary display capital, e.g., on fol. 70, lines 1, 2, and 8 (Pl. 30); here Æ¹ is used side by side angular capital Æ on an alternating basis, and this usage may have been influential in the decision to cut two capital Æ shapes.

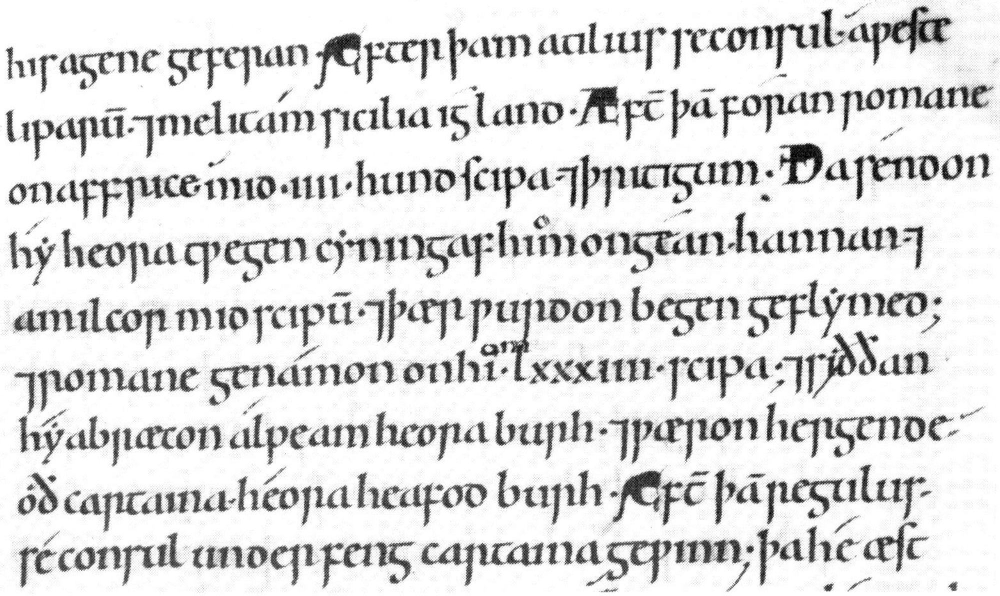

Plate 30   London, British Library, Cotton MS Tiberius B.I, fol. 70, lines 1–9

H, M. Both these forms have not so much a hooked terminal as an attention-seeking twitch at the base of their lower right stem. This feature too is compatible with a Textura face, such as the Pica Textura used for Parker's *Defence of priestes mariages*, and it occurs also in the cadeaulx (i.e. 'quadreaulx', display capitals a quarter of the height higher than those following them) of Geofroy Tory (*Champ Fleury* (1529), sig. O2^r). However, the feature may derive from manuscript usage. (For Uncials used in print cf. Vervliet, *Printing Types* (1968), pp. 208–15.) Twitched M, for example, occurs in Hatton 113, fol. vi^v (see Pl. 29, p. 180 above), and quite frequently in Tiberius B.I, e.g. fol. 63 line 9. Twitched H occurs in Faustina A.IX, fol. 132^v line 22.

X. Although it occurred rarely in proper names ('Xersis' in Tiberius B.I, fol. 37, lines 6, 14) a special sort for this letter was probably cut because of its frequency in the manuscripts as an abbreviation for 'Christ'. A good example, which might have served as a model, occurs in Hatton 113, fol. 56^v (Pl. 26, see p. 177 above, where it is a numeral); for others that are similar cf. Corpus 265, p. 157, line 15, and London, Cotton MS Vespasian D.XIV, fol. 27^v line 5. But in the event this form of abbreviation was not used in print, and so the special sort was to all effects and purposes redundant.

Punctuation

Before the *punctus versus* became available a (?Pica) roman semi-colon was used, as in the *Testimonie* specimen (Pl. 23(a), see p. 161 above).

Appendix 2

A Testimonie of Antiquitie (1566?), *STC* 159.5: Sources of Anglo-Saxon Texts and Passages

References and abbreviations

ASC	*Anglo-Saxon Chronicle.*
Assmann	Assmann, B. *Angelsächsische Homilien und Heiligenleben* (Kassel, 1889).
CCCC	Cambridge, Corpus Christi College.
Clark	Clark, C. *The Peterborough Chronicle 1070–1154* (London, 1954).
CUL	Cambridge, University Library.
Fehr	Fehr, B. *Die Hirtenbriefe Ælfrics* (Hamburg, 1914, repr. suppl. P. Clemoes, Darmstadt, 1966).
Godden	Godden, M. *Ælfric's Catholic Homilies*, EETS (SS), 5 (1979).
Liebermann	Liebermann, F. *Die Gesetzen der Angelsachsen*, 3 vols (Halle, 1903–16).
Liuzza	Liuzza, R. M. *The Old English Version of the Gospels*, EETS (OS), 304 (1994).
Loyn	Loyn, H. R. *A Wulfstan Manuscript Containing Institutes, Laws and Homilies: British Museum Cotton Nero A.I*, EEMF, 17 (Copenhagen, 1971).
OBL	Oxford, Bodleian Library.
Zupitza	Zupitza, J. *Ælfrics Grammatik und Glossar*, Sammlung englischer Denkmäler 1 (Berlin, 1880).

1. Preface

1.1 Sig. A3ᵛ   Ælfric's 'Excusatio Dictantis' (opening statement) at the end of his homily *Depositio S. Martini* (Godden, XXXIV) from CCCC, MS 198, fol. 385ᵛ, lines 5–9;

1.2 Sig. A4   Ælfric's *Grammar*, opening statement from OE Preface presumably quoted from CUL, MS Hh.1.10, fol. 1ᵛ, lines 4–7, beside which there is an annotation by Joscelyn (cf. Zupitza, 2);

1.3 Sig. A6ᵛ–7ʳ   Ælfric's *Grammar*, Latin Preface, quoted from Hh.1.10, fol. 1, lines 12–18, where the reading *scolis uenerabilis aþelwoldi presulis* is distinctive (cf. Zupitza, 1);

1.4 Sig. A8ʳ   Ælfric's *Letter to Sigeferth* preceding homily for 2nd Sunday after Epiphany presumably from BL, Cotton MS Vespasian D.XIV, fol. 6ᵛ, lines 15–21 (Assmann, 13);

1.5 Sig. B4   List of Books given by Leofric to Exeter Cathedral from Exeter Cath. Lib., MS 3501, fol. 1, lines 1–4, 19–22; and fol. 1ᵛ, lines 14–20, where the place of resumption in 14 has been marked with a vertical line and a cross in the margin, presumably by Joscelyn; not from CCCC, MS 101 (transcript *s.* xvi²) as the reading *deorwurþ* is closer to Exeter Cath., 3501 *deorwurðe* than Corpus 101 *deorwurde*;

1.6 Sig. B5ᵛ   Latin quotation of scribal statement from OBL, MS Junius 121, fol. 101, lines 15–18;

1.7 Sig. B7ʳ   Story about wife retention from *ASC* E *s.a.* 1129, OBL, MS Laud Misc. 636, fol. 87, lines 22–4 (Clark, 51).

2. Text

2.1 Sigs C3ᵛ–H3ᵛ   Ælfric's *Sermo de Sacrificio in die Pascae* (Godden, XV) from CCCC, MS 198, fol. 218, line 1–fol. 226ʳ, line 4, with some readings from BL, Cotton MS Faustina A. IX, fol. 131, line 5–fol. 139, line 20; distinctive readings from Corpus 198 (Godden's E) include *heardlice* (20), *tacnie* (37), *swa eac* (66), *hlaf* (75), *sume* (150), *ælcum* (152), *oðære* (159), *ungesewenlice* (194), *he na* (210), *ðe sylf* (216), *efenlæcað* (307–8), *hyrdnysse* (311), *modes* (315); readings taken over from Faustina A.IX (Godden's N) include *race* (34), TAU (54), *manegum* (81), *gehwilcum* (90), *ac* (107), *ðone ylcan* (186), *husel* (225), *ne* (246), *gewistfullian* (267), *mistlicum* (284), *swa* (295), *he* (315), *unscæððigan* (331), *andweardum* (332); CUL, MS Ii.4.6, where this sermon occurs as art. 20, was given to Parker 29 December 1567, too late to be taken into account for this printed version (and the text contains no distinctive readings from it), even though the earliest state of four pages of the book have been bound into it after fol. 156;

2.2 Sigs H5ᵛ–H7ᵛ   Ælfric's letter to Wulfsige III (bishop of Sherborne 992–1002) extracts (Fehr, §§133–42) from MS Junius 121, fol. 109ᵛ, line 23–fol. 110ᵛ, line 5, where the readings *mus oððe nytenu* (§134), *gymene* (§135), *xiiii niht* (§136), *halgan* (§141), and *to his gastlican blode* (§142) are distinctive, and where the end of the passage used has been marked by Parker in the text, with his triquetra mark in the margin to call attention to it; the editors also saw CCCC, MS 190, p. 305, line 20– p. 306, line 17;

2.3 Sigs H8ᵛ–I6ᵛ   Ælfric's second letter to Wulfstan (archbishop of York 1002–23) extracts (Fehr, §§86–95, 97–109) from MS Junius 121, fol. 116, line 8–fol. 118, line 7, where the readings *gefyllað* (§86), *doð unwislice* (§87), *bebead* (§92), *of þam gastlicum stane* (§105), *þa þæt Israhela* (§107), *þeah he* (§108) are distinctive, and where the beginning and end of the passage used are marked with a cross and asterisk respectively, presumably by Joscelyn; the editors also saw Corpus 190, p. 341, line 12–p. 343, line 12. Joscelyn's transcript of this passage from Junius 121 occurs in BL, Cotton MS Vitellius D.VII, fols 5–6 (damaged by fire) see Pl. 21;

2.4 Sigs I8ᵛ–K2ʳ   Latin text (in roman type) of Ælfric's second letter to Wulfstan from CCCC, MS 265, p. 176, line 17–p. 178, line 4 (where the beginning of the passage quoted has been underlined, with Joscelyn's triquetra in the margin), collated with Corpus 190, p. 155, line 1–p. 156, line 22, from which a passage erased in Corpus 265 on p. 177, lines 18–21 has been supplied, with explanatory annotation in the margin by Joscelyn; the readings *est [enim] sanguis* (K1ʳ, line 23) and *qui [pro vobis et] pro multis* (K1ʳ, lines 24–5) are distinctive against Corpus 190 which includes the words in square brackets, although in Corpus 265 the words *vobis et pro* have been supplied above the line by Joscelyn, only to be ignored (assuming they were already there) for the printed text.

3. Editorial statement

3.1 Sig. K6ʳ Ælfric's letter to Wulfsige, extract (Fehr, §§61–2) from MS Junius 121, fol. 105ᵛ, lines 10–16, where the readings *on sunnan dagum* and *andgyt* are distinctive, and where the beginning of the passage has been underlined, with Joscelyn's triquetra in the margin;

3.2 Sigs K6ᵛ–K7ʳ Anglo-Saxon Laws I Cnut 21–22.1 (Liebermann, I, 302) from BL, Cotton MS Nero A.I (Loyn), fol. 13ᵛ, line 10–fol. 14, line 8, where the readings *inweardre, smeagan oft, huru cunne* are distinctive; the reading *geleafan 7 ariht* is correct despite Liebermann's indication that 7 comes from CCCC MS 383; in the reading *smeagan oft* the words '7 swyrian', written by Joscelyn, are indicated for insertion before *oft*, but evidently this collation was done after 1566 (between 1568 and 1580, according to Loyn, 39).

4. Supplementary text

4.1a Sig. K8 OE text of Matthew 6.7–9 (preceding Lord's Prayer, Liuzza, 12) from CUL, MS Ii.2.11, fol. 9ᵛ, line 19–fol. 10, line 1, where the readings *nellon* (2 ×) are distinctive; also distinctive against CCCC, MS 140 (Ker, *Catalogue*, no. 35) are the spellings *gebiddan* (not-*on*), *fæla* (not *fela*), *heora mænig-* (not *hyra menig-*), and *Eornost-* (not *Eornust-*);

4.1b Sigs K8ᵛ–L1ᵛ OE text of Lord's Prayer from BL, Cotton MS Cleopatra B.XIII, fol. 58, lines 15–22, but the reading *þin wylla on eorðan swa swa on heofenū* is apparently from CUL, Ii.2.11 (Cleopatra B.XIII has *Syþin willa swa swa onheofenum swa eac on eorðan*), and *cume þin rice* may also be from the same source, since that MS has *to me be cume* with *to me be* underlined (for omission?) though *ge* has been added above *be* (?*s.* xvi²) to give Cleopatra B.XIII's reading *ge cume*;

4.2 Sigs L1ᵛ–L3ʳ OE text of Creed from Cleopatra B.XIII, fol. 58, line 23–fol. 58ᵛ, line 11;

4.3 Sig. L3ʳ Prologue to Ten Commandments from Ælfric's second (OE) letter to Wulfstan (Fehr, §121), from Corpus 190, p. 344, lines 8–11, collated with Junius 121, fol. 118ᵛ, line 22–fol. 119, line 2; the reading *of þam munte* is a conflation with *of* (not *on*) from Junius 121 and omission of *ylcan* from Corpus 190;

4.4 Sigs L3ᵛ–L5ʳ　Ten Commandments (1st nine only, cf. Liebermann, I, 26–9) from CCCC, MS 173, fol. 36, lines 1–17, where the readings *londe Ꝛ of hiora* (prol.), *noman* (2), *gehalgige, sint* (3), *medder* (4), *dearnenga* (6) are distinctive, but the reading *sealde ðe* (4), which is not in the surviving manuscripts, appears also in Lambarde's *Archaionomia* (1568), G4ᵛ, line 4; BL, Cotton Nero A.I (Loyn) was collated by Joscelyn with readings from Corpus 173, so that the collated text on fol. 51, line 1–fol. 51ᵛ, line 3 could have been the basis of this printed text, but only if the collation was done early enough.

III
Readers as Makers of Texts and Traditions

The Patristic Content of English Book Collections in the Eleventh Century: Towards a Continental Perspective[1]

Teresa Webber

The contents of English book collections in the early twelfth century differed greatly from those of a century before, and it is in their patristic content that the difference is most marked.[2] It is generally accepted that the writings of the Church Fathers copied or acquired by religious houses in the tenth and early eleventh centuries were limited in number and character, and were, for the most part, those which were seen to promote the spiritual and scholarly aims of the tenth-century monastic reform.[3] During the late eleventh and early twelfth centuries large numbers of patristic (and other) texts were acquired, among them a great many that had either not been present or not widely disseminated in England in the preceding century or more. This activity has thus far been interpreted within the context of the impact of the Norman Conquest, as the attempt of ecclesiastics from Normandy to reform English libraries which were, to their eyes, old-fashioned, idiosyncratic and, most important, lacking in the central patristic works of theology, doctrine and exegesis. Lanfranc, in

---

[1] Thanks are due to David Ganz, Michael Gullick and Conrad Leyser for their helpful comments and criticisms of a draft of this essay. Earlier versions of it were presented as papers at the International Medieval Congress, Kalamazoo, and to seminars at the universities of St Andrews, Birmingham, London and Oxford, and at a meeting of the Seminar in the History of the Book. I am also grateful to those attending those seminars for their comments and suggestions. I am alone responsible for the views expressed and the errors that remain.

[2] Ker, *English Manuscripts*; R. M. Thomson, 'The Norman Conquest and English Libraries', in *The Role of the Book in Medieval Culture*, ed. P. Ganz (Turnhout, 1986), II, 27–40; T. Webber, *Scribes and Scholars at Salisbury Cathedral c.1075–c.1125* (Oxford, 1992), pp. 31–43. A rather different picture has recently been suggested by J. F. Kelly, 'The Knowledge and Use of Augustine among the Anglo-Saxons', *Studia Patristica*, 28 (1993), 211–16, but there are several problems with the evidence he presents. He does not distinguish between what was available to Bede and Alcuin and what was still available by the tenth century, and cites as evidence of continued and widespread circulation of certain texts, late-eleventh-century manuscripts which are demonstrably copied from very recently imported continental exemplars.

[3] For the fullest treatment of this aspect of late Anglo-Saxon learned culture, see F. A. Rella, 'Some Aspects of the Indirect Transmission of Christian Latin Sources for Anglo-Saxon Prose from the Reign of Alfred to the Norman Conquest', B.Litt. thesis, University of Oxford (1977). See also Rella's 'Continental Manuscripts Acquired for English Centers in the Tenth and Early Eleventh Centuries: a Preliminary Checklist', *Anglia*, 98 (1980), 107–16.

particular, with his interest in biblical scholarship, theology and canon law, and his known activity in annotating such texts as Augustine, *De ciuitate Dei*,[4] has been viewed as the prime mover behind this initiative. Previous studies have clearly demonstrated that a significant impetus to the importing and production of patristic texts came from Normandy in the wake of the Conquest, but further research, made possible by the ground-breaking work of N. R. Ker and others, indicates that a predominantly Anglo-Norman focus may provide an incomplete context for the changing character of English book collections. An examination of the contents of contemporary continental book collections provides evidence that monasteries and cathedrals in England were by no means alone in possessing only limited numbers of patristic texts prior to the twelfth century. Furthermore, surviving manuscripts and their textual affiliations indicate that non-Norman centres on the continent also played a role in the diffusion of patristic texts to England.

During the early Middle Ages relatively few communities in England or on the continent appear to have considered it necessary, or had the means or opportunity, to acquire a thorough patristic collection consisting of a substantial number of texts in full by all or most of the principal Latin Fathers. Impressive collections were formed from time to time, as at Wearmouth-Jarrow and at York in the eighth century and at the major Carolingian centres, but libraries such as these did not become widespread among religious houses even on the continent until the twelfth century. Carolingian catalogues provide evidence of systematic attempts to acquire thorough holdings of the works of certain authors,[5] but the earliest surviving example of a collection of the 'opera omnia' of an author is the multi-volume collected works of Augustine copied at Clairvaux during the first half of the twelfth century, which, it seems, remained an exception so far as patristic authors are concerned until the printed editions of *opera omnia* initiated by Johann Amerbach at the end of the fifteenth century.[6]

---

[4] M. T. Gibson, 'Lanfranc's Notes on Patristic Texts', *Jnl Theological Studies*, n.s. 22 (1971), 435–50.

[5] A mid-ninth-century cataloguer at Murbach drew up lists of the texts of certain authors (including Cyprian, Ambrose and Augustine) that his abbey wished to acquire, using texts such as Augustine's *Retractiones*, his *Contra Iulianum* (for Ambrose's works), and Book I of Cassiodorus's *Institutiones*, as bibliographical guides: see W. Milde, *Der Bibliothekskatalog des Klosters Murbach aus dem 9. Jahrhundert* (Heidelberg, 1968). For evidence of similar activity at other Carolingian houses, see R. McKitterick, *The Carolingians and the Written Word* (Cambridge, 1989), pp. 169–210.

[6] J. de Ghellinck, 'Une édition ou une collection médiévale des *Opera omnia* de saint Augustin', in *Liber floridus: Mittellateinische Studien P. Lehmann zum 65. Geburtstag gewidmet*, ed. B. Bischoff and S. Brechter (St Ottilien, 1950), pp. 63–82, and De Ghellinck's 'Les éditions des "opera omnia s. Augustini" avant les Mauristes', in his *Patristique et Moyen Age, iii: Compléments à l'étude de la patristique* (Brussels, 1948), pp. 366–411. Collected works were compiled of a few post-patristic authors; for the compilation of the collected works of St Bernard, for example, see J. Leclercq, *Études sur saint Bernard et le texte de ses écrits*, Analecta sacri ordinis cisterciensis, 9 (Rome, 1953), pp. 124–33.

Surviving books and book lists dating from before the twelfth century suggest that the notion of a 'standard' patristic book collection is not one that can be applied to the early Middle Ages as a whole, although a number of Carolingian religious houses came to share very similar objectives in their acquisition and copying of patristic texts.[7] But even during the Carolingian period, when the copying of patristic texts was more intense than at any other time before the twelfth century, certain kinds of text appear to have enjoyed greater popularity than others, and individual houses (or members within them) pursued their own particular interests. The popularity of individual authors and texts did not remain constant throughout the early Middle Ages. M. L. W. Laistner, for example, has shown that interest in the writings of Jerome in the eighth and ninth centuries was focused largely upon his exegetical works (though a greater use was made of certain commentaries than of others) and, to a lesser extent, those of his controversial writings which related to then current doctrinal disputes.[8] Likewise, at Corbie, the theological and doctrinal works of Augustine were subjected to unusually close scrutiny during the ninth century, as a result of the interests of Ratramnus, Paschasius and Hadoard in such issues as the Eucharist and predestination.[9]

Despite the universally acknowledged importance of the writings of the Fathers of the early Church, no single 'canon' of Christian authors or texts was established during the early Middle Ages. Various lists of authors or texts were drawn up from time to time (and especially in times of theological or doctrinal controversy), but whilst they reveal some agreement, they also reveal differences. Bede, so far as we know, was the first writer to single out Ambrose, Augustine, Gregory and Jerome.[10] But it was only from the eleventh century onwards that it was invariably these four writers who were invoked.[11] In 1295 their superior status as the four principal doctors of the Church eventually received papal confirmation in a decretal of

---

[7] McKitterick, *Carolingians and the Written Word*, pp. 165–210.

[8] 'The Study of St Jerome in the Early Middle Ages', in *A Monument to Saint Jerome: Essays on some Aspects of his Life, Works and Influence*, ed. F. X. Murphy (New York, 1952), pp. 233–56.

[9] D. Ganz, *Corbie in the Carolingian Renaissance* (Sigmaringen, 1990), pp. 75–7, 81–92, 97–101.

[10] Bede, *Expositio in Lucae euangelium*, ed. D. Hurst, CCSL, 120 (Turnhout, 1960), p. 7: 'Aggregatisque . . . opusculis patrum quid beatus Ambrosius quid Augustinus quid denique Gregorius uigilantissimus iuxta suum nomen nostrae gentis apostolus quid Hieronimus sacrae interpres historiae quid ceteri patres in beati Lucae uerbis senserint quid dixerint diligentius inspicere sategi.'

[11] Controversy and dispute during the eleventh century gave urgency to appeals to the authority of the Fathers, and no doubt contributed to the frequency of appeals to the writings of the same four authors, Ambrose, Augustine, Gregory and Jerome, as a patristic equivalent of the four evangelists and four major prophets. Berengar, for example, in his controversial writings on the doctrine of the Eucharist in the mid eleventh century, appealed to the authority of the authentic writings of these four authors; Sigebert of Gembloux did likewise in his letter on the question of whether married priests should celebrate Mass, written in the early heat of the Investiture contest: see J. de Ghellinck, 'Les premières listes des docteurs de l'église en occident' in his *Le Mouvement théologique du xiie siècle*, 2nd edn (Bruges, 1948), pp. 514–15.

Boniface VIII.[12] During the early Middle Ages, however, lists of the principal Fathers were not confined to these authors, nor were they necessarily given priority in the order of those named.[13] Cassiodorus, in his guide to the patristic reading which should accompany the study of the Bible, devoted individual chapters to Hilary, Cyprian, Ambrose, Jerome and Augustine.[14] His influence is apparent not only in the canons of the Council of Valence of 855 (provoked by the controversy over the doctrine of predestination), which affirmed submission to these five writers,[15] but also, over two centuries later, in the classification of authors of Haimeric of Angoulême (c.1086), in which, after the authentic canon of the Bible, which represented gold, are listed Cyprian, Ambrose, Jerome, Hilary, Augustine and Gregory, who comprised the silver rank.[16] The early-twelfth-century *Liber pancrisis* began by naming Augustine, Jerome, Ambrose and Gregory, but also named Isidore and Bede, and then struck a new path by adding the names of the modern masters: William of Champeaux, Ivo of Chartres, and the brothers, Anselm and Ralph of Laon.[17]

The diversity of the patristic content of early medieval book collections should be borne in mind when one assesses the character of late Anglo-Saxon book collections. Certainly, by comparison with the great Carolingian libraries, the number and range of patristic texts in religious houses in England on the eve of the Conquest were very limited.[18] A number of texts which had been known to Bede and Alcuin seem no

---

[12] *Liber sextus decretalium*, III, tit. xxii, cap. 1: cited in E. F. Rice, *Saint Jerome in the Renaissance* (Baltimore, MD, 1985), p. 218. 'Egregios quoque ipsius doctores ecclesiae, beatos Gregorium, qui meritis inclytis sedis apostolicae curam gessit, Augustinum et Ambrosium, venerandos antistes, ac Hieronymum, sacerdotii praeditum titulo, eximios confessores summis attollere vocibus, laudibus personare praecipuis et specialibus disponit honoribus venerari. Horum quippe doctorum perlucida et salutaria documenta praedictam illustrarunt ecclesiam, decorarunt virtutibus, et morum informarunt'.

[13] For what follows, see De Ghellinck, 'Les premières listes', pp. 514–17. See also O. Bardenhewer, *Geschichte der altkirchlichen Literatur*, 2nd edn (Freiburg im Breisgau, 1913), I, 44–9.

[14] *Cassiodori senatoris Institutiones*, I, xviii–xxii, ed. R. A. B. Mynors (Oxford, 1937), pp. 58–61.

[15] 'Indubitanter autem doctoribus pie et recte tractantibus verbum veritatis ipsisque sacrae scripturae lucidissimis expositoribus, id est Cypriano, Hilario, Ambrosio, Hieronymo, Augustino, ceterisque in catholica pietate quiescentibus, reverenter auditum et obtemperanter intellectum submittimus, et pro viribus, quae ad nostram salutem conscripserunt, amplectimur.' Cited by De Ghellinck, 'Les premières listes', p. 514.

[16] *Ars lectoria*, ed. C. Thurot, 'Documents relatifs à l'histoire de la grammaire au moyen âge', *Comptes rendus des séances de l'Académie des Inscriptions et Belles Lettres*, n.s., 6 (1870), 249–50.

[17] 'Incipit liber pancrisis, id est, totus aureus, quia hic auree continentur sententie vel questiones sanctorum patrum, augustini, iheronimi, ambrosii, gregorii, ysidori, bede, et modernorum magistrorum willelmi catalaunensis episcopi, iuonis carnotensis episcopi, anselmi et fratris eius radulphi.' Cited by De Ghellinck, 'Les premières listes', p. 516.

[18] For surviving manuscripts, see H. Gneuss, 'A Preliminary List of Manuscripts Written or Owned in England up to 1100', *ASE*, 9 (1981), 1–60. This list is currently being revised. For booklists, see M. Lapidge, 'Surviving Booklists from Anglo-Saxon England', *Learning and Literature in Anglo-Saxon England: Studies Presented to Peter Clemoes on the Occasion of his Sixty-Fifth birthday*, ed. M. Lapidge

longer to have been available in tenth- and early-eleventh-century England. This impression is reinforced by the fact that a significant proportion of the patristic texts which were present in England by the early eleventh century were in books imported from the continent or in copies which had been made from recently imported books. The texts which were imported were limited in both number and character and comprised, for the most part, those which were seen to promote the spiritual and scholarly aims of the tenth-century reform.[19] In theological and exegetical terms at least, these scholarly aims were somewhat limited. Thus several copies of Augustine's introductory text, the *Enchiridion*, survive from late Anglo-Saxon England, but complete copies of his major doctrinal treatises are either very rare indeed or non-existent. The only patristic author whose works are comparatively well represented in full (as opposed to extracts in penitentials and homiliaries) is Gregory. But he is the exception who proves the rule, for his writings were held in the highest esteem by monastic reformers both in England and on the continent because they were seen by the reformers to promote an essentially monastic spirituality.

Carolingian libraries, however, are perhaps an inappropriate standard against which to compare English book collections formed in the tenth and first half of the eleventh centuries. Instead, a more suitable comparison is what can be learned of the reading associated with the monastic reforms of the tenth and early eleventh centuries, and with continental book collections formed during that period. Unfortunately, less research has yet been undertaken on the content of tenth- and early-eleventh-century book collections than on those of the Carolingian period.[20] But my impression is that until around the mid eleventh century the creation of thorough collections of patristic texts was comparatively rare, and that for many

---

and H. Gneuss (Cambridge, 1985), pp. 33–89. The beginnings of an increased interest in patristic texts is apparent in Lapidge's list VIII (books donated by Saewold to Saint-Vaast, Arras, c.1070) and list XIII (a late-eleventh- or early-twelfth-century list probably from Peterborough). For the ongoing project to identify texts known to the Anglo-Saxons, see *Sources of Anglo-Saxon Literary Culture: a Trial Version*, ed. F. M. Biggs, T. D. Hill and P. E. Szarmach (Binghampton, NY, 1990).

[19] See Rella, 'Some Aspects of the Indirect Transmission', p. 95.

[20] On the need for further study of tenth- and early-eleventh-century manuscripts, see R. McKitterick, 'Continuity and Innovation in Tenth-Century Ottonian Culture', in *Intellectual Life in the Middle Ages: Essays Presented to Margaret Gibson*, ed. L. Smith and B. Ward (London, 1992), pp. 15–24; and J. Vezin, 'Les manuscrits en Lotharingie autour de l'an Mil', in *Religion et culture autour de l'an Mil: royaume capétien et Lotharingie*, ed. D. Iogna-Prat and J. C. Picard (Paris, 1990), pp. 309–14. Some important work has already been done: C. E. Eder, *Die Schule des Klosters Tegernsee im frühen Mittelalter im Spiegel des Tegernseer Handschriften*, Studien und Mitteilungen zur Geschichte des Benediktinerordens, 83 (1972), 6–155. The primary focus of both N. Daniel, *Handschriften des zehnten Jahrhunderts aus der Freisinger Dombibliothek* (Munich, 1973) and H. Hoffmann, *Buchkunst und Königtum im ottonischen und frühsalischen Reich*, MGH Schriften, 30 (Stuttgart, 1986), is on the palaeography of the manuscripts rather than their contents. The essential materials for a study of intellectual life at Fleury have been presented in M. Mostert, *The Library of Fleury: a Provisional List of Manuscripts* (Hilversum, 1989), but we await a detailed interpretation of these manuscripts.

religious houses on the continent, as in England, the emphasis was upon a more limited range of texts, and in particular those which promoted the spiritual aims of monastic reform.

An emphasis upon the works of Gregory and other texts considered appropriate for the monastic *lectio* seems to be apparent even in houses such as Gorze and Cluny which by the mid eleventh century did possess fairly extensive holdings of texts by the Church Fathers.[21] A passage in the *Vita* of the monastic reformer, John of Gorze (d. 977), provides a revealing glimpse of the character of patristic reading in the tenth century.[22] John's reading of the Fathers is depicted as being exceptionally wide-ranging by his biographer, yet the lesson to be drawn from the passage seems to be that his omnivorous approach eventually led him astray. According to the *Vita*, John first devoted himself to digesting Gregory's *Moralia in Iob*, until he knew the text by heart, and then read any patristic text he could lay his hands on, including Augustine on John's Gospel and the Psalms, the *De ciuitate Dei* and, finally, Augustine, *De trinitate*.[23] But, in order to understand the logical argument of Augustine's exposition of the doctrine of the Trinity, John realized he would need to acquaint himself with the logical textbooks such as the *Isagoge* of Porphyry, and duly immersed himself in such works. He was reproved, however, by his abbot for engaging in such time-consuming activity, and was instructed to occupy himself with 'sacra lectione'. John therefore returned to the works of Gregory and worked away at his Homilies on Ezekiel until he had virtually committed them to memory.[24] This passage demon-strates well the distinction between the meditative, devotional reading of the Fathers which predominated in reformed monastic houses, and the more intellectual

---

[21] For the eleventh-century catalogue of Gorze, see G. Morin, 'Le Catalogue des manuscrits de l'abbaye de Gorze au xie siècle', *Revue bénédictine*, 22 (1905), 1–10. For the library at Cluny, see V. von Büren, 'Le grand catalogue de la bibliothèque de Cluny', *Le Gouvernement d'Hugues de Semur à Cluny. Actes du colloque scientifique international* (Cluny, 1988), pp. 245–63, and her 'Le Catalogue de la bibliothèque de Cluny du xie siècle reconstitué', *Scriptorium*, 46 (1992), 256–67. Both catalogues begin by listing volumes containing the works of the principal Latin Fathers organized by author. Gorze, in common with most such systematically organized catalogues, begins with Augustine, whose works in any reasonably substantial collection of patristic texts were inevitably the most numerous, but the mid-eleventh-century Corbie catalogue begins with the works of Gregory, which may reflect the special esteem with which he was held in that house.

[22] John of St-Arnulf, *Vita Iohannis abbatis Gorziensis*, ed. G. H. Pertz, MGH Scriptores, 4 (Hanover, 1841), pp. 360–61.

[23] *Vita Iohannis*, ed. Pertz, p. 360: 'In his primum moralia beati Gregorii ordine quam sepissime percurrens, pene cunctas ex eo continentias sententiarum ita memoriae commendavit . . . Nec minor ei Augustini, Ambrosii, Ieronimi, vel si quis antiquorum ad manus venissent, lectio erat; et quia ad id temporis, utpote studiis frigentibus, pene nec ipsi codices inveniebantur, Augustini in Iohannem et psalmos et de civitate Dei integre perlegit, postremum in libris de Trinitate mula intentione sudavit.'

[24] *Vita Iohannis*, ed. Pertz, pp. 360–61: 'Is (Einoldus) . . . tempora eum in his frustra nolens expendere, brevi prohibitione avertit, et ut animum pocius sacra lectione occuparet, ubi satis superque et scientiae et, quod maius est, edificationis ei doctrina suppeteret . . . Praeterea Gregorii in Iezehielem multo usu detrivit, ut pene memoriae commendasse videretur.'

approach to such works which gained more widespread currency during the eleventh and twelfth centuries.[25]

During the eleventh and early twelfth centuries there was a revival of interest throughout western Europe in a number and range of patristic texts which went far beyond what would have been required for monastic *lectio*, and which reflected a more intellectual approach to biblical study, canon law, and questions of theology and doctrine.[26] But such interests, and the acquisition of books to support them, at first took hold only in a small number of centres. Substantial collections of patristic texts were by no means widespread by 1066, even in Normandy, and did not become so on the continent until the first half of the twelfth century. The main phase of manuscript production at the two Benedictine houses at Angers, for example, was the second half, and more particularly, the end of the eleventh century.[27] Nearby, at La Trinité, Vendôme, some limited scribal activity was under way during the third quarter of the eleventh century, but the main campaign of book production can be dated to the abbacy of Geoffrey (1093–1132).[28] The chronology of the acquisition of patristic texts at the Benedictine abbey of Michelsberg, Bamberg (founded in 1015), can be charted with unusual precision from the lists compiled in the mid-twelfth century by the *armarius*, Burchard.[29] The list of books acquired before the twelfth century includes a group of patristic texts comparable in their limited number and range to those of late Anglo-Saxon book collections.[30] More texts were acquired during the abbacy of Wolfram (1112–23), including a number of the major works of Augustine (such as his Commentary on John's Gospel, *De Genesi ad litteram* and *De*

---

[25] On this distinction, see M. B. Parkes, 'The Influence of the Concepts of *Ordinatio* and *Compilatio* on the Development of the Book' (1976) in his *Scribes, Scripts and Readers*, pp. 35–6. On the relationship between different traditions of monastic reform and the content of libraries in the eleventh century, see R. Kottje, 'Klosterbibliotheken und monastische Kultur in der zweiten Hälfte des 11. Jahrhunderts', *Zeitschrift für Kirchengeschichte*, 80 (1969), 145–62.

[26] For a brief survey of such developments, see B. Bischoff, *Latin Palaeography: Antiquity and the Middle Ages*, tr. D. Ó Cróinín and D. Ganz (Cambridge, 1990), pp. 212–23, and B. Munk Olsen, 'Les bibliothèques bénédictines et les bibliothèques des cathédrales: les mutations des xie et xiie siècles', *Histoire des bibliothèques françaises, i: Les bibliothèques médiévales du vie siècle à 1530*, ed. A.Vernet (Paris, 1989), pp. 31–43. On the expansion of the patristic base for canon law during the eleventh and twelfth centuries, see M. Brett, 'Canon Law and Litigation: the Century before Gratian', *Medieval Ecclesiastical Studies in Honour of Dorothy M. Owen*, ed. M. J. Franklin and C. Harper-Bill (Woodbridge, 1995), pp. 24–7. For the analysis of copies of patristic texts for polemical purposes in the late eleventh century, see I. S. Robinson, 'The Bible in the Investiture Contest: the South German Gregorian Circle', in *The Bible in the Medieval World: Essays in Memory of Beryl Smalley*, ed. K. Walsh and D. Wood (Oxford, 1985), pp. 61–84.

[27] J. Vezin, *Les scriptoria d'Angers au XIe siècle* (Paris, 1974).

[28] M.-C. Garand, *Catalogue des manuscrits en écriture latine portant des indications de date, de lieu ou de copiste*, 7 (Paris, 1984), pp. xxxiv–xxxvi.

[29] K. Dengler-Schreiber, *Scriptorium und Bibliothek des Klosters Michelsberg in Bamberg* (Graz, 1979), pp. 147–205.

[30] Ibid., list 2, pp. 160–75. Only one text of Ambrose, for example, is recorded in the list.

Doctrina Christiana).[31] But it was not until the abbacy of Hermann (1123–47) that the abbey acquired (apparently for the first time) a significant number of texts by Ambrose, the biblical commentaries of Jerome and Origen, and other major texts of Augustine, including the Confessions.[32]

In Normandy, as in other regions of western Europe, the chronology of acquisition during the eleventh century differed from house to house, and, as elsewhere, was probably dependent upon the initiative of individual abbots.[33] Only at Mont-Saint-Michel and Fécamp can we be at all confident that there were relatively substantial collections of the works of the Fathers before 1066.[34] According to Orderic Vitalis, scribal activity was under way at Saint-Évroul as early as the abbacy of Thierry (1050–57), but priority was given to copying the books of the Bible and the works of Gregory. Only subsequently did the scribes turn their attention to other patristic authors.[35] Some Norman houses were still in the process of collecting the works of the Fathers at the end of the eleventh century. When English houses in the late

---

[31] Ibid., list 1, pp. 150–59.

[32] Ibid., list 5, pp. 184–95.

[33] The growth of the libraries of eight Norman houses is examined in G. Nortier, *Les Bibliothèques médiévales des abbayes bénédictines de Normandie* (Paris, 1971).

[34] J. J. G. Alexander, *Norman Illumination at Mont Saint Michel 966–1100* (Oxford, 1970). On Fécamp, see Nortier, *Les Bibliothèques médiévales*, pp. 6–13, 26–30; and B. Branch, 'Inventories of the Library of Fécamp from the eleventh and twelfth centuries', *Manuscripta*, 23 (1979), 159–72, and her detailed study of the Fécamp manuscripts, 'The Development of Script in the Eleventh- and Twelfth-Century Manuscripts of the Norman Abbey of Fécamp', PhD thesis, Duke University, NC (1974). The precocity of these two houses in particular can be explained in part by the very close links that existed between them; F. Avril has demonstrated that a number of the Fécamp manuscripts were copied from Mont-Saint-Michel exemplars, and that these Fécamp manuscripts in their turn were later used as exemplars for manuscripts at Jumièges: 'Notes sur quelques manuscrits bénédictins normands', *Mélanges d'archéologie et d'histoire. École française de Rome*, 76 (1964), 491–525, esp. 504–22. Too little survives from Bec to determine how extensive its holdings of patristic texts were by 1066, although some impression may be gained from an examination of the works written by Lanfranc whilst at Bec: see R. W. Southern, *Saint Anselm: a Portrait in a Landscape* (Cambridge, 1990), pp. 53–9.

[35] *The Ecclesiastical History of Orderic Vitalis*, ed. M. Chibnall (Oxford, 1969), II, 48–50: 'Nam Rodulfus nepos eius [i.e. Thierry] Eptaticum scripsit et missalem ubi missa in conuentu cotidie canitur. Hugo autem socius eius expositionem super Ezechielem et Dialogum, primamque partem Moralium; Rogerius uero presbyter Paralipomenon librosque Salomonis terciamque partem Moralium. Praefatus itaque pater [Thierry] . . . omnes libros Veteris et Noui Testamenti omnesque libros facundissimi papae Gregorii Vticensium bibliotecae procurauit. Ex eius etiam scola excellentes librarii . . . processerunt, qui tractatibus Augustini et Ieronimi, Ambrosii, et Isidori, Eusebii et Orosii aliorumque doctorum bibliotecam sancti Ebrulfi repleuerunt.' Orderic's account, as with the many similar accounts found in twelfth-century narratives, needs to be treated with caution; the impression such accounts give of systematic programmes of copying may reflect twelfth-century attitudes and assumptions. It is very difficult to determine how many patristic texts had actually been copied at Saint-Évroul before the end of the eleventh century: for the surviving manuscripts and the problems of dating them, see Nortier, *Les Bibliothèques médiévales*, pp. 99–108, 119–23, esp. 101, n. 21. For modifications to Nortier, see Garand, *Catalogue*, pp. xiii–xiv.

eleventh and early twelfth centuries acquired books which had been made by Norman scribes, these books had been produced, as often as not, by scribes who were working on behalf of Norman as well as English houses. The hands of the same scribes have been identified in manuscripts with such different provenances as Exeter and Durham in England and Lyre and Jumièges in Normandy.[36] Thus while the acquisition of numerous patristic texts in England in the late eleventh century certainly owed a great deal to the initiative of Norman or Norman-trained bishops and abbots, such activity should not be interpreted as a belated attempt to catch up with continental norms, since it coincided with the period when such collections were becoming more widespread both in Normandy and elsewhere on the continent.

Normandy was undoubtedly an important source for the diffusion of patristic texts to England, even though relatively few Norman manuscripts have yet been identified as acting as exemplars for scribes working in England at the end of the eleventh century.[37] Nevertheless, imported manuscripts of non-Norman origin and the textual affiliations of manuscripts copied in England suggest that sources elsewhere on the continent were also used, and that, in the first few decades after the Conquest, the acquisition of books from Normandy was not necessarily the most convenient option.[38] Lanfranc's difficulties in importing books from Normandy are well known from two letters sent to Lanfranc from Anselm who was then at Bec.[39] In the first letter Anselm wrote: 'You asked me for the *Moralia in Iob*. William, abbot of St Étienne, and Arnost have found a scribe, who has begun to copy our manuscript from Bec. I am doing my utmost to get you the [letters of] Ambrose and Jerome; but it is not easy.' But Anselm later wrote of his lack of success. 'There has been a disagreement with the scribe; we have failed to engage the man whom you suggested in Brionne, and no one who is free to do the work here in Bec is sufficiently

---

[36] See, for example, A. de la Mare, 'A Probable Addition to the Bodleian's Holdings of Exeter Cathedral Manuscripts', *Bodleian Library Record*, 11 (1983), 79–88; M. Gullick, 'The Scribe of the Carilef Bible: a New Look at some Late-Eleventh-Century Durham Cathedral Manuscripts', *Medieval Book Production*, ed. Brownrigg, pp. 61–83.

[37] The most well-known example is Cambridge, Trinity Coll., MS B.16.44 (405), a copy of an abbreviated version of Pseudo-Isidore, Decretals and Canons of Councils – the so-called 'Collectio Lanfranci', which Z. N. Brooke argued lay behind the diffusion of this corpus of canon law in England (see his *The English Church and the Papacy*, 2nd edn (Cambridge, 1989), pp. 59–82, 231–5); the manuscript bears an inscription stating that Lanfranc had purchased the book from Bec. For textual relationships between Norman manuscripts and those produced at Rochester and Christ Church, Canterbury, see K. Waller, 'The Library, Scriptorium and Community of Rochester Cathedral Priory, c.1050–1150', PhD thesis, University of Liverpool (1981), pp. 195–206. For a survey of manuscripts imported from Normandy, see M. Gullick, 'Manuscrits et scribes normands en Angleterre', in *Manuscrits et enluminures dans le monde normand xie–xve siècles*, ed. P. Bouet and M. Dosdat (Caen, forthcoming).

[38] A list of manuscripts of non-Norman origin imported to England in the late eleventh and early twelfth centuries has not yet been compiled, nor have such books received much detailed attention.

[39] Anselm, *Epistolae*, ed. F. S. Schmitt, Anselmi Opera omnia, 3 (Edinburgh, 1946), nos 23, 25: see M. Gibson, *Lanfranc of Bec* (Oxford, 1978), p. 179.

competent.' Such problems may account for the comparatively small number of manuscripts from Christ Church which date from Lanfranc's episcopacy.[40] It is also possible that, in these early years, Christ Church may have been experiencing difficulties in borrowing manuscripts to act as exemplars.

The textual affiliations of the manuscripts copied at Salisbury Cathedral (the first house in post-Conquest England to acquire a really thorough collection of patristic texts) suggest that the canons had often to cast much further afield than Normandy to obtain exemplars.[41] For example, a Salisbury copy of a group of Cyprian's treatises and the copy of the Augustinian rule belong to very unusual textual traditions otherwise witnessed only by manuscripts at St Gall and Bobbio respectively. Baldwin, abbot of Bury St Edmunds (1065–1099), almost certainly imported manuscripts from his former monastery of Saint-Denis, near Paris.[42] In addition to a two-volume set of homilies, which includes a sermon for the anniversary of the viewing of the relics of St Dionysius at Saint-Denis, c.1050 (Cambridge, Pembroke College, MSS 23 and 24), Bury also acquired a ninth-century copy of Bede's commentary on Luke (Cambridge, Pembroke College, MS 83), which has been identified as a product of the scriptorium of Saint-Denis.[43] Another ninth-century manuscript owned by Bury in the twelfth century, also of northern French origin, Cambridge, Pembroke College, MS 91 (Jerome on the Psalms), may also have arrived by this route. Other continental manuscripts dating from the ninth century or earlier have been identified as having acted as the archetypes for the diffusion of their contents throughout England during the late eleventh and twelfth centuries, but unfortunately their immediate provenance prior to their arrival in England is not yet known.[44]

It is possible that Norman communities were facing some of the same problems in acquiring texts as those faced by their counterparts in England. This may have been the case even with such texts as Augustine's Confessions (one of the most widely

[40] T. Webber, 'Script and Manuscript Production at Christ Church, Canterbury, after the Norman Conquest', in *Canterbury and the Norman Conquest: Churches, Saints and Scholars 1066–1109*, ed. R. Eales and R. Sharpe (London, 1995), pp. 148–51. Michael Gullick suggests, however, that more of the extant Christ Church manuscripts than was previously thought may date from the 1080s (personal communication).

[41] Webber, *Scribes and Scholars*, pp. 44–81.

[42] T. Webber, 'The Provision of Books for Bury St Edmunds Abbey in the Eleventh and Twelfth Centuries', in *Medieval Art and Architecture at Bury St Edmunds Abbey*, ed. A. Gransden, Trans. British Archaeological Assoc. (forthcoming).

[43] J. Vezin, 'Les relations entre Saint-Denis et d'autres scriptoria pendant le haut moyen âge', in *The Role of the Book*, ed. Ganz, I, 38–39.

[44] For Hereford Cathedral Lib., MS O.iii.2 (Cassiodorus, *Institutiones*, I and other bio-bibliographical texts, *s.* ix), London, BL, Add. MS 23944A (Augustine, *De nuptiis et concupiscentia* and *Contra Iulianum*, *s.* ix), and their English descendants, see Ker, *English Manuscripts*, pp. 11–13. For London, BL, Add. MS 40165A (fragments of works of Cyprian, *s.* iv), see M. Bévenot, *The Tradition of Manuscripts: a Study in the Transmission of St. Cyprian's Treatises* (Oxford, 1961), pp. 9–15: this manuscript and its descendants are Bévenot's E family. For Cambridge, Pembroke Coll., MS 81 (Bede on Habbakuk, *s.* ix), see Thomson, 'The Norman Conquest', p. 35.

read texts of the Fathers in the later Middle Ages and beyond), which one might have assumed were widespread on the continent.[45] The earliest surviving English copies of the *Confessions* date from the late eleventh century and fall into two textual traditions, but neither tradition appears to have circulated in Normandy. Instead, the earliest English witnesses to these two traditions derive at probably just one stage removed from manuscripts each with an eleventh-century Flemish provenance: in one case, Saint-Bertin, in the other, St Peter's Ghent.[46] Eleventh- and early-twelfth-century Norman copies of the *Confessions* are very rare,[47] which may explain why English houses turned to Flanders for exemplars. But other factors, such as contacts with centres elsewhere on the continent, may also have been involved in determining whence manuscripts were imported. Numerous links had, for example, been established between religious houses in southern England and houses in Flanders since the later tenth century.[48] Furthermore, both before and after the Conquest a significant number of the heads of English cathedral and monastic houses, such as Baldwin of Bury, had come from or had spent time at houses on the continent other than those in Normandy.

In his pioneering study of contact between England and Flanders, Philip Grierson concluded:

> there are few lines of research more valuable than that of tracing the interrelationship of manuscripts, of showing how they were loaned from one abbey to another and trying to fill in the gaps in their genealogy . . . It would I think be true to say that only when a systematic study of the textual relationships of early English manuscripts with those in continental libraries has been undertaken, will we be able to form any accurate and precise idea of the relations of England with Flanders, as well as with other parts of the Continent, during the early Middle Ages.[49]

---

[45] For what follows, see T. Webber, 'The Diffusion of Augustine's *Confessions* in England during the Eleventh and Twelfth Centuries', in *The Cloister and the World: Essays in Medieval History in Honour of Barbara Harvey*, ed. J. Blair and B. Golding (Oxford, 1996), pp. 29–45.

[46] Boulogne-sur-Mer, Bibl. mun., MS 46 (from Saint-Bertin), and Paris, BN, MS lat. 1913A (at Ghent by the mid eleventh century).

[47] The only copy known to survive complete is Rouen, Bibl. mun., MS 82 (*s.* xi/xii, from Jumièges). The end of Book XIII survives as part of fragments from a mid-eleventh-century manuscript from Fécamp, now Biblioteca apostolica Vaticana, MS Reg. lat. 755, fols 100–105 (not noticed in my article on the diffusion of the *Confessions*): see Avril, 'Notes', pp. 522-4. The text, however, is not recorded in the mid-eleventh-century Fécamp catalogue.

[48] P. Grierson, 'Relations between England and Flanders before the Norman Conquest', *Trans. Royal Historical Soc.*, 4th ser., **23** (1941), 71–112, and also V. Ortenberg, *The English Church and the Continent in the Tenth and Eleventh Centuries: Cultural, Spiritual and Artistic Exchanges* (Oxford, 1992), pp. 21–40. By confining her study to liturgical and illuminated manuscripts, Ortenberg may underestimate the extent of manuscript exchange between England and not only Flanders but also elsewhere on the continent.

[49] Grierson, 'Relations', p. 112.

An examination of the diffusion of Augustine's Confessions to England has demonstrated the validity of this prediction. Further work on the dissemination of texts may provide more evidence of the importance of what might loosely be described as the Low Countries (from Flanders in the West to Lower Lotharingia in the East) for the diffusion of patristic and other texts to England. Among these different kinds of texts the earliest English copy of Cicero's Tusculan Disputations, for example, an early-twelfth-century manuscript from Salisbury, is most closely affiliated to a manuscript from Gembloux.[50] Scribal evidence also indicates movement between the Low Countries and England in the late eleventh and early twelfth centuries. A scribe who wrote and decorated in a style distinctive of manuscripts from the Meuse region, copied all or parts of several books at Salisbury in the late 1080s and 1090s; his hand has also been identified in a late-eleventh-century copy of Gregory's *Moralia* from Utrecht.[51] Very similar handwriting and decoration is found in several of the small group of manuscripts dating from the late eleventh or early twelfth centuries which have a Bath Abbey provenance.[52] Lastly, the earliest known specimen of written Netherlandish is a late-eleventh-century annotation added to an eleventh-century copy of Old English sermons from Rochester.[53]

Surviving manuscripts and booklists indicate that, by the mid eleventh century, a number of religious houses in the Low Countries had already begun to acquire substantial collections of patristic texts. The library catalogue from Lobbes (on the border between Lotharingia and Hainault) compiled in 1049, can be matched only by the most impressive Carolingian or twelfth-century catalogues in its systematic organization and the extraordinary number and range of patristic texts it lists.[54] Central works of the Latin Fathers also formed a significant proportion of the books produced at Saint-Bertin during the abbacy of Odbert at the end of the tenth and beginning of the eleventh centuries,[55] and of those from Gembloux which date from the abbacy of Olbert (1012–1048),[56] and of the books produced at Saint-Vaast, Arras,

---

[50] Webber, *Scribes and Scholars*, p. 64. For the acquisition of classical texts by Olbert, abbot of Gembloux and St James, Liège, see A. Boutemy, 'Un grand abbé du xie siècle: Olbert de Gembloux', *Annales de la Société archéologique de Namur*, 41 (1934), 43–85.

[51] Webber, *Scribes and Scholars*, p. 14 (on scribe viii). For eleventh- and twelfth-century Mosan manuscripts, see M.-R. Lapière, *La lettre ornée dans les manuscrits mosans d'origine bénédictine* (Paris, 1981).

[52] Compare the reproduction of part of fol. 10 of London, BL, MS Royal 6 B.xi (from Bath) in *Cat. Royal MSS*, IV, Pl. 45c, with reproductions of initials from eleventh-century manuscripts from Gembloux in Lapière, *La lettre ornée*, figs 16–36, 58.

[53] Oxford, Bodl. Lib., MS Bodley 340, fol. 169ᵛ: printed by K. Sisam, 'MSS Bodley 340 and 342: Ælfric's Catholic Homilies', *Review of English Studies*, 9 (1933), 11; see also Ker, *Catalogue*, p. 363.

[54] F. Dolbeau, 'Un nouveau catalogue des manuscrits de Lobbes aux xie et xiie siècles', *Recherches augustiniennes*, 13 (1978), 3–36; 14 (1979), 191–248.

[55] A. Wilmart, 'Les livres de l'abbé Odbert', *Bulletin historique de la Société des Antiquaires de la Morinie*, 14 (1929), 169–88.

[56] Boutemy, 'Un grand abbé', 43–85; Lapière, *La lettre ornée*, pp. 3–41.

during the second quarter of the eleventh century.[57] It may well be no coincidence that the first Norman house to undertake scribal activity on a large scale in the eleventh century, with the production of numerous patristic texts of a fairly advanced kind, was Mont-Saint-Michel, whose manuscripts, as J. J. G. Alexander has demonstrated, exhibit evidence of close contacts with Saint-Bertin and Saint-Vaast, Arras.[58] Lanfranc himself, in his use of patristic authorities in theological debate, was influenced by earlier Lotharingian scholarship. His treatise on the Eucharist, written to refute Berengar, was bolstered by a barrage of patristic quotations, the bulk of which came from Heriger of Lobbes's treatise on the same subject, written in the late tenth century, some 50 years before Berengar and Lanfranc came into conflict.[59] The importance of the Low Countries (most notably Liège), for the study of the classical *auctores* during the eleventh century, has long been recognized. But the content of book collections in the region provides evidence which may be suggestive of other kinds of scholarly activity as well: an interest in the kinds of patristic texts which were associated with a more intellectual approach to the study of the Bible, and questions of theology and canon law. Detailed work on the manuscripts and booklists of this region is required in order to verify this possibility.

The late eleventh and early twelfth centuries were a period of intense scribal activity not only in England but throughout western Europe, an activity in which the copying of patristic texts was a central concern. By the mid twelfth century it had become commonplace for the core of the book collections of any religious house of some size to be comprised of a substantial number of the works of the Fathers. Nevertheless, differences of emphasis still remained, reflecting the particular interests of individual houses. Certain texts remained rare, and appear to have been acquired or sought for by only a comparatively small number of houses. This was the case both in England and elsewhere on the continent. While some texts were diffused throughout England during the late eleventh and twelfth centuries, others were not. Salisbury Cathedral, for example, gained access to an exemplar of Augustine's incomplete commentary on Genesis, the *De Genesi ad litteram imperfectus liber*, from which a copy was made in the early twelfth century (now Salisbury Cathedral Library, MS 197, fols 25–32ᵛ + London, BL, MS Royal App. 1, fol. 15ᵛ). But no other twelfth-century English copies of this text survive, nor is it recorded in any twelfth-century English booklist. Indeed, fewer than twenty manuscripts of the text are known to survive in all, of which the Salisbury copy is the oldest; the only other surviving twelfth-century copy is that in the Clairvaux collection of Augustine's *opera omnia*.[60] As Gorman observes, this

[57] S. Schulten, 'Die Buchmalerei des 11. Jahrhunderts im Kloster St. Vaast in Arras', *Münchner Jahrbuch der bildenden Kunst*, 7 (1956), 49–90.

[58] Alexander, *Norman Illumination*, pp. 61–83.

[59] Gibson, *Lanfranc of Bec*, p. 83.

[60] M. Gorman, 'The Text of Saint Augustine's "De Genesi ad litteram imperfectus liber"', *Recherches augustiniennes*, 20 (1985), 65–86.

particular text appears to have attracted very little attention during the early and central Middle Ages, and only seems to have been of interest in the twelfth century to those who were attempting to collect as many as possible of the works of Augustine. Not all religious houses, then, aimed at comprehensiveness, even during the twelfth century, when most patristic texts had become more widely available. Those that sought to acquire less common texts had to make special efforts. When, for example, during the second quarter of the twelfth century, the abbot of Liessies requested that Clairvaux lend his house copies of some of the rarer texts of Augustine, he was informed by Prior Philip that the only copies that Clairvaux possessed were those in their multi-volume collected works of Augustine, which they were not prepared to loan; instead, a scribe should be sent to Clairvaux to copy the texts *in situ*.[61]

Scholars of various aspects of English history have recently been shifting their focus of attention away from the impact of 1066 and have begun to examine the full range of continental influence and contact during the eleventh century as a whole, as well as the persistence of Anglo-Saxon practice and traditions after 1066.[62] This essay represents another contribution to such an approach: a preliminary attempt to locate the changing character of English book collections within the wider context of developments in learning and the use of the Fathers throughout western Europe during the eleventh and early twelfth centuries. Much more work remains to be done, not only to determine the various factors which shaped the intellectual developments of the eleventh century and the increased interest in the writings of the Fathers that accompanied it but also on manuscript production and the content of book collections on the continent, in order to identify the sources of exemplars and manuscripts imported to England. But I hope that enough has emerged from this preliminary study to indicate the diversity of England's interaction with centres of learning on the continent in the later eleventh century, and to suggest that changes in the size and content of English libraries, whilst facilitated and accelerated by the Conquest, should not be interpreted solely as its 'effects'. In addition, I hope that this overview of the number and range of texts by the Church Fathers present in England during the

---

[61] Cited in J. Leclercq, 'Les manuscrits de l'abbaye de Liessies', *Scriptorium*, 6 (1952), 51–2: 'De operibus eius [Augustine] que uos non habetis inuenimus apud nos libros quatuor, uidelicet adnotationes in Iob, contra Felicem manicheum, contra Pelagium et Celestinum, contra duas epistolas Pelagi . . . Sed et hec uolumina de quibus scribo magnorum uoluminum corporibus inserta sunt, ita ut disiungi non possint nec uobis mitti. Consilium autem nostrum est ut si eos alibi recuperare non potestis et omnino uultis habere, nobis scriptorem et membranas transmittatis ut fiat uoluntas uestra.'

[62] See, for example, C. P. Lewis, 'The French in England before the Norman Conquest', *Anglo-Norman Studies*, 17 (1995), 123–44.

eleventh century (by comparison with what is known of continental book collections) may act as a starting-point for further study. By such means we may gain an understanding of how these works, both collectively and individually, were perceived and used by those who owned or sought to acquire them.

CHAPTER NINE

Medieval Hypertext: Image and Text from York Minster

Vincent Gillespie

For the medieval chroniclers and historians of the cathedral church of York, the major contribution of Archbishop John Thoresby was not his famous pastoral decrees of 1357, nor his mandate to translate them into the vernacular, but rather his major rebuilding of the choir and presbytery of the Minster itself. The fifteenth-century metrical chronicle records:

> Hic novum ecclesiae chorum inchoavit
> Et sic domus Domini decorem amavit.

The fourteenth-century chronicle attributed to Thomas Stubbs makes particular mention of his work on the Lady Chapel: 'Idem vero Archiepiscopus, ut verus amator Virginis, capellam ejusdem Dei genetricis et virginis Mariae mirabili artis sculptura, atque notabili pictura peregit.' This 'new work', initiated in 1362 and probably roofed in by 1371, was sufficiently complete by 1373 for the Archbishop to be buried 'coram altari Beati Virgine Mariam in novo opere chori'.[1]

It may be that the short work edited here for the first time (Appendix) describes an ensemble of text and images which was intended as a contribution to the decorative scheme of Thoresby's new Lady Chapel. Preserved only in Oxford, Corpus Christi College, MS 132, probably written in the second quarter of the fifteenth century, it purports to provide a detailed description of 'þe disposiciun of þe tabyll at our lady auter yn þe cathedrall kyrke of yorke'.[2] In an English marked with some strongly Northern and North East Midland features, it describes five images of the Virgin each supported by three Latin distiches which gloss and comment on each image.[3]

---

[1] *The Historians of the Church of York and its Archbishops*, ed. J. Raine, 3 vols, RS, 71 (1879–94), II, 484, ll. 525–6 and II, 420–21; J. H. Harvey, 'Architectural History from 1291 to 1558', in *A History of York Minster*, ed. G. E. Aylmer and R. Cant (Oxford, 1979), pp. 148–92, esp. 164–9; A. G. Rigg, *A History of Anglo-Latin Literature* (Cambridge, 1992), pp. 293–4.

[2] I am grateful to MBP and Ian Doyle for their opinion of the date of this manuscript, which is mostly the work of a single small Secretary hand, typical of the middle quarters of the fifteenth century, with additional contributions by perhaps two further hands, though one of these might be a version of the main hand. The manuscript was previously owned by Thomas Allen (1540–1632), on whom see A. G. Watson, 'Thomas Allen of Oxford and his Manuscripts', in *Medieval Scribes, Manuscripts and Libraries: Essays Presented to N. R. Ker*, ed. M. B. Parkes and A. G. Watson (London, 1978), pp. 279–314.

[3] The Latin distiches are laid out as verse, and the six verse lines of each section are linked by braces. Throughout this essay I use the term 'image' primarily to describe the visual representation of a

The Corpus text provides an unusually detailed description of a very popular form of late-medieval church decoration, the painted *tabula* or table, which is widely attested in inventories and church descriptions of the period but which have rarely survived because of their portability and vulnerability to damage and destruction.[4]

The term *tabula* refers to one of the most common kinds of portable decoration in medieval churches. Painted wooden tables were used as altar frontals or reredos throughout the medieval period. Other kinds of tables were made of brass, stone or alabaster (the latter increasingly common in late-medieval England which was a leader in the development and manufacture of this kind of imagery). Some reredos tables were made of precious metals, like the 'tabula argentea' commissioned by Bishop Grandisson of Exeter and paid for in 1324–25.[5] Tables could also be made by affixing written or painted parchment to boards. Tables could display simply images, simply texts, or a combination of the two. The Durham Account Rolls offer interesting examples of payment for most kinds of table under discussion here. In 1370–71, 6*s.* was spent 'in pictura cujusdam table pro altare Infirmarie'. In 1418 they record the payment to Dominus Thomas Witton of 6*s.* 8*d.* 'pro factura nove tabule', while in 1441–42 the Infirmarer paid 13*s.* 4*d.* 'pro pictura unius tabule stantis super altare in capella'. The accounts for 1434–35 record payment of 13*d.* 'pro pergameno et scriptura unius tabule et illuminacione ejusdem'. In 1435–36, 9*d.* was spent 'in pergameno, et illuminacione unius tabule', and in 1447–48, 10*d.* was paid to Dominus Johannes Palman 'pro scriptura 4[or] tabularum cum oracionibus de Sco Cuthberto, et cum illuminacione earundem'.[6] Small tables might have been used on the altar as part of the liturgical furniture, but larger tables were displayed as decoration and incitement to devotion and edification.

Marian images were frequently displayed as tables, either in alabaster (a very common medium for images of the Virgin) or as painted boards. Although there are

---

person or object in an artefact, and secondarily to describe the mental recreation of such a visual representation from a description of it. It is not clear from the Corpus text whether the Marian representations are painted (on boards or parchment) or carved (in wood or alabaster), though, as I will argue below, there seems to be no precedent for this unusual kind of Marian imagery in extant alabasters.

[4] On *tabulae* in general, see A. Gransden, *Historical Writing in England, II: c.1307 to the Early Sixteenth Century* (London, 1982), App. E, p. 495; G. H. Gerould, ' "Tables" in Mediaeval Churches', *Speculum*, 1 (1926), 439–40. On panel painting, see P. Binski, *The Painted Chamber at Westminster*, Society of Antiquaries of London, Occasional Paper, n.s., 9 (1986); 'What Was the Westminster Retable?', *Jnl of the British Archaeological Association*, 111 (1987); P. Tudor-Craig, 'Panel Painting', in *Age of Chivalry: Art in Plantagenet England*, ed. J. Alexander and P. Binski (London, 1987), pp. 131–6. I am grateful to Dr David Howlett, editor of the *Dictionary of Medieval Latin from British Sources*, for allowing me access to the dictionary's files on the word *tabula*. This essay is intended as part of a larger survey of *tabulae* in medieval English churches.

[5] *The Accounts of the Fabric of Exeter Cathedral, 1279–1353, part 1*, ed. A. M. Erskine, Devon and Cornwall Record Society, n.s., 24 (1981), 163.

[6] *Durham Account Rolls*, ed. J. T. Fowler, 2 vols, Surtees Soc., 99–100 (1898), I, 115, 227, 275, 263; and II, 468, 469, 473.

no pictures included in the Corpus text, the 'tabyll' it describes is not unusual in its subject-matter. It reveals a comprehensive knowledge of the traditional typological attributes of the Virgin, and employs some unusual iconographic details and combinations.

Corpus 132 is regularly quired in twelves and is substantially the work of a single scribe. Most of its contents are of a scientific nature: the first five quires contain John of Seville's translation of Messahalla's *Secretum philosophorum*, and the manuscript also preserves copies of Richard Lavenham's *De causis naturalibus*, a treatise on astronomy, a *liber alchemicus*, a urinary and other short scientific texts and tables. But it also contains Geoffrey de Vinsauf's *Poetria nova* (in a quire by itself) and part of a commentary on the Song of Songs. Quire six of the manuscript (fols 60–71ᵛ) opens and closes with tables of dates and zodiacal signs but also contains a sequence of three vernacular texts, the last of which is the text edited here.[7]

Each of these short vernacular texts shares a common format: a description of some memorable and striking visual referent supported by Latin scriptural or patristic quotations. The first provides two series of couplets describing the statue in the dream of Nebuchadnezzar, moralized as a mnemonic of the virtues and deadly sins. The second explores the Augustinian Image of Sin to provide guidance in the examination of conscience so as to facilitate the restoration of the Image of God. Both texts draw their inspiration and some of their verbal detail from Walter Hilton's use of these images in *The Scale of Perfection*. Their Latin proof texts are drawn from the pastoral *summa* known as the *Cibus anime*, which has strong links with the northern Carthusians and with the archdiocese of York. These two works are found together in two other manuscripts, one of which gives them the title *Speculum boni et mali*.[8] The third text, describing the 'tabyll' allegedly in the York Lady Chapel, is preserved with them only in this manuscript. The scribal apparatus of Corpus 132 refers to two of the three texts as *tabulae* and links all three together as a sequence.[9] Taken overall, the sequence explores the relationship between the mental recuperation of a visual image and its supporting text in a manner that might be described as medieval hypertextuality.[10]

---

[7] The manuscript lacks a recent description: see H. O. Coxe, *Catalogus Codicum MSS qui in Collegiis Aulisque Oxoniensibus hodie adservantur*, 2 vols (Oxford, 1852), II, iv, 48–9.

[8] Edited, with an account of its manuscripts and sources, by V. Gillespie, 'Idols and Images: Pastoral Adaptations of The Scale of Perfection', in *Langland, the Mystics and the Medieval English Religious Tradition: Essays in Honour of S. S. Hussey*, ed. H. Phillips (Cambridge, 1990), pp. 97–123.

[9] Fol. 69 (at end of the *Speculum boni et mali*): 'Explicit tabula bona', etc.; fol. 70 (at end of the York tables text): 'Explicit quidam tabula et finis.'

[10] Hypertext is a generic computer term that refers to the ability to access, link and jump between non-sequential and non-contingent parts of a computer file, programme or database. In its application to the teaching of literary texts, for example, it allows the user to move between facsimile, transcription, edition, contextual material and notes at the user's own initiative. The texture and detail of a hypertextual experience is largely in the control of the user. By analogy, this seems to me to be similar to a medieval reader's experience of illuminated, illustrated and glossed manuscripts

At the end of the manuscript another scribe has added a further moral text: the complete fourth section of the *Speculum Christiani*, a popular pastoral miscellany of vernacular verse also supported by Latin proof texts, again mostly quarried from the *Cibus anime*, and strongly linked to the secular clergy of York Minster at the turn of the fifteenth century.[11] It is divided into eight sections and covers the basic catechetic syllabus with additional guidance and information for those with the *cura animarum*. Its fourth section characterizes the seven deadly sins in vernacular verse quatrains with appropriate scriptural and patristic citations.

Like the *Speculum Christiani*, and the *Speculum boni et mali*, then, the Corpus trilogy of texts offers a loosely linked sequence of vernacular verse and prose supported by Latin proof texts. It may be that the popularity and influence of the *Cibus anime* and the *Speculum Christiani* among northern religious and secular clergy offers an explanation for the addition to the *Speculum boni et mali* of a text purporting to describe features of the Minster's decoration in a sequence otherwise devoted to images of a catechetic and didactic kind. The presumed physical location of those images in the Minster's Lady Chapel suggests a provenance (and perhaps an audience) for this text that is consonant with that for the other texts in the *Cibus anime/Speculum Christiani* family. The learned scientific, literary and pastoral tastes displayed in the contents of Corpus 132 are in keeping with our knowledge of the intellectual tastes and abilities of some of the Minster clergy in the late fourteenth and early fifteenth century, but no indication is given in the manuscript of the intended audience for these works.[12]

However, the physical and historical status of the Minster images is open to

---

containing different hierarchies of material that can be accessed in various ways. It may also be similar to the viewer's experience of the kind of hybrid amalgam of text and imagery that is edited here. Malcolm Parkes has been exploring medieval hypertextuality in some of his recent publications, see his 'Folia Librorum Quarere: Medieval Experience of the Problems of Hypertext and the Index', in *Fabula in Tabula. Una storia degli indici dal manoscritto al testo eletronnico*, ed. C. Leonardi, M. Morelli and F. Santi (Spoleto, 1995), pp. 23–42.

[11] *Speculum Christiani*, ed. G. Holmstedt, EETS (OS), 182 (1933 for 1929). The eight sections of this text are also known as *tabulae*, and link loosely together like the three texts in the Corpus sequence, or the two texts in the *Speculum boni et mali*. For the provenance and context of the *Cibus anime/Speculum Christiani* group of texts, which seem to have been compiled during the period *c.*1390–1420, see V. Gillespie, 'The Evolution of the *Speculum Christiani*', in *Latin and Vernacular*, ed. A. J. Minnis (Cambridge, 1989), pp. 39–60; '*Cura pastoralis in deserto*' in *De Cella in Seculum: Religious and Secular Life and Devotion in Late Medieval England*, ed. M. G. Sargent (Cambridge, 1989), pp. 161–81, esp. 179–81. J. Hughes, *Pastors and Visionaries: Religion and Secular Life in Late Medieval Yorkshire* (Woodbridge, 1988), pp. 196–7, 179–81, argues for a York Minster provenance for both texts. I am not persuaded that the evidence of York circulation necessarily proves composition there, but there is some evidence of ownership among the Minster clergy: see Gillespie, 'Idols and Images', p. 100.

[12] See Hughes, *Pastors and Visionaries*, pp. 176–229; Gillespie, 'Idols and Images', pp. 97–101; B. Dobson, 'The Residentiary Canons of York in the Fifteenth Century', *Jnl of Ecclesiastical History*, 30 (1979), 145–74.

debate. Despite the survival of quite extensive York inventories and fabric rolls from the late-medieval period, no reference to such a 'tabyll' of images in the Minster's Lady Chapel has been found, and the text itself gives rise to doubts about whether its decorative programme was ever executed. While it may be the case that the Corpus text records a now lost artefact, as it now stands in the manuscript, the text offers itself only as a series of disembodied 'pictures' to be performed and realized in the imagination of its readers. As contextualized by the two vernacular texts that precede it, it is the imaginative and meditative potential and the affective and devotional stimulus of these verbal pictures that is foregrounded in the Corpus manuscript.

Each of the five representations of the Virgin is described in the vernacular. Each image has a double Latin title or *titulus* attached to it, and each purports to have three Latin distiches under her feet, which are transcribed:

> ¶ þys ys þe disposiciun of þe tabyll at our lady auter yn þe cathedrall kyrke of yorke. þat ys for to say þat ower lady ys ymagened in v maner of wysys. þe fyrst ys our lady hauyng yn here hand the tabelis offe moyeses *and* vndir here fete þe berny[n]g buske of moyses *and* also þe figure off þe worlde. And þer scho ys calde Rubus Moisi et Domina Mundi *with* vers wretyn vndyr her fete:

Vt rubus ingne[s]c[i]t et eum vis ingnea nescit,	Exodus 3°
Carne deus latitat sed ca'r'nis opus caro vitat.	
Absque solo vellus maduit sine vellere tellus:	Judices 6°
In signo duplici res apta dei genetrici	
Qua ponat sedem sapiencia construit edem,	In Proverbia 9°
Cum deus hanc condit cuius se ventre recondit.	(lines 1–11)

The representations of the Virgin draw extensively on the well-established repertoire of Marian attributes which had been developed over the preceding two centuries.[13] In

---

[13] For a survey of the tradition in England, see N. Morgan, 'Texts and Images of Marian Devotion in Thirteenth-Century England', in *England in the Thirteenth Century*, ed. M. Ormrod (Stamford, 1991), pp. 69–103. For a survey of the Latin tradition, see A. Salzer, *Die Sinnbilder und Beiworte Mariens in der deutschen Literatur und lateinischen Hymnenpoesie des Mittelalters* (Linz, 1893, repr. Darmstadt, 1967); R. E. Kaske, A. Groos and M. W. Twomey, *Medieval Christian Literary Imagery: a Guide to Interpretation* (Toronto, 1988), pp. 141–6; F. J. E. Raby, *A History of Christian Latin Poetry*, 2nd edn (Oxford, 1953), pp. 365–75; M. Camille, *The Gothic Idol:Ideology and Image Making in Medieval Art* (Cambridge, 1989), pp. 220–41. For a valuable synthesis see J. J. Bourassé, *Summa Aurea de Laudibus Beatae Virginis Mariae*, 13 vols (Paris, 1862), esp. V, cols 1003–36 (on figures and titles of the Virgin) and VI, cols 1035–42 (on Marian iconography), with extracts from texts. Important texts in the formation of the Marian repertoire include *The Liturgical Poetry of Adam of St Victor*, ed. D. S. Wrangham (London, 1881), pp. 164–71, 218–33; Richard of St Lawrence, *De Laudibus Beatae Mariae Virginis* in *B. Alberti Magni Opera Omnia*, 36, ed. A. Borgnet (Paris, 1898), pp. 1–841; and the *Laus Beatae Virginis Mariae*, attrib. Bonaventure, ed. Bourassé, VI, cols 1405–20. Marian hymns often link attributes and epithets applied to the Virgin, see Kaske, *Literary Imagery*, p. 144. For a thirteenth-

the fourteenth century the growing popularity of the Litany of the Virgin helped popularize in schematic form many of these types and attributes.[14] By the fifteenth century this iconographical tradition was outcropping extensively in vernacular texts, such as Marian lyrics, carols and other works, such as the Mary Play of the N-Town plays, and is widely attested in the plastic arts.[15] In the Corpus text, the two titles ascribed to each of the images link together an Old Testament prefiguration or attribute of the Virgin with one of the symbolic names applied to her by the evolving doctrinal tradition. Thus in the first 'Rubus Moisi' is linked with 'Domina Mundi'; in the third 'Arca Testamenti' is balanced by 'Dey Genetryx'; and in the fourth 'Templum Salamonys' with 'Virgo Virginum'. These titles are mostly conventional, although 'Ymparatryx Ynferny' is less commonly found in Marian theology than the others, perhaps because it has no scriptural basis. It has some currency, however, in Middle English vernacular texts of the fifteenth century.[16]

The iconography of each image shows a similar balance between scriptural typology and theology. The fifth image, for example, has 'yn here o hande a

century Latin poem from Yorkshire which uses the attributes, see John of Howden's *Viola*, in *Poems of John of Hoveden*, ed. F. J. E. Raby, Surtees Society, 154 (1939), 194–202; discussed in Rigg (as n. 1 above), pp. 208–15. For a list of references to medieval English artefacts see O. Lehmann-Brockhaus, *Lateinische Schriftquellen zur kunst in England, Wales und Scotland von Jahre 901 bis zum Jahre 1307*, 5 vols (Munich, 1955–60).

[14] See N. Morgan, 'Texts and Images of Marian Devotion in Fourteenth-Century England', in *England in the Fourteenth Century*, ed. D. Williams (Stamford, 1993), pp. 34–57. Other important texts are *Speculum Beatae Mariae Virginis Fr. Conradi a Saxonia*, Bibliotheca Franciscana Ascetica Medii Aevi, 2 (ad Claras Aquas, 1904); *Ludolphus de Saxonia: Vita Christi*, ed. L. M. Rigollet, 4 vols (Paris and Rome, 1878), I, 20–7, 32–5, 94–9. The York liturgy for the Feast of the Assumption, for example, bristles with Sequences using Marian typological attributes and figures, see *Missale ad Usum Insignis Ecclesiae Eboracensis*, ed. W. G. Henderson, 2 vols, Surtees Society, 60 (1874, repr. Farnborough, 1969), II, 81–8.

[15] For texts, see C. Brown, *Religious Lyrics of the Fifteenth Century* (Oxford, 1939), pp. 103–21; *The Early English Carols*, ed. R. L. Greene, 2nd edn (Oxford, 1977), nos 182, 190, 192, 193, 194, 198. For discussion, see D. Gray, *Themes and Images in the Medieval English Lyric* (London, 1972), pp. 84–6; R. Woolf, *English Religious Lyric in the Middle Ages* (Oxford, 1968), chs 4 and 8. On the N-Town play, see *The Mary Play from the N. Town Manuscript*, ed. P. Meredith (London, 1987) and *The N-Town Play*, ed. S. Spector, EETS (SS), 11–12 (1991), esp. play 11; T. Coletti, 'Devotional Iconography in the N-Town Marian Plays', in *The Drama of the Middle Ages: Comparative and Critical Essays*, ed. C. Davidson, C. J. Giankaris and J. H. Stroupe (New York, 1982), pp. 249–71 esp. 267.

[16] A version is found in Latin as early as Adam of St Victor ('Imperatrix Supernorum/Superatrix Infernorum', Wrangham (as n. 13 above), p. 230), but the form 'Imperatrix Inferni' is not found in most of the major Latin repertoires of titles and attributes, though Conrad of Saxony (as n. 14 above) refers to Mary as 'domina infernorum . . . domina daemonum . . . domina in inferno' (pp. 38, 41), and this formula is also found in Ludolph of Saxony (as n. 14 above, p. 34). The N-Town 'Annunciation' play refers to Mary as 'Qwen of Hefne, Lady of Erth and Empres of Helle' (ed. Spector, p. 123; ed. Meredith, p. 76); the title also occurs in *The Pricking of Love*, is common in Lydgate, and is found in Middle English carols (e.g. no. 198, ed. Greene, *Early English Carols*, p. 130) and in *The Book of Margery Kempe*, written in the 1430s: see the discussion in G. McMurray Gibson, *The Theatre of Devotion: East Anglian Drama and Society in the Late Middle Ages* (Chicago, 1989), pp. 137–77.

sprynkyll and a cros yn þe toþir hande' (line 42), with hell and the tree of life under her feet, while in the first image the Virgin has under her feet the burning bush and 'þe figure off þe worlde' (line 4). This iconographical synthesis of types and emblems in each image is unusually rich and imaginative. Moreover the representation of the Virgin holding or standing on her types and attributes (with the possible exception of the lily and the rose) is exceedingly unusual in English Marian iconography of the medieval period.[17]

As in the other texts grouped with it in Corpus, the Latin verses supporting and glossing each image of the Virgin are not, however, original to it. Thirteen of the fifteen distiches are drawn from *Pictor in carmine*, an early-thirteenth-century guide to typology probably composed by an English Cistercian.[18] The particular significance of the use made of *Pictor* in the Corpus text is that M. R. James was unable to point to a single example of the *Pictor* verses occurring in any medieval window or other work of art. The present text, therefore, may be a unique witness to the use of the *Pictor* verses in the literature or visual arts of medieval England. Although there are at least four other medieval English collections of *tituli*, two of which share similar approaches and some verses with *Pictor*, none is as closely related to it as this present text, and none can have been the source of the Corpus verses.[19]

The author of *Pictor in carmine*, possibly Adam, abbot of Dore, declares himself to have been struck with grief at the foolish pictures he found in churches. Despite the iconographical puritanism that characterized his order, Adam recognizes that:

> Since I did not think it would be easy to do away altogether with the meaningless paintings in churches, especially in cathedral and parish churches, where public stations take place, I think it is an excusable concession that they should enjoy at least that class of pictures which, as being books of the laity, can suggest divine things to the unlearned, and stir up the learned to the love of the scriptures.

---

[17] Morgan, 'Texts and Images', pp. 41–2, 47, points out the increasing occurrence of lily pots in annunciation scenes and the frequency of the flower images in English Marian art. I am grateful to Professor Morgan for confirming my sense of the rarity of the conjunction of images, attributes and titles in this text.

[18] See M. R. James, '*Pictor in Carmine*', *Archaeologia*, 94 (1951), 141–66; and D. F. Baker, *Pictor in carmine vel Adaptatio rerum gestarum in Veteri Testamentum ad Nouum: a Critical Edition*, unpublished PhD thesis, University of Toronto (1991), promised for publication in the *Corpus Christianorum* series; D. Park, 'Cistercian Wall Painting and Panel Painting', in *Cistercian Art and Architecture in the British Isles*, ed. C. Norton and D. Park (Cambridge, 1986), pp. 181–210, esp. 199–200. The distinctive and distinct continental circulation of the text has been studied by F. Rohrig, '"Rota in medio rotae": Ein typologischer Zyklus aus Österreich', *Sonderdruck aus Jahrbuch des Stiftes Klosterneuberg*, n.s., 5 (1965), 7–113; 'Der englische Einfluss in der mittelalterlichen Typologie Österreichs', in *Österreich und die angelsächsische Welt*, ed. O. Heisch (Vienna and Stuttgart, 1961).

[19] M. R. James, 'On the Paintings Formerly in the Choir at Peterborough', *Trans. Cambridge Antiquarian Soc.*, Octavo Publications, 3 (1897), 178–94; Baker ('*Pictor in carmine*', pp. 39–62) gives an overview of *tituli* collections. For a list of published English window verses, see *A Dictionary of Medieval Latin from British Sources* (Oxford, 1975), III, lvii.

Regretting the prevalence in church decoration of centaurs with quivers, four-headed lions, headless grinning men and monkeys playing the pipes, he sets out 'to curb the licence of painters, or rather to influence their work in churches where paintings are permitted'. He has drawn up certain symbolic 'applications' from the Old and New Testaments, adding some couplets for each heading. A choice of verses is provided for each heading, he says, so that 'what the shortness of one couplet does not suffice to explain . . . the repetition in different words may supply'. These couplets are designed to be 'inscribed about the Old Testament incident, or about any other mystical or typical [i.e. typological] application'.[20]

Pictor in carmine aims, therefore, to create an unusually literate form of a 'book for the laity'. Although it includes no pictures of its own, it seeks to provide typological cues for the development of appropriate illustrations on scriptural themes, supported by the authority of its distiches. The verses are grounded on the Old Testament types, but link Old and New, and each distich is provided with a marginal reference to its Old Testament source. Other marginalia offer parallel illustrative texts from the Psalms, Prophets and, very occasionally, the New Testament. The only exception to the scriptural basis of the Pictor verses is the occasional inclusion of examples drawn from natural history. One of these examples is included in the Corpus text: the second verse of the second section describes the rhinoceros genuflecting to the Virgin, with a marginal reference to *Natura rerum*:

Artus rinoceros flectit tibi, virgo, severos:	Natura Rerum
Sic deus [e] celis dat se tibi, virgo fidelis.	(lines 17–18)

In Alexander Neckham's topical encyclopedia *De naturis rerum*, Isidore is credited with describing how a virgin is capable of taming and capturing a rhinoceros. This story, clearly a variant on the folklore surrounding unicorns, is then allegorized or adapted to relate to Christ and the Church.[21] The *Pictor* author applies the legend in a more literal way and includes in his section on the Annunciation four verses under the subheading: 'Rinoceros procumbit et obdormit in gremio speciose virginis'.

In its fullest form, *Pictor* lists 138 antitypes and 510 types exemplified by distiches. Of the six manuscripts of this so-called 'longer' version, the four complete copies all derive from England in the thirteenth century. 'Abbreviated' versions are found in five further manuscripts, all now in English collections and apparently of English provenance. Two date from the thirteenth century and three from the fourteenth century.[22] The number of verses associated with the types and antitypes in this

---

[20] Tr. James, '*Pictor in carmine*', 141–2.

[21] *Alexandri Neckam De Naturis Rerum Libri Duo*, ed. T. Wright, RS, 34 (1863), bk 2, ch. 104, p. 187; Salzer (*Die Sinnbilder*), cites Peter of Capua on the same theme (p. 48) and two Latin hymns which use the image (p. 525).

[22] This discussion of the textual tradition of *Pictor* is greatly indebted to Dr Baker's thesis. The abbreviated versions are found in: Lincoln Cathedral Library, MS 222 (art. 16); Durham University Library, MS Cosin V. ii. 5285; Cambridge, Corpus Christi College, MS 217; Cambridge, University

version varies, several copies including only a single verse for each. The example of Lincoln, Cathedral Library, MS 222 (C.4.12) may be significant for the Corpus text: it offers only single verses for each antitype listed and contains no less than 12 of the 13 distiches from *Pictor* included in the Corpus text. Thus although the designer of the Corpus text/images could have made an independent selection from a full copy of *Pictor*, he might have had access to a branch of the 'Abbreviated' tradition similar to Lincoln 222, where the bulk of the selection process had already taken place. Lincoln 222 is a thirteenth-century theological miscellany which is probably of Cistercian origin, so the 'Abbreviated' tradition may have originated within the order. But it probably spread beyond it because Lincoln, Cathedral Library, MS 229 (B.6.7), another 'Abbreviated' version with only single verses for each type and antitype, is a late-fourteenth-century anthology of pastoral and theological material – in fact a fairly typical clerical miscellany of the period. This copy contains 11 of the 13 *Pictor* verses also included in the Corpus text.[23]

If a full version of *Pictor* was used, the Corpus verses are largely drawn from the most obvious sections. Nine distiches are from the chapter devoted to the Annunciation, one from a chapter on the *Canticum Marie*, one from the Nativity chapter and one from the chapter devoted to the visit of the shepherds. But the fact that only one verse is taken from each of the typological subheadings in each chapter support the view that the compiler of the Corpus text used an abbreviated *Pictor*.[24] Whatever version he used, his acquaintance with his source must have extended beyond these early and obviously Marian-oriented chapters. The second distich of the last image returns to Aaron's rod:

> Sub colubro plane colubros sacra virg[a] vorabat
> Quando dolos satane deitas sub carne vocabat. (lines 47–8)

This verse is not associated with Mary in *Pictor*. It occurs in a chapter on the Harrowing of Hell, where it is closely related to Christ's redemption of mankind. Aaron's rod is seen as devouring the evil caused by the serpent in the Garden of Eden.

Library, MS Kk. 5. 10 (not 5. 16 as in James); Lincoln Cathedral Library, MS 229 (art. 4). In the quotations from *Pictor* and in the apparatus of the App. below I follow Baker in using the orthography of the full version in Oxford, Bodl. Lib., MS Rawlinson C. 67, a thirteenth-century copy once in the ownership of Hereford Cathedral, which has a flyleaf ascription to Adam of Dore.

[23] See R. M. Thomson, *Catalogue of the Manuscripts of Lincoln Cathedral Chapter Library* (Cambridge, 1989), pp. 182–4 (MS 222) and 188–9 (MS 229).

[24] Using Baker's chapter and line references to the complete text, the distiches in the York text are found at the following points of *Pictor*: Image 1; verse 1: ch. 4, ll. 27–8; verse 2: ch. 8, ll. 57–8; verse 3: ch. 16, ll. 107–8. Image 2; verse 1: ch. 14, ll. 95–6; verse 2: ch. 20, ll. 137–8; verse 3: ch. 55, ll. 411–12. Image 3; verse 1: ch. 12, ll. 83–4; verses 2 and 3: not in *Pictor*. Image 4; verse 1: ch. 11, ll. 75–6; verse 2: ch. 17, ll. 117–18; verse 3: ch. 51, ll. 377–8. Image 5; verse 1: ch. 1, ll. 7–8; verse 2: ch. 370, ll. 2823–4; verse 3: ch. 30, ll. 231–2.

As well as being prepared to modify and appropriate the typology of *Pictor*, the Corpus compiler also supplied two verses on the woman of Apocalypse chapter 12. All *Pictor*'s verses derive from Old Testament antecedents, and the Apocalypse woman was a somewhat later addition to the repertoire of Marian types (appearing first perhaps in the *Laus beate Mariae Virginis* attributed to Bonaventure).[25] These added verses (lines 26–9) are rather more direct and explicit than those taken from *Pictor*:

> Arca dei visa templo cely reserati
> Et signum grande ⟨mulier⟩ circumdata sole   Apocalypsis 12°
> Sub pedibus luna cuius sunt signa beate
> Virginis et matris que sunt a virgine visa.

The mildly riddling quality of the *Pictor* verses selected for the York scheme contributes to the creative tensions which exist in the iconographical design with its unusual juxtaposition of type, attribute and title. The links are sufficiently clear and conventional to allow for devotion, but sufficiently enigmatic to stimulate reflection or meditation. Hypertextual movement from real or imagined visual image to text, between images and texts and between attributes and types is allowed for and even demanded by the allusive and elliptical concatenation of verbal and visual motifs in each of the five sections. In the second section (lines 12–20), for example, the Virgin holds roses, signifying her typological function as the *rosa inter spinas*, but also by this date carrying traditional connotations from secular love poetry. In her other hand she has the lily of purity, the *lilium sine spinas* of the Song of Songs. Under her feet is the golden gate of Ezekiel 44 and a heaven filled with angels. Her titles are 'Regina Cely' and 'Porta Clausa':

> ¶ þe secunde has yn þe too hand a lily *and* yn þe oþir a brange offe rosys and vndyr here fete a yate of golde sparryd *and* also a heuen full off angelis. And þer scho ys callyd Porta Clausa et Regina Cely *with* þys ve`r´se unþir here fete:

> Invia porta viro domino patet ordine myro,   Ezechiel 44.
> Dum pudor est saluus et pregnans virginis aluus.
> Artus rinoceros flectit tibi, virgo, severos: Natura Rerum
> Sic deus [e] celis dat se tibi, virgo fidelis.
> Fiunt gaudentes Saram peperisse videntes   Genesis 21°
> Sic et pastores ubi gestit virgula flores.

The verses reflect and refract aspects of this visual scheme. The gate under her feet is reflected in the first verse's allusion to the *invia porta* or 'low door' (line 15), perhaps also referring to Mary's theologically significant humility at the Annunciation. The

---

[25] Bourassé, *Laus Beatae*, VI, col. 1411, ch. 19 ('Figurata fuit per mulierem quam vidit Joannes'). The woman of the Apocalypse is included with the other popular types of the Virgin in the early fourteenth-century English preacher's handbook *Fasciculus Morum*, ed. and tr. S. Wenzel (Philadelphia, 1989), pp. 241–9, esp. 245.

lily is also often present in representations of the Annunciation, but has here been placed not in the conventional pot, but in the Virgin's hand to balance the rose. The flowers are recollected by the flowering rod or twig in the last verse (line 20). (The *Pictor* reading of Jesse for 'gestit' is more explicit.) Sara's sustained virginity and her rejoicing parallels the rejoicing shepherds at the flowering of Jesse's rod in the virgin birth. The use of 'virgula' (rod or twig) here deliberately links the tree of Jesse with Aaron's rod, a type explicitly invoked and partly explained in the fourth section, where Mary holds the flowering rod by which Aaron and the Levites were chosen. The rod (bearing nuts as exegetical tradition had come to accept) emblematizes Mary's chosen status and her virginity. Popular legend re-used the flowering staff to describe the choice of Joseph as Mary's husband in a temple ceremony parallel to the choosing of Aaron (as in the Mary Play of the N-Town plays). This may have suggested the elliptical blending of Aaron's staff with Jesse's rod undertaken in the Corpus text, and might explain why the compiler went outside the Marian sections of *Pictor* for this verse in the fourth section. Similarly, the rhinoceros distich (lines 17–18) tangentially engages the allusions to purity in the lily and the rose while reflecting the apocryphal coronation of the Virgin as Queen of Heaven.

The Corpus text offers a verbal description of a coherent and sophisticated series of interrelated visual images and verses, likely to stimulate and edify its audience in a variety of different ways and at a variety of different levels. It is not clear if the images were designed to suit the verses or if the verses were chosen to suit the images: the evidence is equivocal. In addition to its attribution to the Virgin of Aaron's rod, the fourth section offers an alternative iconographical feature, picking up on the final distich from Daniel (lines 38–9) which refers to the stone that was cut without hands: 'Or ellis geue *our* lady yn here hande yn þys place a stone *and* þat ys most *con*uenyent to þys verse'. This might suggest that, at the time of composition or transcription of the Corpus text, the iconographical scheme was not yet fixed. Alternatively, the inclusion of non-*Pictor* verses from the Apocalypse might suggest that verses were being subsequently fitted to pictures. Taking, for the moment, its alleged location in the Lady Chapel of York Minster at face value, how well would it have fitted into the decorative context of newly remodelled fabric of the cathedral?

Tables in churches fulfilled a range of functions for a range of audiences, from the actively literate and educated clergy to the illiterate or passively literate laity. Imagery could become the subject of veneration, superstition and decoration; text tables could inform and admonish and educate. Benefactors could be commemorated (as they often still are) by tables displayed in an institution: early in the fifteenth century, a *tabula* listing the books in Cobham's library was set up on the wall of the University Church in Oxford. In 1483, the chantry deed of James Terumber for St James, Trowbridge listed the merchants and gentlemen who had contributed to the rebuilding of the church, who 'should be comprised in a table hanging in the high altar of Jhesu exhorting the people present devoutly to say *Pater Noster* and *Ave Maria*'.[26] Major churches often used such tables to display their privileges or to recount highlights of their history for the benefit of pilgrims and visitors: the *magna tabula* from Glastonbury Abbey (now in the Bodleian Library, Oxford) is one such object.[27] The Augustinian priory at Stone in Staffordshire had tables recording the legends of St Wulhed and St Ruffin, another recording the history of the house and its benefactors down to the time of Henry IV and another with the names of the Norman lords who came over with William the Conqueror. Twenty-nine rhyme-royal stanzas constituted a guide to the tombs in Worksop priory in Nottinghamshire.[28] Text tables were found at pilgrim shrines, such as those of Henry VI and St Walstan of Bawburgh.[29] Verses from Lydgate formed part of the decorative scheme of the Clopton chapel in the richly decorated (and unusually well-documented) church at Long Melford: some were painted on wooden *tabulae* just below ceiling level; others were placed on structural timbers.[30] Chaucer's Latin epitaph by the mid-fifteenth-century Italian humanist poet Stephen Surigo was displayed on a table near his tomb in Westminster Abbey; early in the sixteenth century John Skelton wrote elegies for Margaret Beaufort and Henry VII, which were displayed on tables close to their tombs in the Lady Chapel of the Abbey.[31] Between 1299 and 1321, Abbot Godfrey of Peterborough gave various images to his Lady Chapel and 'unam tabulam quae vocatur lignum scientiae bonum et mali', which was presumably either a diagram or a text table and which hung over the altar. Such diagrammatic representations of doctrine are perhaps now best attested in those manuscript 'spiritual encyclopaedias' studied by Fritz Saxl, or in the repertoires of schematic instruction preserved in works such as the *Speculum theologie*, which radically blur the distinction between image and text.[32] But they must have been a significant feature of many great medieval

---

[26] M. B. Parkes, 'The Provision of Books', in *The History of the University of Oxford*, 2, *Later Medieval Oxford*, ed. J. I. Catto and T. A. R. Evans (Oxford, 1992), pp. 407–83, esp. 472; A. D. Brown, *Popular Piety in Late Medieval England: the Diocese of Salisbury 1250–1550* (Oxford, 1995), pp. 118–19.

[27] Oxford, Bodl. Lib., MS Lat. hist. a. 2; J. A. Bennett, 'A Glastonbury Relic', *Somerset Archaeological and Natural History Society's Proc.*, 34 (1888), 117–22 (with pl. preceding title page).

[28] Gerould, 'Tables'; Gransden (as n. 4 above), p. 495 adds further examples of chronicle tables (dating from the eleventh century onwards) from Durham, St Paul's, Lincoln and Lichfield Cathedrals.

[29] E. Duffy, *The Stripping of the Altars: Traditional Religion in England 1400–1580* (London, 1992), pp. 198 and 201ff, pl. 77.

[30] J. B. Trapp, 'Verses by Lydgate at Long Melford', *Review of English Studies*, n.s., 6 (1955), 1–11.

[31] The Chaucer epitaph is pr. and tr. in full in *Chaucer: the Critical Heritage*, ed. D. Brewer (London, 1978), I, 77–80; for the Tudor royal tables, see D. R. Carlson, *The Latin Writings of John Skelton, Studies in Philology*, Texts and Studies 88.4 (1991), items XVI (datable 1512); XX (datable 1516); XXIII (datable *c.*1522); XXIV (datable *c.*1522); App. 4, pp. 115–21. P. Tudor-Craig, 'The Embellishment and Furnishings of the Medieval Church', in C. Wilson, P. Tudor-Craig, J. Physick and R. Gem, *Westminster Abbey* (London, 1986), p. 105 notes that in 1272 a Peter de Hispania was paid for two 'well-painted tables' for the Altar of St Mary, valued at the large sum of £80.

[32] Lehmann-Brockhaus, *Lateinische Schriftquellen*, item 3510; F. Saxl, 'A Spiritual Encyclopaedia of

churches (an example from York is discussed below), and something of their effect can be gauged from those manuscripts and from the tables of the Decalogue and evangelical precepts set up in churches by the sixteenth-century reformers. Text tables were apparently a significant feature of the fifteenth-century decoration of the church at Sheen Charterhouse, according to William Worcestre in his *Itineraries*:

> Memorandum that on the walls on each side of the nave of the church hang many devotions and good reminders to devotion and the arousing of all good Christian souls to God, both smaller and larger tables written in good text hand and in bastard letter to the number of 34, nor have I seen in any other monastic church even the twentieth part of these tables so fully written.

Worcestre is able to make a palaeographical distinction between those tables in 'good text hand' and those others, presumably more recently executed, in the fashionable Burgundian 'bastard letter'.[33]

In the sixteenth century, an 'erroneous' table containing prayers and an account of the Rood of Ashford was corrected, by a reformer, by the deletion of offensive words, but the priests of the church wrote them back in. In the 1530s John Warde made a picture table of St Christopher with details of his life for display in his own pew. Single tables with images were also commonly displayed on altars.[34] Durham Cathedral provides a fine, late description of a single image table in a closing mount:

> Also yer was standing on ye alter . . . a most curiouse and fine table wth ij leues to open and clos againe all of ye hole Passion of or Lord Jesus christ most richlye and curiously sett furth in most lyvelie coulors all like ye burninge gold . . . The wch table was alwaies lockt vp but onely on principall daies.[35]

Such tables were vulnerable to decay, to disappearance and to destruction. Their very portability could be a mixed blessing.[36] Roger Parkyn, the Yorkshireman dubbed 'the

---

the Later Middle Ages', *Jnl Warburg and Courtauld Institutes*, 5 (1942), 82–134. For the diagrams and images of the *Speculum theologie*, see L. F. Sandler, *The Psalter of Robert de Lisle in the British Library* (Oxford, 1983), pp. 23–7 and App. III.

[33] *William Worcestre: Itineraries*, ed. J. H. Harvey (Oxford, 1969), p. 270. Worcestre also records (p. 112) Latin verses he saw on a table in Tavistock church. I owe this reference to MBP.

[34] Duffy, *Stripping*, pp. 419, 166.

[35] *Rites of Durham*, ed. J. T. Fowler, Surtees Society, 107 (1902), p. 33. Fowler also prints (p. 40) a description of 'an alter wth a faire Allabaster table above yt' on the north side of the church.

[36] Iconoclastic legislation at the Reformation frequently specifies that *tabulae* are to be removed, defaced or destroyed. See M. Aston, *England's Iconoclasts*: vol. 1, *The Laws Against Images* (Oxford, 1988), pp. 210–94; R. Whiting, *The Blind Devotion of the People: Popular Religion and the English Reformation* (Cambridge, 1989), pp. 206–10. In 1552, Archbishop Holgate of York enjoined the Minster to replace the images on its walls with verses of Scripture, while Cranmer's 1548 articles for Canterbury Diocese included the question: 'Whether you know any that keep in their houses undefaced, any abused or feigned images, any tables, pictures, paintings or other monuments of feigned miracles, pilgrimages, idolatry or superstition', see *Visitation Articles and Injunctions of the Period of the Reformation*, ed. W. H. Frere and W. McClure Kennedy, 3 vols, Alcuin Club, 14–16

last medieval Englishman', recalled that in Lent 1547: 'All ymages, pictures, tables, crucifixes, tabernacles, was utterly abolischide & takyn away furth of churches.'[37] Reflecting on the waves of iconoclasm that he had lived through in the sixteenth century, Roger Martin of Long Melford (d. *c*.1580) recalled that:

> There was in my Ile, called Jesus Ile, at the back of the Altar, a table with a crucifix on it, with the two thieves hanging, on every side one, which is in my house decayed, and the same I hope my heires will repaire and restore again, one day.[38]

Single alabasters were sometimes placed in wooden mounts, often with doors, and these frameworks themselves became the vehicle for verses or further decoration to be added to create a hypertextual ensemble.[39]

Single tables, whether painted or in alabaster or metal, could easily be joined together to make repertoires of imagery (and sometimes text) of varying sizes from diptychs upwards. The Lady Chapel at Evesham was rebuilt and redecorated between 1282 and 1316, and the new decorative programme included 'duas . . . tabulas sumptuose depictas et deauratas ante et super altare ibidem stantes'.[40] These were presumably a frontal and retable. Work on royal palaces regularly included commissions for and purchases of single tables and repertoires of tables, intended for display in chapels and on altars as well as in public and state rooms.[41] The inventory of Westminster Abbey in 1388 records two tables hinged together and well painted, with a crucifixion scene, the Virgin with Christ on her knees and images of John the Baptist and Katherine on one leaf (apparently divided in two parts), and an Annunciation and Nativity on the two parts of the other leaf. It also records a

---

(London, 1910), II, 189, 320. 'Superstitious' tables were often replaced by more edifying material, also displayed in tabular form, such as the Decalogue. In York, Grindal's 1572 Injunctions instructed the Dean and Chapter to erect 'a fair table . . . written without blot or rasure' concerning the sermons to be had, made and continued in the Cathedral. It was to be placed in the choir or chancel 'where it may easily be seen and read' to remind clergy of their duty as preachers; ibid., III, 346.

[37] A. G. Dickens, 'Robert Parkyn's Narrative of the Reformation', in his *Reformation Studies* (London, 1982), pp. 287–312, esp. 295.

[38] 'Ancient Ceremonies at Melford Church, Suffolk', *Gentleman's Magazine*, September 1830, pp. 204–7. For a recent account of Long Melford's decoration and its destruction, and new editions of the documents, see D. Dymond and C. Paine, *The Spoil of Melford Church: the Reformation in a Suffolk Parish* (Ipswich, 1989); Duffy, *Stripping*, pp. 37–9.

[39] See the example discussed (with plates) by W. H. St John Hope in *Proc. Society of Antiquaries*, 25 (1913), 79–84; for a recent survey, see F. Cheetham, *English Medieval Alabasters* (Oxford, 1984), pp. 11–30; *Age of Chivalry*, items 699–707.

[40] Lehmann-Brockhaus, *Lateinische Schriftquellen*, item 1656; cf. items 2123; 4091; 3425; 4924 and the numerous references to gold and silver tables.

[41] *The History of the King's Works, parts 1 and 2: The Middle Ages*, ed. H. M. Colvin (London, 1963): e.g., the Royal House at Guildford (p. 952); the Royal Castle at Nottingham (pp. 759–60); Westminster Palace (pp. 502–3); Carmarthen (p. 601); St Stephen's Chapel, Westminster (pp. 518–19).

'tabula plicabilis' containing 'octo ymagines eburnee'. Four tables of the Virgin survive from the Lady Chapel at Ranworth church.[42] Altar retables could be created by assembling alabasters and mounting them together (like the Swansea altarpiece), as well as by assembling painted panels, as in the five panels of the Despencer retable from Norwich.[43] Indeed five panel paintings of scenes from the life of the Virgin are a common subject for altar decoration: outstanding English examples are the Cluny frontal (which has a Marian programme) and the Thornham Parva retable. Such Marian programmes often present the five Joys of the Virgin or scenes from her life, both scriptural and apocryphal.[44] So the description in the Corpus text of five tables designed for the Lady Chapel altar is not in itself unusual or significant. What is much more significant is that there is no evidence of linked Marian types and attributes of the kind found in the Corpus text figuring in such sequences of altar tables.

The late-medieval Minster at York certainly displayed a full range of *tabulae* in its internal decoration. The Minster Library still preserves a set of text tables recording church and political history, often erroneously described as the Tables of the Vicars Choral. Consisting of parchment mounted on boards, and dating from between 1377 and 1381, they were probably displayed in the Minster for the edification and information of pilgrims and visitors. The text, closely geared to the historical power of York, and (like the Glastonbury *magna tabula*) part of a process of historical self-justification, is not supported by any kind of illustration. The *Chronicon metricum ecclesiae Eboracensis* is explicitly designed for display on such a text table:

> Haec ex archivis de multis paucula scripsi
> Ne lateat latebris, tabula sic publice fixi.[45]

---

[42] J. W. Legg, 'On the Inventory of the Vestry in Westminster Abbey, taken in 1388', *Archaeologia*, 2nd ser., 52 (1890), 240; Duffy, *Stripping*, p. 181 and pl. 74.

[43] On repertoires of alabasters, see P. Nelson, 'The Woodwork of English Alabaster Retables', *Trans. Historical Society of Lancashire and Cheshire*, 72 (1920), 50–60; P. Sheingorn, 'The Te Deum Altarpiece and the Iconography of Praise', in *Early Tudor England*, ed. D. Williams (Woodbridge, 1989), pp. 171–82; Cheetham, *English Medieval Alabasters*, pp. 20–28; *Age of Chivalry*, items 706 (alabaster) and 711 (Despencer retable); W. H. St John Hope, 'On a Painted Table or Reredos of the Fourteenth Century, in the Cathedral Church of Norwich', *Norwich Archaeology*, 13 (1898), 293–14. As at Long Melford, the Despencer table survived, in this case by being inverted and disguised as a (horizontal) table.

[44] C. Norton, D. Park and P. Binski, *Dominican Painting in East Anglia: the Thornham Parva Retable and the Musée de Cluny Frontal* (Woodbridge, 1987); cf. C. Grössinger, *North-European Panel Paintings: a Catalogue of Netherlandish and German Paintings before 1600 in English Churches and Colleges* (London, 1992); L. E. Plahter, E. Skaug and V. Plahter, *Gothic Painted Altar Frontals from the Church of Tingelstad* (Oslo and Bergen, 1974).

[45] 'From many deeds I've written just a few/And placed them on a board in public view', tr. Rigg, *Anglo-Latin*, pp. 293–4; Raine, *Historians of York*, II, 446; J. S. Purvis, 'The Tables of the York Vicars Choral', *Yorkshire Archaeological Jnl*, 41 (1966), 741–8; B. Dobson, 'The Later Middle Ages, 1215–1500', in Aylmer and Cant, *York Minster*, p. 108, dismisses the association with the vicars choral, arguing that the tables were for the edification of pilgrims and visitors.

By 1408, the material recorded in the York tables had been incorporated into a *Liber cosmographiae* by John de Foxton, a diocesan chaplain, and extracts were later used in the Sherborne Missal.[46] This pattern of transmission from *tabula* to manuscript provides a possible analogue for the origins of the Corpus text. Foxton's book used the resources of the great library of the Augustinian priory in York, quoting from John Ridwall's *Fulgentius metaforalis* and adding more mythographic material of his own.

These York history tables were still on display in 1534, when John Leland visited the Minster with Sir George Lawson, the treasurer of Berwick, who recounted the visit in a letter to Thomas Cromwell:

> Sir, as Maister Leylond and I did walke in the Cathedrall Churche of Yorke he perceyved a table hangyng upon a walle within the said Churche and ther found the reigne of divers kinges of this realme emonges which he found one lyne of a king that took the kingdome of the pope by tribute to hold of the Churche of Roome, which I cutt oute of the said table and raysed the same and herein I send you the title thereof as it was in the said table.

A text table of the Miracles of St William of York hung in the Minster revestry.[47] Elsewhere in the Minster, the Pater Noster Guild manifested and encouraged devotion to the Lord's Prayer by maintaining a candelabrum of seven lights in honour of the seven petitions of the prayer. It was also responsible for a *tabula* 'de toto processu utilitatis oracionis dominice', which hung from a nearby column. Such a table probably reflected in schematic form the popular collocation of the seven petitions with the Deadly Sins, Beatitudes (skilfully reduced), Gifts of the Spirit and Virtues. Such schematisations readily lent themselves to visual display in stained glass or tabular format, and could form part of the didactic scheme of a church's decoration. Once again, they most commonly survive through manuscript versions. Diagrammatic representations of these septenaries are found, for example, in manuscripts of Robert Grosseteste's *Templum Dei* (described as a 'tabula de tota cura officii pastoralis'), and there is a vernacular version in the Vernon Manuscript. Their influence can be detected in texts such as *Piers Plowman*, but they may have been a common part of the didactic experience of the medieval churchgoer.[48]

---

[46] J. B. Friedman, *John de Foxton's Liber Cosmographiae (1408): an Edition and Codicological Study* (Leiden, 1988), and his ancillary studies: 'John de Foxton's Continuation of Ridwall's *Fulgentius Metaforalis*', *Studies in Iconography*, 7 (1981), 65–79; 'John Siferwas and the Mythological Illustrations in the *Liber cosmographiae* of John de Foxton', *Speculum*, 58 (1983), 391–418.

[47] J. S. Purvis, 'A Leland Discovery', *Antiquaries Jnl*, 31 (1951), 200–201. The transcription of the text of the Miracles of William was collected by the antiquarian Roger Dodsworth (d. 1654) in Oxford, Bodl. Lib., MS Dodsworth 125, fols 132–142ᵛ, 'out of a table in ye Revestry in ye Cathedrall Church of York' (fol. 132). Pr. Raine, *Historians of York*, II, 531–43.

[48] For the Pater Noster Guild returns, see *Records of Early English Drama: York*, ed. A. F. Johnston and M. Rogerson (Manchester, 1979), II, 646–7 (Latin) and 864 (tr.). On the schematic representation

Although such text tables were common enough in medieval churches, most references to tables in York Minster describe the pictorial images that were found on them.[49] By 1390, an inventory of the chantry of St John the Baptist lists the purchase of a veil to hang before the 'tabulam depictam' and in 1483 the chantry had a table painted with an image of the Trinity. By 1360, the chantry of St Nicholas had a small 'pulcra et decora' table above the altar, and another 'cum imaginibus eburneis', valued by estimation at 30 shillings.[50] An inventory of c.1500–10 lists 'una tabula argenti deaureati cum ymagine B.M. enamyld', and the use of precious metals is paralleled in a 1465 inventory from the York Corpus Christi Guild which lists: 'Item j tabelett de auro cum ymagine sancte Trinitatis, Christofere & sancte Barbare', which was valued at 22 shillings.[51]

The comprehensive chantry inventory of the early 1520s records numerous tables, including 'j tabyll of the vernakyll' in St Lawrence's chantry, 'a tabyll of ix partes' in St Blase and six tables in St Christopher, picturing Our Lady; Jesus, Mary and John (presumably a crucifixion scene); St Peter; St George; St Christopher; and St John. The altar of Saints Agatha, Lucy and Scholastica had a 'tabula depicta' with the Trinity and other images. The Name of Jesus chantry, which was next to the Lady Chapel in the east end of the presbytery, is also recorded as having 'ij tabyls'. The Lady Chapel, or chantry of St Mary the Virgin, was probably the most distinguished chantry in the Minster, and was proportionately well endowed with decorations. Fifteenth-century inventories include gold crowns for the images of the Virgin and Child kept there, as well as various alabaster panels, including 'una ymago B.M. sedentis cum filio suo de alabaustro' and a 'tabula alba picta' which showed the coronation of the Virgin.[52] But no mention is made in any of the published inventories or fabric rolls of the tables described in the Corpus text.

Superficially at least, the extensive tradition of decorative *tabulae* provides a satisfactory context for the Corpus text. It describes image and text tables presented

---

of didactic material, see A. I. Doyle, *The Vernon Manuscript: a Facsimile of Bodleian Library, Oxford, MS. Eng. Poet. a. 1* (Cambridge, 1987), p. 9; A. Henry, '"The Pater Noster in a table ypeynted" and Some Other Presentations of Doctrine in the Vernon Manuscript', in *Studies in the Vernon Manuscript*, ed. D. Pearsall (Cambridge, 1990), pp. 89–113; V. Gillespie, 'Thy Will Be Done: *Piers Plowman* and the *Paternoster*', in *Late Medieval English Texts and Their Transmission: Essays in Honour of A. I. Doyle*, ed. A. J. Minnis (Cambridge, 1994), pp. 95–119. On the link between schematic didactic materials displayed in churches and religious drama, see M. D. Anderson, *Drama and Imagery in English Medieval Churches* (Cambridge, 1963), pp. 60–84; A. F. Johnston, 'The Plays of the Religious Guilds of York: the Creed Play and the Pater Noster Play', *Speculum*, 50 (1975), 55–90.

[49] C. Davidson and D. E. O'Connor, *York Art: a Subject List of Extant and Lost Art Including Items Relevant to Early Drama* (Kalamazoo, 1978) lists many items from the Minster; *The Fabric Rolls of York Minster*, ed. J. Raine, Surtees Society, 35 (1858) edits a selection of the medieval fabric rolls.

[50] Ibid., pp. 290–91, 298.

[51] Ibid., p. 223; *Records of Early English Drama: York*, App. II, p. 635.

[52] *Fabric Rolls*, pp. 293, 279, 280, 304, 294–7.

on an altar in a recently refurbished and redecorated chapel in a metropolitan church containing many well-documented images of a similar kind. Moreover, the text's description of five representations of the Virgin might support the contention that the text refers to a Marian altarpiece. The failure of the images to survive or to be mentioned in documentary records is hardly surprising given the depredations suffered by such classes of art and by the records themselves.

There are, however, a number of circumstances, both internal and external to the text, which raise serious doubts about whether such a work of art ever existed. In the first place, the iconography offers an unusually dense synthesis of images, types, attributes and titles, which is possibly unique among English Marian altarpieces. Each image represents an amalgam of typological attributes which is not related to any phase or sequence of the life of the Virgin, scriptural or apocryphal, unlike the normal iconographic representation of scenes from the Life of the Virgin. Moreover the density of iconographical allusion is not common among single images of the Virgin either: I have, for example, been unable to find any reference to any extant Marian alabaster which treats the Virgin in the eclectically typological and non-narrative manner described in the Corpus text.

Secondly, internal evidence suggests that the 'tabyll' may not have been executed at the time that the text was first composed. This argument hinges on some notably ambiguous terminology used to describe the five images. The text purports to describe the 'disposiciun' of the 'tabyll'. Although this can mean 'the way in which the material has been disposed according to a plan', the primary sense in Middle English seems to be 'the preparation, planning or arrangement of something, or a plan of arrangement' (*MED*, s.v. 1 (a), (b)), prior to its execution. Similar ambiguity is found in the peroration: "¶þys ys þe consayte offe þe tabyll, aftyr þe consayte offe sum pepyll, *and* so Amene' (line 51). 'Consayte' is being used in at least two different senses here. The first refers to the appearance of the images (*MED*, s.v., 4 (d)). But parallel senses muddy the semantic waters: 4(b), the conception or plan (of a treatise); 4(c) a summary or digest (of a subject). Thus although the text may be describing an actual object, it may equally well be describing a planned object that has not (yet) been created. Similarly 'þe consayte offe sum pepyll' might refer to the plan for the images, drawn up by others but not yet executed, or to a 'summary' supplied by others. Two further senses are possible: a 'concept, idea, thought, notion or opinion; (*MED*, 2 (a)) of the 'tabyll' or 'an opinion entertained concerning' the 'tabyll' (*MED*, 3 (a)). The Corpus text could thus be describing an extant work of art as envisaged or summarized by others, or a planned work of art as conceived by others, possibly those who commissioned the work, whoever they might be.

At the outset, the text says that the Virgin is 'ymagened in v maner of wysys'. Although this might seem to incline the argument in favour of an 'imaginary' text, not yet 'performed', it is important to note that 'ymagened' can be the preterite of the verb 'imaginen'. Now, although this has 'to imagine' as its primary sense, a cognate noun 'imaginour/imaginer' means one who makes statues or images. 'Ymagened' might, by analogy, be extended to mean 'imaged or pictured'. Thus the text's semantics allow the Virgin to be both physically 'pictured' and/or mentally 'imagined' in five different ways.

Perhaps the most telling evidence against this being a description of an actual art object is the final sentence of the description of the fourth image: 'Or ellis geue *our* lady yn here hande yn þys place a stone *and* þat ys most *con*uenyent to þys verse' (lines 40–41). This suggests that the images had not yet been executed, and that the realization and performance of the 'consayte' remained open to variation. There are several possible explanations for this. The text may represent a record of an uncompleted commission ('aftyr þe consayte offe sum pepyll'); or it may predate the execution of a table that was subsequently lost; or the text records a completed commission with a view to soliciting similar commissions, while allowing for some typological and iconographical variation to suit taste and circumstances, assuming the selection of verses to be more or less final.

Whatever the historical reality may have been, the preservation of the text in its current form, out of its apparently intended architectural context, and as the third and final in a series of vernacular discussions of different kinds of images, shows that it was capable of adaptation and function in a context that explores hypertextual links between words and pictures. As a textual artefact rather than a pictorial artefact, the images it describes must indeed be 'ymagened' without the benefit of an actual visual referent (unless the reader could be assumed to know the actual pictures). The scheme of iconography must be performed in the imagination of its reading or listening audience; the pictures must be realized through the generation of mental imagery. As a verbal manifestation of a visual object, the 'performance' of each image must resonate against its verses in a more private way; each link and paradox must be interrogated in the hypertext created by the reader's psyche.

Here too the Corpus text can be provided with a context, albeit a more speculative one than for its plastic manifestation. This is the tradition of 'Roman' pictures, allegorical descriptions of pagan deities and, increasingly, of virtues and vices, popularized in the fourteenth century by the English classicizing friars John Ridwall and Robert Holcot, and echoed in derivative works like the *Imagines Fulgentii* and preaching aids such as the *Fasciculus morum*.[53] It is interesting to note that John de

---

[53] On mythography, see Kaske, *Literary Imagery*, pp. 104–29. On friars and Roman pictures, see B. Smalley, 'Robert Holcot O.P.', *Archivum Fratrum Praedicatorum*, 26 (1956), 5–97, esp. 65–82; and her *English Friars and Antiquity in the Early Fourteenth Century* (Oxford, 1960); N. F. Palmer, '"Antiquitus depingebatur": the Roman Pictures of Death and Misfortune in the *Ackermann aus Böhmen* and *Tkadleč*, and in the Writings of the English Classicizing Friars', *Deutsche Vierteljahrs Schrift*, 57 (1983), 171–239; J. B. Allen, *The Ethical Poetic of the Latin Middle Ages: a Decorum of Convenient Distinction* (Toronto, 1982), pp. 222–4; M. *Robert Holkoth . . . in librum Sapientiae regis Salomonis praelectiones* and *Moralizationum moralium*, ed. J. Ryter (Basle, 1586); *Fulgentius Metaforalis: Ein Beitrag zur Geschichte der Antiken Mythologie im Mittelalter*, ed. H. Liebeschütz,

Foxton's *Liber cosmographiae*, composed early in the fifteenth century from resources in the Minster and the Augustinian Priory in York, uses Ridwall's *Fulgentius metaforalis* and adds more material of a similar kind. The book may have been commissioned as a presentation copy by John Erghome, the bibliophile Augustinian friar at the York priory. His book shows that York had materials for the study of such texts, and clergy who, whether as commissioner, scribe or recipient, were interested in such study, within 20 years of the Corpus text being written.[54]

Although classical deities form the bulk of Ridwall's and Holcot's work, the *Imagines* in particular includes more overtly medieval and moral images, for example, the constellation Virgo moralized as the Virgin and Child. (Interestingly, Wyclif likened images of the Virgin to the image of Artemis/Diana defended by the silversmiths of Ephesus in Acts chapter 19.)[55] The characteristic features of Holcot's *Moralitates* have much in common with the Corpus Marian images. Consider, for example, the *moralitas* of Richness:

> The state of richness was depicted as a fickle woman, a crown on her head, with covered eyes, holding a royal sceptre and a peacock in her hands, clothed with various garments and sitting in a chariot pulled by truculent and most savage lions.[56]

Holcot presents a simple image 'fanciful indeed, but easily grasped and capable of being drawn or painted'. He uses verses or *tituli* to point the moral of the picture and the image is composed of striking and memorable attributes, often held by the subject. Thus, for example:

> The likeness of Penance, which the priests of the goddess Vesta painted, according to Remigius. Penance used to be painted in the form of a man, his whole body naked, who held a five-thronged scourge in his hand. Five verses or sentences were written on it.[57]

Similarly many of Ridwall's female deities in the *Fulgentius metaforalis*, such as Venus, Minerva, Juno and Cybele are presented as holding symbolic objects or as seated or standing in symbolic postures. Juno is seated on a throne, holding a sceptre in her left hand, with a veiled head, crowned with a diadem, and with peacocks at her feet. Minerva, similarly, was depicted by the poets ('pingebatur a poetis') as an

---

Studien der Bibliothek Warburg, 4 (1926); *Fasciculus Morum*, ed. Wenzel, e.g., pp. 329, 631; S. Wenzel, *Verses in Sermons:* Fasciculus Morum *and its Middle English Poems* (Cambridge, MA, 1978), pp. 57–9.

[54] Friedman, *John de Foxton*.

[55] Palmer, 'Roman Pictures', p. 176. Wyclif's comment is quoted by Aston, *England's Iconoclasts*, p. 107.

[56] *Holkoth*, ed. Ryter, p. 742: 'Status divitiarum depingebatur ut mulier vaga, habens coronam in capite, oculis velata, sceptrum regale tenens et pavonem in manu, variis vestimentis induta, sedens in curru quem trahebant leones truculenti et immanissimi' (my translation).

[57] *Holkoth*, ed. Ryter, pp. 728–9; tr. Smalley, *English Friars*, p. 165.

armed woman ('in similitudinem domine armate') with a lance in the left hand and a crystalline shield in the right.[58]

The 'Roman' picture tradition has much in common with the rhetorical tradition of artificial memory: both depend on the artful 'disposition' (to use a technical rhetorical term as well as a term from the Corpus text) of images to stimulate retention and manipulation of material. The *Ad Herennium* gives the classic description of the process:

> We ought, then, to set up images of a kind that can adhere longest in memory. And we shall do so if we establish similitudes as striking as possible; if we set up images that are not many or vague, but active (*imagines agentes*); if we assign to them exceptional beauty or singular ugliness; if we ornament some of them, as with crowns or purple cloaks, so that the similitude may be more distinct to us.

These precepts were adapted by Thomas Aquinas, here as distilled in a fourteenth-century preacher's handbook:

> There are four things which help a man to remember well. The first is that he should dispose those things which he wishes to remember in a certain order. The second is that he should adhere to them with affection. The third is that he should reduce them to unusual similitudes. The fourth is that he should repeat them with frequent meditation.[59]

Characteristic of the processes of artificial memory is the disposition of images in *loci*. Although the absence of *loci* in the 'Roman' picture tradition has been said to set it apart from memory systems, it is worth noting that some of Holcot's *Moralitates* use actual locations:

> The goddess Vesta used to be painted with a lily having five leaves, and a verse written on each, which the priests of the temple would expound in the concourse of people in the goddess Vesta's temple.

Moreover, Thomas Bradwardine's treatise *De memoria artificiali* specifically recommends that:

> the places should be real rather than mostly imagined or made-up, for real places one can frequently inspect and thus through repetition shape and firm-up an habitual knowledge of them.[60]

---

[58] See Ridwall, *De deorum imaginibus libellus*, in *Fulgentius Metaforalis*, ed. Liebeschütz, pp. 118–21.

[59] On the tradition of artificial memory, see F. Yates, *The Art of Memory* (Harmondsworth, 1969); for the *Ad Herennium* quotation, see pp. 25–6; for the Thomistic paraphrase, see p. 96. M. Carruthers, *The Book of Memory: a Study of Memory in Medieval Culture* (Cambridge, 1990), pp. 229–42 discusses mental pictures (including those of Holcot and Ridwall) and offers a more rigorous and scholarly account of the medieval psychology of mental imagery.

[60] Smalley, *English Friars*, p. 165; Bradwardine, *De Memoria Artificiali*, ed. and tr. Carruthers (*Book of Memory*), App. C, pp. 281–88, esp. 281–3.

Bradwardine also argues that the image should have attributes in left and right hands (as in the Corpus text), and that three, five or seven images work best for optimal retention of the material (Corpus has five).

In its literary manifestation, therefore, the Corpus text offers many similarities with this mnemonic tradition of 'literary' pictures. It envisages a specific *locus* (the York Minster Lady Chapel), as well as component *loci* (cf. line 40: 'yn þys place'); it offers a clear disposition of the imagery; it is 'ymagened' (cf. Holcot's 'depingebatur'); it offers pictorial descriptions of subjects holding and standing on familiar attributes grouped in unfamiliar synthesis; it describes itself as a 'consayte' to be 'ymagened'; its reference to 'þe consayte offe sum pepyll' is similar to the vague references in Holcot and Ridwall to 'the painting by poets'. Like those memory pictures, it exploits hypertextual links between text and image, inviting meditation and rumination by the enigmatic and allusive links between the iconography and the verses. As in the *Imagines Fulgentii*, the allegorical and typological force of the iconography is teased out by these verses.

Perhaps this desire to create *imagines agentes* explains the alternative iconography offered at the end of the fourth image (lines 40–41): 'Or ellis geue our lady yn here hande yn þys place a stone *and* þat ys most conuenyent to þys verse.' Although it may originate as an instruction to the painter or patron, the imperative 'geue' now emphasizes the performative role to be played by the reader of the text as opposed to the viewer of the table. This permissive provision is certainly within the spirit of the author of *Pictor in carmine*, who wrote: 'It was not my business to arrange for those who supervise such matters that all should be painted; let them look to it themselves as fancy takes each, or as he abounds in his own sense.' As Bradwardine put it:

> For trained memory, two things are necessary, that is, firm locations and also images for the material; for the locations are like tablets on which we write, the images like the letters written on them.[61]

In their written manifestation, in the Corpus text, the York Lady Chapel images balance provocatively on the threshold between the literal and the figurative resonances of Bradwardine's analogy. Neither verified as artefact, nor self-sufficient as text, they exist now only in the hypertextual synapses of our imaginative recuperation, 'aftyr þe consayte offe sum pepyll'.

---

[61] *Pictor*, tr. James (1951), p. 142; Bradwardine, tr. Carruthers, p. 281.

Appendix: Oxford, Corpus Christi College, MS 132, fols 69ᵛ–70

Editorial method

Expansions of the Middle English text are italicized; Latin abbreviations are silently
expanded. Orthography of the Middle English is preserved; the Latin has been
checked and occasionally emended against the full copy of *Pictor in carmine*
preserved in Oxford, Bodleian Library, MS Rawlinson C. 67, which supplies the
readings in the apparatus. U/V has been normalized in the Latin. Scribal insertions
are marked ` . . . ´. Editorial additions and emendations are enclosed in square
brackets. Erasures, text over erasures, and other deficiencies are enclosed in angle
brackets. Manuscript capitalization and paraphs are preserved. Punctuation and line
numbering are editorial, and the manuscript lineation has not been preserved. The
Latin distiches are laid out as verse and the six lines of each section are linked by
braces in the manuscript, which are not preserved here.

[fol. 69ᵛ]

¶ þys ys þe disposiciu*n* of þe tabyll at o*ur* lady auter yn þe cathedrall kyrke of
yorke. þ*at* ys for to say þ*at* ower lady ys ymagened in v maner of wysys. þe fyrst
ys o*ur* lady hauyng yn here hand the tabelis offe moyeses *and* vnd*ir* here fete þe
berny[n]g buske of moyses *and* also þe figure off þe worlde. And þ*er* scho ys
5   calde Rubus Moisi et Domina Mundi w*ith* vers wretyn vndyr her fete:

     Vt rubus ingne[s]c[i]t et eum vis ingnea nescit,   Exodus 3°
     Carne deus latitat sed ca`r´nis opus caro vitat.
     Absque solo vellus maduit sine vellere tellus: Judices 6°
     In signo duplici res apta dei genetrici
10   Qua ponat sedem sapiencia construit edem,   In Proverbia 9°
     Cum deus hanc condit cuius se ventre recondit.

¶ þe secu*n*de has yn þe too hand a lily *and* yn þe oþir a brange offe rosys and
vndyr here fete a yate of golde sparryd *and* also a heuen full of a*n*gelis. And þ*er*
scho ys callyd Porta Clausa et Regina Cely w*ith* þys ve`r´se unþir here fete:

15   Invia porta viro domino patet ordine myro,   Ezechiel 44.
     Dum pudor est saluus et pregnans virginis aluus.
     Artus rinoceros flectit tibi, virgo, severos: Natura Rerum
     Sic deus [e]celis dat se tibi, virgo fidelis.
     Fiunt gaudentes Saram peperisse videntes   Genesis 21°
20   Sic et pastores ubi gestit virgula flores.

¶ þe thyrd ys o*ur* lady w*ith* her sch[il]de yn here arme *and* vnþir here fete þe
mone *and* þe arke offe the holde testame*n*t. And þ*er* scho ys callyd Dey Genetryx
et Arca Testamenti w*ith* þys 1 verse wretyn vnd*ir* here fete:

	Cuntis crede tronis prestare tronum salamonis,	Reges 3 11°
25	Et plus felicem cuntis dei genetricem.	
	Arca dei visa templo cely reserati	
	Et signum grande ⟨mulier⟩ circumdata sole	Apocalypsis 12°
	Sub pedibus luna cuius sunt signa beate	
	Virginis et matris que sunt a virgine visa.	

30 ¶ þe 4 has yn here hand þe wande of aron florischyng [fol. 70] *and* beryng almundys *and* hath undyr here fete a tempyll and many virgynys. And þer scho ys callyd Templum Salamonys et Virgo Virginum w*ith* þys verse wretyn vndyr here fete:

	Nec sonus auditur in templo quando politur,	Reges 3 6°
35	Nec pudor atteritur dum virgo parens reperitur.	
	Sponsi missa manus sentitur ventre tremente,	Canticum 5°
	Cum deus humanus fit, virgine suscipiente.	
	Mons lapidem iecit quem nulla manus patefecit:	Daniel 2°
	Virgo deum gestat quam nulla libido molestat.	

40 Or ellis geue o*ur* lady yn here hande yn þys place a stone *and* þat ys most con*u*enyent to þys verse.

¶ þe 5 lady has yn here o hande a sprynkyll *and* a cros yn þe toþ*ir* hande and v*n*dyr here fete þe tre offe lyfe *and* helle. And þer scho ys callyd Ymparatryx Ynferny et Lignum Vitae w*ith* þys verse v*n*dyr here fete:

45	Serpentis fragile teritur caput a muliere,	Genesis 3°
	Dum cor habens humile cupit innuba ventre tumere.	
	Sub colubro plane colubros sacra virg[a] vorabat	Exodus 7°
	Quando dolos satane deitas sub carne vocabat.	
	Laude fit eximia merso duce prima maria,	Exodus 15
50	Sic fit iocunda Zabulo pereunte secunda.	

¶ þys ys þe co*n*sayte offe þe tabyll, aftyr þe consayte offe sum pepyll, *and* so Amene.

---

4 *berny[n]g*] MS bernyg.   6 *ingne[s]c[i]t*] MS ingnect; *Pictor* ignescit.   9 *In signo*] *Pictor* Est signo.   18 *deus [e] celis*] so *Pictor*; MS deus celis.   20 *gestit*] *Pictor* Iesse. 21 *sch[il]de*] MS schade.   37 *suscipiente*] *Pictor* concipiente.   47 *virg[a]*] so *Pictor*; MS virgo.   48 *vocabat*] *Pictor* necabat.

CHAPTER TEN

History and Legend at Kirkstall in the Fifteenth Century

Jeanne E. Krochalis

In *Medieval Libraries of Great Britain*, Neil Ker listed eight manuscripts from the Yorkshire Cistercian house of Kirkstall, near Leeds.[1] In the course of this essay, I would like to add five manuscripts to Ker's list, and then look closely at the work of three scribes who appear in several Kirkstall manuscripts, most notably in London, BL, Cotton MS Titus A.XIX and Oxford, Bodleian Library, MS Laud Misc. 722. Ker placed Laud at Kirkstall, but did not mention Titus. However, while cataloguing the contents of the latter (in the course of editing the *Pilgrim's Guide to Compostela*) I found that three of the hands which appear in the Laud manuscript, writing some texts and annotating others, also appear in Titus. The manuscript contains a great deal of local Kirkstall material.[2] Cumulatively, the evidence for its Kirkstall provenance is convincing. Several of the texts in Titus by one of the scribes I am considering, whom I shall call hand 1, are unprinted, and two of its most interesting texts are edited in the Appendix at the conclusion of this essay.

Many of the walls of the numerous buildings which comprised Kirkstall Abbey are still standing, but the placement and physical extent of its library is a problem. In the original excavation, W. H. St John Hope noted a small cupboard for book storage in the cloister, off the south transept of the church. He thought that there, as at Meaux, the room behind this aumbry was also devoted to books. It is still a small space, but he compared it to the similarly placed room at Meaux, which we know from Meaux's catalogue must have contained over 200 volumes.[3] Perhaps, as

---

[1] Ker, *MLGB*, p. 107. It seems appropriate to begin an essay for Malcolm Parkes with a reference to the distinguished palaeographer who was his teacher, and also mine, and whose work remains central to subsequent studies in English manuscripts. For fruitful discussion about the manuscripts cited here, I am indebted, as always, to Malcolm Parkes, and also to Ruth Dean, Robert Frank, W. Gerald Heverly, Michael Robson OFM and Alison Stones. The manuscript libraries of the British Library, Bodleian Library, the University Library in Cambridge, Sidney Sussex College, and Jesus College, Cambridge, and the staff of the Rare Book Room, Pennsylvania State University were helpful as always. The computer staff at Clare Hall, Cambridge, were particularly supportive in 1995.

[2] A. Stones and J. Krochalis, *The Pilgrim's Guide to Compostela*, II: *Manuscripts and Readers* (London, forthcoming). Titus appears in manuscripts considered but rejected in Watson, *Supplement*, p. 41.

[3] W. H. St John Hope, *Architectural Description of Kirkstall Abbey*, Thoresby Society, 16 (1907), 29 and fig. 23. If the books were stored flat, rather than upright, it is difficult to see how 200 could have been accommodated in the space. According to the current guide, the room held only the books for

happened at other Cistercian houses, part of the original sacristy off the transept was added to the book room at the back, or additional bays between the original aumbry and the chapter house door might have been used for books.[4] Later, without explanation, Hope labelled the room over the infirmary, built c.1220, as 'library'. It would be long and narrow, and, if windowed, could well have made a library cum scriptorium.[5] More recent excavations have concentrated on the kitchen area, and contain no mention of a library, nor any book or writing related finds.[6] But there is evidence for a lively intellectual life at Kirkstall in the fifteenth century, when the monastery was again enjoying some prosperity after troubled times in the late fourteenth century, and in the aftermath of the Black Death. It must have continued to be a viable foundation until the Dissolution in 1539, when it had an abbot, a prior, a sub-prior and 29 monks. Among Yorkshire foundations of comparable size and antiquity, Fountains had the same number; Meaux had an abbot and 24 monks, and Rievaulx an abbot and 22 monks.[7]

Four volumes from the twelfth or early thirteenth centuries survive: Oxford, Bodleian Library, MS Laud Misc. 216 is a twelfth-century copy of Bede; MS Laud lat. 69 an early copy of Hugucio, *Magnae derivationes*; MS e Mus. 195 contains Smaragdus. Liège, University Library, MS 369C (which I have not seen) is a twelfth-century copy of Eutropius. All have *ex libris* inscriptions and notes in later medieval hands which suggest that texts in earlier manuscripts continued to be read. None of these are exceptional works to find in a Cistercian library.[8]

These are books which were at Kirkstall, and were demonstrably read there, but to say that books which can be convincingly associated with the house were necessarily written there is a tricky proposition. No scriptorium appears in Hope's reconstructed plan, although there must have been a place for writing, if only for keeping accounts. We too often forget that monasteries had various ways of acquiring books, of which in-house copying was only one.[9] Two later volumes, Cambridge, Jesus College, MS

---

reading in the cloister. See J. Spence and B. Spence, *The Medieval Monasteries of Yorkshire* (Helmsley, 1981), p. 57.

[4] D. Knowles, *The Religious Orders in England II: the End of the Middle Ages* (Cambridge, 1957), pp. 351–2.

[5] Hope, *Kirkstall*, p. 42. Knowles notes that a room designated as a scriptorium appears only a century after the Conquest, and that a library often appears in English monasteries only in the late fourteenth or fifteenth centuries. Before then, we assume that the monks read and wrote in the cloisters; see Knowles, 'The Monastic Buildings of England', in *The Historian and Character and other Essays*, ed. C. N. L. Brooke and G. Constable (Cambridge, 1963), pp. 192–3.

[6] *Kirkstall Abbey Excavations 1950–1954*, ed. D. Owen, Thoresby Society, 43 (1955).

[7] For figures at the Dissolution, see *Letters and Papers Foreign and Domestic of the Reign of Henry VIII*, XIV, ed. J. Gairdner and R. H. Brodie (London, 1895), II, p. 198, no. 567 (Kirkstall); pp. 208–9, no. 587 (Fountains); p. 234, no. 670 (Meaux); I, p. 67, no. 185 (Rievaulx).

[8] See C. R. Cheney, 'English Cistercian Libraries: the First Century', in *Medieval Texts and Studies* (Oxford, 1973), and D. Bell, *The Libraries of the Cistercians, Gilbertines, and Premonstratensians*, Corpus of British Medieval Library Catalogues 3 (Oxford, 1992).

[9] See J. Sheppard, 'The Twelfth-Century Library and Scriptorium at Buildwas: Assessing the

75, from the thirteenth and fourteenth centuries, and Sidney Sussex College, MS 85, from the fourteenth century, illustrate this point.

Sidney Sussex 85 begins with *Barlaam et Josaphat* (fols 2–74ᵛ), and contains a number of other devotional texts.[10] The manuscript originally belonged to Simon Gowshill, a canon of Chicksands which was a Gilbertine double priory in Bedfordshire. He has not been traced, but he copied many of the texts in this manuscript, in a mid-fourteenth-century hand. The texts copied by him include the *Summa* of John de St Edmund, on fols 123ᵛ–142. According to Emden, an Augustinian friar of that name was in Cambridge from 1345 to 1356, though he does not credit him with this work.[11] If the friar were indeed the author of the *Summa*, it would provide a *terminus a quo* for the text. Another candidate, mentioned by James, is a Johannes a Fano Eadmundi of Ipswich (fl. *c.*1350). As it is, the only certain *terminus a quo* is provided by the account of a miracle of the Virgin involving Richard of Leicester, who was chancellor of Cambridge University by 1222. Gowshill's *ex libris* is in the volume, and he wrote a note about a copy of the Institutes of John Cassian belonging to Warden in Bedfordshire on fol. 79ᵛ. Warden is a Cistercian foundation (a daughter house of Rievaulx) and about five miles from Chicksands, south-east of Bedford. In the 1330s, Chicksands fell on hard times, and had to send some of its canons and nuns elsewhere. Fifteenth-century buildings suggest a later more prosperous period, but at the Dissolution there were only six canons and 18 nuns.[12] Did Gowshill in the mid fourteenth century perhaps take refuge with the nearby Cistercians of Warden? Or could Chicksands have sold some of its library? A Warden destination would put this manuscript in the Cistercian orbit, with Yorkshire connections at Rievaulx.

However it reached there, the volume was certainly at Kirkstall in the fifteenth century, judging by the inscription 'Constat Johanni Stamborn monacho de kyrkestall' on fol. 1ᵛ. There is another erased inscription in which the name of Kirkstall can be made out (on fol. 4ᵛ) in a different fifteenth-century hand. In addition, an early-sixteenth-century Anglicana hand which occurs in other Kirkstall manuscripts has been at work here. John Taylor calls this the 'backwards' hand, because it consistently has a slight back slant, as if the writer were left-handed.[13] This 'backwards' hand left notes in the margins and on blank folios in both Titus and Laud, and wrote a quire of four leaves in Titus (fols 59–62), containing the history of the abbey up to its dissolution: 'Supprecio ʽet eiusdemʼ domus de kyrkestall die

Evidence', *England in the Twelfth Century: Proceedings of the 1988 Harlaxton Symposium*, ed. D. Williams (Woodbridge, 1990), pp. 193–204. Some of the Buildwas books she discusses (pp. 196–8) must have been written and glossed in Paris.

[10] M. R. James, *A Descriptive Catalogue of the Manuscripts in the Library of Sidney Sussex College, Cambridge* (Cambridge, 1895), pp. 68–71.

[11] A. B. Emden, *Biographical Register of the University of Cambridge* (Cambridge, 1963).

[12] S. Houfe, 'The Builders of Chicksands Priory I', *Bedfordshire Magazine*, 16 (1977), 186.

[13] J. Taylor, *The Kirkstall Abbey Chronicles*, Thoresby Society, 42 (1952), introduction.

sabbati anno domini m° ccccc° xxxix° die Sancte Cecelie dicata x° kalendas decembris littera dominicalis. E.' (fol. 62^v). The same 'backwards' hand added interlinear glosses in Sidney Sussex 85 on fols 5^v, 6, 10, 10^v, and 84.

The 'backwards' hand also occurs in Jesus 75, which was given to the monks of Kirkstall by the otherwise unknown frater Johannes de Driffeld, Ascension day, 1344, 'ad memoriam inter fratres perpetuandam et animam precibus deo commendandam' (fol. 1). This manuscript begins (fols 1–61) with one of the texts copied by Gowshill in Sidney Sussex 85 (fols 147–190^v): the *Tractatus de oculo spirituali*. Gowshill's and the hand of the text in Jesus 75 are contemporary. Could Sidney Sussex have been borrowed from Chicksands or Warden, and then not returned after the Jesus scribe made his copy? Jesus 75 is a careful production, accompanied by a table, and two of its other main texts are also devotional works: the *Medulla philosophorum*, accompanied by a table, and a text on the virtues beginning 'Notandum quod aristoteles determinat in libro primo Ethicorum de virtute ipsa tamen ad quatuor'.[14] The sixteenth-century writer of the 'backwards' hand evidently at least glanced at both copies of *De oculo spirituali*. There are several *nota* markings by him in Sidney Sussex: by a passage on the eremetical life (fol. 155); by a passage about women being caught by sight, like a tiger who sees its image in a mirror, and is distracted from its prey (fol. 169^v); and by the account of Socrates throwing money in the sea to indicate the evil of riches (fol. 173). In Jesus 75, he noted only one passage, a discussion of prelates as the spiritual eyes of the church (fol. 44).

Jesus 75 is also noteworthy because it is the only Kirkstall manuscript to preserve its medieval binding: brown leather with a stamped border of 16 roses, four to each side, within a frame, with a central cross pattern, made up of four roses in lozenges around a central rose in a circle. The spine has been rebacked, and the clasp is missing.

The 'backwards' hand also appears in Cambridge, Sidney Sussex College, MS 47, a twelfth-century collection of early saints' lives, including Jerome's Life of St Paul the Hermit, and lives of Anthony, Hilarion, Appolonius and Jerome. Like Sidney Sussex 85, it was given to the college by Samuel Ward of Durham in 1643. There is no *ex libris* but among the names on the end leaf is *gabriell losthus* in a sixteenth-century Secretary hand. A Gabriel Lostens was among the Kirkstall monks pensioned on 22 November, 1539.[15] We may assume that a book which was used by Kirkstall monks almost certainly belonged at Kirkstall. The interlinear glosses in the 'backwards' hand (on fols 5^v, 6, 10, 10^v, 12 and 84) look as though the scribe was collating the text with another copy.

Who was the 'backwards' hand? He nowhere signs his name but he is likely to have been a monk at Kirkstall to have had such access to its books before and at the

---

[14] See M. R. James, *A Descriptive Catalogue of the Manuscripts in the Library of Jesus College, Cambridge* (Cambridge, 1895), p. 112.

[15] *Letters and Papers . . . Henry VIII*, XIV, pt ii, p. 198, no. 567.

Dissolution; what happened to him later? Many of the monks had local names and were likely to have stayed in the area, although the only identifiable former monk of Kirkstall that I could trace in the local records, at the Borthwick Institute, was Thomas Rawson who had been at Kirkstall since 1508. After the Dissolution the abbey property was bought by Robert Payman but it continued to be managed by Rawson who had been the abbey's bursar. He must have known the 'backwards' hand scribe. When John Thorneton, vicar of Leeds, tried to collect tithes from the abbey lands in the 1540s, Payman and Rawson took him to court, on the grounds that no such demands had ever been made of any of the abbey lands in any parish; Rawson claimed then, 'that he was a monke in Kyrkestall by the space of xxxi[ty] yeares and Bursar of the same howse by the space of tenne or twelfe yeeres before the surrenderinge of the same.'[16] In 1557, John and Walter Rawston [sic] were fighting the same issue for the same property; perhaps Thomas had married and had had sons.[17]

Three other manuscripts may be attributed to Kirkstall although the 'backwards' hand does not occur in any of them. London, BL, Cotton MS Domitian A.XII, part 1, though not in Ker, has sometimes been described as a Kirkstall book, and can now be confidently assigned there. It contains two chronicles, the second being a text usually known as the Long Chronicle of Kirkstall (fols 57–138).[18] The noted Yorkshire antiquary, Roger Dodsworth (1585–1654), who transcribed part of it and was normally careful in identifying his sources, refers to it as 'chronica de Kirkstall'.[19] This chronicle, however, as Dugdale pointed out, concerns itself with national rather than local events.[20] It is, in fact, a condensed version of Higden's *Polychronicon*, extended from 1346 to 1430. This continuation is identical with the Whalley Abbey continuation in London, BL, MS Harley 3600, which also puts it in a Yorkshire Cistercian orbit.[21] It seems not unlikely that Kirkstall could have had a copy of a Whalley text, as Cistercian chronicles circulated from one house to another.[22] The

---

[16] York, Borthwick Institute: York Cause Papers G 866/2. Rawson is not on the list of monks receiving pensions; perhaps this was because he had property instead.

[17] Borthwick Institute: York Cause Papers G /438.

[18] Taylor, *The Kirkstall Abbey Chronicles*; N. Denholm-Young and M. V. Clarke, 'The Kirkstall Chronicle 1355–1400', *Bulletin of the John Rylands Library*, 15 (1931), 100–137. The text is on fols 121–37. The manuscript is in two parts; part 2 is a twelfth-century copy of Ivo of Chartres. There is no indication whether this was part of the same manuscript as the chronicle before Robert Cotton acquired them; it has no *ex libris*, and no glosses. The following remarks therefore, apply only to the Kirkstall Chronicle section of Domitian A.XII.

[19] Oxford, Bodl. Lib., MS Dodsworth 88, fol. 10.

[20] William Dugdale, *Monasticon Anglicanum*, ed. J. Caley, H. Ellis and B. Bandinel (London, 1817–30), V, 326.

[21] For the relationship of the texts, and a partial edn (1399–1430), see C. L. Kingsford, *English Historical Literature in the Fifteenth Century* (Oxford, 1913), pp. 278–91.

[22] See the examples in R. Barber, 'Was Mordred Buried at Glastonbury? An Arthurian Tradition at Glastonbury in the Later Middle Ages', *Arthurian Literature*, 4 (1985), 43–44.

fact that Dodsworth, who could not have concluded its provenance from its contents alone, referred to it as a Kirkstall chronicle, is surely important. But Dugdale's doubts have carried more weight among subsequent scholars than Dodsworth's certainty. Furthermore, the manuscript has no Kirkstall *ex libris*, and scholars who have worked on it have been reluctant to assign it there. However, close codicological examination reveals that Domitian A.XII was written on the same paper as the first quire, and fols 76–80 (containing the life and miracles of St Kentigern) of Titus A.XIX. Portions of the same unidentified watermark, can be seen on Domitian A.XII, fols 57, 64, 65, 80 and 82 and Titus A.XIX, fols 8, 11, 53, 56, 65–67, 71, 76 and 77. The paper stock was not exclusive to Kirkstall: it also appears in Oxford, Bodleian Library, MS Digby 186, which is probably from York. But in Domitian, the leaves are the same size as those in Laud Misc. 722 (240 × 140mm) while the ruling is the same simple pencil frame and line (ruled to the same dimensions, 225 × 130mm) as the Kentigern section of Titus. The Kentigern hand also appears in Oxford, Bodleian Library, MS Dodsworth 140 (fols 98–109), writing the *Historia de Kirkstall*, and in Laud Misc. 722 (fols 129–38), writing the *Fundatio Kirkstall*.[23] This is suggestive, but what establishes Domitian at Kirkstall with greater probability is the appearance in it of the Titus hand 1, glossing and correcting, adding historical information, such as the dates of crusaders' battles (including the capture of Antioch in 1097, on fol. 75) and the death of Queen Matilda in 1117, on fol. 75^v. On fols 79^v–80, in an account of the consecration of Theobald as archbishop of Canterbury in 1139, hand 1 noted 'Rogerus archiepiscopus Ebor. presens fuit, sed manum non apposuit'. Further notes throughout contain general historical information, but also demonstrate a careful reading of the main text, and an ability to augment it from another source. Hand 1 may be dated to the late fifteenth century. It also appears in Laud Misc. 722 which was at Kirkstall at that time; therefore Domitian was certainly used at Kirkstall in the late fifteenth century.[24]

London, BL, MS Arundel 248 (thirteenth century), which contains Arnold of Brescia's *De forma vitae*, an anonymous *De amore et dilectione Dei et Christi* and some Middle English lyrics (including a text of 'hende' Nicholas's sequence 'Angelus ad Virginem') may also have come from Kirkstall. In the seventeenth century, Henry Savile of Banke acquired the manuscript from Thomas Foxcroft of Kirkstall; previously it had belonged to Thomas Bromhead of Bramley, which is within two miles of Kirkstall.[25] And if Ushaw, St Cuthbert's College, MS 6, a late-twelfth-century

---

[23] *The Foundation of Kirkstall Abbey*, ed. and tr. E. Kitson Clark, Thoresby Society, 4 (1892–95), 169–208, with a pl. from Laud Misc. 722, fol. 136.

[24] The first chronicle in Domitian A.XII, which goes from Brutus to Edward III, was no. 78c in the collection of Henry Savile of Banke, who also owned Arundel 248, see below. But no identifiable Kirkstall hand appears in it. See A. G. Watson, *The Manuscripts of Henry Savile of Banke* (London, 1969), p. 34. Savile, like Cotton, combined manuscripts on occasion, so there is no clear evidence that all the items in Savile's no. 78 were at Kirkstall.

[25] Ibid., no. 103, pp. 48–9.

volume, also comes (as Levison suggested) from Kirkstall, this would put the works of Geoffrey of Monmouth and Henry Huntingdon on the abbey's shelves. Levison noted the name 'Thomas Kilingbecke' on fol. 242^v in a sixteenth-century hand; a Robert Killingbeck was abbot of Kirkstall *c*.1499–1501, and other Killingbeckes were tenants and post-Dissolution owners of the abbey's lands at North Allerton and Chapel Allerton, also near Leeds. Fourteenth-century annotations suggest an interest in northern affairs.[26]

That the library at Kirkstall continued to expand until the Dissolution is evidenced by its possession of four early printed books: Oxford, Corpus Christi College, Δ.10.4 (Petrus Crinitus), printed in Paris, 1508 and three works bound into the back of Laud Misc. 722 – a copy of Albertus Magnus, *Secreta*, Edmund Rich, *Speculum ecclesiae*, STC 965 (1521) and an early printed account of Columbus's voyage to the New World, *Epistola de insulis noviter repertis*.[27] Acquisition of the latter suggests an interest in contemporary international discoveries which would be somewhat surprising in a Yorkshire Cistercian house. (However, there are no Kirkstall hands annotating it.)

What can we deduce from its manuscripts about historical compilation and composition at Kirkstall in the late fifteenth century? We have several chronicles and two composite volumes (Laud Misc. 722 and Titus A.XIX), probably fragments shored against the ruin by a monk after the Dissolution, which indicate that in the century before that, Kirkstall monks were actively preserving history, copying the texts of the *Fundatio*, *Historia*, and the two chronicles already mentioned. The *Fundatio* and *Historia* are largely of local interest, but the Short Chronicle was certainly written for a wider posterity. It is, to quote John Taylor, 'a highly illuminating account of the reign of Richard II, concentrating its narrative dramatically upon the final years of Richard's reign. It is in fact a brief fragment of contemporary history from the very end of the fourteenth century.'[28] The main focus of the remainder of this essay is a group of texts from Kirkstall, which are historical or legendary and are found in Titus A.XIX copied by the two scribes whom I call hand 1 and hand 2.

Titus must have come from Kirkstall since it contains texts in three hands which also occur in Laud; and the 'backwards' hand which annotated other Kirkstall manuscripts appears in it. Like Laud Misc. 722, Titus A.XIX is a composite volume; it is not certain that it formed a fifteenth-century collection but it can be established that each section of it was at Kirkstall before the Dissolution. The absence of an *ex libris* inscription, found in earlier Kirkstall manuscripts, can be explained by the

---

[26] Cf. W. Levison, 'A Combined Manuscript of Geoffrey of Monmouth and Henry of Huntingdon', *English Historical Review*, 58 (1943), 41–51; J. Crick, *The Historia Regum Britannie of Geoffrey of Monmouth III: a Summary Catalogue of the Manuscripts* (Woodbridge, 1989), no. 210, pp. 317–18.

[27] For the Albertus and the Columbus see R. Proctor, *An Index to the Early Printed Books in the British Museum: from the Invention of Printing to the year MD* (London, 1898), nos 1114 and 7988.

[28] J. Taylor, *English Historical Literature in the Fourteenth Century* (Oxford, 1987), p. 21.

absence of original endleaves; the volume has been re-bound and each leaf is now mounted separately. The original make-up of Laud is also uncertain and the extent to which each section in both manuscripts was self-contained is problematic. For that reason I have used the term 'unit' rather than 'booklet' in the discussion of Titus which follows.[29]

Both volumes are mainly collections of historical works. As well as a history of Jerusalem and saints' lives, Laud Misc. 722 contains the Long Chronicle of Kirkstall (fols 33–88) and the *Fundatio Kirkstall* (fols 129–140).[30] The hand of the *Fundatio* also wrote a life of St Kenelm in Titus and the *Historia de Kirkstall* in Domitian A.XII. Laud has been extensively annotated by the 'backwards' hand who added various details concerning the Lacy family (on fols 97ᵛ, 98ᵛ, 111ᵛ–112ᵛ, 126ᵛ). He copied the same notes in Titus on fols 59–61. Henry de Lacy had founded the community in 1147. There is also a note about the capture of the Scots pirate, Andreas Barton, at Flodden Field in 1513, written by 'Antonius Adyl, monachus de kyrkestall' on fol. 102ᵛ. Notes and texts added by Titus hand 1 include: the names of the Apostles (fol. 89); a tract against evil prelates (fols 93–97); historical notes on events up to 1489 (fol. 111); an account of Bruno, founder of the Carthusian order (fol. 112 bis); historical details about the Carmelites, up to 1298 (fols 124ᵛ–125); and a version of *Amis and Amile*. The Short Chronicle of Kirkstall (now Dodsworth 140, fols 98–109) may also once have been part of this volume.[31] The state of the binding suggests that leaves have been removed from Laud between folios 88 and 89. The miscellaneous nature of its contents is paralleled in Titus A.XIX.

Titus contains the work of at least a dozen different scribes but the combination of their stints and differing watermarks enable one to establish that it was made up of ten separate units: fols 3–15, 16–47, 48–49, 50–58, 59–62, 63–73 + 76–81; (74–75 is an inserted bifolium); 82–100, 101–116, 117–152 and 153–156.[32] The presence of the 'backwards' hand in each of them establishes that this volume had been put together by the 1540s. Those units which chiefly concern us here are the first and the second.

Hand 1 wrote the first unit which contains a copy of Simeon of Durham's brief account of the archbishops of York to 1140, an account of the bishops of Lincoln (an extract is edited at the end of this essay), a poem on the history of the church at York (also found on wooden tablets made during Arundel's archiepiscopate (1388–96) which still survive in the Minster library)[33] and an incomplete text on the antiquities of Rome.

---

[29] See P. R. Robinson, 'The "Booklet": a Self-Contained Unit in Composite Manuscripts', *Codicologica*, 3 (1980), 46–69.

[30] H. O. Coxe, *Bodleian Library Quarto Catalogues II: Laudian Manuscripts*, ed. R. W. Hunt (Oxford, 1973), no. 722 and pp. 581–2.

[31] Denholm-Young and Clarke, 'Kirkstall Chronicle', p. 105.

[32] A complete description of Titus will appear in Stones and Krochalis, *Pilgrim's Guide*.

[33] J. Raine, *The Historians of the Church of York, and its Archbishops*, 3 vols, RS, 71 (1886), II, 446–63.

Hand 1 wrote a very individual, irregular Anglicana with looped ascenders, backwards **e**, '8' shaped **g** and long **r**. His writing varies considerably in size and tends to slant upwards or downwards to the right of the page; although letters within a word are widely spaced there is little space left between words or lines. As noted, he describes events up to the year 1489 in Laud Misc. 722. His list of archbishops of York in Titus (fol. 4) ends with William Booth, archbishop 1452–65. However, a later list of archbishops (fol. 150) includes Thomas (1480–1500); perhaps because hand 1 was uncertain of the surname he left a blank here which was filled by the writer of the 'backwards' hand. We can therefore date hand 1's activity to the period *c.*1460–90 or a little later.

The second unit in Titus consists of the so-called Glastonbury quire (fols 16–23)[34] and folios 24–47 which contain the *Pseudo-Turpin* and a partial copy of the *Pilgrim's Guide*. This unit was written by hand 2 in a somewhat larger and more regular hand than hand 1's, using Anglicana and Secretary forms. Hand 2's letter forms include single-compartment **a** and slant-backed **d**, looped ascenders to letters such as **b** and **l**, the occasional long **r** (descending well below the line), open-tailed **g** and long **s** at the beginnings and in the middle of words (round **s** appears only at the ends of words); double-compartment **a** appears only in capital letters, or initially in prepositions such as 'Ab' or 'Ad'. The duct is very upright with little use of splay. Although this hand has been dated early-fifteenth-century,[35] the watermarks in the paper hand 2 wrote on indicate that he cannot have been working here before *c.*1460. Hand 2 must be contemporary with hand 1 since the latter wrote in spaces left blank by hand 2, who annotated text copied by hand 1 in John Stafford's verse chronicle beginning on fol. 105.

When one looks at much of the material copied by these two scribes one discovers a substantial admixture of the legendary side of medieval historical and quasi-historical texts, including stories about Arthur and about Merlin, and the *Pseudo-Turpin*, a highly romantic account of Charlemagne's campaign in Spain. In establishing how each scribe went about assembling material (blending 'history' and 'legend') and arranging stories it will be useful to look first at the activity of hand 2 who was mainly responsible for the texts about Charlemagne, Arthur and the legendary history of Britain. These projects were shared with hand 1 who may also have intended to contribute the Carolingian legend of Amis and Amile, which he copied in Laud Misc. 722 (fol. 127), to the Charlemagne stories collected together in Titus. The treatment of these texts establishes a method shared by both scribes in assembling and reworking their different kinds of historical materials. The distinctions between history and legend were not clear-cut in the Middle Ages. Saints' lives

---

[34] M. Lapidge, 'Additional Manuscript Evidence for the *Vera Historia de Morte Arthuri*', *Arthurian Literature*, 2 (1982), 163–8; esp. 164.

[35] Ibid., p. 164, citing Julian Brown; for the manuscript's contents see H. D. L. Ward, *Catalogue of Romances in the Department of Manuscripts in the British Museum*, I (London, 1883), pp. 578–80.

inhabit the borderland: after his canonization in the late twelfth century, we find accounts of Charlemagne in lectionaries, to be read on his feast.[36] However, the standard text is a condensed version of the *Pseudo-Turpin*, rather than the more recognizably historical accounts of his life by Einhard or Notker. *Pseudo-Turpin* was probably composed at St Denis in the 1130s; it circulated widely in both Latin and French. About a hundred Latin copies survive, over thirty of which are in England. Most belong to one of two identifiable groups, but Titus does not fit either. In both groups, for instance, the description of the representation of the liberal arts, painted in Charlemagne's palace at Aachen, is briefer.[37] The text in Titus seems to go back directly, though with at least one careless intermediary, to the text in the *Codex Calixtinus* written at Compostela *c.*1138, and is the only English manuscript in which *Pseudo-Turpin* is followed by the *Pilgrim's Guide* to Compostela. We do not know where hand 2 got his exemplar from, although, in the northern Cistercian orbit, Meaux had a copy.[38] We cannot know exactly what was in the Meaux manuscript. The Kirkstall *Pseudo-Turpin* includes two texts not found elsewhere with it in any of the other surviving manuscripts. The first is an account of Charlemagne's journey to the Holy Land, and his return with numerous relics. (There are several versions of this story, but hand 2 ascribes the one here to Helinand of Froidmont.)[39] The second is from Alexander Nequam, and concerns Ogier the Dane.[40] They are inserted into the *Pseudo-Turpin* where they belong in the chronological sequence of events.

There is one other Charlemagne/Roland text in Titus A.XIX, also in hand 2, the unique *Carmen de prodicione Guenonis* (fols 153–5), a verse account of the treachery of Ganelon (Gueno) and the death of Roland.[41] The author is anonymous, but the

---

[36] Gloucester Cathedral MS 1 is one such; Oxford, Bodl. Lib., MS Bodley 240 is another.

[37] The manuscript tradition of *Pseudo-Turpin* is complicated. The most recent classifications, dealing with the greatest number of manuscripts, is in A. de Mandach, *Naissance et developpement de la Chanson de Geste en Europe*, I, *La Geste de Charlemagne et de Roland* (Geneva and Paris, 1980), App. G. See also A. Hämel, *Überlieferung und Bedeutung des Liber Sancti Jacobi und des Pseudo-Turpin* (Munich, 1950); 'Los manuscritos latinos del falso Turpino', *Estudios dedicados a Menéndez Pidal*, 4 vols (Madrid, 1953), IV, 67–85; *Der Pseudo-Turpin von Compostela, aus dem Nachlass von A. de Mandach* (Munich, 1965); and C. Meredith-Jones, *Historia Karoli Magni et Rotholandi ou Chronique du Pseudo-Turpin* (Paris, 1936, repr. Geneva, 1972).

[38] Numerous other English libraries had copies, but usually of *Turpin* on its own, or with other historical texts. One other possible source was the Premonstratensian abbey of Titchfield, where *Historia Turpini Archiepiscopi* (no. 167), was certainly a pseudo Turpin; *Gesta Karoli Francie in quaterno* (no. 224), could have been Einhard, or Notker, or a later version of *Pseudo-Turpin*. For both Meaux and Titchfield, see Bell, *Libraries of the Cistercians, Gilbertines & Premonstratensians*.

[39] Although Titus hand 2 ascribes his version to Helinand, it differs in details from that in the printed version of the Chronicle of Helinand. See Helinandus, *Chronica*, in *PL*, **212**, 845.

[40] See *Alexandri Neckam De Naturis Rerum*, ed. T. Wright, RS, 34 (1863). The text was written *c.*1200–1204.

[41] See G. Paris, '*Le Carmen de proditione Guenonie* et la légende de Ronceveaux', *Romania*, **11** (1882), 465–518; see also F. Michel's edn, *La chanson de Roland* (Paris, 1837), App. 2, pp. 228–42.

poem is unlikely to have been composed as late as the fifteenth century; it may have been a twelfth-century Yorkshire composition. The canonization of Charlemagne in the late twelfth century might have provided an impetus for a new version of the story.

What hand 2 assembled is an anthology of all the available information about Charlemagne and his knights. If the events of the *Pseudo-Turpin* are arranged as a chronicler would arrange them, in chronological order, the *Carmen* also indicates an interest in variant versions of the story, which is similarly the mark of a good historical sense. I have already suggested that hand 1 copied *Amis and Amile* (in Laud Misc. 722, fol. 127) for inclusion in this collection of Carolingian legends.

How the Charlemagne material was handled makes the Kirkstall treatment of Arthurian material clearer, for the other group of texts copied by hand 2 concerns King Arthur. These occur on fols 16–23, the 'Glastonbury Quire', so-called because it seemed for the most part to contain material found only at Glastonbury.[42] When Richard Barber analysed it, he numbered the items, and reference will be made to his numbers in my discussion below. Barber thought it an autograph compilation, assembled as the basis of a new history of Glastonbury Abbey.[43] This is quite possible, though the sense of scribal freedom to adapt a text was not as great as Barber thought. He missed one source which supplies exact texts for many, though not all, passages: the Glastonbury *Magna Tabula*, made sometime between 1382 and 1420, during the abbacy of John Chinnock. This large wooden box containing six mounted pages of text on Glastonbury's history, now Oxford, Bodleian Library, MS Lat. hist. a.2,[44] was kept in the abbey for pilgrims to read until the Dissolution.

The texts copied in Titus by hand 2 are seemingly in random order: two tales about King Arthur (nos 1–2); two accounts of the discovery of his tomb (nos 3–4); one of the arrival of Joseph of Arimathea in AD 63 (no. 5); of his descendants, including both Arthur and Galahad (no. 6); and of the arrival of the companions of St Philip and St James, and subsequently of Phagan and Deruvian in the second century (no. 7); an account of the churches on the site (no. 8); a section on St Benignus, sixth-century abbot (no. 9); a list of famous visitors who were buried at Glastonbury, including Arthur (no. 10); an account of the translation of Dunstan from Canterbury, a persistent Glastonbury legend (no. 11); an account of a group of miraculous statues and crosses (nos 12–15); and a relic list (no. 16). The scribe has gone through all these items, and put small letters in the margin, as scribes often did for a rubricator. Hand 2 himself left guide letters which have subsequently been painted over. However,

---

For discussion, see also J.-L. Picherit, *The Journey of Charlemagne to Jerusalem and Constantinople* (*Le Voyage de Charlemagne à Jerusalem et à Constantinople*) (Birmingham, Alabama, 1984).

  [42] Lapidge, 'Additional Manuscript Evidence', pp. 163–8.

  [43] Barber, 'Was Mordred Buried at Glastonbury?', pp. 37–63, esp. 37–8. He also thought the comment on fol. 18ᵛ, 'Ego henricus non concedo', supplied the name of the scribe, but this is in another hand.

  [44] See further J. Krochalis, '*Magna Tabula*: The Glastonbury Tablets', pt 1, *Arthurian Literature*, 15 (1997), 93–138; pt 2, *Arthurian Literature*, 16 (1998).

although this quire is rubricated, the small marginal letters have no correspondents within the text. Barber ignored them. But if one uses these letters, in alphabetical order, to rearrange the sequence of the texts, it becomes clear that hand 2 was thereby arranging the material in chronological order, thus:

A. *Joseph of Arimathea at Glastonbury* (fols 18ᵛ–19); Barber, no. 5. *Gospel of Nicodemus*, chapters 11–13, much condensed, to which has been added material about Joseph's arrival at Glastonbury in AD 63, drawn from the Vulgate cycle of Arthurian romance. This is the first text on the *Magna Tabula*.[45]

B. *Disciples of St Philip and St James at Glastonbury* (fols 19ᵛ–20); Barber, no. 7. *Magna Tabula*, top of tablet 2. From William of Malmesbury, *De antiquitate*, pp. 42–47.[46] Inspired by the archangel Gabriel, they build the wattled church.

C. *On the Churches Built at Glastonbury* (fol. 20–20ᵛ); Barber, no. 8. This text was copied from a brass tablet on a pillar in the church at Glastonbury, which recorded the building of the original church, the church of the followers of the second-century missionaries Phagan and Deruvian, the chapel of King Ine, and that from the time of King David, which Christ himself consecrated. It concludes with a note on the dimensions of the old church.[47]

D. *Two brief stories from the Lancelot and the Quete del Saint Graal, about Lancelot and Gawain* (fol. 19); Barber, no. 6. *Magna Tabula*, centre of tablet 1. These tales come from the *Vulgate cycle of Arthurian romance*; John of Glastonbury turned the French into Latin.[48] They might logically come later, but relate to the genealogies of Arthur and Galahad below.

E. *Four short texts on Joseph of Arimathea's descendants* (fol. 19–19ᵛ); Barber, no. 6, as part of the preceding item; from the bottom of tablet 1. The first is the Prophecy of Melkin about the coming of Arthur.[49] The second contains verses on

---

[45] John of Glastonbury, *The Chronicle of Glastonbury Abbey: an Edition, Translation and Study of John of Glastonbury's Cronica sive Antiquitates Glastoniensis Ecclesie*, ed. J. P. Carley, tr. D. Townsend (Woodbridge, 1985), ch. 18; see also Carley's notes. The version on the tablets has an extra concluding sentence not in John about Celidon, son of Nascien, who married the king of Persia's daughter and was given the Kingdom of Wales. This information is also in the *Estoire del Saint Graal*, John's source for his account of Joseph's British adventures, but occurs much later on. The tablet compiler consulted the *Estoire* separately. See *The Vulgate Cycle of Arthurian Romance*, 8 vols, ed. H. O. Sommer (Washington, DC, 1908–16), I, 143–293.

[46] *The Early History of Glastonbury: an Edition, Translation and Study of William of Malmesbury's De antiquitate Glastonie Ecclesie*, ed. J. Scott (Woodbridge, 1981).

[47] The tablet survived the Dissolution, and was first printed by Archbishop James Ussher in his *Britannicarum ecclesiarum antiquitates* (Dublin, 1639), p. 9 (see London 1689 (same pagination), repr. Westmead 1970). See also J. Goodall, 'The Glastonbury Abbey Memorial Plate Reconsidered', *The Antiquaries' Jnl*, 66 (1986), 364–7, and pl. LXII.

[48] *The Vulgate Cycle*, III, *Livre de Lancelot*, pp. 455 and 464–8; VI, *Queste del Saint Graal*, pp. 24–7; I, *Estoire*, p. 285. See John of Glastonbury, *Chronicle*, p. 52.

[49] J. P. Carley ed., in 'Melkin the Bard and the Esoteric Tradition at Glastonbury Abbey', *The Downside Review*, 99 (1981), 10–17. See also John of Glastonbury, *Chronicle*, p. 54.

Joseph of Arimathea from Peter Riga's *Aurora*.[50] The third, praises of Joseph of Arimathea, is headed: *Item versus reperta in quibusdam cronicis ubi agitur de rege Arvirago*, one of these chronicles being John of Glastonbury's.[51]

F. *Abbreviated early history of Glastonbury* (fols 21–22ᵛ); Barber, no. 10. *Anno ab incarnatione domini lxiii° et assumpcione beate marie xv°, Sanctus Philippus episcopus . . . .* Some of the material is from William of Malmesbury's *De antiquitate*, ch. 1. The list of saints who visited Glastonbury, or whose relics were there, does not match exactly any of the extant Glastonbury relics lists, but it must date from after 1382, as it mentions that Abbot John Chinnock (1375–1420) renovated the chapel where Joseph of Arimathea's relics were kept in that year. It includes the verse epitaph of Arthur, which is repeated in the margins of the chronicle below, in hand 2.[52] This is followed by a list of royal visitors to and burials at Glastonbury. A shorter account of the chapel, mentioning Chinnock, is on *Magna Tabula* 6. Item F includes a prayer for benefactors, which may be taken from Glastonbury's *Liber memorialis*.

G. *Liturgical Readings for St Benignus* (fols 20ᵛ–21); Barber, no. 9. A lection, with collect and hymn. The feast of St Benignus was celebrated on 9 November; his translation was celebrated only at Glastonbury, on 27 June.[53] Like the use of the brass tablet text for C (fol. 20), these texts indicate strongly that the scribe assembled much of his material at Glastonbury.

H. *The translation of St Dunstan, and other texts* (fol. 22ᵛ); Barber, no. 11; *Magna Tabula* 3. The account of the translation is abbreviated from William of Malmesbury, *De antiquitate*, ch. 23. It is followed by four short texts on miraculous images. The first three, on two crosses and an image of the Virgin (Barber, nos 12–14), are from *De antiquitate*, chs 27–29, and repeated in John of Glastonbury's *Chronica*, ch. 17; they are all found in the same order on the bottom third of the *Magna Tabula* 3. The fourth text (fol. 23; Barber, no. 15), on another image of the Virgin which, according to the fourteenth-century Glastonbury monk Edmund Stowrton, bowed to the choir when the *Salve Regina* was performed, is found only in John's *Chronica*. The version on the third leaf of the *Magna Tabula* is condensed from John, and Titus follows this. *The relics of St David, and churches at Glastonbury* (fol. 23); Barber, no. 16. Some items are mentioned on *Magna Tabula* 3, but this text is an amalgam of information found in *De antiquitate*, ch. 16, followed by an excerpt from ch. 40 on the churches founded in the Isle of

---

[50] *Aurora Petri Rigae Biblia Versificata, A Verse Commentary on the Bible*, ed. P. Beichner, 2 vols (Notre Dame, IN, 1965), *Evangeliarum*, II, 531–2, lines 2807–8, 2813–16, 2819–20.

[51] John of Glastonbury, *Chronicle*, ch. 20, p. 50.

[52] M. Brown and J. Carley, 'A Fifteenth-Century Revision of the Glastonbury Epitaph to King Arthur', *Arthurian Literature*, 12 (1993), 179–91. Arthur's epitaph on *Magna Tabula* 3 has two variant readings: line 1, *regni* (T: *mundi*); line 2; *mores* (T: *morum*), so it is likely that another source was used.

[53] See *Acta Sanctorum*, Nov. IV, p. 188, on the cult of St Benignus at Glastonbury. The prayer, collect and hymn used as an *Oratio* are unidentified.

Avalon. Like item F, this is either a Glastonbury text which does not survive elsewhere, or a compilation made by the scribe from material at Glastonbury.

I. *An Arthurian Miracle, 'Quedam narracio'* (fols 16–16ᵛ); Barber, no. 1. The story is a Glastonbury tale, about King Arthur and a miraculous vision at the chapel at Beckery, near Glastonbury, which led to his adoption of arms with the Blessed Virgin on them. It is not on the tablets but manuscripts containing this story were available at Glastonbury, and possibly at York. Besides being incorporated into the chronicle of John of Glastonbury, ch. 34, *Quedam narracio* is found in Oxford, Bodleian Library, MS Digby 186, fols 23–24ᵛ from St Mary's, and an historical miscellany, containing Arthur and Merlin material, in the library of the York Austin friars, contained a text listed as *quedam narraciones*.[54]

K. *The Vera Historia of Arthur* (fols 16ᵛ–17ᵛ); Barber, no. 2. This is not a Glastonbury text. In this version Arthur is buried in Avalon, a tradition not associated with Glastonbury; it must have been a text with which the compiler supplemented his Glastonbury material, and may well have come from the library of the Austin friars at York.[55]

L. *Finding of the bodies of Arthur and Guinevere at Glastonbury* (fol. 17ᵛ–18); Barber, no. 3. The text comes from Ralph Higden, who used Giraldus Cambrensis.[56] Neither this, nor text M, is on the *Magna Tabula*, which gives its own account of the graves of Arthur and Guinevere on tablet 4.

M. *Chronicle of Margam Abbey. A variant account of the discovery of the tombs of Guinevere, Arthur, and Mordred* (fol. 18); Barber, no. 4. This text is not on the *Magna Tabula*. The burial of Mordred at Glastonbury is not part of the Glastonbury tradition.[57] The inclusion of Mordred is unusual; his burial place is not usually recorded.

---

[54] J. P. Carley, 'A Glastonbury Translator at Work: *Quedam narracio de nobili rege Arthuro* and *De origine gigantum* in their Earliest Manuscript Contexts', *Nottingham French Studies*, 30 (1991), 5–12. On the York manuscript, see Lapidge, 'Additional Manuscript Evidence', pp. 163–8, and M. R. James, 'The Catalogue of the Library of the Augustinian Friars at York', *Fasciculus Iohanni Willis Clark dicatus* (Cambridge, 1909), pp. 35–6, no. 256c.

[55] M. Lapidge, 'An Edition of the *Vera Historia de Morte Arthuri*', *Arthurian Literature*, 1 (1981), 79–93 (from London, BL, Cotton MS Cleopatra D.III and Gray's Inn MS 7; and 'Additional Manuscript Evidence', pp. 163–8 (readings from Titus). R. Barber, 'The Manuscripts of the *Vera Historia de Morte Arthuri*', *Arthurian Literature*, 6 (1986), 163–4, added to the list of manuscripts.

[56] *Polychronicon*, bk vii, ch. 23. The passages from Giraldus are included in Barber, 'Was Mordred Buried at Glastonbury?', pp. 55–9.

[57] On Margam, see *Annales Monastici*, ed. H. R. Luard, 5 vols, RS, 36 (1864–9), I, 21–2. For the derivation of this passage in the chronicle from a Glastonbury source, see A. Gransden, 'The Growth of the Glastonbury Traditions and Legends in the Twelfth Century', *Jnl of Ecclesiastical History*, 27 (1976), 337–58, esp. 354 and 356, where she posits that a common source, probably originating at Glastonbury, lay behind the Margam entry and the similar account in Ralph of Coggeshall. See also Barber, 'Was Mordred Buried at Glastonbury?' for the probable development of the text.

Hand 2 copied texts from the *Magna Tabula* more or less in the order in which they appear there. Material from other sources preceded and followed. These include the brass tablet on a pillar in the chapel and one or two liturgical books from Glastonbury. The texts in Titus, which have been carefully and accurately copied from these sources, imply that either their scribe, hand 2, or perhaps the scribe of his immediate exemplars, had actually been at Glastonbury at some time. The feast of the translation of St Benignus (27 June) was unique to Glastonbury; the simplest way for a visitor to become aware of this feast was to be at Glastonbury while it was being celebrated. (The saint's day was 9 November.) If our northern historian was likelier to visit during the summer we may imagine him browsing among the monuments and muniments of Glastonbury in the month of June some time between 1460 and 1489.

He assembled several accounts of the burial of Arthur. None corresponds exactly with either John of Glastonbury's *Chronica* or the *Magna Tabula*. The first account from Higden is based on Giraldus Cambrensis; the second, from the Chronicle of Margam Abbey in Glamorgan, adds Mordred to the royal Glastonbury burials. However, given the geographical closeness of Margam, this text may well have been available at Glastonbury. The *Vera Historia* (probably from York), records Arthur's burial at Avalon, which is not identified with Glastonbury. The Arthurian material gathered together in Titus does not all agree, but our compiler has kept it all.

Hand 1 in Titus also gathered Arthurian material, and added to this Arthur/ Merlin project from other sources. On fols 101–102^v he copied a verse epitome on Wales, in 406 lines compiled from Giraldus Cambrensis, *Descriptio Cambriae* and *Itinerarium Cambriae*. We do not know where hand 1 got his exemplar for Titus from, although the text was included by Higden in his *Polychronicon*, which had a wide circulation and was a source for other texts copied in Titus.[58] While not concerned exclusively with Arthur, the poem includes material about Merlin, and may have been copied for that reason. On fols 74 and 75, hand 1 copied – or perhaps even composed from oral sources – three unique Tales of Merlin and Lailoken.[59]

Hand 1 also copied the verses on fols 105^v–114^v which chronicle events from the time of Brutus to the fourteenth century. The Chronicle, ascribed here by a later hand, in the margin, to John Stafford, is usually anonymous in the manuscripts. Titus is a unique expanded version of the text, which probably came from St Peter's, York.[60] It was thus a British historical text within the orbit of the Kirkstall scribes.

---

[58] *Ranulphus Higden Polychronicon*, RS, 41 (1865), I, ed. C. Babington, bk I, ch. 38. See the Grosseteste material below, and also fols 57–8.

[59] H. D. Ward, ed., 'Lailoken (or Merlin Silvester)', *Romania*, 22 (1893), 504–26; tr. in B. Clarke, *Geoffrey of Monmouth, Life of Merlin: Vita Merlini* (Cardiff, 1973). See also Ward, *Catalogue of Romances*, I, 290–91; and A. Jarman, 'The Welsh Myrddin Poems', *Arthurian Literature in the Middle Ages: a Collaborative History*, ed. R. Loomis (Oxford, 1960), pp. 20–30.

[60] A. G. Rigg, *A History of Anglo-Latin Literature 1066–1422* (Cambridge, 1992), pp. 204–5 and 371, notes 163–5.

The chronicle is prefaced by two sets of verses, on London trade and English cities, which are not found elsewhere. They are edited at the conclusion of this essay.

In gathering other British material, for example, the *De origine Gigantium* (the story of the foundation of Britain, and the tale of Brutus' descendants – Albinia and her 30 sisters, fol. 103)[61] – hand 1 also seems to have resorted to Glastonbury sources. Like the Vulgate cycle stories and the *Quedam narracio*, the *De origine* story had been translated from French into Latin. Perhaps this made it look more ancient and authoritative; perhaps Latin was still more accessible than French for Glastonbury's international visitors.

Hand 1's account of the history of Lincoln shows the same kind of careful, chronological assembly work, and lively interest in the anecdotal and miraculous, as his Charlemagne and British material. The text, on fols 4–5, begins with Geoffrey of Monmouth's etymologies for the name of Lincoln. It continues with an account of the bishops of Lincoln, drawing on the life of the first bishop, Remigius, and his immediate successors, by Giraldus Cambrensis. But it also made use of Henry of Huntingdon's *Chronicle* and his *Epistola de contemptu mundi* which discusses Remigius and his successor Robert Bloet. On Bloet, the compiler also consulted either William of Malmesbury's *Gesta Pontificum*, or, more probably, Higden's *Polychronicon*.

The account in Titus A.XIX shows no knowledge of later Lincoln sources.[62] (Nor does it make any use of Giraldus's separate life of St Hugh, or the *Magna vita Hugonis*.) There are anecdotes about several bishops later than those covered by Giraldus, but the most detailed account is of Robert Grosseteste, which is extracted and edited below. It includes his usual morning prayer, *Jhesu mercy, Jhesu grant mercy*; and a story about his sister's impregnation by his chamberlain, the chamberlain's confession, the couple's marriage, and the chamberlain's restoration to office. An account of Grosseteste's death at Woodstock in 1253 is followed by his epitaph. None of this material is in any of the extant lives of Grosseteste, including the 1503 version by Richard of Bardsey in verse.[63] Nor is it drawn from Friar Hubert's 192-line elegiac lament.[64] The death is followed by a detailed account of his stormy relations with Pope Innocent IV (1243–54), partly but not entirely drawn from Higden's *Polychronicon*, and of his trials with the curia, and its failure to

---

[61] J. P. Carley and J. Crick, 'Constructing Albion's Past: an Annotated Edition of *De Origine Gigantum*', *Arthurian Literature*, 13 (1993), 41–103, with discussion of all other manuscripts.

[62] *Giraldus Cambrensis, Opera*, ed. J. S. Brewer, J. F. Dimock and G. F. Warner, 8 vols, RS, 21 (1861–91), VII (1877), xlii–xliii.

[63] Richard of Bardsey (c.1503), in *Anglia Sacra*, I, ed. H. Wharton (London, 1750), pp. 32–41. The manuscript is London, BL, Cotton Otho C.XVI, fols 29–54, which had belonged to Henry Savile of Banke. See Watson, *Henry Savile*, no. 144, p. 46.

[64] For Friar Hubert, see R. W. Hunt, 'Verses on the Life of Robert Grosseteste', *Medievalia et Humanistica*, n.s., 1 (1970), 241–51; there is a brief discussion in Rigg, *Anglo-Latin Literature*, pp. 158–9.

approve his canonization.[65] Two visions of the pope are included; one is also found in Higden, and variant versions of both occur in Matthew Paris. In a separate text, at the end of the letter collection (fols 99–100ᵛ), hand 1, also copied a letter of Innocent, secretary to Innocent IV, sent to Grosseteste, and his reply.[66]

None of the material seems to make any use of the fourteenth-century compilation of lives of Lincoln bishops by John de Schalby.[67] But other material must have come from Lincoln. How did the Titus scribe acquire his information? Several York–Lincoln links are possible. The archbishop of York was among those approached to write letters for Grosseteste's canonization in 1286–87; could Titus reflect in part a copy of materials sent at that time?[68] Two successive archbishops of York, Thomas Rotherham or Scott (1480–1500; he used both surnames) and Thomas Savage (1501–1508) were translated from Lincoln to York. Rotherham was a learned man, and interested in books. He might well have brought texts on Lincoln history with him.[69] But it is also possible that someone connected with Kirkstall made a trip to Lincoln himself.

We know that there were tablets on display in Lincoln Cathedral, though no record survives to tell us what they contained. Could this unique Grosseteste material have come from such *tabulae*, like the York and Glastonbury material which follows it in Titus?[70] It does seem to be material which must have emanated from Lincoln. (The use of a specific tablet text might also explain the very slight mention of St Hugh; there would have been an account of his life and miracles on a separate tablet at his tomb and shrine in Lincoln.)

Both hand 1 and hand 2 are associated with the copying of Glastonbury and other British historical and legendary texts. Their stints show a pattern of activity which involved gathering as much as possible of such material from Latin sources and of subsequent efforts (most noticeable in the Titus Glastonbury quire) to arrange it within a clear chronological framework. If their arrangement of the Charlemagne and Arthurian materials ever achieved its final form, that volume has not survived. But the pieces that do survive enable us to see and comprehend their working process. They were each engaged in the activity delineated by Malcolm Parkes in his classic study of *ordinatio* and *compilatio*.[71]

---

[65] For some of this material, cf. J. Strawley, *Robert Grosseteste, Bishop of Lincoln 1235–1253* (Lincoln, 1957).

[66] Both letters printed in *Robert Grosseteste Episcopi quondam Lincolniensis Epistolae*, ed. H. R. Luard, RS, 25 (1861), 432–7.

[67] Cf. *The Book of John de Schalby, Canon of Lincoln 1299–1333, Concerning the Bishops of Lincoln and their Acts*, tr. J. Strawley (Lincoln, 1952).

[68] E. Kemp, 'Appendix II. The attempted Canonization of Robert Grosseteste', in *Robert Crosseteste Scholar and Bishop*, ed. D. A. Callus (Oxford, 1955), pp. 241–6; see p. 244.

[69] R. B. Dobson, 'The Educational Patronage of Archbishop Thomas Rotherham of York', *Northern History*, 31 (1995), 65–85.

[70] A. Gransden, *Historical Writing in England*: II, *c.1307 to the Early Sixteenth Century* (Ithaca, NY, 1982), p. 495; Raine, *Historians of York, and its Archbishops*, introduction.

[71] M. B. Parkes, 'The Influence of the Concepts of *Ordinatio* and *Compilatio* on the Development of

Appendix: Unpublished texts copied in London, BL Cotton MS Titus A.XIX by hand 1

Editorial method

In the following texts all abbreviations have been expanded silently; **u** and **v** have been normalized; and punctuation has been modernized. The scribe, hand 1, used punctuation sparingly, the *punctus elevatus* and the *punctus* indicating pauses. He used the *virgula suspensiva* only when transcribing verse. He used few capitals, but the text below capitalizes personal and place names for ease of reading. Words enclosed in ` ´ indicate scribal interlineations. Marginal additions, which often repeat names and dates in the text, have been put in footnotes. Where text is damaged and the reading is conjectural, words are enclosed in ⟨ ⟩. Emendations, which are rare, are in parentheses, and are discussed in footnotes. Editorial commentary has been kept to the minimum.

Extract from The History of the Bishops of Lincoln, *fols 4–5*

The text has been discussed above, pp. 245–6. It gives a fairly full account of Remigius, the first bishop (d. 1092), drawing largely on Giraldus Cambrensis, *Vita S. Remigii* and Higden's *Polychronicon*. For Remigius's successor, Robert Bloet (1094–1123), it quotes the verse epitaph composed by Henry of Huntingdon, *Historia Anglorum*.[72] Thereafter entries are largely formulaic beginning 'Cui successit . . .' and give only the bare details of bishops from Alexander (1123–48) to Hugh of Wells (1209–35) and from Henry Lexington (1254–58) to William of Alnwick (1436–49). One notice of possible interest to an historically minded Kirkstall monk is the mention of Aaron the Jew of Lincoln, in the account of the episcopacy of Geoffrey Plantegenet (1173–82), who is said to have redeemed pledges made to Aaron by his predecessor, Robert de Chesney. Aaron was a well-known figure, whose extensive list of creditors had included Kirkstall Abbey.[73] Apart from this fact, most other notices are only one or two lines in length. Only Robert Grosseteste, bishop 1235–53 and chancellor of the University of Oxford, merits fuller treatment. Much of what is related about him is legend. The story of the bishop's sister and his chamberlain is found nowhere else and is improbable, in that the officials in Grosseteste's household

---

the Book' (1976), in *Scribes, Scripts and Readers*, pp. 35–70. 'The compiler adds no matter of his own (unlike the commentator) but compared with the scribe he is free to rearrange (*mutando*)' (p. 59).

[72] T. Arnold, ed., RS, 74 (1879), 244–5. The epitaph also appears in Henry's *Epigrammata*, ed. T. Wright, *Anglo-Latin Satirical Poets of the Twelfth Century*, 2 vols, RS, 59 (London, 1872), I, 168. See also Rigg, *Anglo-Latin Literature*, pp. 36–7.

[73] See J. W. F. Hill, *Medieval Lincoln* (Cambridge, 1965), pp. 217–20.

were all in clerical orders.[74] Moreover, so far as we know, Grosseteste had no sister
except the nun Juetta.[75] The story of Pope Innocent's IV vision is paralleled by a story
told by Matthew Paris in his *Chronica Majora*,[76] in which a similar vision comes to a
cardinal after Innocent's death. In Paris's version, the cardinal sees Innocent kneeling
before Mary, God, and Ecclesia, who accuse the pope of three major crimes: having
released church lands; having cared too much about money, and not enough about the
salvation of souls; and having taken a church founded in firmness of faith, justice and
truth, and left it weakened, its justice subverted, and its truth shadowed. The devil is
not said to appear. The variations in the versions suggest an oral transmission. Paris
also has a version of the story of the pope's death in which the pope wanted
Grosseteste's bones dug up and thrown out of the church for his disobedience. That
night, in a dream, Grosseteste appeared in his episcopal robes, accused the pope
furiously, and wounded the pontiff in the side. The pope awoke, groaning; and the
wound gave him the fever from which he died.[77] The account here concludes with a
verse epitaph for Grosseteste which is not found elsewhere.[78]

> [Fol. 4ᵛ] Cui successit sanctus Robertus Grosted. 'dicto Grossum capud'
> archidiaconus Leycestre, consecratus a Sancto Edmundo Cantuariensium, vir
> magne sanctitatis et inter doctores Anglorum famosior. De isto refertur Roberto
> quam cum mane fuisset excitatus a sompno; dicebat *Ihesu mercy. Ihesu grant
> mercy.* Primum pro peccatorum yemia, secundum pro adhibita nocturna in
> custodia. Et tunc idem nomen fronti ori et pretori inscribebat cum pollice et
> cuius nomen sibi imprimebat pro divina tutela ante oculos cordis sui constitu-
> ebat. Item legitur quod ipse habuit unicam sororem quam mirabiliter multum
> dilexit, cui per camerarium suum sibi magis inter alios specialem. pecuniam.
> vestes. et alia bona frequenter misit. Tandem contigit quam ille Camerarius
> episcopi sororem impregnavit. Hoc facto, ali⟨ud⟩ nescivit remedium quam
> domino suo episcopo in confessione suum denudare delictum. Venit igitur
> quadam die ad episcopum et peciit sibi confiteri. Episcopus aut admirans
> quam pocius tunc quam antea ab eo peteret confessionem. Dixit sibi quam
> confiteretur cuicumque vellet ex parte Dei. Ipse autem instanter rogans, votum
> episcopi optinuit. Dixit enim sibi: 'Veni, fili, in nomine Domini.' Alius statim
> dixit sibi: 'Domine, ego fateor me delequisse multum contra Deum et contra vos.
> Nam ego, instigante diabolo, sororem vestram impregnavi.' Cui statim dixit
> bonus homo: 'O fili, Deus remittat tibi. Si enim hoc esset notum episcopo, ipse

---

[74] See K. Major, 'Appendix I: The Familia of Robert Grosseteste', in *Robert Grosseteste Scholar and Bishop*, ed. D. A. Callus (Oxford, 1955), pp. 216–41.

[75] For whom see *Grosseteste . . . Epistolae*, ed. Luard, pp. 43–4.

[76] See *Chronica Majora*, ed. H. R. Luard, RS, 57 (1880), 471–2, and also S. Pegge, *The Life of Robert Grosseteste, the Celebrated Bishop of Lincoln* (London, 1793), App. iv, pp. 309–10.

[77] *Chronica Majora*, pp. 429–30; Pegge, App. iv, pp. 309–10. Innocent died 7 December 1254, at Naples, while fighting for the possession of the two Sicilies.

[78] His tomb does not survive; it was destroyed by Cromwell; for an eighteenth-century account of the remains, see J. F. Hill, 'Appendix 3: The Tomb of Robert Grosseteste with an Account of its Opening in 1782', in *Robert Grosseteste*, ed. Callus, pp. 246–50.

forte tibi offenderetur, et te extra officium tuum confusione expelleret.[79] Consulo enim quam antequam episcopus hoc percipiat, eam in uxorem ducas.' Quod ita factum est. Quibus episcopus multa bona contulit, et Camerarium hoc non obstante, in officio suo retinuit. Anno domini 1253 obiit sanctus Robertus, qui postquam plura gloriose perpetravit; viii° Idus Octobris, apud Wodestoke.[80] Post cuius obitum cum Dominus Papa Innocencius Quartus quem dictus Robertus in quasdem sermocinacionibus suis vehementer commoverat, de morte eiusdem in vocem audiretur, vere inquit 'Mortuus est et sepultus in inferno.' Cui, nocte sequenti soporato, idem sanctus Robertus pontificalibus decenter ornatus per visionem pape apparuit, dicens: 'Surge, miser. Veni ad iudicium. Hesterno in die dixisti me',[81]

[fol. 5] ' "Vere mortuum et in inferno asseruisti sepultum." Sed ego quidem nunc vere vivo, et tu mortuus sepelieris in inferno.' Et compulit eum venire. Qui surgens, videbatur astare coram iudice Christo. Sedente ex una parte beata virgine Maria, et ex altera Sancta Ecclesia sub specie cuiusdam nobilis domine. Que dixit: 'Domine, vindica me de isto misero, qui me vititur in terram confundere.' Astitit, et diabolus iudicem hiis verbis alloquens: 'Cum tu sis verax `iudex´, iustusque per omnia, iudex `vindex´, in hanc animam miseri quam peto redde mihi.' Et respondetur papa: 'Cum tu sis clemens, pius et mitis, miserere. Iudicium nollo, sed peto, pie, parce mihi.' Et dixit illi iudex, 'Te nec apex nec opes[82] nec opus rediment; ego vindex.' Convertens Dominus se ad diabolum, dixit: 'Hanc animam pape quam petis, ecce; cape.' Evigilans aut papa, plurimum contristatus est. Fecitque postea constitucionem ut Ytalicus non succederet ultra Ytalico.[83] Solebat aut predictus papa prelatis Anglicis mandare ut tali clerico vel tali providerent in tot marceratis vel libratis beneficii ecclesiastici. Alioquin se noscerent ab illo die suspensos. Et hoc rep(re)hendebat[84] dictus Robertus Lincolniensis asserens hoc esse contra ius et honestatem ecclesie, necnon auctoritati prelatorum plurimum derogare.[85]

---

[79] That is, presumably, if the bishop had to take official notice of the chamberlain's actions, outside the seal of the confessional, he would have had to dismiss the man.

[80] For variations in the date of Grosseteste's death, see *Giraldus Cambrensis Opera*, VII, App. E, p. 205 n. 2. Schalby gives 'VI Id. Octob.', but the date given here 'viii Id.' is also found in the Peterborough Chronicle and the Spalding Chronicle.

[81] MS: the last two words are the catchword on fol. 4ᵛ. They are not repeated at the top of fol. 5, but the text seems to be continuous. This seems to indicate a scribe working rapidly, as usually the catchwords (which hand 1 put at the bottom of the verso of most leaves) were repeated.

[82] MS corrected above the line to 'opex nec apes', which does not make sense.

[83] Grosseteste had sent Innocent a letter in 1245 arguing against putting Italians in English sees (*Grosseteste . . . Epistolae*, ed. Luard, pp. 338–9; for the date, see S. Harrison Thomson, *The Writings of Robert Grosseteste, Bishop of Lincoln 1235–1253* (Cambridge, 1940), p. 211, and again in 1253 protesting against the appointment of Innocent's nephew to a canonry at Lincoln (pp. 432–7). Papal policy remained unchanged; see J. R. Wright, *The Church and the English Crown 1305–1334* (Toronto, 1980), pp. 287–308.

[84] MS abbreviation for 'per'.

[85] Cf. the language of Grosseteste's letter to the citizens of London, *Grosseteste . . . Epistolae*, ed. Luard, pp. 442–4.

Item Ranulphus Cestrensis, hic Robertus in cunctis liberalibus artibus excellit; erudituis in logica, ethica precipue et astrologia florens plurima commentatus est.[86] Ad Innocencium quoque papam misit epistolam invectivam satis tonantem que sic incipit: *Deus noster Ihesus Christus pro eo* quam ecclesias Anglicanas indebitis et insolitis exaccionibus gravare videretur.[87] Et eciam quia nepotulo suo puerulo contulerat canonicatum cum proxima vacatura in ecclesia Lyncolniensis, quem eum Robertus iste admittere detrectavit, rescribens pape se nec velle nec debere tales ad curam animarum admittere qui se nescirent regere. Hac de causa Robertus iste ad curiam vocatus et excommunicatus; appellavit a curia Innocencii ad tribunal Christi. Unde contigit quam Roberto in Anglia obeunte, apparuit ipsi pape de nocte in stratu suo quiescenti pontificalibus indutus sic inquiens, 'Surge miser. Veni ad iudicium.' Que vox audita in curia pape, et statim cum baculo pastorali pupigit latus sinistrum ipsum usque ad cor. Unde lectiscerium pape repertum est mane cruentatum, et ipse papa defunctus est. Hiis de causis, licet perspicuis effulserit miraculis iste Robertus translari tamen et in catholigo sanctorum poni non est a curia permissus.[88]

'Versus'
Anni tamen Domini transissent mille ducenti
Quinquagenta duo vir transiit iste sequenti,
hunc decimi mensis octava dies tumulavit
Qui ter sex annis et semis et pontificavit.
Lyncolniense tumulatur.

Translation

[Hugh of Wells] was succeeded by saint Robert Grosseteste, called big head, the archdeacon of Leicester, consecrated by St Edmund of Canterbury, a man of great holiness and very famous among the English doctors. It is said of this Robert that when in the morning he was roused from sleep, he said, 'Jesus Mercy! Jesus grant Mercy!' The first for the forgiveness of sins, the second for keeping night thoughts under guard. And then he would inscribe the same name on the brow of his face as a guard with his thumb, and the name which he imprinted on himself was fixed firmly before the eyes of his heart by divine tutelage. Item, one reads that he had one sister, whom he loved wonderfully much; through his chamberlain, he frequently sent her, among other things, money, clothes, and other goods. Nevertheless, it happened that his Chamberlain

---

[86] Cf. *Higden Polychronicon*, VIII, (1882), ed. J. R. Lumby, pp. 240–42. From here to the epitaph the language is close to Higden's but not exactly copied from him. This incident is also recounted in Henry Knighton's *Chronicon* (ed. J. R. Lumby, 2 vols, RS, 92 (1889–95), I, pp. 219–20), but in several places (e.g. for 'cruentatum', 'sanguinolentem'), the version here is closer to Higden.

[87] *Grosseteste . . . Epistolae*, ed. Luard, no. 128, pp. 432–7. The phrase does not begin the letter but is found in the second paragraph.

[88] See E. W. Kemp, 'Appendix 2: the Attempted Canonization of Robert Grossetesste', in *Robert Grosseteste*, ed. Callus, pp. 214–46.

got his sister pregnant. Having done this, he knew no other remedy than to disclose his dereliction to his lord bishop in confession. One day, therefore, he came to the bishop and asked to confess to him. The bishop, wondering that he should seek confession from him then, rather than before, said to him that he could confess to whomever he wished, on behalf of God. Instantly pleading, he obtained the bishop's promise. He said to him: 'Come, my son, in the name of the Lord.' The other immediately said to him: 'Lord, I confess that I have sinned greatly against God and against you. For, urged on by the devil, I have got your sister pregnant.' The good man immediately said to him: 'O son, God will forgive you. If, however, this should be known to the bishop, he himself might well be offended by you, and expel you from your office in disarray. Therefore, I counsel you that, before the bishop finds this out, you marry her.' He did so. The bishop gave them many good things, and the chamberlain not objecting, kept him in office.

In the year of the Lord 1253, on 8 Ides October, saint Robert died at Woodstock, who afterwards perpetrated even more glorious deeds. After his death, when the Lord Pope Innocent IV, whom the said Robert had violently attacked in certain sermonizing works, heard about his death, he actually said, 'He is dead and buried in hell.' On the following night, while he was sleeping, saint Robert appeared to the pope in a vision, appropriately clad in his episcopal robes, saying: 'Rise, wretch. Come to judgement. Yesterday you said to me, [fol. 5] '"You are truly dead and have earned a grave in hell." But now truly I live, and you, the dead one, will be buried in hell.' And he compelled him to come. Rising, [the pope] saw himself standing before Christ the judge. Seated on one side was the Blessed Virgin Mary, and on the other Holy Church in the form of a certain noble lady. She said, 'Lord, avenge me for this wretch, who has viciously tried to confound me on earth.' And the devil stood up, speaking to the judge in these words: 'Since you are a true judge, and just in all ways, a righteous judge, give me that which I ask for – the soul of the wretch.' And he is answered by the pope, [speaking to Christ] 'Since you are merciful, pious and gentle, have mercy. I do not wish a judgement, but I beseech you, o holy one, spare me!' And the judge said to him, 'Neither power nor works nor wealth shall save you; I avenge.'

And the Lord, turning to the devil, said, 'Behold this soul of the pope, which you seek; seize it.' And the pope, waking, was greatly grieved. Afterwards he made a constitution that an Italian should not succeed to a post outside Italy. For it had been the custom of the aforesaid pope to command English prelates to provide the whole income in marks or pounds of an ecclesiastical benefice for this or that cleric. But from that day they found themselves released from the practice. And the said Robert of Lincoln had reprehended this practice, asserting it to be against the law and the honest custom of the church, if not indeed derogatory to the authority of most prelates.

Item, Ralph [Higden] of Chester has commented that this Robert excelled in all the liberal arts; he was most erudite in logic, outstanding in ethics, and had his greatest flowering in astrology. He sent Pope Innocent a letter of thundering invective, which begins thus: *Our God Jesus Christ, for him*, which showed the English churches to be weighed down by debts and unreleased obligations. And also because [the pope] had demanded a canonry at the next vacancy in the church of Lincoln for his nephew, a little boy, whom that Robert declined to admit, responding to the pope that he neither wished to, nor ought to admit such people to the cure of souls who did not know how to rule themselves. For this reason, Robert himself was called to the curia and excommunicated. He appealed from the curia of Innocent to the tribunal of Christ. So it happened that, when Robert was going back into England, he appeared to the pope lying quietly in his bed at night, garbed in his bishop's robes, waking him thus: 'Rise, wretch. Come to judgement.' His voice was heard in the papal curia. And immediately he struck the [pope's] left side to the heart with his pastoral staff. In the morning, the pope's bedding was found bloody, and the pope himself was dead. This Robert shone by conspicuous miracles, and was permitted to be translated, but nevertheless, for this reason, he was not permitted by the curia to be placed in the Catalogue of Saints.

Verse:
A thousand years had passed; two hundred went
Then fifty-two; one more; a man died then.
In the tenth month's eighth day they buried him;
Thrice six years and a half he'd bishop been.
He was buried at Lincoln.

Prefatory poems to John Stafford's verse chronicle, fol. 105

This folio has the same heading 'de Anglia' as the following text, the verse chronicle beginning 'Anglorum regum cum gestis nomina scire'. Poems in praise of a country are an old tradition. Curtius traces the presence of such a poem as a preface to a chronicle to Isidore of Seville.[89] Some praise landscape; more religiously oriented poems may praise saints and martyrs. What is remarkable about the poems in Titus is their praise of trade: England's exports and imports. The list of the latter differs from the imports given in a verse section of William FitzStephen's description of London, which has the same exotic flavour.[90]

Where were these poems written? The chronicle is generally assumed to be from the York area. But these prefatory verses have several specific echoes in three twelfth-century poems on England possibly composed by Richard of Cluny, or, as Longleat MS 27 has it, by Hugh, first the prior of the Cluniac foundation of Montacute, near

---

[89] E. R. Curtius, *European Literature and the Latin Middle Ages*, tr. W. Trask (New York, 1953), pp. 157–8.

[90] This description formed the preface to FitzStephen's life of Becket, see *Materials for the Life of Thomas Becket*, ed. J. G. Robertson, 7 vols, RS, 67 (1875–85), III, 7–8; tr. H. E. Butler in F. M. Stenton, *Norman London: an Essay*, Historical Association Leaflets 8 (London, 1934), repr. J. Krochalis and E. Peters, *The World of Piers Plowman* (Philadelphia, 1975), p. 30.

Glastonbury, and afterwards abbot of Muchelney, Somerset. There was a Hugh, abbot of Muchelney, in 1166 and a second Hugh, after a vacancy, in 1175.[91] Muchelney, like its neighbour Glastonbury, was a prosperous Benedictine abbey, mitred before 1341, though not later. In 1328, it provided a place of retirement for the king's harper.[92] One harper does not make a literary tradition, but cultural contact with Glastonbury in the later Middle Ages seems probable. Such Somerset texts could easily have been available at Glastonbury, which we know supplied other additions to the chronicle. There are lines borrowed from each of the first two poems, which are cited in the notes, and a part of the third could have given our poet the germ of his idea:

> Istic invenies venalia tanta, quod omnes
> expositas merces vix sibi mundus emat[93]

> (Here will you find such lavish goods from all
> the distant marts, that scarce the world itself could purchase them).

Hand 1 may have found the verses ready-made at Glastonbury, but they rather suggest the world of the secular cleric. It is noteworthy that all the cities mentioned are cathedral towns, which such a cleric might have occasion to visit. The knowledge of trade it shows is general – French goods rather than Fitzstephen's wine – and it is impossible to locate the poet.

[fol. 105]

[i]   *De Anglia. Comoditates aliarum nacionum.*

> ¶ Ergo ut semediam solio dedit aduolat omnis.
> Terra simul. tuncque suos provincia fructus
> Exposuit, fert Indus ebur. Caldeus amomum.[94]
> Assirius gemmas. Seire vellera.[95] thura Sabeus.
> Attis mel. Fenix palmas.[96] Lacedemon olivum,
> Aurum Lidus. Arabs guttam. Panchara mirram.[97]

---

[91] A. B. Scott, 'Some Poems Attributed to Richard of Cluny', in *Medieval Learning and Literature: Essays Presented to Richard William Hunt*, ed. J. J. G. Alexander and M. T. Gibson (London, 1976), pp. 181–99; for the two Hughs, see pp. 192–3. The attribution to Hugh is accepted without question by Rigg, *Anglo-Latin Literature*, pp. 135–6.

[92] R. Midmer, *English Mediaeval Monasteries 1066–1540: a Summary* (Athens, GA, 1979), p. 224.

[93] Scott, 'Some Poems', App. II, no. 3, lines 13–14.

[94] Cf. 'India mittit ebur, molles sua turra Sabaei,
at Chalybes nudi ferrum, virosaque Pontus
castorea, Eliadum palmas, Epiros equarum' (Virgil, *Georgics*, I, 57–9).

[95] Cf. 'velleraque ut foliis depectant tenua Seres' (*Georgics*, II, 121). The Romans thought that silk came from the tree, not the worms

[96] Pliny, *Natural History*, I, 29.56, refers to the date-palm as 'phoenix'.

[97] 'totaque turiferis Panchaia pinguis harensis' (*Georgics*, II, 139). Cf. Ovid, *Metamorphoses*, X, 309. Panchaia is an imaginary island in the Indian ocean.

Arma Calibs. frumenta Libeus. Campanus Yachum.
Archas equos. Epirus equas. peonaria Gallus.
Pontus castorea. blateram Tyrus. aera Corintus.
Sardinia argentum. naves Hispania defert.

[ii]   ¶ Anglia terra ferax et fertilis angulus orbis[98]
Anglia plena iocis gens libera digna iocari
Libera gens, cui libera mens et libera lingua
Sed lingua melior, liberiorque manus.[99]
Anglia terrarum decus, et flos finitimarum,
Et contenta sui fertilitate boni.
Externas gentes consumptis rebus egentes.
Cum fames. ledit. recreat et reficit
Commoda terra satis mirande fertilitatis
Prosperitate viget, cum bona pacis habet
Anglorum portus occasus novit et ortus
Anglica classis habet quam loca multa iuvet,
Est cibus et sensus magis hoc convivis habetur
Nam de more viri sunt ibi magnifici.
Illa quidem longe celebri splendore beata
Globis lacte fanis freminet insula cunctis
Testes Londonie ratibus.[100] Wyntonia bacho
Herefordia grege, Wircestria fruga redundat
Batha lacum. Saresbiria feris. Cantuaria pisce.
Ebraucus silvis. Excestria clara metallis.
Norwicum Dacis. Hibernis Cestria. Gallis.
Cicestria. Nowagenis Dunelmia propinquans.
Insula predives que toto 'unde'[101] non eget orbe
Et cuius totus indiget orbis ope
Insula predives cuius miretur et optet
Delicias Salomon. Octavianus opes.[102]
Anglia munitur nec idem pare reperitur
Acrinis milicia sensu probitate sophia.

There is a note in the bottom margin, also in hand 1, introducing the Chronicle:

[iii]   Te quicumque bene si vis noscere reges
Anglos ut leges hec iterando leges
Reges maiores referam sive nobiliores
Quanto regnarunt et ubi gens hos tumularunt
Mille quater decabis sit Adam Bruto prior annis.

---

[98] Cf. Scott, 'Some Poems', App. II, no. 2, line 1.
[99] Cf. ibid., no. 1, lines 51–2.
[100] Ibid., no. 3, praises 'dives Londonia', but there are no close verbal echoes.
[101] This word is not in Scott's text.
[102] Cf. Scott, 'Some Poems', App. II, no. 2, lines 9–12.

Translations

(i)   Therefore, as all things turn, to every farm
the sowing season comes; the land brings forth
its fruits from every province; ivory
from India, from Chaldee spicy amomum;
Assyria sends gems, the Chinese silk;
incense from Sabea comes, and honey
from the Attic lands; Phoenicia sends palm trees
Oil from Sparta, gold from Lydia,
the gum of Araby, Panchaian myrrh.
Chalybean arms, the grain of Lybia.
Campanian ware,[103] and steeds from Arcady,
Epirus sends us mares, and Wales its flocks;
Pontus the beaver's musk; the purple dye
from Tyre; from Corinth brass, and from Sardinia
comes silver; ships are dispatched from Spain.

(ii)   England is a fruitful land, a fertile corner of the world.
Full of pleasant things is England; a liberal race, well worth enjoying;
a liberal race, a liberal mind, a liberal tongue
but sweeter than the tongue, the hand stretched out to give.
England, loveliest of lands, flower of its neighbours
Content in the fertility of its own goods,
when famine starves, she makes to grow again
the foreign nations lacking goods.
A spacious land, wondrous in its fertileness,
flourishing in prosperity, since it has the gift of peace.
The port of England knows both East and West;
The English fleet gives help to many places,
There's food, and a great sense of fellowship.
Men have the habit of magnificence.
For long, in famed and blessed splendour,
She's teemed with milk for the world, this templed isle.
Witness the ships from London, wine from Winchester,
Hereford's sheep; Worcester is filled with fruits,
Bath with waters; Salisbury with game, Canterbury fish,
York with forests, Exeter bright with metal.
From neighbours – Norwich from Danes, Chester from Eire,
From Wales does Chichester, from Norway Durham draw.
The richest isle, none in the whole world greater,
whom the whole world needs for merchandise,
this richest isle is much admired, and can supply

---

[103] MS 'campanus yachum'. Perhaps 'the bell from Jacca', but 'Campanus' in the masculine refers to Campagna, in Italy, which gave its name to bells made there.

delights of Solomon, wealth of Octavian.
With these is England furnished, nor has she equal here
in military strength, sense, probity or wisdom.

(iii)   If you should wish your English kings to know,
as you read here, read over, say them slow;
The greater kings, the nobler, shall I show,
and when they reigned, and where interred below;
a thousand years, four decades twice, from Adam unto Brutus go.

IV
Ideas of Authors and Authorities

The Author's Two Bodies? Authority and Fallibility in Late-Medieval Textual Theory

A. J. Minnis

In his second 'familiar letter' to Cicero, Francis Petrarch assured his ancient addressee that he was eminently capable of distinguishing between life and literature: 'It was your life I criticized, not your ingenuity (*ingenium*) or your eloquence, for I admire the first, while the second strikes me dumb with wonder'.[1] Cicero's *vita* was marred by weakness in adversity and inconstancy, Petrarch believed. Yet the achievement of the 'great founding father of Roman eloquence' was considerable, and Petrarch fulsomely acknowledged his own debt: 'it is under your auspices that I have attained my present skill in writing'. Several decades later, in a different country and within a quite different society, Geoffrey Chaucer had the most offensive character on his Canterbury pilgrimage present the case that an immoral man can tell a moral tale: 'For though myself be a ful vicious man, /A moral tale yet I yow telle kan'.[2] These statements belong within a complicated medieval matrix of ideas concerning the relationship between authority and fallibility (including downright deviancy). Its distinctive discourses are evident in many spheres of social, political, and ecclesiastical/theological theory and practice, as I hope to show. My main concern will be with the apparent division – sometimes it looks like a wide gulf – between the two facets which, following medieval culture's dualistic categorization, came to constitute the 'authority': the authority as figure worthy of respect, belief and obedience, and the authority as fallible human being. He seemed to have two types of existence, two distinct natures – or, indeed, two bodies, to borrow a phrase

---

[1] *Le Familiari*, xiv, 4; tr. in A. J. Minnis and A. B. Scott with D. Wallace, *Medieval Literary Theory and Criticism c.1100–c.1375: The Commentary Tradition*, rev. edn (Oxford, 1991), p. 417.

[2] *Canterbury Tales*, VI, 459–60. All Chaucer quotations are from *The Riverside Chaucer*. The Pardoner is, of course, not an *auctor* in the sense that he has inscribed his allegedly authoritative teaching, for within the frame of Chaucer's Canterbury fiction the narration for which he demands respect remains oral, unrecorded. My intention is to bring together Cicero (as constructed by Petrarch) and the Pardoner (as constructed by Chaucer) as authority figures among others, the fundamental point of this essay being to highlight the similarities between prestige-claims which might, on the face of it, seem to derive from utterly different systems of valuation and acclamation. In fact, medieval authorities of many kinds – whether kings, popes, priests, preachers or 'literary' practitioners (including writers) – manifestly shared crucial discourses of authority. (I am fully aware that the term 'literary' as used here is an anachronism, but it is useful as a sort of shorthand in implicating matters poetical, rhetorical and hermeneutic.)

from Ernst H. Kantorowicz, whose study *The King's Two Bodies* was the inspiration for the title of this essay.[3]

Petrarch's segregation of Cicero's *vita* and literary virtuosity may be seen as a move away from some of the values of the medieval 'ethical poet', to use the late Judson Allen's felicitous term.[4] In the *accessus* or 'academic prologues' to glosses on the Latin canonical texts studied in the grammar schools, the 'branch of philosophy' to which those books belonged was regularly discussed, to establish their ideological credentials and justify their inclusion in a Christian curriculum.[5] In the case of a wide range of syllabus authors (Aesop, Ovid, Horace, Juvenal, Virgil, among others) the subject-matter treated was usually identified as moral philosophy or ethics, and so those authors became regarded as authorities in the study of human behaviour. By these means such texts were 'authenticated' in the medieval sense of the term, their prestige and *auctoritas* being secured. The concomitant was that the poets had to be of good character, men worthy of respect and belief. Hence the learning and prophetic powers of vatic Virgil, and the social outrage of satirists like Horace and Juvenal at the evils of their age, were emphasized. Ovid, the expert on sex and seduction, was a particularly difficult case, but a measure of moral conformity was imposed on his poems. The *Amores* and *Ars amatoria* remained resistant, but their damage was limited through the construction of a *vita Ovidii* which claimed that the poet, exiled by the Emperor Augustus on account of his scurrilous verses, had repented of what he had written and produced other texts (particularly the *Remedium amoris*) which asserted his change of heart. According to this interpretative model, Ovid had left his youthful misdemeanours behind him, and attained that wisdom which age (and painful experience) brings.

Fascinating problems arose when, in the later Middle Ages, certain vernacular writers (Dante most of all) sought to locate and empower their writings and those of distinguished contemporaries in relation to the systems and strategies of textual evaluation which scholasticism had produced.[6] Their sense of the worth of the vernacular in general and their own writing in particular impelled them irresistibly in that direction. But there was a major stumbling block; the shade of Ovid, as it were, haunted such attempts at valorization. Vernacular secular literature had human love as a major subject, and how could a poet who wrote about love, and/or expressed his

---

[3] *The King's Two Bodies: a Study in Medieval Political Theology* (Princeton, 1957). Inevitably, this seminal work is now somewhat dated, and should be read in the light of subsequent scholarship, particularly that of C. J. Nederman. See especially his 'The Physiological Significance of the Organic Metaphor in John of Salisbury's *Policraticus*', *History of Political Thought*, 8 (1987), 211–23.

[4] As employed throughout his book *The Ethical Poetic of the Later Middle Ages* (Toronto, 1982).

[5] For discussion and references see A. J. Minnis, *Medieval Theory of Authorship: Scholastic Literary Attitudes in the Later Middle Ages*, 2nd edn (Aldershot, 1988), pp. 23–7; Minnis and Scott, *Medieval Literary Theory*, pp. 2, 11, 13–14, 15, 26, etc.

[6] This paragraph is based on the fuller discussion in my 'Authors in Love: the Exegesis of Late-Medieval Love Poets', in *The Uses of Manuscripts in Literary Studies: Essays in Honor of Judson B. Allen*, ed. C. Morse, P. Doob and M. Woods (Kalamazoo, 1992), pp. 161–91.

own (limiting and probably demeaning) emotional experiences, be trusted as a fount of wisdom, accepted as a figure worthy of respect and belief? An *auctor amans* was an utter paradox, almost a contradiction in terms.

Dante met the problem with typical forcefulness. His *Convivio*, which is ostentatiously based on the medieval genre of the commentary on an *auctor*, elaborately brings out the profoundly scientific subject-matter of three of his *canzoni*. The point is being made loudly and clearly that Dante's vernacular works merit the full scholarly apparatus of commentary which for generations had been lavished on Latin *auctores*. Moreover, given that a (would-be) *auctor* has to have an impeccable character, Dante is anxious to emphasize that his life is not letting down his lyrics. The reader of these *canzoni* may have formed the impression that he had pursued a great passion of love, Dante admits. But in fact virtue was the 'moving cause', as, he promises, the subsequent expositions will make clear.[7] Any potential threat to the authority of the text or the good character of its author is refined out of existence by the techniques of allegorical exegesis.

However, in his *Trattatello in laude di Dante* Giovanni Boccaccio chose not to adopt such a defensive strategy. Instead he flatly declares that all his life Dante suffered from licentiousness: 'Amid such virtue, amid such learning as we have noted there to have been in this magnificent poet, lust (*lussuria*) found most ample space.'[8] Moreover, this was 'not just in his youthful years', when the emotion was more understandable and perhaps more excusable, 'but also in maturity'. 'But who', Boccaccio asks, 'among mortals can play the just judge in condemning it? Not I'. The attractions of the female sex are very powerful, as is proved by both secular and sacred literature. No reasonable person can gainsay the testimony of holy Scripture, which offers the *exempla* of Eve's persuasion of Adam, David's adultery with Bathsheba and murder of her husband, and the story of the wise Solomon who, 'to please a woman', kneeled down and worshipped Baalim. Dante, then, may not be excused, but some comfort may be found in the fact that many other great writers experienced similar difficulties. The clear implication is that *amor* need not necessarily destroy *auctoritas*; the moral virtue of a text may survive the lapses of its author.

Those 'sinful authors' Solomon and David are invoked to similar effect in what is probably the most daring defence of Jean de Meun to figure in the famous *querelle de la Rose* of the early fifteenth century. In a letter which he wrote at the end of the summer of 1402, Jean's staunch defender Pierre Col went beyond all analogies with Ovid – a major strategy in the *querelle* – to appeal to the precedent of biblical lovers.[9] Chancellor Jean Gerson had attacked the *Rose* on the grounds that 'he who

---

[7] *Il Convivio,* I, 2, ed. B. Cordati (Turin, 1968), p. 12.

[8] Tr. Minnis and Scott, *Medieval Literary Theory,* pp. 502–3.

[9] *Le Débat sur le Roman de la Rose,* ed. E. Hicks (Paris, 1977), p. 94; cf. '*La Querelle de la Rose*': *Letters and Documents,* tr. J. L. Baird and J. R. Kane (Chapel Hill, NC, 1978), pp. 97–8. See further

made it was a foolish lover'. Why then, Col retorts, does Lady Eloquence – a personification in Gerson's *Traité contre le Roman de la Rose* – not first draw such conclusions against Solomon, David, and other foolish lovers, who lived long before Jean de Meun, 'whose books are made a part of holy Scripture and their words a part of the holy mystery of the Mass'? It was 'a foolish lover' (David) who 'caused Uriah the good knight to be killed by treachery in order to commit adultery with his wife'. It was 'a foolish lover' (Solomon) 'who caused the temples with the idols to be built for the love of strange women'.

Col proceeds to extol the advantages of knowing one's enemy by personal experience. Saints Peter and Paul were more firm in the faith after they had sinned, he declares; similarly, Jean de Meun, because he had been a foolish lover, was very firm in reason, for the more he knew by his own experience the folly which is in foolish love the more he was able to despise it and praise reason. When he wrote the poem he was no longer a foolish lover, and had repented of having been one.[10] This is indicated by the fact that he speaks so well of reason, for a foolish lover is unable to do this. The voice of 'Raison', it would seem, is in large measure the voice of Jean de Meun.[11]

The ingenious appeals to the Bible by Boccaccio and Col echo a long-running controversy in biblical exegesis, over how the deviancy of major scriptural *auctores* could be reconciled with their undeniable authority. Theologians had for generations attempted to cope with unpalatable historical facts concerning the lives of Kings David and Solomon.[12] Twelfth-century biblical commentators had allegorized David as Christ, Bathsheba as the Church, and Uriah as the devil. Their successors, some of whom seem to have been worried by the obvious clash between the literal and spiritual meanings here, were willing to accept that David, Solomon (and, in a very

---

A. J. Minnis, 'Theorizing the Rose: Commentary-Tradition in the *Querelle de la Rose*', in *Poetics: Theory and Practice in Medieval English Literature*, ed. P. Boitani and A. Torti (Woodbridge, 1991), pp. 13–36.

[10] Col supports this argument by citing Jean de Meun's own *Testament*, in which, he declares, Jean admits that in his youth he made 'many works through vanity', these being 'various ballades, rondeaux and virelais that we do not have in writing' – which are not to be confused with that later, mature work, the *Rose*. Hicks, *Débat*, p. 95; cf. Baird and Kane, *Letters and Documents*, p. 98. It may be suggested that Jean de Meun, in his *Testament* and indeed within the *Rose* itself, had engaged in Ovidian self-fashioning, interpreting his own writings in a way which his later supporters were to adopt and amplify. Similarly, Giovanni Boccaccio 'constructed details of his own "vita" in accordance with what he found in Ovid's', as has been demonstrated by R. Hollander, *Boccaccio's Two Venuses* (New York, 1977), pp. 112–16.

[11] That point of view has been echoed by such recent readers of the *Rose* as D. W. Robertson, *A Preface to Chaucer: Studies in Medieval Perspectives* (Princeton, NJ, 1962), p. 199, and J. Fleming, *The Roman de la Rose: a Study in Allegory and Iconography* (Princeton, NJ, 1969), pp. 107, 132–5. I find the text's meaning far more elusive; see A. J. Minnis, 'Lifting the Veil: Textual/Sexual Nakedness in the *Roman de la Rose*', King's College London, Centre for Late Antique and Medieval Studies, Occasional Publications, 1 (London, 1995).

[12] For discussion and references see Minnis, *Medieval Theory of Authorship*, pp. 103–8.

different capacity, St Paul) had indeed sinned, but translated these figures into *exempla* of what to do and what not to do. St Bonaventure, writing *c.*1254–57 in his commentary on Ecclesiastes (then supposed to be by Solomon), affirmed that this work was written not by a sinner but by a penitent man who regretted his sins.[13] Similarly, the English Dominican Thomas Waleys, commenting on the Psalter in the early fourteenth century, described David and St Paul as having passed through a state of sin; they were writing not as sinners but as men who had once been sinners, and hence one can have confidence in what they wrote.[14] Arguments like this were obviously in Col's mind when he wrote the above passage. His position here seems to be that a writer's amatory experience does not necessarily invalidate his work – providing that he has put his *amours* behind him (like David, and indeed like the chastised Ovid).

But what if a writer does not leave his love behind? If, as in the case of Dante as described in Boccaccio's *Trattatello*, the emotion persists? That is a far more difficult proposition to defend. But Col, to his intellectual credit, tries to do just that in a later passage of the letter quoted above.[15] First he argues that in itself to be a clerk, a philosopher or theologian is not irreconcilable with being a foolish lover – witness the examples of David, Solomon and others. Indeed, he adds, some clerics even say that Solomon wrote the Song of Songs on account of his love of Pharaoh's daughter. ('Scarcely a Catholic view', Gerson was to declare in his reply.[16]) One could bring forth, Col exclaims, 'more than a thousand examples of people who were clerks and at the same time foolish lovers'. These roles are as compatible with one another 'as being at once clerk and knight', as were Pompey, Julius Caesar, Scipio and Cicero.

Gerson's problem, Col continues, is that he believed everyone to be like himself: because he was a clerk, philosopher and theologian without being a foolish lover, he thought that all others were like him. This is manifestly not the case. Moreover, even if the great Gerson himself were, in the future, to become a foolish lover, this would not make him any the less a clerk – at least, not at the beginning of this passion. That last remark perhaps implies that when it took proper hold it could well interfere with his proper functioning as a clerk, philosopher and theologian.

This vacillation is fascinating. On the one hand, Col does not want to set aside the argument that Jean composed his poetry not as an actual lover but as a repentant one: 'when he made this book of the *Rose*, he was no longer a foolish lover, and had repented of being one'. On the other, he is tempted to go for the more daring proposition that even if Jean had written his poem while under the influence of foolish love, this would not have interfered with the text's clerkly, philosophical and theological achievements. And here perhaps he comes close to Petrarch's attitude

---

[13] Tr. Minnis and Scott, *Medieval Literary Theory*, pp. 232–3; cf. the discussion on pp. 207–9.

[14] *Postilla super primos xxxviii psalmos Davidicos Thomae Iorgii* (London, 1481), [pp. 1–3].

[15] Hicks, *Débat*, p. 97; cf. Baird and Kane, *Letters and Documents*, pp. 100–101.

[16] Hicks, *Débat*, p. 168; cf. Baird and Kane, *Letters and Documents*, p. 149.

regarding Cicero, as quoted at the very beginning of this essay. A man can do his job and exercise his professional skills whether or not he is weak in adversity, inconstant in his loyalties, or in love/lust. By the same token, the intellectual and rhetorical skills necessary to produce brilliant poetry or prose are not destroyed by an author's moral deficiencies.

The full significance of this and related issues can be appreciated better if we move beyond the specifics of textual authorship and authority to consider the wider context in which they belong. For medieval *auctor*-theory did not occupy some sort of autonomous, specially privileged site of its own ('aesthetic', literary-critical/ theoretical or whatever) but rather partook of discourses which feature crucially in accounts of the formation of the king, the pope, the bishop, the priest, the preacher, and others. As John Guillory has emphasized, in terms of authority, 'canonical authors are not markedly different . . . from their contemporary workers in the medium of power; they have only chosen a strangely durable medium, the text'.[17] This point may be substantiated in the first instance with reference to the 'political theology' behind the notion of 'the king's two bodies'.

Writing around 1100 in his *De consecratione pontificum et regum*, the 'Norman anonymous' speaks of the 'twin person' of the king, 'one descending from nature, the other from grace.' In one sense, he was, by nature, an individual man (*individuus homo*); in another he was, 'by grace, a Christ-like figure, that is, a God-man (*Christus, id est Deus-homo*)'.[18] To put it another way, in terms of his *officium* ('office', public role, vocation) the king is the very image and figure of God.[19] Kantorowicz suggests that such a 'yoking of two seemingly heterogeneous spheres' had 'a particular attraction for an age eager to reconcile the duality of this world and the other, of things temporal and eternal, secular and spiritual'. With the late-medieval secularization of many aspects of society various dualities were to emerge relating to the 'professional' and 'personal' capacities of human beings.

After the time of the 'Norman anonymous' the relevant discourses pulled in two directions: on the one hand a 'more theocratical-juristical idea of government' emerged within the political sphere, whilst on the other notions relating to the 'quasi-priestly and sacramental essence of kingship' evolved into the late-medieval theory of kingship by 'divine right'.[20] Future formulations are intimated in the *Policraticus* of John of Salisbury, who holds a view of the ruler in 'a new juristic sense' as 'the very Idea of Justice which itself is bound to Law and yet above the Law because it is the end of all Law. Not the Prince rules, but Justice rules through or in a Prince who is the instrument of Justice'.[21] John of Salisbury made the crucial point in

---

[17] *Poetic Authority: Spenser, Milton and Literary History* (New York, 1983), p. vii.
[18] Quoted by Kantorowicz, *King's Two Bodies*, p. 47.
[19] Ibid., p. 48.
[20] Ibid., p. 93.
[21] Ibid., pp. 96–7.

these terms: 'the prince is the public power and a certain image on earth of the divine majesty'; 'in all matters' he 'prefers the advantage of others to his private will (*privata voluntas*)', and indeed 'in public affairs' he is 'not permitted his own will unless it is prompted by law or equity'.[22] As the bearer of the *persona publica* the prince 'punishes all injuries and wrongs, and also all crimes', not incurring individual blame for the blood which is shed in the process.[23] Similarly, in his *Summa theologica* Thomas Aquinas argued that a private person (*persona privata*) has no authority to compel right living; rather the power of compulsion belongs either to the community as a whole or to its *persona publica*, i.e. its ruler who has the duty of inflicting punishments.[24]

Parallel distinctions between 'public' and 'private', the 'official' and the 'individual', emerged in medieval valuations of the figure of the pope. Walter Ullmann has explained how Leo I (who died in 461) used Roman law to clarify the issue of papal power, identifying as a major change 'the separation of the (objective) office of the pope' which originated with St Peter 'from the (subjective) personality of the pope'. For governmental purposes, Ullmann continues, 'it was the office of the pope, the papacy as such, which mattered'; the issue of whether someone was a 'good' or 'bad' pope was not crucial. 'The pope as office holder was conceived to be an instrument to execute the office, that is, to translate the abstract programme of the papacy.' Thus,

> subjective standards and personal qualifications were irrelevant as far as the scope and extent of the office were concerned. In other words, within the terms of papal primatial doctrine the validity of a papal act or decree or judgment did not depend upon the morality or sanctity or other subjective-moral standards applicable to the person of the pope, but solely upon whether or not the judgment or decree was legally valid . . . The office, in a word, absorbed the man.[25]

Here there is, perhaps, an inclination towards a sort of Monophysitism: on the analogy with the heresy which denied the human nature in the person of the incarnated Christ it might be said that such a view of the *officium papae* tends to have the higher, divine element override the lower, human one. However, in the later Middle Ages there were substantial challenges to this dichotomy. The 'intellectual revolution' (as Ullmann terms it) of Aristotle's teachings, particularly on ethics and politics, contributed to the emergence of 'the conception of the individual as a

---

[22] *John of Salisbury: Policraticus*, ed. and tr. C. J. Nederman (Cambridge, 1990), pp. 28, 30.

[23] Ibid., p. 31.

[24] *Summa theologiae*, 1a 2ae, 90, art. 3, ad 2um; as in the Blackfriars edn (London and New York, 1963–80), XXVIII, 12–15.

[25] *A Short History of the Papacy in the Middle Ages* (London, 1972), pp. 20–21. The fact that the office of pope, and the medieval papacy as an institution, 'suffered no damage from popes of extremely dubious or criminal character', Ullmann continues, 'was certainly due to the operation of this principle which disregarded the personality of the pope and concentrated solely on the papal office as a thing inherited from St Peter'.

citizen' with specific rights and responsibilities rather than as a mere 'subject' who received 'doctrine clothed in the law' which had to be obeyed.[26] At the end of the thirteenth century a 'subjective point of view' regarding the papacy became clearly visible. The distinction 'between office and person was now beginning to be reversed': 'What began to matter was the personality of the pope, was whether he was a morally "good" or "bad" pope'.[27]

Some of the sharpest testimonies of this development are found in the writings of men who placed themselves outside the orthodox church through their dissent. For example, in his polemical treatises William of Ockham deduced various radical consequences from the principle that all the power which God had given to men is limited, such as the notion that certain restrictions had been imposed on the power of St Peter, which should not be transgressed by his successors. As a mortal man and hence imperfect, there is no way in which the pope can possess all the power which Christ, even as mortal man, possessed.[28] Far from being irrefutable, the pope 'may not add any "novelties" to the evangelical law, especially such as would be grave or onerous. Indeed, without the consent of the faithful he cannot regularly command any special fast or abstinence.'[29] Ockham goes so far as to say that, in the interests of the greater good of the universal Church, circumstances might arise whereby it was better for it not to be ruled by any pope – or, alternatively, to be ruled by many popes.[30] Such remarks are devoid of any belief in the mystical inevitability of the figure and office of the pope.

---

[26] Ullmann, *Short History of the Papacy*, p. 268.

[27] Ibid., p. 269. Writing around 1280, Petrus Joannis Olivi stated that an error by a pope 'could be merely personal or it could be "magisterial", i.e. it could be merely an individual opinion or it could be proposed as a public teaching which would affect the faith of others'. However, Olivi felt 'it was not sufficient to distinguish between the pope's private and public capacities', because the horrifying prospect remained of a person making pronouncements from the papal throne who was a pope 'only in name and appearance'. B. Tierney, *Origins of Papal Infallibility, 1150–1350. A Study on the Concepts of Infallibility, Sovereignty and Tradition in the Middle Ages* (Leiden, 1972), pp. 120–21. Tierney regards Olivi's contribution as crucial in the development of the doctrine of papal infallibility.

[28] J. J. Ryan, *The Nature, Structure and Function of the Church in William of Ockham* (Missoula, MT, 1979), p. 9.

[29] Ryan, *The Church in Ockham*, p. 10. On Ockham's views on papal infallibility (or, more accurately, fallibility) see especially J. Kilcullen, 'Ockham on Infallibility', *Jnl Religious History*, 16 (1991), 387–409. This article offers an important critique of the views of Tierney, *Origins of Papal Infallibility*, pp. 205–37. See further the exchange between Ryan and Tierney in *Franciscan Studies*, 46, Annual 24 (1986), 285–94 and 295–300. Their disagreement turns on the technical meaning of 'infallibility'. If we take Ryan's definition ('not able to fail, err, mistake') then Ockham certainly did not believe in papal infallibility (*Franciscan Studies* (1986), 290). Tierney, on the other hand, argues that Ockham's version of the doctrine – which accommodates the belief that 'any particular occupant of the Roman see could profess heresy and, in doing so, show himself to be no true pope' – is quite consonant with the views of certain thinkers from our own century, who nevertheless purport to accept the Vatican I (1870) definition of papal infallibility (*Franciscan Studies* (1986), 298–9).

[30] Ryan, *The Church in Ockham*, p. 20.

Remarkably similar discourses and dilemmas characterize the medieval history of the 'office of preacher'. Here the term 'office' denoted at once a vocation and an honour or privilege conferred (and controlled) by the Church, whereby *inter alia* an individual was licensed to preach in public. The *officium praedicatoris* was described in the most glowing terms. According to Humbert of Romans (*c.*1200–77), who was elected Master-General of the Order of Preachers in 1254, it is apostolic, angelic and divine; in its foundation, which is holy Scripture, it excels all the other sciences.[31] What, then, of those cases in which a preacher's *vita* did not live up to the high office which he held? Late-medieval schoolmen agonized over that issue. To take but one example among many, a *quaestio* included in the *Summa de arte praedicandi* of Thomas of Chobham (*c.*1158/68–*c.*1233/6)[32] considers the proposition that to preach while in a state of mortal sin is itself a mortal sin. In resolving the problem, Thomas draws distinctions between preaching *ex officio* and preaching in special circumstances, and between sins which are public knowledge and those which are secret. The sinner who, not required to preach by virtue of office, actually does so out of devotion or owing to the wish of another, does not sin by preaching, providing that his sinful state is concealed and private. If, however, his sin is public knowledge, then, irrespective of whether he is preaching *ex officio* or not, he sins mortally on account of the scandal he creates.[33]

The distinction between what might be termed 'public' as opposed to 'private' sin is treated more elaborately in Henry of Ghent's *quaestio* on whether or not a sinner can be a teacher (*doctor*) of theology.[34] Henry asks, is the deviant teacher's sin

---

[31] *Liber de eruditione praedicatorum*, I, ed. J. J. Berthier, *B. Humberti de Romanis, De Vita regulari* (Rome, 1888–89), II, 374–6; cf. the tr. (from his forthcoming edition) by S. Tugwell in *Early Dominicans: Selected Writings* (London, 1982), pp. 184–5.

[32] *Thomae de Chobham, Summa de arte praedicandi*, ed. F. Morenzoni, CCCM 82 (1988), 59, 61–3; this is identical with the anonymous *quaestio* from Paris, BN, MS lat. 3108 transcribed by J. Leclercq, 'Le magistère du prédicateur au XIIIe siècle', *Archives d'histoire doctrinale et littéraire du moyen âge*, 21 (1946), 129–30. On Thomas's life see the Introduction to his *Summa confessorum*, ed. F. Broomfield, Analecta mediaevalia Namurcensia (Louvain and Paris, 1968), pp. xxviii–xxxviii. He seems to have read arts and theology at Paris before joining the episcopal *curia* of the bishop of London; sometime between October 1206 and *c.*1208 he was appointed sub-dean of Salisbury.

[33] Here 'scandal' has the sense of something which occasions a general feeling of outrage or indignation, causes a public affront. The modern 'tabloid' sense of sexual revelation is not relevant. On medieval uses of the term see further K. Gill, '*Scandalia*: Controversies concerning *clausura* and Women's Religious Communities in Late Medieval Italy', in *Christendom and its Discontents: Exclusion, Persecution, and Rebellion*, ed. S. L. Waugh and P. D. Diehl (Cambridge, 1996), pp. 177–203.

[34] 'Utrum homo peccator possit esse doctor huius scientiae', being Art. XI, qu. 5 of the prologue to the *Summa quaestionum ordinariarum*. First written at Paris *c.*1275–76, the prologue was revised towards the end of Henry's career in 1289. Here and below I use two early printed editions: *Summa quaestionum ordinariarum* (Paris, 1520, repr. Louvain and Paderborn, 1953), and *Summa in tres partes praecipuas digesta* (Ferrara, 1646). For Art XI, qu. 5 see Paris edn, fols 70ʳ–81ʳ; Ferrara edn, pp. 199–201. On Henry's hermeneutics see my 'The *Accessus* Extended: Henry of Ghent on the Transmission

hidden, the man himself being of good reputation? Or is it manifest, the man being infamous on account of his evil life? If it is hidden, the sinner may be teaching to flatter and please, or out of vainglory; here we are dealing with sins perpetrated in the very act of teaching (*ex ipso actu docendi*). Alternatively, he may be a sinner on account of another kind of act (*ex actu alio*), for example because he is covetous, lustful, or the like. Henry goes on to argue that if the teacher's hidden sin is nothing to do with the very act of teaching itself, providing that such a person does not teach anything against Christian truth (in contrast with the heretic) his doctrine can be of use to others, even though he secretly fails to follow his own advice. By contrast, the teacher whose wicked life is manifest and infamous should not, insofar as it lies within his own power, teach at all, because by so doing he will scandalize his audience. However, on account of the faithful (but not on his own account) he may be heard, providing that he has sound doctrine and is permitted to teach by the Church, not having been removed from his office. If, however, such a person is rejected by the Church, he should not be listened to by any means.

The Carmelite theologian Gerard of Bologna, who produced his *summa* between 1313 and 1317, felt that Henry of Ghent had not made himself clear in treating of the case where a teacher of theology sins in the actual act of teaching.[35] He seems to have been concerned that Henry was underrating the culpability of the sinful preacher who sins through another kind of act (*ex alio actu*).[36] Sins of both types can be hidden, Gerard argues, and it cannot be said that a man is preaching from wicked intention more in one case than in the other. Why should the preacher who sins *ex actu praedicandi* be deemed to be committing mortal sin while the preacher who sins in a different way be regarded as liable to benefit spiritually from the help which he gives others through his doctrine? Gerard inclines to the view that in neither case should the sinful preacher be able to benefit. Discussions such as these seem to indicate the very tentative nature of scholastic speculation regarding the 'non-public' (to use the safest term) ethics of the public man.[37]

---

and Reception of Theology', in *Ad Litteram: Authoritative Texts and their Medieval Readers*, ed. M. Jordan and K. Emery (Notre Dame, IA, and London, 1992), pp. 275–326; and 'Medium and Message: Henry of Ghent on Scriptural Style', in *Literature and Religion in the Later Middle Ages: Philological Studies in Honor of Siegfried Wenzel*, ed. R. Newhauser and J. Alford (Binghamton, NY, 1994), pp. 209–35.

[35] He does not name Henry at this point, but the verbal echoes of Henry's treatment are unmistakable, as has been pointed out by B. Smalley, 'Gerard of Bologna and Henry of Ghent', *Recherches de théologie ancienne et médiévale*, 22 (1955), 125–9. It should be emphasized, however, that despite this and other criticisms Gerard is heavily dependent on Henry, as Smalley notes.

[36] *Summa Gerardi Bononiensis*, quaestio VI, art. 2, published by P. De Vooght, *Les sources de la doctrine chrétienne d'après les théologiens du XIVe siècle et du début du XVe* (Paris, 1954), pp. 373–4.

[37] For Gerard's views on the immoral preacher see further his brilliant *quodlibet* 'Utrum melius sit praedicare et facere contrarium eius qui praedicat quam omnino tacere', printed from Paris, BN, MS lat. 17485 by Leclercq, 'Le magistère du prédicateur', pp. 124–7.

Moreover, they mark just how important it is to avoid anachronism in seeking to interpret what, in medieval terms, belongs to the 'public' and 'private' spheres. Kantorowicz has rightly warned us against deducing, from the evidence presented by medieval constructions of the king's two bodies, the existence of the concept of the 'king as a purely private person'. For him the line of distinction should rather be drawn 'between the king alone in his relations to individual subjects, and matters affecting all subjects, the whole polity'.[38] And when medieval writers spoke of the performance of the *officium praedicatoris* as a public duty they had in mind matters relating to location (preaching as an activity conducted in church) and audience (preaching as a performance which was, in theory, open to all, whatever one's status, sex or ability, offering instruction of a kind which was necessary to help all Christians towards salvation). This contrasted with 'private' or 'extra' teaching in special circumstances, which could involve one-to-one instruction or addresses to small groups, and did not always require the services of an ordained priest. Examples of 'private' instruction included an abbess teaching her nuns, a layman instructing his wife or familiars in the rudiments of the faith, and a mother educating her children in like manner. These activities were confined within the supposedly 'private', domestic or reserved (because removed from public view) spaces of family home or nunnery, with proper hierarchical relationships being maintained within each sphere. Women could teach other women or children; it was not permitted for them to teach mixed audiences which included men, since provocative female speech would inflame them with lust. Besides, so the argument ran, men would regard it as unseemly and shameful to be instructed by women. They lacked the authority to preach on account of their inferior subject-position; their bodies were blemished with natural weakness and impurity, and besides only the male form could sacramentally image Christ: hence the ordination of women was impossible.[39] What, then, of those female prophets referred to in the Bible? They were given their gift for private rather than public instruction, declares Henry of Ghent, and if men were taught thereby this was by a special dispensation, wherein divine grace did not respect sexual difference. Similarly, Thomas Aquinas argued that women can teach privately, in the sense of 'familiarly conversing' with a few others, but not publicly, in church. By the same token, a layman could teach his servants and family, but (unless specially licensed) not a gathering of all-comers in a public place, far beyond the walls of the house wherein he ruled as *paterfamilias*. Hence Georges Duby can say that 'the opposition between private life and public life is a matter not so much of place as of

---

[38] Kantorowicz, *King's Two Bodies*, p.172.

[39] These comments regarding female teaching are based on my article, '*De impedimento sexus*: Women's Bodies and Medieval Impediments to Female Ordination', forthcoming in *Medieval Theology and the Natural Body*, ed. P. P. A. Biller and A. J. Minnis. See further J. H. Martin, 'The Ordination of Women and the Theologians in the Middle Ages', *Escritos del Vedat*, 16 (1986), 115–77, and A. Blamires, 'Women and Preaching in Medieval Orthodoxy, Heresy, and Saints' Lives', *Viator*, 26 (1995), 135–52.

power',[40] though I myself would wish to emphasize the conjunction rather than the disjunction of place and power.[41]

It should be noted that when the schoolmen spoke of the 'secret' sins of priests they generally did not have in mind the notion of misdemeanours perpetrated within the boundaries of what we might call 'personal or private morality', but rather sins of which a priest's congregation was ignorant. Of course, Henry of Ghent's treatment of sins which are perpetrated in the very act of public teaching (including vainglory and flattery) as opposed to those which are not (including covetousness and lust) raises larger issues. But, *pace* Gerard of Bologna, Henry did not actually say that it is worse for a preacher to be vainglorious than to be lecherous; neither does the notion of 'privacy', as known to (say) nineteenth-century English bourgeois culture, apply here. For if the lecherous behaviour of a preacher were to become known, it would scandalize the members of his congregation, who would justifiably feel that he was failing to 'practise what he preached'.[42] And in the eyes of his superiors and ultimately of God a sinful priest was just as culpable for his 'private' failings as for those committed in the exercise of his office. In short, here we are largely dealing with matters relating to public and private places, information and power, rather than to public and private life as envisaged in later centuries.

However, in the scholastic treatments of the effect which a person's human fallibility (or downright deviancy) has, or does not have, on the high office which he holds, we do seem to enter the realm of subjectivity – though it should be recognized that it is the individual's display or *performance* of subjectivity, and the public's *perception* of it, which is fundamentally at stake. Once again, Thomas of Chobham is an efficient guide to the major issues. His *quaestio* on whether preaching while in a state of mortal sin is itself a mortal sin offers a distinction between the respective roles of the *praedicator* and the *lector*.[43] The preacher, because of his particular office, is bound to the cure of souls, and therefore he owes his flock his devotion. A lecturer or master in a school, by contrast, does not have the cure of the souls of his

---

[40] 'Private Power, Public Power', in *A History of Private Life*, vol. 2: *Revelations of the Medieval World*, ed. G. Duby (Cambridge, MA, and London, 1988), p. 7.

[41] More precisely, Duby posits two different kinds of power: 'Think of two realms in which peace and order were maintained in the name of different principles. In both the individual was disciplined, supervised, corrected, and punished, but correction and punishment were administered by different authorities. In one the purpose was to govern the *res publica*, the *populus*, the group of men (women had no place here) who, assembled, constituted the state, administered communal property, and shared responsibility for the common good' (ibid., p. 7). From the public 'corporations' of schools and universities, women were similarly excluded. And in the other realm, of 'private' power, the purpose was to govern the *familia*. Moving from the secular to the sacred, Duby describes 'Christians of the feudal era' as 'aspiring to enter into God's private realm, his *familia*, but with a rank appropriate to the order to which they belonged – at the bottom of a hierarchy of submission. They sought to assume a position in one of the interlocking networks of subordinate territories in God's private domain' (p. 25).

[42] Cf. Matthew 23:3; encapsulated by Jerome, *Epistola* lii, in *PL*, 22, 533.

[43] *Summa de arte praedicandi*, ed. Morenzoni, pp. 61–2.

students, and therefore if he is a sinner he is not depriving them of anything because he does not owe them his devotion, and so in his lecturing activity he does not sin mortally. Furthermore, lecturing is not the purely spiritual work that preaching is, whence a layman may lecture on Scripture; the office of lecturer (*officium lectoris*) is not primarily conducive to the *salus animarum* but rather to the instruction of the auditors in some science. The *lector's* brief is simply to improve the minds, rather than save the souls, of his auditors. Knowledge (*scientia*) is not a moral virtue, Thomas declares, because, as Aristotle says, it does little or nothing to lead one to the virtues: 'Scire aut parum aut nichil prodest ad virtutes.'[44]

That dictum from Book 2 of Aristotle's *Ethics*, where the distinction between art and virtue is described, was to resonate through generations of scholastic treatments of the nature of ethics, of the relative merits of intelligence and action, of the qualities essential for the Christian teacher. Averroes, commenting on the relevant passage, had explained that for a craftsman to attain perfection in his art it suffices that the artefacts he produces should be good.[45] By contrast, for a man to lead a virtuous life he must be virtuous in himself *and* perform virtuous actions, these things being equally necessary. Similarly, Thomas Aquinas, in his exposition of the same passage, explains that in the sphere of morality, action and perseverance really matter.[46] Doing is more important than knowing. By performing just and temperate actions a man becomes just and temperate; thereby the moral *habitus* or fixed disposition is established. Hence, 'knowledge has little or no importance in a person being virtuous', this being Thomas's phrasing of Aristotle's statement that mere knowledge has little or no importance as far as the virtues are concerned.

This may be identified as the dominant intellectual tradition to which belongs Thomas of Chobham's distinction between the different offices of the *lector* and the *praedicator*. The work of the *lector* is an activity involving that understanding and knowledge which is specific to a given human discipline, the exercise of specialized skills. The work of the *praedicator* involves, in addition to possession of the relevant knowledge and skills, a propriety of behaviour which may be quite crucial for the successful discharge of his office. The same discourses are present in the two definitions of the term *doctor* which Henry of Ghent provides. The teacher may be regarded either as someone who is capable of teaching because he has the requisite *habitus* of knowledge, or as someone who exercises the 'office of teaching' with the trust and co-operation of the taught. In the first sense, one is a *doctor* by dint of his established, settled state or condition (*habitus*) of knowledge and consequent ability to teach. Such a *habitus* is not dismissed by the act of sinning, any more than it is acquired by virtuous action. In this sense a man who is evil and a sinner can be called a *doctor* of the science of theology, for he is able to have correct doctrine just like the

---

[44] *Nicomachean Ethics*, II, 4 (1105a).

[45] *Aristotelis opera cum Averrois commentaria* (Venice, 1562–74), III, 22ᵛ.

[46] *Super Ethicam*, II, 4, ed. R. M. Spiazzi (Turin and Rome, 1949), p. 80; tr. C. I. Litzinger, *St Thomas Aquinas: Commentary on the Nicomachean Ethics* (Chicago, 1964), p. 130.

righteous man, and indeed he may be better educated than the righteous man in respect of the relevant *habitus* of knowledge. Hence he may function as the *doctor* of another person because of his possession of the *habitus* of the science in question, and may be compared to the craftsman (*artifex*) who practises his skill in accordance with the *habitus* of that art. Aristotle is quoted as saying that it is not necessary for the craftsman to be morally virtuous in order to exercise his craft.[47] In order that an artisan might make good knives, Henry elaborates, he requires not moral virtue but mere proficiency in the art of knife-making. The inference is that the good *doctor* (on this first definition) does not have to be a morally good man, but simply be good at his job.

However, the second sense in which someone may be said to be a *doctor* relates to the audience's reception of the teacher rather than to the teacher's mental state and personal abilities. For someone who holds the office of public teaching (*officium publice docendi*) the approval of his *auditores* is essential. Here the analogy is with the doctor of medicine rather than with the craftsman. No matter how experienced he may have been in his profession, or however good were the medicines he dispensed, a medical doctor would not be acceptable to his patients if he were not disposed to make them well. So, if he were irascible, and thereby provoked all his patients to anger, which inevitably would endanger their health, he would not be permitted to practise. Likewise with the *doctor* of theology: no matter how skilled he may be, if he cannot exercise his *officium doctoris* without imperilling his clients, then he should by no means be allowed to teach them. Therefore it is necessary that the teacher of theology should have both the *habitus* of knowledge (as explained in relation to Henry's first definition) and a good reputation. As St Gregory says, the *magisterium* of pastor is confounded when one thing is done and another is taught; consequently, when someone's life is despised it follows that his preaching will be condemned.[48]

'When someone's life is despised it follows that his preaching will be condemned': that statement could well have been made about Chaucer's Pardoner; it certainly fits his character as presented in the *Canterbury Tales*. The *quaestor* who tells the story of the quest for death has himself incurred spiritual death by his mortal sin of unworthy preaching. But is there some sense in which we can find truth in the Pardoner's claim that he, though an immoral man, can tell a moral tale and thereby turn others from sin? Perhaps there is. After all, Henry of Ghent assures us that, considered from the point of view of his state (*habitus*) of knowledge, a clever sinner can be a teacher of Scripture. And the weighty authority of *the* philosopher, Aristotle,

---

[47] *Politics*, I, 13 (1260a–b).
[48] *Regula pastoralis*, I, 1–2 (*PL*, 57, 14–16).

could be cited in support of the view that a person did not have to be virtuous in order to be knowledgeable. But the total context of Henry's statement must, of course, be remembered. And we have seen how Thomas of Chobham emphasized that the university lecturer or teacher (unlike the preacher) was under no obligation to have as his particular objective the moral, as opposed to the intellectual, improvement of his audience. Since the Pardoner has presumed to preach,[49] surely he must be judged according to the terms of reference of the *officium praedicatoris*, not those of the *officium lectoris*.[50]

Should we therefore dismiss the Pardoner and refuse to listen to him? The orthodox late-medieval response to these questions would seem to be in the negative. Typically, Henry of Ghent argued that the mercenary preacher is to be tolerated. Similarly, in his *Summa praedicantium* (written in the second quarter of the fourteenth century)[51] the English Dominican John Bromyard advised against condemning preachers with personal shortcomings; that is something which one should not take upon oneself, because of the risk of slander, and also because the doctrine preached by a sinful preacher is not the sinner's but God's.[52]

This is all very well, it could be responded, as long as the sin of the preacher is secret. As we have seen, the traditional line was that an immoral preacher can have a good effect on his audience, provided that (or especially if) they are ignorant of his sin. If, however, the sin is or becomes public knowledge, then the preacher constitutes a source of scandal and endangers the spiritual welfare of his flock. Henry of Ghent's partial defence of the *mercenarius* seems somewhat less tolerant when it is realized that he seems to have in mind an individual whose wrongdoing is not known to his congregation. In the case of the preacher whose immorality was notorious, Thomas of Chobham spoke for many of his contemporaries in declaring

---

[49] It should be noted that, in fact, pardoners were not generally licensed to preach, and therefore it is possible to argue that Chaucer's character has usurped an office to which he has no legal right (quite apart from his moral unworthiness for the task). This is one – albeit the most obvious one – among several priestly functions which the Pardoner confidently professes, and constitutes the main basis of his authority-claim. Cf. A. J. Minnis, 'Chaucer's Pardoner and "The Office of Preacher"', in *Intellectuals and Writers in Fourteenth-Century Europe*, ed. P. Boitani and A. Torti (Tübingen and Cambridge, 1985), pp. 88–119.

[50] Given that certain pardoners were laymen, it could casuistically be argued that if Chaucer's creation was a layman then he does not owe his audience his devotion. But that would be to underline, yet again, the point that the Pardoner does not have the right to preach, not having been 'sent' in the official manner intimated by Romans 10:15. Cf. Minnis, 'Chaucer's Pardoner', pp. 99–100.

[51] In the judgement of G. R. Owst, the *Summa praedicantium* 'presents us with the gathered fruits of Mendicant preaching in England throughout the fourteenth century and even earlier': *Literature and Pulpit in Medieval England* (Oxford, 1966), p. 224. On Bromyard's intellectual milieu see P. Binkley, 'John Bromyard and the Hereford Dominicans', in *Centres of Learning, Learning and Location in Pre-Modern Europe and the Near East*, ed. J. W. Drijvers and A. A. MacDonald (Leiden and New York, 1995), pp. 255–64.

[52] *Summa praedicantium* (Venice, 1586), II, 261^v–62^r (s.v. *praedicator*).

that such a man sinned mortally on account of the scandal he created. And surely it is significant that the Bromyard excursus quoted above completely avoids the subject of scandal; it may be suggested that it is only through the exclusion of the contrast between good *verba* and bad *vita* that he can argue as he does. Instead Bromyard narrowly concentrates on the *verba* themselves and their ultimate authorship: they belong to an authority higher than the weak vessel in which they have been placed.

Moreover, the Pardoner's main sins are definitely not of the type which one might describe as being 'non-public' in the sense explained above. For the Pardoner sins in his very act of preaching, due to his vainglory and greed for gain. (Of course, he sins *ex alio actu* as well.) And the major problem he presents is that he makes no secret of his moral deviancy. Indeed, he positively revels in exhibiting it to the audience of Canterbury pilgrims; given this ostentatious public display, the risk of scandal is great. If the standard scholastic critique were applied, it could be said the effect of his preaching is thereby destroyed, since the pilgrims are bound to take more notice of his bad personal example than of his good narrative *exemplum*. Little wonder, then, that after his tale is told he receives insults rather than alms.

Chaucer's Pardoner's Prologue and Tale leaves many questions open. Does the moral tale have a power of its own, an efficacy which functions independently of the teller's immoral life? That is how the issue has usually been formulated in modern criticism, but it misses the point that the Pardoner's skill in tale-telling issues from a certain intellectual *habitus* or body of established knowledge which exists despite his blatant lack of moral virtue. There is no doubting the Pardoner's credentials as a good *artifex*, but rather more is required to make a 'good' preacher. It would seem that Aristotle, who expressed what might be called the 'clever bastard' theory better than anyone, was absolutely right: *Scire aut parum aut nichil prodest ad virtutes*. One could go a stage further and say that Chaucer presents the prospect of 'the author's two bodies'.[53] As the bearer of authoritative information and moral narration the Pardoner constitutes a sort of *persona publica*. This abstract programme exists over and above the individual's ability to execute the office he has assumed (or, more accurately in this case, usurped). As a *persona privata*, however, the Pardoner is clearly deviant, guilty of the sins of greed, lust, hypocrisy, blasphemy, etc. This proposition, it could be argued, is quite in accord with the orthodox Creed and recognized medieval dogma, which no doubt is how Thomas of Chobham and Henry of Ghent would have seen themselves as acting in their discussions of the *officium praedicatoris/doctoris*. However, the risk of a sort of 'Nestorianism' (with two *separate* persons being postulated) was always present in medieval thought which followed the 'two bodies' model.[54] And in Chaucer's text that risk amounts to a direct challenge.

---

[53] On the Pardoner as authority figure, cf. nn. 2 and 49 above.

[54] Cf. Kantorowicz, *King's Two Bodies*, p. 17, who suggests that in discussions of the king's two bodies the 'danger of a royal "Nestorianism"' was 'great at all times'.

This challenge becomes even more acute when it is realized that in Chaucer's day not everyone was prepared to accept the orthodox doctrine regarding the immoral preacher. The schoolmen we have cited had carefully demarcated the qualities of the office and the qualities of the man – Lollard theology brought them together with a vengeance. Above, the possibilities of latent 'Monophysitism' and 'Nestorianism' were tentatively explored in various late-medieval attempts to reconcile abstract authority with human fallibility. There is nothing tentative about the relevant statements of John Wyclif and his followers: here we are dealing with blatant 'Donatism', the belief that if ministers are unworthy, the ecclesiastical offices they hold, and the sacraments they perform, are thereby devalued. Among the heretical views attributed to Wyclif at the London Blackfriars in May 1382 was the proposition 'quod si episcopus vel sacerdos existat in peccato mortale: non ordinat, conficit, nec baptizat'.[55] Conversely, every member of the true Church, being one of the elect and a recipient of divine grace, 'was *ipso facto* more priest than layman, ordained of God'.[56] A version of this doctrine emerges in, for example, one of Wyclif's *Responsiones ad argumenta Radulfi Strode*, Strode having been a Fellow of Merton College before 1360 and probably to be identified with the 'philosophical Strode' who is one of the addressees of Chaucer's *Troilus and Criseyde*.[57] Wyclif declares that the faithful who by true belief and love are members of Jesus Christ (who is the archpriest) are themselves *sacerdotes*, thanks to the spiritual oil of predestination. The implication being that in this respect they do not need to receive the material oil traditionally used in the ordination service. The office of priest is often bestowed on those who are unfit for it, continues Wyclif, and it may be right for the true sons of God to perform that office, even though they may not have been consecrated by a bishop, and lack the priestly tonsure and the *character* (or sacred imprint) which ordination imposes.

This association of authority with personal worthiness has been described as 'the single most destructive and heretical feature of Wyclif's teaching'.[58] It was one of the

---

[55] *Fasciculi zizaniorum Magistri Johannis Wyclif*, ed. W. W. Shirley, RS, 5 (1858), p. 278; cf. p. 320.

[56] G. Leff, *Heresy in the Later Middle Ages*, 2 vols (Manchester and New York, 1967), II, 520.

[57] *Opera minora*, ed. J. Loserth (London, 1913), pp. 177–8; cf. *Troilus and Criseyde*, V, 1856–7.

[58] By Leff, *Heresy*, II, 520. However, M. Wilks, 'Predestination, Property, and Power: Wyclif's Theory of Dominion and Grace', *Studies in Church History*, 2 (1965), 226–7 is able to cite passages from Wyclif which seem to indicate that he wished to preserve the dignity (*dignitas*) of the offices of priest and prince: although vicious prelates and tyrannical rulers have technically disempowered themselves, if they are challenged confusion and scandal may result. However, it is going too far, I believe, to suppose that 'Wyclif took particular pleasure in indulging in lengthy speculation about divine possibilities . . . but knowing full well that this speculation was to have no immediate results for human life' (Wilks, 'Predestination', p. 228; cf. Leff, *Heresy*, II, 549). For more nuanced assessments see A. Hudson, *The Premature Reformation: Wycliffite Texts and Lollard History* (Oxford, 1988), pp. 359–62; J.-P. Genet, 'Ecclesiastics and Political Theory in Late Medieval England: the End of a Monopoly', in *The Church, Politics and Patronage in the Fifteenth Century*, ed. R. B. Dobson (Gloucester, 1984), pp. 30–31; A. Kenny, *Wyclif* (Oxford, 1985), pp. 42–55. At any rate, the

consequences of his theory of dominion. *Dominium* meant divine right of possession: the right to hold power, whether spiritual or secular, depended on grace. Hence only the elect, those predestined to be saved, can legitimately perform priestly functions. By the same token, no king had true dominion over his kingdom whilst he was in a state of mortal sin. The implications for the sinful preacher were obvious. The conventional argument that he could preach provided his sin was not public knowledge was brushed aside. Such a man, Wyclif declared, should not preach in any circumstances. Traditionally, the mercenary preacher was to be tolerated; the office should be respected even if the office-holder cannot be. But according to Wyclif, such a man should be shunned by his congregation and be subject to punishment. In *De veritate sacrae scripturae*, for example, it is argued that prelates who live an ungodly life should forfeit their sacerdotal privileges.[59] Similarly, John Purvey held that the priest who did not implement his office in his life, by setting a good example, effectively excommunicated himself.[60] It was even claimed that the value of the Mass and the worth of the Host vary in accordance with the spiritual condition of the priest. Hence the anonymous Lollard author of the treatise 'Of Prelates' declares that 'a prest may be so cursed & in heresie þat he makiþ not þe sacrament'.[61]

Archbishop Arundel's *Constitutions* of 1409 sought to eradicate all the erroneous Wycliffite opinions here described. They clamped down on unlicensed preaching, banned mention of the sins of the clergy or anything which might undermine orthodox instruction on the sacraments in sermons aimed at the general public, and forbade all other teachers from concerning themselves with disputatious matters of theology. Unlicensed translation of biblical passages into English was also forbidden – and this applied not only to the 'Lollard Bible' in whatever version, in part or entire, but also to extracts from the holy Scriptures as included in vernacular books and treatises, and indeed those vernacular books and treatises themselves. Moreover, the ownership of an English Bible translation made in the time of Wyclif or later was prohibited, except in the case in which special diocesan permission had been given.[62]

These prohibitions raise issues wider and more varied than those relating to 'the

---

opinions I attribute to Wyclif here are expressed unambiguously in certain Lollard writings, so we are on safe ground there. It must be recognized that Wyclif's followers, and indeed his opponents, frequently made blunt instruments out of his subtle (and often shifting) speculations.

[59] Ed. R. Buddensieg, 3 vols (London, 1905–9), III, 67–8.

[60] *Fasciculi zizaniorum*, ed. Shirley, p. 390.

[61] 'Of Prelates', in *The English Works of Wyclif*, ed. D. F. Matthew, EETS (OS) 74 (1880), 102. For Wyclif's own (much more subtle and complex) view on the immoral celebrant see for instance his *De Eucharista*, ed. J. Loserth (London, 1892), pp. 112–15; cf. H. B. Workman, *John Wyclif: a Study of the English Medieval Church* (Oxford, 1926), II, 13, 41–4.

[62] See A. Hudson, 'Lollardy: the English Heresy?', in her *Lollards and their Books* (London and Ronceverte, 1985), pp. 141–63; and N. Watson, 'Censorship and Cultural Change in Late Medieval England: Vernacular Theology, the Oxford Translation Debate and Arundel's *Constitutions* of 1409', *Speculum*, 70 (1995), 822–64.

authority's two bodies', yet for our purposes they will help locate that particular matrix of ideas within late-medieval English culture. In the Oxford translation debate of *c*.1401 scholars had clinically debated if knowledge of God should hierarchically proceed from the Latinate clergy to the laity, if layfolk could cope with a text so stylistically difficult as the Bible, and if the barbarous English language was capable of serving as a vehicle for the communication of divine truth.[63] When issues of social control impinged on the consciousness of the Church authorities, however, the situation acquired a new urgency. They 'came to see that the vernacular lay at the root of the trouble', 'that the substitution [of English for Latin] threw open to all the possibility of discussing the subtleties of the Eucharist, of clerical claims, of civil dominion, and so on'.[64] In such a climate, all English writings, no matter how much or how little theology they contained, no matter how unimpeachable their orthodoxy may have been, inevitably fell under suspicion. In the later fifteenth century a copy of the *Canterbury Tales* was produced for the prosecution during a heresy trial. As Anne Hudson says, if this manuscript 'had included, for instance, the Pardoner's Tale, or, even more, the Parson's Tale, it could on a rigorous interpretation' of the relevant Constitution have been 'regarded as indicative of heresy'.[65] One might also mention the Wife of Bath's Prologue and Tale, which features a woman who is very competent in the academic discipline of disputation and adept at deploying authorities from the Bible and the writings of the Church Fathers – and, it may be added, who tells a tale in which the social order is challenged to the extent that a poor woman of low birth manifests moral dominion over a churlish aristocrat. Nicholas Watson makes the point well that the *Canterbury Tales*, 'playing, as they so disruptively do, with the most important contemporary arguments over teaching and religious authority', are 'a product' of 'a world which is crucially pre-Arundelian'.[66]

The post-Arundelian world was very different. Its culture of control and repression inhibited the development not only of what Watson has called 'vernacular theology' but also of 'vernacular commentary tradition' in general, by which I mean commentary, both in Latin or *in vulgari*, on texts of all kinds – secular and religious – which were composed in English. This point is given more force by the fact that much Middle English biblical exegesis produced in the late fourteenth and early fifteenth centuries was of Wycliffite origin (including the 'Glossed Gospels' and the prefatory material included in the various versions of the Lollard Bible, particularly the 'General Prologue'). The contrast with the situation in France in the age of Charles V is most telling. Charles commissioned 'over thirty translations of authoritative classical and medieval works as part of a conscious policy to legitimate

---

[63] See A. Hudson, 'The Debate on Bible Translation, Oxford 1401', in her *Lollards and their Books*, pp. 67–84.

[64] Hudson, 'The English Heresy?', p. 145.

[65] Ibid., p. 149.

[66] Watson, 'Censorship and Cultural Change', p. 858.

the new Valois dynasty'.[67] Most notable among them are Nicole Oresme's vernacular versions, including commentary, of Aristotle's *Politics, Nicomachean Ethics* and *On the Heavens* along with the pseudo-Aristotelian *Economics*.[68] *Li Livre des Problems de Aristote*, a translation of the Latin text accompanied by a long vernacular commentary, was contributed to Charles's translation programme by his physician, one Evrart de Conty (*c.*1330–1405). To Evrart we also owe a long exposition of an anonymous poem on 'The Chess of Love' (the *Eschez amoureux*),[69] which appears to be the first French full-scale commentary on any French text. Here the move has easily been made from translating existing academic commentary on an authoritative Latin work to providing academic-style commentary on a work written originally in the vernacular.

The progress Evrart made towards a 'secular' mythography is especially intriguing. In particular, he drew selectively on Pierre Bersuire's *Ovidius moralizatus* (a work which Bersuire himself sought to justify in terms of its usefulness to preachers), with the allegorical material which refers to prelates or prelatical theology being systematically reduced.[70] In similar vein, though far more adventurously, those most innovative of medieval literary theorists, Dante, Petrarch and Boccaccio, drew on religious hermeneutics as they forged their apologies for poetry. However, such practice was scarcely credible in the England of Thomas Arundel and Henry V. When Bishop Reginald Pecock set out to produce a body of orthodox doctrine in English to counteract the Wycliffite corpus he met with strong opposition and finally with condemnation, and it should be noted that his general educational programme – for that is how he saw it – included philosophy (largely of the kind which we might call 'general knowledge') as well as theology. Such a climate of repression, involving both church and state, of theological and philosophical thinking and writing *in vulgari* was inimical to the emergence in England of a vigorous tradition of vernacular textual commentary. Little wonder, then, that there is no mythographic commentary on the *Parliament of Fowls* of the type produced by Evrart de Conty, or a *querelle* over *Troilus and Criseyde*, despite Chaucer's attempt to provoke one in the prologue to his *Legend of Good Women*. By the same token, when certain textual-theoretical implications of 'the authority's two

---

[67] C. R. Sherman, *Imaging Aristotle: Verbal and Visual Representation in Fourteenth-Century France* (Berkeley and Los Angeles, 1995), p. 6.

[68] On Oresme's milieu and works see Sherman, *Imaging Aristotle*, pp. 6–33; *Maistre Nicole Oresme: Le Livre de Politiques d'Aristote*, ed. A. D. Menut (Philadelphia, 1970), pp. 5–33.

[69] For the proof of Evrart's authorship see F. Guichard Tesson, 'Evrart de Conty, auteur de la *Glose des Echecs amoureux*', *Le Moyen français*, 8–9 (1981), 111–148. For Evrart's literary theory see A. J. Minnis, 'Late-Medieval Vernacular Literature and Latin Exegetical Traditions', in *Text und Kommentar: Archäologie der literarischen Kommunikation IV*, ed. J. Assmann and B. Gladigow (Munich, 1995), pp. 311–31. I am grateful to Bruno Roy for kindly providing me with typescript extracts from the forthcoming edition of Evrart's *Eschez amoureux* commentary which he is publishing in collaboration with F. Guichard Tesson, and for answering several queries concerning this work.

[70] See F. Guichard Tesson, 'La *Glose des Echecs amoureux*: Un savoir à tendance laïque: comment l'interpréter?', *Fifteenth-Century Studies*, 10 (1984), 229–60.

bodies' doctrine show themselves in Chaucer's work, it is in association with a figure who has appropriated the *auctoritas* and the methodology characteristic of the preacher's role, rather than as part and parcel of an apologia for some *auctour newe* in the vernacular. And when that extraordinary instance of Italian self-commentary and self-promotion, Dante's *Convivio*, impacted on Middle English literature it was as the source for quite traditional (though perhaps n'er so well expressed) teaching on true nobility, as featured in The Wife of Bath's Tale, rather than as the model for auto-exegesis by Chaucer or any of his English contemporaries or successors.

Chaucer's French contemporaries spoke a very different language. Nicole Oresme, following Cicero, stated that 'matters which are weighty and of great authority are delightful and agreeable to people when written in the language of their country'.[71] Christine de Pisan, enthusing about Charles V's translation programme, declared that 'it was a noble and perfect action' to have major works 'translated from Latin into French to attract the hearts of the French people to high morals by good example'.[72] She then develops the *translatio studii* theme, to make the point that France has now taken possession of a heritage which in days of yore had passed from Greece to Rome. But in the realm of Henry V, the English language could hardly function in the same way within orthodox promotion of a transfer of learning and power as expressed in works written in the vernacular. The *translatio studii* topos had been tainted by the Lollards. And the fate of Reginald Pecock hardly bode well for any other ambitious attempt to reclaim the vernacular for orthodoxy. It is not surprising, then, that there is no affirmation of the *translatio auctoritatis* from Latin into English of the type which, most memorably, Dante had been able to make for his own 'illustrious vernacular'.[73]

Medieval textual theory never generated the specific notion of 'the author's two bodies', but the thinking underlying this notion to some extent did exist, and appeared in various guises. In France and Italy it figured within sophisticated discussions of the ethical credentials of vernacular authors and texts. In England it manifested itself in a particularly dangerous form, within a dialectic which questioned the efficacy of the words and sacramental actions of a man of great authority if his life did not accord with his official status. This may to some extent account for the different textual cultures of Petrarch's Italy and Chaucer's England. At the very least it helps to explain the differences between Petrarch's Cicero and Chaucer's Pardoner, in the light of their shared discourses of authority.

---

[71] *Le Livre de Politiques*, ed. Menut, p. 44.

[72] *Chemin de long estude*, quoted by Sherman, *Imaging Aristotle*, p. 7; see also p. 9.

[73] By the term *translatio auctoritatis* I mean the process whereby literary prestige moved from Latin into the European vernaculars. See further my '*De Vulgari Auctoritate*: Chaucer, Gower, and the Men of Great Authority', in *Chaucer and Gower: Difference, Mutuality, Exchange*, ed. R. F. Yeager (Victoria, BC, 1991), pp. 36–74.

CHAPTER TWELVE

'Mind in Character': Ancient and Medieval Ideas about the Status of the Autograph as an Expression of Personality

David Ganz

When those two accomplished English palaeographers Mistress Ford and Mistress Page compared their letters from Sir John Falstaff, they had no difficulty in identifying the same writer's hand.[1] Other characters in Shakespeare's plays readily recognize the handwriting of their correspondents.[2] Paradoxically Shakespeare's fullest description of the features of an individual's handwriting occurs in a case of mistaken identity, when Malvolio incorrectly identifies the handwriting of Olivia on a letter sent to deceive him.[3] The assumption that a reader will recognize the identity of the writer from the handwriting of someone whom that reader knows well seems self-evident, but finding evidence for recognition of handwriting has proved harder. To examine accounts of the handwriting of individuals, and to explore what medieval readers described when they looked at autographs brings us to an uncharted area where personality and style are interlaced. I hope that the beginnings of such an investigation will prove an appropriate tribute to a scholar who has consistently shown how palaeography is too important to be treated as a branch of empirical learning, and whose work is a continual reminder of the necessity for range of expertise, precision of detail, and above all generosity in the encouragement which spurs and trains future colleagues.

---

[1] Shakespeare, *The Merry Wives of Windsor*, II, I, 72: 'Why this is the very same: the very hand: the very words.' For this and subsequent quotations from Shakespeare's plays see the First Folio edn (1623). I have tried consistently to use 'handwriting' for the script of an individual, and 'script' for the palaeographical categories of kinds of handwriting; 'hand' is normally used only to translate quotations.

[2] *Much Ado about Nothing*, V, 4, 86 and 89 (Beatrice and Benedict writing sonnets to one another): 'For heres a paper written in his hand.' 'Here's our owne hands against our hearts.' Cf. *Merchant of Venice*, II, 4, 12; *Hamlet*, IV, 7, 50; and *King Lear*, I, 2, 61, 'You know the character to be your Brothers?'

[3] *Twelfth Night*, II, 5, 70ff. (Malvolio, reading Maria's letter imitating Olivia's handwriting): 'by my life, this is my Ladies hand: these bee her very C's, her U's, and her T's, and thus makes shee her great P's. It is in contempt of question her hand.' The matter is righted at V, 1, 332: 'Alas Maluolio, this is not my writing,/ Though I confesse much like the Character:/ But out of question, 'tis Marias hand.'

Julius Victor's brief account of letters in his treatise on rhetoric, generally dated to the fourth century, affirms that ancient practice was to write autograph letters to one's friends. He states that the ancients used to write to those dearest to them in their own hands or frequently to add a *subscriptio*.[4] Roman practice as evidenced in surviving letters, and literary accounts of Roman practice, confirm and amplify Victor's account.

In Plautus' comedy *Bacchides*, composed before 184 BC, the slave Chrysalus tells Mnesilochus to write to his father and explains that if Mnesilochus writes the letter himself his father will recognize the letters and will be more likely to respond favourably to the request.[5] Most Roman correspondence was copied by a professional scribe, who was often a slave. But the person sending the letter was accustomed to add a line of greeting in his own handwriting, just as today we might add a postscript to letters which we have had typed or printed.

The fullest literary evidence for such personal additions is found in the correspondence of Cicero. It has references to autograph additions in letters either for confidential material which the writer did not wish to entrust to a secretary, or as a sign of affection towards the recipient. In letters to Atticus of 6 August 47 BC, Cicero explains that he is writing in his own hand to ensure the secrecy of the subject-matter: 'But here I go back to my own hand, for what follows is confidential'.[6] For the same reason a piece of information (about the manoeuvrings of a possible husband for Atticus' daughter) was added by Cicero, in his own hand, at the end of a letter of 26 May 45.[7] A postscript written in Pompey's own hand, at the end of a letter Pompey sent him during the Civil War in February 49 BC, suggested to Cicero that Pompey had given up the towns and the coast for lost.[8]

Writing all of the letter in one's own hand, when the writer was at leisure, was a sign of affection.[9] A letter to Atticus written on 28 March 45 BC begins, 'I write this in my own hand'.[10] Cicero wrote to Appius Pulcher, his predecessor as governor of

---

[4] 'Observabant veteres karissimis sua manu scribere, vel plurimum subscribere', Julius Victor, *Ars rhetorica*, ed. R. Giomini and M. S. Celentano (Leipzig, 1980), *cap.* 27, *de epistolis*, p. 106.

[5] 'nam propterea te volo scribere, ut pater cognoscat litteras' (Plautus, *Bacchides*, 729–30).

[6] 'sed ad meam manum redeo, erunt enim haec occultius agenda' (Cicero, *Ad Atticum*, XI, 24, 2). Cf. Symmachus, *Epistolae* II, 31 (written in 390 to Flavius), and an autograph passage added at the end of *Ep.* II, 30: 'Hoc enim manu sua subter adiecit.' For a Christian letter where the autograph was used to ensure secrecy cf. Ambrose: 'Postremo scribo manu mea quod solus legas' (I will write in my own hand what you alone may read.) *Ambrosii epistulae*, 3, ed. M. Zelzer, CSEL, 82 (1982), Ep. 11 (14), p. 217.

[7] *Ad Atticum*, XIII, 28.

[8] 'in ea Pompeii epistola erat in extremo ipsius manu: Tu censeo Luceriam venias, nusquam eris tutius' (ibid., VIII, 1, 1).

[9] See ibid., V, 14, 1.

[10] 'haec ad te manu mea' (ibid., XII, 32, 1). Cf. the opening of V, 19, written en route to Laodicea: 'I had already sealed the letter . . . written in my own hand and containing all my news, when Apella's courier suddenly arrived with a letter from you' (ibid.).

Laodicea, about a meeting before he took on the governorship: 'Accordingly I altered my plan and immediately dispatched a letter to you in my own hand.'[11] A letter to his brother Quintus, dated 17 January 56 BC was dictated: 'Contrary to my habit when writing to you I am dictating this letter instead of writing it myself, not because of pressure of business (though busy I certainly am) but because I have a touch of ophthalmia.'[12] Dictation saved time and energy, but close friends expected an autograph. A long letter sent to Quintus in September of 54 BC gives details of how it was written: 'After I had written these last lines which are in my own hand your son came over to us for dinner . . . He gave me your letter to read . . . I dictated the above to Tiro at dinner, in case the different handwriting may surprise you.'[13] Quintus was expected to notice the change of hand, and presumably might have worried about his brother's health.

Cicero also reveals how a reader reacted to autograph letters. He wrote to Atticus:

> I come to your letters, a spate of which reached me simultaneously, each more agreeable than the last – those, that is, which were in your own hand. I liked Alexis' hand because it so nearly resembles your own, but again I didn't like it because it showed you were unwell.[14]

One of the duties of the secretary was always to imitate his master's hand.[15] But this could lead to forgery, and the autograph affirmed the authenticity of the document sent. 'The first glance at it [your letter] gave me pleasure, for the writing was your own.'[16] The pleasure of recognizing the handwriting of a close friend, which Cicero mentioned in his letter to Atticus, is discussed in detail by Seneca. 'For that which is sweetest when we meet face to face is afforded by the impress of a friend's hand upon his letter – recognition.'[17]

---

[11]   *Ad familiares*, III, 6, 2, to Appius Pulcher.

[12]   'parvula lippitudine aductus sum, ut dictarem hanc epistolam, et non, ut ad te soleo, ipse scriberem' (*Ad Quintum fratrum*, II, 2). Cf. 'When you get a letter from me in the hand of one of my secretaries you are to infer that I did not have a minute to spare; when in my own, that I had – a minute!' (ibid., II, 16).

[13]   'cum scripsissem haec infima, quae sunt mea manu' (ibid., III, 1).

[14]   'epistolas tuas . . . accepi, aliam alia iucundiorem, quae quidem erant tua manu' (*Ad Atticum*, VII, 2, 3).

[15]   For Roman secretaries see H. Teitler, *Notarii and Exceptores* (Amsterdam, 1985), and F. Millar, *The Emperor in the Roman World* (London, 1992), pp. 69–110. For an account of the varied tasks of the secretary in a better documented period, cf. H. R. Woudhuysen, *Sir Philip Sidney and the Circulation of Manuscripts* (Oxford, 1996), pp. 69–87 (for imitation of hands, see p. 388). For a telling modern instance, cf. C. Hamilton, *The Robot that Helped to Make a President. A Reconnaissance into the Mysteries of John F. Kennedy's Signature* (New York, 1965).

[16]   'e quibus hanc primo aspectu voluptatem cepi, quod erant a te ipso scriptae' (*Ad Atticum*, VII, 3, 1).

[17]   'Quanto iucundiores sunt litterae, quae vera amici absentis vestigia, veras notas adferunt Nam quod in conspectu dulcissimum est, id amici manus inpressa praestat, agnoscere' (Seneca, *Epistulae morales*, 40, 1).

But issues of status might also be involved. Between AD 143 and 175 Fronto wrote to his pupil the emperor Marcus Aurelius who had taken the trouble to copy out a speech by Fronto in his own hand and to send it to Fronto. In his reply Fronto affirms that those who despise the speech (*orationem*) will admire the script (*litteras*), while those who dislike the writing (*scripta*) will still admire the writer (*scriptorem*).[18] A letter written in the emperor's own hand is for Fronto a sign of special favour.[19] Roman scribes were of low status, so that for a person of higher status to write in his own hand revealed a bond which challenged perceived hierarchies.

The personal autograph postscript or subscription seems to have been standard practice in Roman letters. The evidence from Vindolanda is summarized by Bowman and Thomas: 'It is only rarely that the end of a letter is preserved. When it does survive it almost always shows the writer adding a brief greeting in what we take to be his own hand.'[20] Such greetings are most frequently extremely brief and they have a standard form.[21] Most celebrated is an autograph salutation at the end of an invitation to a birthday party.[22] Other original letters on papyri preserve comparable autograph salutations at the ends of the letters.[23] One such, a second-century letter in Greek, suggests that the expression of pleasure on recognizing the handwriting of a close friend was not simply a literary topos. Apion, a young Egyptian recruit who had crossed the sea to Italy, asked his father Epimachus for a letter: 'I beseech you therefore, my lord father, write unto me a little letter, first of your health, secondly of that of my brother and sister, thirdly that I may do obeisance to your hand, because

---

[18] Fronto expresses his pleasure in an autograph copy of his work made by Marcus Aurelius: 'Enimvero quibus ego gaudium meum verbis exprimere possim, quod orationem istam meam tua manu descriptam misisti mihi? . . . Mea oratio extabit M. Caesaris manu scripta. Qui orationem spreverit, litteras concupiscet: qui scripta contempserit, scriptorem reverebitur' (Fronto, *Ad M. Caesarem*, I, 7).

[19] 'Sed acceptis litteris tuis ea re iam primum bona spes mihi ostentata est, quod tua manu scripseras . . . diluisse te in id tempus, quo mihi scribebas, litterae declarent' (ibid., II, 6).

[20] A. K. Bowman and J. D. Thomas, *Vindolanda: the Latin Writing Tablets* (London, 1983), p. 50.

[21] *The Vindolanda Writing Tablets (Tabulae Vindolandenses II)*, ed. A. K. Bowman and J. D. Thomas (London, 1994), see no. 248, letter from Niger and Brocchus to Cerealis, 'optamus frater bene valere te domine'; no. 250, letter to Cerialis, 'vale frater manus'; and cf. nos 242, 252, 255, 256, 258 and 264. See also no. 247, letter to Cerialis (with greetings to his wife), 'vale mi domine frater karissime'. Cf. nos 292, 295.

[22] Ibid., no. 291, a letter of Claudia Severa to Sulpicia Lepidina, wife of Cerealis, has two subscriptions: 'sperabo te soror' and 'vale soror anima mea ita valeam karissima et have'.

[23] P. Cugusi, *Corpus epistularum Latinarum papyris tabulis Ostracis servatarum* (Florence, 1992), nos 147, 161, 191, 199. New Haven, Yale University, P. Dura 64 in *Chartae Latinae Antiquiores: Facsimile–edition of the Latin Charters prior to the Ninth Century*, ed. A. Bruckner and R. Marichal (Olten and Lausanne, 1954–), VI, 319, dating to AD 221 (Cugusi, *Corpus*, no. 237); cf. London, BL, P. Lond. 1767, a letter with remarkably poor orthography apparently written to a Christian cleric dating to the fourth century, illust. in *Chartae Latinae Antiquiores*, III, 211, 'optinem cum domino . . . deus omnipotes plurimos constodire dignetur' (*sic*). (That I may obtain that Almighty God be pleased to protect thee brother.)

you trained me well.'[24] Apion's letter is considered an autograph, and given his low status his respect for his father's autograph seems unlikely to have been a literary convention. An autograph message could also provide reassurance about the health of the writer. Thus Symmachus reassured his daughter after an illness by writing her an autograph letter.[25]

Christian writers were well aware of the importance of the personal salutation.[26] It is frequent in the letters of Paul who writes 'in my own hand' at the end of letters written by a secretary, as at Galatians 6:11: 'See what large letters I make when I am writing in my own hand.'[27] 1 Corinthians 16:21 is the only place where Paul mentions his name in such a salutation. Other letters ending with greetings in Paul's name, but now generally thought not to be authentic, are Colossians 4:18, and 2 Thessalonians 3:17 ('I, Paul, write this greeting with my own hand. This is the mark in every letter of mine; it is the way I write'). The Epistle to Philemon ends with formal business language and the signature is regarded as a part of that formality, as is shown by contemporary Jewish practice: 'I, Paul, am writing this with my own hand: I will repay it.' These autograph subscriptions of Paul and of the pseudo-Pauline letters are taken by modern exegetes as the expression of the desire to give a legal status to what was said in the letter.[28] 'The primary purpose of the autograph greeting was not to testify to the Pauline authorship of the letter, but rather to emphasize the authority of the letter and the need for its contents to be obeyed.'[29] The signature served to affirm Christian doctrine, and could be seen as authenticating the document which it endorsed although the signature was never of any formal legal status. The names of the witnesses on Roman legal documents were not signatures, and the security against forgery of such documents was the seal, not the signature. Minors however needed a master to sign for them; the signature was regarded as a sign of maturity.[30]

Patristic commentary on the Pauline letters treated Paul's autograph subscription as providing a proof of the letters' authenticity, and this was probably the reason that the authors of the pseudo-Pauline letters had supplied subscriptions. Jerome sets out this view clearly in his commentary on Colossians:

---

[24] Berlin GU II, 423, as tr. and illust. in A. Deissmann, *Light from the Ancient East* (New York, 1927), pp. 179–80.

[25] Symmachus, *Ep.* VI, 16 (AD 397). Cf. Cicero's letter n. 13 above.

[26] See O. Roller, *Das Formular der Paulinischen Briefe. Ein Beitrag zur Lehre vom antiken Briefe*, Beiträge zur Wissenschaft vom Alten und Neuen Testament, IV, 6 (Stuttgart, 1933), pp. 70–8.

[27] On Paul's letters cf. F. Schneider and W. Stenger, *Studien zum Neutestamentlichen Briefformular* (Leiden, 1987) and J. A. D. Weima, *Neglected Endings: the Significance of the Pauline Letter Closings* (Sheffield, 1994), pp. 118–35.

[28] Schneider and Stenger, *Studien*, p. 160.

[29] Weima, *Neglected Endings*, p. 207.

[30] C. G. Bruns, 'Die Unterschriften in den römischen Rechtsurkunden', *Kleinere Schriften*, 2 (Weimar, 1882), pp. 37–118. For later practice cf. H. Bresslau, *Handbuch der Urkundenlehre für Deutschland und Italien*, 2 (Berlin, 1931), p. 206.

So that he [Paul] should remove all the letter which he sent from the suspicion of forgery he subscribed it in his hand at the end, saying, 'The greeting of Paul in my hand which is the sign in every letter: thus I write, the grace of Lord Jesus Christ be with all of you.' The letters which he dictated to the Colossians he subscribed with his hand in the same way, 'the salutation by the hand of me Paul. Remember my bonds.' And wherever he knew that there were false teachers who might sow new dogma on the authority of the Apostle he subscribed the letter with his own hand . . . so that when they recognized the strokes of the letters they thought they could see him who had written them.[31]

Augustine has a similar view of the meanings of the *subscriptio*: 'Your amen is your subscription, your consent, your agreement.'[32] Thus Augustine assures Jerome that autograph subscriptions on a group of his letters relating to the Pelagian controversy, which he is sending, attest to their authenticity and completeness.[33]

In addition to authentication, the autograph was considered the token of Christian friendship. Thus the Carolingian commentary on the Pauline Epistles by Haimo of Halberstadt quotes Jerome to affirm that the autograph was a sign of Paul's affection for his correspondent. 'I, I say, who do not write my other letters but dictate them, for the sake of your love, that I might obtain what I ask, I wrote this to you.'[34] The Church Fathers generally dictated their letters to a secretary, but sometimes wrote in their own handwriting. Ambrose in his letter to Sabinus explains:

I feel that it is far more suitable that I put my own hand to the stylus, not to appear to be lustily pouring forth words, but concealing them, so that I will not

---

[31] 'Et ut totam epistolam quam mittebat, suspicione erueret falsitatis, manu sua in fine subscribit, dicens: salutatio mea manu Pauli, quod est signum in omni epistola: ita scribo: gratia domini nostri Iesu Christi cum omnibus vobis. Ad Colossenses etiam quas dictaverat litteras, manu sua similiter subnotavit: Salutatio mea manu Pauli: Memores estote vinculorum meorum. Et ubicumque sciebat falsos adesse doctores, qui possent per Apostoli auctoritatem nova dogmata seminare, epistolam manu propria subscribebat . . . ut dum litterarum apices recognoscunt, ipsum se putarent videre, qui scripserat . . . Et quia necessitas expetebat, ut manu sua epistolam subscriberet, contra consuetudinem curvos tramites litterarum, vix magnis apicibus exprimebat' (Jerome, *PL*, 26, 434–5).

[32] 'amen vestrum, subscriptio vestra est, consensio vestra est, adstipulatio vestra est' (Augustinus, *Sermo*, 348A, *PL*, 39, 1721).

[33] 'quaecumque autem mihi occasio proxima occurerit omnium carundem epistolarum exemplaria manu mea subnotata, quam confido tibi esse notissimam, tuae germanitati adiuvante domino curabo dirigere, ut scias mihi quae rescribas, utrum ad te non solum cuncta sed etiam integra et vera pervenerint' (*Augustini epistolae*, ed. J. Divjak, CSEL, 88 (1981), Ep. 19, p. 93). Cf. *Hieronymi epistulae*, ed. I. Hilberg, CSEL, 55 (1912), Ep. 105, p. 243: 'epistulam meam videras et notae tibi manus in subscriptione signa deprehendas, ut tam facile amicum laederes et alterius malitiam in meam verteres contumeliam?' After an orthodoxy trial the defendant was required to sign his confession with his own hand, see *PL*, 65, 23. For the diplomatic of such letters cf. Bresslau, *Handbuch*, II, 450.

[34] 'Ego, inquam, qui alias epistolas meas non scribo, sed dicto, causa amoris tui ut obtinere possim quod postulo, scripsi ipsam tibi.' (Haimo, *In Epistolas Pauli ad Philemon*, *PL*, 117, 819.) Haimo is quoting Jerome, cf. *PL*, 26, 651. See also Primasius *In Epistolas Pauli*, *PL*, 68, 649, and Atto of Vercelli, *PL*, 134, 723.

have to be ashamed in the presence of another who is doing the writing, but conscious only of myself, without a witness, and weighing with the ear and also with the eye the things I write. The Apostle Paul also used to write with his own hand, as he himself says: 'I am writing to you with my own hand.' He said this for reasons of honour, but we because of shame.[35]

Ambrose is apologizing for his lack of wordiness, but his language depends on a convention that the autograph is a sign of intimacy, even the intimacy of incoherence rather than an epistolary formula. Elsewhere Ambrose notes that the Emperor Gratian took the trouble to write him an autograph letter: 'You wrote the entire letter with your own hand, so that the very letters speak your faith and piety.'[36]

Manuscripts which have preserved collections of ecclesiastical letters sometimes include the formula *et alia manu*, noting that the original of the letter copied bore an autograph subscription. The earliest instance seems to be a letter dating to 320 by the Donatist Bishop Sabinus: '*And in another hand* I wish you to be well in the Lord and remember us. Farewell, but I beg you, let no one know.'[37] The greeting added was often as standardized as in the formulae of the Vindolanda letters. In the *Collectio Avellana*, a collection of early-sixth-century papal letters, at the end of a letter from Pope Hormisdas to Epiphanius of Constantinople, the pope thanks the archbishop for a gift of liturgical vessels to St Peter's '*And in the pope's hand*: We received a gold chalice with gems, and another silver chalice and two veils for the office of the basilica of St Peter which your charity sent.'[38] Imperial letters contained a similar standard formula, and copies preserved in this collection prefaced the emperor's *subscriptio* with the phrase *et manu divina*.[39] For example the Novella I, 3 of

---

[35] 'aptius videtur propriam manum nostram affigere stilo, ut non tam deflare aliquid videamur quam abscondere neque alterum scribentem erubescamus, sed ipsi nobis conscii sine ullo arbitrio non solum auribus, sed etiam oculis ea ponderemus quae scribimus . . . Apostolus quoque Paulus sua scribebat manu, sicut ipse ait: Mea manu scripsi vobis, ille propter honorificentiam, nos propter verecundiam.' *Ambrosii epistulae*, CSEL, 82/2, Ep. 37, p. 21.

[36] 'Scripsisti tua totam epistolam manu, ut ipsi apices fidem tuam pietatemque loquuntur', CSEL, 82/3, Ep. 12, p. 220; cf. Fronto in n. 19 above.

[37] 'et alia manu Opto te in domine bene valere et nostri memoriam esse, vale, sed rogo te, nemo sciat.' *Optati Milevitani libri*, ed. C. Ziwsa, CSEL, 26 (1893), 192. The *opto te bene valere* subscription was frequently used by Cyprian (cf. *Opera*, ed. G. Hartel, CSEL, 3/2 (1871), 509, 547). In the ninth-century Cyprian manuscript (Oxford, Bodl. Lib., MS Laud Misc. 105) these subscriptions are copied in red ink.

[38] 'et manu pape Suscepimus calicem aureum gemmatum, patenam argenteam et alium calicem argenteum et vela duo ministerio basilicae beati Petri apostoli profutura a caritate tua directa', *Epistulae imperatorum pontificum aliorum*, ed. O. Guenther, CSEL, 35 (1895), no. 239, p. 739.

[39] See Largus to Bishop Aurelius of Carthage: '*Et alia manu*: Incolumem te divinus favor praestet annis compluribus, domine pater merito honorabilis' (ibid., p. 82). For other greetings by emperors and ecclesiastics in the *Collectio Avellana* see: Maximus to Pope Siricius, '*Et manu imperatoris* Divinitas te servet per multos annos' (ibid., no. 40, p. 91); Justinian to Pope John, 'Divinitas te servet per multos annos, sancte et religiosissime pater' (ibid., no. 84, p. 325); and 'Vegetum te nostrique memorem

Valentinian III dating from 450 reads: '*Et manu divina*: Optamus vos felicissimos et florentissimos nostrique amantissimos per multos annos bene valere. sanctissimi ordinis p(atres) c(onscripti).'[40] A similar formula is found at the end of some letters in a manuscript of Augustine's letters.[41]

Copies of papal letters often include the note *et alia manu* separating the *subscriptio* from the text of the letter.[42] Similar formulae were used by bishops and other signatories. Thus the *Collectio Avellana* records how letters from Pope Vitalian to the Emperor Justinian included a formula 'Et manu domni Pape' followed by the subscription of the patrician Dominicus. The copyist, a chancery official, took pains to record where the original copied had received an autograph salutation by the pope.[43] Several sixth-century manuscripts transcribe these salutations in a distinctive cursive, half-uncial script only used to copy the papal *salutatio* formula: *Deus vos incolumes custodiat fratres carissimi*, including those found at the end of several papal letters to Gaul included in the sixth-century manuscript of canonical collection, Paris, BN, MS lat. 12097.[44] The words *et alia manu* preceding these salutations were read out by the official who read the letter aloud, and established that the reader held the original version of the letter. This is confirmed by a letter of Pope Leo the Great recording that the priest Atticus had signed a formula submitting to the Council of Chalcedon: 'adiecta subscriptione propriae manus, quae in ecclesia christiano populo praesente recitetur'.[45]

Most medieval letters, like these papal letters, were dictated and so seldom autograph.[46] Influential figures had secretaries to write, and sometimes to draft, their

---

praestet omnipotens deus, domine frater (ibid., no. 85, p. 330); cf. the African bishops' letter to Pope John (ibid., no. 85, p. 328). Also, Justinian to Pope Agapetus, 'Diuinitas te servet per multos annos, sancte et religiosissime pater' (ibid., no. 89, p. 340); and John of Constantinople to Pope Hormisdas, 'Incolomes in domino orate pro nobis, amabilis deo et sanctissime frater' (ibid., no. 182, p. 638), cf. nos 183, 195 (pp. 639, 654).

[40] *Theodosiani libri XVI*, ed. T. Mommsen and P. Meyer (Berlin, 1905), II, 76. *Manu divina* is also found in Valentinian, Novellae 17 and 19 (ibid., 103, 106) and is equivalent to the formulae *Et manu imperatoris*, and *Et alia manu principis* used in canon law.

[41] *Augustini epistulae*, 3, ed. A. Goldbacher, CSEL, 44 (1904), 39; the signatures of Aurelius of Carthage and Silvanus in letter 129 are written *et alia manu*. In letter 125 the Monte Cassino manuscript (Monte Cassino, MS 162) records that Augustine's signature was *alia manu*, ibid., p. 92. Pope Innocent greeted Augustine and others: 'Et alia manu deus vos incolomes custodiat, fratres karissimi' [*Collectio Avellana*] CSEL, 35, p. 96.

[42] See P. Silva-Tarouca, 'Nuovi studi sulle antiche Lettere dei Papi IV: Il problema critico delle piu antiche lettere pontificie (sec. IV–VI)', *Gregorianum*, 12 (1931), 349–86, esp. 361–74.

[43] CSEL, 35, p. 739.

[44] See Silva-Tarouca, 'Nuovi studi', p. 351. Cf. E. A. Lowe, 'The Script of the Farewell and Date Formulae in Early Papal Documents', in his *Palaeographical Papers 1907–1965* (Oxford, 1972), II, 450–58, noting the use of different scripts for the dating formulae in manuscripts of the letters of Pope Leo I (Munich, Clm 14540 and Vatican, Bibl. apost., MS Reg. lat. 1997, fol. 78), and in the oldest manuscripts of Bede's *Historia Ecclesiastica*.

[45] See Silva–Tarouca, 'Nuovi studi', pp. 364–6.

[46] H. Hoffmann, 'Zur mittelalterlichen Brieftechnik', in *Spiegel der Geschichte Festgabe für Max*

letters and those letters were authenticated with a seal rather than a subscription. The transition can be followed from the late-antique letters of Isidore, and Desiderius of Cahors, to the correspondence of twelfth-century authors. In the seventh century the personal subscription was still used between friends or relatives. Isidore of Seville wrote 'Ora pro nobis, beatissime domne et frater' with his own hand on a letter to his brother Braulio, and Braulio used a similar formula, which copyists of the letters note was written *et manu sua* at the ends of their letters.[47] Letters of the seventh-century Merovingian bishop, Desiderius of Cahors, to Grimoald, the mayor of the palace, include reference to a subscription *manu propria*: 'incolomem excellentiam vestram superna pietas tueatur'.[48] The life of Desiderius also includes such subscriptions in the texts of his letters: 'May the Lord keep you safe and choose to make you heirs of his kingdom.'[49] Other letters in this collection record the *salutatio* formula written *manu propria*.[50]

In the letters of Boniface we find the last instances of the late-antique *propria manu* formula. A letter of Bishop Lul, Boniface's successor, to Bishop Gregory of Utrecht includes the notice: 'I have added this in my own hand: Observe what has been ordered and you will be saved'.[51] A letter of Bishop Daniel of Winchester to Boniface ends: 'Vale vale centupliciter carissime mihi et alia manu.'[52] Here it seems that the copyist misplaced *et alia manu*, which originally identified an autograph *subscriptio* of Daniel with its hundredfold greeting. St Bernard also regarded a personal note at the end of a letter which he had dictated as a sign of affection. 'I dictated these things but I wanted you to recognize my love by a handwriting known to you.'[53] Both Cicero and St Paul would have shared this feeling.

Braubach zum 10 April 1964, ed. K. Repgen and S. Skalweit (Munster, 1964), pp. 141–70. Cf. *Gli autografi medievali: problemi paleografici e filologici*, ed. P. Chiesa and L. Pinelli (Spoleto, 1994), esp. J. Hamesse, 'Les autographs à l'époque scholastique' (pp. 179–205) which provides a full account of medieval terminology for autographs.

[47] *Epistolario de S. Braulio de Zaragoza*, ed. J. Madoz (Madrid, 1951), Ep. III and IV, VI, VIII (pp. 78, 79, 88, 89).

[48] *Epistulae Sancti Desiderii Cadurencsis*, ed. D. Norberg (Stockholm, 1961), Ep. 1, 2, p. 12.

[49] 'incolomes vos dominus custodire et heredes regni sui praeparare dignetur', *Vita Desiderii, cap.* 10, MGH, Scriptores Rerum Merovingicarum, 4 (1902), 540. Bishop Leodegar of Autun included an autograph 'amen' in a prayer in a letter to his mother: 'Sanctus Christopherus martyr inclytus sit pro te intercessor assiduus. Amen'. The 'Amen' was copied in Uncials in one manuscript, see MGH, Epistolae III, *Epistolae Merowingici et Karolini aevi*, 1 (1892), p. 467.

[50] Sulpicius of Bourges to Desiderius, '(Istud manu propria fecit) aeternis temporibus vestrae gratiae servire merear, mihi particularis domine' (*Epistulae S. Desiderii*, ed. Norberg, Ep. 2, 1, p. 42); for discussion see ibid., p. 73.

[51] 'Propria manu subscripsi haec: Observa quae precipiuntur et salvus eris', MGH, Epistolae selectae I, *Die Briefe des heiligen Bonifatius und Lullius*, ed. M. Tangl (1916, repr. 1955), Ep. 92, p. 212. For *propria manu* in royal charters cf. Bresslau, *Handbuch*, II, 163–70.

[52] *Bonifatius*, ed. Tangl, Ep. 64, p. 136.

[53] 'Haec ipse dictavi, sic me habens, ut per notam vobis manum agnoscatis affectum. Verumtamen rescripsisse, quam scripsisse maluerim' (*PL*, **182**, 514).

One of Bernard's secretaries, Nicholas of Montiéramey, was accused of forging letters in Bernard's name. His subsequent career supplies other instances of how handwriting was studied, and when the author of a letter copied out all of its text. Bishop Arnulph of Lisieux in his letter 66 written to Nicholas *c.*1170 explained that he had received letters supposedly from Henry the Liberal, count of Champagne, which he believed to have been composed by Nicholas.[54] He based this conclusion largely on his recognition of the letter forms which he compared with those in other letters in Nicholas's hand:

> The letters are full of that style of your learning and the letter forms are like those which I lately received from your holiness; and to me they reveal the identity of the hand with reliable evidence.[55]

Arnulph was also aware of earlier alleged frauds by Nicholas. Comparing letter forms was the standard test for forgery in Roman law.[56]

Nicholas himself wrote letters to Peter of Celle which include statements that they were autograph. Nicholas explains that he copied the letter himself lest it come to the eyes of others: 'Close this letter for your own eyes and those of your staff. I wrote it with my own hands so that it would not be seen by other people.'[57] A later letter in the same correspondence again requests confidentiality:

> Conceal this letter from everyone but you and your Thomas, and don't lead me into the open . . . For that reason I wrote it with my own hands while I was worn out with a headache. I didn't even show it to the most familiar of my familiars in case I might arouse suspicion.[58]

---

[54] On Nicholas of Montiéramey, see G. Constable, *The Letters of Peter the Venerable* (Harvard, 1967), App. P, II, 316–30, and J. F. Benton, 'The Court of Champagne as a Literary Center', *Speculum*, 36 (1961), 555–7. Nicholas's own letters emphasize that dead letters cannot convey his feelings (see *PL*, 196, cols. 1597, 1606, 1648, 1652).

[55] 'Porro littere ille stilum vestre peritie redolebant, apicesque his, quos noviter a vestra sanctitate recepi, identitatem manus michi certis indiciis penitus expresserunt.' *The Letters of Arnulf of Lisieux*, ed. F. Barlow, Camden Society, 3rd ser., 61 (London, 1939), no. 66, p. 117.

[56] See *Codex Theodosianus*, 2, 27, 1, *Theodosiani libri*, ed. Mommsen and Meyer, I, 117–19. The procedure is discussed most fully in a capitulary of Charlemagne (MGH, Capitularia Regum Francorum (1883, repr. 1960), I, 215, c. 7) where at least two other charters are to be compared. For the fullest account of the palaeographical examination of medieval charters see H. U. Kantorowicz, 'Schriftvergleichung und Urkundenfalschung. Beitrag zur Geschichte der Diplomatik im Mittelalter', *Quellen und Forschungen aus Italienischen Archiven und Bibliotheken*, 9 (1906), 38–56.

[57] 'Claudite epistolam hanc vestris et vestrorum oculis:quam idcirco propriis manibus exaravi, ne in oculis aliorum incideret.' *PL*, 202, 479, cf. *PL*, 202, 494. On Peter, cf. Benton, 'Court of Champagne', pp. 557–8.

[58] 'Claude epistolam nisi tibi et Thomae tuo, nec me perducas in publicum . . . Propterea enim haec propriis manibus scripsi cum nimia vertigine capitis fatigarer. Nec etiam familiarissimos familiarium meorum admisi, ne forte vel ad curiositatem vel ad suspicionem juveniles et ferventes animos mutarem' (*PL*, 202, 505).

Writing a personal letter oneself concealed private business from unreliable secretaries. For reasons of confidentiality the autograph signature, rather than the signature of a secretary, might prove essential in official correspondence. The most telling instance is the letter sent by Edward III to Pope John XXII, copied by Richard de Bury. The pope had wished to have a private sign by which he might know which of the king's requests were to be taken as coming from the king's heart and which might be disregarded. This letter is signed by Edward III with a motto *Pater sancte* in the king's own handwriting, which was to be used on all requests from the heart.[59]

In his treatise on the Trinity, Anselm of Havelburg (d. 1158), gives a full account of the process of moving from deciphering letters to understanding.

> Visible forms of letters are formed visibly on visible parchment and silently they speak and speaking they are silent, and again by the same visible forms of letters an invisible understanding is formed in the mind of the reader.[60]

The process of 'invisible understanding' is more than mere 'silent speech', and Anselm's formulation expresses a new attitude to the perception of writing. As written words were regarded as something other than speech, discussion of handwriting explored its individual and personal features.

A few medieval texts give an account of the experience of reading a letter from a friend. The teacher Goswin wrote to his former pupil Walcher at Liège, probably between 1066 and 1070 explaining how the poor letter forms of Walcher's letter would once have been punished:

> In earnest my mind rejoices . . . for I once would have beaten you for your poorly made letters and the other things of that kind by which tender age sins just as I thought . . . the wealth of leaves on our trees an excess but now rejoice in its increase and fruit.[61]

Medieval romances record the special pleasure of receiving an autograph letter from the beloved. Iseult felt comforted to have a letter from Tristan.[62] When Tristan accused Iseult of loving Kehedin he regarded apparent autograph letters as an

[59] *The Liber Epistolaris of Richard de Bury*, ed. N. Denholm-Young, Roxburghe Club (Oxford, 1950), pl. 1. Edward characterizes the letters as 'os quelles soyent escrites cestes paroles de nostre main'. I owe this reference to Pamela Robinson.

[60] 'Formantur etiam visibiliter visibiles litterarum apices in visibili membrana, et tacendo loquuntur et loquendo tacent. Et rursus per eosdem apices visibiles formatur invisibilis intellectus in anima legentis' (*PL*, **188**, 1187).

[61] 'Serio vero triumphat animus, quod rudes articulos tuos aliquando ipse manu mea ad scribendum direxerim quod que male tornatos apices ceteraque id genus quae tenera peccat aetas super dorsum tuum cuderim, ut scilicet de arbuscula nostra putans superfluum mergitum et foliorum luxuriem, postmodo de cremento et fructu eius gauderem', *Goswinus epistola*, CCCM, 62 (Turnhout, 1975), 11.

[62] 'Qe porrai penser ne dire quant je celui ne puis avoir qi cest brief escrist de ces propres mains? Nul reconfort ne me vausist tant.' See E. P. Ruhe, *De Amasio ad Amasiam: zur Gattungsgeschichte des mittelalterlichen Liebesbriefes* (Munich, 1975), p. 350.

aggravation of her offence.[63] In Wolfram von Eschenbach's *Parzival* (composed *c.*1210) Gawain sent a letter to Arthur's queen Ginover who recognized his handwriting when the letter was brought to her by a messenger.

> He gave her the letter and she examined the script; she recognized it immediately before the servant who was kneeling there could name his master. The queen spoke to the letter: 'Well the hand that wrote you!'[64]

There are classical analogies for such associations in Ovid's *Heroides*, fictitious verse letters from great lovers in legend and Antiquity. *Heroides* XV opens with the lover's speculation about whether her handwriting will be recognized.

> Tell me when you looked at the letters of my eager right hand, did your eye know instantly whose they were? Or unless you had read their author's name, Sappho, would you fail to know from where these brief words come?[65]

Petrarch recognized individual handwriting: 'I wish I could think that the complaints in your letter were someone else's; instead the writing gave evidence that they were written by your own fingers.'[66] The correspondence of Petrarch provides detailed accounts of how Petrarch assumes that some of his friends will recognize his handwriting, and frequent apologies for the quality of that handwriting. He gave the first explanation of the circumstances which produced his poor handwriting:

> I might add that, if this rather uncultivated writing of mine offends your eyes, accustomed to artificial and contrived lettering, you must blame a broken country seat, thick ink, rough paper, and a rural pen. I do however ask for forgiveness; may your politeness have pity on my fingers.[67]

---

[63] *Le Roman de Tristan*, 3, ed. R. L. Curtis (Woodbridge, 1985), p. 143: 'Vez ci le brief, vez ci les lettres que vos feistes de vos mains et le madastes à Kehedin.'

[64] *Parzival*, bk 13, 644, 27–30:
einen brief si nam ûz sîner hant
dar an sie geschriben vant
schrift, die si bekante
ê sînen hêrren nante
Der knappe den si knien dâ sach.
diu kunegin zem brieve sprach
ôwol der hant diu dich schreip!

[65] Ecquid ut adspecta est studiose littera dextrae
Protinus est oculis cognita nostra tuis
an nisi legisses auctoris nominis Sapphus
hoc breve nescires unde movetur opus?
(Ovid's authorship of this poem has been questioned.)

[66] 'et non propriis tuis digitis querulum illud cyrographum constaret' (*Epistolae ad familiares*, II, 6 to Giovanni Colonna), F. Petrarca, *Le Familiari*, I–III ed. V. Rossi, IV ed. V. Rossi and U. Bosco (Florence, 1933–42), 1 (1933), 82; cf. 'amici digitum et anulum nosti, intactas abicere amor et verecundia non sinent'.(*Ep. fam.*, III, 20 to Lello di Pietro Stefano dei Tosetti), ibid. p. 145.

[67] 'Reliquum est ut si oculos tuos artificiosis literarum tractibus assuetos scriptura incultior offendit,

Another letter conveys an elaborate response to the personality of handwriting:

> Your letter, written in haste and on the spur of the moment, was nevertheless pleasing to my eyes and mind, indeed even more so; its appearance was like that of a rather disheveled woman to her eager lover . . . It bore witness to its hasty stuffing into an everyday dress and to its command to come to me in that fashion, as you were rising from dinner, with Ceres and Bacchus struggling within you, to use your joking phrase. Yet its style revealed a sober and fasting author.[68]

On another occasion he wrote: 'I admit that it would be proper to recopy this but let my weakness and affairs and the weariness of the flies excuse me. You will receive the additions and erasures as signs of familiarity and whatever faults you find, in writing or in style, I have no doubt you will take in good part.'[69] Petrucci has written of how Petrarch's letters display 'una vasta esperienza del fatto grafico'.[70]

Erasmus in his *De recta Latini Graecique sermonis pronuntiatione dialogus* is eloquent about the nature of our response to a letter in handwriting which we recognize:

> Not to mention how much a hand that is recognized contributes either to confidence or to pleasure as the case may be. It is significant that the apostle Paul penned his letter to the Galatians entirely in his own hand. Who would not respect a king who dispatches a letter that he himself has written. How warmly we respond whenever we receive from friends or scholars letters written in their own hands! We feel as if we were listening to them or seeing them face to face . . . A man's handwriting, like his voice, has a special, individual quality (*Habet enim singularum ut vox ita manus quoque quiddam suum et peculiare*).[71]

Erasmus frequently ended his autograph letters with the phrase 'You will recognize the hand of your friend',[72] sometimes with more (or less) confidence. In the last year of his life he wrote: 'I have affixed my seal, because some people have begun to

---

montanum claudicans sedile et concretum atramentum et palustris papirus et pastoralis calamus culpentur.' *Ep. fam.*, XIII, 4 (ibid., 3 (1937), 65).

[68] 'Tumultuariam et festinatam epystolam tuam legi, que non minus ideo grata oculis meis atque animo, sed prope gratior fuit; talis illa michi qualis amanti cupido incomptior amica . . . Ipsa se forte, dum a prandio consurgis, Cerere, ut iocando ais, Liberoque certantibus, raptim quotidiana veste suffarcinatam et sic ad me venire iussam affirmabat.' *Ep. fam.*, XVIII, 7 to Francesco of the Church of the Holy Apostles (ibid., p. 285).

[69] 'Erat urbanum, fateor, hanc rescribere, sed fragilitas et occupatio et muscarum tedia excusent. Tu additiones et lituras quasi signa familiaritatis/accipies et quicquid aut in scriptura vitii erit, aut in stilo, boni consules et in meliorem omnia partem trahes, non sum dubius.' (*Ep. seniles*, XII, 1), dated July 1370, *Francesco Petrarca, Epistole Autografe*, ed. A. Petrucci (Padua, 1968), p. 51 and pl. XVII.

[70] A. Petrucci, *La Scrittura di Francesco Petrarca*, Studi e testi, 248 (Vatican, 1967), p. 62.

[71] *Collected Works of Erasmus*, 26, ed. J. K. Sowards (Toronto, 1985), p. 391. Latin text ed. J. Kramer, Beiträge zur Klassischen Philologie, 98 (Meisenheim, 1978), p. 52.

[72] Ep. 1603 to Pirckheimer, 28 August 1525, *Collected Works of Erasmus*, 11, ed. A. Dalzell (Toronto, 1994), p. 257.

imitate my handwriting, so successfully that forgery can scarcely be detected. Erasmus of Rotterdam, with my own hand.'[73] Like Cicero, he assumed his autographs would be valued for their author's sake: 'Even though I am overwhelmed rather than occupied with work yet I am sending you an autograph letter for I assume that it would be dearer to you.'[74]

However, this fuller discussion of the warmth of feeling with which an autograph letter was received comes at a time when the scripts which were required for letters were expected to differ according to the status of the recipient. Since the late thirteenth century it had been assumed that a letter writer needed to be a master of at least three different scripts, suited to different types of letter.[75] The Swiss *scholasticus* at the cathedral of Zurich, Konrad von Mure, in his *Summa de arte prosandi* written in 1275, had discussed the appropriate script for letters in a chapter *De Forma carte et scriptura*.[76]

In 1599 the great Dutch writing master Jan van der Velde affirmed that a writing master must teach a range of scripts:

> Pareillement il ne suffit pas aussi à un Maistre de Plume, de scavoir escrire simplement une main ou deux, ains faut necessairement qu'il en sache plusieurs divers sortes, pour en satisfaire a tous venants, tant des lettres curieuses et mignardes, que les hommes les affecteront diversement, comme nous voyons que l'un veut une lettre Italique ou Espaignole, et l'autre une lettre d'Estat ou Marchande.[77]

In 1579 the Italian writing master Giovanni Cresci had made the same point: 'Now it is not right that one should have to use the same script for privileges as is employed in ordinary correspondence. And even in correspondence, it is no more necessary to cling always to the same script.'[78]

So the individual quality which Erasmus admired in a man's handwriting must also be seen within the context of mastery of a hierarchy of scripts. Edmund Spenser signed a letter he had written in Secretary script with an Italic signature, and other

---

[73] Ep. 3028 (dating to 1535), in *Erasmi epistolae*, ed. P. S. Allen, 6 (Oxford, 1947), p. 145.

[74] Dedicatory letter to Maximilian of Burgundy, cf. Latin text in Kramer's edn (as n. 71 above), p. 2.

[75] 'There are many male and female scribes who can form letters well or adequately in quires, but scarcely any know how to train their hand to writing letters. So we can say that in letters a good, better and best hand is needed. The good hand writes legibly and with good spelling, legal sententiae need a better hand, but for indulgences, privileges, confirmations and decrees the best hand is needed' (cf. *Konrad von Mure, Summa de arte prosandi*, ed. W. Kronbichler (Zurich, 1968), p. 64. For the range of documents in medieval formularies cf. *Liber Epistolaris*, ed. Denholm-Young.

[76] 'Scriptura littere regulis orthographie observatis una manu et eadem sine omni vitio rasure in loco suspecto . . . ductu scribatur lineali, grossetur legibiliter, comprimatur, ut nec sit nimium sparsa, nec nimium compressa, nec deformis, set correcta et equalis' (p. 62).

[77] Jan van den Velde, *Lettre defensive, pour l'art de bien escrire* (Rotterdam, 1599).

[78] G. F. Cresci, *Il perfetto cancelleresco corsivo* (Roma, 1579), as tr. A. S. Osley, *Scribes and Sources: a Handbook of the Chancery Hand in the Sixteenth Century* (London, 1980), p. 119.

contemporaries observed the convention of using Italic for Latin and Secretary for the vernacular in correspondence.[79] The use of two or more scripts by one individual writer was commonplace throughout the sixteenth century in England. And, as Greg pointed out, the playwright Thomas Dekker (1570?–1632) 'wrote two, or really three, distinct hands' (i.e. different scripts).[80] Writing masters, as we have seen, not only prided themselves on the range of scripts which they could teach but also aspired to a discipline in which every pupil would attain an identical quality of handwriting in each script. In 1628 the Scots writing master David Browne worried that if everyone learned to write in the same way it would 'make the Subscription of Evidence doubtfull'.[81] Cresci had earlier recognized that individual personality meant that such uniformity would not be attained.

> Men's hands do not all possess the same natural constitution; it happens that one
> is suited to writing with or without flourishes, while another man who has less of
> a gift for the profession of writing will succeed only at one kind of chancery style
> – one without flourishes, as this is easier.[82]

The professional writing master finds personality in the choice of an appropriate script which corresponds to the individual's capacities.

The hand did not authenticate a document: in France the signature was only required as a means of authentication after the Ordonnance de Fontainbleau, 1554, which decreed that all contracts, obligations, receipts and private acts must be signed by consenting parties.[83] (Earlier notaries had used a sign manual rather than a signature, and these were often drawn as punning rebuses upon the notaries' names.[84])

Paintings which include depictions of letters, and the use of signatures on pictures, offer additional evidence for attitudes to individual handwriting. Artists originally signed pictures painted for export in order to authenticate them, as when Konrad Witz, working in Basel, signed an altarpiece painted for Geneva: 'Hoc opus pinxit

---

[79] A. G. Petti, *English Literary Hands from Chaucer to Dryden* (Cambridge, 1977), p. 19. W. W. Greg ('Derby his Hand and Soul', *The Library*, 4th ser., 7 (1926–7), 39–45) discusses the problem of identifying an individual hand amid English and Italian scripts.

[80] W. W. Greg, *English Literary Autographs*, 3 (Oxford, 1932), no. 9.

[81] David Browne, *The New Invention, Intituled Calligraphia: or, the Arte of Faire Writing* (St Andrews, 1622), p. 188.

[82] *Il perfetto cancellaresco corsivo*, tr. Osley, *Scribes and Sources*, p. 119.

[83] See A. Giry, *Manuel de Diplomatique* (Paris, 1894), p. 610; B. Fraenkel, *La signature genèse d'un signe* (Paris, 1992), pp. 24–5. The edict was renewed in 1560, 1572, 1579 and during the French Revolution.

[84] Ibid., p. 10. For more facs. of these sign manuals see M.-C. Guigue, *De l'origine de la signature et de son emploi au Moyen Age* (Paris, 1863).

magister conradus sapientis de basilea 1444.' Frequently the artist gives his place of origin: 'Hanssen muoltscheren vo richehofe' (1437) for a sculpture by Hans Multscher.[85] Jan van Eyck regarded his signature on his paintings as a form of attestation; calligraphic signatures by Van Eyck in a Bastarda script are found on paintings dated between 1432 and 1440, sometimes accompanied by his device 'Als ich Can' which affirmed his mastery.[86] Petrus Christus also signed his paintings in a calligraphic script, sometimes on a *trompe-l'oeil* frame.[87]

Albrecht Dürer seems to have been the first artist to monogram not only paintings and engravings, but also his sketches. The artist's sign establishes the right of property in the engraving. The records of a Venetian lawsuit clarify how this sign was understood. Marcantonio Raimondi had produced a pirated edition of the woodcut series 'The Life of the Virgin and The Great Passion', complete with Dürer's monogram. The Signoria in Venice decided 'that Marc' Antonio should no longer use the name or the above mentioned signature [the monogram] of Albrecht in his work'.[88] In 1512 the Nuremburg council decreed that a

> foreigner, who sold prints before the town hall, some with Albrecht Dürer's monogram that were fraudulently copied from him, shall be bound by oath to remove all the said monograms and sell none of them here, and if he refuses, all his said prints shall be confiscated as counterfeit [*ain falsch*] and taken into the hands of the council.[89]

J. L. Koerner comments: 'If we follow a medieval definition of counterfeiting as "making something appear other than it is", then the only thing that is truly Dürer's, and that can be protected as such, is his name, or better, what is criminal about replicating the monogram is the false appearance the copy conveys that it is the immediate product of Dürer's hand.'[90] While Van Eyck and Christus regarded the signature as a statement of achievement, Dürer enforced his right to his monogram as the proof of authenticity of his works. Dürer brings us into a world in which the

---

[85] M. Baxandall, *The Limewood Sculptors of Renaissance Germany* (New Haven, 1980), p. 245, cf. pp. 120–21.

[86] R. W. Scheller, 'Als Ich Can', *Oud-Holland*, 83 (1968), 135–9. The most celebrated signature is the inscription 'Johannes van Eyck fuit hic' above the mirror on the Arnolfini portrait in the National Gallery in London.

[87] See M. W. Ainsworth, *Petrus Christus Renaissance Master of Bruges* (New York, 1994), pp. 27–33. I am grateful to James Marrow for discussion of artists' signatures; the best introduction to the medieval evidence is P. C. Clausen, 'Kunstlerinschriften', in *Ornamenta Ecclesiae: Kunst und Kultur der Romanik*, 1, ed. A. Legner (Cologne, 1985), pp. 263–76. (Painted autograph letters bearing the artists' signatures are found held by the subjects of portraits by Titian, Velazquez and Goya, among others (illust. in *Revue de l'art*, 26 (1974), 38).

[88] See J. L. Koerner, *The Moment of Self-Portraiture in German Renaissance Art* (Chicago, 1993), p. 209 (quoting Vasari).

[89] Ibid., p. 209 and n. 35.

[90] Ibid.

scribal signature has lost many of its earlier features. His engravings can be so successfully imitated that they lack a 'personal' style, and his signature (or monogram) can also be imitated. Only by enforcing rights to a mechanically reproduced monogram could Dürer exclude others from his share of the market for his work.

One of the earliest, realistic, painted depictions of specific handwriting which is not the artist's handwriting is found on a letter held by the Venetian ambassador to London, Marco Barbarigo, in a portrait attributed to the school of Van Eyck, now in the National Gallery, London. The ambassador holds a letter addressed to him in London from his brother Franciscus, who was Procurator of Venice, and is so described on his letter.[91] Presumably the London based artist chose (or was commissioned) to depict an authentic letter.

Barbarigo's portrait is comparable to the celebrated double portrait of Erasmus and Pieter Gilles, by Quinten Metsys, sent as a gift to Thomas More in September 1517.[92] Erasmus is shown copying the opening of his *Paraphrasis* of St Paul's Epistle to the Romans, and Julian Brown has affirmed that 'those words are written in a close imitation of Erasmus' own hand. He holds the reed pen he insisted on using'. In the companion portrait Pieter Gilles is shown holding a letter from More, and while the painting is now so overpainted that the handwriting cannot be identified, earlier transcriptions read: 'Viro Illustrissimo Petro Egidio Amico charissimo Atverpias.' The portrait is exceptionally well documented, and so is More's reaction to the handwriting. He wrote to Gilles:

> My dear Pieter, marvellously as our Quinten has represented everything, it shows above all what a wonderful forger he would have made! He has imitated the address on my letter to you so well that I do not believe I could make a better job if I tried to repeat the original inscription myself. And so, unless he wants it for some purpose of his own, or you are keeping it for your own ends, do please let me have the letter back: it will double the effect if it is kept handy alongside the picture. If it has been lost, or if you have a use for it, I will see whether I in my turn can imitate the man who imitates my hand so well.[93]

More is responding to a world in which the skilled artist, or the accomplished secretary, can imitate faithfully, and he raises questions of authenticity which seem close to our own worries about identity.

In 1523 Holbein painted Erasmus writing the paraphrase on St Mark in a painting now in the Louvre, of which there is a copy in Basle. Holbein's sketches of Erasmus' hands survive. In the sketches the right hand holds a pen, but there is no attempt to reproduce any writing, so for the painting presumably Holbein had access to text

---

[91] M. Davies, *The National Gallery, Early Netherlandish School* (London, 1968), pp. 56–7.

[92] L. Campbell, M. Mann, H. Schute Herbruggen and J. B. Trapp, 'Quentin Matsys, Desiderius Erasmus, Pieter Gillis and Thomas More', *Burlington Magazine*, 120 (1978), 716–24.

[93] More's letter is included in Erasmus' Ep. 684, see *Erasmi epistolae*, ed. P. S. Allen, 3 (Oxford 1913), p. 107. Cf. Erasmus' worries about forgery of his handwriting in Ep. 3028.

written by Erasmus.[94] As in Metsys's picture, the handwriting of Erasmus was regarded as authenticating the portrait by adding to its verisimilitude. Comparable fidelity in the depiction of an individual's handwriting for the sake of verisimilitude is seen in the portrait of a merchant, perhaps to be identified with Jerome Sandelin, by Jan Gossart in the National Gallery, Washington, dating c.1530.[95] On the wall behind him hang two large bundles of documents. The left-hand group has a cover sheet with the caption 'Alrehande Missiven' and the right-hand pile has a sheet with the caption 'Alrehande Minuten'. The merchant has his left hand on a ledger, and with his right hand he is writing on a sheet resting on a folded quire. Similar realistic representation of legible scripts is found in the series of paintings attributed to Marinus van Reymersvaele. One, in the National Gallery, London (c.1540) shows two officials apparently using the tax registers of Reymersvaele. A second group of paintings, depicting the calling of Matthew, shows a tax collector's office with tax returns.[96] A third painting, now in New Orleans, shows two lawyers in an office full of legible documents in different handwriting.

Some individual hands lacked the craft which a writing master might strive to teach, and a secretary strive to imitate. Their differences could be celebrated as distinctive signs of individuality. Montaigne described how he wrote letters.

> J'escris mes lettres tousjours en poste, et si précipiteusement que, quoy que je peigne insupportablement mal, j'ayme mieux escrire de ma main que d'y en employer un'autre, car je n'en trouve poinct qui me puisse suyvre, et ne les transcris jamais. J'ay accoustumé les grands qui me conoissent, à y supporter des litures et des trasseures, et un papier sans plieure et sans marge.[97]

Montaigne, 'the first modern man in his intense awareness of and passionate interest in the individuality of himself and of all other human beings', recorded the details of his bad handwriting in an essay on style which started from Cicero.[98] Racine, in a letter of 4 October 1692 to his son Jean Baptiste, knew that we recognize the handwriting of our intimates, and therefore charged him to 'leave out all the ceremonial of "Your humble servant". I even know your handwriting well enough for you not to be obliged to include your name.'[99] The loving father sees individual identity in handwriting: identity and style have fused. Our notion of character rightly

---

[94] E. Foucart Walter, *Les peintures de Hans Holbein le jeune au Louvre* (Paris, 1985).

[95] J. O. Hand and M. Wolff, *Early Netherlandish Painting* (National Gallery of Art, Washington, DC, 1986), pp. 103–7.

[96] Davies, *Early Netherlandish School*, pp. 82–5. This was a popular subject of paintings by Reymersvaele, cf. L. Campbell, *The Early Flemish Pictures in the Collection of Her Majesty the Queen* (Cambridge, 1985), pp. 114–18.

[97] *Essais*, I, 40 (ed. P. Villey (Paris, 1965), p. 253).

[98] The description of Montaigne is from Leonard Woolf's *The Journey not the Arrival Matters* (London, 1969), p. 19.

[99] 'Quand vous m'écrivez, vous pouvez vous dispenser de toutes ces cérémonies de Votre très

affirms that the features of a line of writing express the features of personality. 'Charactering precepts', as Polonius would have us remember, has been Malcolm Parkes's distinctive contribution to palaeography.

Postscript: collecting autographs

There is literary evidence for autograph collecting in Antiquity. The elder Pliny records having seen autographs of the Gracchi, Cicero and Virgil.[100] Aulus Gellius claimed to have seen works of Cicero copied by his slave Tiro,[101] and the autograph of *Aeneid*, Book II[102] as well as a copy of Ennius corrected by the grammarian Lampadio.[103] Fronto speaks of the value conferred on a manuscript written in Lampadio's or Tiro's hand.[104] Quintilian discussed the spelling of Cicero and Virgil on the basis of supposedly autograph manuscripts.[105] Possidius, Augustine's biographer, recorded that the church at Hippo preserved a quire which Augustine had written in his own hand.[106]

Surviving manuscripts regarded in the Middle Ages as autographs of Bede include: a Northumbrian Gospel book (Durham, Dean and Chapter Library, MS A.II.16), described as *Quattuor Evangelia de manu Bedae* in the 1391 catalogue; a glossed manuscript of the Pauline Epistles (Cambridge, Trinity College, MS B.10.5 (216)); and an abridgement of Cassiodorus on the Psalms (Durham, Dean and Chapter Library, MS B.II.30) similarly ascribed *de manu Bedae*.[107] The autograph manuscripts of personalities were prized in the twelfth century. Orderic Vitalis noted the manuscripts copied by Theoderic of Jumièges, abbot of Saint Evroul.[108] The life of Hildegard of Bingen records that she wrote the accounts of her visions in her own hand.[109]

---

humble serviteur. Je connais même assez bien votre écriture sans que vous soyez obligé de mettre votre nom' (*Oeuvres completes*, ed. P. Clarac (Paris, 1962), p. 548).

[100] Pliny, *Historia naturalis*, XIII, 83.

[101] Aulus Gellius, *Noctes Attici*, I, 7; XIII, 21. Cf. J. Zetzl, 'Emendavi ad Tironem', *Harvard Studies in Classical Philology*, 77 (1973), 227–45. See also M. McDonnell, 'Writing, Copying, and Autograph Manuscripts in Ancient Rome', *Classical Quarterly*, 46 (1996), 469–91.

[102] Gellius, *Noctes Attici*, IX, 14, 7.

[103] Ibid., XVIII, 5, 11; cf. L. Holford Strevens, *Aulus Gellius* (London, 1988), pp. 139–41.

[104] Fronto, *Ad M. Caesarem*, I, 7, 4.

[105] Quintilian, *De institutione oratoria*, I, 7, 20.

[106] 'Quaternio unus quam propria manu sanctus episcopus Augustinus initiavit', *Indiculus*, X, no. 15; see E. Dekkers, 'Les autographes des pères latins', *Colligere fragmenta: Festschrift Alban Dold* (Beuron, 1952), pp. 127–39.

[107] For all these see *Catalogi veteres librorum ecclesiae cathedralis Dunelmensis*, ed. J. Raine, Surtees Society, 7 (1838), 16, 18.

[108] The books are listed in *Ecclesiastical History of Orderic Vitalis*, ed. M. Chibnall (Oxford, 1969–80), III, 48, and mentioned in Orderic's epitaph (ibid., VI, 336). Guibert of Nogent notes that he wrote his commentary on Hosea, Amos and Lamentations himself (see *PL*, 156, 340).

[109] 'manu propria scripsit, et ore edidit' (*PL*, 197, 101). Cf. the account of how St Euphraxia wrote a

Autographs recovered their textual importance in the Renaissance. Humanist scholars consulted the autographs of Petrarch's poems; Niccolo Niccoli transcribed the *Africa* from an autograph manuscript in Padua, and a copy of the *Canzoniere* in the Vatican has a colophon saying that it was collated with the original autograph.[110] Pietro Bembo owned Petrarch's autograph of *Canzoniere* and Poggio's transcript of the *De Legibus*.[111] But the development of extensive autograph collections seems to have started in the seventeenth century and the fullest discussion of a collection is Goethe's.[112] His collection of autographs numbered 1,862 items (the earliest dating from 1552) and included autographs of Beethoven, Davy, Euler, Haydn, Hegel, Kant, Melanchton, Mozart, Nelson and Washington.[113] His reflections on the power of the autograph are perhaps views we share: 'For since visual experience is indispensable for me, remarkable men are made present to me in a magical way through their handwriting.'

---

letter in her own hand, in the seventh-century Latin tr. of the fifth-century Greek *Vita S. Euphrasia* (*PL*, 73, 629).

[110] Vatican, Bibl. apost., MS Vat. lat. 4786 is a copy of Petrarch's *Canzoniere* with a colophon saying 'sumpte dal originale del Petrarcha e con quello fedelmente scontrate'.

[111] See C. H. Clough, 'The Library of Bernardo and Pietro Bembo', *The Book Collector*, 33 (1984), 305–31. For Bembo's interest in Petrarch autographs see *P. Bembo, Lettre*, ed. E. Trari, 2 (Bologna, 1990), no. 911, p. 545, and *Lettre*, 4 (Bologna, 1993), nos 2220, 2246 (pp. 333, 506–7).

[112] 'denn da mir die sinnliche Anschauung durchaus unentbehrlich ist, so werden mir vorzügliche Menschen durch ihre Handschrift auf eine magische Weise vergegenwärtigt'. Letter to Jacobi, 27 April 1806. (Goethe was influenced by the Physiognomy of Lavater.)

[113] H.-J. Schreckenbach, *Goethes Autographensammlung Katalog* (Weimar, 1961). I am deeply grateful to Rivkah Zim for her expert editing and amending of this essay.

A Bibliography of the Published Writings of M. B. Parkes

Rivkah Zim

Items marked * are reprinted in *Scribes, Scripts and Readers* (1991).

1955
'Manuscript fragments of English Sermons Attributed to John Wyclif', *Medium Ævum*, 24 (1955), 97–100.

1958
A Provisional Handlist of the Principal Records of the Vicar-General's Office [Province of Canterbury], [London, Lambeth Palace Library, 1958], 13 pp. [typescript].

Guide to the Records of the Faculty Office [Province of Canterbury], [London, Lambeth Palace Library, 1958], 10 pp. [typescript].

*'Fragments of Medieval Manuscripts', App. 1 in *Guide to the Kent County Archives Office*, prepared by Felix Hull (Maidstone, Kent County Council, 1958), pp. 227–30.

1961
*'A Fifteenth-Century Scribe: Henry Mere', *Bodleian Library Record*, 6 (1957–61), 654–9, + 2 pls.

Review: Istvan Hajnal, *L'Enseignement de l'écriture aux universités médiévales*, 2nd edn, revised and added to by Laszlo Mezey (Budapest, 1959), *Medium Ævum*, 30 (1961), 61–4.

1962
Review: *Catalogue des manuscrits en écriture latine portant des indications de date, de lieu, ou de copiste*, ed. C. Samaran and R. Marichal, 1 (Paris, 1959), *English Historical Review*, 77 (1962), 129–30.

1965
'The Manuscript Collections of Keble College', *Keble College Record* (1965), 8–11 [unsigned].

1969

English Cursive Book Hands 1250–1500, Oxford Palaeographical Handbooks (Oxford, Clarendon Press, 1969).

1972

*'The Manuscript of the Leiden Riddle', *ASE*, 1 (1972), 202–17, + 1 pl.

1973

*'The Literacy of the Laity', in *Literature and Western Civilization: the Medieval World*, ed. David Daiches and Anthony Thorlby (London, Aldus Books, 1973), pp. 555–77.

1976

*'The Influence of the Concepts of *Ordinatio* and *Compilatio* on the Development of the Book', in *Medieval Learning and Literature: Essays Presented to Richard William Hunt*, ed. J. J. G. Alexander and M. T. Gibson (Oxford, Clarendon Press, 1976), pp. 115–41, + 8 pls.

*'The Palaeography of the Parker Manuscript of the *Chronicle*, Laws and Sedulius, and Historiography at Winchester in the Late Ninth and Tenth Centuries', *ASE*, 5 (1976), 149–71, + 3 pls.

*'The Handwriting of St Boniface: A Reassessment of the Problems', *Beiträge zur Geschichte der deutschen Sprache und Literatur*, 98. Band, 2. Heft (1976), 161–79, + 13 pls.

1978

'Palaeographical Description and Commentary', in *Geoffrey Chaucer, Troilus and Criseyde: a Facsimile of Corpus Christi College Cambridge MS 61, with Introductions by M. B. Parkes and Elizabeth Salter* (Cambridge, D. S. Brewer, 1978), pp. 1–13.

'Punctuation, or Pause and Effect', in *Medieval Eloquence: Studies in the Theory and Practice of Medieval Rhetoric*, ed. James J. Murphy (Berkeley, Los Angeles, London, University of California Press, 1978), pp. 127–42.

[with Andrew G. Watson], *Medieval Scribes, Manuscripts and Libraries: Essays Presented to N. R. Ker*, ed. M. B. Parkes and Andrew G. Watson (London, Scolar Press, 1978).

[with A. I. Doyle], 'The Production of Copies of the *Canterbury Tales* and the *Confessio Amantis* in the Early Fifteenth Century', in *Medieval Scribes, Manuscripts and Libraries*, pp. 163–210.

1979

[with A. I. Doyle], 'Palaeographical Introduction', in *Geoffrey Chaucer, The Canterbury Tales: a Facsimile and Transcription of the Hengwrt Manuscript* [Aberystwyth,

National Library of Wales, MS Peniarth 392], *with Variants from the Ellesmere Manuscript*, ed. Paul G. Ruggiers with introductions by Donald C. Baker and by A. I. Doyle and M. B. Parkes, A Variorum Edition of the Works of Geoffrey Chaucer, 1 (Norman, University of Oklahoma Press and Folkestone, Wm Dawson and Sons, 1979), pp. xix–xlix.

The Medieval Manuscripts of Keble College, Oxford. A Descriptive Catalogue with Summary Descriptions of the Greek and Oriental Manuscripts, compiled by M. B. Parkes (London, Scolar Press, 1979).

Medieval Manuscripts from Keble College Oxford [Oxford, Keble College], 18pp. incl. 16 pls [unsigned].

English Cursive Book Hands 1250–1500 (London, Scolar Press, 1979) [corrected repr. of 1969 edn with index added].

[contributor to] *La Ponctuation: Recherches historiques et actuelles*, fascicule 2, Actes de la Table ronde internationale CNRS, de mai 1978 (Paris and Besançon, Centre nationale de la recherche scientifique, 1979), p. 276 [in French].

1980

[*English Cursive Book Hands 1250–1500* (Berkeley, Los Angeles, University of California Press, 1980)], North American edn, cf. 1979.

[with Richard Beadle], 'Commentary', in *Geoffrey Chaucer, Poetical Works: a Facsimile of Cambridge University Library MS Gg.4.27* with introductions by M. B. Parkes and Richard Beadle, 3 vols (Cambridge, D. S. Brewer, 1979–80), 3 (1980), pp. 1–68.

'Books and Aids to Scholarship of the Oxford Friars', in *Manuscripts at Oxford: an Exhibition in Memory of Richard William Hunt*, ed. A. C. de la Mare and B. C. Barker-Benfield (Oxford, Bodleian Library, 1980), pp. 57–9.

1981

*'A Note on MS Vatican, Bibl. Apost., Lat 3363', in *Boethius: his Life, Thought and Influence*, ed. Margaret Gibson (Oxford, Basil Blackwell, 1981), pp. 425–7.

1982

The Scriptorium of Wearmouth-Jarrow (Jarrow Lecture, 1982), 32 pp. incl. 7 pls.

1983

*'On the Presumed Date and Possible Origin of the Manuscript of the "Orrmulum"': Oxford, Bodleian Library, MS Junius 1', in *Five Hundred Years of Words and Sounds: A Festschrift for Eric Dobson*, ed. E. G. Stanley and Douglas Gray (Woodbridge, D. S. Brewer, 1983), pp. 115–27.

*'A Fragment of an Early-Tenth-Century Anglo-Saxon Manuscript and its Significance', *ASE*, 12 (1983), 129–40, + 4 pls.

Review: Bernhard Bischoff, *Paläographie des römischen Altertums und des abendländischen Mittelalters*, Grundlagen der Germanistik, 24 (Berlin, Eric Schmidt, 1979) in *Beiträge zur Geschichte der deutschen Sprache und Literatur*, 105. Band, 2. Heft (1983), 292–6.

'Howard Millar Nixon', *Keble College Record* (1983), 22–3 [obituary notice].

1984

Editor, *Keble College Record* [unsigned].

1985

*'The Date of the Oxford Manuscript of *La Chanson de Roland* (Oxford, Bodleian Library, MS. Digby 23)', *Medioevo romanzo*, 10 (1985), 161–75, + 8 pls.

1986

'Introduction' to 'The Making of the Book', in *The Role of the Book in Medieval Culture*, Proceedings of the Oxford International Symposium, 26 September–1 October 1982, 2 vols, ed. Peter Ganz, vol. 1, Bibliologia, 3 (Turnhout, Brepols, 1986), 11–16.

1987

*'The Contribution of Insular Scribes of the Seventh and Eighth Centuries to the "Grammar of Legibility"', in *Grafia e interpunzione del latino nel medioevo*, Seminario Internazionale, Roma, 27–29 settembre 1984, ed. Alfonso Maierù, Lessico Intellettuale Europeo, 41 (Rome, Edizioni dell' Ateneo, 1987), pp. 15–30, + 1 pl.

1988

[with Bernhard Bischoff], 'Palaeographical Commentary', in *The Épinal, Erfurt, Werden and Corpus Glossaries*, ed. Bernhard Bischoff, Mildred Budny, Geoffrey Harlow, M. B. Parkes and J. D. Pheifer, EEMF, 22 (Copenhagen, Rosenkilde and Bagger, and Baltimore, Johns Hopkins University Press, 1988), pp. 13–25.

*'Book Provision and Libraries at the Medieval University of Oxford (Robert F. Metzdorf Memorial Lecture, 1987)', *The University of Rochester Library Bulletin*, 40 (1987–88), 28–43.

1989

[with Rivkah Zim], '"Sacvyles Olde Age" A Newly Discovered Poem by Thomas Sackville, Lord Buckhurst, Earl of Dorset (c.1536–1608)', *Review of English Studies*, n.s., 40 (1989), 1–25.

*'Tachygraphy in the Middle Ages: Writing Techniques Employed for "Reportationes" of Lectures and Sermons', *Medioevo e Rinascimento*, Annuario del Dipartimento di Studi sul Medioevo e il Rinascimento dell' Università di Firenze, 3 (1989), 159–69, + 2 pls.

1990

'Stephen Wall: a Tribute', *Keble College Record* (1990), 17–19.

1991

Scribes, Scripts and Readers: Studies in the Communication, Presentation and Dissemination of Medieval Texts (London and Rio Grande, OH, Hambledon Press, 1991) [contains revised or augmented versions of items marked * in this list].

1992

Pause and Effect: an Introduction to the History of Punctuation in the West (Aldershot, Scolar Press, 1992).

'Produzione e commercio dei libri manoscritti', in *Produzione e commercio della carta e del libro secc. xiii–xviii*, Atti della 'Ventitreesima Settimana di Studi', 15–20 aprile 1991, ed. Simonetta Cavaciocchi, serie ii – Atti delle 'Settimane di Studi' e altri Convegni, 23, Istituto internazionale di storia economica 'F. Datini', Prato (Florence, Le Monnier, 1992), pp. 331–42 [in English].

'The Provision of Books', in *The History of the University of Oxford*, ii, *Late Medieval Oxford*, ed. J. I. Catto and Ralph Evans (Oxford, Clarendon Press, 1992), 407–83, + 8 pls.

[with Peter Ganz], *Das Buch als magisches und Repräsentationsobjekt*, ed. P. Ganz and M. B. Parkes, Wolfenbütteler Mittelalter-Studien, 5 (Wiesbaden, Harrassowitz Verlag, for Herzog August Bibliothek, 1992).

1993

[*Pause and Effect: an Introduction to the History of Punctuation in the West* (Berkeley, Los Angeles, University of California Press, 1993)], N. American edn, cf. 1992.

1994

'Le pratiche di lettura', in *Lo spazio letterario del medioevo, 1. Il medioevo latino*, ed. Guglielmo Cavallo, Claudio Leonardi and Enrico Menestò, ii, *La circolazione del testo* (Rome, Salerno Editrice, 1994), pp. 465–86 [in Italian].

'Latin Autograph Manuscripts: Orthography and Punctuation', in *Gli autografi medievali: problemi paleografici e filologici*, Atti del convegno di studio della Fondazione Ezio Franceschini, Erice, 25 settembre–2 ottobre 1990, ed. Paulo

Chiesa and Lucia Pinelli, Quaderni di cultura mediolatina, 5 (Spoleto, Centro Italiano di Studi sull'alto Medioevo, 1994), 23–36.

'The Scriptorium of Wearmouth-Jarrow', in *Bede and his World: the Jarrow Lectures 1958–1993* (Aldershot, Variorum, 1994), pp. 555–86 [repr. from 1982].

'Punctuation and the Medieval History of Texts', in *La filologia testuale e le scienze umane*, Convegno Internazionale, Accademia Nazionale dei Lincei, Roma, 19–22 aprile 1993, Atti dei Convegni Lincei, 111 (Rome, Accademia Nazionale dei Lincei, 1994), 265–77.

1995

'*Folia librorum quaerere*: Medieval Experience of the Problems of Hypertext and the Index', in *Fabula in tabula. Una storia degli indici dal manoscritto al testo elettronico*, Atti del Convegno di studio della Fondazione Ezio Franceschini e della Fondazione IBM Italia, Certosa del Galluzzo, 21–22 ottobre 1994, ed. Claudio Leonardi, Marcello Morelli and Francesco Santi, Quaderni di cultura mediolatina, 13 (Spoleto, Centro Italiano di Studi sull'alto Medioevo, 1995), 23–41, + 8 pls.

'Leggere, scrivere, interpretare il testo: pratiche monastiche nell'alto medioevo', in *Storia della lettura nel mondo occidentale*, ed. Guglielmo Cavallo and Roger Chartier (Rome and Bari, Laterza, 1995), pp. 71–90 [in Italian, the original English version, based on a paper delivered to the Colloquium of the Center for Medieval Studies, University of Minnesota, 1991, is otherwise unpublished].

'Patterns of Scribal Activity and Revisions of the Text in Early Copies of Works by John Gower', in *New Science out of Old Books: Studies in Manuscripts and Early Printed Books in Honour of A. I. Doyle*, ed. Richard Beadle and A. J. Piper (Aldershot, Scolar Press, 1995), pp. 81–121.

'The Planning and Construction of the Ellesmere Manuscript', in *The Ellesmere Chaucer: Essays in Interpretation*, ed. Martin Stevens and Daniel Woodward (San Marino, CA, Huntington Library, and Tokyo, Yushodo Press), pp. 41–7.

1996

[with Judith Tschann], *Facsimile of Oxford, Bodleian Library, MS Digby 86*, with an introduction by Judith Tschann and M. B. Parkes, EETS (SS), 16 (Oxford University Press, for EETS, 1996).

'Buchversorgung und Buchgebrauch in den Ordenshäusern der Oxforder Universität', in *Der Codex im Gebrauch*: Akten des 2. internazionalen Kolloquiums des Sonderforschungsbereichs, 231, ed. C. Meier, D. Hüpper and H. Keller, Münstersche Mittelalterschriften, 70 (Munich, Wilhelm Fink Verlag, 1966), 109–26 [in German].

1997

'Archaizing Hands in English Manuscripts', in *Books and Collectors 1200–1700: Essays Presented to Andrew Watson*, ed. James Carley and Colin G. Tite (London, British Library Publications, 1997), pp. 101–41.

'Lire, écrire, interpréter le texte: pratiques monastiques dans le haut Moyen Age', in *Histoire de la lecture dans le monde occidental*, ed. Guglielmo Cavallo and Roger Chartier (Paris, Editions du Seuil, 1997), pp. 109–23 [in French, cf. Italian version, 1995].

'Punctuation in Copies of Nicholas Love's *Mirror of the Blessed Life of Jesus Christ*', in *Nicholas Love at Waseda*, ed. Shoichi Oguro, Richard Beadle and Michael G. Sargent (Woodbridge, Boydell and Brewer, 1997), pp. 47–59.

'Rædan, areccan, smeagan: How the Anglo-Saxons Read', *ASE*, **26** (1997), 1–20.

'Stephan Batman's Manuscripts', in *Medieval Heritage: Essays in Honour of Tadahiro Ikegami*, ed. Masahiko Kanno, Hiroshi Yamashita, Masatoshi Kawasaki, Junko Asakawa and Naoko Shirai (Tokyo, Yushodo Press, 1997).

Forthcoming

'Medieval Punctuation and the Modern Editor', in *Filologia classica e filologia romanza: esperienze ecdotiche a confronto*, ed. Anna Ferrari (Spoleto, Centro Italiano di Studi sull'alto Medioevo).

'The Compilation of the Dominican Legendary', in *Proceedings of the 36. Wolfenbütteler Symposion, 1994*, ed. K. Elm, Wolfenbütteler Mittelalter-Studien.

'Of the making of books there is no end.'

I am grateful to the following for assistance and information received in the preparation of this bibliography: Dr A. I. Doyle, Mr Benjamin Keene and MBP.

V
Notes on Contributors
Index of Manuscripts
General Index

Notes on Contributors

Richard Beadle is a University Lecturer in English and a Fellow of St John's College, Cambridge. In 1979–80 he co-edited with MBP *Geoffrey Chaucer: Poetical Works. A Facsimile of Cambridge University Library MS Gg.4.27* (Cambridge: D. S. Brewer, 3 vols), and in 1995 he edited (with A. J. Piper) *New Science out of Old Books: Studies in Manuscripts and Early Printed Books in honour of A. I. Doyle* (Scolar Press).

A. I. Doyle, F.B.A., Honorary Reader in Bibliography and former Keeper of Rare Books, University of Durham, was Lyell Reader in Bibliography, University of Oxford, 1967. He is co-author, with MBP, of 'The Production of Copies of the *Canterbury Tales* and the *Confessio Amantis* in the Early Fifteenth Century' in *Medieval Scribes, Manuscripts and Libraries: Essays presented to N. R. Ker*, ed. M. B. Parkes and A. G. Watson (Scolar Press, 1978), and of the 'Palaeographical Introduction' to *Geoffrey Chaucer, The Canterbury Tales: A Facsimile and Transcription of the Hengwrt Manuscript*, A Variorum Edition of the Works of Geoffrey Chaucer, I (Norman, Oklahoma, 1979).

David Ganz is Professor of Medieval Latin and Latin Palaeography at the University of North Carolina at Chapel Hill, and Professor of Palaeography (elect), King's College London. He is the author of *Corbie in the Carolingian Renaissance* (Sigmaringen, 1990), and one of the editors of the series *The Medieval Book* published by the University of Notre Dame Press. MBP examined his doctoral thesis and has long been a source of unstinting critical advice.

Vincent Gillespie is a Lecturer in English and a Fellow of St Anne's College, Oxford. He works on the development and transmission of Middle English devotional literature and is the author of 'Vernacular Books of Religion' in *Book Production and Publishing in Britain 1375–1475*, ed. J. Griffiths and D. Pearsall (Cambridge, 1989). He began his career as an undergraduate at Keble College where MBP was his tutor and also helped supervise his doctoral thesis.

Helmut Gneuss, F.B.A., is Emeritus Professor of English Philology at the University of Munich. He is the author of *Hymnar und Hymnen im englischen Mittelalter*, Buchreihe der Anglia, 12 (Tübingen, 1968), and of *Language and History in Early England* and *Books and Libraries in Early England*, both published by Variorum (1996). He became acquainted with MBP through their mutual interest in Anglo-Saxon manuscripts.

Jeanne E. Krochalis is Associate Professor of English at Pennsylvania State University. While she was a B.Phil. student at Oxford, MBP was her tutor and later also an informal advisor for her Harvard doctoral dissertation. She is the author of *The Pierpont Morgan Library MS M. 817*, A Variorum Edition of the Works of Geoffrey Chaucer, IV (Norman, Oklahoma, 1986), and (with Alison Stones) of *The Pilgrim's Guide to Compostela*, 2 vols (Harvey Miller, forthcoming).

Peter J. Lucas, Statutory Lecturer in Old and Middle English at University College Dublin, read English at Keble College, where his interest in medieval studies was aroused by MBP. He has published editions of the Old English poem *Exodus* (Methuen, 1977; rev. edn, Exeter University Press, 1994) and of John Capgrave's *Abbreviacion of Cronicles*, EETS (OS) 285 (1983). His book on *Medieval Publication*, based on his work on Capgrave, is published by University College Dublin Press, 1997.

A. J. Minnis is Professor of Medieval Literature at the University of York. As a research student at the Queen's University of Belfast, he was matriculated at Keble College as a 'migrant student', with MBP as a supervisor. He regards this period as one of the most stimulating and formative periods of his life. He is the author of *Medieval Theory of Authorship: Scholastic Literary Attitudes in the Later Middle Ages* (Scolar Press, 1984) and *The Oxford Guide to Chaucer: The Shorter Poems* (1995).

Jean F. Preston was formerly Curator of Manuscripts at the Huntington Library in California, 1960–77, and at Princeton University, 1977–93, and became acquainted with MBP through his many visits to the United States. She is the co-author (with Laetitia Yeandle) of *English Handwriting 1400–1650* (Binghamton, NY, 1992) and (with Jeanne Krochalis) of *Finding Western Medieval Manuscripts in North American Collections* (Kalamazoo, 1988).

P. R. Robinson is Lecturer in Palaeography at the Institute of Romance Studies, School of Advanced Study, University of London, and was a graduate student of MBP. She is the author of 'The "Booklet": A Self-Contained Unit in Composite Manuscripts', *Codicologica*, 3 (Leiden, 1980), and the *Catalogue of Dated and Datable Manuscripts c.737–1600 in Cambridge Libraries* (Cambridge, 1988).

Jean Vezin, Director of Studies in the École pratique des hautes études, Section des sciences historiques et philologiques, Paris, is the author of *Les scriptoria d'Angers au XIe siècle* (Paris, 1974). He edited (with H.-J. Martin) *Mise en page, mise en texte du livre manuscrit* (Paris, 1990), and (with H. Atsma) published Merovingian and Carolingian documents produced before AD 800 in *Chartae latinae antiquiores*, XIII–XIX (Dietikon-Zurich, 1981–87). He became acquainted with MBP through a mutual interest in the history of punctuation.

Teresa Webber is a Lecturer in the Department of History, University of Southampton, and Lecturer in Palaeography (elect), University of Cambridge. She was a graduate student of MBP. She is the author of *Scribes and Scholars at Salisbury Cathedral c. 1075–c. 1125* (Oxford, 1992) and (with A. G. Watson) has just completed an edition of the medieval library catalogues of the Augustinian canons in England and Wales for the British Academy/British Library Corpus of British Medieval Library Catalogues.

Rivkah Zim is a Lecturer in English at King's College London and a former College Lecturer in English at Keble College. She is the author of *English Metrical Psalms: Poetry as Praise and Prayer 1535–1601* (Cambridge, 1987) and co-editor, with MBP, of '"Sacvyles olde age": a newly discovered poem by Thomas Sackville, Lord Buckhurst, Earl of Dorset *c*.1536–1608', *Review of English Studies*, n.s. 40 (1989). There are grateful acknowledgements to MBP in all her published work.

Index of Manuscripts

Figures in bold type refer to plate numbers

General Index

This is an index of places and names of persons living before 1800 (including book collectors from all periods); early medieval persons are indexed by given first name. See also separate Index of Manuscripts.